Past and Present Publications

*The First Modern
Society*

Past and Present Publications

General Editor: PAUL SLACK, *Exeter College, Oxford*

Past and Present Publications comprise books similar in character to the articles in the journal *Past and Present*. Whether the volumes in the series are collections of essays – some previously published, others new studies – or monographs, they encompass a wide variety of scholarly and original works primarily concerned with social, economic and cultural changes, and their causes and consequences. They will appeal to both specialists and non-specialists and will endeavour to communicate the results of historical and allied research in readable and lively form.

For a list of titles in Past and Present Publications, see end of book.

Lawrence Stone

The First Modern Society

Essays in English History in Honour of LAWRENCE STONE

Edited by
A. L. BEIER
DAVID CANNADINE and
JAMES M. ROSENHEIM

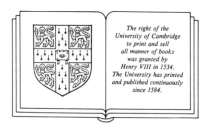

The right of the University of Cambridge to print and sell all manner of books was granted by Henry VIII in 1534. The University has printed and published continuously since 1584.

CAMBRIDGE UNIVERSITY PRESS

Cambridge
New York New Rochelle Melbourne Sydney

Published by the Press Syndicate of the University of Cambridge
The Pitt Building, Trumpington Street, Cambridge CB2 1RP
32 East 57th Street, New York, NY 10022, USA
10 Stamford Road, Oakleigh, Melbourne 3166, Australia

First published 1989

Printed in Great Britain at the University Press, Cambridge

British Library cataloguing in publication data

The first modern society: essays in English
history in honour of Lawrence Stone –
(Past and present publications).
1. England, history.
I. Beier, A. L. II. Cannadine, David, 1950–
III. Rosenheim, James M. IV. Stone, Lawrence. V. Series.
942

Library of Congress cataloguing in publication data

The first modern society: essays in English history in honour
of Lawrence Stone / edited by A. L. Beier, David Cannadine,
and James M. Rosenheim.
   p.   cm. – (Past and present publications).
'Lawrence Stone: a bibliography, 1944–87': p. 597.
Includes index.
ISBN 0 521 36484 1.
1. Great Britain – History – Modern period, 1485–
2. England – Social conditions. 3. Stone, Lawrence.
I. Stone, Lawrence. II. Beier, A. L. III. Cannadine, David, 1950–
IV. Rosenheim, James M.
DA300.F57 1989.
941 – dc19   88-29236   CIP

ISBN 0 521 36484 1

... how and why did Western Europe change itself during the sixteenth, seventeenth and eighteenth centuries so as to lay the social, economic, scientific, political, ideological and ethical foundations for the rationalist, democratic, individualistic, technological industrialised society in which we now live? England was the first country to travel along this road ...

Lawrence Stone, *The Past and the Present Revisited*
(London, 1987), p. xi.

Contents

List of illustrations   *page* xii
List of tables   xiv
Notes on contributors   xvi
Preface   xxi

PROLOGUE: LAWRENCE STONE – AS SEEN
BY OTHERS   1

The myth and the man   3
JULIAN MITCHELL

The enfant terrible?   9
C. S. L. DAVIES

'Il Magnifico'   15
MIRIAM SLATER

The eminence rouge?   21
JOHN M. MURRIN

I THE CROWN, THE ARISTOCRACY AND
THE GENTRY   31

1   Lineage and kin in the sixteenth-century aristocracy: 33
some comparative evidence on England and
Germany
JUDITH J. HURWICH

2   Public ceremony and royal charisma: the English   65
royal entry in London, 1485–1642
R. M. SMUTS

3   County governance and elite withdrawal in Norfolk,   95
    1660–1720
    JAMES M. ROSENHEIM

4   The last Hanoverian sovereign?: the Victorian   127
    monarchy in historical perspective, 1688–1988
    DAVID CANNADINE

5   The gentrification of Victorian and Edwardian   167
    industrialists
    RICHARD TRAINOR

II POWER AND SOCIAL RELATIONS   199

6   Poverty and progress in early modern England   201
    A. L. BEIER

7   Ambiguity and contradiction in 'the rise of   241
    professionalism': the English clergy, 1570–1730
    MICHAEL HAWKINS

8   Bourgeois revolution and transition to capitalism   271
    ROBERT BRENNER

9   Crowds, carnival and the state in English executions,   305
    1604–1868
    THOMAS W. LAQUEUR

10 Interpersonal conflict and social tension: civil   357
    litigation in England, 1640–1830
    C. W. BROOKS

11 Church and state allied: the failure of parliamentary   401
    reform of the universities, 1688–1800
    JOHN GASCOIGNE

III URBAN SOCIETY AND SOCIAL CHANGE   431

12 Resistance to change: the political elites of   433
    provincial towns during the English Revolution
    ROGER HOWELL, Jr

13 The London Whigs and the Exclusion Crisis   457
    reconsidered
    GARY S. DE KREY

14 Cultural life in the provinces: Leeds and York,   483
    1720–1820
    J. JEFFERSON LOONEY

15 The dynamics of class formation in   511
    nineteenth-century Bradford
    THEODORE KODITSCHEK

16 The community perspective in family history: the   549
    Potteries during the nineteenth century
    MARGUERITE DUPREE

EPILOGUE: Lawrence Stone – as seen by himself   575

APPENDIX: Lawrence Stone: a bibliography,
1944–87

    Index   613

Illustrations

Frontispiece   Lawrence Stone. Photo reproduced by
permission of the Ford Foundation, Villa Serbelloni,
Ballagio, Italy

1.1   Genealogy of the Zimmern family   *page* 62

5.1   The Black Country and its vicinity in the later   170
nineteenth century

7.1   Numbers of ordinations of deacons in the Diocese   253
of Peterborough, 1570s to 1720s

9.1   'View of Tyburn Towards Hyde Park', 1785   310
(British Museum, Department of Prints and
Drawings, Crace Collection xxx/2)

9.2   'View of Tyburn Towards Hyde Park', 1810   312
(British Museum, Department of Prints and
Drawings, Crace Collection xxx/1)

9.3   'An Interesting and Heartrending Account of a   314
Dreadful and Unnatural Murder Committed by
Jessy Dalton Upon the Body of Her Mother', early
nineteenth century (St Bride Printing Library)

9.4   Thomas Rowlandson, 'An Execution outside   316
Newgate Prison', 1790s

9.5 and 9.6 Two versions of a standard early nineteenth-   318
century execution scene

9.7   William Hogarth, 'The Idle 'Prentice Executed   333
at Tyburn', 1747

9.8   'The Life, Trial, and Execution of R. Cooper',   334
1862 (Guildhall Library)

9.9   'The Sorrowful and Weeping Lamentation of   335
Four Lovely Orphans Left by J. Newton' (St Bride
Printing Library)

9.10	'Hanging in Chains of Francis Fearn, on Loxley Common, Near Sheffield'	336
9.11	'Preparing for an Execution'	338
9.12	'The Trial and Sentences of All the Prisoners . . . Old Bailey, September 1822'	339
9.13	Breughel's 'Christ Carrying the Cross'	342
9.14	Jack Sheppard as Harlequin Jack Sheppard, 1724	343
9.15	'The Funeral Procession of the celebrated Mr. Jonathan Wild Thief Taker General of Great Britain and Ireland' (British Library, Sat. 1751)	344
9.16	'The Tub Preacher and the Mountebank', 1696/1724 (Bancroft Library, University of California, Berkeley)	345
10.1	Cases in advanced stages in King's Bench and Common Pleas, 1640–1830	362
10.2	Number of cases sent for trial at Assizes, Common Pleas, 1672–1830	363
13.1	Institutions and personnel of Corporation of London Governance	468
16.1	Standard of living by life-cycle for various occupations of husbands: Potteries sample, 1861	571

Tables

1.1   Sons and daughters in thirteen southwestern   *page*   46
German noble families who survived until the age
of fifteen between 1400 and 1599

3.1   Claims on the Pipe Rolls for Norfolk justices   108
attending sessions, 1660–1685

3.2   Norfolk justices' attendance at quarter sessions,   108
1660–1718

6.1   Mean household sizes   206

6.2   Social structures and levels of need, 1582–1630   207
(in %)

6.3   Age-structures in English communities,   213
1587–1695

6.4   Sexes and ages of the poor, 1587–1629   216

7.1   Educational qualifications of ordinands to the   254–5
diaconate in the diocese of Peterborough, 1570s
to 1720s

7.2   Educational qualifications of deacons in the   257
diocese of Peterborough, 1570s to 1720s

7.3   Percentage of deacons obtaining Masters'   259
degrees in the diocese of Peterborough, 1570s to
1720s

7.4   Ages of ordinands in the diocese of   260
Peterborough, 1570s to 1720s

7.5   Ordinations as priests of deacons ordained at   261
Peterborough, 1570s to 1720s

7.6   Geographical origins of ordinands to the   262
diaconate in the diocese of Peterborough, 1570s
to 1720s

7.7	Location of clerical employment of Peterborough ordinands, 1570s to 1720s	263
7.8	Career patterns of Peterborough deacons, 1570s to 1720s	264
7.9	Known social origins of Peterborough deacons, 1570s to 1720s	267
10.1	Common Pleas. Numbers of cases sent for trial at assizes in the office of a single prothonotary, 1645–62	361
10.2	Number of bills entered in the Court of Chancery, 1673–1809	361
10.3	Geographical distribution of litigation in King's Bench and Common Pleas, 1606–1750	370
10.4	Actions in the Newcastle town courts, 1665–1830	373
10.5	Social status of litigants in Common Pleas, 1640 and 1750	384
10.6	Forms of action at common law, 1640–1750	388
13.1	Nonconformist Common Councilmen in London, 1664–83	464
16.1	The employment of children and the presence and occupation of fathers: Potteries, 1861	560
16.2	The employment of unmarried daughters (aged fifteen and over), and the presence of parents and occupation of fathers: Potteries, 1861	562
16.3	The employment of wives and occupation of husbands: Potteries, 1861	564
16.4a	Determinants of family standard of living for families headed by married men in various occupations: Potteries, 1861	569
16.4b	Mean values of each of the three variables used in Table 16.4a for married men in various occupations who headed households: Potteries, 1861	569

Notes on contributors

A. L. BEIER completed his Princeton Ph.D. under Lawrence Stone's supervision in 1969. He is Lecturer in History at the University of Lancaster, the author of *Masterless Men. The Vagrancy Problem in England, 1560–1640* (London, 1985), and a co-editor of and contributor to *London 1500–1700. The Making of the Metropolis* (London, 1986).

ROBERT BRENNER, whose graduate work was directed by Lawrence Stone at Princeton, was awarded a Ph.D. there in 1970. His important articles on the rise of capitalism are collected in the volume *The Brenner Debate. Agrarian Class Structure and Economic Development in Pre-Industrial Europe*, ed. T. H. Aston and C. H. E. Philpin (Cambridge, 1985). He is Professor of History at the University of California, Los Angeles.

C. W. BROOKS graduated in 1970 from Princeton University, where his interest in English social history was stimulated by the writings and undergraduate teaching of Lawrence Stone. He completed an Oxford D.Phil. on early modern attorneys in 1978 and has published *Pettyfoggers and Vipers of the Commonwealth: The 'Lower Branch' of the Legal Profession in Early Modern England* (Cambridge, 1986). He is Lecturer in Modern History at the University of Durham.

DAVID CANNADINE is Professor of History at Columbia University. He studied with Lawrence Stone at Princeton in 1973–4 as a Procter Fellow, and is the author of *Lords and Landlords: The Aristocracy and the Towns, 1776–1967* (Leicester, 1980) and *The Pleasures of the Past* (London, 1988).

C. S. L. DAVIES, an undergraduate and graduate student of Lawrence Stone's, has been Fellow of Wadham College, Oxford since 1963. He has written articles on fifteenth- and sixteenth-century history and a book entitled *Peace, Print and Protestantism* (Paladin History of England, 1976). He is currently writing a volume in the *New Oxford History of England* for the years 1461–1547.

GARY S. DE KREY's Ph.D. research was supervised by Lawrence Stone at Princeton. He is Associate Professor of History at St Olaf College and has published *A Fractured Society: The Politics of London in the First Age of Party: 1688–1715* (Oxford, 1985). His new research is on dissent and politics in English towns from 1660 to 1715.

MARGUERITE DUPREE studied as a graduate student with Lawrence Stone at Princeton and has been a Fellow of Wolfson College and Emmanuel College, Cambridge. She is currently a Research Fellow of the Wellcome Unit for the History of Medicine at the University of Glasgow and is the editor of *Lancashire and Whitehall: The Diary of Sir Raymond Streat, 1931–1957*, 2 vols (Manchester University Press, 1987). Her study of *Family Structure in the Staffordshire Potteries, 1840–1880* is to be published by Oxford University Press.

JOHN GASCOIGNE studied as a graduate student with Lawrence Stone at Princeton. He completed his Ph.D. on Newtonian natural philosophy and Latitudinarian theology at Cambridge in 1981 and is currently completing a book on science and natural theology at Cambridge from 1660 to 1880. He lectures at the University of New South Wales.

MICHAEL HAWKINS, Reader in History at Sussex University, studied with Lawrence Stone both as an undergraduate and as a postgraduate. He has published on the Court of Wards in the early seventeenth century and was a contributor to *Origins of the English Civil War*, ed. C. Russell (London, 1973) and to the *Dictionary of British Seventeenth-Century Radicals*, 3 vols (London, 1982).

ROGER HOWELL, Jr, who is William R. Kenan, Jr, Professor of Humanities in the Department of History, Bowdoin College, studied with Lawrence Stone at Oxford. He is the author of

Newcastle-upon-Tyne and the Puritan Revolution (Oxford, 1967), *Sir Philip Sidney: The Shepherd Knight* (London, 1968), *Cromwell* (London, 1977), and *Puritans and Radicals in North England: Essays on the English Revolution* (Lanham, MD, 1984). He is currently working on seventeenth-century urban history.

JUDITH J. HURWICH's Ph.D. on Nonconformity in Warwickshire from 1660 to 1720 was supervised by Lawrence Stone at Princeton and was completed in 1970. She has published several articles on dissenters and Catholics, and her present research is on the history of the family in early modern Europe. She has been chairman of the Department of History of the Greenwich Academy, and currently teaches at Fairfield University.

THEODORE KODITSCHEK completed his Princeton Ph.D. in 1981 under Lawrence Stone's direction. Its subject was class formation in the city of Bradford from 1750 to 1850. He is now revising this study for publication, after which he plans to extend the research to 1914. He is Assistant Professor at Worcester Polytechnic Institute.

THOMAS W. LAQUEUR is Professor of History at the University of California, Berkeley. As a graduate student he was supervised by Lawrence Stone at Princeton, where he received his Ph.D. He has published numerous articles and a book entitled *Religion and Respectability: Sunday Schools and Working Class Culture, 1780–1850* (New Haven, 1976).

J. JEFFERSON LOONEY is associate editor of the Thomas Jefferson Papers and the co-author of *Princetonians: A Biographical Dictionary, 1784–1794*. His Princeton Ph.D. (1983) was supervised by Lawrence Stone and was on the subject of advertising and leisure in the eighteenth century. His most recent research is on literary societies at American universities from 1783 to 1800.

JULIAN MITCHELL is the author of six novels, and many plays for the stage and television, including *Another Country*. His first scholarly articles have recently appeared in *The Welsh History Review* and *The Monmouthshire Antiquary*, proving that his three years under Lawrence Stone as an undergraduate, and four as a graduate student (D.Phil. uncompleted), were not entirely wasted.

JOHN MURRIN, a specialist in American colonial history, has been a colleague of Lawrence Stone's at Princeton since 1973. He completed his Ph.D. at Yale University and his publications include an essay in the collection *Three British Revolutions, 1641, 1688, 1776*, J. G. A. Pocock, ed. (Princeton, 1980). He has also co-edited and contributed to two books, *Colonial America: Essays in Politics and Social Development* (New York, 1983) and *Saints and Revolutionaries: Essays on Early American History* (New York, 1984).

JAMES M. ROSENHEIM, currently Assistant Professor of History at Texas A & M University, worked with Lawrence Stone at Princeton University and received his Ph.D. in 1981, writing a thesis on the gentry of Restoration Norfolk. His book, *The Townshends of Raynham: Nobility in Transition in Restoration and Early Hanoverian England*, will be published in 1989 by Wesleyan University Press.

MIRIAM SLATER, until recently Dean of the School of Sciences at Hampshire College, is Harold F. Johnson Professor of History there. She studied with Lawrence Stone as a graduate student at Princeton; her Ph.D. thesis, a study of the Verney family, was published in a revised version as *Family Life in the Seventeenth Century* (London, 1983). She has also published articles on English and American materials, and most recently a book with P. Glazer, *Unequal Colleagues: Women's Entrance into the Professions* (Rutgers University Press, New Brunswick, 1987).

R. MALCOLM SMUTS is Associate Professor of History at the University of Massachusetts (Boston) and the author of several articles on the court of Charles I. His research degree was supervised by Lawrence Stone at Princeton, and his book on *Court Culture and the Origins of a Royalist Tradition* (University of Pennsylvania Press) appeared in 1986. His current research is on the court, the gentry and urban society in the West End between 1600 and 1642.

RICHARD TRAINOR is Lecturer in Economic History at Glasgow University and Director of the Design and Implementation of Software in History Project there. He studied as a graduate student with Lawrence Stone at Princeton and was a Junior Research Fellow of Wolfson College, Oxford. A revised version of his 1981 Oxford D.Phil. thesis is being published by Oxford University Press as *Black Country Élite: the Exercise of Authority in an Industrialised Region, 1830–1900*.

Preface

These essays, by former students of Lawrence Stone on both sides of the Atlantic, are gathered together to celebrate his seventieth birthday, and to mark his retirement from the Dodge Professorship of History at Princeton University. They are offered as an appreciative and affectionate tribute to one of the towering figures of our profession, whose insatiable curiosity about the past, refreshing openness to new ideas, unerring instinct for raising large issues, prodigious creative energies, and robust delight in controversy, have been an example to us all – and a reproach and provocation to many others.

No single volume of essays could hope to do full justice to the breadth of his interests, ranging as they do across a millennium of the British past – in political, economic, social, family, cultural, educational and architectural history, and in sociology, statistics, demography, economics and anthropology. But all the essays collected here owe much to his inspiration and his influence. To these are added four appreciations by friends and colleagues from Oxford and Princeton, and a little-known but highly revealing piece of autobiography by Lawrence Stone himself, which was originally given as the third Charles Homer Haskins Lecture under the title 'A Life of Learning,' and is reprinted here by kind permission of the American Council of Learned Societies.

The editing of this volume has been a memorable and educational experience for us all, and we have shared its burdens equally. We are extremely grateful to our fellow contributors for their forbearance and co-operation, to Kenneth E. Hendrickson for his assistance in compiling the bibliography, and to the Department of History and the College of Liberal Arts at Texas A & M University, and the Department of History at the University of

Lancaster, for their generous financial support. We owe particular thanks to Joan Daviduk, Ted Rabb and Jeanne C. Fawtier Stone for their crucial – but necessarily clandestine – contributions. William Davies and the staff of Cambridge University Press have been unfailingly helpful, and we are very grateful to Angela Coss for undertaking the mammoth task of compiling the index. But our greatest debt of all is to Lawrence Stone himself.

A. L. BEIER
DAVID CANNADINE
JAMES M. ROSENHEIM

Prologue
Lawrence Stone – as seen by others

The myth and the man

JULIAN MITCHELL

I knew Lawrence Stone as a myth before I knew him as a man. In the 1950s, although many of us had done National Service, and so had some experience of the outside world, undergraduates felt considerable awe in the presence of their tutors, and spoke of them amongst themselves, at least till they got to know them, as beings of a superior order. It was a quiet and obedient time, and we brought to Oxford the respect for teachers we had learned at school – respect still being as important a part of the curriculum at some schools as learning. Like any other under-class, we mixed prurient gossip with our awe. There was much speculation about the Fellows' personal habits and sexual tastes, and their alleged sayings were repeated and analysed like sacred texts. Above all we liked them to be 'characters'. This was perhaps especially so at Wadham, where the College was presided over by Maurice Bowra, one of the most formidable Oxford 'characters' of the century, a ferocious wit whose *bons mots* (and they were excellent, unless you were their victim) were meant to be repeated in the smartest London drawing-rooms.

The Wadham historians, graduate and undergraduate, proudly claimed Lawrence as a 'character' to outdo any other in the College. Where Pat Thompson was comfortably pipe-smoking and relatively gentle in his treatment of incompetence, Lawrence was a dragon-tutor whose lightest breath would scorch your essay to a pile of ash. It was known that he had published an article while on a destroyer in the Atlantic during the war, and a whiff of depth-charge hung about him still. The fact that the article was about the Armada added a romantic glow, a touch of Elizabethan privateer. His intolerance of idleness was terrifyingly naval and upper-deck, while his use of the vernacular was unsettlingly lower – dons didn't habitually use rude words to undergraduates in those days. Naturally his pupils adopted his language and tried to outdo him, but this could be risky. One undergraduate dashingly described Northumberland as a Fascist beast. Lawrence thought only for a moment, then said Northumberland wasn't a Fascist beast but a bloody shit; not the same thing at all. The speed of judgement was almost more awe-inspiring than the judgement itself.

Everything about Lawrence was swift. Tall, thin, rangy, he loped about Wadham like a long-legged lurcher, a squash- or tennis-racquet in his hand, a hard stare behind a long nose perpetually questing for facts. Even his car was an Allard, a very rare and piratical sports car which seemed perfectly suited to his impetuous character. But of course in Oxford impetuosity is called rashness, and by the time I arrived at Wadham Lawrence was already embroiled in the great row over the Rise of the Gentry. In our eyes this made him a specially glamorous figure, but some of his colleagues in the university were spiteful. I remember overhearing a conversation about him in the King's Arms one lunchtime. Two dons were cutting him up over a hot pie. 'The trouble with Lawrence Stone', said the female of the pair, 'is he's the sort of man who will stick that long nose of his *into* things.' The man sighed, then said, with the malicious satisfaction that distinguishes so much Oxford conversation, 'He will get it bitten.' It was dangerous talk in the Wadham pub, for we were fiercely loyal to our tutors, especially those under fire, but I dare say the pie did for the dons what I would like to have done. Those pies were lethal.

By then, after an idle and unhappy first year, I had abandoned PPE and been allowed to do history instead. But before I could start, I had to resit my Prelims, as I'd wholly failed to grasp the elementary principles of economics, and to this day cannot see what Perfect Competition has to do with anything in the real world. This economic blindness meant I had temporarily to suspend what I considered my serious work at Oxford, which was in writing and the theatre. However I did allow myself the luxury of appearing in a Wadham revue, called, I'm almost sure (it almost always was), 'WADS and Sods'. The Wadham Amateur Dramatic Society was then under the benign leadership of Michael Barnes, a history graduate as tall and thin as Lawrence himself, and now a powerful figure in the artistic life of Northern Ireland. Among the sketches was one in which he played a history tutor, who peered down a cardboard tube at a hapless undergraduate whose essay on the reforms of Thomas Cromwell consisted of the single magnificently irrefutable sentence: 'Henry VIII came to the throne in 1509.' In this important role, I was directed to read the sentence with the solemnity of a great scholar announcing a major discovery. There was a long silence. Then Michael, who had been gazing out of the window through his tube, turned, and with all the affronted incredulity which Lawrence brought to the fallen world of undergraduate essays, said '*Is that all?*'

It brought the house down, and I thought I knew what I was in for if I did manage to satisfy the examiners in economics. '*Is that all?*' was Lawrence's motto, according to his pupils, and even members of the Boat Club trembled before climbing the narrow stone stair to his room over the main gate. This room seemed physically set apart from the rest of the College – like a turret employed for particularly gruesome tortures; or so one felt on first entering. In fact it was high and handsome, with a grand fireplace and two big windows. I was much too frightened to think so at the time, but it now seems significant that it was, or seemed to be, the only one in college which looked out as much as in. What did seem appropriate, even then, was that it was the room in which the Royal Society was supposed to have been founded in the 1650s. For in spite of his critics, Lawrence's approach to the truth about the past seemed fundamentally scientific rather than literary, which so much of the history we had done at school still was. The counting of manors, or the manner of counting them, might have gone astray, but among the young there was never anything wrong with the idea that you should bring modern methods to the study of the past.

The Royal Society's foundation in Wadham during the Interregnum was a direct link to the period of British history which seemed in the 1950s of most relevance to our own time. Intellectual Britain was obsessed with class; the Rise of the Gentry, or their Decline, or whatever *did* happen to them, was almost painfully important to us. The debate about the origins of the English Civil War was confused in our minds with Nancy Mitford's notorious article on the use of U and Non-U, published in the smart new intellectual magazine, *Encounter*. Undergraduates discussed class day and night, with arrogance or fear according to their confidence in their own place in the existing scheme of things and their hopes for the future. People like myself, from a solid professional background, were challenged to produce a working-class ancestor to appease the new left, and longed for at least an Honourable one as well in order to feel at ease in Christ Church and Trinity. The submerged subject of the rancorous debate in the *Economic History Review*, or so it felt to us, was the future of Britain. I'm not sure we weren't right. Nothing else can satisfactorily explain the wholly disproportionate anger which the subject inspired.

Of course we undergraduates loved the intemperance of the row. The idea of the pages of academic history journals being stained with modern blood gave us huge delight, and we thought of Trevor-Roper as a Cavalier and Lawrence as a Roundhead. Whether it was actually so or not, Trevor-Roper seemed utterly Christ Church – a hunting Tory, with the aristocratic brutality in argument brought to perfection, if that's the word, by Evelyn Waugh – who himself contributed to the U and Non-U debate. Lawrence was Roundhead, as we were – Wadham prided itself on its radicalism then, as it does today, though Lawrence, as it happened, had been an undergraduate at Christ Church under Trevor-Roper. The long nose, poking into aristocratic archives, the expressions of outrage at what he found there in the way of idleness, immorality, extravagance and incompetence, the impatience with detail in the desire to get to the truth, the withering '*Is that all?*' – all these made him definitely of the godly party. The fact that he was anything but a literal iconoclast, that he'd actually written a book about early sculpture in Britain, was difficult to reconcile with the myth, so we tended to ignore it. What mattered was the English Revolution. If we could only properly understand what produced that upheaval then, perhaps we could understand what was happening to our own class-ridden society now, and, by not making the same mistakes, make sure the new revolution lasted. Happy days.

After the myth, the reality, when I at last came face to face with it, was distinctly disappointing. Lawrence did not set fire to one's essay in front of one's face, and a cautious scrutiny of his room showed no evidence of human blood. He did, it's true, sometimes gaze at the New Bodleian through a cardboard tube, like Michael Barnes, he did prowl about the room, and he did occasionally swish his squash-racquet, but there were no mutilated academic journals and no evidence of angry inkpots hurled at recalcitrant students or nit-picking opponents. Furthermore he was extraordinarily open-minded about the controversies in which he was engaged. He made us read the evidence for ourselves and come to our own conclusions. His passion was evident, but it was not for personalities but for truth, whatever, in history, that may be. The aggression was there all right, and a passionate desire that his pupils should make an effort and *understand*, that we should *think* – but in this form they were not frightening but stimulating.

Now that I've known Lawrence for thirty years, I see why the superficial characteristics were the ones we first latched on to. They can still be alarming. His croquet, even in his sixties, is furiously competitive. He challenges his opponent at every turn, questions and tries to bend the rules, accuses everyone else of cheating, and wreaks terrible revenge on those who dare to dismiss him to the rose-bed. One might be in the presence of a dangerous psychopath. Listening to him ordering Jeanne how to play her shots, one cannot imagine how the marriage has survived. He is intolerant, aggressive, argumentative – and then he laughs. As he did in tutorials. There would be intense concentration as he developed an idea, then a sudden shrug and smile, and the dismissal of everything that had gone before as possible nonsense. After wreaking havoc on a jejune answer in my Collection paper, he typically added at the bottom, in his hurried handwriting, 'A silly question, anyway.' That a don could undercut his own authority like that seemed quite astonishing. But then he never really seemed like a don, or, when it came to it, a 'character'. He was too direct, too busy to play up to our idea of him. Not the least important thing I learned from Lawrence was that myths and appearances aren't nearly so interesting as realities.

The enfant terrible?

C. S. L. DAVIES

My own credentials for this appreciation consist in being an undergraduate pupil of Lawrence's at Wadham between 1956 and 1959, and being supervised by him as a research student between 1959 and 1962; and, to my surprise, being elected to succeed him at Wadham in 1963.[1] Lawrence took his interrupted final examination in 1946, and was immediately elected to the Bryce Research Studentship. In 1948 he began a teaching career by becoming a Lecturer at University College, Oxford; and in 1950 he was appointed Fellow of Wadham, remaining there until 1963 when he moved to Princeton.

Those who have known Lawrence since 1963 will not be surprised to learn that he was not a pillar of the Establishment. But what may surprise them is that for most of the time at least he was not particularly prominent as an agitator for reform. Oxford is very good at defusing the potential trouble-maker – partly because of the diffusion of power between colleges and the university, partly because of the democratic nature (as far as teaching staff are concerned) of the university's organization. Syllabus reform, for instance, involves constructing a scheme which will avoid offending too many interest groups, piloting it through or past the labyrinthine committees of the Faculty Board, only, for the most part, to have it rejected in the Faculty Meeting by an unholy coalition of conservatives opposing change generally and radicals opposing this particular change.

Rebels rarely have the temperament; Lawrence, perhaps least of all. But, more fundamentally, it was not until the end of the 1950s, that Lawrence's dissatisfaction with 'a curriculum stifling both in its

[1] Especially valuable have been conversations with Mr J. O. Prestwich and Mr A. F. Thompson.

national insularity and in its limited late Victorian conception' of history seems to have come to a head.[2] Before that time he had, no doubt, grumbled; had been involved in an abortive attempt, in 1957–8, to introduce what now seem very limited reforms; but, in this realm, as in so much else, the existing system seemed unshakable. Fundamental reform was as inconceivable as, say, throwing the ancient colleges open to women.

I suspect Lawrence would not in any case have wanted to establish a following among undergraduates. As a tutor he was not given to expounding his own views. He would challenge the logic of our argument, demand evidence for unsubstantiated statements, express his amazement at any suggestion that public life might be conducted on any but the lowest principles. Above all, he would try to provoke us to fight back: disconcerting, even demoralizing for some, but for those of us who understood the game that was being played, not too hazardous, especially as a parry was often enough to send Lawrence scuttling back to his corner. He would provide an efficient, up-to-date and realistic set of books to read, but leave it to us to work out our own interpretation – no mini-lecture to expound his own views, no careful feeding of dollops of recent discoveries to stimulate the imagination or help fool the examiners. It was an astringent regime. Of course, college tutors also delivered lectures to the history students of the university at large. Unfortunately I took too literally Lawrence's own advice not to go to lectures, anachronistic as an art-form since the time of Caxton, and so missed his own: a survey of the main issues of Tudor and Stuart politics, I gather, the progenitor, without the sociological vocabulary, of *The Causes of the English Revolution*.

There was little in the way of a graduate school in history in Oxford in the 1950s. Lawrence had I think only three graduate students of his own, all of them represented in this volume, all of them in fact formerly undergraduates of Wadham. Graduate students were relatively thin on the ground, but I suspect that part of the reason may have been the general impression following the 'Gentry' controversy that Lawrence was 'unsound'. Lawrence did not aspire to the American or Germanic views of the role of supervisor (much in evidence in Tudor studies in London and Cambridge). He did not regard his students' work as ancillary to his own, did not attempt to influence what one wrote, let one make

2 See below, pp. 583–4.

one's own mistakes. His only requirement, and that a salutary one, was to insist on regular production of written work; in effect, a thesis chapter per term. As with undergraduate essays criticism was confined largely to style and internal logic.

Lawrence's intervention in university affairs seems to have been concerned mainly with practical aesthetics. He cared about the fabric of Oxford's buildings, protesting at over-zealous restoration by both university and colleges. He had, I suspect, more institutional loyalty than he would readily admit. At Wadham he did a superb and rather thankless job in sorting and cataloguing the college archives.[3] He avoided college office otherwise, and carefully rationed his time so as to press on with *The Crisis of the Aristocracy*; aided here by the willingness of his colleague A. F. (Pat) Thompson to spend hours in administration and dealing with the foibles of the young.

Lawrence's teaching, although not allowed to encroach into research time, was never skimped; and he cared about the quality of student entry and performance in History Schools. At college meetings he was a vigorous but (fortunately) unsuccessful critic of investment policy. Wadham in the 1950s was a convivial and intellectually stimulating place, the cracking pace set by its legendary warden Sir Maurice Bowra. The fellowship numbered about fourteen, almost all of them Lawrence's own generation and sharing in the general progressive optimism of those years of broad political consensus. Lawrence played his full part in the social life of the college; while the bonds created in the (male-only) Senior Common Room were reinforced by strenuous entertaining by Jeanne of colleagues and colleagues' wives (and indeed of pupils) in their house in Woodstock Road.

Not, it seems, until Lawrence's visit to Princeton in 1960 did serious dissatisfaction with Oxford set in. On his return he wrote in the *Oxford Magazine* about the diminishing enthusiasm of 'most of us who have been doing the job for nearly twenty years' (a splendidly characteristic piece of Lawrentian hyperbole) for undergraduate teaching. He wanted a switch of emphasis to graduate studies. To effect this, Oxford should revert to the pre-war practice of choosing only a minority of its undergraduates on grounds of academic merit, reserving the rest of its places for 'good college

---

[3] See *A Catalogue of the Muniment of Wadham College*, produced for the Historical Manuscripts Commission, National Register of Archives, 1962.

men' (i.e. sportsmen, actors, and so forth), a proposal which must have put Lawrence in the unfamiliar company of a declining band of reactionaries lurking in the darker corners of the university. In turn, this would help appease the fears of other English universities that Oxford and Cambridge were denuding them of their best students – itself a rather remarkable example of Oxonian condescension.[4]

As it happened this coincided with the foundation of the 'new universities' which were to shake, for a while at least, Oxford's self-confident assumption of its own superiority. Instead of plodding like their predecessors through years of apprenticeship to the University of London, Sussex, York, Lancaster, Kent and Essex were to spring into being as fully fledged universities, determining their own syllabuses and with a mission 'to make the map of knowledge'. Heading a history department (or whatever it might now be called) might be a challenge, might also be an opportunity, especially as ambitious and publicity-seeking vice-chancellors were determined to recruit young and radical senior staff. Change was in the air in Oxford as well. For the first time undergraduates launched a campaign for reform of the syllabus; prominent amongst them were such luminaries as Tim Mason, Brian Harrison and (a new graduate) Peter Burke. Lawrence gave conspicuous support. In the short run, at least, nothing came of it. Expectations roused, then dashed, accounted in classic 'J-curve' fashion for Lawrence's accepting the offer of the Dodge Chair at Princeton.

It is, fortunately, premature to review Lawrence's scholarly work; nor would I be the person to do so. His production record while he undertook his tutorial stint (a minimum of fourteen hours a week, sometimes as much as twenty) was amazing, in bulk and range; not only *Palavicino* and *Sculpture in Britain: The Middle Ages*, but *Crisis of the Aristocracy*, the typescript handed in just before his departure for Princeton. I was given a draft of the chapter on 'Violence' to read. It was a revelation in its demonstration that, far from being cured by Edward IV or Henry VII (we used to debate which), 'bastard feudalism' was alive and kicking until late in Queen Elizabeth's reign. Indeed, while Stone was shattering the legend of a Tudor peace, K. B. McFarlane was taking the violence out of the fifteenth century. The dialectic of historical controversy produced the apparent paradox of a sixteenth century

[4] *Oxford Magazine*, 28 October 1961.

more violent than the fifteenth; McFarlane's responsible noblemen would hardly, one feels, countenance the sort of armed mayhem in Fleet Street perpetuated by Lawrence's Lord Rich and his twenty-five armed retainers. Both writers, reacting against the conventional wisdom on their subject, were overstating their case. *Crisis*, however, by breaking out of the economic strait-jacket in which it was conceived, helped in turn to smash the assumption on which the Oxford History School was implicitly based, even for would-be reformers: that English history was an intelligible unity, that the political story would be underpinned, not undermined, by uncovering its economic sub-structure. We are still picking up the pieces.

'Il Magnifico'

MIRIAM SLATER

I walked along the corridor in McCosh looking for Lawrence
Stone's office and finally arrived at the appropriate number. Where
his name should have appeared on a neatly printed plaque some
wag had pasted, rather crookedly, a hand-lettered card which read
'Lorenzo Il Magnifico'. I smiled to myself at the bravado of one of
my fellow first-year graduate students. In the first weeks of our
seminar on Tudors and Stuarts the exact identity of the person or
persons who relabelled the office door was a matter of some
concern and speculation among all eleven new students in the
history department. As the term progressed, the nickname took on
meaning and nuance and carried that complicated mixture of awe,
admiration, ambivalence and fear which many of us felt for the new
professor in the department.

Certainly, it relieved my nervousness somewhat to see the
irreverent little nameplate as I walked into Lawrence's office on the
day of our first private meeting. It reassured me to know that other
students were also searching for their places in the scheme of
things. Actually, I had met Lawrence for the first time at the initial
meeting of our graduate seminar a few weeks before. That introduction was the culmination of two years of battling to be allowed
to enter the then male bastion of the university. Fortunately for
my prospects of success, Lawrence had come to Princeton from
Oxford the previous year. Only his willingness to have me as a
student made it possible for me to gain entrance into the graduate
programme. Of course, he never mentioned to me that his support
had been essential to my acceptance; others told me of his role in
that peculiar debate and of his conviction that teaching a woman
was nothing out of the ordinary.

Princeton had steadfastly refused to take women undergraduates and had been largely successful in keeping otherwise eligible women out of the graduate school. The university had been known to make rare exceptions in exotic fields, but they were loath to agree to admitting someone for the more popular courses on sixteenth- and seventeenth-century England. Lawrence may have had a casual attitude toward the prospect of teaching a woman, but the university authorities did not. Many were afraid that accepting me would set a precedent – a prospect ordinarily so feared among academics as to be virtually the death blow to any new idea or departure from the norm.

But in their determination to demonstrate their pleasure in his appointment they agreed to allow him to take on this one, eager woman despite the institution's stated and public preferences for young, single, male candidates. Those who were against the decision believed, as the catalogue firmly asserted, that the graduate curriculum was too demanding to be successfully negotiated by anyone who was not male, undistracted by the demands of matrimony, and unencumbered by progeny. I flunked on all points. But they capitulated to the extent that they allowed me entrance as an 'incidental student' and, confidently believing in their own catalogue prose, were certain that I would fail in any case.

That first class meeting of the seminar was also my first time on campus. I had never met the tall, smiling man who came right up to me and offered his hand, his head characteristically cocked to one side. I had been told that he was a brilliant scholar, was new to Princeton and to the States. He behaved as if it were the university that had been most fortunate in having attracted me to its halls. I was desperate to do well and fearful at bottom that 'they' might be right. My youngest child was fourteen months old. But I liked Lawrence immediately and was relieved by his obvious willingness to treat me as he did his other students. And I was considerably cheered by his sense of humour, which contrasted markedly with my own tendency, at the time, to be overly serious in the hope of being taken seriously.

All the students shared the opinion that Lawrence was not only extraordinarily erudite and intellectually exciting but a marvellous seminar leader. By the second year we were all calling him by his first name to his face, and the 'Lorenzo' tag slipped away, unneeded. Good as the seminars were, we all looked forward, in our callous way, to the coffee-breaks, when the conversation was more spirited, wide-ranging and relaxed. At these times the students jockeyed for position and conversation. He made time for everyone and alerted them by his treatment of me to the fact that I was their colleague. Typically, when we moved to the adjoining room for the break, a dozen men circled Lawrence. The first time we went through this ritual I was uncertain about whether I should enter the charmed circle or not and timidly decided that since I was there on sufferance I would sit across the room. Lawrence signalled to them and me that I was not 'incidental' at all by sitting down next to me so that the group formed around the two of us. In the years before the women's movement had been heard of at Princeton, or elsewhere for that matter, his gesture was not only one of politeness and consideration, but one that signified precisely that kind of inclusion of women that subsequently was to become central to feminist ideas of equality.

Concern with the position of women was not a high priority at the university. One of our seminars met in the engineering building and in those days there were plaques on the walls in the entrance hall which cautioned that 'no women were allowed in this building after 10 p.m.'. I was reliably informed afterward that this was an attempt to keep the male undergraduates from enjoying illicit female companionship of an evening. No one at the time thought that this was in any way inappropriate, and I could not repress the feeling that it might equally well have read 'before 10 p.m.' and evoked no comment. Lawrence was way ahead of his time in his sensitivity to these issues.

Lawrence Stone's directness is legendary, but his kindness and thoughtfulness, not as apt to be the stuff of good stories, is perhaps less talked about than it should be. Those who know him only by his work and from public appearances frequently express curiosity about what he is 'really like', especially as a thesis director. The answer is that his help, concern and generosity to his doctoral students are well known among them. Of course, he does belong to what one journalist writing about him recently called the 'slash and burn' style of intellectual engagement. I have two comments on that. One is that while it is true that there were occasions after he had gone over one of my essays when I was certain that I would be able to exit without opening the office door and simply scuttle out under the crack when it came time to leave, I soon learned that he did not reserve this treatment solely for powerless graduate students. When it came to intellectual matters the great and mighty were treated the same way. Secondly, I learned a great deal from those office meetings not only about how to do history and judge historical work, but how to separate my ego from the work, a useful and necessary skill in this profession.

Furthermore, when one became his student one was also the recipient of his endless willingness to exchange and examine one's ideas. Since I was married to a farmer and we lived outside of Princeton, I did not have many opportunities to share in the casual intellectual exchange of the university community. But early on, Lawrence encouraged me to call him on the phone, at home or in the office, if I had a question or if I wanted to discuss some idea. Once when I was doing some research I came across a particularly revealing letter and wanted to tell him about it. I telephoned, and without any preliminaries except 'Hello Lawrence, it's me, just listen to this,' I read the letter out loud and told him what I made of it. He responded with similar interest and enthusiasm. As a non-resident, those phone calls were my lifeline to the intellectual ferment of the university and it was a measure of his unusual accessibility that this kind of interaction should have become natural to his students.

For his part, Lawrence never seemed hurried or too busy. I marvelled at that even then. It seems even more amazing now that I know the range of demands that he must have had in the mid- to late 1960s, publishing his magisterial studies of the aristocracy, taking over the chair of the department, creating the Davis Center, and building a national reputation in the United States.

He and his wife Jeanne were and are extraordinarily generous and hospitable people. We graduate students and our spouses are invited frequently. We were welcomed to their home in England as well. Another married student went over to do some research one summer with his wife and small child. The Stones had invited them to stay for a few days and they arrived with a croupy and sick baby. I remember that upon their return, they told me how wonderfully helpful the Stones had been and how graciously they had been treated, sick baby and all.

When I began my thesis I went to England to work in the muniment room of the family whose history I was researching. When I returned I met with Lawrence and he greeted me with that glorious invitation to first-time-abroad travellers: 'Tell me everything you saw and did.' I proceeded to do just that for the better part of two hours, with the kind of enthusiasm and enjoyment that subsequent trips, however satisfying, cannot evoke. What a generous gift of time and caring he gave me that day.

Some colleagues have told me that their thesis directors never saw their work until it was in the final stages; by contrast, Lawrence helped each of us at every stage of the work. Sometimes he would invite me to show him the written work, but he would also encourage me to meet and simply talk over my ideas. Occasionally I could not arrange for a babysitter. I would bring my pre-school child to the office with some toys and he would play on the floor while Lawrence went over my chapter with me. I recall the bemused and even hostile stares I occasionally received from others when I walked down the austere halls of McCosh with a three-year-old in tow. But Lawrence always took it all in his stride, and both my children, now grown, still have warm memories of their visits to the campus and to the Stones' home.

In the late 1960s the Princeton history department began to build the impressive reputation it enjoys today. It was an exciting and unique time to be a graduate student there. Lawrence legitimized interdisciplinary approaches, introduced us to the ideas of *les annalistes*, made us alive to various models of causation and the process of breaking them down with merciless critiques – it was a rich, demanding and exhilarating education. He taught us to do social history and to move beyond narrative chronology to analysis, and also to find in these endeavours our connection to historical development and its meaning for our lives. The late 1960s was also a time of challenge to the university and to its traditions in other ways. Lawrence enjoyed the political debates and knew many of the student activists; he admired their idealism and was saddened by the gradual allegiance of some of them to the immovably doctrinaire. But he was always certain of their right to challenge and debate and was a vigorous defender of the legitimacy of the need to air all points of view.

By the summer of 1970 both the new left and the feminist movement had made their marks on the university and I was half-way through the final draft of my dissertation. At this point a personal crisis occurred, when my husband became suddenly and critically ill. I called Lawrence in England to tell him that my thesis would be delayed and why. He told me not to worry about it at all, he would be back in the States in a month, to call him collect if he could do anything at all, and did I need any money to tide me over? When he returned I had no new work to show him, but my husband was at home recuperating slowly. Lawrence called and invited me to come to Princeton for lunch and conversation. It was so important to be able to reach out again and resume some part of an ordinary life. Lawrence had sensed this and his invitation was most welcome and perfectly timed. For the first time since my husband's illness I talked about the future; I began to feel that we had a future. I resumed work on my thesis.

Nowadays, when people ask what kind of thesis director was Stone anyway, I tell them that he was quite out of the ordinary in every way and a wonderful model for all his students. But those of us who were his students in the 1960s knew from the beginning that he was *Il Magnifico*.

The eminence rouge?

JOHN M. MURRIN

I first met Lawrence Stone in the spring of 1964. J. H. (Jack) Hexter invited him to give a lecture at Washington University in St Louis where I was a new assistant professor. As a graduate student I had read several of Stone's essays and particularly admired one of his earliest and most controversial efforts, 'The Anatomy of the Elizabethan Aristocracy' (1948), for which he had absorbed a great deal of acrimonious criticism from his former tutor, H. R. Trevor-Roper, from Hexter, and others.[1] Hexter's famous *Encounter* piece, 'Storm over the Gentry', had tried to leave Stone's argument in ruins, but Hexter's attack had been a model of decorum compared with some of the exchanges that followed in later issues of that journal. When Stone tried to distinguish carefully between those points on which he and his mentor, R. H. Tawney, agreed and disagreed, J. P. Cooper likened his tactics to 'those of some sort of academic boa-constrictor which surrounds its victim and patron with tangled coils of imitative flattery and settles down to a life-long feast. When after a few years the meal proves hopelessly indigestible, it bravely announces that it prefers independence and will fend for itself, though still hoping that a few fragments may prove nutritious.'[2]

Few academics have received comparable abuse. To me it seemed from a distance that some of Stone's English colleagues

---

[1] Lawrence Stone, 'The Anatomy of the Elizabethan Aristocracy', *Economic History Review*, 18 (1948), pp. 1–53.

[2] J. H. Hexter, 'Storm over the Gentry', *Encounter*, 10, No. 5 (May 1958), pp. 22–34. A fuller version is in Hexter, *Reappraisals in History: New Views on History and Society in Early Modern Europe* (Evanston, 1961), pp. 117–62, which also contains a full bibliography of the Stone and Trevor-Roper exchanges. Stone's reply to Hexter is in *Encounter*, 11, No. 1 (July 1958), pp. 73–4; and Cooper's is in *Encounter*, 11, No. 3 (September 1958), pp. 73–4.

were trying to drive him completely out of the profession. I also knew that Stone had recently moved from Wadham College, Oxford, to Princeton. As I strolled towards the lounge where the lecture would be held, I could not help wondering what sort of man I was about to meet. Had he fled in defeat across the Atlantic to a genteel retreat at Princeton, leaving Trevor-Roper in full command of the sixteenth and seventeenth centuries at Oxford? Hexter's invitation was undoubtedly some sort of peace-offering to one of the many victims of his scalding wit. Was it also an act of expiation toward a destroyed scholar? Did Stone still have something fresh to say, and even if he did, would he still dare make the arresting generalizations I had admired for years?

My musings were extremely naive. Only somebody who did not know the man at all could envision him in full retreat. As Hexter explained when he introduced Stone, the manuscript of *The Crisis of the Aristocracy, 1558–1641* had recently gone to Oxford University Press and would appear in 1965. Stone's lecture, one of the most fascinating performances I had ever witnessed, compressed his chapter on 'Power'. He revealed no scars. He betrayed no hint of defeat. He thoroughly enjoyed the vigorous discussion that his talk provoked. I was the youngest faculty member in the room and had not even completed my Yale dissertation. Yet when I asked a question and made an observation that I hoped was deeply penetrating, Stone *took notes*. The man, we all agreed, possessed a natural eloquence matched by few others. Even more telling, he knew how to listen. And he had learned from his own mistakes.

The Princeton history department fully realized what it was doing when it approached Stone, who had met most of its members in 1960–1 when he had been a visiting fellow at the Institute for Advanced Study a short distance from the university. The department's needs seemed particularly acute when the chairman, Jerome Blum, first wrote to him about an appointment on 18 January 1963. Elmer Beller, who taught early modern European history, was about to retire, and E. Harris Harbison, already suffering from the illness that would kill him a year later, could teach only half-time. Early in these brief negotiations Robert R. Palmer announced his resignation to become dean of the faculty at Washington University. Palmer's decision left the Dodge chair of history vacant. Because 'Englishmen have a fondness for titles', one of the younger full professors brightly suggested, the 'special distinction' of this chair 'might help persuade Stone to accept our offer', which Stone received in mid-February. He had already made it clear that the salary had to be high enough to permit annual research trips to England, and now he asked to visit the campus from 1 to 5 March. Blum agreed and also sent him instructions on how to take a bus from the Port Authority in New York City to Cox's on Nassau Street in Princeton. Stone came to satisfactory terms during his brief stay, at a cost to the university's travel budget of $423.34. He insisted that the library's holdings in English history needed drastic and rapid improvement, and he requested a house with at least five bedrooms.[3]

The second demand worried Blum more than the first. 'It is really extremely important to us that he get a house of the right size', Jerry explained to the dean of the faculty. 'We *need* this man, and I fear that if he does not get a suitable house we may not be able to hold him here. He has no reason yet to be loyal to Princeton', Blum explained, 'and I am certain that when some of our competitors learn that he is here they will begin to make him offers. If he is unhappy here, he will accept one of the bids. And that will mean that one of your "bread and butter" departments (to quote you) will suffer another body blow.'[4] Nassau Hall responded with atypical swiftness, and within a week the Stones were assigned a large house on Mercer Street next door to Arthur Link.

Thus at age forty-three, Lawrence Stone finally left Oxford. He and Jeanne, with their fourteen-year-old daughter Elizabeth and their four-year-old son Robert, moved to America in the summer of 1963, although the family retained its home in Oxford, to which Lawrence and Jeanne still return every June as they continue their joint research. Although Stone had assured Blum that 'I am a dyed-in-the-wool European, indeed an Englishman, rooted in this crumbling old island, and with the usual love-hate feelings about America which Europeans tend to have', he soon became a citizen

[3] Jerome Blum to Lawrence Stone, 18 January 1963; Stone to Blum, 26 January 1963; Blum to President Robert F. Goheen, 11 February 1963; Stone to Blum, 17 February 1963; Blum to Stone, 20 February 1963; Blum to J. Douglas Brown, 5 March 1963; Blum to William S. Dix, 6 March 1963; Stone to Blum, 6 March 1963; Blum to Brown, 11 March 1963; Blum to Stone, 11 March 1963, all in Lawrence Stone personnel file, Department of History, Princeton University.
[4] Blum to Brown, 5 March 1963, Lawrence Stone personnel file, Department of History, Princeton University.

of the United States.[5] Much of Lawrence's affection for his adopted country stems from his experiences during World War II. His education had omitted many elementary episodes in American history. Once in 1944 he and Jeanne happened to be entertaining an American bomber pilot who made some remark about the British burning of Washington in 1814, an incident that Jeanne had absorbed from history lessons in the French schools she had attended. Rather startled, Lawrence admitted to complete ignorance on this subject. 'It was part of the War of 1812,' Jeanne explained.

'The War of 1812?' replied Lawrence. 'What did Britain and America have to fight about in 1812?'

When Lawrence was reassigned to the Pacific, his commanding officer explained the decision and then inquired, 'Stone, the British Empire has a powerful and dangerous enemy in the Pacific. Can you tell me who it is?'

'Yes sir! The Japanese Empire, sir,' responded Lawrence.

'Stone, you are wrong. The major enemy of the British Empire in the Pacific is the United States Navy. They intend to take our colonies away from us. Go out there and make sure they don't.'

'Yes sir!' snapped Lawrence as he did an about face and marched smartly from the room, wondering whether he would be spending the next several months sabotaging American aircraft carriers. Instead he acquired a deep admiration for the American navy which was, he insists, the most efficient institution he had ever encountered. 'I could not believe it,' he once explained. 'The Americans would command 400 ships to appear off some abscure island at 4 a.m. on the same morning and to open fire an hour later.' He paused. 'And they were all there!' he added.

Blum was absolutely correct about the danger of competing offers. After *The Crisis of the Aristocracy* appeared in 1965, Nottingham, Pittsburgh, Johns Hopkins, the University of California at Los Angeles, Yale (in 1969 and again in 1976), Edinburgh, and the Massachusetts Institute of Technology all approached him, but he chose to stay at Princeton, where he and Jeanne had rapidly

---

[5] Stone to Blum, 17 February 1963, Lawrence Stone personnel file, Department of History, Princeton University.

made numerous friends.[6] Though as busy as any university couple, they entertain more frequently than anyone else in the history department. Jeanne sets an elegant table, and the conversation is the best around.

Blum had asked Stone to prepare a general undergraduate course on early modern Europe from 1558 to 1715, and Stone declared that he would concentrate on 'the development of, and crisis in the history of, the modern state; growth, then stagnation, in population, trade, and industrial output; the scientific revolution, such as it was; the rise of Calvinism, and the limited spread in England and the Netherlands of notions of liberty and representative government; the changes in the nature and scale of war, and its attendant consequences'. But because moving his household across the Atlantic would absorb all of his available time over the summer, Stone asked that for his first year only he be permitted to lecture on 'England 1460–1660: Reformation and Revolution', a variation of what he already taught at Oxford.[7]

The department never got the course that Lawrence boldly outlined for Blum. With the title altered to 'The First Road to Modernization: England, 1470–1690' (the dates have varied) and the lectures and readings frequently revised, Lawrence has taught the English history course ever since. Theodore K. Rabb and Natalie Z. Davis have filled the university's needs in early modern European history. Stone also offers a graduate seminar nearly every semester. Many students who have taken his seminars have since established formidable reputations of their own.

His growing eminence earned him added responsibilities within the Princeton community. In 1971–2 he served on the faculty advisory committee that helped to choose William G. Bowen as president of the university, and in 1986–7 he played a similar role in the selection of Harold Shapiro to succeed Bowen. He has always been a powerful voice in departmental appointments but by no means omnipotent. His opposition to a candidate can be fatal, but his advocacy of someone is not sufficient in itself to over-ride resistance from colleagues. As chairman of the history department from 1967–70 (he sacrificed a semester's leave to accept that responsibility), Lawrence helped to lure Carl Schorske to Prince-

---

[6] Correspondence about these offers is in Lawrence Stone personnel file, Department of History, Princeton University *passim*.

[7] Stone to Blum, 12 March 1963, Lawrence Stone personnel file, Department of History, Princeton University.

ton from Berkeley and to attract Robert Darnton as an assistant professor. He also presided over a dramatic democratization of departmental procedures. Not only did the university go co-educational during this period, but both junior faculty and students acquired the right to be consulted within the department about curriculum and most personnel decisions. This process culminated in a written constitution for the department, largely drafted by Stone and implemented in 1971. It standardized these procedures and redefined roles so that the faculty became only the 'executive committee' of a department that incorporated both undergraduate and graduate students as integral members. Junior faculty won the right to participate in the hiring of new assistant professors, a decision that still disturbs Nassau Hall.

The most significant professional accomplishment of Stone's chairmanship was, however, the creation of the Shelby Cullom Davis Center for Historical Studies, of which he has been director since 1 July 1968. Resources for the centre came from the exceptionally generous donation of over $5 million to the history department by Mr Davis in 1964. When Stone became chairman, he discovered that because the department had devised no explicit and specific use for this gift, the university was merely expending it to replace the general funds which had supported the department before 1964. In effect the Davis largesse was benefiting other programmes, not history. By 1968, standard accounting procedures had already absorbed about half of it. Stone favoured the creation of some kind of centre for the study of history that would not duplicate what the department or other research institutes were already doing. After pondering advice from such sources as the Institute for Advanced Study in Princeton and Harvard's Charles Warren Center for Studies in American History, Stone chose a format that has proved to be distinctive.

A Davis Center committee, consisting of faculty members from quite different historical fields, selects a topic for study over a period of several years – initially four, now two. The committee tries to identify themes that are eliciting the most imaginative scholarship in the entire discipline of history. Subjects have included the history of education, popular culture, history of the family, the professions, political power and ideology, war and society, charity and welfare, and currently (1986–8) the transmission of culture. Advertisements describing the theme for the coming year appear in major journals and urge interested scholars to apply for fellowships. Competition is open to specialists in all geographical regions and chronological periods of history and also to scholars in related disciplines. In a typical semester four or five fellows will be in residence who under normal circumstances would not have the opportunity to study together. Each must present a paper to the weekly seminar and participate in the other sessions. Any member of the history department may also give a paper. The remaining slots go to outsiders who are asked to share their research with the regular participants. Sometimes the weekly seminars are supplemented by a colloquium of one or two days that looks intensively at a more specialized aspect of the general theme. Two years of exposure to current scholarship on a given topic usually provide a thorough introduction to the subject. Stone then asks a member of the department, sometimes an assistant professor, to put together the best essays, or those that most successfully address related themes, and publish them after the authors have had the opportunity to revise their contributions. The list of Davis volumes is impressive and still growing.[8]

The heart of the Davis Center is its Friday morning seminar. Open to everyone with an interest in the subject matter, it usually draws two or three dozen participants to a session, all of whom are expected to have read in advance the paper under discussion. University faculty, graduate students and sometimes even undergraduates gather with the Davis fellows and other participants from the New York–Philadelphia corridor and occasionally more distant locales. Stone introduces the author of the paper and permits him or her to spend five or ten minutes placing the essay in whatever broader context he or she chooses. Most authors explain how their current effort will fit into a larger book. Stone then presents his critique of the paper, although he sometimes assigns this function to another participant. After a brief response from the writer, other

---

[8] Lawrence Stone, ed., *The University in Society*, 2 vols (Princeton, 1974); James Obelkevich, *Religion and the People, 800–1700* (Chapel Hill, 1979); Gerald L. Geison, ed., *Professions and Professional Ideologies in America* (Chapel Hill, 1983); Gerald L. Geison, ed., *Professions and the French State, 1700–1900* (Philadelphia, 1984); Sean Wilentz, ed., *Rites of Power: Symbolism, Ritual, and Politics since the Middle Ages* (Philadelphia, 1985); John M. Murrin, ed., *Violence and Voluntarism: War and Society in America from the Aztecs to the Civil War* (Philadelphia, forthcoming); Peter Brown, ed., *The Uses of Charity: The Poor on Relief in the Nineteenth-Century Metropolis* (Philadelphia, forthcoming).

people join in. But Stone insists on a *disciplined* discussion. He cuts off individuals whose remarks are irrelevant and asks others, whose observations or questions are pertinent but not quite on target at that moment, to wait fifteen or twenty minutes until the group can give undivided attention to their concern. In this way he guides the analysis through a set of specific issues. Somewhere around noon, he calls a halt and gives his own synopsis of what has happened. His mastery of the art of impromptu summation continues to amaze even those who have been attending for ten or fifteen years. Quite often the discussion continues informally but at a vigorous pace over lunch at Prospect, the Princeton faculty club.

The result is nearly always an intense intellectual engagement with a problem that truly matters. For the author this experience can range from exhilaration to despair. High points in the seminar include the paper that made the central argument for Carlo Ginzburg's *The Cheese and the Worms*, Inga Clendinnen's 'The Cost of Courage in Aztec Society' and E. P. Thompson's acute and witty challenge to both Stone and Jack Hexter, who happened to be a fellow at the Institute for Advanced Study that year. Toward lunchtime in the Thompson session, Lawrence tried to deliver a death blow. Quoting a string of about a dozen scurrilous terms that Thompson had inflicted upon Sir Robert Walpole and the Whig oligarchy, Stone asked, 'Is this history? Is this kind of language even helpful, much less objective?' Thompson had a reply waiting. 'Why Lawrence, a new deity has recently been erected in the land, and it is called "political stability" ', he smiled disarmingly. 'When someone creates new gods, the only proper response is – BLASPHEMY!'[9]

On the other hand, some writers have discovered that their own approach, whatever it happens to be, is hopeless. Their only rational choice is as to the method by which they can commit

---

[9] Carlo Ginzburg, 'Cheese and Worms: The Cosmos of a Sixteenth-Century Miller', in Obelkevich, ed., *Religion and the People, 800–1700*, pp. 87–167, which was later expanded into *The Cheese and the Worms: The Cosmos of a Sixteenth-Century Miller*, translated by John and Anne Tedeschi (Baltimore, 1980); Inga Clendinnen, 'The Cost of Courage in Aztec Society', *Past and Present*, 107 (May 1985), pp. 44–89. E. P. Thompson's essay never appeared in print in the form in which he presented it to the Davis Center, but most of his arguments are in his 'Eighteenth-Century English Society: Class Struggle without Class?' *Social History*, 3 (1978), pp. 133–65.

intellectual suicide. Lawrence asked one author, the director of an extremely expensive social history project that had produced few publishable results, whether the man did not feel like the last dinosaur in the coming academic ice age. 'Aren't you', he inquired, 'devouring all of the remaining provender that might otherwise sustain dozens of smaller but better conceived studies?' Most authors, of course, have fallen between these extremes. In a typical week they learn how to strengthen their argument, and they are usually grateful for the opportunity. Regular participants, whether or not they give a paper, acquire an extraordinary education after several years' exposure to the seminar.

Despite heart attacks in September 1973 and early 1975, Stone's research and publications have continued without pause. He even used his period of enforced rest in Princeton Hospital during the fall of 1973 to read more than a hundred diaries, journals and memoirs that provided much of the personal evidence for his *The Family, Sex and Marriage in England, 1500–1800* (New York, 1977). As his national and international stature grew, he acquired a regular platform in *The New York Review of Books* and other periodicals, and the Davis Center drew increasing attention in intellectual circles. In England, Keith Thomas called Stone 'the leading figure' in one of the world's 'most thrusting and innovative . . . history departments', and he described the Davis Center as 'a celebrated arena for historical pugilism, where visiting historians defend their papers against aggressive attack over several long and punishing hours'.[10] In America, the Center even began to win a reputation among some people for what it emphatically did *not* do. Norman Cantor, a medievalist at New York University, traced the resurgence of Marxism in historical studies in the United States to Stone and the Davis Center. Although Davis seminars have indeed been open to Marxists, as well as liberals and conservatives and the politically uncommitted, this claim irritated Lawrence, who is widely known throughout the profession for his liberal, anti-Marxist views. Rather than reply in person, he encouraged such conservative friends as Hexter and Gertrude Himmelfarb to explain to the readers of the conservative journal in which the controversy occurred that Cantor ought not to pontificate until he

---

[10] Keith Thomas, review of Lawrence Stone, *The Past and the Present* (London, 1981), in *The Times Literary Supplement*, 30 April 1982, p. 479.

discovers the difference between a radical and a liberal, a lesson that the man seems determined not to master.[11]

From 1988 through 1990 the Davis Seminar will turn to the subject of 'power and the responses to power', with emphasis upon political and cultural imperialism and the reactions, both imitative and hostile, that it has generated among affected populations in different times and places. As with previous Davis topics, the challenge will be huge, and Stone plans to be there, in charge as always. Jeanne, now that diminished family responsibilities have given her more time, has increasingly become Lawrence's colleague in research and his co-author.[12] She has even led him gently into the era of computers and word-processors, a major step for a man who never mastered the typewriter. No doubt they will continue to hold their delightful dinner-parties for guest participants in the seminar.

Lawrence will turn seventy in December 1989, and he plans to retire the following June. But he has no intention of giving up research and writing. Through regular swimming, careful diet and adequate rest, he seems healthier now than a decade ago. His energy level remains awesome. He and Jeanne are now well advanced on a study of divorce in early modern England. Their friends and colleagues wish them many more years of productive scholarship together. Even in retirement, Lawrence will continue to be a dynamic presence within the history department and the university, and a creative force within the intellectual community of the Atlantic world.

11 Norman Cantor, 'The Real Crisis in the Humanities Today', *The New Criterion* (June 1985), pp. 1–11; for the replies, see *ibid.*, March 1986, pp. 84–8. More recently Cantor has used the occasion of an obituary tribute to Joseph R. Strayer to attack Stone through his mentor, R. H. Tawney, the Christian socialist whom Cantor describes as a 'British Marxist and advocate of the welfare state'. Cantor also claims that Natalie Z. Davis gets her inspiration from 'Mikhail Bakhtin, the Soviet theoretician of the Stalinist era' (*Princeton Alumni Weekly*, 30 September 1987, p. 4). For several replies, see *ibid.*, October 28, 1987, pp. 1–2; *ibid.*, November 11, 1987, pp. 6–7.

12 See Lawrence Stone and Jeanne C. Fawtier Stone, *An Open Elite? England, 1540–1880* (Oxford, 1984).

I

The crown, the aristocracy and the gentry

1. *Lineage and kin in the sixteenth-century aristocracy: some comparative evidence on England and Germany*

JUDITH J. HURWICH

Lawrence Stone has played a key role in the 'new' history of the family which combines the techniques of historical demography developed by Louis Henry and by the Cambridge Group with the study of attitudes or *mentalités* pioneered by Philippe Ariès. Stone's *The Family, Sex and Marriage in England 1500–1800* (London and New York, 1977) was the first important synthesis of the 'new' family history to appear in English, and it has had a strong influence on the work of English-speaking historians of the family, whether their research deals with England, America or continental Europe.[1] He describes the major change in the English family between 1500 and 1800 as 'the growth of affective individualism': an increasing emphasis on the nuclear family as a focus of the individual's loyalty and an increasing emphasis within the nuclear family on personal autonomy and affectionate relationships. The baseline from which he measures this change is the traditional family of the late Middle Ages and sixteenth century, which he calls the 'Open Lineage Family'.[2] He tends to emphasize the negative aspects of this 'traditional' family form in order to dramatize the growth of individualism and affection in the late seventeenth and eighteenth centuries.

Stone's writings have been influential in reinforcing the view that the family in the period between 1450 and 1650 was 'patriarchal in

---

[1] Lawrence Stone, *The Family, Sex and Marriage in England, 1500–1800* (New York, 1977). On Stone's influence on the history of the family in America, see Michael Gordon, ed., *The American Family in Social-Historical Perspective*, third edition (New York, 1983), pp. 9–10. Marshall's research on the family in the Netherlands also owes its initial impetus to Stone, although she disagrees with many of his conclusions: Sherrin Marshall, *The Dutch Gentry 1500–1650: Family, Faith and Fortune* (New York, 1987), pp. xvii, 168.

[2] Stone, *The Family . . . in England*, pp. 6–7.

authority, lacking in affective relationships between husband and wife and between parent and child, and that the lineage [was] more important than either the individual or the nuclear family'.[3] However, his thesis has been sharply criticized on the grounds that it both underestimates the amount of affection within the nuclear family and overestimates the importance of ties to extended kin. Most of the criticism has focused on the question of affection within the nuclear family; historians who specialize in the late Middle Ages and sixteenth century have argued that it is misleading to judge the sources from this period by the standards of the more literate and demonstrative eighteenth century.[4] The question of whether the individual's loyalties were focused primarily on the nuclear family or on the extended kin group has attracted less attention. However, this issue has been raised by historians using the techniques of social anthropology to study village communities and kin inter-action. Alan Macfarlane noted that the diary of the seventeenth-century clergyman Ralph Josselin made relatively few references to extended kin, and Macfarlane made the primacy of ties to the nuclear family one of the central arguments in his *Origins of English Individualism* (1979). The question has been further exam-ined in two of the most important recent general studies of the family in early modern England: Keith Wrightson's *English Society 1580–1680* (New Brunswick, N.J., 1982) and Ralph Houlbrooke's *The English Family 1450–1700* (London, 1984).[5] Houlbrooke's book, the first comprehensive synthesis of research on the early modern English family to appear since Stone's, may be considered a revisionist manifesto. Rejecting Stone's view of evolution through a series of family types, Houlbrooke argues that continuity rather than change has been characteristic of the English family:

[3] Marshall, *The Dutch Gentry*, p. xvii.

[4] Ralph Houlbrooke sums up these arguments in *The English Family 1450–1700* (London, 1984), p. 15; in chapters 4–8 he cites many of the specialized studies on this period which take issue with Stone's thesis. See also the critique of Stone's views on parent–child relationships in Linda Pollock, *Forgotten Children: Parent–Child Relationships from 1500 to 1900* (Cambridge, 1983), chapter 2. Historians of the family in Germany and the Netherlands have also criticized Stone's thesis and stressed the presence of affection within the nuclear family: Steven Ozment, *When Fathers Ruled: Family Life in Reformation Europe* (Cambridge, Mass., 1983), pp. 59–61, 116–17, 154; Marshall, *The Dutch Gentry*, pp. 8–9, 14–19, 168.

[5] Alan Macfarlane, *The Family Life of Ralph Josselin, A Seventeenth-Century Clergyman: An Essay in Historical Anthropology* (Cambridge, 1970); *The Origins of English Individualism: The Family, Property and Social Transition* (New York,

the elementary or nuclear family typically occupied a central place in the life and aspirations of the individual between 1450 and 1700 as it still does today ... the momentous developments of this period, although certainly affecting family life, brought no fundamental changes in family forms, functions, or ideals.[6]

More recently, David Cressy has argued for a less drastic interpretation of the evidence of village studies; he accepts Macfarlane's basic classification of the English kinship system but believes the extended kin network is much deeper and richer than Macfarlane admits.[7]

The issue of ties to kin beyond the nuclear family is closely related to the question of the basic structure of the English kinship system: is it patrilineal (tracing descent through the male line), as Stone implies, or bilateral (tracing descent through both male and female lines), as the revisionists maintain? This article will first examine Stone's views of family structure and extended kin ties in the 'Open Lineage Family' and the revisionists' critique of these views. It will show that the apparent conflict between the two points of view can best be resolved by adopting a comparative perspective: the kinship structure of the English landed elite, like that of continental aristocracies, contained a mixture of patrilineal and bilateral elements. Secondly, the article will draw on research on the sixteenth-century German aristocratic family as depicted in the *Zimmerische Chronik* (*Chronicle of the Counts of Zimmern*) to analyse the obligations of extended kin and the sense of identification with the lineage in a kinship system in which the mixture of patrilineal and bilateral elements is more obvious than it is in England.[8] (For a discussion of the chronicle and the Zimmern family, see Appendix at end of chapter.)

1979). Keith Wrightson, *English Society 1580–1680* (New Brunswick, N.J., 1982). For Houlbrooke see note 4 above.

[6] Houlbrooke, *The English Family*, pp. 14–15.

[7] David Cressy, 'Kinship and Kin Interaction in Early Modern England', *Past and Present*, 113 (1986), pp. 38–69.

[8] I have relied primarily on the most recent edition: *Die Chronik der Grafen von Zimmer*, ed. Hansmartin Decker-Hauff, 3 vols (Sigmaringen, 1964–72), hereafter cited as *ZC* (Decker-Hauff). For the concluding portion of the chronicle, which has not yet appeared in the Decker-Hauff edition, I have used the older Barack edition: *Zimmerische Chronik*, ed. Karl Barack, 4 vols (Tübingen, 1869), vol. 4; hereafter cited as *ZC* (Barack). For further references on the chronicle see note 57 below.

The field of the history of the family is less developed in Germany than in England or France, and it is therefore difficult to say how far the Zimmern may be

I

According to Stone, the 'Open Lineage Family' of the late Middle Ages and sixteenth century persisted until the mid-seventeenth century among the aristocracy and had two major characteristics: first, the nuclear family must compete with extended kin or with neighbours for the loyalty and affection of its members; and second, the members of the nuclear family are subordinated to the will of the patriarchal head and are not closely bonded to one another by emotional ties.[9] Stone sees ties to extended kin as more important among landed elites and ties to neighbours as more important among the lower classes, but in neither case does he believe that the nuclear family of parents and children was the primary focus of the individual's loyalty and affection. Since his own research is on the aristocracy, he deals chiefly with the aristocratic family and with ties to extended kin.

In his *Crisis of the Aristocracy* (Oxford, 1965), Stone describes the medieval and modern English family as 'patrilinear' (= 'patrilineal', tracing descent through the male line), in that 'it was the male line whose ancestry was traced so diligently by the genealogists and the heralds, and in almost all cases via the male line that titles were inherited'. Although he does not use the term 'patrilinear' in *The Family . . . In England*, he emphasizes the role of the lineage, the group which traces its descent in the male line from a

considered representative of the sixteenth-century German nobility. The best overview of recent research on the history of the family in Germany is Michael Mitterauer and Reinhard Sieder, *Vom Patriarchat zur Partnerschaft: Zum Struckturwandel der Familie* (Munich, 1977). The English translation updates the bibliography to 1979; *The European Family: Patriarchy to Partnership from the Middle Ages to the Present*, tr. Karla Oosterven and Manfred Hörzinger (Chicago, 1982). The only demographic study of the nobility which includes the fifteenth and sixteenth centuries is Michael Mitterauer's study of Lower Austria: 'Zur Frage des Heiratsverhaltens im österreichischen Adel', in Heinrich Fichtenau and Erich Zollner, eds. *Beiträge zur neueren Geschichte Österreichs* (Vienna, Cologne and Graz, 1974), pp. 176–94. Gregory Pedlow's study of Hessian knights deals with a later period but provides a useful analysis of partible inheritance strategies among the nobility: 'Marriage, Family Size and Inheritance among Hessian Nobles, 1650–1900', *Journal of Family History*, 7 (1982), pp. 333–52. David Sabean has studied inheritance and kinship practices and popular culture among the peasantry of southwestern Germany, the region depicted in the *Zimmerische Chronik*: 'Aspects of Kinship and Property Behavior in Rural Western Europe before 1800', in Jack Goody *et al.*, *Family and Inheritance* (Cambridge, 1976), pp. 96–111; and *Power in the Blood: Popular Culture and Village Discourse in Early Modern Germany* (Cambridge, 1984).

[9] Stone, *The Family . . . in England*, pp. 6–7.

common ancestor and bears a patrilineally-inherited surname. Stone defines 'lineage' as 'relatives by blood or marriage, dead, living, and yet to be born, who collectively form a "house" identified by a common surname'. Since he defines 'kin' as 'those members of the *lineage* (emphasis added) who are currently alive', he implies that ties to extended kin are limited to members of the lineage. By using such terms as 'clan heads' and 'family councils', Stone implies that the lineages or 'houses' of the English aristocracy were formally organized corporate descent groups like those found in non-Western patrilineal societies.[10]

Macfarlane and the revisionists, on the other hand, maintain that the English kinship system is fundamentally different from the patrilineal societies of Asia and Eastern Europe. On the basis of their community studies, they see the kinship system as a bilateral one (tracing descent through both male and female lines) in which the nuclear family is the focus of individual loyalty and affection, ties to extended kin are flexible and relatively weak, and there are no formally organized corporate descent groups. Macfarlane believes that English society is uniquely individualistic in its values, and he sees this individualism as a direct result of the bilateral kinship system. Whereas patrilineal societies are 'ancestor-oriented', with the individual placing himself in a line of descent from a particular ancestor, the English kinship system is 'ego-centered', with the individual tracing kin ties outward from himself.[11] Since every individual in a bilateral kinship system has a unique set of relatives traced through both the male and the female lines, extended kin groups in such systems lack persistence over time and cannot be formally organized like the lineages and clans of patrilineal societies. Macfarlane declares that the English kinship system is uniquely individualistic as far back as records permit us to trace it: 'Within the recorded period covered by our documents, it is not possible to find a time when an Englishman did not stand alone. Symbolized and shaped by his ego-centered kinship system, he stood alone in the center of his world.'[12]

Macfarlane, Wrightson and Houlbrooke interpret the absence of formally organized corporate descent groups in a bilateral society

[10] Stone, *The Crisis of the Aristocracy 1558–1641*, abridged edition (Oxford, 1967; original edition 1965), p. 271; *The Family . . . in England*, p. 29.

[11] Macfarlane, *The Origins of English Individualism*, pp. 144–7; Wrightson, *English Society*, p. 46.

[12] Macfarlane, *The Origins of English Individualism*, pp. 32–3.

to mean that extended kin beyond the nuclear family played a minor role in the life of the individual. They believe that only the parents and siblings of nuclear family members played a significant role (i.e. grandparents, uncles, in-laws). 'Assertions of the importance of wider kindred in late medieval England are based on long exploded myths', says Houlbrooke; 'they fly in the face of the facts that there were no clearly defined groups of kinsfolk or obligations to them'.[13] Wrightson and Houlbrooke do note that members of the landed elite recognized a larger number of distant kin than did members of lower social classes, and that they also maintained effective kin ties with more of their distant kin through visits and mutual aid.[14] However, the revisionists argue that even in the landed elite, loyalties outside the nuclear family could never take priority over an individual's self-interest and his desire to advance the interests of his direct descendants. 'Belonging to a well-established or famous family was often a matter of pride', says Houlbrooke, 'but the fact of family membership did not, as some romantic descriptions have suggested, bind kinsmen together in a loyalty to name and blood which transcended the interests of the individual and his nuclear family'. Indeed, Houlbrooke dismisses the concept of lineage loyalty (defined as a sentiment of 'special solidarity with dead ancestors and descendants yet unborn') as a mere rationalization for the selfish desire to expand one's holdings and to pass them on to one's direct descendants rather than to collateral relatives.[15]

If one looks only at the evidence from historians of the English family, it seems impossible to reconcile Stone's view of a patrilineal aristocracy dominated by loyalty to the lineage with the revisionists' view of a bilateral and individualistic kinship system. In order to resolve the paradox, one must adopt a comparative perspective, drawing on the findings of anthropologists and also placing the English landed elites in the context of the historical development of other western European aristocracies. The revisionists, feeling that earlier attempts to draw parallels between England and the societies of Asia and Eastern Europe had led to misinterpretations of the English kinship system, have rejected comparisons of England

---

[13] Houlbrooke, *The English Family*, pp. 14–15.
[14] Wrightson, *English Society*, pp. 47–8; Houlbrooke, *The English Family*, pp. 19, 40.
[15] Houlbrooke, *The English Family*, pp. 40–1.

with other societies.[16] This has led them to overstate the uniqueness of the English kinship system and to ignore elements in the aristocratic family which are inconsistent with a bilateral kinship system.

Both Stone and the revisionists imply that ties of affection and obligation to members of the extended kin exist only within the bounds of formally organized descent groups such as lineages or clans. Yet anthropologists studying societies which have such groups have long emphasized that ties of affection and obligation are *not* limited to members of the lineage or the clan, although in cases of conflict of loyalty one must support the member of one's own descent group.[17] To show that formally organized corporate descent groups did not exist in early modern England does not, in and of itself, prove that extended kin played no significant role in the life of the individual.

Extended kin do indeed play a significant role in many bilateral societies which lack formally organized descent groups. Bilateral extended kin groups (technically known as 'kindreds') have overlapping memberships, and it is more difficult for them to mobilize all their members for collective action than it is for patrilineal lineages or clans. Nevertheless, kindreds perform the same basic functions in bilateral societies that lineages and clans do in patrilineal societies: they define permissible marriage partners and establish the obligation to aid and defend kinsmen.[18]

As Andrejs Plakans points out in *Kinship in the Past* (1984), anthropologists studying kinship today are increasingly turning away from the view that kinship is a set of fixed obligations between persons who stand in a certain genealogical relationship to each other. Rather, they see kinship ties as part of an individual's broader social network, and analyse particular social transactions to see 'who does what with whom'. This 'network' approach is similar to that used by the revisionists in their community studies, which rely heavily on the evidence of wills and legal transactions.

---

[16] Macfarlane, *The Origins of English Individualism*, pp. 32–3; Wrightson, *English Society*, pp. 50–1.

[17] George Murdock, *Social Structure* (New York, 1962; first published 1949), p. 16; William J. Goode, *The Family*, second edition (Englewood Cliffs, N.J., 1982), p. 115; Jack Goody, *The Development of the Family and Marriage in Europe* (Cambridge, 1983), p. 225.

[18] On the role of kindreds in bilateral societies, see Murdock, *Social Structure*, pp. 44–62.

But as Plakans notes, it is very difficult when using the 'network' approach to identify collective kinship groups – especially since the historian, unlike the anthropologist, cannot supplement his observations of interactions with interviews of the participants.[19] David Cressy, who accepts Macfarlane's basic view of the English kinship system as 'egocentric and bilateral, contextual and informal', notes that the type of evidence used can lead to radically different assessments of the importance of extended kin: the quantitative evidence of wills shows few bequests outside the nuclear family, but qualitative evidence such as letters shows 'a vibrant kinship system'. Cressy concludes that in early modern England, even below the level of the landed elite,

> A dense and extended kindred was a store of wealth, like a reserve account to be drawn upon as needed. For most people, for most of the time, their dealings were limited to those closest to them, but the potential existed to bring even distant and latent kin into a close and effective relationship.[20]

Even if the basic structure of the English kinship system is bilateral, then, we must be cautious about asserting on the basis of negative evidence that extended kin played no significant role. We must be even more cautious about asserting that the English kinship system created a uniquely individualistic set of values. Many of the 'individualistic' features of the English kinship system, including its kinship terminology and the predominance of nuclear family households, are shared with many other bilateral societies. Bilateral kinship itself is not unique to England but is part of the Germanic heritage of northern and western Europe; many specific features cited by the revisionists, such as medieval changes in kinship terminology, have parallels in other western European societies or were actually introduced from other parts of western Europe.[21] Only a comparison of England with related societies can demonstrate which features are unique to England and should be attributed to a specifically English character or to a specifically English historical development.

19 Andrejs Plakans, *Kinship in the Past: An Anthropology of European Family Life 1500–1900* (Oxford, 1984), pp. 251, 259.
20 Cressy, 'Kinship and Kin Interaction in Early Modern England', pp. 59, 69.
21 For a critique of Macfarlane's thesis of the uniqueness of the English kinship system, see Jack Goody, *The Development of the Family and Marriage in Europe*, pp. 231–2, 262–78. Goody discusses changes in kinship terminology in detail in Appendix 1; *cf.* Murdock, *Social Structure*, pp. 141–2.

Recent research on Germanic kinship systems and on the rise of continental aristocracies is particularly relevant to resolving the conflict between Stone's patrilineal aristocracy and the revisionists' bilateral kinship system. It is now generally believed that the areas of western Europe settled by the Germanic tribes adopted a bilateral kinship system, and that formally organized descent groups survived only on the Celtic fringe (e.g. Scottish and Irish clans). The 'houses' or 'lineages' of the medieval nobility differed in many respects from the patrilineal descent groups in non-Western societies which anthropologists term 'lineages'.[22]

According to David Herlihy, the kinship system of medieval Europe combined two distinct elements: a bilateral system which was common to all early Germanic societies (including Anglo-Saxon England), and a patrilineal system which was superimposed upon it by the landed elite in the high Middle Ages in order to control access to office and to preserve landed property. This process of 'lineal consolidation' in the nobility has been described in detail for France by Georges Duby and for Germany by Karl Schmid.[23] As Herlihy points out, the older Germanic system favoured the 'kin' (the living relatives) at the expense of future generations and emphasized the equality of all members of the sibling group. It practised partible inheritance, dividing property equally among all siblings; daughters shared equally with sons in the inheritance. The new system practised by the nobility, on the other hand, benefited the 'lineage' (those tracing descent in the male line from a common ancestor) at the expense of some of the living kin, and created inequality among members of a sibling group. Inheritance practices favoured sons over daughters and one

---

[22] Goody, *The Development of the Family and Marriage in Europe*, pp. 17–19. Mitterauer attacks the 'myth of the sib' and argues that, contrary to the beliefs of nineteenth-century historians, the Germanic *sippe* ('sib', 'clan') was not a formally organized descent group: Mitterauer and Sieder, *The European Family*, pp. 11–13.

[23] David Herlihy, 'The Making of the Medieval Family: Symmetry, Structure and Sentiment', *Journal of Family History*, 8 (1983), pp. 116–30; Georges Duby, 'Lineage and Nobility in the Twelfth Century', in Robert Forster and Orest Ranum, eds., *Family and Society: Selections from the Annales* (Baltimore and London, 1976), pp. 16–40; Karl Schmid, 'Zur Problematik von Familie, Sippe und Geschlect, Haus und Dynastie beim mittelälterlichen Adel', *Zeitschrift für die Geschichte des Oberrheins*, 105 (1957), pp. 14–56. For a discussion of Schmid's thesis and its critics, see John Freed, 'Reflections on the Medieval German Nobility', *American Historical Review*, 91 (1986), pp. 560–3.

son (usually the eldest) over the others.[24] When carried to its logical conclusion, this trend resulted in impartible inheritance with the title and ancestral lands descending to the eldest son alone – that is, primogeniture as practised by the English landed elite.

Even among the nobility, however, the new system was merely superimposed upon the older system which reckoned descent through both the male and the female lines. The most important functions of kinship, those of regulating marriage and defining obligations to aid kinsmen, continued to be defined in terms of the bilateral kinship group: the 'prohibited degrees of marriage' continued to be calculated through both the male and female lines of descent, as did obligations to feud and blood-money. Ties to the 'extended kin' (reckoned bilaterally) were thus *not* synonymous with loyalty to the 'lineage' (reckoned through the male line), as Stone implies. In a feud between two noble houses, a nobleman related to one house through the male line and to the other through the female line was faced with a conflict of loyalties, and medieval legalists did not assume (as they would have in a truly patrilineal system) that he had a superior obligation to the house to which he was related in the male line.[25]

This combination of bilateral and patrilineal elements in the aristocratic family posed a serious dilemma in family strategy, for the two systems required different solutions to the problem of obtaining political allies and property through marriage and yet preserving property for future generations. The bilateral system placed the highest priority on obtaining alliances for the living kin; this was facilitated by a partible inheritance system which gave several sons and daughters the property necessary for a marriage settlement. The patrilineal system, in contrast, placed the highest priority on passing ancestral property intact to future generations; this was facilitated by a system of impartible inheritance which kept the property undivided, but which also left many younger sons and daughters without the resources necessary for marriage alliances.[26]

---

24 Herlihy, 'The Making of the Medieval Family', p. 124.
25 Marc Bloch cites the thirteenth-century French legalist Beaumanoir on the case of such a conflict: 'Wisely, Beaumanoir's choice is to side with the nearest relative, and if the degrees [of relationship] are equal, to stand aloof. Doubtless in practice the decision was often dictated by personal preference.' Marc Bloch, *Feudal Society*, tr. L. A. Manyon, 2 vols (Chicago, 1961; original French edition 1940), vol. 2, p. 138.
26 Herlihy, 'The Making of the Medieval Family', p. 124.

Stone recognizes this same dilemma of family strategy among the English aristocracy. However, by the sixteenth century the patrilineal elements had so completely triumphed in the English aristocratic inheritance system that there was no question which goal was more important. Primogeniture was universal among the English landed elite, and even among the lower social classes partible inheritance was confined to a few isolated regions and was dying out by the end of the seventeenth century. Cressy states that 'a patrilineal lineage bias affected the transmission of property' in all social classes, even though he believes that 'in other respects the [English kinship] system was fluid and flexible';[27] this paradox deserves more investigation than it has thus far received. The process of 'lineal consolidation' had gone so far in England by the sixteenth century that writers on the early modern period simply take primogeniture for granted and do not feel it necessary to account for its presence.

Primogeniture has, however, been emphasized as the primary determinant of family relationships within the early modern aristocratic family, and especially as the cause of estrangement between brothers. Stone emphasizes the negative effects of primogeniture both on elder sons, who led a 'shadow existence' while waiting to come into their inheritance, and on downwardly mobile younger sons.[28] Houlbrooke also stresses the downward mobility of younger sons under primogeniture and uses it as a major argument for the weakness of extended kin ties in England. In his view, the widening economic and social gap between the heir and his descendants on the one hand, and the younger sons and their descendants on the other, tends to destroy any sense of loyalty to the common lineage.[29]

If one looks at England in comparative perspective, one must ask why the process of lineal consolidation and the victory of primogeniture were so much more complete among the English landed classes than among the French and German nobility. Nineteenth-century legal historians viewed primogeniture as the result of the early centralization of political authority in England and the interest of strong monarchs in regulating succession to fiefs.

[27] Stone, *The Family . . . in England*, pp. 43–4; Cressy, 'Kinship and Kin Interaction in Early Modern England', pp. 67–8.
[28] Stone, *The Family . . . in England*, pp. 87–8.
[29] Houlbrooke, *The English Family*, pp. 48–9, 58.

However, Duby's and Schmid's analysis of lineal consolidation in France and Germany suggests that the internal social dynamics of the nobility were also important; this aspect deserves further investigation by English medievalists. Moreover, one must be cautious about attributing all the emotional strains in English families to the existence of primogeniture and about assuming *a priori* that primogeniture causes greater psychological tensions and greater estrangement among siblings than do other inheritance systems. Reinhard Sieder, who has studied both partible and impartible inheritance practices among German peasants, suggests that the formal relationship between siblings which prevails under primogeniture is less destructive of sibling affection than is the fierce rivalry which ensues when the inheritance system does not designate the heir or heirs at an early stage.[30] This implies that primogeniture might actually reduce tension within the nuclear family and lead in the long run to more amicable relationships with siblings and collateral relatives.

The co-existence of bilateral and patrilineal elements in the aristocratic kinship system, which is obscured in England by the triumph of primogeniture, is easy to see in Germany, where lineal consolidation had not proceeded so far. Only a few of the greatest princely houses of Germany practised primogeniture in the six-teenth century. Smaller princes continued to divide not only their personal lands but their territorial states among several sons well into the eighteenth century, and partible inheritance remained the general rule among the German nobility even though a trend toward primogeniture was evident in some regions such as Aus-tria.[31] However, estates divided over generation after generation might soon become too small to support a noble style of life. This dilemma was particularly acute for nobles in regions such as the Rhineland and southwestern Germany, where noble estates were usually small and incomes were derived largely from fixed rents and dues whose value fell during the inflation of the early sixteenth century. Nobles in these regions found it essential to supplement their landed income by securing lucrative ecclesiastical prebends or by becoming professional army officers; the very poorest nobles

[30] Mitterauer and Sieder, *The European Family*, pp. 99–100.
[31] Hajo Holborn, *A History of Modern Germany: The Reformation* (New York, 1959), p. 33; Mitterauer, 'Zur Frage des Heiratsverhaltens im österreichischen Adel', pp. 188–9.

became the notorious 'hedge-knights' for whom highway robbery was 'halfway between a profession and a pastime'.[32] Although some nobles of the Rhineland (e.g. Hesse) continued to practise completely partible inheritance, with all sons (though not all daughters) inheriting equal shares in the estates,[33] the *Zimmerische Chronik* shows the nobles of southwestern Germany evolving a mixed inheritance system which combined partible and impartible elements. This mixed system provides a particularly clear example of the co-existence of patrilineal and bilateral elements in the kinship system.

The customary law of southwestern Germany provided for completely partible inheritance, with daughters sharing equally with sons. Nobles in the *Zimmerische Chronik* nevertheless excluded dowered daughters from further claims on the estate as early as 1381. By the fifteenth century dowered daughters, as well as children who entered the church, were required to make legal renunciations of all claims to the landed estates.[34]

The nobles of southwestern Germany sought to limit the number of possible claimants on the estates by forcing many children to remain unmarried, especially during the economic hard times of the fifteenth and early sixteenth centuries. The number of heirs which an estate could support varied greatly from generation to generation. Once the estate had been divided, it might take several generations before a branch could accumulate enough property to afford another division; on the other hand, many branches died out within one or two generations and their estates reverted to col-

---

[32] Ernst Zeeden, *Deutsche Kultur in der frühen Neuzeit* (Frankfurt, 1968), pp. 36–7. Froben von Hutten, the godfather of the chronicler Froben Christoph von Zimmern, was one of these 'hedge-knights' (*heckenreuter*). On the economic problems of the German nobility, which in many ways resembled Stone's 'crisis of the aristocracy' in England, see *ibid.*, p. 28, and Holborn, *A History of Modern Germany: The Reformation*, pp. 31, 54–5, 60–1.

[33] Pedlow, 'Marriage, Family Size and Inheritance among Hessian Nobles', pp. 345–9.

[34] On family and inheritance law in southwestern Germany in the sixteenth century, see Rolf-Deter Hess, *Familien- und Erbrecht im württembergischen Landrecht von 1555* (Stuttgart, 1968). The main features of the inheritance law are summarized in Sabean, *Power in the Blood*, pp. 167–8. Renunciations by dowered daughters were difficult to enforce in court if an excluded child challenged the renunciation after her parents' death, for the courts tended to interpret inheritance cases in terms of the customary law, which favoured equality of all siblings and the claims of surviving daughters over those of the male line (sons of a deceased son). For examples of such inheritance cases, see *ZC* (Decker-Hauff), vol. 1, pp. 130–1, 150–1; vol. 3, pp. 23–5.

Table 1.1. *Sons and daughters in thirteen southwestern German noble families who survived until the age of fifteen between 1400 and 1599*

	Sons				
	N	Entered church		Married		Mean number marrying per sibling group
		N	%	N	%	
1400–1449	73	26	36	32	44	1.2
1450–1499	46	11	24	25	54	1.0
1500–1549	59	10	17	34	57	1.4
1550–1599	40	2	5	32	80	1.9
Total, 1400–1599	218	49	22	123	56	1.4
	Daughters				
	N	Entered church		Married		Mean number marrying per sibling group
		N	%	N	%	
1400–1449	53	17	32	36	68	1.3
1450–1499	44	12	27	29	66	1.2
1500–1549	74	23	31	48	65	2.0
1550–1599	61	13	21	42	69	2.6
Total, 1400–1599	232	65	28	155	67	1.7

lateral branches. When divisions did take place, they were by no means equal. One son – usually though not invariably the eldest – received the most important ancestral estates, and it was unusual for more than two sons to share in the division even if three or more sons survived. Sons who did not inherit land found themselves in a position similar to younger sons under the English system of primogeniture. They were forced either to enter the church or to take service under a greater noble (or later, to serve the emperor or territorial princes as army officers or court officials). Such knights and courtiers could rarely afford to marry unless their patron rewarded them with the hand of a widow or an heiress.

An examination of the genealogies of the Zimmern and of twelve other noble families with whom they intermarried shows that slightly more than half of the sons who survived to adulthood in the fifteenth and sixteenth centuries married, while about two-thirds of the surviving daughters married (see Table 1.1).[35] The proportion of women who married changed little over the period 1400–1600, and almost all of the daughters who did not marry became nuns. Among men, however, the proportion entering the church fell drastically, from 36 per cent in the early fifteenth century to only 5 per cent in the late sixteenth century. The proportion of men marrying rose from 44 per cent in the early fifteenth century to 80 per cent in the late sixteenth century, with an especially sharp increase after 1550. Since all of these families remained Catholic, these changes in family strategy cannot be attributed to religious changes. It is more likely that increased opportunities to earn income (in professional armies and especially through court office) made these nobles less dependent on ecclesiastical prebends as a source of support for landless sons. The general recovery in the economic fortunes of the German nobility in the late sixteenth century would also help to explain the increase in the proportion of sons marrying.[36]

Limiting the number of sons who married would reduce the pressure to sub-divide estates; nevertheless, these thirteen families divided their estates in twenty-one out of the fifty-four cases in which there were two or more surviving sons.[37] Since over a third of all the estate-holders in these families had no sons or only one son, divisions actually occurred about once in every four generations. Divisions were most common among the wealthier and higher-ranking families: the record was set by the Counts (*grafen*) von

[35] The genealogies of the thirteen families are printed in Wilhelm Karl von Isenburg, *Europäische Stammtafeln: Stammtafeln zur Geschichte der Europäischen Staaten*, second revised edition, 5 vols (Marburg, 1975; first published 1953). The families are as follows: Bickenbach (vol. 5, table 107), Eberstein (vol. 4, tables 132–3), Erbach (vol. 5, tables 22–3), Fürstenberg (vol. 4, table 127), Geroldseck (vol. 5, table 122), Gundelfingen (vol. 5, table 125), Henneberg (vol. 3, table 76), Kirchberg (vol. 5, table 122), Leuchtenberg (vol. 4, table 107), Limpurg (vol. 3, tables 93–5), Oettingen (vol. 5, tables 150–1), Zimmern (vol. 5, table 123) and Zollern (vol. 5, tables 152–5). From the second half of the sixteenth century onwards, these genealogies list offices held under the Hapsburgs, though they do not usually list offices held under other German princes.

[36] On the increasing importance of court office to the German nobility and the economic recovery of the nobility in the late sixteenth century, see Holborn, *A History of Modern Germany: The Reformation*, p. 56; Zeeden, *Deutsche Kultur in der frühen Neuzeit*, pp. 26–7, 30–1.

[37] There were eighty-nine men in these families who inherited land, of whom fifty-four had two or more sons surviving to adulthood. In fifty of these cases at least two sons who remained laymen were still alive at the time of the father's death, so that a division of the estates was actually possible.

Oettingen, who divided their estates on seven out of the nine occasions when they had two or more sons, including a division among four heirs in 1423 and one among three heirs in 1602. Fathers evidently had considerable freedom to select heirs based on their fitness (or on parental favouritism) rather than strictly on the order of birth: five of the fifty-four men who had more than one son as a potential heir passed over their eldest sons, sending them into the church and making younger sons heirs to their estates.

The inheritance system practised by the nobles of southwestern Germany seems almost designed to maximize uncertainty, for it was not clear at an early stage how many heirs there would be in a given generation, nor which of the sons would inherit. If Sieder's theory about the effect of inheritance systems on family relationships is correct, this uncertainty should have produced great tension and rivalry among siblings. But despite the disadvantages of this system, with its mixture of partible and impartible inheritance, these nobles showed no inclination to adopt a more consistent strategy of impartible inheritance. The number of sons marrying per generation increased in the sixteenth century rather than decreasing as it would have under a strategy of impartible inheritance, and divisions among more than two heirs became more common after 1550. The priorities of the southwestern German nobles were those of the older bilateral kinship system rather than those of the newer patrilineal system: when economic circumstances permitted, they preferred to increase the number of marriage alliances rather than to maximize the amount of ancestral property transmitted undivided to future generations. The triumph of impartible inheritance and of primogeniture is thus less inevitable than it might seem to one familiar only with the English evidence. It would be interesting to compare German-speaking regions such as Austria, where a trend toward primogeniture developed in the sixteenth century, with those such as Hesse and southwestern Germany, where it did not. This would help to identify the factors promoting primogeniture and could prove useful for comparisons with England at an earlier period.

II

The debate between Stone and the revisionists over the importance of ties beyond the nuclear family in England has been confused by the failure to distinguish between the 'kin' (the living relatives on both the father's and the mother's sides) and the patrilineal 'lineage'. Stone's definitions erroneously imply that ties beyond the nuclear family were limited to the lineage, and the revisionists believe that by proving the absence of formally organized patrilineal descent groups they have proved the insignificance of ties to kin beyond the nuclear family. Since early modern Germany possessed distinct terms for the bilateral extended kin group (*freundschaft*) and the lineage (*geschlecht*), it is easier to distinguish between the two. Seing how 'kin' and 'lineage' functioned in the life of an individual in the German nobility can serve as a useful comparison with England. Two major differences between the two countries need to be noted. First, the weakness of central government in Germany (especially in the southwest), might be expected to increase the importance of the extended kin group, as it did in the border regions of England. Second, the German nobles might be expected to have a weaker sense of lineage than did the English aristocracy because of the persistence in their inheritance system of bilateral elements which emphasized the sibling group rather than the lineage.

The *Zimmerische Chronik* provides an unusually detailed account both of a nobleman's expectations with regard to kin obligations and of the actual behaviour of relatives toward each other. The chronicle, written by Count (*graf*) Froben von Zimmern in the 1560s, is anecdotal in nature and draws extensively on personal reminiscences as well as documents in the family archives. The bulk of the chronicle covers the period from the 1480s to the 1560s, covering three generations and narrating the fall and rise of the Zimmern family's fortunes. In 1488 the chronicler's grandfather Johann Werner I von Zimmern was placed under the imperial ban; his estates were confiscated and given to his old foe(and third cousin) Count Hugo von Werdenberg. Repeated petitions to the Emperor failed to recover the estates, but Johann Werner's sons recaptured them by armed raids, and in 1504 the ban was officially lifted. The three surviving sons quarrelled among themselves and were forced to sell many of the ancestral estates to pay debts. However, the chronicle ends on a note of triumph as the Zimmern succeeded in recovering their lands through lawsuits, managed them shrewdly, gained the favour of Emperor Charles V, and were raised from the rank of baron to that of count.

Two aspects of these events are particularly interesting for issues of kin and lineage relationships: the role played by relatives in the crisis after the confiscation of the Zimmern estates, which bears on the obligations of extended kin; and the relationship between the three sons of Johann Werner I, which bears on the question of lineage loyalty. The chronicler constantly laments the lack of help from relatives and the absence of unity within the Zimmern family. Taken at face value, his complaints suggest a pattern of behaviour similar to the revisionists' view of the English kinship system, in which individuals place their own interests and that of their direct descendants ahead of any obligations to extended kin or of loyalty to the lineage. A closer investigation is needed to see whether his gloomy view was borne out by the actual events.

The view that one could rely only on one's relatives for assistance and emotional intimacy is seen in the use of the term 'friends' to designate kinsmen. This usage, common in medieval France and England as well, remained standard in Germany until the eighteenth century, and the normal term for the bilateral extended kin group was *die Freundschaft*. The *Freundschaft*, corresponding to the English 'kin', included relatives by blood and by marriage on both the father's and the mother's side.[38] It continued to play a quasi-official role in protecting its members well into the sixteenth century, although the old Germanic tribal obligations of feud and blood-money had long been obsolete. Individual kinsmen or groups of kinsmen were given official status as imperial commissioners to arbitrate quarrels among noblemen which threatened to disturb the peace, and in the era of personal violence which lasted until at least the 1520s, the obligation to support a kinsman in a petition or lawsuit carried with it the very real possibility of using armed force.

The chronicler Froben von Zimmern felt that the relatives of his grandfather, Johann Werner I, had not lived up to their obligations

---

[38] On the use of the term 'friends' for kinsmen in medieval France and Germany, see Bloch, *Feudal Society*, vol. 2, pp. 123–4; on its use in England to denote kinsmen, especially parents and uncles, see Stone, *The Family . . . in England*, pp. 97–8. In German, '*die Freundschaft*' originally meant 'blood relatives', but the term was also used more loosely to include relatives by marriage. By the eighteenth century, '*Verwandten*' had become the standard term for blood relatives, and '*Freunde*' came to be used principally for relatives by marriage. See Ingeborg Schwarz, *Die Bedeutung der Sippe für die Öffentlichkeit der Eheschliessung im 15. un 16. Jahrhundert* (Tübingen, 1959), p. 12; Sabean, *Power in the Blood*, p. 31.

to support his family in time of crisis and to help him recover his confiscated estates; personal friends had shown themselves more loyal during his exile.[39] However, the Zimmern were unusually vulnerable during the crisis, because they had few kinsmen to call upon for assistance. They had never established any collateral lines and thus had few paternal relatives. Johann Werner's father, Werner, was dead, and his uncle Gottfried, an eccentric old bachelor, was ill-prepared to take on the leadership of the family during the crisis. (Johann Werner's wife Margarethe von Oettingen proved far stauncher than Gottfried in her determination not to give in to the Werdenbergs). Nor did Johann Werner I have many close relatives on his mother's side, and the scandalous circumstances of his parents' marriage meant that these relatives could not automatically be counted as allies. Werner von Zimmern had fallen in love with Countess Anna von Kirchberg while she was married to Count Johann von Fürstenberg; he killed her husband in a duel and married her a few months later. Thus the marriage did not further an existing friendship or political alliance between the bride's and the groom's families, and it does not appear that the mere fact of the marriage created any such alliance. In 1488 the Kirchberg family was headed by Count Philip von Kirchberg; he was first cousin to Johann Werner, yet he did not give the Zimmern any aid in their petitions. Under the circumstances, it is scarcely surprising that the Fürstenbergs gave the Zimmern no aid. However, they remained neutral and later tried to help arbitrate the quarrel in conjunction with Werner von Zimmern's good friend (and second cousin) Eitelfriedrich von Zollern.[40]

The closest relatives who actively aided the Zimmern were the knightly family of Klingenberg, who were first cousins of Werner and Gottfried von Zimmern on their mother's side. When Gottfried asked Albrecht von Klingenberg to plead the Zimmern cause before the Reichstag, 'he did it to the best of his ability because he was so closely related to the Zimmern family'.[41] Albrecht von Klingenberg also participated in the armed raids which recovered the Zimmern estates; his brother Wolfgang acted as an elder

---

[39] *ZC* (Decker-Hauff), vol. 1, p. 307; vol. 2, p. 86.

[40] *Ibid.*, vol. 1, 300–7. Fürstenberg and Zollern were appointed imperial commissioners to arbitrate the quarrel in 1497 because they were 'trusted by and related to both sides'; the treaty they negotiated was signed at Kirchberg, so the Kirchbergs may also have been friendly neutrals.

[41] *Ibid.*, vol. 1, p. 261.

statesman and adviser to Johann Werner's sons and carried out the division of the Zimmern estates in 1508. The Klingenberg brothers were only remote relatives of Johann Werner's sons (first cousins twice removed), so it is clear that, as Cressy says of England, 'the potential existed to bring even distant and latent kin into a close and effective relationship'.[42]

Relatives by marriage were reluctant to help the Zimmern, at least as long as Johann Werner I was alive and under the imperial ban. His brothers-in-law Count Wolf von Oettingen and Schenk Albrecht von Limpurg refused to support him in his petitions to the emperor for the return of the estates. Limpurg excused himself on the grounds that he was related to both sides in the quarrel (his son was married to a Werdenberg), while Oettingen was willing to negotiate for the return of property which belonged to his sister (Johann Werner's wife), but not for Johann Werner's own estates. However, the chronicler exaggerates when he claims that after the death of Johann Werner in 1495, 'other members of the family did not take up [his sons'] cause but left the boys to shift for themselves and to do the best they could'.[43] Oettingen and Limpurg actually became much more active in petitioning the emperor once they no longer risked political disfavour by association with a proscribed 'traitor'. They also used their influence to place Johann Werner's two youngest sons at princely courts for their education.

This crisis illustrates the different kinds of aid which could be expected from kin, as well as the limits of the kin group from which aid was expected. Blood relatives (the Klingenbergs) took greater physical and political risks than relatives by marriage (Oettingen and Limpurg). The latter gave little help to Johann Werner himself and confined their assistance chiefly to his wife and children, who were their own blood relatives. The most distant kin to whom Gottfried von Zimmern, as acting head of the Zimmern family, appealed for help were first cousins on his mother's side. Second and third cousins played no role in the crisis at all, unless they happened to be close personal friends as well. Even the relationship of first cousin carried no absolute obligations of aid: the Klingenberg brothers regarded themselves as obligated to help their Zimmern cousins because they were 'so closely related', but Philip von Kirchberg ignored his first cousin Johann Werner von

[42] Cressy, 'Kinship and Kin Interaction in Early Modern England', p. 69.
[43] ZC (Decker-Hauff), vol. 2, p. 297.

Zimmern. Moreover, the crisis illustrates the conflicts of loyalty inherent in a bilateral kinship system. Johann Werner von Zimmern and his arch-enemy Hugo von Werdenberg were themselves distantly related (third cousins). Many of the relatives to whom the Zimmern might have turned for aid had equally close genealogical ties to the Werdenbergs and could therefore declare themselves neutral. It appears that ties of kinship obligation were stronger between blood relatives than between relatives by marriage, but the circle even of blood kin who were obligated to help in a serious crisis was quite restricted.

Armed support was no longer an obligation of kin in sixteenth-century England, at least outside the border regions. In other respects the assistance supplied by kin in the *Zimmerische Chronik* is similar to that described for England: providing advice and financial aid, acting as executors of wills and guardians of minor children, and helping to secure places at court and advantageous marriage alliances.[44]

In Germany the guardianship of minor children was a responsibility of the father's lineage; neither the emperor nor the territorial princes exercised rights of wardship as the Crown did in England. Since the children were members of their father's lineage, the widow lost physical custody of them if she remarried and severed her connection to the lineage. After the mother's remarriage, the children resided with their guardian, who was normally the father's father or father's brother. A remote collateral relative might serve as guardian if no closer paternal relative was available. There are a few cases in the *Zimmerische Chronik* of maternal uncles serving as guardians, either because the mother's family was of higher rank or because the paternal relative originally appointed as guardian had betrayed his trust.[45] In these cases the children continued to reside with their mother.

The duty of giving advice and arbitrating quarrels fell primarily

---

[44] *Cf.* Wrightson, *English Society*, pp. 44–50; Houlbrooke, *The English Family*, pp. 45–50; Cressy, 'Kinship and Kin Interaction in Early Modern England', p. 68.

[45] A case which demonstrates most of these features of the guardianship system is that of Katharina and Anna von Erbach, daughters of Schenk Erasmus von Erbach who died in 1503. When their mother remarried a few months later, guardianship of the two girls passed to their distant cousin Schenk Eberhard von Erbach, who had inherited their father's title. After Eberhard attempted to seize the girls' estates for himself, their maternal uncle Christoph von Werdenberg forcibly ousted him from the role of guardian and assumed it himself.

upon the 'elder statesmen' and those of highest rank and greatest political influence among the *freundschaft*. These might be blood relatives in either the male or female line (grandparents, great-uncles and great-aunts, uncles and aunts) or affines (chiefly fathers-in-law and brothers-in-law). There was no formal family council, but respected and influential kin were consulted individually on important decisions such as a child's career or a marriage alliance. The chronicler Froben von Zimmern says that he was given a free choice in his own marriage, and he did in fact reject a match proposed by his uncle. However, he began his own search for a bride by asking several other relatives to recommend candidates.[46] Elder kinsmen sometimes acted in concert to settle disputes, as when Froben's uncle and father-in-law arbitrated a quarrel between Froben and his two brothers over their father's estate.

Probably the most important aid given by kin in the *Zimmerische Chronik* was in the education and advancement of children. Grandparents, aunts and uncles might actually bring up a child from an early age, either because the child's father was dead or because a widow or childless couple wanted the companionship of a child. Grandparents were usually dead by the time that decisions had to be made about a child's career or marriage, so the crucial advice and aid in adolescence was more likely to come from uncles and aunts. Daughters who were 'fostered out' in their teens as the equivalent of sending a son to court were usually sent to the household of an aunt or uncle. Uncles were key figures in securing placement for their nephews at princely courts, as we have seen in the case of Oettingen and Limpurg. When university education began to replace court service in the sixteenth century, it was again uncles who helped to underwrite the costs. Gottfried Werner and Wilhelm Werner von Zimmern agreed to finance the university careers of Froben and his brothers when the boys' father refused to spend any more money on their education. In all of these cases, aid came from grandparents and uncles – the only relatives outside the

---

[46] In this search for a bride, Froben did not raise any questions about the appearance or personality of the prospective bride, though he was concerned about rumours of scandal in one family and the poor health of another candidate. The relatives who were most influential in arranging possible matches were not the oldest members of the family but the affines with the highest rank and greatest political influence: Friedrich von Fürstenberg (son-in-law of his great-uncle Christoph von Werdenberg) and Jos Niklaus von Zollern (son-in-law of his uncle Gottfried Werner von Zimmern). ZC (Decker-Hauff), vol. 3, pp. 285–7.

nuclear family whom the revisionists see as important in the life of an individual. However, the *Zimmerische Chronik* also records services provided by more remote kin connections, including some designated only as *vetter* (= 'cousin', used for any blood relative) or *schwager* (= 'brother-in-law', used for any relative by marriage), whose exact relationship cannot be determined. These distant kin were asked to board the boys during their travels abroad, to provide social introductions for them, and to help secure ecclesiastical preferments for them.

The only kin function which belonged specifically to the patrilineal lineage was the guardianship of minor children, and as we have seen, exceptions occurred even here. All other kin functions were performed by relatives on either the mother's or the father's side. It was thus the bilateral extended kin group (*Freundschaft*) and not the lineage which played the most important role in the day-to-day life of the individual and provided advice and support on major decisions. Nevertheless, the nobles in the *Zimmerische Chronik* also felt a strong sense of identification with their lineage or *geschlecht*. The rules regarding guardianship show that children were regarded in a sense as 'possessions' of the lineage who were not to be placed under the control of males from another lineage. The very existence of family chronicles such as the *Zimmerische Chronik* testifies to a sense of identification with the lineage. In Germany, as in England, nobles attempting to vindicate their privileges in the face of challenges from lesser landowners and the bourgeoisie fell back upon the antiquity of their lineage to justify their status. Genealogy, heraldry and family chronicles blossomed in the sixteenth and seventeenth centuries, all glorifying the great deeds of the 'house' which bore a common surname and stressing the descent in the male line from an illustrious ancestor. Genealogies and family chronicles typically dealt only with the male line of descent, though connection through females was sometimes invoked to explain the descent of an estate or to claim a kin connection to a famous person.[47]

---

[47] On the development of genealogy, heraldry and family chronicles in German-speaking lands, see Wilhelm Karl von Isenburg, 'Die geschichtliche Entwicklung von Sippenkunde und Sippenforschung bis zum Ende des dreissigjährigen Krieges', *Historisches Jahrbuch der Görregesellschaft*, 60 (1940), pp. 1–13, and Beat Jenny, *Graf Froben Christoph von Zimmern: Geschichtsschreiber – Erzähler – Landesherr* (Lindau and Constance, 1959), Part I. *Cf.* Stone, *Crisis of the Aristocracy*, pp. 16–17.

'It was this relationship of the individual to his lineage which provided a man of the upper classes ... with his identity', says Stone;[48] and the chronicler Froben Christoph would certainly have agreed. He was brought up from infancy by his maternal grandmother, a member of the Werdenberg family who had been such bitter enemies of the Zimmern, and he apparently never saw any of his Zimmern relatives until he was twelve years old. Yet by identifying himself wholeheartedly with the interests of the Zimmern (both through lawsuits to recover ancestral lands and through writing the family history), he was able to establish his position in the lineage and thus to define his position in society. As a champion of the Zimmern interests, he was also justified in denigrating his father Johann Werner II, a spendthrift who had sold off ancestral lands and who had also ignored Froben himself. Clearly the chronicle could provide much material for the psychohistorian; here we need only note the Biblical passage which Froben wrote on the wall after a particularly bitter quarrel with his father: 'The stone which the builders rejected is become the head of the corner.'[49]

When the chronicler refers to the Zimmern 'family', he means the lineage or house identified by the patrilineally-inherited surname. He uses the term *geschlecht* ('lineage') interchangeably with the phrase *stam und nam*, which emphasizes the identification with the surname. The worth of an individual is stated in terms of his contribution to the wealth and honour of his lineage. Even Count Hugo von Werdenberg, 'although he was the greatest enemy of the Zimmern and also wanted to destroy this family [*stammen und namen*]' is called 'a worthy, wise count' because 'he brought great honour and wealth to those of his family [*geschlecht*]'.[50]

The chronicler conceives of the interests of the family in terms of the patrilineal line of descent, and he frequently laments the insistence of brothers on dividing the estates and diminishing the wealth of the lineage. 'Unity among brothers' – i.e. willingness to maintain the estate undivided – is the key to the prosperity of a family. He imagines that such unity was common in the Middle Ages and cites the legendary ten Zimmern brothers, who in the eleventh century restored the family fortunes by keeping the

[48] Stone, *The Family ... in England*, p. 29.
[49] *ZC* (Decker-Hauff), vol. 3, p. 145.
[50] *Ibid.*, vol. 2, p. 31.

estates undivided. However, he admits that such co-operation is rare in his own day, when 'we have many examples of disunity among brothers but few of unity', and 'love and unity among brothers is a rare bird'.[51] Here the chronicler clearly finds his own sense of priorities (lineage over kin) at odds with the partible inheritance system which prevailed in southwestern Germany.

The quarrels among the sons of Johann Werner I vividly illustrate 'the damage which could be done to lineage interests by disunity among brothers in a partible inheritance system. In 1508 the Zimmern estates were divided between the two elder sons, Johann Werner II and Gottfried Werner. The youngest son Wilhelm Werner was persuaded to renounce his claims to the estate 'out of brotherly love and loyalty and regard for his impoverished family [*geschlecht*] so that the two brothers could maintain themselves in a respectable manner befitting their descent'.[52] He expected to enter the church but turned to the law when he failed to receive the prebend he had been promised.

Bitter quarrels followed the division of the lands. Gottfried Werner, a shrewd manager, manoeuvred his feckless older brother into an exchange of estates. Johann Werner, feeling he had been swindled, began to sell off ancestral estates just to spite his brother. The elevation of the Zimmern brothers to the rank of count in 1538, which came as a reward for Wilhelm Werner's services as an imperial judge, completed the estrangement among them. Johann Werner disliked the new-fangled coat of arms quartering the lions rampant of Zimmern with those of Wildenstein, and adopted his own personal arms instead. A courtier remarked to Froben that the new Zimmern coat of arms aptly symbolized the dissension within the family, for the four lions rampant appeared to be grimacing and clawing at each other. 'There was no unity or loyalty in the Zimmern family', laments the chronicler; 'each one had his own state [*republicam*]'.[53]

This unedifying series of quarrels seems at first to demonstrate the absence of any sense of loyalty to the lineage. Yet a closer look at these events shows that the chronicler was not the only one who

---

[51] *Ibid*, vol. 1, p. 62; vol. 2, pp. 113, 115. The chronicle does record one notable recent case of brothers who held their estates undivided: Christoph von Werdenberg and his brothers Johannes and Felix. However, two of the brothers were childless and resided at distant courts or on their wives' estates, so that only Christoph resided on and managed the ancestral estates at Sigmaringen.

[52] *Ibid.*, vol. 2, pp. 36–7.   [53] *Ibid.*, vol. 2, p. 110; vol. 3, pp. 22, 132.

thought in terms of the interests of the lineage, and that the two younger brothers voluntarily sacrificed their own interests and those of their direct descendants to the interests of the lineage.

The first test of lineage loyalty came when the patron of Johann Werner II tried to help restore the Zimmern finances by arranging a match with a rich widow from the urban patriciate. Johann Werner II was reluctant to accept the match despite the urging of friends and relatives, who argued that the widow's fortune would enable his brothers to marry according to their rank. Froben praises his father for rejecting the match (even though this act cost him the favour of his patron and seriously damaged the financial interests of the Zimmern in the short run), for he upheld the honour of the Zimmern lineage by maintaining the purity of its noble descent.[54] Here Johann Werner II and his son clearly saw the good of the lineage as taking priority over the good of the living kin, but the appeal to lineage interests does smack strongly of individual self-interest.

The youngest brother Wilhelm Werner acted more altruistically, for he did renounce his own claim to the inheritance in order to allow his two older brothers to maintain a noble style of life. His position was similar to that of a younger son under the English system of primogeniture, and he certainly had no personal reason to favour inheritance systems which favoured one heir at the expense of his brothers. Yet when he arbitrated a quarrel over Johann Werner II's estate, he persuaded Froben's two brothers to give up all claims to the property 'in order to keep the estates undivided and in better condition for the honour of the family [*stam und nam*]'.[55]

Gottfried Werner went further than his childless brother and actually sacrificed the interests of his own daughter in order to benefit the sons of Johann Werner II, the brother from whom he was bitterly estranged. Although he was a notoriously indulgent father to his daughter Anna, he refused to make her his heiress since this would allow the estates to pass out of the Zimmern family: 'He saw no use in saving up for the benefit of sons-in-law.'[56] He left his estates to his nephew Froben instead, in a clear victory for lineage interests at the expense of his direct descendants.

It is possible that a partible inheritance system made the

---

[54] *Ibid*, vol. 1, pp. 358–60.   [55] *ZC* (Barack), vol. 4, p. 123.
[56] Jenny, *Graf Froben Christoph von Zimmern*, p. 109.

Zimmern more willing to sacrifice their own interests to those of their brothers than English nobles would have been. However, the Zimmern brothers referred in each instance to the interests of the lineage (*geschlecht, stam und nam*) to justify their decisions, and Johann Werner II specifically rejected arguments based on advancing the interests of brothers. For Johann Werner II and his son Froben, 'the good of the lineage' may indeed have been a mere rationalization for their own self-interest. But this cannot be the case for the two younger brothers, who acted contrary to their own self-interest and the interests of their direct descendants in order to benefit the sons of a brother whom they thoroughly disliked. The inheritance system and the values of the nobles of southwestern Germany were more ambivalent than those of England about the priority of lineage interests over the interests of living kin. Nevertheless, 'loyalty to the lineage' was to them not a meaningless phrase, but an ideal for which they were willing to make genuine sacrifices.

III

What does this comparative evidence from Germany suggest for future research on the early modern English aristocratic family?

Viewing the English aristocratic family in comparative perspective helps to resolve the apparent contradiction between Stone's view of a patrilineal 'Open Lineage Family' permeated by the influence of extended kin and the revisionists' view of an individualistic bilateral kinship system. Both patrilineal and bilateral elements co-existed in the kinship system of the English aristocracy, as they did in continental aristocracies. One question raised by this comparative perspective is why lineal consolidation proceeded so much further in England than on the continent. The case of southwestern Germany shows that the trend toward impartible inheritance was not irresistible, even among landed elites. The universality of impartible inheritance and primogeniture among the English landed elite, and the diffusion of this inheritance system to other social classes, certainly does not accord with the revisionists' view of the English kinship system as uniquely flexible and individualistic.

Failure to distinguish between the patrilineal lineage and the bilateral extended kin group has caused much confusion in the discussion of the role of extended kin in England. Differences in the types of sources used have also contributed to the discrepancy between Stone's views and those of the revisionists on the importance of extended kin ties. Elites are more likely than lower social classes to leave documentary evidence of their ideals and expectations regarding kin behaviour, and the qualitative sources which are more abundant for elite groups make it easier to identify collective kin groups than do the quantitative sources which are the basis of many community studies. More systematic use of network analysis to study interactions with extended kin on both the father's and the mother's side in aristocratic families would facilitate comparisons with the community studies in which this network approach has been used, and would show whether there is in fact a marked difference between the kinship system of the aristocracy and that of other Englishmen.

A case study of nobles in southwestern Germany, where the co-existence of bilateral and patrilineal elements in the kinship system is more obvious than it is in England, suggests that lineage was a more important focus of the individual's loyalty than the revisionists are willing to admit. On the other hand, it also suggests that an individual's relations with kin beyond the nuclear family focused more on the bilateral extended kin group than on the lineage, and that these relationships were more flexible and carried fewer binding obligations than Stone implies.

The German evidence contradicts the revisionists' argument that lineage loyalty and ties to kin beyond the nuclear family were insignificant in societies which lacked formally organized descent groups. Clearly the lineage was a significant focus of loyalty for the Zimmern, even though the kinship system of the southwestern German nobility was more ambivalent than the English one about giving priority to lineage interests over the interests of living kin. Nor was the sense of solidarity with ancestors and with descendants yet unborn limited to the heirs for whom lineage loyalty so conveniently coincided with self-interest. Ties beyond the nuclear family did, at least on occasion, transcend the interests of the individual and his direct descendants.

However, the case study of the Zimmern suggests that the circle of extended kin who had binding obligations to help in a serious crisis was more restricted than Stone implies. This is the case even though the weakness of political authority in southwestern Germany meant that the extended kin group continued to perform protective functions which it had largely lost in England by this date. Remote kin ties could indeed be activated into effective relationships when they were needed. Nevertheless, if collaterals and affines as close as first cousins and brothers-in-law had no absolute obligation to give aid in a serious crisis, one must view extended kin relationships as fairly flexible and personal even in the aristocracy. Grandparents and uncles played an ongoing role in the lives of individuals in the *Zimmerische Chronik*. Support from more distant collaterals and affines was invoked in certain circumstances, especially those requiring patronage or political influence. However, this support was not automatic; the genealogical relationship had to be reinforced with ties of personal friendship. In many respects the extended kin relationships in the *Zimmerische Chronik* resemble those of English villagers as described by the revisionists (who stress the centrality of grandparents and uncles) and by Cressy (who stresses the importance of more distant extended kin as a reservoir of support upon which the individual could draw). Closer examination of the social networks of individuals in English aristocratic families may show a similar pattern: perhaps members of the English landed elite spent a good deal of time and effort *cultivating* ties to extended kin precisely because the mere fact of genealogical relationship was not enough to ensure support.

We still know little about the English aristocratic family in the fifteenth and early sixteenth centuries in comparison with the better-documented seventeenth and eighteenth centuries. It is to be hoped that the recent upsurge of interest in the early Tudor nobility will produce more case studies of individual families focusing on their family values and kin relationships. Only an analysis of the actual interactions of individuals with their kin and the choices they made when lineage interests conflicted with self-interest can answer the question of whether the loyalties of the individual in the early modern English aristocracy lay primarily with his lineage or with his nuclear family.

APPENDIX: THE *ZIMMERISCHE CHRONIK* AND THE ZIMMERN FAMILY

The *Zimmerische Chronik*, written by Count (*graf*) Foben Christoph von Zimmern (1519–66/7) in the 1560s, has long been recognized as an

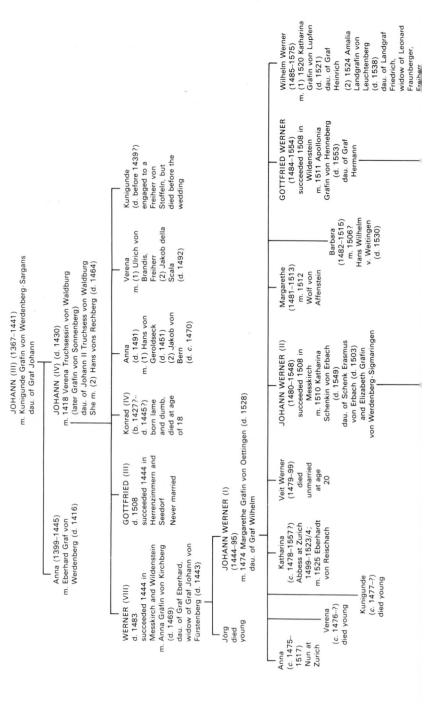

JOHANN (III) (1367–1441)
m. Kunigunde Gräfin von Werdenberg-Sargans
dau. of Graf Johann

Anna (1399–1445)
m. Eberhard Graf von
Werdenberg (d. 1416)

JOHANN (IV) (d. 1430)
m. 1418 Verena Truchsessin von Waldburg
(later Gräfin von Sonnenberg)
dau. of Johann II Truchsess von Waldburg
She m. (2) Hans vons Rechberg (d. 1464)

Kunigunde
(d. before 1439?)
engaged to a
Freiherr von
Stoffeln, but
died before the
wedding

Verena
m. (1) Ulrich von
Brandis,
Freiherr
(2) Jakob della
Scala
(d. 1492)

Anna
(d. 1491)
m. (1) Hans von
Geroldseck
(d. 1451)
(2) Jakob von
Bern
(d. c. 1470)

Konrad (IV)
(b. 1427?–
d. 1445?)
born lame
and dumb,
died at age
of 18

GOTTFRIED (III)
d. 1508
succeeded 1444 in
Herrenzimmern and
Seedorf
Never married

WERNER (VIII)
d. 1483
succeeded 1444 in
Messkirch and Wildenstein
m. Anna Gräfin von Kirchberg
(d. 1469)
dau. of Graf Eberhard,
widow of Graf Johann von
Fürstenberg (d. 1443)

JOHANN WERNER (I)
(1444–95)
m. 1474 Margarethe Gräfin von Oettingen (d. 1528)
dau. of Graf Wilhelm

Jörg
died
young

Katharina
(c. 1478–1557?)
Abbess at Zurich
1499–1523/4;
m. 1525 Eberhardt
von Reischach

Veit Werner
(1479–99)
died
unmarried
at age
20

JOHANN WERNER (II)
(1480–1548)
succeeded 1508 in
Messkirch
m. 1510 Katharina
Schenkin von Erbach
(d. 1549)
dau. of Schenk Erasmus
von Erbach and Elizabeth Gräfin
von Werdenberg-Sigmaringen

Margarethe
(1481–1513)
m. 1512
Wolf von
Affenstein

Barbara
(1482–1515)
m. 1506?
Hans Wilhelm
v. Weitingen
(d. 1530)

GOTTFRIED WERNER
(1484–1554)
succeeded 1508 in
Wildenstein
m. 1511 Apollonia
Gräfin von Henneberg
(d. 1553)
dau. of Graf
Hermann

Wilhelm Werner
(1485–1575)
m. (1) 1520 Katharina
Gräfin von Lupfen
(d. 1521)
dau. of Graf
Heinrich
(2) 1524 Amalia
Landgräfin von
Leuchtenberg
(d. 1538)
dau. of Landgraf
Friedrich,
widow of Leonard
Fraunberger,
Freiherr

Verena
(c. 1476–?)
died young

Kunigunde
(c. 1477–?)
died young

Anna
(c. 1475–
1517)
Nun at
Zurich

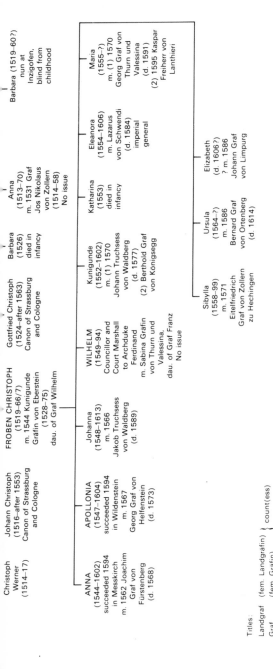

Titles:

Landgraf (fem. Landgräfin) } count(ess)
Graf   (fem. Gräfin)
Freiherr (fem. Freifrau)   = baron(ess)
Truchsess (fem. Truchsessin)   = steward
Schenk   (fem. Schenkin)   = cupbearer

This genealogy is based on the one given by W. K. von Isenburg, *Europäische Stammtafeln: Stammtafeln zur Geschichte der Europäischen Staaten*, second revised edition, 5 vols (Marburg, 1975; original printing 1953), vol. 5, Table 123, with corrections based on the *Zimmerische Chronik* itself and on Beat Jenny, *Graf Froben Christoph von Zimmern*. Names in capital letters are those who inherited estates. The Roman numerals are those used by Barack in the index to his edition of the *Zimmerische Chronik* to differentiate between men bearing the same name, whether or not they inherited estates. It should be noted that noble titles descended to all the sons and daughters of the titleholder, and that women continued to be styled by the rank and title of their family of birth even after their marriage.

Figure 1.1 Genealogy of the Zimmern family

important source for the social history and popular culture of sixteenth-century Germany.[57] The narrative framework of the chronicle, tracing the Zimmern from their legendary origins down to the author's death, is based on the family archives. About two-thirds of the chronicle's 2,000 pages deal with the period from the 1480s to the 1560s; in this portion of the chronicle the documents are supplemented by the personal recollections of participants in the events. In addition to the narrative of the Zimmern family, the chronicle contains a vast amount of incidental material, including genealogies and histories of local noble families, anecdotes about acquaintances, jokes, legends and folklore. It is this incidental material which has made the chronicle such a gold-mine for students of popular culture. The anecdotal nature of the chronicle also makes it a particularly valuable source for the history of the family, for it provides a wealth of detail on events in everyday family life – including visits to kin, marriage negotiations, child-rearing and sexuality – which is rare in sixteenth-century sources.

The Zimmern themselves, whose seat was at Messkirch about fifty miles south of Stuttgart, were one of the numerous families of small independent nobles in the politically fragmented southwest.[58] The family first appears in legal documents in the eleventh century; its members bore the rank of barons (*freie herren*) until 1538, when they were elevated to the rank of counts (*grafen*). Although the Zimmern belonged to the higher nobility (*Reichsadel*), they were more comparable in wealth and social position to the English county gentry than to English peers. The most famous member of the family was the jurist and historian Wilhelm Werner von Zimmern (1485–1575); several other members of the family were minor patrons of humanist literature and Renaissance art in Swabia. The Zimmern remained Catholic but avoided taking sides in the wars of the Reformation era in order not to jeopardize their estates. The family became extinct in the male line in 1594.

[57] The best guide to the *Zimmerische Chronik* is Jenny, *Graf Froben Christoph von Zimmern*, which contains an extensive bibliography. Jenny traces the development of the family chronicle as a genre in sixteenth-century Germany. He also gives a detailed analysis of the sources of the *Zimmerische Chronik* and evaluates the chronicler's reliability in handling his evidence.

[58] For a brief outline of the family history based on legal documents, see Johann Siebmacher, *Grosses und Allgemeines Wappenbuch*, 6 vols (Nuremberg, 1856–1908, with later additions), vol. 6, part 2, pp. 112–13. A biography of Wilhelm Werner von Zimmern appears in *Allgemeine Deutsche Biographie* (Leipzig, 1875–1900), vol. 45, pp. 303–4. For the family's cultural contributions, see Josef Nadler, 'Die Herren von Zimmern: eine schwäbische Familie von Dichtern und Geschichtsschreibern', *Der Schwäbische Bund*, 3 (1920–1), pp. 296–305. Jenny, *Graf Froben Christoph von Zimmern*, gives detailed biographies of the male members of the family in the sixteenth century.

2. Public ceremony and royal charisma: the English royal entry in London, 1485–1642

R. MALCOLM SMUTS

Despite the recent flurry of interest in the court cultures and royal cults of Tudor Stuart England, remarkably little has been written about how rulers in this period presented themselves to popular audiences during great ceremonial occasions. The symbolism of masques, portraits and outdoor entertainments has been analysed with great care, but the public rituals of kingship, and the behaviour of rulers before large crowds, have received much less attention. Virtually all modern accounts convey the impression that monarchs sought to influence the public primarily through visual, dramatic and poetic images, so that to understand a royal cult we must first unravel its symbolism.[1] Clifford Geertz has neatly encapsulated the assumptions underlying this approach in an essay

Earlier versions of this paper were delivered at the annual meeting of the Conference of British Studies in Washington, D.C. in October 1983 and at the Tudor Stuart seminar at the Institute of Historical Research, London, in the spring of 1984. The author wishes to thank members of the audiences on both occasions for stimulating suggestions. In addition he would particularly like to thank Tim Harris, Mark Kishlansky, Linda Peck, A. J. Slavin, Richard Strier and John Watanabe for reading and commenting helpfully on earlier drafts.

[1] See in particular Sydney Anglo, *Spectacle, Pageantry and Early Tudor Policy* (Oxford, 1969); David Bergeron, *English Civic Pageantry* (Columbia, S.C. and London, 1971); D. J. Gordon and Stephen Orgel, *The Renaissance Imagination* (Berkeley, Los Angeles and London, 1980); Stephen Orgel, *The Jonsonian Masque* (Cambridge, Mass., 1965), *The Illusion of Power* (Berkeley, Los Angeles and London, 1975); Stephen Orgel and Roy Strong, *Inigo Jones and the Theatre of the Stuart Court* (London, 1972); Roy Strong, *Splendour at Court* (London, 1973), *The Cult of Elizabeth* (London, 1977); Frances Yates, *Astrea* (London, 1975). For two more general discussions of royal cults principally in the Stuart period, see Graham Parry, *The Golden Age Restored* (Manchester, 1981) and R. Malcolm Smuts, *Court Culture and the Origins of a Royalist Tradition in Early Stuart England* (Philadelphia, 1987). Judith Richards, '"His Nowe Majestie" and English Monarchy: The Kingship of Charles I before 1640', *Past and Present*, 113 (1986), pp. 70–96, is the most striking and original departure from the approach defined by the foregoing works.

comparing royal processions in Renaissance England, pre-colonial Bali and nineteenth-century Morocco. In each of these places, he argues, processions expressed a ruler's 'charisma' through a distinctive 'idiom', which operated within a particular 'cultural frame'. In Elizabethan England the idiom was allegory and the 'cultural frame' was a concept of royal authority as a projection of abstract ideals of piety and justice. Elizabeth's 'whole public life – or more exactly, that part of her life the public saw – was transformed into a kind of philosophical masque in which everything stood for some vast idea and nothing took place unburdened by parable'.[2] When Geertz describes an Elizabethan procession he accordingly devotes almost all his attention to street pageants, in which this transforming symbolism was expressed.[3]

Although Platonic ideals and allegorical modes of thought certainly shaped Elizabethan political culture, there are a number of reasons to question whether the public saw Elizabeth and other English monarchs of the sixteenth and seventeenth centuries in quite the way Geertz describes. To begin with, public allegorical pageants centring on royalty were much less common than he implies, even in London where the court normally resided. Pageant scenes accompanied Elizabeth's coronation entry in 1559, and entries by James I in 1604 and 1606, but there were no street pageants directly associated with reigning monarchs between 1559 and 1603, nor between 1606 and the Civil War, although rulers did appear in public on numerous occasions during these intervening periods.[4] Moreover, even when pageants did take place their allegorical meaning would have been less clear to most spectators than it is to modern scholars. Scholars can work with printed accounts which describe all the pageants accompanying events like coronation processions in detail, complete with full transcripts of recited speeches. Except for those actually in the royal procession,

---

[2] 'Centers, Kings and Charisma: Reflections on the Symbolics of Power', most conveniently available in *Local Knowledge* (New York, 1983), p. 129.

[3] Geertz's preoccupation with the street pageants follows a tradition defined, especially, by Anglo, *Spectacle and Tudor Policy* and Bergeron, *English Civic Pageantry*.

[4] There were also river processions in 1610 and 1617 associated with Prince Henry and Prince Charles. All these pageants are recorded in John Nichols, *Progresses of Queen Elizabeth*, 3 vols (London, 1823) and *Progresses of James 1*, 3 vols (London, 1828). For modern accounts see Bergeron, *English Civic Pageantry*, chapters 1 and 2, and for James's coronation entry, Parry, *The Golden Age Restored*, chapter 1.

contemporaries had to content themselves with a much more fragmentary view. At best they could see and hear a single pageant in the series placed along the monarch's route. Yet even this was difficult, since painted emblems could not always be seen clearly from a distance and the noise of the crowd frequently drowned out recited speeches.[5]

Geertz and others have failed to recognize, in short, that the elaborate allegorical schemes recorded in printed accounts of royal processions often bear little relationship to what most spectators actually saw. They have also failed to give more than cursory attention to aspects of these ceremonies that vividly impressed contemporaries. Eye-witness descriptions of royal processions that were not written for publication almost invariably pay less attention to parables than to the sheer spectacle of the court as it moved along public thoroughfares. Whether they included allegories or not, royal processions were always displays of majesty – gorgeous assemblages of all the trappings of wealth, rank and power known to society. This above all made them effective vehicles for the royal charisma. As the Earl of Newcastle put it in a letter to his royal ward, Prince Charles:

> What protects you kings more than ceremony: the distance people are with you, great officers, heralds, drums, trumpeters, rich coaches ... Marshal's men making room ... I know these [things] master the people sufficiently. Aye even the wisest ... shall shake off his wisdom and shake for fear of it, for this is the mist is cast before us and masters the commonwealth.[6]

Everyone recognizes, of course, that gorgeous display was an inseparable feature of Renaissance kingship. Yet there persists a largely unspoken assumption that such display becomes worthy of serious attention only when it can be related to poetry, art, drama or some other form of high culture.[7] I wish to argue that this

---

5 There are numerous accounts of songs or verses being drowned out by the crowds during royal processions. See, for example, *The Royal Passage of her Majesty from the Tower of London, to her Palace of Whitehall* (London, 1559), Bi-Bii; Nichols, *Progresses of James I*, vol. 2, p. 68.

6 BL Harl. MS. 6988, fo. 112. I have modernized the spelling and punctuation.

7 At least in English historiography. Students of continental pageantry have sometimes taken an approach less indebted to the traditional methods of literary critics and art historians. See, for example, the essays in Sean Wilentz, ed., *Rites of Power* (Philadelphia, 1984). Lawrence M. Bryant, *The King and the City in the Parisian Royal Entry Ceremony: Politics, Ritual, and Art in the Renaissance* (Geneva, 1986) provides an extensive survey of the French royal entry.

approach is limiting and fundamentally misleading. Much of the idiom used to convey the charisma of Tudor and early Stuart monarchs owed little or nothing to artists and poets. It derived instead from social and religious conventions deeply embedded within English culture, which orchestrated the majestic ceremonies enveloping the monarch and shaped public reactions to the ruler's presence. The present essay has two goals. It seeks, first, to elucidate this idiom, and the cultural frame which defined it, through a 'thick description' of the most common of the great public rituals of Tudor monarchy, the royal entry into London.[8] To do this we will need to examine both the symbolism of the entry itself and the responses and expectations of those who watched it, for the full meaning of the royal entry becomes evident only if we recognize that it embodied not only courtly and aristocratic forms of display but genuinely popular elements, to express a rich and subtle image of kingship. Second, the essay seeks to explain how the royal entry declined under the Stuarts, so that by the eve of the Civil War Charles I almost never appeared in the streets of his capital. I hope to show how an essentially medieval ritual, encompassing a set of traditional attitudes about the royal office, retained its vitality down to the late sixteenth century, across the great watershed of the Reformation, and then gradually disintegrated. The result was to weaken the royal charisma, at least in the London area, in ways that help to explain Charles I's inability to control his capital on the eve of the Civil War.

I

The Tudor royal entry belonged to a family of rituals inherited from the Middle Ages, during which the Lord Mayor and a delegation of leading citizens formally greeted the monarch before a large audience.[9] These rituals often took place some distance from London, when the King or Queen approached the city after a military campaign or summer progress. Thus when Henry V returned from Agincourt, the Lord Mayor and Aldermen in scarlet

---

[8] See Clifford Geertz, 'Thick Description: Toward an Interpretive Theory of Culture', in *The Interpretation of Cultures* (New York, 1973).

[9] Bryant, *The Parisian Royal Entry Ceremony*, chapter 3, provides an illuminating account of the French royal entry in the Middle Ages. There is no comparable work for England, although a comparative study would be most valuable.

robes, and 300 mounted citizens dressed in coats of murrey (dark purple) with gold chains around their necks, rode out to meet him at Blackheath and accompanied him back to Westminster.[10] More than a century and a half later, in 1584, Elizabeth returned from a progress to an essentially similar welcome.[11] The city also frequently escorted monarchs as they moved through the immediate London area while travelling between palaces. If the journey took place on the Thames, the brightly decorated barges of the city's livery companies took the place of a citizens' cavalcade.[12] In all cases, however, the ritual assumed the form of a grand procession, in which both the court and London dignitaries joined.

A formal entry occurred only when the King or Queen actually set foot in London. When this happened the civic elite did not form its own procession, but instead assembled along the monarch's route through the city. The ceremonies surrounding the royal procession, however, became much more elaborate. Hall's account of Henry VIII's coronation illustrates the essential features:

> His grace with the Queen departed from the Tower through the City of London, against whose coming the streets where his grace should pass were hanged with tapestry ... cloth of Arras ... [and] cloth of gold. And the streets [were] railed and barred, on the one side ... where every occupation stood, in their liveries in order, beginning with base occupations, and so ascending to the most worshipful crafts: highest and lastly stood the Mayor, with the Alderman. The goldsmith's stalls unto the end of the Old Change being replenished with virgins in white, with branches of white wax: the priests and clerks, in rich copes, with crosses and censers of silver ... censing his grace and the Queen as they passed.[13]

The virgins in white appear to have been unique to this procession and after the Reformation the clergy with their censers withdrew, but in virtually all other respects Hall's description could apply to any royal entry from the late Middle Ages to the reign of James I.

10 Edward Hall, *Chronicle, Containing the History of England* (1809; facsimile reprint, New York, 1965), pp. 72–3.
11 John Stow, *Annales* (1631 edition), p. 700.
12 I have not discovered any formal limits to the geographic area in which these escorts were provided, and it is possible that formal limits were never defined. Barge processions often went as far up as Chelsea, but to my knowledge never proceeded on to Richmond or Hampton Court.
13 Hall, *Chronicle*, p. 507.

Sometimes additional embellishments were provided, such as pageants and triumphal arches along the route. But in essence a royal entry was always a procession by the monarch and the court, through streets decorated with tapestries, silks and cloth of gold. The livery companies and the Lord Mayor and aldermen always stood at the front of the crowd, the former dressed in dark robes with hoods trimmed in red; the latter in robes of crimson and scarlet. In front of these dignitaries stood whifflers or guards, while overhead fluttered banners bearing the arms of London and its guilds.

This ceremony is best approached as a fusion of two distinct species of processional rites, each possessing its own idiom and cultural frame. A royal entry was, first, an especially lavish progress, such as occurred whenever the monarch or any other great figure travelled along a public road.[14] Progresses were framed by the assumption that the size and quality of a great man's entourage directly reflected his status or, in contemporary parlance, his honour.[15] The concept of honour encompassed personal qualities like courage, prowess, honesty and loyalty, but it also involved an ability to demonstrate authority over others. A progress did this by parading a great man's affinity of servants, retainers, friends and and allies, in a spectacular display of prestige and power.

The idiom of progresses consisted of certain well-established emblems of rank, including heraldic banners to proclaim the great man's ancestry, trumpeters or ushers to announce his coming and clear his path, an entourage of mounted gentlemen and a foot guard of liveried yeomen. In a royal entry all these features reappeared on an exceptionally grand scale. Instead of being attended by fifty or a hundred horsemen monarchs sometimes entered London accompanied by 500 or 1,000, including some of the realm's greatest noblemen. The guards and trumpeters were also more numerous than in private progresses, and their liveries

---

[14] For Elizabethan royal progresses, see Lawrence Stone, *The Crisis of the Aristocracy* (Oxford, 1965), pp. 451–4. For aristocratic progresses in the late Middle Ages, see Mark Girouard, *Life of the English Country House* (New Haven, 1978), pp. 14–15. The tradition Girouard describes survived in its essentials down to the late sixteenth century and, in some cases, beyond.

[15] For a general discussion of the concept of honour in English political culture see Mervyn James, *English Politics and the Concept of Honour, 1485–1642*, Past and Present Supplement no. 3 (1978), reprinted in *Society, Politics and Culture* (Cambridge, 1986), pp. 308–415.

were especially splendid. In addition monarchs rode beneath red or gold canopies, a symbol reserved for royalty.[16]

Perhaps the single most impressive expression of royal grandeur, however, was ornate clothing. In Tudor England the sight of rich silks, brocades and jewels was a compelling expression of prestige and power. The moralist Stubbes concluded a diatribe against luxurious dress by exempting noblemen and gentlemen from his strictures, since they 'ought to wear [sumptuous] attire . . . for the distinction of them from the inferior sort'.[17] Elizabethan portraitists often depicted costumes with more care and attention than faces, while both poets and letter-writers frequently commented at length upon the sartorial splendour of the great, especially when describing ceremonies. Shakespeare's description in *Henry VIII* of the Field of Cloth of Gold, for example, is almost entirely preoccupied with competitive displays of clothing:

> today the French
> All clinquant, all in gold, like heathen gods
> Shone down the English; and tomorrow, they
> Made Britain India; every man that stood
> Show'd like a mine. Their dwarfish pages were
> As cherubins, all guilt: the madams, too,
> Not used to toil, did almost sweat to bear
> The pride upon them.[18]

Although less eloquent, accounts of royal entries sometimes convey much the same impression. The 'whole court so sparkled with jewels and gold collars', the Venetian ambassador wrote at Elizabeth's coronation entry, 'that they cleared the air, though it snowed a little'.[19] Few things expressed the majesty of kingship more vividly than the sight of hundreds of brilliantly dressed men and women, walking or riding with solemn dignity around an even more resplendent monarch.

On one level, then, a royal entry asserted the monarch's position as the greatest lord in the realm, through an idiom rooted in the

[16] For all these features see, for example, the Venetian ambassador's description of Elizabeth's coronation entry in *Calendar of State Papers Venetian*, vol. 2, p. 12.

[17] Frederick J. Furnivall, ed., *Anatomy of Abuses in Shakespeare's Youth* (London, 1877), p. xii.

[18] I. i. 18–26.

[19] *CSP Ven.*, vol. 7, p. 12. *Cf.* Hall's description of Henry VIII's coronation entry (*Chronicle*, p. 507).

neo-feudal conventions of great medieval households. The royal entry also belonged, however, to a family of civic processions, such as took place not only in London but in other English boroughs and many European cities. In this case the frame consisted of a conventional view of urban society as an organic hierarchy rooted in the mysteries of various industrial crafts. Membership in the guilds which regulated these mysteries also conferred the 'freedom' of the city: the right to trade within its boundaries and to vote in civic elections. At the head of each guild stood a livery company of prosperous, senior members. The liveries formed an elite of 'worshipful' citizens, who employed poorer artisans and journeymen, while also dominating neighbourhood offices and forming the pool from which the city selected its magistrates.[20] The magistracy – consisting of a Mayor, a court of aldermen and, in the case of London, a recorder and two sheriffs – formed the apex of the urban pyramid. In a normal civic procession the magistrates marched first, followed by the livery companies in an order reflecting the superiority of some crafts and the relative inferiority of others. The rest of the population stood to the side and watched. The procession thereby articulated the hierarchical structure of the community's elite, while at the same time emphasizing the broad distinction between that elite and everyone else.[21]

In a royal entry this whole configuration was altered by the presence of the monarch, who stood outside the urban community, but who also represented the ultimate source of its corporate privileges. Yet the basic distinctions displayed in a more normal civic procession remained. The special place of the Lord Mayor and aldermen was emphasized not only by their ceremonial robes, but by a rite that took place as the monarch reached the point along the procession's route where the magistrates stood.[22] The magistrates always stepped forth from the crowd, whereupon the City Recorder delivered a speech expressing the citizens' loyalty and asking the ruler to be a good and gracious sovereign. As he did so he presented a sword or sceptre. The ruler took the sceptre and

---

[20] In London and many other cities this pool was limited specifically to members of the most prestigious liveries.

[21] The best discussion is Charles Phythian-Adams, 'Ceremony and the Citizen: The Communal Year at Coventry', in *Crisis and Order in English Towns*, ed. Peter Clark and Paul Slack (London, 1972).

[22] This could be the point at which the King entered the city, or some conspicuous place within London.

handed it to the Mayor, while verbally expressing confidence in the city's magistrates and the citizens' loyalty. The Mayor then proceeded to carry the sceptre before the monarch for the remainder of the procession.[23] His position as the crown's trusted representative within the city was thus acted out before the assembled crowds. The aldermen also joined the procession further to the rear, symbolizing the fact that they too were royal magistrates.

The livery companies were pushed out of the procession itself, but they occupied a place of honour at the front of the audience, where they formed a symbolic buffer between the royal court and the mass of ordinary spectators watching from windows, rooftops and other vantage-points further back. This position emphasized the liveries' role as a responsible urban elite, to whom the ruler looked for the maintenance of order. The presence at the front of the companies of whifflers or footguards, with staffs of authority, further underlined this role. At the same time the sober, uniform appearance of the liverymen's robes must have made a striking contrast to the far more colourful and individualized clothes of the court. The liverymen enjoyed a corporate dignity, differing from the more individualistic and assertive ethos of the great noblemen around the monarch.[24] The whole arrangement of a royal entry thus expressed the coming together of two distinct hierarchies, one based on the wealth created by London's crafts, the other anchored in the traditions of the royal court and the kingdom's great feudal families.[25] The ruler occupied a position at the apex of both

23 For a good example see Wriothesley's description of the presentation of the sceptre at Mary's first entry (*Camden Society Publications*, new series, 20 (1877), p. 93). Unlike their French counterparts, English monarchs did not specifically confirm the privileges of the rulers of their capital city during royal entries. Instead they promised to remember the citizens' loyalty and to rule graciously over the city. In general French entries appear to have involved efforts to dramatize fairly precise legal and constitutional relationships, whereas English entries emphasized a more generalized ethos of loyalty and royal benevolence.

24 On this point *cf.* James, *Society, Politics and Culture*, pp. 35–6.

25 The emphasis on the fusion of different groups into a unified body under the Crown seems to have been a distinctive feature of English entries. In French royal entries, by contrast, representatives of the city of Paris and of the clergy (and eventually also of the University and the Parlement) confronted the King separately, at different points along his route. Interestingly this situation changed in several entries staged during the English occupation of Paris in the 1420s and early 1430s, when for the first time the representatives of the city, the clergy and the Parlement jointly paid homage to Lancastrian monarchs and their representatives. (On this point see Bryant, *Parisian Royal Entry Ceremony*, pp. 82–8). Here again one can detect a difference between the French emphasis on

hierarchies, mediating between them, as the ultimate source of unity and authority.

II

An ordinary Londoner who witnessed a royal entry would therefore be forcefully reminded of his subordination to a massive, multi-layered system of authority, ascending from his wealthier liveried neighbours and employers, through the Lord Mayor and aldermen, to the resplendent royal court and half-deified monarch. From this vantage-point royal entries appear as classic examples of rituals which demonstrate and define power and status. Such a conclusion is tempered, however, if we turn our attention to the behaviour of the crowd of ordinary Londoners and people up from the country that watched from vantage-points behind the livery companies. If an entry was simply an assertion of power and status, we should expect the crowd to have assumed a passive and deferential posture. Instead it always aggressively asserted its presence, treating the monarch less as an awesome symbol of authority than as a popular hero.

The most obvious way in which the crowd did this was by making an enormous amount of noise. Especially during a monarch's first entry, spectators always cheered loudly, adding to the sound of artillery salutes and the pealing of the bells of London's 104 parish churches. Spectators often pushed and shoved each other in their efforts to get a better view and sometimes threw their hats into the air as the ruler passed by. The effect impressed witnesses as one of deliberate pandemonium: during Mary's coronation entry the noise sounded 'like an earth quake'; at Elizabeth's acclamation, 'it seemed as if the world were come to an end'.[26] It is more difficult to find descriptions of crowd behaviour during entries by crowned monarchs, but the few accounts that have survived indicate that these also took place in an atmosphere of boisterous holiday revelry, which occasionally threatened to degenerate into real disorder.

particular corporate rights and duties, which separately defined the relationship to the Crown of each group within the realm, and the English stress on a common, transcendent bond of loyalty.

[26] *Wriothesley's Chronicle*, p. 95; *CSP Ven.*, vol. 7, p. 17. During her coronation entry Elizabeth had to ask the crowd to be quiet so she could hear the speeches delivered in the pageants.

The single most revealing account of a London crowd watching a great procession in our period was recorded by the Venetian, Orazio Busino, after the Lord Mayor's Day Pageant of 1617. He described a carnivalesque atmosphere, with apprentices jumping up to hitch rides on coaches of aristocrats who had come to watch the pageant, pelting with rocks and mud any coachman who tried to drive them off.[27] The climax to the pageant was the appearance of a float bearing an actor parodying a Spanish courtier, who brought roars of appreciative laughter from the crowd. When a real Spaniard appeared in the street a detachment of apprentices, urged on by a ferocious matron, scooped up rocks, dirt and refuse and took off after him.

This vignette is fairly late in date and it does not concern a royal entry, but it none the less shows how the crowd might decisively alter a procession's flavour and significance. The official account of this particular Mayor's Day Inauguration underlines the point: it mentions the Spanish courtier briefly as part of a 'Pageant of several Nations', which purportedly represented 'the prosperity of love, which by the virtue of traffic [trade] is likely to continue' between different peoples.[28] He seems a minor part of a day-long celebration of such conventional themes as 'Peace, Prosperity, Love, Unity, Plenty and Fidelity'. Only Busino's account reveals that the crowd seized upon this little piece of theatre to demonstrate its hatred of Spain and, by implication, its disapproval of James I's pro-Spanish policies. An allegory that was supposed to celebrate Anglo–Spanish friendship instead became the centrepiece for a nasty display of xenophobia, which inverted the pageant's ostensible message.

Subversive behaviour by the crowd or by individuals within it was rare during Tudor royal entries, but it did occur. When Mary travelled through the city after asking for its support during Wyatt's rebellion one onlooker shouted at her that she should send her priests and bishops to fight the rebels.[29] During Anne Boleyn's

---

27 *CSP Ven.*, vol. 15, p. 60; 'We noticed but few coaches . . . for the insolence of the mob is extreme. They cling behind the coaches and should the coachman use his whip, they jump down and pelt him with mud . . . In these great uproars no sword is ever unsheathed, everything ends in kicks, fisticuffs, and muddy faces.

28 Thomas Middleton, *The Tryumphs of Honour and Industry* (London, 1617).

29 John Proctor, *The History of Wyates Rebellion* (London, 1554), pp. 54–55. The protesting individual, who was rumoured to be a Protestant hosier, was confined to Newgate.

coronation entry in 1533, the crowd stood mute. When a servant of the Queen exhorted the spectators to cheer he was told that 'no one could force the people's hearts, not even the King'.[30] This was, of course, true: at least in principle every royal entry ran the risk of encountering a sullen or hostile reception. But this fact must have enhanced the impact of the more normal, enthusiastic cheers and the monarch's gracious responses to them. The intended effect of such exchanges was, in the words of one Elizabethan, to convert London to 'a stage wherein was showed the wonderful spectacle of a noble hearted princess toward her most loving people, and the people's exceeding comfort in beholding so worthy a sovereign'. Such demonstrations of popular devotion were especially significant against the background of threatened rebellions and invasions which characterized so much of the Tudor period. During a crisis the ruler's ability to command the loyalty of the urban populace could prove decisive, as Wyatt's rebellion showed. Even when no immediate threat existed, vocal popular support enhanced a ruler's reputation, as James acknowledged when London greeted him after the failure of the Powder Plot. He told the crowd that 'these signs [of devotion] were the more welcome to him for that foreign ambassadors might see the vanity of those reports that were spread abroad in other countries of mislikes and distastes twixt him and his people'.[31]

III

A royal entry thus presented a curiously dualistic image of king-ship, by emphasizing both the majesty that separated the monarch from ordinary subjects and the emotional bonds that united them. One way to interpret this duality is in terms of Victor Turner's argument that ritual frequently expresses a dialectical tension between what he calls 'structure' and 'communitas'. Structure, for Turner, designates 'all that holds people apart, defines their differences and constrains their actions', whereas communitas represents 'the desire for a total, unmediated relationship between person and person, a relationship which nevertheless does not

---

[30] Sydney Anglo, *Spectacle and Early Tudor Policy*, p. 259. I have translated the quotations from a French manuscript that Anglo quotes.
[31] Norman McClure, *The Letters of John Chamberlain* (Philadelphia, 1939), vol. 1, p. 223.

submerge one in the other but safeguards their uniqueness in the very act of realizing their commonness'.[32] Tudor entries can certainly be seen in this way. To be sure, the monarch never established a truly egalitarian and unmediated relationship with onlookers: the ruler's superiority was always acknowledged, even in the most friendly interactions.[33] But the crowd's cheers undeniably had the effect of breaking through formal ceremonial barriers, making possible, in however tenuous and fleeting a manner, some sort of direct contact between the ruler and ruled. Contemporary descriptions, moreover, indicate that monarchs themselves sometimes deliberately promoted a sense of oneness and fellowship with plebeian spectators. During her coronation entry Elizabeth

> did not only show her most gracious love to her people in general, but also privately, if the baser personages had either offered her grace any flowers or such like, as a signification of their good will, or moved her to any suit, she most gently, to the common rejoicing of all the lookers-on . . . staid her Chariot, and heard their requests.[34]

These gestures emphasized the Queen's basic humanity and accessibility, thereby counterbalancing the formidable display of authority and status which the royal procession embodied. Power was given a friendly human face, so that even the humble could vicariously share in its splendour.

We also need to ask, however, whether the concept of communitas cannot be translated into sixteenth-century terms. Every student of the period is familiar with concepts of hierarchy, subordination and obedience which underlay a Tudor Englishman's belief in 'structure'; but the notion that a ruler might have participated in a 'total unmediated' relationship with ordinary subjects may seem to contradict the whole tenor of sixteenth-century political thought. What sort of cultural frame encompassed the

---

[32] Victor Turner, *Dramas, Fields and Metaphors* (Ithica, N.Y., 1974), p. 274. See also *The Ritual Process* (Chicago, 1969).

[33] Nothing in the Tudor royal entry corresponds to the liminal phases in many of the rituals Turner studies, in which participants are systematically stripped of rank and status and placed in a special position at the boundary of society. Pure communitas does not appear in the royal entry. What does exist, I am arguing, is an important dimension of communitas, wrapped up within a ritual that in most respects remained an expression of hierarchical rank and power.

[34] *Royal Passage*, fo. Aii.

mutual expressions of goodwill that monarchs exchanged with their subjects during royal entries? Was there in fact a sense of human solidarity implicit in the entry ritual?

Part of the answer lies in the ancient custom of the acclamation, which in a remote period had expressed the idea that the assembled people must assent to the making of a King. In the Tudor period this was no longer true, but the notion persisted that monarchs ought to rule with their people's unforced obedience. By appearing to show that this was the case, a royal entry reinforced the aura of legitimacy. There is also some evidence that royal entries reflected the bastard feudal concept of good lordship. Elizabeth promised to be a 'goodlady' to the city during her coronation entry.[35] She also stopped along her route to hear petitions, and promised to remember – and thus, implicitly, to reward – the city's devotion. These gestures emphasized the reciprocal character of the bonds between the Queen and her subjects: the notion that in return for loyalty and service she would provide protection, justice, charity to the needy and patronage for the elite.[36] A concept of government was being acted out, not only in the allegorical street pageants, but in the unrehearsed speeches and gestures of the Queen and her audience.[37]

At its deepest level, however, the human bond between ruler and people was conceived in religious terms. The crowd's cheers were actually a blessing, expressed with great emotional intensity. Von Wedel wrote that when Elizabeth entered London in 1585 'she sat alone [in an open chariot] ... and addressed the multitude, saying "God save my people" ... the latter answering "God save her grace" ... The people said this very often, falling on their knees.'[38] A sympathetic French ambassador no doubt had such scenes in mind when he said that 'he had often seen the Queen on her way through the city receive such blessings from the people as though she had

---

[35] *Ibid.*, Eiii.   [36] For charity see *ibid.*, Div-Ei.

[37] Indeed on at least one occasion a street pageant provided a cue for a demonstration of mutual goodwill between Elizabeth and her people. A child recited a speech concluding with the words 'God thee preserve, we pray, and wish thee ever well.' At this point 'the whole people gave a great shout, wishing with one assent as the child had said. And the Queen's Majesty thanked most heartily both the City for this her gentle receiving ... and also the people for confirming the same' (*ibid.*, Aiii). Note the distinction made by Elizabeth between the welcome of the city, embodied in the pageant, and the welcome of 'the people', expressed through the crowd's shout.

[38] *Transactions of the Royal Historical Society*, new series, 9 (1895) p. 256.

been another Messiah'.[39] This was not simply an Elizabethan custom, however; Wriothesley recorded that during Mary's first entry the streets were 'full of people shouting and crying Jesus save her Grace . . . weeping tears of joy'.[40]

Although the expression 'God save the Queen' is still a commonplace expression of English patriotism, in the Tudor period the words possessed a deeper resonance. Especially before the Reformation the public exchange of blessings between Prince and people would have called to mind numerous other ritualized expressions of religious solidarity which punctuated the city's public life.[41] In the early sixteenth century the pursuit of salvation was frequently a collective activity, bound up with the quest for peace and unity within the community. People prayed for each other's souls, pooled their resources to support masses for the dead and joined together to honour the saints and worship God. Quarrelling neighbours refrained from taking the sacrament until they settled their differences. During holidays wealthy citizens set out tables of food in the streets, where their poorer neighbours might gather together in a spirit of festive goodwill. On joyous occasions like the birth of an heir to the throne citizens made bonfires at which, according to Stow, feuding neighbours were 'by the labour of others reconciled, and made of bitter enemies loving friends'.[42] Behind all these practices lay the central ideal of charity, the belief that to worship God properly one also had to love one's neighbours and obey the moral commandments which assured civic peace.

The way in which the royal entry fitted into this pattern appears with special vividness in Hall's account of London's reception of Henry VII, after his victory on Bosworth Field.

> The king removed . . . toward London, and even as he passed, the rustical people . . . assembled in great numbers, and with great joy clapped their hands and shouted, crying King Henry, King Henry. But when he approached near the city the Mayor, the Senate [aldermen] and the magistrates . . . met him at Shoreditch, and not only saluted and welcomed him with one voice in general, but every person particularly pressed and advanced himself, gladly to touch and kiss [those] victorious

[39] *CSP Ven.*, vol. 8, p. 115.   [40] Wriothesley's *Chronicle*, p. 95.

[41] On this point see, especially, Susan Brigden, 'Religion and Social Obligation in Early Sixteenth-Century London', *Past and Present*, 103 (1984), pp. 67–112.

[42] Quoted in Phythian-Adams, 'Ceremony and the Citizen', pp. 65, 66.

hands which had overcome so monstrous and cruel a tyrant . . .
And with great pomp and triumph he rode through the city to the
Cathedral church of St. Paul where he offered his three standards.
[After giving thanks Henry dined at the Bishop of London's
palace], during which time plays, pastimes and pleasures were
shown in every part of the city. And to the intent that their good
mind toward God should not be put in oblivion, they caused
general processions solemnly to be celebrated.[43]

Religious and secular elements blended in a general celebration
of love and thanksgiving that reached upward to embrace the
King and downward to engulf the humblest urban residents. This
celebration, in turn, expressed the providentialist message that
Henry's victory had come as a divine mercy upon the kingdom. To
reject that message, by casting doubt on Henry's otherwise tenuous
claims to legitimacy, meant placing oneself outside the Christian
fellowship which the day's rituals defined.

In most early Tudor entries liturgical elements and popular
celebrations were less prominent, but the same general effect was
none the less intended. Several contemporary descriptions underline this point by describing the people, the ruler, or both as
'rejoicing' during an entry. During Elizabeth's coronation entry 'on
either side there was nothing but gladness, nothing but prayer,
nothing but comfort. The Queen's Majesty rejoiced marvellously
to see . . . so earnest love of subjects, so evidently declared even
unto her Grace's own person, being carried in the middest of them.
The people again were wonderfully ravished with the loving
answers and gestures of their Princess.'[44] Even if such accounts
greatly exaggerated, they demonstrate the attitudes and expectations which lay behind the interactions between rulers and crowds.
An entry publicly celebrated the Christian love that united ruler
and ruled in a well-governed commonwealth. It reflected the
medieval conviction that, however unequal people may be in this
world, they are both equal and interdependent in God's eyes. For
all his grandeur, a King belonged to a Christian community of
fallible men and women. The English expected his public conduct
to show an awareness of this fact.

In post-Reformation England the religious context of the royal

---

[43] *Chronicle*, pp. 492, 493.
[44] *Royal Passage*, fo. A2. For examples from other reigns see *The L'Isle Letters*, 6
vols (Chicago, 1981), vol. 3, p. 576; Wriothesley's *Chronicle*, p. 28.

entry was drastically altered, as the emphasis upon communal worship and mutual spiritual interdependence that had characterized late medieval urban piety gradually gave way before more individualistic Protestant concepts of salvation. Yet in royal entries the emphasis on religious solidarity not only persisted; it sometimes took on aggressively Protestant overtones. Elizabeth's first entry featured pageants which made thinly-veiled allusions to her adherence to the Reformation. Thus on Fleet Street the Queen encountered a representation of Deborah, 'the judge and restorer of the house of Israel,' and a transparent symbol for Elizabeth herself. The real meaning of this pageant emerges only against the background of tension and manoeuvring between Roman Catholics and religious reformers which followed Mary's death. Spectators were in effect being given the choice of applauding a Protestant restoration or insulting both the city, which had supervised the planning of the street pageant, and the new Queen, whose gracious response indicated her sympathy with its message. At Temple Bar, as a pageant character delivered speeches advocating the 'maintenance of truth and rooting out of error', Elizabeth 'now and then held up her hands to heavenward and willed the people to say Amen'.[45] Everyone present must have suspected that in the new reign 'truth' would be associated with some as yet undefined form of Protestantism and 'error' with the purported superstitions of the old church. Conventions rooted in medieval piety were being manipulated to promote a Protestant redefinition of the English Christian community.

Thereafter religious imagery was normally absent, although an entry following the Armada's defeat is a notable exception. On this occasion Elizabeth made a formal entry into London and proceeded to St Paul's cathedral, where she knelt on the ground before her subjects, humbled herself to God and offered thanks for the victory. Fifty clergymen in full liturgical garments then escorted her into the cathedral to hear a sermon. As in 1559 the Queen identified herself with the lowest common denominator of Protestant sentiment. In most Elizabethan entries there were no pageants and no sermons, but the Queen herself remained the primary symbol of England's resistance to popery, rebellion and foreign domination. The blessings she gave and received during royal entries reinforced

---

[45] *Ibid.*, Eii.

the peculiar amalgam of patriotism and Protestantism so essential
to her cult.

IV

The Stuart dynasty thus inherited a vital tradition of processional
rituals, which James I's magnificent coronation entry continued.
Within a few years, however, a marked falling off in the level of
public royal ceremonies became evident. James made another
formal entry into London in 1606, but subsequently did so only
once more during the remaining nineteen years of his reign.[46]
Prince Henry was fond of public ceremony and for a time it
appeared that he might remedy his father's neglect. But his
premature death, shortly after his installation as Prince of Wales,
prevented this from happening. Charles avoided making any
entries into London, either as Prince or King, until 1638, when his
mother-in-law, the Queen Dowager of France, arrived in England
and etiquette demanded that he accompany her as she passed
through London en route to her lodgings in St James's Palace.[47]
Even then he rode in a closed coach, instead of on horseback, in the
traditional manner. No other public ceremony took the royal
entry's place, especially in Charles's reign. Public royal ceremonies
simply became less frequent and less magnificent, until in the 1630s
Charles virtually withdrew from his people's gaze.[48] Much has been
made of the 'theatrical quality' of early Stuart kingship. But outside
the walls of their palaces James I engaged in noticeably less public
display than his predecessor, while Charles I was the least theatrical
English monarch since at least Henry VI.

Why did this dramatic curtailment in public ceremony occur? It is
tempting to seek at least part of the explanation in the increasingly

---

[46] The 1606 entry celebrated the arrival of his brother-in-law, Christian IV of
Denmark, on a visit to England. For this and the coronation entry see Nichols,
Progresses of James I, vol. 1, pp. 325–424, and vol. 2, p. 68. James also appeared
before London crowds after the failure of the Powder Plot in 1605, although I
have not found any record of a formal entry. The last Jacobean entry came in
1620 when James worshipped in St Paul's Cathedral, in an effort to encourage
donations for its restoration.

[47] The entry is described and illustrated in Jean Puget de la Serre, *Histoire de la
reine mere du roy très chrestien dans la Grande Bretagne* (London, 1639).

[48] Richards, 'Kingship of Charles I', provides much more elaboration on this point.
Charles did continue to touch for the King's Evil, but he restricted access to this
ceremony as well.

modern and Protestant character of London. The royal entry was in essence a medieval ceremony, deriving partly from the quasi-feudal traditions of the royal progress and partly from an urban ceremonial culture rooted in late medieval Catholicism. It has been shown that in other English cities, notably Coventry and Bristol, the Reformation undermined a rich processional culture inherited from the fourteenth and fifteenth centuries.[49] Specifically religious processions were already under attack in the 1540s and mostly perished before or during the early years of Elizabeth. Processions that were partly secular in character, such as those accompanying the inauguration of a new Mayor, often survived somewhat longer; but these had also disappeared before the early seventeenth century. The old Catholic emphasis on charity and communality was subverted by Protestant ideals of discipline, by increasingly acute class divisions, and by a more restrictive code of decorum. The result, as Phythian-Adams writes of Coventry, is that 'ceremony and religion together withdrew indoors from the vulgar gaze'.[50] Broadly similar changes also took place in London, where traditional outdoor religious ceremonies also disappeared and the tremendous variety of processional rituals that had existed in the early sixteenth century was drastically reduced.

Yet the record does not support the view that the royal entry declined because of a change in civic culture. On the contrary, whenever a Stuart monarch appeared in London both the city corporation and the urban populace responded enthusiastically. London prepared the traditional coronation pageants for Charles I's entry in 1625 and continued to await the event until the court cancelled it the next spring. The city began preparations again when he returned from a progress to Scotland in 1633, and was again disappointed. Moreover in London the most important traditional civic processions, the annual Lord Mayor's Pageants, did not die out in the seventeenth century. Instead they became even more elaborate, by absorbing the street pageants and some other elements which had previously distinguished the greatest royal entries.[51] The Lord Mayor became a surrogate for the King,

---

[49] Phythian-Adams, 'Ceremony and the Citizen', pp. 57–85; David Harris Sachs, 'The Demise of the Martyrs: The Feasts of St. Clement and St. Katherine in Bristol, 1400–1600', *Social History*, 11 (1986), pp. 141–70.

[50] Phythian-Adams, 'Ceremony and the Citizen', p. 80.

[51] The fullest treatment is Bergeron, *English Civic Pageantry*, pp. 123–308.

allowing the traditions of the royal entry to survive even in the monarch's absence.[52]

The great royal processions finally died, not because of a shift in religious climate or a waning of interest on the part of the citizenry, but because the court withdrew from them. The crucial problem is therefore to explain the behaviour of James and Charles. Why, despite their exalted view of the monarchy, did they fail except on rare occasions to assert their charisma in the accustomed public manner? The traditional answer to this question, insofar as one exists at all, is that James's distaste for plebeian crowds caused him to minimize his contact with the public, and that in this respect Charles followed his father's lead. There is undoubtedly something to this. James's distaste for crowds may have been exaggerated by a few contemporaries and by later historians, but there is abundant evidence that he sometimes became uncomfortable in public and behaved very ungraciously. Sir Simonds D'Ewes found it worthy of remark that in 1621 the King responded courteously to the cheers of spectators watching him as he went to open Parliament, 'contrary to his former hasty and passionate custom, which often in his sudden distemper would bid a p— or a plague on such as flocked to see him'.[53]

Historians have been too willing, however, to attribute James's behaviour to his alleged neuroses, without enquiring into what else may have lain behind it. It is far more plausible to seek an explanation in the frustration of a Scottish King unaccustomed to the peculiar conventions of English monarchy.[54] Paradoxically it

---

[52] See, for example, Anthony Munday's description of the torchlight procession that was the culmination of the Lord Mayor's Pageant, *Metropolis Coronata*: 'The way being somewhat long, the order of the march appeared the more excellent . . . even as if it had been a Royal Masque prepared for the marriage of an immortal deity; as in like nature we hold the Lord Mayor to be this day solemnly married to London's supreme dignity, by representing the awful authority of Sovereign Majesty.' The parallel between civic pageants and court theatricals, and the position of the Lord Mayor as a symbolic substitute for the King, could hardly be clearer.

[53] *Autobiography and Correspondence*, ed. James Orchard Halliwell, 2 vols (London, 1845), vol. 1, p. 170. *Cf.* the anonymous 'Advertisement of a Loyal Subject to his Sovereign, Drawn out of his Observation of his People's Speeches', in SP14/2, piece 26. Citations on this point could be multiplied.

[54] The following discussion is indebted to Jenny Wormald, 'James VI and I: Two Kings or One?', *History*, 68 (1983), pp. 187–209. I disagree, however, with Wormald's contention that Elizabeth's more gracious public behaviour reinforced a mystique which distanced the Queen from her people, for reasons that should, by now, be clear.

was the very grandeur and formality of English court ceremonies that enabled Elizabeth to step outside the role of royal demigod and make contact with her people. Those ceremonies were so imposing and the deference accorded the Queen so profound that neither her people's boisterous enthusiasm nor her own affability could jeopardize her status. In Scotland, on the other hand, an elaborate court ceremonial never developed. There James had ruled, in his own words, as 'a King without state, without honour, without order, where beardless boys would brave him to his face'.[55] No doubt because of this background he shrank from public events which seemed disorderly and undignified. He did not object to adulation as such, but he felt profoundly uncomfortable contending with the throng of raucous plebeians that greeted him whenever he ventured into London.[56] Nor was he the only Scot who found English crowds indecorous and annoying. 'When hereafter [the King] comes by you,' one of his countrymen admonished the Londoners in 1604, 'do as they do in Scotland, stand still, see all, and use silence.'[57]

Further, James's disdain for crowds was more in tune with dominant European attitudes than Elizabeth's graciousness. The Venetian ambassador who watched Elizabeth's coronation thought she was too affable and had compromised her dignity. In the seventeenth century public royal ceremonies were curtailed in many parts of Europe, including Spain and France.[58] The Stuarts were in the vanguard of this movement: in France the royal entry survived into the early years of Louis XIV.[59] But their withdrawal from the public conformed to a general European trend toward isolating monarchs from anything that savoured of popularity. Almost everywhere kingship became more autocratic in tone and kings tended to retreat within a courtly, aristocratic milieu. Older rituals which stressed the reciprocal nature of the bond between

---

[55] He made this statement at the Hampton Court Conference. See J. R. Tanner, *Constitutional Documents of the Reign of James I, 1603–1625* (Cambridge, 1961), p. 60.

[56] For an example see Gilbert Dugdale's account of James's unsuccessful attempt to examine the arches being prepared for his coronation 'privately at his own pleasure' (Nichols, *Progresses of James I*, vol. 1, p. 413).

[57] Quoted, *ibid.*, p. 414.

[58] On this point see Ralph E. Giesey, 'Rulership in French Royal Ceremonial', in Wilentz, *Rites of Power*, especially pp. 58–9; Bryant, *Parisian Royal Entry*, chapter 10.

[59] Giesey, 'Rulership in French Royal Ceremonial', p. 58.

monarchs and subjects were abandoned, in favour of more un-
compromising assertions of absolutism.

In England the shift toward a more aloof and reserved style of
kingship may have been accelerated by larger political developments. Elizabeth's entries took place against a background of
threatened Catholic rebellions and foreign invasions, which
reinforced patriotic devotion to the Queen while also making
public demonstrations of that devotion seem more essential. Even
after her death and the conclusion of peace in 1604, fear of
Catholics and Spaniards could produce reflexive surges of loyalty.
James's momentary popularity after the Powder Plot illustrates the
point, as does an incident of 1606. One evening when the King was
away hunting in the countryside a rumour swept the city that
Spaniards or Jesuits had murdered him. In the ensuing panic
citizens began erecting barricades, until James returned the next
day to a hero's welcome.[60] Seen against this background the
demonstration witnessed by Busino takes on added significance.
For many Londoners hatred of Spain and loyalty to the sovereign
appear to have formed two elements in a single emotional
compound.

James's friendly relations with Spain ran directly counter to this
attitude. Between 1618 and 1623, during negotiations for the
notorious Spanish Match for Prince Charles, Londoners abused
and even violently assaulted members of the Spanish embassy, so
infuriating James that he once threatened to revoke the city's
charter if its magistrates could not control popular demonstrations.[61] In the late 1620s the populace was equally demonstrative in its hatred of Buckingham.[62] Of course the crowd's hostility
was directed against foreigners and royal favourites, rather than
against the monarchs themselves. But the knowledge that many
Londoners disapproved vehemently of their policies and their
favourites can only have reinforced the aversion both James and
Charles felt for the city's crowds.

For two reasons, however, Stuart distaste for shouting plebeians
and distrust of London opinion cannot fully explain the royal
entry's decline. First, we have seen that the royal entry did not

[60] Nichols, *Progresses of James I*, vol. 2, pp. 38–43.
[61] Nichols, *Progresses of James I*, vol. 3, p. 662.
[62] For the abuse of Spaniards see, for example, BL Harl. MS. 389, fos. 48v and
61. The crowd's dislike of Buckingham, and the murder of one of his followers,
Dr Lambe, by a London mob is well known.

collapse abruptly after 1603: James entered London less frequently than Elizabeth, but he did not refrain altogether from doing so. At least two of the entries he did make were, moreover, extraordinarily lavish. Henry's installation as Prince of Wales in 1610 and Princess Elizabeth's wedding in 1613 also gave rise to spectacular public celebrations. Thereafter the level of public ceremony fell off somewhat, but events like the opening of Parliament continued to bring James, and later Charles, into the streets. Only in the 1630s did public appearances by the monarch virtually cease. The very gradual nature of the decline of public ceremonies, and the few spectacular revivals of public display under James I, suggests that more complex causes than the King's own prejudices were at work.

Secondly, royal entries demonstrated not only the monarch's 'popularity', but also his majesty and his sovereignty. Why did the Stuarts not modify the ceremony, curtailing its popular features while amplifying its formality and grandeur, instead of allowing it to lapse? The reason appears to be twofold: the royal entry had become both prohibitively expensive and increasingly out of step with changing attitudes toward conspicuous consumption among the landed elite.[63] Its demise can be related to the complex series of changes Lawrence Stone has traced in the public life of the aristocracy, which signalled a fundamental 'readjustment in values by which emphasis was laid less on publicity and display and numerical quantity and more on privacy and luxury and aesthetic quality'.[64]

In the early seventeenth century aristocratic households generally became smaller as peers dismissed superfluous servants. Great men started travelling in private coaches rather than on horseback, attended by a score or two of liveried retainers. After the 1610s funerals were usually more modest. It is important to realize that at court the story was far more complex than this bald summary suggests. Some courtiers continued to engage in traditional forms of display long after most noblemen had abandoned them. As late as 1638 the Duchess of Buckingham departed from London accompanied by 'a hundred horse . . . bravely set forth for her own followers [and] wagons for her stuff, covered with

---

[63] *The Crisis of the Aristocracy* (Oxford, 1965), p. 584. However much controversy still surrounds some of Stone's conclusions, the mass of evidence he has assembled on this point is overwhelming.

[64] *Ibid.*, chapter 10.

embroidered cloths'.[65] Nevertheless, by the second quarter of the century a marked decline had become evident in the scale on which most courtiers engaged in public display, particularly as they travelled. In 1560 the Duchess's grand departure from London would have seemed relatively commonplace. In 1638 it was described as occurring 'with such pomp of provision and equipage as our age hath not seen'.[66]

Yet it was precisely 'pomp of provision and equipage' which characterized the royal entry. That ceremony was becoming increasingly out of step with dominant aristocratic attitudes. If the King had wished to preserve or revive the ancient medieval traditions of his nobility this might not have mattered, but James showed no particular fondness for ornate ceremonies of any sort, and he had little sympathy for the bellicose culture of the medieval nobility. Charles was more warlike and more conscious of the importance of ritual, but his tastes ran to more up-to-date forms of display, such as indoor masques. Neither of the early Stuarts sympathized very deeply with the old traditions which entry processions embodied.

This change in cultural outlook might not have been decisive, however, if financial considerations had not reinforced it. Whatever broad cultural changes occurred among the aristocracy, the King had special ceremonial obligations which made it unusually difficult for him to abandon traditional forms of ostentation. On the other hand, the crown also had special incentives to curtail public display. Stone has argued that noblemen jettisoned traditional forms of conspicuous consumption partly because they could not afford them after the inflation of the sixteenth century decreased the real value of rents. Inflationary pressures affected few landlords as severely as the King, however, who had to maintain by far the most lavish neo-feudal household in the realm on increasingly inadequate revenues. Precisely because they were monarchs, James and Charles had to make their public appearances as spectacular as possible. As court ritual grew ever more elaborate, and as each successive public ceremony set higher standards of comparison, the cost of mounting such events rose to staggering levels. James's coronation procession cost him over £36,000. The

---

[65] PRO C115/N8/8822.
[66] *Ibid.* The comment was that of Sir John Finett, the court's Master of Ceremonies; he, of all people, should have known.

record, however, was set by the wedding of Princess Elizabeth. On this occasion the crown spent £4,800 producing a mock naval battle on the Thames, which failed to impress the spectators, £2,800 on fireworks, and an incredible £6,252 on the Princess's 'apparel and other necessaries'. The bill for gold and silver lace alone came to more than £1,700. The total expense, including the cost of entertaining the groom and his train and defraying the expenses of the nobles who escorted the couple to Heidelburg after the wedding, was £93,293.[67]

Even James I appears to have recognized that ceremonies on this scale represented an intolerable drain on the crown's ordinary revenues.[68] It is scarcely surprising that a few years later Charles's investiture as Prince of Wales was done privately, 'without cost', or that in 1626 the Venetian ambassador reported that the King had cancelled his coronation entry because he thought it a waste of money.[69] From the crown's point of view the royal entry had become a prohibitively expensive example of an increasingly obsolete form of conspicuous consumption, which both James and Charles happened to dislike.

V

The decline of the royal entry thus resulted from a combination of mutually reinforcing circumstances. The personal preferences of both James and Charles, financial constraints and broad changes in cultural attitudes, both in England and throughout Europe, all tended to undermine the greatest public royal ceremony. Since no adequate substitute was developed, the King became increasingly

---

67 All these figures are from BL Add. MS. 58833 except for the cost of gold and silver lace, for which see PRO E/405/265. I wish to thank Conrad Russell for the first reference.

68 In his speech to Parliament of 1610 James mentioned his coronation entry into London, his reception of foreign princes and the installation of Henry as Prince of Wales among the circumstances which had caused him to pile up the debts which Parliament was being asked to clear (Charles McIlwain, ed., *The Political Works of James I* (Cambridge, Mass., 1918), p. 319). The implication of the speech is that the Crown could not afford to go on defraying the costs of such events from its own revenues. It is possible, although I have found no direct evidence on this point, that the failure of the 1610 and 1614 Parliaments helps explain why great public rituals became so rare in the latter part of the reign.

69 G. Gerard to Sir Dudley Carleton, 11 June 1616, *Calendar of State Papers Domestic*, vol. 9, p. 373; *CSP Ven.*, vol. 19, p. 464. Cf. Richard Perrinchief, *The Royal Martyr* (London, 1676), p. 21.

less visible to the London populace. At least one royalist commentator, looking back from the perspective of the 1650s, thought this development had contributed materially to the collapse of royal authority. He was Laud's former chaplain, Peter Heylin. Elizabeth, he wrote,

> did very seldom end any of her summer progresses but she would wheel about to some end of London, to make her passage to Whitehall through . . . the City . . . By means whereof she did not only preserve that Majesty which did belong to a Queen of England, but kept the Citizens (and consequently all the subjects) in a reverent estimation of her . . . But these [ceremonies] being laid aside by King James . . . and not resumed by King Charles . . . there followed first a neglect of their persons, which Majesty would have made more sacred, and afterwards a mislike of their government, which a little popularity would have made more grateful.[70]

Was Heylin correct? This question is perhaps the most difficult of all to answer, since it raises fundamental issues concerning the nature of royal power. Many political historians would argue that rituals ultimately made little difference to the King's ability to govern; that in the final analysis coercion rather than rhetorical display and popular support exacted obedience. In early modern England the crown had to enlist at least minimal co-operation from traditional elites in order to coerce. But so long as that co-operation was forthcoming, it can be argued, public ritual and popular sentiment were largely irrelevant. At least up to a point the force of this contention must be granted. It would be very difficult to argue that in the 1630s Charles's neglect of his public role made much practical difference to the conduct of government. If he had succeeded in making prerogative rule permanent, the decline in public ritual might appear as a natural outgrowth of the rise of English absolutism.

To view the politics of his reign entirely from this perspective, however, is to miss the point that prerogative rule eventually did collapse, and in the ensuing political struggle London opinion acquired a decisive strategic importance. The decline of the royal entry had nothing to do with the crisis in Scotland or the summoning of the Long Parliament, but it is relevant to the events which

---

[70] *A Short View of the Life and Reign of King Charles* (London, 1658), p. 228.

followed, in particular the street demonstrations of the spring and autumn of 1641.

This is not to suggest that a few public ceremonies would, by themselves, have made Charles popular in London. Heylin drastically oversimplified the reasons for the 'neglect' of royal authority and 'mislike' of royal government by Londoners at the outset of the Civil War. Among other things he ignored the suspicions swirling around Laud and Henrietta Maria and the grass roots support and organization of disaffected clergy and their radical lay allies.[71] The point remains, however, that the crisis of the 1640s overtook a monarch whose charisma had already been weakened by his own failure to uphold the peculiar combination of 'majesty' and 'popularity' which the English had traditionally associated with their monarchs. Instead of a visible symbol of the religious and patriotic values uniting England, Charles I had ruled as a remote source of authority, who seemed indifferent to his people's love.

Only in the autumn of 1641, after returning from Scotland where he had failed to rally a party to his side, did Charles finally enter London. Significantly, even at this late date the royal entry evidently had an appreciable effect on the capital's mood. 'I am glad we are thus dutiful,' one of the King's sympathizers wrote as preparations got under way, 'it makes the sectaries to look about them, and certainly the consideration of his Majesty having the love of able citizens will conduce much to the management of his affairs.'[72] As the King approached London 500 mounted citizens and thousands of spectators went out to greet him; when he accepted the gift offered by the Lord Mayor the crowd was reported to have 'shouted forth as if in a solemn passion ... the Lord preserve our dread sovereign King Charles'.[73] The King, the Queen and the Prince of Wales then entered London in the full Elizabethan manner.[74] 'All the way that their Majesties passed,' one contemporary reported, 'the people [greeted them] with loud and joyful acclamations, crying God bless and long live King Charles and Queen Mary, and their majesties reciprocally and

---

[71] Valerie Pearl, *London and the Outbreak of the Puritan Revolution* (Oxford, 1965), chapter 4, especially pp. 122–32; Brian Manning, *The English People and the English Revolution* (London, 1975), chapters 1–4.

[72] Thomas Wiseman to Admiral Pennington, 18 November 1641, SP16/485 piece 92.

[73] Lawrence Price, *Great Britain's Time of Triumph* (London, 1641), p. A3.

[74] See *ibid.* for a description.

heartily bless[ed] and thank[ed] the people, with as great expressions of joy.'[75]

Yet even this entry was not an unequivocal expression of the old ideals of harmony and solidarity. Both the corporation and Charles himself used the occasion to emphasize the divisions between London's more affluent citizens – who were presumed to be loyal – and plebeian groups who were blamed for the recent upheavals. In welcoming the King the Recorder alleged that the crowds which had recently demonstrated against the court had consisted predominantly of poor residents from the suburbs, over which the corporation had no control. As Charles entered London a mounted horse guard was deployed along the streets, a far more visible and formidable force than the traditional whifflers, which must have emphasized the court's fear of the massed spectators. And at the conclusion of the day's events the King remarked, 'now I see that all these tumults and disorders have arisen only from the baser sort of people, and that the affections of the better and main part of the City have ever been loyal'.[76] One can perhaps understand why, at this juncture, Charles did not want to pass unescorted through London crowds, and why he resented the role of the 'baser sort' in the events of the past few months. The fact that some Londoners, including the city's MP, John Venn, had opposed giving the King a lavish reception may also help to explain Charles's caution.[77] It is nevertheless striking that at a time when he plainly needed to garner as much support in London as possible Charles gratuitously emphasized his distaste for the city's plebeians. Nearly a century earlier Queen Mary had saved her crown by courageously appealing to the London populace, assembled on the hustings outside the Guildhall, as Wyatt's forces neared the city.[78] Charles proved unwilling to undertake a similar risk.

It is arguable that by November 1641 no amount of pageantry and royal graciousness could have regained the capital. But one needs to ask what might have happened if Charles had shown more skill and energy in appealing to popular loyalist sentiment – and if he had not waited until the eleventh hour before doing so at all. In November of 1641 Charles did not need to regain the full allegiance of London; he only needed to neutralize the capital's highly

[75] *Octavio Carolina* (1641), p. 16.   [76] SP16/485 piece 110.
[77] Anthony Fletcher, *The Outbreak of the English Civil War* (London, 1981), p. 162.
[78] Wriothesley, *Chronicle*, pp. 108, 109.

partisan crowds. There is no sure way of knowing whether he could have done so by a determined campaign, involving direct personal appeals to the urban populace. But it surely tells us much about both Charles himself and the royalist cause that such a campaign was never seriously attempted. In London as elsewhere the King refused to make even symbolic gestures that might have provided a rallying point for popular royalism. He relied entirely on the efforts of 'the better sort', as if those outside the traditional elites did not matter. Unfortunately for the crown, at this juncture the 'baser sort' in London did matter, since their numbers and their support for Parliament severely restricted the King's options, weakening him in his struggle against opponents whose parliamentary majorities and upper-class support appeared increasingly vulnerable. It is scarcely an exaggeration to say that Charles needed to raise an army in the spring of 1642 because, during the previous months, he had become the first English monarch since the Middle Ages to lose even the passive loyalty of his own capital.

The collapse of royal government that precipitated the Civil War cannot be fully explained in terms of political events being played out between the royal court, the parliamentary leadership, and the local elites of the counties and leading boroughs. It is also necessary to explain why Charles found it so difficult to inspire loyalty, not only from gentry and urban oligarchs, but also from those outside the political nation.[79] To do this, in turn, requires that attention be given to the cultural significance of kingship among people beyond the reach of courtly genres like masques and Van Dyck portraits. The evidence presented here shows that at least in London the early Stuarts, and particularly Charles I, simply failed to project an effective public image. For some years before 1642 the King had ceased to demonstrate his sense of membership in a civic and national community, or to assert publicly his commitment to the religious and secular values which should have united the realm. As a result traditional feelings of devotion to the reigning monarch became increasingly attenuated, and dark suspicions concerning the popish and tyrannical proclivities of the royal court could strike root more easily. The defence of the community and its faith no longer appeared to entail devotion to the King. That is one reason why royal authority collapsed.

---

[79] The fullest discussion is Joyce Malcolm, *Caesar's Due: Loyalty and King Charles, 1642–1646* (London, 1983). Some of Malcolm's arguments have been criticized but the perspective she advances remains an important and provocative one.

3. *County governance and elite withdrawal in Norfolk, 1660–1720*

JAMES M. ROSENHEIM

One well-recognized but still improperly studied feature of the social polarization of early modern England is the withdrawal of the nation's elite from close engagement with much of the society around it, a process that began under the Tudors and was completed by the eighteenth century, when the gap between plebeian and patrician culture had grown to nearly unbridgeable proportions.[1] On the whole, what we know of this withdrawal is largely inferential. Specific indices of involvement are difficult to come by, but participation in local government provides one measure, and Lawrence and Jeanne Stone have recently documented the abdication of local government responsibility by country-house owners in eighteenth-century Northamptonshire and Hertfordshire. Such a study is especially useful because elite withdrawal has not adequately been reconciled with the equally commonplace depiction of gentlemen as deeply immersed in local government.[2] The essay here, an examination of the workings as well as the personnel of local government in Norfolk between 1660 and 1720, reveals a surprising degree of distancing at an earlier date than that indicated by the Stones. The county displays a pattern of elite involvement

I am grateful for the helpful comments of Mark Fissel, Cynthia Herrup, Larry Yarak and Andrew Rosenheim, as well as my co-editors. An early version of this essay was presented in October 1987 at the Western Conference on British Studies in Lincoln, Nebraska. Some of the research upon which this study was based was made possible by a Fellowship for College Teachers from the National Endowment for the Humanities. I am also grateful to the Marquess Townshend of Raynham for kind permission to consult and cite from manuscripts at Raynham Hall.

[1] This polarization is a basic theme of K. Wrightson, *English Society 1580–1680* (London, 1982). See also A. Fletcher and J. Stevenson, eds., *Order and Disorder in Early Modern England* (Cambridge, 1985), pp. 10–11; P. Burke, *Popular Culture in Early Modern Europe* (New York, 1978), pp. 270–81.

[2] L. Stone and J. C. F. Stone, *An Open Elite? England 1540–1880* (Oxford, 1984), pp. 269–75.

extending for three decades after the Restoration, followed by withdrawal from the routine of county administration commencing in the reign of William III – not as a consequence of the Hanoverian ascendancy, but occurring long before. Thus, even before an era of putative political stability might have encouraged them, English landowners were stepping back from day-to-day participation in the local affairs that had so engaged their forefathers.

Such withdrawal and its accompanying cultural polarization are evident in many facets of elite life, from architecture to social ritual. The growth of a London 'season', for example, created a different annual rhythm for the gentry from that of their country neighbours.[3] The grand occasions of country life that gentlemen sponsored dwindled in the eighteenth century to an occasional ox roast, peal of bells or bonfire, and in these the squire himself (like as not in London or Bath) rarely participated. A growing desire for privacy informed the decline of such events and also the new style in country-house building that separated owners from their followers and servants. The Stones have noted the elite's fashionable pursuit of 'detachment and splendid isolation', reflected in the choice of building sites removed from surrounding villages and towns. There the gentry's houses were set in walled parks and surrounded by extensive gardens, both of which protected the elite from the world outside and provided visible symbols of separation and withdrawal, as well as of wealth and authority.[4] On a different plane, elite withdrawal is found in the gentry's rejection of once common beliefs and attitudes – whether toward magic, suicide, insanity or the church.[5] It is also seen in a disillusionment with past efforts to reform society and in the channelling of reformist energies away from individual cases in particular villages and into Societies for the Reformation of Manners or wholesale efforts at badging of the poor.[6] Even where scholars have noted the con-

---

[3] Stone and Stone, *An Open Elite?* pp. 324–6; see P. Jenkins, *The Making of a Ruling Class: The Glamorgan Gentry 1640–1790* (Cambridge, 1983), chapter 9, esp. pp. 239–50, for the draw of London among the gentry of Glamorgan.

[4] M. Girouard, *Life in the English Country House: A Social and Architectural History* (New Haven, 1978), chapter 5, esp. pp. 136–43; Stone and Stone, *An Open Elite?* pp. 329–30; J. Bassin, 'The English Landscape Garden in the Eighteenth Century: The Cultural Importance of an English Institution', *Albion*, 11 (1979), pp. 26–7.

[5] Fletcher and Stevenson, *Order and Disorder*, pp. 12–14.

[6] A. Fletcher, *Reform in the Provinces: The Government of Stuart England* (New Haven, 1986), chapter 8, esp. pp. 262–81.

tinuing high visibility of specific gentry functions, especially governmental ones, the gentry's physical withdrawal from daily encounters with local residents is still emphasized. Whether motivated by the fear of criminal interlopers or by fashion in landscaping, the landed elite interposed agents between themselves and the lower orders, whom they increasingly met only on formal occasions and on their own terms.[7]

Scholars have stressed the formidable nature of these occasions, their ritual and theatrical element, arguing implicitly that their awe-inspiring, even oppressive majesty made up for and derived from their infrequency.[8] Meetings such as quarter sessions were significant moments in the routine of country life, and, at least on Kent's eighteenth-century bench, justices used 'manners, ceremony, and formality to create awkwardness, to emphasize the social distance between the sovereign's commissioners and those they were commissioned to govern'.[9] Women and men a hundred years before probably found the formal occasions of local government less awe-inspiring than historians once imagined, since they regularly confronted single justices or groups of magistrates in scheduled divisional meetings. Justices were also encountered on more flexible and less domineering terms than was once thought to be the case, especially in petty sessions.[10] But by the eighteenth century there was a greater distance between magistrate and supplicant or criminal, even if 'public demonstrations of the gentry's "cultural hegemony" ... were [not] new to the Hanoverian period'.[11]

One feature of such public occasions that historians have failed fully to explore is the question of who actually attended. It is stressed that the semi-annual assizes and even the quarter sessions were notable county events, boasting impressive gatherings of county grandees at substantial dinners and elegant balls. Yet

---

[7] E. P. Thompson, 'Patrician Society, Plebeian Culture', *Journal of Social History*, 7 (1973–4), p. 389.

[8] *Ibid.*, and D. Hay, 'Property, Authority and the Criminal Law', in D. Hay *et al.*, *Albion's Fatal Tree: Crime and Society in Eighteenth-Century England* (New York, 1975), pp. 26–30.

[9] N. Landau, *Justices of the Peace, 1679–1760* (Berkeley, 1984), p. 204; Fletcher, *Reform in the Provinces*, p. 88.

[10] C. Herrup, 'New Shoes and Mutton Pies: Investigative Responses to Theft in Seventeenth-Century East Sussex', *Historical Journal*, 27 (1984), pp. 811–30; Fletcher, *Reform in the Provinces*, pp. 134–5.

[11] Fletcher and Stevenson, *Order and Disorder*, p. 21.

patterns of attendance varied from county to county, depending within each upon roads and weather, the centralized or decentralized nature of county government, and on the conviviality likely to be provided.[12] Such vagaries, combined with the distraction of London life and the apparent desire for less contact with the lower orders, help to explain why elite attendance at the formal proceedings of sessions and assizes was in decline. Overall, the elite movement away from local administration in the Augustan era coincides with the picture of a social group increasingly distanced physically from the local community, aesthetically from traditional culture, and psychologically from the obligations of good lordship and hospitality characteristic of an earlier landowning elite. As withdrawal from government business shows, the elite gentry's yearning for isolation – or their fear of contact with the raucous populace – extended beyond the realm of their personal lives and had consequences for public life: the Augustan age saw both their disengagement from the lives of those they governed and a disengagement from local government itself.

A recent analysis of provincial government convincingly argues that the priority of local initiative and of provincial resistance to central interference helped to determine the profile and character of seventeenth-century local administration. This was necessarily the case if 'face-to-face confrontation with complainants, witnesses and suspected culprits in the intimate surroundings of the manor-house hall or parlour was the essence of magistracy'.[13] But with the rise of petty sessions such direct meetings became rarer, and by the end of the seventeenth century there are signs that Augustan magistrates were losing their taste for that essence: the attraction of county business may never have been great, but it grew especially weak for those late Stuart gentry who hoped to make something of themselves outside the county arena.

In one scholar's words, the 'patriarchal paternalist', immediately concerned with the well-being of a local community that largely defined his status, was becoming a 'patrician paternalist', who participated in a superior culture different from that of his neighbourhood.[14] In concrete terms, by the mid-eighteenth century the justice's role as arbitrator was diminished from its seventeenth-

[12] Fletcher, *Reform in the Provinces*, pp. 97–103.
[13] Fletcher, *Reform in the Provinces*, p. 79 and chapter 2 in general.
[14] Landau, *Justices of the Peace*, pp. 3–5.

century height; by 1800, much of the administration that had been a gentry monopoly in Elizabethan and Stuart days had devolved upon clerical justices, urban trading justices and finally even stipendiary magistrates.[15] In the 1660s, however, the avid attendance and application to business of greater gentry justices in Norfolk suggest anxiety to prevent a return to the spirit of the 1640s and 1650s and to maintain the re-established political order. A society secure in its social peace did not simply replace one riddled with fear of disorder in 1660: the activity of the Norfolk magistracy and lieutenancy testifies to the work that had to be done.[16]

The withdrawal of grandees from active participation thirty years later points up the accomplishment, as well as a number of changes that were transforming the workings of English local government. On one level, disengagement speaks of the routinization (even trivializing) of court business and the diminished significance of individual actors in the magistracy, as crimes the sessions had once addressed were now dealt with summarily (as with game offences) or by assizes (as with virtually all felony charges).[17] Withdrawal also depended upon the recruitment of reliable replacements to conduct the business of local government: those who stood back from provincial administration after the 1690s demonstrated their confidence in their replacements as active administrators and in the durability and adaptability of existing institutions.

Paradoxically, disengagement occurred precisely during that time which has been identified as one flaming with party rage, when every institution of power might be expected to have been exploited for party advantage. Indeed, it is well known that places on the commission of the peace were so exploited, and the gentry elite recruited and relied on agents to uphold the interests of themselves and their party at public events in the county. But withdrawal also testified to the compelling pull of London, which drew grandees away from the county, to return (at least for political reasons) only for the truly significant occasions represented now above all by elections, rather than by the meeting of county courts. Had the gentry seen the *business* of the bench – as opposed to its

---

15 Landau, *Justices of the Peace*, pp. 142–3, 184–6, 194–5, 362; J. M. Beattie, *Crime and the Courts of England 1660–1800* (Oxford, 1986), pp. 62–5.

16 The activity is discussed in *Norfolk Lieutenancy Journal 1660–1676*, ed. R. M. Dunn, *Norfolk Record Society*, 45 (1975), as well as my forthcoming study of Horatio, first Viscount Townshend.

17 Beattie, *Crime and the Courts*, pp. 16–17; Landau, *Justices of the Peace*, p. 263.

membership – primarily as a matter for political manipulation, it is scarcely credible that they would have withdrawn from it at a time of pronounced political volatility.

I

The story of the later Stuart commission of the peace is one of growth. Although uneven, increase in the size of the bench was common to all English counties between 1660 and 1714, testifying to the 'determination of the gentry to keep the day-to-day enforcement of local government above party'.[18] On the face of it, the commission's increasing size provided enough men to undertake thorough and effective local administration, even if many justices looked upon appointment as an honour that required no active labour.[19] The difficulties of the Norfolk magistracy in obtaining adequate administrative coverage of the county belie this impression. Lack of attendance by the justices was best met by efforts to promote men to the bench who it was thought would give adequate geographical coverage within the county.[20]

Defects in geographical coverage in Norfolk were common enough. In 1676, in the wake of purges to the commission, a recommendation to the new lord lieutenant of a possible justice featured as a prime qualification his residence close to the port of Wells, a fractious town otherwise unserved by a local magistrate. The candidate's additional credentials as a counsellor at law were no more important than where he lived.[21] During the reign of James II, when the magistracy was nationally transformed, Sir Francis Jerningham of Costessey, a newly-appointed Roman Catholic justice for Norfolk, lamented the consequences of a recent purge of magistrates who had refused to co-operate in the King's

[18] Fletcher, *Reform in the Provinces*, p. 372; see Landau, *Justices of the Peace*, Appendix A, for numbers of justices.

[19] The growth of the Elizabethan bench in Norfolk also owed much to the demands of honour and did not guarantee the activism of justices: A. H. Smith, *County and Court: Government and Politics in Norfolk 1558–1603* (Oxford, 1974), chapter 4.

[20] Concerns with geographical coverage were not new. The Elizabethan privy council in 1587 sought 'a reasonable geographical distribution of magistrates', and in 1599, H. Holdiche was recommended as a likely Norfolk justice, 'there being noe other within eight miles of his residence': *ibid.*, pp. 70, 79–80.

[21] R. Coke to Lord Yarmouth, 9 July 1676, Norfolk Record Office (hereafter NRO), Bradfer-Lawrence I, c, 'Historical Original State Letters', v. i.

campaign to repeal the Test Act. Blaming these men for their own dismissal, Jerningham also complained that 'our Norfolk gentry . . . have . . . left their county almost naked', forcing on him and two other justices the administration of two hundreds in south Norfolk, which were inconveniently distant from their homes.[22] In the same year, the bench was said to need three men in the area around King's Lynn, where all but one magistrate (who was dying) had recently been displaced.[23] Politically-motivated alterations to the bench thus might at least temporarily disrupt effective administration, but the routine of parliamentary life, which became regular and predictable with the advent of annual sessions, also sometimes stripped the provinces of resident justices. In 1705 Sir Charles Turner called for the appointment of a magistrate as 'absolutely necessary . . . for this corner where I live', complaining to Robert Walpole that 'now you are gone from amongst us, I am sure you ought to give us who are left all possible assistance'.[24]

Beyond the acknowledgement made by individuals, the bench as an institution revealed an awareness of the problems caused by absences and by insufficient numbers of active justices in particular areas. The first sessional orders made in Restoration Norfolk to cope with inadequate magisterial coverage were drawn up at the end of the seventeenth century, as the problem became serious. During an extraordinary meeting held at Norwich in late 1698, the court was informed of a lack of justices in four southeastern hundreds of the county. To remedy the defect in part, a justice living near two of the hundreds was specifically requested to join in the petty sessions and any other business there.[25] At the regularly-scheduled Epiphany sessions of the Norwich bench a month later, a similar deficiency of magistrates was noted in other areas, and again a neighbouring magistrate was named to join the single justice active in the affected sub-division. In the context of magisterial bi-partisanship, it is notable that a long-serving Whig magistrate,

---

[22] Sir F. Jerningham to Sir J. Holland, 19 March 1688, Bodleian Library, MS Tanner 259, fos. 63v–64.

[23] G. Duckett, ed., *The Penal Laws and the Test Act* (London, 1883), p. 312.

[24] Sir C. Turner to R. Walpole, 2 July 1705, Cambridge University Library, Cholmondeley (Houghton) correspondence 420. As noted below, Walpole's most frequent attendance at Norfolk sessions occurred betwen 1710 and 1714, when he not coincidentally enjoyed no public office.

[25] Order of 10 December 1698. Specific orders are referred to here only by date; they may be found in NRO, C/S2/4–8 for the years 1689–96, 1697–1707, 1707–15, 1715–18 and 1718–20 respectively.

Francis Long, was asked in this instance to co-operate with the lonely Thornhagh Gurdon, an equally long-serving Tory.[26] By 1702, inadequacy of coverage had reached a point where a sessions meeting at Little Walsingham – a region of the county distant from those affected by the orders of 1698–9 – 'did fall for want of justices of the peace'.[27] The embarrassment caused by such default can be imagined: if sessions provided an occasion for theatrical display of the elite's position of cultural and political hegemony in society, this occasion surely disappointed the house.

In response to such shortcomings, the court did what it could, assigning particular justices to supply local defects where possible; where names are mentioned, they are often of men diligent in sessions work. It only made sense to designate those upon whom the court could rely. In July 1704, Sir John Holland, 2nd Bt., was requested to attend public meetings of justices in Diss and Depwade hundreds in the south of the county, just as a year later Henry Negus and John Berney were ordered to act and actually appoint petty sessions meetings in East and West Flegg, north of Great Yarmouth, because of a 'defect' of justices in the area.[28] In the latter case, the two justices' impact was impermanent, for in 1716 Negus and the energetic Francis Long were assigned to act in East and West Flegg, settling overseers accounts, licensing victuallers and generally transacting necessary business, 'there being no justices at this present [time] residing there'.[29] The examples could be multiplied.[30]

The court also sometimes needed to act systematically to co-ordinate justices' assignments and arrange petty sessional meetings, which were especially important in a decentralized county, where the sessions met every quarter in three nominally equal meetings.[31] The boundaries linking the thirty-three hundreds into petty sessions and other administrative divisions were redefined, meetings of the

---

[26] Order of 10 January 1699.

[27] The sheriff having made provision for a meeting as usual, the Norwich court ordered him to be reimbursed for his outlay: order of 14 April 1702.

[28] Orders of 11 July 1704 and 9 January 1705: this latter arrangement was made at the request of Sir Isaac Preston, who had presumably been acting alone hitherto.

[29] Order of 10 April 1716.

[30] See orders of 5 October 1714, 10 July 1716 and 14 January 1718.

[31] In fact the first and best-attended meeting was always held at Norwich, thereafter by adjournment for the King's Lynn division (which met there or at Swaffham) and the Fakenham division (which met there or at Little Walsingham and later at Holt as well).

quarter sessions adjournments were shifted, and efforts were taken to maintain the decentralized divisional jurisdictions that had been set up in the 1690s to cope with alehouse licensings (and probably tax appeals as well).[32] Administrative arrangements probably never became uniform for all of Norfolk's petty sessional divisions, but those that were worked out suggest a very different situation from the politically charged and highly manipulated one that existed in eighteenth-century Kent, where petty sessions particularly served to demonstrate party dominance.[33] In Norfolk the business of the sessions was less politics than governance. Even the existing documented divisional rivalries in the county have an ambiguous political content. Their seriousness is revealed in the role the lord lieutenant played in several cases, but they were not party clashes.

In one instance, a controversy arose when justices who met at Norwich passed an order in January 1685 regulating county pensions.[34] The order – elicited by apparent improprieties in the payment of pensions – stipulated that no money would in future be paid from any county treasury except by authority of the justices who sat at Norwich, rather than those of the King's Lynn and Fakenham divisions. The justices outside the Norwich area were offended by the order, which they condemned as illegal, arguing that the Norwich meeting had no special status and had overstepped its authority. These dissatisfied magistrates turned in the spring to Horatio, first Viscount Townshend, former lord lieutenant, as their champion, since he too lived in one of the maligned, implicitly second-class divisions. Willingly, he rallied to the defence of his and the other justices' rights, privileges and honour. At their urging, he

---

[32] In 1711, for example, eight different justices were assigned by the bench to act in five different divisions: order of 10 April 1711. See also orders of 11 December 1714, 21 January 1715 and 19 April 1716. J. Wrott to R. Walpole, 7 and 21 May 1703, Cambridge University Library, Cholmondeley (Houghton) correspondence 305, 307 discussed tax appeals and Wrott's inability to prevail on Sir Charles Turner, a justice, to attend a local appeals meeting.

[33] Landau, *Justices of the Peace*, chapter 7, especially pp. 232–6. Landau does note, however, the emergence among Kent's magistrates of a 'collegial spirit' that altered 'the model of a model justice' (especially one of modest status) to exclude 'those exhibitions of pride, temper, or dominance' which had earlier been acceptable for justices: p. 236. One might suggest that exhibitions of excessive partisanship might have been equally impermissible.

[34] What follows is based on Sir J. Holland's copy correspondence in Bodleian Library, MS Tanner 259, fos. 1–10.

'espoused the business & gave out that if those justices of the peace of the Norwich division did not revoke this order that he would bring the complaint before the king & council'.[35] After long negotiation, Townshend and Sir John Holland, 1st Bt., the Norwich division's spokesman, achieved a compromise that was adopted at quarter sessions a year after the matter first arose.

Holland and Townshend had previously been Whiggish allies, and their correspondence suggests that reputation was at stake more than party advantage in this affair, but Townshend's recent attempt to ingratiate himself with the new King James II, even by exertions on his behalf in parliamentary elections, cautions against ignoring a political element in the quarrel.[36] Perhaps the two motives mixed, with Townshend hoping to resolve the dispute and demonstrate both to county and central government the strength of his interest in Norfolk. In any event, Holland's justification for the offending order – that it had been sanctioned by an eminent sergeant-at-law present at Norwich sessions – was guaranteed to infuriate Townshend. Although the justices in other divisions had no such legal experts, he said, they tried their best to serve King and country, as men of standing they would not act as 'clerks of ease' to the Norwich magistrates, whose order was unreasonable, unprecedented, illegal and insulting. Conceding that the Norwich meeting attracted the largest attendance of justices, Townshend none the less argued that the county's western magistrates made up in substance what they lacked in numbers.

For Townshend the magnate, the issue at stake had little to do with the efficiency of the bench but rather with maintaining an interest by standing up for his neighbourhood; in his eyes, as a result, any solution to the quarrel had to preserve his side's honour. A decision not to repeal the original order but to pass a new one superseding it achieved this end. Of greatest consequence for the present discussion is that the new order protected the administrat--ive goal that had prompted the original Norwich order, by prescribing that pension orders henceforth be signed by ten justices at the

---

[35] Sir J. Holland's note (damaged), prefacing the copy correspondence concerning this dispute, Bodl., MS Tanner 259, fo. lv.

[36] (Draft) Lord Townshend to the Earl of Rochester, 10 February 1685, Raynham Hall (Norfolk), box files (hereafter RBF), '1st Viscount Townshend, 1650s–87'. NRO, L'Estrange P20, fo. 110v; *CSPD Feb–Dec. 1685*, p. 21; BL, Add. MS 15892, fo. 194.

sessions meeting that authorized them.[37] Whatever political conflict had been involved in the divisional dispute, it was sufficient to polarize the county magistracy and undo this step toward greater accountability and efficiency in the bench's operation.

Half a century later, a similar, potentially disruptive dispute shows resistance on the part of some magistrates to the interjection of party considerations into what they deemed administrative matters. In 1738, the third Viscount Townshend – grandson of Horatio, son of Robert Walpole's colleague Charles, and current lord lieutenant – responded to the promptings of interested inhabitants of Fakenham. To forestall the pending authorization of funds to build a sessions house at Holt, he campaigned to transfer the sessions meeting from Holt to its former location at Fakenham.[38] Townshend claimed that he was simply seeking for residents near the town 'that common ease and conveniency which the whole county have allowed us ... till within these very few last years' by holding in Fakenham one of the adjourned sessions meetings.[39] By insisting that the bench at Norwich consider the request, he acknowledged the dominance that group effectively exercised over the other justices, a concession his grandfather would not have made, but he also turned the issue into a county rather than a divisional matter and set up a test of strength with Sir Robert Walpole, who opposed removing the meeting back to Fakenham.

Walpole castigated Townshend's behaviour as 'precipitate', deplored his involvement with sessions business in his capacity as lord lieutenant and *custos rotulorum*, and lectured him like a schoolboy. 'No man ... is above taking the advice of friends', the great man pontificated, chiding Townsend for listening to those who sought 'to divide him from his real friends'. 'I am sorry', Walpole went on, 'that you think the cause of any market town in the county of consequence enough to make such a division in the [Whig] party, which you are at the head of, & may, if you please, continue so',[40] hyperbole calculated to remind Townshend of the

37 For the new order, see BL, Add. MS 41656, fo. 64 and Bodl., MS Tanner 259, fos. 20v–21; for its acceptance by the other two divisions, (copy) I. Motham to Sir J. Holland, 25 January 1688, *ibid.*, fos. 19v–20.
38 (Copy) Lord Townshend's general letter to the Norfolk justices, 20 December 1738, and Townshend to unknown, 5 July 1739, RBF, 3rd Viscount, 1723–63.
39 (Copy) Townshend to Lord Walpole, 21 December 1738, *ibid.*
40 Sir R. Walpole to Lord Townshend, 26 December 1738, NRO, uncatalogued mss, box M, P168C.

commoner's dominant place in the county. Townshend, however, rejected Walpole's interpretation of his behaviour and, naive, disingenuous, or both, professed amazement that 'it could . . . have entered into the mind of anyone to have called this a party cause'.[41] What Townshend failed to accept was that justices' affairs had party implications, even when no national issues were involved.

At the Norwich sessions which considered Townshend's pro-posal, twenty-three justices, acting in concert after a pre-sessions caucus, voted to keep the sessions at Holt; only eight supported Townshend.[42] The Viscount responded to Walpole's part in the defeat he suffered with a vow of vengeance to rectify 'the greatest instance of ingratitude that ever I heard of'.[43] More significant as an indicator of the Viscount's attitude toward the affair was his response to 'the gentlemen who live in the Holt corner' when he first heard of their objections to his plan. Avowing his aim to 'do *all* which lies in my power to obtain [the change in venue] without any partiality to party', he sought to remind the justices 'of one thing, which is that the country was not made for the justices of peace, but that the justices were appointed for the benefit of the country'.[44] This may not have been a view of which party men like Walpole approved, but it is one that the actions of the bench often, if not infallibly, endorsed.

II

Divisional disputes and questions of adequate geographical cover-age arose as much as anything from poor attendance by those made justices of the peace. Although justices from any social background could readily find reasons to avoid the burden of acting as a magistrate, the inactivity of Norfolk's greater-gentry justices stands out. It is not just that the bench, as it grew in size, was recruited

---

[41] Lord Townshend to unknown, 5 January 1739, RBF, 3rd Viscount 1723–63; two days earlier Townshend wrote to M. Branthwaite and T. Cooke, 'I do think that election affairs ought not to overthrow and subvert matters which do affect the necessary conveniency of a county': NRO, uncatalogued mss, box M, P168C.

[42] 'Question whether the sessions held by adjournment shall be continued as they are or be altered', n.d., *ibid*. See letters to Lord Townshend concerning this matter from eighteen justices, *ibid*.

[43] Lord Townshend to Major N. Symonds, 10 January 1739, *ibid*.

[44] (Copy) Lord Townshend to Lord Lovell, 20 December 1738, RBF, 3rd Viscount 1723–63. Emphasis in the original.

from lower down the social scale,[45] but also that among the most elite fewer actually served or served actively. At the end of the seventeenth and beginning of the eighteenth century, men with long-standing connections to the bench and men from the highest ranks of society partook less in provincial administration than they had just after the Restoration, a surprising development considering the 'persistent vein of genuine anxiety about lesser gentry taking the reins' of county government after the 1690s.[46] By withdrawing themselves from active involvement in government, the greater gentry left the reins to be grasped.

This withdrawal can be shown in several ways in Norfolk. Attendance at sessions and assizes, however imperfectly recorded, provides one guide, and evidence of magistrates' judicial activism (although difficult to assess) helps to measure the extent of elite disengagement from the Norfolk bench. Central government records provide information on appointments,[47] those who took out their dedimuses (which gave them authority to act on their commissions),[48] and some notion of those attending assizes.[49] The court of quarter sessions' formal records, both order books and sessions books, broadly show which justices were actively at work, by recording those who attended sessions, those who were assigned administrative tasks, those whose prisoners appeared at sessions and whose orders were (haphazardly) brought to the court's attention on appeal.[50] Together, these sources show the decreasing

---

[45] *Cf.* Landau, *Justices of the Peace*, chapter 10.

[46] Fletcher, *Reform in the Provinces*, pp. 35–6, where he says that the 1690s brought 'a distinct and permanent change in the character of the commissions of the peace', as they grew in size and became diluted by 'gentry of varying wealth and standing'.

[47] PRO, C 234/26 for fiats to issue Norfolk commissions and C 231/7 for Crown Office doquet books with warrants for commissions. The doquet books cease to include names of individuals to put in or out of new commissions by 1708.

[48] This information survives for Norfolk for the years from 1701–13: PRO, C 193/43.

[49] PRO, ASSI 16/3–59 and ASSI 35/133–47. The surviving run of assize *nominae ministrorum*, which include lists of justices, theoretically required to attend assizes, is by no means complete between 1660 and 1720.

[50] The sources for this information are the court's sessions books and order books, C/S1/8–11 and C/S2/2–8. No sessions book survives for 1676–83, 1693–1710, 1718–20 and no order book for 1683–9.

The evidence of attendance these books provide is inevitably imperfect, if only because the clerk of the peace invariably ended his list of justices at sessions with the notation 'et alii', indicating that other justices than those named may have been present. Still, the congruity between the pipe roll figures and those derived

Table 3.1. *Claims on the pipe rolls for Norfolk justices attending sessions, 1660–1685*

Years	Average no. of JPs in commission	Average no. of JPs claimed	Average % attending	Average no. of days attended
1660–1669	82	46	56	9.2
1670–1679	80	40	50	9.1
1680–1685	83	37	45	10.3

Source: PRO, E372/504–530

Table 3.2. *Norfolk justices' attendance at quarter sessions, 1660–1718*

Years	Average no. of JPs in commission	Average no. of JPs in attendance	Average % attending
1660–1675	79	40	51
1689–1693	90	30	33
1710–1718	133	32	24

Source: Attendance derived from Norfolk Record Office, quarter sessions order books C/S2/2–8, and sessions books C/S1/8–11. Only those years for which both sessions and order books survive have been included in the table.

proportion of magistrates who came to and did the work of sessions (see Tables 3.1 and 3.2).[51]

These tables provide the best surviving information about attendance at sessions. After the mid-1680s, the sheriff's claims to 4s *per diem* for justices present at sessions (which are recorded in the pipe rolls) deteriorate,[52] but up to that point they show a modest

from sessions records is reassuring, and where attendance figures based on attendance lists and names of justices signing orders at sessions can be compared with other evidence, the accuracy is high: see for example references in the notebook of R. Doughty, NRO, Aylsham 829.

[51] The absence of petty sessions records hinders an exact recovery of justices' activity, but in a decentralized county like Norfolk, where the sessions met quarterly in three different venues, petty sessions were not (as they were in eighteenth-century Kent) 'the prime focus of judicial power': Landau, *Justices of the Peace*, p. 209. Landau further notes that 'it is quite probable that the administrative powers of even late seventeenth-century petty sessions were insignificant compared with those wielded in the eighteenth century': *ibid.*, p. 214.

[52] As early as 25 Charles II, moreover, all claims for days attended were entered as multiples of two, indicating some decay in the records' accuracy.

decrease in the number of magistrates who turned up and a marginal increase in the average number of days they attended. The attendance figures derived from quarter sessions records more clearly suggest that as the commission grew larger, proportionately (and absolutely) fewer of the Norfolk gentry appointed justices of the peace found it worthwhile to attend. Where half the commission had done so at the Restoration, one-fourth did so around the accession of George I, and this at a time when the size of the commission of the peace was expanding throughout the nation.[53] Attendance at assizes shows similar decrease: rates diminished from 50 per cent of the bench (nearly attained as late as 1688) to 15 to 20 per cent in the 1690s. Thereafter records are sparse, but in 1724, only nine of 115 justices turned out (8 per cent), although attendance recovered to nearly 30 per cent by 1734.[54]

Such a pattern of declining attendance is not unique to Norfolk, but most evidence from the best-studied county, Kent, belongs to the late 1730s and after,[55] and attendance varied from county to county according to whether the bench met quarterly in one location or many and according to regional geography.[56] Whether regionally unique or not, declining attendance indicates a new attitude to the meaning and importance of sessions, which seem to have been perceived as a less significant forum for the exercise of power, creation of interest or maintenance of reputation than had been the case in Elizabethan or early Stuart Norfolk.

Somehow the commission was filled up, and many justices (even if a minority) attended sessions. But justices could not be forced to participate actively in the sessions meetings or easily be bullied into assuming the burdens of magistracy outside sessions. Although contemporaries complained that areas of the county were left uncovered because of the accidents of death, the politics of purge or by the central government's omission, lack of administrative coverage was most justly attributed to the unwillingness of resident justices to be active. In Norfolk, this reluctance drew substantial

---

[53] Landau, *Justices of the Peace*, Appendix A.
[54] Only 10 *nominae ministrorum* survive from 1699 through 1738 and none between 1707 and 1724: PRO, ASSI 35. Most *nominae* before this date are in PRO, ASSI 16; several *nominae* are among the Norfolk sessions records in NRO, C/S3.
[55] Landau, *Justices of the Peace*, pp. 261–2 and tables E–1 and E–2; assize attendance diminished from over half to around twenty per cent between the 1670s and Anne's reign: p. 39.
[56] Fletcher, *Reform in the Provinces*, pp. 100–2, 108–10, 157.

adverse comment in the early eighteenth century. Young Robert Walpole's steward, John Wrott, reported that the sessions at Little Walsingham in January 1701 saw 'a very small bench' of merely two justices, for which the disappointed Wrott blamed the poor weather ('much snow with frost') and several justices' 'pretended illness'.[57] Robert Britiffe, attorney for Norfolk's lord lieutenant, Viscount Townshend, heartily approved several new appointments to the bench in 1707, especially considering the 'great fault [of] Mr Windham, Dr Doughty & other gentlemen' who were inactive in the area where the appointees lived. Britiffe (although himself not a justice) spoke later with one of the new magistrates and 'insisted upon it that he must act'.[58] It was through similar 'great importunities' by three Norfolk justices that Harbord Harbord, having been in the commission for three years, was prevailed upon to swear the oaths of the peace in 1714. The fact that he was enlisted two days later to participate in a meeting to sign 'articles for the assizes' testifies to the urgency with which his colleagues sought his assistance.[59] And seven years later the Bishop of Norwich commented on the 'thin appearance' of magistrates at midsummer sessions in the city.[60]

There was nothing new about non-appearance of justices, nor about the assumption of the major burden of work on the part of a few men. The pattern is evident from Tudor Suffolk to late Stuart Yorkshire.[61] But analysis of the fifty-six most active Norfolk

[57] J. Wrott to R. Walpole, 27 January 1701, Cambridge University Library, Cholmondeley (Houghton) correspondence, 95.

[58] R. Britiffe to Lord Townshend, 17 March 1707, RBF, '3rd Viscount Townshend, Britiffe et al.'. Peter Wilson, the new justice, took out his dedimus some time between his appointment and 1710 but before Ashe Windham did. Robert Doughty never took out a dedimus in the Lord Chancellor's office: PRO, C 193/43.

[59] A. Windham to [Lord Townshend], 14 March 1714, B.L., Add. MS 63079, fo. 18; R. Britiffe to same, 16 March 1714, RBF, '3rd Viscount Townshend, Britiffe et al.'

[60] Charles Trimnel, Bishop of Norwich, to [the Duke of Newcastle], 17 July 1721, B. L., Add. MS 32686, fo. 174.

[61] See, for example, D. MacCulloch, *Suffolk and the Tudors: Politics and Religion in an English County 1500–1600*, (Oxford, 1986), Appendix 1: only twenty of sixty JPs in the commission in 1601 apparently attended sessions. G. C. F. Forster notes that 'the work of quarter sessions throughout the [seventeenth] century fell on small groups of J.P.s': *The East Riding Justices of the Peace in the Seventeenth Century*, East Yorkshire Local History Series, no. 30 (York, 1973), p. 32. In the North Riding of Yorkshire, as many as ten justices rarely attended any adjourned meeting between 1660 and 1716 except for those held twice yearly at Thirsk:

justices between 1660 and 1720 (men set apart by heavy attendance, frequent committee appointments, and recurrent service as
treasurer and as sessions chairman) shows a pattern to activity that
reinforces the picture of an early surge of activity followed by elite
inattendance and withdrawal.[62]

Among the active magistrates, one-third (nineteen) were deputy
lieutenants, a position of substantial status, and just five of them
began their tenure on the bench after 1690. Nineteen active justices
were knights or baronets: fourteen began their service as magistrates in the 1660s, but only three became justices after 1700 and
only four even sat after 1710. Titled men, MPs (including knights of
the shire), and men with predecessors on the bench all served more
often before 1690 than after as one of the six county treasurers
appointed annually from the bench.[63] After 1700, the calibre of
treasurers altered, and greater gentry like Sir John Holland, Sir
John Hobart and Sir Peter Gleane were no longer willing to
undertake such an administrative task, or at least not more than
once or twice. Instead, men from Norwich and its neighbourhood –
like Waller Bacon, Thornhagh Gurdon, Henry Davy, John Peck,
George Warren and Francis Long – brought legal training and
energy (but few family connections) to their duties as treasurer.[64]
Those prominent on the bench no longer bore the ancient pedigrees
of the Spelmans, Gawdys, L'Estranges and Calthorpes, but were
names newer to the county. Moreover, this development occurred
not because members of old families were absent from the commission (although the proportion with ancestors on the bench did

Quarter Sessions Records, ed. J. C. Atkinson, *North Riding Record Society*, vol.
6, *1658–77* (1888) and vol. 7, *1677–1716* (1889).

[62] The East Riding saw a far greater proportion of active justices in the 1660s–70s,
when between sixteen and nineteen of about thirty justices attended at least once
a year, more than in the preceding two decades: Forster, *East Riding Justices*, p. 32.

[63] In the former period nine baronets and three knights served as treasurers a total
of twenty-nine times; in the latter, four baronets and three knights served sixteen
times. Sir Roger Potts, who served as treasurer in both periods (1675, 1689, 1690
and 1692) has been excluded. Two treasurers each were appointed for the
prisoners in the Castle, for the King's Bench and Marshalsea and for maimed
soldiers and mariners. In Kent, justices did not serve as treasurers: Landau,
Justices of the Peace, pp. 255–6. They did, however, in Nottinghamshire; H. H.
Copnall, *Nottinghamshire County Records* (Nottingham, 1915), p. 13.

[64] Of sixteen men who were treasurers three or more times between 1700 and 1720,
five came from Norwich itself and another four from a radius of five to six miles
away.

decrease)[65] but because their representatives apparently preferred to take little or no part in its business.

Across the generations, service within eminent families diminished. Among those who represented Norfolk's most prominent families, few were active on the bench by the turn of the eighteenth century. In 1711, at a time when the commission numbered about 130,[66] twenty-five justices, most of them newly appointed, took out their dedimus to act: the group's lack of social standing is reflected in the fact that only four ranked as high as thirty-one in the commission's order of precedence, while the remaining twenty-one averaged a spot 109 places down the commission. The same pattern holds true for the other twenty-six men who obtained dedimuses between 1701 and 1713.[67]

In short, the siblings and children of the county's titled and politically dominant families no longer helped to build and maintain the family interest by an active presence at sessions. Where exemplary fathers had led the way under Charles II and James II, their sons and grandsons were less ardent: Sir John Hobart, a Whig knight of the shire in the Exclusion era and an active justice, was followed by an inactive son (who died at forty) and a grandson who worked far harder as deputy lieutenant than as justice. Sir John Holland, 1st Bt., veteran of the Long Parliament and an aggressive and innovative magistrate even in his mid-eighties, was succeeded by a grandson who participated with much less zeal, distracted by his position as knight of the shire, privy councillor and Controller of

---

[65] In January 1661, 45 per cent of the bench lacked connection to justices appointed before 1640. For the 62 justices whose Hearth Tax assessments are known, those 37 with ancestors on the bench had houses averaging over 24 hearths, those 25 without ties had houses that averaged under 14 hearths. By September 1689, the proportion without ties had fallen to 41 per cent, but another 23 per cent had ties only with justices appointed since the Restoration, so that nearly two-thirds of the bench was comprised of relative newcomers to the magistracy. In October 1714, 30 per cent of the bench was comprised of absolute newcomers and an additional 32 per cent were linked only to justices appointed after 1660.

[66] A commission issued in February had 127 members; one issued in June had 135: NRO, T287A.

[67] Dedimus book, PRO, C 193/43. Justices taking out their dedimus were not necessarily a representative sample of magistrates, since use of the writ was 'reserved for magistrates unable to attend assizes' to be sworn by the judges there: T. Barnes and A. H. Smith, 'Justices of the Peace from 1558 to 1688 – a Revised List of Sources', *Bulletin of the Institute of Historical Research*, 32 (1959), pp. 226–7. Yet the bias in this sample of magistrates might arguably be toward those of high social status, most likely to be absent from the county, and not in the direction of the socially inferior figures noted here.

the Household. Sir Robert Kemp, another exclusionist knight of the shire, produced a less-than-energetic son; the heir of Sir Peter Gleane (himself a regular attender at sessions from 1660 to 1670 and thrice a county treasurer) made his only mark with the county court by petitioning it for financial assistance when imprisoned in the Fleet for debt. Sir Ralph Hare, an assiduous justice until his death in 1672, was succeeded by a son who never went to sessions and by a grandson who became only marginally active when he took out his dedimus at least nine years after appointment to the bench.

There are perhaps reasons to argue that decreasing activism across generations might be a common and understandable phenomenon, resting primarily on the success of earlier family members in founding secure fortunes. Yet there seems to be more involved, and the instances of Robert Walpole father and son, used by the son's biographer thirty years ago to reveal a generational and societal change,[68] remain illustrative. Walpole the elder, like his son a member of parliament and a man of influence, none the less found ample time for attendance at quarter sessions, assizes and lieutenancy meetings; his son Robert was far more busy in London. The father, between 1673 and his death in 1700, attended forty lieutenancy gatherings and at least sixty-seven sessions meetings, although – as a squire from the west of the county – only two recorded ones at Norwich. His son between 1701 and 1720 went to just five meetings of the deputy lieutenants and three dozen sessions. Six of these sessions were in Norwich, too, as young Robert sought the larger arena offered by the county town more than did his father.[69]

Of course, the younger Robert was a member of parliament virtually from the date he became a justice, whereas his father only sat from 1689. It might appear that the young man simply had less time for the county than his father, but that conclusion begs the question of how each man valued time spent respectively in the province and at the centre. The pair set their priorities differently, and that fact in itself reflects part of the altered character of elite life

[68] J. H. Plumb, 'The Walpoles: Father and Son', in J. H. Plumb, ed., *Studies in Social History: A Tribute to G. M. Trevelyan* (London, 1955), pp. 179–207.
[69] For lieutenancy attendance, see *Norfolk Lieutenancy Journal 1660–1676*, ed. R. M. Dunn, *Norfolk Record Society*, 45 (1975); Norfolk Lieutenancy Journal 1676–1715, NRO, NRS 27276, 372x7; Norfolk Lieutenancy Journal 1715–50, NRO, NRS 27308, 447x.

in Augustan England. The early beneficiaries of the Restoration settlement combined activities as legislators and magistrates, in part because the demands of the former role were still relatively limited and occasional, at least compared with the time when annual sessions became the norm. Beyond this, however, men like the elder Walpole remained imbued with and affected by older notions of prestige and local obligation, which meant that they could not be effective as legislative politicians at the centre without at least titular service in the provinces.[70] The case of young Robert Walpole shows how times changed: he was present at only four quarter sessions meetings between 1706 and 1711, while the Whigs held sway in Parliament and he held office, but he attended fourteen meetings in the next two years, when out of office and less bound to life in the capital. In fact, Walpole testified to his long-standing detachment from the business of magistracy when he became caught up in the county dispute about a changed venue for sessional meetings in the late 1730s, confessing that the observations he made now were more on 'the subject of justices of the peace than I have said or thought these twenty years'.[71]

The experiences of the first and second Viscounts Townshend, Norfolk's lords lieutenant between 1661–76 and 1701–30,[72] run parallel to the Walpoles. Horatio Townshend personally attended twenty-seven meetings of the Norfolk lieutenancy during fifteen years as lieutenant; his son, preoccupied with central office, attended only ten meetings of his lieutenancy between 1701 and 1720, and none at all between 1720 and 1730.[73] The first Viscount even appeared at quarter sessions a dozen recorded times, his son but two. The second Viscount's attenuated personal involvement in local administration is plain. Although in the last year of his life he was sufficiently concerned to take depositions in a case of accused theft,[74] he revealed his underlying thoughts about local administration in 1725 when in Hanover as secretary of state. Writing anxiously to the Duke of Newcastle about pending elections for the

---

[70] I owe this insight to Cynthia Herrup.

[71] Sir R. Walpole to third Viscount Townshend, 26 December 1738, NRO, uncatalogued mss, box M, P168C.

[72] The second Viscount was temporarily displaced, 1713–14.

[73] See note 69 above for attendance. The figures exclude two times each man held a meeting by himself at Raynham Hall.

[74] Informations of 7 and 9 June 1738, assize files for July 1738, PRO, ASSI 35/178/16.

London sheriffs, Townshend reminded the Duke how important it was to intervene directly with 'the persons one would engage' in the affair. Disgusted with the meagre attention he believed Newcastle and Robert Walpole were directing to so crucial a matter, he could not 'help [but] imagine that Claremont [Newcastle's country home] and Norfolk take up a large share of your grace's and my brother Walpole's thoughts', as a consequence of which 'we cannot be able to carry but one sheriff in the city'. County business was potentially a distraction from affairs that mattered more.[75]

III

This was especially so because county business was not always the occasion for the working out of party rivalries or for demonstrations of party dominance. There is no question that politics played their part in the Norfolk commission; to stress the existence of bi-partisanship on the bench is not to deny the magistracy's politicization. In the 1680s, rather than debating matters before the court, the Norfolk justices moved directly to partisan votes.[76] In the reigns of both William III and Anne there were politically motivated manipulations of the commission's membership, and after 1715, Whigs visibly dominated the bench and the thirty-three new appointments made to the commission before 1722.[77] Of the most assiduous attenders at quarter sessions from the accession of George I until 1720, ten of nineteen are identifiable Whigs and only two clear-cut Tories. Over the same period, both county treasurers and sessions chairmen were also predominantly Whigs. The evidence of Whig domination on the Norfolk bench is clear.

But if party considerations overwhelmed the selection of key personnel in county administration at a time when the power of one party had been crippled,[78] ironically the earlier period of party rage in the reigns of William and Anne saw signs of a bi-partisan or non-partisan approach to quarter sessions business. Bi-partisanship

[75] 18–29 June 1725, BL Add. MS 32687, fo. 87.
[76] *Calendar of State Papers Domestic 1682*, pp. 54–5. See also Fletcher, *Reform in the Provinces*, p. 91.
[77] Fiats for new commissions, PRO, C 234/26.
[78] Even then, the purges of 1715–16 removed only twelve Tories, eleven of them justices placed on the commission at a time of Tory manipulation in 1711. Just sixteen magistrates in all (other than those who had died) were removed from the Norfolk commission between 1715 and 1722.

provided a valuable element of administrative stability and continuity. As Fletcher points out, those involved in Stuart government
'shared a sense of the limits to the disruption of good government
that personal antagonisms could be allowed to inflict'.[79] The same
strictures applied to excessive partisanship on the bench, because it
could destroy good government. If a relatively objective criterion
such as legal training counted less than 'accumulated wisdom and
devoted service . . . [or] continuity and stability of membership' in
making the bench effective,[80] the same might be said for the
subjective matter of political affiliation.

The evidence of bi-partisanship in the Norfolk sessions appears
among other places in committee membership. A handful of
partisan committees existed before 1715. One committee,
appointed in January 1711 to inspect constables' accounts and
ferret out defaulters, included eight Whigs out of nine members:
what this means during a time of national Tory dominance is hard
to decipher. A committee appointed a year later, to put in effect the
act concerning a highway from Attleborough to Wymondham,
consisted of six Tories.[81] More significant than these, however,
were the mixed committees that appeared even at times of high
partisan feeling and of one party's apparent numerical domination
of the bench. They include two important highway committees
named ten years apart, three major accounts committees, a causeway committee, and a body named in 1714 to investigate the
continuing dispute between the county and the city of Norwich over
bridges they shared.[82] On none of these bodies was there a
preponderance of identifiable partisans of one political party.

'General' committees were also established, embracing, for
example, all justices in a given division of the county or those living
within so many miles of Norwich. They suggest that party affiliation
meant little in relatively non-controversial county business like
bridge repair or highway maintenance.[83] This is not to deny what
held true in Kent, that in so far as the decisions of two justices

[79] A. Fletcher, 'Honour, Reputation and Local Officeholding in Elizabethan and
   Stuart England', in Fletcher and Stevenson, *Order and Disorder*, p. 115.
[80] Fletcher, *Reform in the Provinces*, pp. 38, 372.
[81] Orders of 9 January 1711, 15 January 1712.
[82] Orders of 11 July 1699, 22 April and 7 October 1707, 12 July 1709, 15 July 1712,
   14 July 1713, and 6 April 1714.
[83] See assignments made 10 January and 10 April 1716, 7 February (which also
   pertains to a criminal matter) and 6 October 1719.

acting together could easily affect local rates and therefore individuals' tax burdens, they were open to political influence.[84] But there is no reason to assume that the principal consideration for justices when making *collective* administrative decisions in sessions was the economic impact they might have on the allegiance of potential voters.[85]

A clearer indication than committee composition that the bench was only a partly-politicized institution is the retention on the commission, regardless of party purges, of insubstantial but active justices. When it came to purging,[86] thoroughgoing eradication of all political opponents was simply infeasible, first because it was always possible that men not purged might in gratitude shift allegiances but also because it was unthinkable to displace wholesale one group of 'natural rulers', especially those who had shown themselves energetic administrators of local government. Given these two criteria, one might expect that the most prominent justices of a party out of power would retain places on the commission during partisan purges, while those most dispensable (even if retention might arguably help sway their party allegiance) would be men placed low on the commission, those without claims to special consideration because of their status, connections or family tradition of service.

Purges in Norfolk under William III were few: most of the names omitted from commissions between 1689 and 1701, excluding the large number of James II's aberrational appointees who were purged, were left out because they had died.[87] In all, fourteen men were left off the commission for reasons other than death. Yet they were not a group easily dismissable because of their low standing: they were preponderantly (nine out of fourteen) non-attenders at sessions, and whatever the cause, their dismissals would have little

---

[84] Landau, *Justices of the Peace*, pp. 32–8.

[85] John, 1st Baron Ashburnham, showed a keen sensitivity to the level of local assessments and rates, not for party interest but for pure self-interest: C. Brooks, 'John, 1st Baron Ashburnham, and the State, c. 1688–1710', *Historical Research, The Bulletin of the Institute of Historical Research*, 60 (1987), pp. 64–79, esp. 67–71.

[86] Fletcher, *Reform in the Provinces*, pp. 29–30; L. K. J. Glassey, *Politics and the Appointment of Justices of the Peace 1675–1720* (Oxford, 1979), pp. 171 ff.

[87] Deterioration of the records makes it difficult to identify precise dates of exclusion, and men dying shortly after their last appearance on a list of justices, when no other list intervenes, may have been excluded because they were dead.

affected the business of the bench. Here is a demonstration that the lesson of the 1680s had been learned: that undifferentiated and widescale purges were to be avoided, because they necessarily entailed 'the loss of men who were outstandingly competent and experienced'.[88]

Under Anne purges were equally restrained. Thirteen justices were put off for reasons other than death, all presumable Whigs who suffered between 1711 and 1713. But only five of the thirteen were even regular attenders at sessions, so that non-attenders continued to make up the bulk of magistrates singled out for punishment, and of the five, four ranked in the upper one-third of the commission in terms of precedence: their dismissals were intended to send clear political messages. To put the purges under Anne in another light, eleven of the fifty-six most active justices in Augustan Norfolk began their tenure before and finished it after Anne's reign: only two had it interrupted by political purges during her reign.

Retention of minor justices seems to have been the result of a largely unspoken acknowledgement of the need to get business done, regardless of justices' political allegiances. Matters of good government could over-ride party concerns; this at least is the best explanation to provide for the two-party composition of committees in the Norfolk magistracy, as well as for the retention on the bench of so many active justices, regardless of party allegiance. Not only were minor figures coming to the fore in county business, but their party allegiance seemed to matter less than the perspicacity and commitment they brought to their work. The retention of numerous minor figures between 1689 and 1715,[89] despite manipulations both Tory and Whig, represents an acknowledgement of the value these men possessed as workhorses of sessions, party men perhaps, but useful beyond their party roles.

IV

The reluctance to dismiss partisan but hard-working minor judicial figures was an obvious concomitant of the retreat of the greater

---

[88] Fletcher, *Reform in the Provinces*, pp. 23, 26.
[89] These include men like Francis Long, Henry Negus, Thomas Tanner, Thornhagh Gurdon, Sir Isaac Preston, Sir Charles Turner, Edmund Wodehouse, Ralph Hare of Harpham, James Hoste, Hatton Berners and John Knyvett.

gentry from prominent roles on the bench.[90] From the late seventeenth century, many of Norfolk's greater gentry abandoned even an adjunct role in the magistracy, despite the continued anxiety expressed throughout the nation over the inflation of the commission's size and debasement of its status.[91] For these men, the prospect of a socially inferior magistracy did not move them to participate in the way that fear of new social or political disorder had spurred their energetic counterparts in the 1660s and early 1670s. Moreover, competing activities and new attitudes diminished the attraction of the labours of magistracy. The increasingly common experience of a European tour changed the outlook of some.[92] For others, the demands and joys of house and estate ultimately outweighed a sense of public duty,[93] and anxieties about the state of the county were likely to be forgotten or ignored in the whirl of London.

One development that diminished the dangers inherent in this shift in administrative control was the emergence of increasingly professional methods and attitudes toward sessional business,[94] whether reflected in efforts to maintain decorum in the court or in efforts to rationalize sessions business. This growing professionalization, as much as a shift away from general to petty sessions as the arena in which to transact business,[95] accounts for the declining participation of the greater gentry in the formal meetings of provincial government. As recognized routines were established to cope with settlement appeals, bridge repairs, highway surveys – business that virtually crowded out criminal matters at sessions in the eighteenth century[96] – the personnel involved in making and implementing decisions mattered less.

[90] It was also common even in Elizabethan Norfolk for relatively minor gentry to play a role in the magistracy disproportionate to their status: Smith, *County and Court*, p. 90.

[91] Fletcher, *Reform in the Provinces*, pp. 35–6.

[92] See A. W. Moore, *Norfolk & the Grand Tour: Eighteenth-Century Travellers Abroad and their Souvenirs* (Fakenham, 1985).

[93] William Windham, an unsuccessful Whig candidate for MP, admitted that he did not mind losing, since he took 'so much delight in my nursery and garden': R. W. Ketton-Cremer, *Felbrigg, the Story of a House* (London, 1982), p. 68.

[94] Fletcher, *Reform in the Provinces*, pp. 368–71; Landau, *Justices of the Peace*, pp. 253–4.

[95] *Ibid.*, chapter 7, esp. pp. 213–20. Fletcher, *Reform in the Provinces*, p. 133, notes that the extensive, early development of petty sessions in Kent may well be unique.

[96] Landau, *Justices of the Peace*, pp. 241–5; Beattie, *Crime and Courts*, pp. 5–6.

In Norfolk, the county treasurerships provide one example of the institutionalization of sessions. By the early eighteenth century, at least ten justices served an obvious 'rotation' through the three county treasuries in successive years. From 1707 the first signs appear of what became a similarly routine arrangement in selecting sessions chairmen.[97] Another sign of the bench's growing corporate awareness appears in the accommodation made several times to delay sessions meetings when their scheduled date fell before the end of Trinity term, which would allow counsel and otherwise-occupied persons a chance to attend.[98] Beginning in 1707, careful attention was bestowed on the needs of bridewells at Norwich, Aylsham, Swaffham and Wymondham, care that extended for four years and entailed authorization of over £1,300 to pay for repairs.

The court attempted also to regulate the conduct of those who came in contact with it. In April 1707 the Norwich bench forbade those having business with the court to stand on the tables during sessions; perhaps inspired by this effort to establish an atmosphere of propriety, the Little Walsingham sessions three years later demanded that all counsel appear before it in gowns, 'in like manner as they do in Norwich division'.[99] After 1715 steps to expedite business followed rapidly.[100] Justices' clerks were ordered to bring in their recognizances on the first day of sessions; appeals of justice's orders were also to be dealt with on the first day or not at all.[101] Gaolers were required to provide the clerk of the peace with the preceding session's gaol calendar at least a week before every sessions. Alehouse-keepers' recognizances were to be engrossed and returned with the signatures of the justices before whom they had been taken. The court condemned constables who failed to return lists of potential jurors or omitted from them the names of qualified men, and it tried to check the 'irregularities' of bailiffs who failed to serve the court's processes with sufficient vigilance or who served fraudulent ones to promote their own interests.

---

[97] Order of 22 January 1712. On the significance of the chairman, see Fletcher, *Reform in the Provinces*, pp. 166–9.

[98] Orders of 3 May 1709, 18 April 1710, 29 April 1712.

[99] 22 April 1707 and 19 January 1710.

[100] For what follows, see orders of 11 January, 4 October, 19 November 1715, 2 August 1716, 30 April 1717, 14 January 1718, and 13 January 1719.

[101] In Surrey, a similar order concerning appeals was issued only in 1754: Beattie, *Crime and Courts*, p. 392.

The justices further kept an eye on the implementation of their orders, notably by appointing committees to inspect repairs to county buildings and by reviewing the ranks of the county pensioners.[102] The court had formerly examined the accounts of its treasurers, who were chosen from among the justices, but because each of the three treasuries had two treasurers (for the 'home' and 'foreign' divisions into which the county was split), gathering the accounts, much less reconciling them, was a major task made greater by the fact that treasurers were replaced each year. An examination begun in 1681 (one of the earliest signs of rationalization from the bench) dragged on for five years until the court, probably at the instigation of the indefatigable octagenarian, Sir John Holland, appointed an auditor to look into the county treasuries.[103] This official had little success in ferreting out the treasurers' accounts, but Holland resolved 'not to let the matter slide', hounding fellow justices – as well as the court's employees – year after year. Only as late as 1692 did the auditor finally present his accounts to the justices, at which point the court issued a set of systematic directions to guide him, the treasurers and their clerks, and the chief constables responsible for paying in money to the treasuries.[104]

In similar fashion, a review of pensions was ordered in 1715, 'at which time [pensioners were] to appear in person or to send authentic certificates or some persons to give the court satisfaction viva voce of their being alive & of their several conditions & circumstances'.[105] The pious thought was later translated into action by the appointment of a large committee of thirteen justices

[102] Orders of 26 July 1715 and 7 October 1718.

[103] A committee of four to examine the treasurers' accounts was appointed 12 April 1681, but Sir John Holland was not among the members: NRO, C/S2/3. Given his assertion at the end of 1686 that he had been trying to clear the accounts for six years (Bodl., MS Tanner 159, fo. 45v), he was presumably appointed some time after October 1681, the start of an eight-year gap in the quarter sessions order books.

[104] According to Holland, *ibid.*, fo. 67v, the order instructed the auditor to examine accounts between Midsummer and Michaelmas and report to the Michaelmas sessions; chief constables were to pay in money quarterly, clearing their accounts at Easter, so no arrears would be carried on to newly-elected treasurers' accounts. Treasurers' clerks were to deliver to the sessions chairman a quarterly account of constables in arrears, so the latter could account to sessions for deficiencies. The treasurers' clerks then had to move against defaulting constables for their arrears, upon pain of losing the fees for their work. See in general *ibid.*, fos. 41–67v, also orders of 12 July and 4 October 1692.

[105] It is not clear that this review in fact took place.

in January 1718, when concern had mounted over the fiscal burden of the pensions and the apparent fraud in their administration. The committee was ordered to investigate 'all particular matters & things ... needful for detecting all fraud and evil practices'. Pensioners were summoned to the Easter sessions at Norwich, and 'upon full debate & due consideration of the whole matter in open court', three pensioners were discovered to be dead, fifteen pensions were suspended temporarily or entirely revoked, and thirty-eight were continued. By these actions, the court reduced pension costs by £100 a year (leaving a total burden of £208 outstanding) and demonstrated the benefits to the county that concerted action could bring.[106]

V

The gentry of eighteenth-century England have commonly been portrayed as keenly attuned to local life and closely involved in the maintenance of local order. Yet this essay shows that greater-gentry dominance of local government was achieved by indirection much less than by active intervention. There were many reasons why the elite was able to abandon its active role at a time when the tumultuous conditions of local politics might have called for frequent (theatrical) appearances by them in the local community. The explanations, as argued here, include the increasing routinization of justices' business, the institutionalization of the bench's procedures, even a measure of professionalization to service in the magistracy.

Others may be suggested. If the elite were to withdraw from participation in local governance, new and socially less substantial men had to be brought on to the bench, a development that took place nationally from the 1690s.[107] Lesser gentry, whose importance as a group had been sometimes frighteningly demonstrated by their role in the interregnum, were again brought into the process of governance, but this time elite influence saw to it that the reins of government were put into reliable hands. Many of those recruited to the Norfolk bench who lacked the 'natural' qualifications of

[106] Orders of 26 July 1715 and 22 April 1718.
[107] Fletcher, *Reform in the Provinces*, pp. 15–19, 32–5. In Norfolk, even if the magistracy was being recruited from lower down the social scale than hitherto, only one parish clergyman sat on the bench before 1720 (although the diocesan chancellor and the cathedral's dean also normally belonged to the commission).

leadership (traditions of family service or ancient stature in the county) enjoyed compensatory legal qualifications or experience. Service on the assize grand jury evidently assisted in gauging the suitability of prospective justices.[108] Reliance on connections, in a less bureaucratically rational manner, might also ensure a dependable commission: the Norfolk bench in the fall of 1714 boasted fourteen justices who were tenants or relatives of either Robert Walpole or the second Viscount Townshend.[109] Such magistrates sat on the bench in part merely as clients of their patrons; in some measure their presence is evidence of the co-opting power of a culturally as well as politically dominant elite. But when they served actively it was not merely to ingratiate themselves with their patrons. They also sought to extract every ounce of the residual honour and reputation that still accrued to the office of magistrate, something they needed and were able to do because they retained links to the local community which their greater gentry counterparts now lacked, ties, moreover, that helped make these new recruits effective governors as well.

The emergence of the lieutenancy was another factor that balanced elite withdrawal from county governance. The coincident timing of lieutenancy meetings with quarter sessions may testify to the continued vitality of the latter in county life but also suggests that the one way to bring elite justices to sessions was to schedule the more weighty lieutenancy meeting at the same time.[110] The importance of the lieutenancy, symbolically and really, has not yet been fully explored by historians,[111] perhaps because its early eighteenth-century duties seem so mundane. But in Norfolk it brought together a small coterie of leading figures, individuals who almost to a man possessed strong links with the metropolis; they served as the lord lieutenant's agents in the county, as conduits for central government authority and as transmitters of metropolitan culture, values and concerns. The symbolic importance of the lieutenancy and the militia it oversaw is nowhere better expressed

---

108   Of 399 identifiable grand jurors in the period between 1661 and 1707, 143 [36 per cent] were justices, 83 of whom [58 per cent] served on the jury prior to appointment to the bench: PRO, ASSI 16 and 35 and NRO, C/S3 for jury lists.
109   The full commission is listed in the fiat for this date: PRO, C 234/26.
110   In early eighteenth-century Norfolk, often only two or three deputies attended lieutenancy meetings; the same men also attended sessions.
111   But see Fletcher, 'Honour, Reputation and Local Officeholding', pp. 106–9, and *Reform in the Provinces*, chapter 9.

than in the widespread late seventeenth-century adoption of military honorifics, evident even in the Norfolk sessions records.[112]

Elite withdrawal in every avenue in which it occurred was voluntary rather than forced; since the greater gentry remained on the commission, they were at any time free to resume an active role on the bench. If we are to speculate on what led them into withdrawal beyond a general inclination toward separation from the mundane, then one factor is perhaps the stultifying nature of judicial routine.[113] Another was surely the changing perception of the honour and reputation to be gained by service, probably a more important consideration, since a conscientious justice's business had never been riveting.[114] Yet a third explanation for withdrawal is the elite's confidence in the stability and durability of local government without their participation. In addition, it might be suggested that the issues that most engaged men of substance in the years after 1689 were not entirely of the sort that focused their attention on the county. If the first part of the eighteenth century saw the final stage in the creation of a truly national genteel class, it is understandable that the greater gentry lost interest in county affairs, which now had little consequence to men whose self-identity derived no longer from victory in precedence battles on the commission of the peace but instead from association with national issues, connections and parties. The withdrawal provides further evidence of the unlooked-for alterations to patterns of elite life that the late seventeenth century brought about, an orientation away from the county and outward toward the nation.[115]

In this respect, the structure of politics portrayed in Norfolk at the end of the sixteenth century had been nearly reversed. Then, county issues fed into, indeed often generated, discussion of central government issues. This was not the case a hundred years later.

[112] Titles first appear in the sessions book 1684–93, NRO, C/S1/10.
[113] G. C. F. Forster, 'Government in Provincial England under the Later Stuarts', *Transactions of the Royal Historical Society*, 5th ser., 33 (1983), pp. 34–7.
[114] Landau argues that by the mid-eighteenth century local office would only 'enhance whatever natural authority [a gentleman] already possessed; he could not entertain hopes of gain, material or immaterial, not already inherent in his station in private life': *Justices of the Peace*, p. 325. This is an opposite view to that portrayed by Fletcher for Elizabethan and Stuart justices: 'Honour, Reputation and Local Officeholding'.
[115] Jenkins's *The Making of a Ruling Class* illuminates both this political shift and the many others which together characterized the creation of a truly national ruling class.

'There is no doubt', we are told, 'that gentry in late sixteenth-century Norfolk regarded local politics and parliamentary business as two aspects of a continuing process.'[116] And from the 1620s through the 1650s, issues raised by privy council orders, by administration of the militia or impressment and billeting, by Ship Money and assessments, not to mention religion and concern with moral reform, all impinged most immediately upon life in the county.[117] After 1690, the localist issues of public life were joined, perhaps even overshadowed, by ones distinctly national and even foreign: the future of overseas commerce, the question of succession, the virtues of a land war against a sea war, the Bank of England. If these issues had local resonances, their sound none the less emanated from the centre. So the greater gentry understandably focused their attentions outside the county arena.

Evidence of elite withdrawal from local governance ultimately raises questions about the nature of England's political stability, which, this retreat suggests, may have stemmed less from party hegemony after 1725 than from administrative efficiency in the preceding fifty years. This essay underscores the need to reassess the timing of that stability's emergence, not just in the centre of English life,[118] but in the provinces, where examining the interaction of party politics with provincial administration may modify the view of an elite world so intensely politicized that the very fabric of local administration was imprinted with the pattern of Tory–Whig rivalry. The withdrawal of the greater gentry from local government, without any appreciable harm to provincial administration, suggests that despite party differences, there existed an under-appreciated but substantial level of unanimity, solidarity and capacity for compromise among all levels of the county elite of Augustan England.

[116] Smith, *County and Court*, pp. 335–6.
[117] See G. Owens, 'Norfolk 1620–41: Local Government and Central Authority in an East Anglian County', unpublished Ph.D. dissertation, University of Wisconsin, 1970.
[118] See L. Colley, *In Defiance of Oligarchy: The Tory Party 1714–60* (Cambridge, 1982), chapter 1.

4. The last Hanoverian sovereign?: the Victorian monarchy in historical perspective, 1688–1988

DAVID CANNADINE

It is not easy to make the study of Queen Victoria yield significant difficulties.[1] What, indeed, is there to say about the bourgeois gloriana, the gas-lit faery, the matriarch of empire, and the grandmother of Europe, which has not been said already? The appearance of Lytton Strachey's biography established the contours of her life: 'the sheltered, rather down-trodden princess, the gay young queen, the devoted wife, the abject widow, and finally the symbol of British glory at its zenith'.[2] And the publication of the Queen's letters defined the phases of her reign: from her accession to the death of Albert; from 1861 until the eve of her first Jubilee; and from 1886 up to the very end of her life.[3] Even historians find little to debate or dispute. There may be differences of emphasis and degree, but there is a remarkable consensus that by the end of her reign, the monarchy was less powerful, more

[1] Earlier versions of this essay have been presented to the seminars in modern British political history held at Oxford and Cambridge Universities, to a meeting of the Historical Association in London, and to a symposium sponsored by the British Institute of the United States in New York. I am most grateful for the many useful comments which were made on these occasions, and especially to Professor L. J. Colley for her careful scrutiny of the whole text, and to Dr David Reynolds for help with particular references. Some of the arguments advanced here were first outlined in the following three articles: 'The Ideal Husband', *New York Review of Books*, 31 (8 November 1984), pp. 22–4; 'The Merry Wives of Windsor', *New York Review of Books*, 33 (12 June 1986), pp. 15–17; 'The Brass Tacks Queen', *New York Review of Books*, 34 (23 April 1987), pp. 30–1.

[2] L. Strachey, *Queen Victoria* (London, 1921); R. Fulford, *Hanover to Windsor* (London, 1966), p. 38.

[3] A. C. Benson and Lord Esher, eds., *The Letters of Queen Victoria*, 1st series, 3 vols, *1837–61* (London, 1907); G. E. Buckle, ed., *The Letters of Queen Victoria*, 2nd series, 3 vols, *1862–85* (London, 1926); G. E. Buckle, ed., *The Letters of Queen Victoria*, 3rd series, 3 vols, *1886–1901* (London, 1932); hereafter referred to as *Letters*.

popular, more splendid and more imperial than it had been at the beginning.[4]

Above all, it remains a widely held view that from the outset, Victoria and Albert broke completely with the recent royal past – dynastically, politically and socially – and thus immediately established a new conception of monarchy which has endured essentially unaltered until our own time, based on political impartiality and a happy family life. Accordingly, the Queen and the Prince Consort continue to receive the gratitude of posterity for having been the architects of that great national success story, the modern British constitutional monarchy. Although they present much evidence which runs contrary to this interpretation, this remains the received view in almost every recent biography of the royal pair: of Eyck, Bennett, Hobhouse and Rhodes James in the case of the Prince Consort,[5] and of Woodham-Smith and Weintraub in the case of the Queen.[6] And the same disparity between evidence and interpretation may even be found in the writings of such distinguished

---

[4] See, for example: G. H. L. Le May, *The Victorian Constitution* (London, 1979), chapter 3; F. M. Hardie, *The Political Influence of Queen Victoria, 1861–1901* (London, 1935); N. J. Grossman, 'Republicanism in Nineteenth-Century England', *International Review of Social History*, 7 (1962), pp. 47–60; F. D'Arcy, 'Charles Bradlaugh and the English Republican Movement, 1868–78', *Historical Journal*, 25 (1982), pp. 367–83; G. Stedman Jones, 'Working-Class Culture and Working-Class Politics in London, 1870–1900: Notes on the Re-making of a Working Class', *Journal of Social History*, 7 (1974), pp. 460–508; R. I. McKibbin, 'Why was there no Marxism in Britain?', *English Historical Review*, 99 (1984), pp. 297–331; D. Cannadine, 'The Context, Performance and Meaning of Ritual: The British Monarchy and the "Invention of Tradition", *c.* 1820–1977', in E. Hobsbawm and T. Ranger, eds., *The Invention of Tradition* (Cambridge, 1983), pp. 101–64; J. Cannon, 'The Survival of the British Monarchy', *Transactions of the Royal Historical Society*, 5th series, 36 (1986), pp. 143–64; T. Nairn, 'The House of Windsor', *New Left Review*, 127 (May–June 1981), pp. 96–100; F. Harcourt, 'The Queen, the Sultan and the Viceroy: A Victorian State Occasion', *London Journal*, 5 (1979), pp. 35–56, and 'Gladstone, Monarchism and the New Imperialism', *Journal of Imperial and Commonwealth History*, 13 (1985), pp. 133–62.

[5] F. Eyck, *The Prince Consort* (London, 1959), pp. 9, 23–4, 26, 254; D. Bennett, *King Without a Crown: Albert, Prince Consort of England, 1819–1861* (London, 1977), pp. 127, 154, 377–80; H. Hobhouse, *Prince Albert: His Life and Work* (London, 1983), pp. viii, 39; R. Rhodes James, *The Prince Consort: A Biography* (London, 1983), pp. 111, 167.

[6] C. Woodham-Smith, *Queen Victoria: Her Life and Times*, vol. 1, *1819–1861* (London, 1972), pp. 199–200; S. Weintraub, *Victoria: Biography of a Queen* (London, 1987), pp. 143, 153, 165. The conspicuous and honourable exception to this is E. Longford, *Victoria R. I.* (London, 1966), pp. 711–12.

historians as G. B. Henderson, C. H. Stuart, Norman Gash and Lord Blake.[7]

The purpose of this essay is to reconsider this most powerful, popular and pervasive myth of the Victorian monarchy's instant, deliberate and successful modernity. It begins by providing the familiar evidence for the view that Victoria and Albert immediately brought about a sudden break with the past, and thus instituted in all its fundamentals the essentially 'modern' monarchy. It then explores the many ways in which this was not actually so: the tenacity of the Hanoverian influences and temperament in the case of the Queen herself; the backward-looking concept of monarchical power and functions entertained and promoted by Albert; the highly traditional mode of family life and matrimonial arrangements which characterized the royal pair; and the degree to which these pre-modern features have survived, more tenaciously than is usually recognized, even down to the monarchy of our own times. It then considers the ways in which, nevertheless, the late nineteenth-century monarchy did indeed change into something recognizably more modern, one aspect of which was the invention of the myth – to which so many historians and biographers still adhere – that it had, in fact, been like that from the very beginning of the Queen's reign.

As such, this essay's particular aim is to explode the widespread myth of the Victorian monarchy's premature modernity.[8] But more generally, it seeks to show how we might begin to understand that institution historically, as well as biographically, in its own time, rather than anachronistically. The difficulty with the study of the British royal family since 1837 is that there has been too much chronicle and too little history, a surfeit of myth-making and a dearth of scholarly scepticism. The following pages try to correct

---

[7] G. B. Henderson, 'The Influence of the Crown, 1854–1856', in his *Crimean War Diplomacy and Other Essays* (Glasgow, 1947), esp. pp. 96–7; C. H. Stuart, 'The Prince Consort and Ministerial Politics, 1856–9', in H. Trevor-Roper, ed., *Essays in British History presented to Sir Keith Feiling* (London, 1964), pp. 268–9; N. Gash, *Reaction and Reconstruction in English Politics, 1832–1852* (Oxford, 1965), p. 27; R. Blake, 'The Prince Consort and Queen Victoria's Prime Ministers', in J. A. S. Phillips, ed., *Prince Albert and the Victorian Age* (Cambridge, 1981), pp. 30–1, 36, 42.

[8] For the royal family's own continued belief that Queen Victoria and Prince Albert modernized the British monarchy, especially in its constitutional and familial aspects, see the remarks of the King of the Belgians and the Duke of Gloucester in Phillips, *Prince Albert*, pp. viii, 17–18, 21, 24–5, 28.

that imbalance by taking the monarchy seriously, by treating it as an historical problem and as an historical phenomenon. And as such, they are also offered as an appropriate tribute to the historian who has done incomparably the most in his generation to explore the sinews and substance of elite existence in the British past.

I

It has often been argued – by contemporaries then and by historians since – that from the very moment that she acceded to the throne, Queen Victoria was, as *The Times* described her at her death, 'a ruler of a new type'.[9] Her youth, her gender and her purity stood in marked contrast to her three predecessors, George III, George IV and William IV, who were respectively, but not respectfully, described as 'an imbecile, a profligate and a buffoon'; and with the advent of this new queen from a new generation, there was a widespread hope for something different and something better.[10] Indeed, Victoria and Albert consciously sought to satisfy these expectations, and were determined to introduce a new style of monarchy, based on decency, dutifulness and decorum, in contrast to the debts, divorces and debauchery of their predecessors. In this sense, so the argument runs, the years 1837 to 1840 mark the great divide between the old and the new monarchy, and bring us at once into a royal world which has more in common with that of the fifth and sixth Georges than with the era of the first four.

Beyond question, there is much evidence for this view. Dynastically, their break with the past was the greatest since the Hanoverian succession in 1714. Victoria's father may have been the Duke of Kent and son of George III, but her mother was Princess Victoria, from the minor German house of Coburg, after whom the Queen herself was named. When challenged on the subject of her parents, Victoria always claimed that she inherited 'more from my dear mother' than from her father.[11] Moreover, her mother's brother, Prince Leopold of Coburg, had been married to Princess Charlotte, daughter of the Prince Regent and heir to the British throne, who had died in 1817. In 1831, Prince Leopold was elected King of

9 *The Times*, 23 January 1901.
10 Longford, *Victoria*, p. 77; Fulford, *Hanover to Windsor*, p. 42; R. Ormond, *The Face of Monarchy: British Royalty Portrayed* (Oxford, 1977), p. 35.
11 Longford, *Victoria*, p. 22.

Belgium, and together with his adviser Baron Stockmar, he remained the most influential family figure in Queen Victoria's life until his death in 1864. Even more important, Prince Albert came from the same stock, being the nephew of both Princess Victoria and King Leopold. So Victoria herself was at least half Coburg, while her descendants were much more so.

Not surprisingly, the surviving members of the Hanoverian, or 'old', royal family, much resented this dynastic takeover by the Coburgs. George IV disliked Prince Leopold and the Duchess of Kent intensely, and it was only the Prince's generosity which enabled the widowed Duchess to bring up the future Queen Victoria in England at all. Likewise, William IV deeply disapproved of the dynastic machinations of the Coburgs, and in the 1830s did his best to find an alternative marriage partner for the young Victoria from the House of Orange.[12] And after Victoria's marriage, the Dukes of Cambridge, Cumberland and Sussex, who were the surviving sons of George III, despised Albert as a parvenu and impoverished adventurer, constantly sought to deny him his rightful precedence immediately after his wife, snubbed him on every possible social occasion, and tried to prevent him from being sole regent in the event of Victoria's incapacity or death. It was even rumoured that the King of Hanover was behind some of the early assassination attempts on the Queen and the Prince.[13]

This hostility was heartily reciprocated by the new royal pair. The Queen despised her remaining Hanoverian relatives as her 'wicked uncles', and many of her later actions derived from her impassioned desire to distance herself from them as completely as possible. Both Victoria and Albert were 'disgusted' by Brighton Pavilion, 'a strange, Chinese-looking thing, haunted by ghosts best forgotten', and were happy to dispose of it to the local corporation.[14] And while members of the 'old' royal family had been buried in St George's Chapel, Windsor, Victoria constructed a new mausoleum at Frogmore to house her own relatives. But it was in the names they gave their children that they rejected the past most emphatically. Traditional Hanoverian appellations like George and Frederick, Caroline and Charlotte, virtually disappeared,

[12] Weintraub, *Victoria*, p. 88.
[13] Woodham-Smith, *Victoria*, pp. 213, 233, 239; Longford, *Victoria*, pp. 170, 180–1; R. Fulford, *The Prince Consort* (London, 1949), pp. 63, 66.
[14] Rhodes James, *Prince Consort*, p. 139; A. Hardy, *Queen Victoria was Amused* (London, 1976), p. 65.

while the Queen insisted that all their own descendants should bear the name Albert or Victoria until the end of time.[15] Likewise, when she bestowed dukedoms on her sons, she refused to revive such old and discredited titles as York or Cumberland or Sussex, but preferred new names like Connaught, Albany and Edinburgh instead.

This new beginning seems to have been equally manifest in the realm of political behaviour, where the constitutional role of the monarchy was apparently revolutionized. The previous Hanoverian monarchs and their heirs had been violent and influential partisans in the political battle, ardently supporting some administrations but implacably hostile to others. Initially, Queen Victoria herself inclined to the same stance, with her fervent support of Melbourne. But the combined Coburg pressure soon began to make for a very different royal posture, of a monarchy no longer involved in the party-political battle, but floating serenely above it. 'Your part', King Leopold explained to Victoria, very soon after her accession, 'must be . . . to remain as long as possible agreeable to all parties.'[16] Baron Stockmar insisted that the crown must work with the ministry of the day, regardless of its political affiliations, until such time as it was replaced by a government formed by another party, to whom the same support must then be extended. But above all, it was Albert who wooed the Queen away from her early infatuation with Melbourne, towards a more measured and moderate mode, 'calm and free from party spirit'. As Albert was able to write to Stockmar in 1852, with pardonable pride, 'constitutional monarchy marches unassailably on its beneficent course'.[17]

As well as pioneering fundamentally new and different rules of royal political behaviour, Victoria and Albert also profoundly adjusted the whole relationship between the crown and the nation. George III may, in his demented dotage, have been called 'the father of his people', and George IV may have visited Scotland and Ireland; but no Hanoverian brought the monarchy close to the lives of ordinary subjects, nor sought to align the institution so emphatically with the major developments of the day. Under Albert's direction, this changed dramatically. The monarch and her consort

[15] Fulford, *Hanover to Windsor*, p. 60.
[16] King Leopold to Queen Victoria, 15 June 1837, in *Letters*, 1st series, vol. 1, p. 92.
[17] Prince Albert to Baron Stockmar, 6 January 1846 and 15 October 1852, both published in K. Jagow, ed., *Letters of the Prince Consort, 1831–1861*, trans. E. Dugdale (London, 1938), pp. 99, 185.

went out among the people, to centres of industry and population like Leeds, Liverpool, Manchester and Birmingham.[18] They identified themselves very closely with the new, burgeoning bourgeoisie, and Albert was untiring in his support of improved housing for the working classes. And as the inspirer of the Great Exhibition, the chairman and president of innumerable societies and organizations, as the friend and patron of artists, scientists and craftsmen, the Prince kept his finger on the pulse of national life to an extent that had never been known before in a sovereign or consort.[19]

At the same time, the Victorian monarchy was made both more economical and more efficient than its immediate predecessors. The debts and financial embarrassment of the later Hanoverians gradually but inexorably disappeared, as Albert greatly improved the crown's financial position, husbanded the revenues of the duchy of Cornwall, and completely reorganized the administration and the staffing of the royal palaces.[20] Above all, the Prince brought to the conduct of official royal business a new sense of order and endeavour. He rose with the dawn and was an indefatigable worker; he bombarded successive governments with thousands of memoranda on every conceivable subject of public importance; he wrote his own speeches and maintained a massive private and official correspondence; he assimilated endless state papers, read newspapers avidly and devoured statistics voraciously; and all incoming and outgoing letters were scrupulously annotated and filed. He was, as the Queen admitted (and sometimes resented), a 'terrible man of business', 'torn to pieces' with work of every kind, something which had never been said in the days of George IV or William IV.[21]

To this was added a 'moral court and a happy domestic home', as Victoria and Albert were determined that the debauchery which had so undermined the standing of the monarchy in previous reigns should be brought to an end.[22] They were both utterly faithful to

---

18 Bennett, *King Without a Crown*, p. 335.
19 Rhodes James, *Prince Consort*, pp. 191, 201; Eyck, *Prince Consort*, p. 163.
20 Longford, *Victoria*, pp. 208–10; Woodham-Smith, *Victoria*, pp. 262–5.
21 Woodham-Smith, *Victoria*, p. 391; Rhodes James, *Prince Consort*, p. 212;
    A. Briggs, *The Age of Improvement, 1783–1867* (London, 1959), pp. 456, 458;
    P. Colson, *Their Ruling Passions* (London, 1949), p. 33.
22 Queen Victoria to the Princess Royal, 27 February 1858, in R. Fulford, ed.,
    *'Dearest Child': Private Correspondence of Queen Victoria and the Crown
    Princess of Prussia, 1858–1861* (London, 1964), p. 63.

each other, and they were as devoted at Albert's death as they had been at their wedding. Beyond doubt, their marriage was one of the great romances of history, movingly captured in Victoria's widowed recollection 'when in those blessed arms clasped and held tight in the sacred hours at night, when the world seemed only to be ourselves'.[23] And as the devoted parents of nine children, they seemed to embody a new ideal of a happy and decorous family. At Osborne and Balmoral, they created a private, intimate and cosy life, where the children caught butterflies, where Victoria sketched, and where Albert played hide and seek. The shift from Brighton to Osborne – 'a place of one's own, quiet and retired' – speaks volumes for the new domesticity which they had so success-fully introduced.[24]

Nor was this probity confined to the private sphere, for Victoria and Albert expected the same good character from those at court and in public life. In the case of the Flora Hastings affair, the Queen thought the worst of her lady-in-waiting because she expected the best. One of the reasons why Palmerston was so unacceptable was because he was 'a man of expediency, of easy temper, of no very high standard of honour, and not a grain of moral feeling'.[25] And on the formation of the Tory ministry in 1852, Prince Albert witheringly described Lord Derby's nominations for household appointments as 'the dandies and roués of London and the turf'. 'Rakishness', which Lord Melbourne thought 'refreshing', was now dismissed as 'melancholy' and 'bad'. In despair at this new prim-ness, the Prime Minister sighed that 'this damned morality will ruin everything'. But others took a different view. After watching Sarah Bernhardt give one of her more passionate performances as Cleo-patra, one Victorian lady remarked, with evident relief, 'How different, how very different, from the home life of our own dear queen.'[26]

---

[23] Queen Victoria to the Princess Royal, 18 December 1861, in R. Fulford, ed., *'Dearest Mama': Private Correspondence of Queen Victoria and the Crown Princess of Prussia, 1861–1864* (London, 1968), p. 23.

[24] Weintraub, *Victoria*, p. 182; Woodham-Smith, *Victoria*, p. 274.

[25] Prince Albert to Lord John Russell, 2 April 1850, in B. Connell, ed., *Regina versus Palmerston: The Correspondence between Queen Victoria and her Foreign and Prime Minister, 1837–1865* (London, 1962), p. 115.

[26] Bennett, *King Without a Crown*, p. 228; Eyck, *Prince Consort*, pp. 191–2; Briggs, *Age of Improvement*, p. 455; Rhodes James, *Prince Consort*, p. 110; Longford, *Victoria*, p. 715.

II

In all these ways, it seems clear that Victoria and Albert deliberately and successfully rejected the modes and methods, the morals
and *mentalité* of their immediate royal predecessors. There was a
new generation with a new style; there was a new dynasty with a
new name; there was a new attitude to politics and politicians; there
was a new concern about the state of the nation; and there was a
new stress on family and fidelity. All this was brilliantly captured in
the pictures of the royal family by Landseer and Winterhalter,
which conveyed so vividly the intimate, private and responsible
regime which the new royal couple had established.[27] But like most
royal portraiture, these paintings were carefully contrived and
stage-managed, and concealed as much as they gave away.[28] For all
the novelty and modernity of the Queen and the Prince Consort,
for all their wish to break with the wicked uncles and their terrible
forbears, the family background kept reasserting itself in the lives
and actions of the Queen and her children. Time and again,
Hanoverian nature triumphed over Victorian intention.

Ironically enough, the very notion of rebelling against the past
was itself a quintessentially Hanoverian characteristic. There was
nothing unusual about rejecting one's immediate forbears in the
British royal family. From the reign of George I to that of George
III, the heir to the throne had turned against the King, and the
loathing had in each case been heartly reciprocated.[29] In every
generation, the homes of successive Princes of Wales, at Leicester
House and Carlton House, had become the focus for political
opposition and dissident society. Indeed George III had so hated
his grandfather, George II, that on his accession in 1760, he had
flatly refused to live in any of his predecessor's houses. Instead of
residing at Hampton Court, Kensington Palace and St James's
Palace, each of which was haunted by the ghosts of his grandfather,
he preferred to live at Kew, at Windsor and at Buckingham

---

[27] W. Gaunt, *Court Painting in England from Tudor to Victorian Times* (London,
1980), pp. 211–14; Ormond, *Face of Monarchy*, pp. 34–6; R. Ormond *et al.*, *Sir
Edwin Landseer* (London, 1981), pp. 14–15, 143–65; C. Lennie, *Landseer: The
Victorian Paragon* (London, 1976), pp. 97–106, 115–23, 140–2, 182–3.

[28] S. Schama, 'The Domestication of Majesty: Royal Family Portraiture, 1550–
1850', *Journal of Interdisciplinary History*, 17 (1986), pp. 157–8.

[29] R. Sedgwick, ed., *Letters from George III to Lord Bute, 1756–1766* (London,
1939), introduction, pp. xi–xix.

Palace.[30] So, in reviling her predecessors, and in preferring Balmoral to Brighton, Victoria was merely recapitulating an eighteenth-century royal theme in a nineteenth-century setting. It was a well-attested Hanoverian tradition to want to be new.

Moreover, Victoria herself was quintessentially Hanoverian – rather than Coburg – in physique and personality. At her birth, she was described as being the very image of her grandfather, King George III. Like all Hanoverians, she was short of stature: in her case, less than five feet tall. Like them, she grew fat as she grew older, and in later life weighed well over eleven stone.[31] Like them, again, she was possessed of very blue and very protuberant eyes, of a hawk-like nose, of a receding chin and of heavy jowls. As with all the first four Georges, she possessed what Greville called 'great animal spirits' – abundant stamina and amazing zest for life. From an early age she adored riding, dancing, eating and parties, and could make do with very little sleep. She loved the fresh air, and constantly discomfited her servants and courtiers by insisting that the windows at Balmoral be kept open, or no fires be lit at Osborne, in the chilliest of weather. 'I always feel so brisk', was her explanation.[32] And, like all Hanoverians, she was highly-sexed: one of her most heart-rending letters is her lament, after Albert's death, that it was not the day, but 'above all the night', which was now 'too sad and weary'.[33]

Indeed, her temperament was as Hanoverian as her body. Like George II and George III, she was extremely long-lived, with a tenacious hold on life. 'I do not cling to life, you do', was one of Albert's last and truest remarks. As the Queen admitted, he 'died from want of what they call pluck'. But no one could have accused her of being deficient in that. 'My poor old birthday, my 74th', she noted in 1893. 'I wish now it was instead 64th.' Like the Hanoverians again, she was extremely obstinate and bad-tempered: even with Albert, she could fly into paroxysms of apparently uncontrolled and uncontrollable rage, at little or no provocation.[34] To

[30] J. H. Plumb, *New Light on the Tyrant George III* (Washington, D.C., 1978), p. 6.
[31] Fulford, *Hanover to Windsor*, p. 40; Woodham-Smith, *Victoria*, p. 93; Weintraub, *Victoria*, pp. 4, 127.
[32] Hardy, *Queen Victoria was Amused*, pp. 26, 134.
[33] Queen Victoria to the Princess Royal, 18 December 1861, in Fulford, *'Dearest Mama'*, p. 23.
[34] Longford, *Victoria*, pp. 391, 654; Weintraub, *Victoria*, p. 56; Queen Victoria to the Princess Royal, 27 December 1861, in Fulford, *'Dearest Mama'*, p. 30.

Albert, to Stockmar, to Sir James Clark and to Lord Clarendon, this betokened a temperament so unstable that there were fears that the assumed insanity of her grandfather might reappear in her. Throughout her life, she had a horror of madness; when she collapsed hysterically at the news of her mother's death, the rumours of her insanity were widespread; and when she shut herself away for years at Albert's demise, there were constant whispers that 'hereditary eccentricities' were again working themselves out.[35]

In the same way, the Queen's personal and political preferences were very like those of her grandfather. Like him, her father died when she was young, and her infatuation with Lord Melbourne during her early years on the throne closely resembles George III's obsession with Lord Bute: in each case the search for the father they never knew.[36] Like George III (and his two immediate predecessors) she was much concerned about medals and uniforms, the award of honours and decorations, church patronage and military appointments, genealogy and precedence, order and routine.[37] Like George III again, she was essentially stubborn and intransigent in her political opinions, opposed to 'revolutionary and extreme views' anywhere, to the education and improvement of the lot of women, and to the reform of the army. Above all, her impassioned, unyielding opposition to Gladstone's policy of Irish Home Rule was remarkably reminiscent of George III's hostility to the rebellion of the American colonies one hundred years before. Like her grandfather, she was not prepared to countenance any steps – from within or without – to break up the empire or break down the established order.[38]

---

[35] Longford, *Victoria*, pp. 115, 143, 220, 326; J. R. Vincent, ed., *Disraeli, Derby and the Tory Party: The Political Journals of Lord Stanley, 1849–69* (Hassocks, 1978), p. 180, entry for 16 December 1861.

[36] Gash, *Reaction and Reconstruction*, p. 23.

[37] J. H. Plumb, *The First Four Georges* (London, 1966), p. 69; J. B. Owen, 'George II Reconsidered', in A. Whiteman, J. S. Bromley and P. G. M. Dickson, eds., *Statesmen, Scholars and Merchants: Essays in Eighteenth-Century History Presented to Dame Lucy Sutherland* (Oxford, 1973), pp. 120–2; R. Pares, *King George III and the Politicians* (Oxford, 1967), p. 64; Fulford, *Hanover to Windsor*, p. 71; Le May, *Victorian Constitution*, pp. 73–86; D. W. R. Bahlman, 'Politics and Church Patronage in the Victorian Age', *Victorian Studies*, 22 (1979), pp. 253–96.

[38] Queen Victoria to Cardwell, 24 January 1871, and to Gladstone, 31 December 1881, in *Letters*, 2nd series, vol. 2, pp. 114–15, vol. 3, pp. 249–50; Queen

So, despite her Coburg mother, the Hanoverian blood pulsed powerful and passionate through the Queen's veins. And, despite his Coburg father, the same blood pulsed with equal vigour through the veins of her eldest son, the Prince of Wales. Predictably, it was the aim of the educational system devised for him by Albert and Stockmar that there should be no repetition of the mistakes that George III had made in the schooling of his sons, and also that any lingering traces of the Georges' temperament should be eradicated.[39] But even in the next generation, Hanover again triumphed over Coburg. From an early age, the hereditary characteristics were once more apparent: Bertie possessed a 'painfully small head ... immense features, and a total want of chin'; he was fat, fond of food, wine and women; he was so bad-tempered that there were fears for his sanity; and he was slow to learn, 'very dull', and totally without intellectual curiosity.[40] It was not just that the Prince of Wales was no Albert: it was also, as the Queen had the humility and perception to recognize, that 'Bertie is my caricature.' And Stockmar agreed: 'he is an exaggerated copy of his mother'. She was the image of George III, and the Prince of Wales was a parody of her.[41]

As Bertie grew up, his disappointed parents were further appalled by the prospect that his life was indeed becoming that of the Queen's 'wicked uncles' reincarnated. Even as an adolescent, he began to run up debts, to associate with the fast set, and to have affairs. In his greed, his gluttony and his gambling, he seemed more akin to a Regency rake than to a Victorian worthy. Albert, during the last years of his life, and the Queen ever after, were obsessed with the fear that 'the country could never bear to have George IV as Prince of Wales again'. Yet this seemed to be precisely the horror in prospect. Bertie, with his pronounced Hanoverian blood, would undo all the work they had done to restore and re-establish the monarchy. Accordingly, Albert's over-reaction to Bertie's affair with Nellie Clifden was prompted by the fear that it would

Victoria to Goschen, 17 and 24 January 1886, and to Gladstone, 6 May 1886, in *Letters*, 3rd series, vol. 1, pp. 10, 16–17, 118–19.

[39] P. Magnus, *King Edward VII* (Harmondsworth, 1967), p. 19; P. Crabites, *Victoria's Guardian Angel: A Study of Baron Stockmar* (London, 1937), pp. 142–5.

[40] Magnus, *Edward VII*, pp. 25, 32; Queen Victoria to the Princess Royal, 27 November 1858 and 4 December 1858, in Fulford, *'Dearest Child'*, pp. 147, 149.

[41] Magnus, *Edward VII*, p. 45; Rhodes James, *Prince Consort*, p. 243; Queen Victoria to the Princess Royal, 27 April 1859, in Fulford, *'Dearest Child'*, p. 187.

lead to public scandal reminiscent of an earlier generation.[42] And in Victoria's eyes, it was her husband's subsequent visit to the Prince of Wales at Cambridge, at the very time when his own health was already seriously troubled, which led directly to his own death. In the appropriately rotund shape of Bertie, the Hanoverian 'wicked uncles' had taken their terrible revenge.

III

From this eighteenth-century dynastic perspective, it is arguable that the Victorian monarchy looked backwards at least as much as it moved forwards: like most royal pairs, Victoria and Albert were prisoners of their ancestry more than they wished, and more than they knew. But this argument may be carried one stage further. For although it is frequently claimed that Albert was the creator of modern constitutional monarchy, that Victoria learned the lesson her husband taught her, and that she then passed it on to her successors, the evidence suggests that this interpretation of their aims and actions is little more than anachronistic invention.[43] Beyond question, both Albert and Victoria frequently spoke of 'constitutional monarchy', and of placing the crown above party. In retrospect, it is easy to see this as anticipating the formulation of royal power subsequently adumbrated by Walter Bagehot. But if these remarks are considered in the context of their own time, then a very different picture emerges. For the ambitions which Albert cherished for the monarchy looked back to the eighteenth century rather than forward to the twentieth.

Historically speaking, a crown above parties and a 'constitutional' monarchy do not necessarily mean a sovereign with no governing power. Of course, this is the formulation which has been accepted in the aftermath of Bagehot, yet this was not at all how it appeared in the time of Victoria and Albert. Many previous rulers had urged that the crown should be above party, but they had done so with a view to *increasing* the sovereign's governing power, not reducing it. William III hated parties, aspired to end them, and regarded them at best as a regrettable aspect of political life. Queen Anne saw party as a threat to royal power and to national unity,

[42] Rhodes James, *Prince Consort*, p. 268; Magnus, *Edward VII*, p. 168; Longford, *Victoria*, p. 347.
[43] See the references cited earlier in notes 5, 6 and 7.

believed that ministers ought to be her servants, and constantly strove to create mixed administrations which would give her the maximum freedom of manoeuvre.[44] George III set out 'to put an end to those unhappy distinctions of party', 'to recover monarchy from the inveterate usurpation of oligarchy', and to institute a revived and reinvigorated version of personal sovereignty and personal rule. And in 1834 and 1836, William IV sought to 'bring about a union of parties' and to promote broad-bottomed coalition governments.[45]

As exemplified by these sovereigns, the conventional royal wisdom on constitutional monarchy in 1837 and 1840 was thus as follows. Party was essentially anathema: it gave too much scope for self-seeking politicians to place their individual interests before the good of the nation as a whole; it made it impossible to form an administration of all the best men, who would be loyal and obedient to the sovereign, and who would put the country first; and it meant that the power of the monarch to be centrally, creatively and actively involved in the governing process was fatally circumscribed as a result. For pre-Bagehot kings and queens, this is what a constitutional monarchy above party actually meant: a ruler who was emancipated from the politicians, rather than fettered by them; a crown that was influentially, not impotently, above the battle; a sovereign who governed as well as reigned. And it is clear that this is very much what it meant to Albert and to Victoria as well.

Nor should this come as any surprise, since this view corresponded very closely to the opinions held by those two men who gave them so much 'constitutional' advice: Stockmar and Leopold. Stockmar was a doctor by profession, had learned about the English constitution from theory and history rather than from practice and experience, and – as befitted the chief adviser to the Coburgs – believed that monarchs should be the chief repositories of political power. He despised the House of Commons as a talking shop which had usurped too much influence since the Reform Act. He regarded most British party politicians as discredited and discreditable. Even Prime Ministers came and went in rapid

---

44 E. L. Ellis, 'William III and the Politicians', in G. Holmes, ed., *Britain After the Glorious Revolution, 1689–1714* (London, 1969), pp. 117–2; E. Gregg, *Queen Anne* (London, 1980), pp. 134–8, 141–7, 403–5.

45 J. Brewer, *Party Ideology and Popular Politics at the Accession of George III* (Cambridge, 1976), pp. 116–17, 132–36; Gash, *Reaction and Reconstruction*, pp. 7, 14; Le May, *Victorian Constitution*, p. 33.

succession.[46] Accordingly, it was the monarchy, as the only fixed and disinterested part of government, which should reclaim supreme power, and reassert itself as the 'permanent premier who takes rank above the temporary head of the cabinet'. Here was a picture of an active and energetic sovereign, which would have meant much more to George III than to George V: the very antithesis of 'a mandarin figure, which has to nod its head, in assent or denial, as his minister pleases'.[47]

Gladstone believed that Stockmar's views were 'only an English top dressing on a German soil', but there is no doubt that the Prince 'heartily agreed' with them.[48] Words and phrases which appear one day in a Stockmar memorandum re-emerge shortly after in an Albert letter or a royal communication. Moreover, King Leopold of Belgium was parlaying very similar advice, based on his own experience as the 'constitutional' monarch of Belgium. As an 'upright, firm, active, intelligent king', he was 'given to believe that he must rule the roast [sic] everywhere'.[49] Especially during the earliest years of his reign, Leopold was as much chief executive as he was head of state. He rose early and worked extraordinarily hard; he personally appointed carefully mixed administrations; he himself presided over the council of ministers once a week; he regarded foreign affairs as his exclusive preserve; and he jealously safeguarded the royal prerogative. 'A Minister', he once remarked, 'only has authority in so far as he is Minister of the King.' For thirty-four years, as a self-styled 'constitutional' monarch, Leopold not only reigned: he governed.[50]

Likewise, in Britain itself, it is not mere coincidence that Albert's favourite public man – Sir Robert Peel – shared this essentially executive view of politics. In part, there was a real temperamental affinity between the Premier and the Prince: both worked obsessively hard, were high-minded, dutiful, earnest and insecure. But what really marked Peel out in Albert's eyes was that he seemed to

[46] Crabites, *Victoria's Guardian Angel*, pp. 214–15, 248–9.

[47] Eyck, *Prince Consort*, pp. 199–201; Longford, *Victoria*, pp. 299–300; Crabites, *Victoria's Guardian Angel*, pp. 184, 197, 213, 216, 220.

[48] Sir L. Woodward, *The Age of Reform, 1815–1870* (2nd edn., Oxford, 1962), p. 107; Prince Albert to Baron Stockmar, 24 January 1854, in Jagow, *Letters of the Prince Consort*, p. 204.

[49] Weintraub, *Victoria*, p. 116; Baron E. von Stockmar, *Memoirs of Baron Stockmar*, ed. F. Max Muller, 2 vols (London, 1872), vol. 1, p. 203.

[50] J. Richardson, *'My Dearest Uncle': A Life of Leopold, First King of the Belgians* (London, 1961), pp. 132–7, 172, 195, 220–1.

be putting the country and the national interest before personal advantage and party calculation. As such, Peel was the patriot minister to Albert's patriot king: 'a great statesman, a man who thinks but little of party and never of himself', in whose hands 'the interests of the crown were most secure'.[51] In their exaltation of the executive, their contempt for mere party politicians, and their concern with the 'national interest', Peel and Albert spoke the same language, not just metaphorically, but literally as well. Indeed, on Peel's death, Albert felt 'dreadfully' that 'he has lost a second father', and Stockmar composed an appreciation which was quite unprecedentedly effusive.[52]

It is in this context – of existing historical precedent, of Stockmar's theorizing, of Leopold's practice and of Peel's support – that Albert's notion of the Victorian monarchy must be set. And it must also be remembered that he himself was the son of a German ruling prince, whose control of his duchy was absolute: parties, democracy and representative institutions had no place in the political and constitutional world in which Albert grew up.[53] Nor did they have much in his more mature thinking. 'Composed as party is here of two extremes,' he once wrote, 'both must be wrong.' In contrast, 'our chief wish and aim is, by hearing all parties, to arrive at a just, dispassionate and correct opinion upon all the various political questions'. And this was made the more necessary because ministers were merely 'the favourites, for the time being, of the public'.[54] In short, Albert, like his predecessors, wished to make the monarchy independent of party and of politicians, not because he regarded parties and politicians as an essential part of national life, but because he regarded their existence as regrettable. His aim was not to diminish the power of

51 Bennett, *King Without a Crown*, p. 202; Briggs, *Age of Improvement*, p. 457; N. Gash, *Sir Robert Peel* (London, 1972), pp. 259–62, 290–4, 555–9, 670–1.
52 Stockmar, *Memoirs*, vol. 2, pp. 419–26. Compare these two remarks. Here is Peel: 'I cannot charge myself with having taken any course inconsistent with conservative principles, calculated to endanger the privileges of any branch of the legislature, or any institutions of the country.' And here is the Prince: 'I must rest mainly upon a good conscience and the belief that during the fifteen years of my connection with this country, I have not given a human soul the means of imputing to me the want of sincerity or patriotism.' (Gash, *Peel*, p. 590; Rhodes James, *Prince Consort*, p. 225).
53 Bennett, *King Without a Crown*, p. 180
54 Rhodes James, *Prince Consort*, p. 105; Eyck, *Prince Consort*, p. 76; Prince Albert to Lord Palmerston, 9 August 1846, in Jagow, *Letters of the Prince Consort*, p. 106.

the crown, but to enhance it. As a man who believed that William III was 'the greatest monarch the country has to boast of', he was bound to pitch the sovereign's claims high.[55]

Beyond doubt, Albert entertained no personal ambitions, sought 'no power by himself or for himself', but sincerely wished to sink his own identity 'entirely' into that of the Queen. But as 'the constitutional genius of the Queen', as her 'sole confidential adviser in politics', her 'private secretary' and her 'permanent minister', he was determined that the monarchy should be part of the efficient, rather than the decorative, side of the constitution. He believed the sovereign was 'necessarily a politician', with the duty to 'watch and control' ministers, to be centrally and creatively involved in the governing process.[56] He asserted that the crown had the right to share in the making of all government decisions, could recommend and veto all cabinet appointments, and could even dismiss ministers if the occasion arose. He regarded foreign affairs as the crown's special preserve, and conducted private correspondence with other crowned heads, independent of the Foreign Office, in which he did not hestitize to criticize his own government. Trained by Stockmar and Leopold, it was Albert's wish, not to create a new and impotent monarchy, but to revive a more energetic crown on an older model. He was looking backwards to Blackstone rather than forwards to Bagehot.[57]

This is clearly shown by the way in which Victoria and Albert actually behaved. The Prince Consort was as ardent in his support of Peel as the Queen had hitherto been in favour of the Whigs, visiting Drayton and appearing in the gallery of the Commons at a crucial juncture in the debate on the Corn Laws. He made plain his disapproval of Russell's lethargic mode of doing business, bombarded him with numerous memoranda and press-cuttings on economic questions (which he did not believe the Prime Minister understood), and insisted on seeing Cabinet papers before decisions were reached, so that he might be an active participant in the

[55] Rhodes James, *Prince Consort*, p. 167; Colson, *Their Ruling Passions*, p. 28.
[56] Prince Albert to the Duke of Wellington, 6 April 1850, in Jagow, *Letters of the Prince Consort*, pp. 156–8; Rhodes James, *Prince Consort*, p. 218; Eyck, *Prince Consort*, p. 138.
[57] Fulford, *Prince Consort*, pp. 128–33; Connell, *Regina versus Palmerston*, p. 61; Prince Albert to King Frederick William IV of Prussia, 2 April 1847, in Jagow, *Letters of the Prince Consort*, p. 109.

discussions.[58] His personal disapproval of Palmerston was reinforced by what he regarded as the Foreign Secretary's wayward European policy, and by his obstinate refusal to submit diplomatic despatches to Buckingham Palace for clearance before they were sent off. In December 1851, the Queen and the Prince Consort effectively forced Palmerston out of office, and in 1853, when Lord Aberdeen became Prime Minister almost by court diktat, the royal pair celebrated 'the realisation of our own ... most ardent wishes' by virtually choosing his Cabinet for him.[59]

Nor were these authoritarian views foisted by the Prince Consort on an unwilling wife, for Victoria also believed that the monarchy's powers were 'her appenange by gift of God', and that they must be preserved and handed on 'unimpaired' to her successors.[60] Almost immediately after his death, during the crisis over Schleswig-Holstein, she played a vigorous and decisive part in the Cabinet's policy-making, over-riding the views of her Prime Minister and Foreign Secretary.[61] For the remainder of her reign, any politician who put the House of Commons and the party first, rather than the country, was bound to incur her wrath. Part of the attraction of Disraeli was that he constantly reassured her that 'the course of the ministry depends upon the will of the Queen'. As late as the 1880s, she was still protesting that 'she cannot, and will not be the queen of a democratic monarchy', and Gladstone himself 'would never be surprised to see her turn the government out, after the manner of her uncles'. She never disavowed her rights to make and unmake not only individual ministers, but also entire administrations, and even in 1893, she was prepared to consider a peremptory dissolution of Parliament to thwart Home Rule.[62]

It was this shared and exalted conception of the power and purposes of the monarchy which also explains the arduous edu-

---

58 Fulford, *Prince Consort*, pp. 114–16; Prince Albert to Baron Stockmar, 17 December 1843, in Jagow, *Letters of the Prince Consort*, p. 87.

59 Fulford, *Prince Consort*, pp. 151–2; Bennett, *King Without a Crown*, p. 244.

60 Longford, *Victoria*, p. 711; Lord Esher, *Queen Victoria's Journals: Some Unpublished Extracts* (London, 1909), pp. 15–16.

61 W. E. Mosse, 'Queen Victoria and Her Ministers in the Schleswig-Holstein Crisis, 1863–1864', *English Historical Review*, 78 (1983), pp. 263, 281–3; K. A. P. Sandiford, 'The British Cabinet and the Schleswig-Holstein Crisis, 1863–1864', *History*, 57 (1973), pp. 360, 380–3.

62 Le May, *Victorian Constitution*, p. 34; Longford, *Victoria*, p. 647; Weintraub, *Victoria*, p. 348; Queen Victoria to W. E. Forster, 25 December 1880, and to Earl Granville, 22 October 1883, in *Letters*, 2nd series, vol. 3, pp. 165–6, 447.

cational scheme which the Queen and the Prince – aided and abetted by Stockmar – devised for the Prince of Wales. The training was uniquely arduous because his future position was held to be uniquely demanding and important. By definition, since Bertie might be called upon 'at any moment to take over the reins of government in an empire where the sun never sets', his education was 'a public matter, not unconnected with the present and prospective welfare of the nation and the state'.[63] As the future 'executive governor of the state', one of those 'enlightened princes' whose task would be to save Europe from 'the danger inherent in a democratic age', it was necessary to make him 'the most perfect man', of 'calm, profound, comprehensive understanding'. And it was with the same end in view that Albert was 'gradually amassing a treasure of political knowledge which grows daily more valuable to us, and which we hope one day to hand down to the Prince of Wales ... as the best endowment for his future kingly office'.[64]

Nowhere is the essentially backward-looking conception of monarchy entertained by Victoria and Albert – part absolute ruler, part philosopher sovereign, part patriot king – more fully laid bare. No wonder, too, that Albert himself toiled so unceasingly at his desk, and likened himself to the hawk who could never sleep because he was always on the watch.[65] In common with those other workaholic sovereigns Joseph II and Philip II from an earlier era, and Leopold I and Franz Josef from his own day, he wanted to be the flywheel, not the figurehead, of government. And there can be no doubt that he made his impact felt. Lord John Russell believed that Albert was truly 'an informal but potent member of all cabinets', while Lord Clarendon thought he knew more about the workings of government than most ministers. In seeking 'the exaltation of royalty', Albert was playing for very high stakes indeed: he wanted 'more power and influence in the conduct of affairs', not less.[66] Seen in this light, Disraeli's observation, that had the Prince lived, he

[63] Magnus, *Edward VII*, p. 51; Rhodes James, *Prince Consort*, pp. 232–5; Bennett, *King Without a Crown*, p. 327.

[64] Magnus, *Edward VII*, pp. 19–20; Rhodes James, *Prince Consort*, p. 235; Sir S. Lee, *King Edward VII*, 2 vols (London, 1925–7), vol. 1, p. 27; Prince Albert to King Frederick William IV of Prussia, 2 April 1847, in Jagow, *Letters of the Prince Consort*, p. 108.

[65] Rhodes James, *Prince Consort*, p. 266.

[66] Magnus, *Edward VII*, pp. 17, 34; Fulford, *Prince Consort*, p. 277; Rhodes James, *Prince Consort*, p. 228; Prince Albert to Baron Stockmar, 6 January 1846, in Jagow, *Letters of the Prince Consort*, p. 99.

would have given Britain 'the blessings of absolute government' while 'retaining all constitutional guarantees', seems far less 'dubious', 'facile', 'extravagant' and 'misleading' than is generally admitted.[67]

IV

If the constitutional conception of the monarchy entertained by Victoria and Albert was as exalted and as authoritarian as these remarks imply, this in turn must have influenced their personal relations within the royal family. For ambition and affection rarely co-habit easily, even in the best-regulated of households, and they did not do so in this case. Just as it is mistakenly anachronistic to depict Victoria and Albert as pioneering a modern constitutional monarchy, so it is misleading to see their royal menage as being the prototypical modern happy family.[68] For all the carefully cultivated image of Albert and Victoria as devoted parents, presiding over a household almost middle-class in its friendship and intimacy, living a cosy existence in the sequestered seclusion of Osborne and Balmoral, the reality was in many ways inevitably rather different. As Stanley Weintraub has recently and rightly remarked, 'the charms and delights of Queen Victoria's private life' had another and less attractive side to them, namely 'an insensitivity to their children that flies in the face of the *gemütlich* image that has come down to us'.[69]

In Albert's case, it is clear that, for all his love of games and of Christmas trees, he was in many ways a stern, unbending and dictatorial father. Lord Clarendon was not alone in thinking that the Prince's treatment of his children was definitely 'injudicious'. He wanted them all to be paragons, but in practice only Vicky, the eldest daughter, actually was. Yet even she was made to suffer: when once caught telling a lie, she was 'imprisoned with tied

---

[67] Longford, *Victoria*, p. 381; Eyck, *Prince Consort*, p. 253; Fulford, *Prince Consort*, pp. 237–9; Blake, 'The Prince Consort and Queen Victoria's Prime Ministers', p. 47. But consider also these words of Lord Stanley, in Vincent, *Disraeli, Derby and the Tory Party*, pp. 180–1: 'The Prince had undoubtedly a fixed determination to increase the personal power of the Crown: had he lived to add to his great industry and talent the weight which age and long experience would have given in dealing with statesmen of his own standing, he might have made himself almost as powerful as the Prime Minister of the day.' The entry is for 16 December 1861.

[68] Fulford, *Prince Consort*, pp. 95, 235.   [69] Weintraub, *Victoria*, p. 226.

hands'.[70] As for the rest, in one way or another all were a disappointment to him, and he made his displeasure abundantly, sarcastically and terrifyingly plain. They were regularly whipped, their nursery was freezing, and their diet was at best frugal. Apart from Vicky, all the children were frightened of him, and with good reason. Lord Lincolnshire later recalled that the Prince of Wales 'was afraid of his father, who seemed a proud, shy, standoffish man, not calculated to make friends easily with children'.[71] He was far from being the quintessential 'family man' of popular myth.

In the case of the Queen herself, this coldness and hostility was if anything even more marked. 'It is indeed a pity', Albert once scolded, 'that you find no consolation in the company of your children.'[72] Although she clearly enjoyed sex, she viewed pregnancy with 'totally insurmountable disgust', and regarded childbirth as the basest and most degrading feminine and human endeavour, 'more like a rabbit or a guinea pig'. And she was 'no admirer of babies generally', with their animal functions and their 'terrible froglike action'.[73] Even when her children grew up, she 'felt no especial pleasure or compensation' in their company, and found 'intimate intercourse' with them neither 'agreeable' nor 'easy'. Apart from Arthur, all of her sons were a disappointment to her, and her daughters squabbled incessantly among themselves. Most of them lived in dread and fear of her temper and her selfishness, and throughout her life she was able to manipulate their feelings with consummate and almost sadistic skill.[74] When, in turn, they began to produce their own offspring, she was even more disparaging and discouraging: 'our children have (alas!) such swarms of children'; 'it seems to me to go on like the rabbits in Windsor Park'.[75]

[70] Woodham-Smith, *Victoria*, p. 267; Crabites, *Victoria's Guardian Angel*, p. 162.
[71] Magnus, *Edward VII*, pp. 31, 37.   [72] Rhodes James, *Prince Consort*, p. 244.
[73] Queen Victoria to the Princess Royal, 24 March 1858, 14 April 1858, 21 April 1858, 15 June 1858, 4 May 1859, 1 August 1860, in Fulford, *'Dearest Child'*, pp. 77–8, 90, 94, 115, 191, 195; Queen Victoria to the Princess Royal, 22 February 1865, in R. Fulford, ed., *'Your Dear Letter': Private Correspondence of Queen Victoria and the Crown Princess of Prussia, 1865–1871* (London, 1971), p. 18; Queen Victoria to the Princess Royal, 27 October 1872, in R. Fulford, ed., *'Darling Child': Private Correspondence of Queen Victoria and the German Crown Princess, 1871–1878* (London, 1976), p. 159.
[74] Rhodes James, *Prince Consort*, p. 245; Weintraub, *Victoria*, pp. 273, 331–2, 363, 436, 541.
[75] Queen Victoria to the Princess Royal, 10 July 1868 and 1 November 1870, in Fulford, *'Your Dear Letter'*, pp. 210, 306.

This uncaring attitude emerged most forcibly in their heartless, cruel and insensitive treatment of the Prince of Wales. For reasons which need not be laboured, it was the Queen's deepest wish that he should 'resemble his angelic father in every respect, both in body and mind'.[76] But the relentless system of education which was devised for him was quite ineffectual, since it presupposed the existence of gifts which the Prince simply did not possess. Yet his parents persisted, and merely became irritated, then disappointed, and finally enraged when he did not match up to their unrealistically high demands. Albert thought him 'a thorough and cunning lazybones', and reprimanded him with irony and sarcasm, while the Queen described him as 'idle and weak', made her 'sorrow and bitter disappointment' abundantly plain, and regarded the prospect of his succeeding her as 'too awful a contemplation'.[77] After Albert's death, she 'never could look upon him without a shudder', and she deliberately refused to allow him access to any official papers, or to sanction any proposed scheme of employment for him. 'I often pray', she wrote in 1876, 'he may never succeed me, for I know not what would happen.'[78]

Accordingly, the underlying realities of the royal family's emotional life were still largely determined by the traditional forces by which such households had always been controlled: demographic constraints and dynastic considerations. Like its predecessors, the Victorian monarchy was in many ways a brass tacks affair, in which the elemental facts of birth and copulation, death and disease, were paramount. Victoria herself only acceded by the sheer accident that her parents won the game of reproductive roulette played by George III's descendants. For the first part of her reign, she was almost fully preoccupied in producing children: nine of them in seventeen years. Even at the age of forty, she had never seen a death bed.[79] But thereafter, disease and death emphatically took over. In 1861, both her mother and her husband died, and during the rest of her reign, the royal reaper never let up. Three

---

76 Rhodes James, *Prince Consort*, p. 240.
77 Magnus, *Edward VII*, pp. 43–5, 51; Queen Victoria to the Princess Royal, 31 March 1858, 26 May 1858, 1 December 1858, 9 April 1859, in Fulford, *'Dearest Child'*, pp. 81, 108–9, 144, 148, 174.
78 Queen Victoria to the Princess Royal, 15 January 1862 and 7 November 1876, in Fulford, *'Dearest Mama'*, p. 40; Fulford, *'Darling Child'*, p. 231.
79 Queen Victoria to the Princess Royal, 2 January 1861, in Fulford, *'Dearest Child'*, p. 296.

children, three sons-in-law and several grandchildren predeceased her, while her eldest daughter, Vicky, only outlived her by a few months. Towards the end of the Queen's life, there was scarcely a day on her calendar which was not the anniversary of a family death.

Within these powerful constraints of disease and demise, Victoria and Albert manipulated their children as determinedly and dynastically as they themselves had been manipulated in their own youth. For while their marriage may have become one of the great love matches of history, its origins were far less roseate. Well before Victoria and Albert had ever met, that resourceful trio of Coburg intriguers, the Duchess of Kent, Prince Leopold and Baron Stockmar, had resolved to promote this union.[80] Leopold had hoped to project the Coburgs on to a wider European stage by marrying Princess Charlotte, the heir to the British throne; but her early death in 1817 ruined these plans, and he was obliged to resort to other means. From 1835, there was a sustained and successful Coburg campaign to ensure – despite the opposition of William IV – that Albert married Victoria. The contrived meetings and the psychological pressure exerted by this dynastic trio ensured that the marriage came about. And with this background to their own union, it is hardly surprising that Albert and Victoria treated their own children in exactly the same way.

In the case of their eldest (and most gifted) child, Princess Vicky, the marriage was fixed up with almost indecent haste. One of the deepest ambitions cherished by Albert and Stockmar was that of a unified Germany, under Prussian leadership, tied to England by bonds of friendship and shared liberal constitutional ideals.[81] And the coping stone of this policy was to be Vicky's marriage to Prince Frederick, the nephew and eventual heir of the King of Prussia. They were introduced at the time of the Great Exhibition, when Vicky was only ten years old, and in 1855 Fritz was invited to Balmoral, where the engagement was rushed through – even though Vicky was not yet of age – for fear of competitors for his affections.[82] Although Fritz and Vicky soon became as devoted as Victoria and Albert, and although both the Queen and the Prince

[80] Bennett, *King Without a Crown*, p. 16; Fulford, *Prince Consort*, p. 42.

[81] For the background, see Eyck, *Prince Consort*, chapter 6.

[82] See Prince Albert to Baron Stockmar, 20 September 1855, and to Prince William of Prussia, 21 September 1855, in Jagow, *Letters of the Prince Consort*, pp. 236–7.

Consort felt genuine regret at the departure of their favourite daughter, the deliberate ruthlessness with which they promoted the union cannot be questioned. As Vicky herself later wrote to her father, 'a useful alliance was the real reason for this marriage'.[83]

With Bertie, their eldest son, the ambitions were less political, but an arranged marriage was nevertheless deemed to be crucial.[84] By the late 1850s, it was clear that the plan of education had failed, and that the only hope for Bertie was to find him a good woman, 'pretty, quiet, clever and sensible'. In growing desperation, because the matter was so urgent and the choice 'so circumscribed', his parents, aided by Vicky in Berlin, scanned the *Almanack de Gotha* and compiled a list of 'candidates'.[85] Elizabeth of Wied and Anna of Hesse were soon eliminated, but then they came across Princess Alexandra of Denmark. Photographs were inspected, Bertie was urged to take an interest, and a meeting was arranged. 'We dare not let her slip away', Albert cautioned. Initially, Bertie did not respond as hoped, and it was feared that if news of the Nellie Clifden affair leaked out, his chances would be further harmed. But eventually Bertie realized where his duty lay, duly proposed, and the couple had little alternative but to become engaged. To his mother's and elder sister's great relief, 'the jewel' was thus 'secured'.[86] Once again, it was an arranged marriage, well within the dictates of dynastic tradition.

Thereafter, the marriages of the Queen's children followed a similar pattern, the essential features of which may be easily summarized. When Victoria decided the time was ripe, she drew up a shortlist of names, usually in consultation with Vicky. Investigations were then made, and some were eliminated on the grounds of their appearance, their family or their nationality. When the final list was settled, the candidates were invited to Windsor or Osborne or Balmoral, and the son or daughter in question was allowed to decide. As the Queen herself admitted: 'My course is simply to say, there are these few unmarried Protestant princesses whom I hear generally well spoken of. Choose for yourself

[83] Longford, *Victoria*, p. 329; Eyck, *Prince Consort*, p. 238.
[84] For a full account, see Magnus, *Edward VII*, pp. 65–73.
[85] Queen Victoria to the Princess Royal, 31 March 1858, 6 February 1861, 25 February 1861, Princess Royal to Queen Victoria, 20 April 1861, in Fulford, *'Dearest Child'*, pp. 81, 312, 314, 323.
[86] Queen Victoria to the Princess Royal, 12 November 1862, in Fulford, *'Dearest Mama'*, p. 130.

amongst them.'[87] Of course, this did not always work. Sometimes the Queen pushed only one candidate particularly hard (as with Prince Leopold). Sometimes there was a refusal to accept any of the shortlist (as with Prince Alfred). And sometimes she was too late (as with Prince Arthur).[88] But in most cases, it was the Queen who effectively determined her children's marriage partners. The media may have said that they married for love; but the realities were usually far less romantic.

V

In all these ways, the early Victorian monarchy, like the early Victorian age, had more in common with what had gone before than with what was to come after. Despite the wish of Victoria and Albert to break with the Hanoverian past, the forces of heredity reasserted themselves in a remarkably abiding way. Although many commentators have subsequently claimed that Albert was the pioneer of a modern constitutional monarchy, the evidence is clear that he was actually seeking to revive a much older notion of personal royal rule. And while there were undoubtedly some aspects of the Queen's and the Prince's existence which seemed cosy, comfortable and *gemütlich*, the dynamics of their family life were virtually indistinguishable – in their fundamentals – from other royal houses abroad and earlier royal dynasties at home. Accordingly, to depict the years of Victoria and Albert as the prototypical modern monarchy – suddenly and successfully breaking with the past, detached in its politics, and middle-class in its relationships – misleads more than it illuminates.

Moreover, in many ways, this essentially pre-modern monarchy endured, not only into the late Victorian era, but even beyond it. In terms of personal appearance and family relations, the Hanoverian inheritance lingered – and lingers – on. That was obviously so in the case of Edward VII, with his corpulence, his garrulousness and his

---

[87] Queen Victoria to the Princess Royal, 25 October 1872, in Fulford, *'Darling Child'*, p. 65.

[88] Queen Victoria to the Princess Royal, 14 November 1866 and 7 August 1867, in Fulford, *'Your Dear Letter'*, pp. 105–6, 147; Queen Victoria to the Princess Royal, 27 November 1872, 12 July 1873, 12 March 1878, in Fulford, *'Darling Child'*, pp. 70, 101, 285–6; Queen Victoria to the Princess Royal, 29 November 1881, in R. Fulford, ed., *'Beloved Mama': Private Correspondence of Queen Victoria and the German Crown Princess, 1878–1885* (London, 1981), p. 112.

rages. George V, Edward VIII and George VI were all small men, with receding chins, bright blue eyes and bad tempers. Even among the present members of the royal family, these characteristics remain pronounced, among both the women and the men. Likewise, the family life created by George V and Queen Mary was no more idyllic than that of Victoria and Albert.[89] Once again, they made terrible, intimidating and distancing parents, and once again, the children suffered. The Prince of Wales and his father never saw eye to eye. The Duke of York stammered, smoked and suffered from a duodenal ulcer. The Duke of Kent was reputedly a bisexual drug addict. And the Duke of Gloucester was peppery and bad-tempered in a quintessentially Hanoverian way, and was known to his friends as 'Potty'.[90]

In other ways, too, pre-Coburg characteristics were amply manifest. From his earliest days, Edward VII was obsessed with 'clothes and again clothes', in a manner reminiscent of George IV, was much concerned about the granting of honours, and loved to return from foreign visits with new uniforms and orders. George V regularly rebuked Cabinet Ministers if he saw them wearing what he deemed to be improper attire, and went to great lengths to ensure that the members of the first Labour government should be correctly turned out.[91] Even in the darkest days of the Second World War, George VI was equally punctilious about matters of dress, and was delighted to regain control of the Orders of the Garter and the Thistle from the Labour government in 1947. And as the Duke of Windsor, King Edward VIII wrote a book about clothes and loved dressing up.[92] Like George III, these monarchs were obsessed with routine, discipline and punctuality: they liked their lives to run in a secure and pre-ordained path.[93] And their

---

[89] K. Rose, *King George V* (London, 1983), pp. 52–60; F. Donaldson, *Edward VIII* (London, 1976), pp. 8–14.
[90] Rose, *George V*, p. 303; Donaldson, *Edward VIII*, p. 14; Sir J. Wheeler-Bennett, *King George VI: His Life and Reign* (London, 1958), pp. 27–8, 84–5, 99, 103–4; M. Thornton, *Royal Feud: The Queen Mother and the Duchess of Windsor* (London, 1985), pp. 396–7; P. Brendon, *Our Own Dear Queen* (London, 1986), p. 130.
[91] Magnus, *Edward VII*, pp. 45, 308, 373–8, 447, 467, 481; Rose, *George V*, pp. 184, 233, 306, 331.
[92] Brendon, *Our Own Dear Queen*, pp. 149–50, 153; Wheeler-Bennett, *George VI*, pp. 755–60; Donaldson, *Edward VIII*, pp. 43–4, 83, 399–400.
[93] Plumb, *George III*, pp. 11–17.

excessive interest in order and orders, in time and titles, was but one aspect of this.

Another was their generally held belief that, in both domestic and international affairs, any change was by definition change for the worse. Edward VII thought that many members of his last Liberal government were not even gentlemen, was strongly opposed to the Morley-Minto reforms which he felt undermined the Raj, and was deeply distressed by the violent attacks on the House of Lords at the end of his reign.[94] George V regarded the strikes of 1911 and 1926 as the portents of revolution, and took an attitude to his empire, according to the Colonial Secretary Leopold Amery, which was closely reminiscent of George III. He was much put out by the growth of dominion autonomy in the aftermath of the Balfour Declaration and the Statute of Westminster, and his view of Indian self-government was reminiscent of his grandmother's on Ireland, and of his great-great-grandfather's on America. 'Remember, Mr Gandhi', he remarked, after entertaining the 'rebel fakir' to tea at Buckingham Palace, 'I won't have any attack on my empire.' And when Indian independence was finally achieved, the loss of his imperial title upset George VI very deeply.[95]

Not surprisingly, these monarchs had as little time for party politics as Victoria and Albert and their predecessors. In telling the young Winston Churchill that the essence of statesmanship was 'putting country before party', King Edward VII merely reiterated the centuries-old royal view. George V placed 'little faith in democracy', and backed the generals against the politicians during the First World War. And George VI was much happier when coalition governments were in power.[96] But it was in the future King Edward VIII that this traditional royal distrust of Parliament, politicians and party re-emerged most strongly. By the late 1920s and early 1930s, there was widespread disillusionment with democracy in Britain, which the young Prince of Wales fully shared. He had no time for the 'Old Gang' as represented by Baldwin and Macdonald; he was an ardent admirer of the Hitler and Mussolini regimes; and he looked forward to playing a positive part in the

[94] Magnus, *Edward VII*, pp. 429, 437–9, 520–1, 551.
[95] Rose, *George V*, pp. 67, 342–3, 348, 353; Brendon, *Our Own Dear Queen*, p. 153.
[96] Magnus, *Edward VII*, p. 432; Rose, *George V*, pp. 201, 376, 382; Wheeler-Bennett, *George VI*, p. 631.

formation of government policy, especially with regard to foreign affairs. 'I shouldn't be surprised', Henry Channon observed, 'if he aimed at making himself a mild dictator.' Although these sentiments are usually described as embodying a total and regrettable aberration from the constitutionalist royal tradition, the evidence presented here suggests that they were more unusual in degree than they were in kind.[97]

In the same way, the peculiar needs of royalty have continued to influence their matrimonial arrangements, often at the expense of emotional preference. The most famous example of this concerned the abortive marriage of the Duke of Clarence in 1892.[98] The eldest son of the Prince of Wales, and thus the heir to the throne, was so lazy, shy, backward, vague and lethargic that – like his father – he was thought to need 'a good, sensible woman, with some considerable character'. After some searching, it was decided by Queen Victoria and by the Prince and Princess of Wales that Princess Mary of Teck was a suitable candidate. Fortunately, she did not 'make any resistance', and Prince Eddy was 'told he must do it . . . for the good of the country'. But although the engagement was thus arranged in the usual manner, the Duke of Clarence died on the eve of his wedding. Unabashed, his parents persuaded Princess Mary to transfer her affections to his younger brother, Prince George, who was now heir to the throne, which she obligingly did. As he later admitted to her, with almost artless candour, 'when I asked you to marry me, I was very fond of you, but not very much in love with you', a view with which Princess Mary herself fully concurred.[99]

Likewise, opportunities for dynastic aggrandizement have still been taken, as is shown by the rise to royal prominence of the Battenburgs. As with the Coburgs, they were obscure, impoverished German princelings, further tainted by the stain of morganatic

---

[97] Donaldson, *Edward VII*, chapter 15; R. Rhodes James, ed., *'Chips': The Diaries of Sir Henry Channon* (London, 1967), p. 84.

[98] For full accounts of this, see: Magnus, *Edward VII*, pp. 275, 299–303; Rose, *George V*, pp. 22–33; J. Pope-Hennessy, *Queen Mary, 1867–1953* (London, 1959), chapters 8–12.

[99] Pope-Hennessy, *Queen Mary*, p. 279. There was an exact precedent for this match in Princess Alexandra's family. Her sister Minnie, Princess Dagmar of Schleswig-Holstein, was first engaged to Grand Duke Nicholas, the heir to the Russian throne. But he died in 1865, and in the following year she married his younger brother, who became the Emperor Alexander III. See Magnus, *Edward VII*, pp. 126–7.

blood.[100] But during the late nineteenth century, they married their way into the royal houses of England, Russia and Scandinavia, and in Lord Mountbatten boasted a twentieth-century operator who combined the ambitions of Leopold with the skills of Stockmar. Despite the opposition of King George VI, he planned and promoted the marriage of his nephew, Lieutenant Philip Mountbatten, to Princess Elizabeth. On Elizabeth's accession in 1952, Mountbatten was thus able to claim triumphantly that the Battenburgs were now the reigning English family; and since 1960 the name of Britain's royal house has been officially recognized as Mountbatten-Windsor.[101] Indeed, if Lord Mountbatten had succeeded in his last dynastic ambition, of marrying off his granddaughter Amanda Knatchbull to Prince Charles, his dynastic takeover of the house of Windsor would have been complete.

VI

Viewed in this light, the history of the modern royal family remains the history of successive waves of parvenu German invaders. In the eighteenth century, it was hijacked by the Hanoverians; in the nineteenth, it was commandeered by the Coburgs; and in the twentieth, it has been mugged by the Mountbattens. Nevertheless, despite the tenacious survival of some of these pre-modern elements down to our own time, it remains clear that by the end of Queen Victoria's reign the British monarchy had indeed been fundamentally transformed into an institution which had at least as much in common with what was to come after as with what had gone before. As the Victorians themselves were only too well aware, the twenty-year period of royal seclusion following Albert's death effectively separated the early and later periods of the Queen's reign. And it was this, combined with more deeply-rooted changes at home and abroad, which meant that the late nineteenth-century monarchy was in many ways a very different institution from that which had existed during the years of Victoria and Albert. It was not merely, as Lord Salisbury said on her death, that the Queen 'has bridged over that great interval which separates old

---

100 P. Ziegler, *Mountbatten: The Official Biography* (London, 1985), pp. 21–5.
101 Brendon, *Our Own Dear Queen*, p. 157; Rhodes James, *'Chips'*, pp. 286–7, 328, 386; Ziegler, *Mountbatten*, pp. 523, 681–2.

England from new England'; she had also bridged that same great interval which separated the old monarchy from the new.[102]

One aspect of this was that the power to influence political events, and to mould and control government, which had been so cherished and desired by Albert, did not long survive his death. Even during his own lifetime, his remarkable degree of involvement was only made possible by the very fluid nature of the party system in the aftermath of the Tory split over the Corn Laws; he and the Queen nevertheless suffered successive defeats at the hands of Palmerston; and his substantive influence on the political process was never in practice as great as he wished or supposed. Thereafter, the Queen remained opinionated and obstructive, exerted undeniable influence over Schleswig-Holstein and the Third Reform Act, and made difficulties for Gladstone, Salisbury and Rosebery.[103] But the growth of democracy and of the party system, combined with her inability to work as hard and as intelligently on the papers as Albert had done, meant that, during the last years of her reign, she was no longer performing the central, creative and controlling functions that Albert had sought and sometimes fulfilled. Personal monarchy, as the Prince Consort had understood and envisaged it, was no more.

Since then, the attenuation of royal power has continued inexorably. King Edward VII was untrained in statecraft, loathed paperwork, and was abroad for three months of the year. He did not see ministers individually, and was merely informed of Cabinet decisions when they had been reached. With the role of the monarchy so reduced, it was perhaps as well that he had rebelled against Albert's rigorous educational scheme, for the skills which that remorseless regime was designed to promote were now no longer needed in a constitutional sovereign. Indeed, one of the reasons why Lord Esher was so anxious to publish Queen Victoria's early correspondence in the 1900s was to show how much more active the monarchy had been then, with the clear implication that this role should be claimed once again.[104] But this has not happened: no subsequent monarch, from George V to our present Queen, could be described as 'watching and controlling govern-

---

[102] *Parliamentary Debates*, 4th series, vol. 89, col. 10.

[103] See the references cited in note 61, and C. C. Weston, 'The Royal Mediation in 1884', *English Historical Review*, 82 (1967), pp. 296–322.

[104] Magnus, *Edward VII*, pp. 347–51.

ment' in the manner envisaged by Albert. At most, they are occasionally obliged to intervene – as in 1910, 1923 and 1931 – when the constitution cannot work without them.[105] Even if the present Queen wields more influence than it is fashionable to suppose, she is clearly not 'an informal but potent member of each cabinet'. And no one has yet said of Prince Philip that 'He governs us, really, in everything.'[106]

In other words, this particular brand of 'constitutional monarchy', which has evolved since 1861 and which is rightly described as a monarchy 'above parties', is not so much the *fulfilment* as the *negation* of the ideal of sovereignty which Albert and Victoria entertained. Ironically enough, it was in Germany, rather than in England, that Albert's ambitious concept of monarchy found its fullest – if much perverted – expression, for in many ways the personal rule of the Kaiser bore a closer resemblance to Albert's aim of watching and controlling everything than did the limp and lethargic regime of Edward VII across the North Sea.[107] However much Wilhelm revolted against his parents' liberal and constitutionalist values, and however much of a disappointment he was to his mother, he did indeed inherit her forceful, strong, assertive and independent personality, which was given full scope when he became German Emperor. Contemporaries like Holstein and Eulenburg fully endorsed the Kaiser's view that 'My mother and I have the same characteristics.' And of all the Queen's children, it was Vicky who possessed her 'father's ... mind and genius'. Albeit in militaristic rather than liberal guise, the Coburg conception of monarchy came closest to realization in Berlin rather than at Windsor.[108]

In other ways, too, the monarchy of Victoria and Albert was soon overturned by events. For Albert, the institution was rational,

---

[105] This, of course, was Professor Pares's point about George III, who had 'to do for his country what it had not yet the means of doing so well for itself'. Pares, *George III and the Politicians*, p. 207.

[106] Fulford, *Prince Consort*, p. 181.

[107] P. Kennedy, 'The Kaiser and German *Weltpolitik*: Reflections on William's Place in the Making of German Foreign Policy', in J. G. C. Rohl and N. Sombart, eds., *Kaiser Wilhelm II: New Interpretations* (Cambridge, 1982), pp. 153–5.

[108] T. A. Kohnt, 'Kaiser Wilhelm II and his Parents: An Inquiry into the Psychological Roots of Germany's Policy Towards England Before the First World War', in Rohl and Sombart, *Wilhelm II*, pp. 80–2; Queen Victoria to the Princess Royal, 24 May 1863, in Fulford, *'Dearest Mama'*, p. 216.

practical, down to earth: the veneration, the hyperbole and the quasi-religious language which were unfurled so fulsomely from the end of the nineteenth century formed no part of his essentially utilitarian conception. Nor does the monarchy as a predominantly ceremonial and theatrical institution fit in with Albert's scheme of things. His provincial visits were not primarily social functions or decorative tableaux, but were fact-finding missions, so he could go back to London to govern the country better. For Albert, the prime purpose of the monarchy was that it should be fundamental, not ornamental. And although Victoria herself became the cynosure of late nineteenth-century pageants, she never really regarded the prime purpose of the monarchy as ceremonial.[109] 'Bartering substance for show' was the last thing either of them had ever wanted or intended. Accordingly, it is difficult to resist the conclusion that the monarchy's subsequent development into a spectacular and matriarchal soap opera would have been for both of them the negation of all they most strongly believed in.[110]

One further irony is that the descendants of Victoria and Albert repudiated their parents' conception of monarchy more successfully and more completely than they themselves had turned their backs on the Hanoverians. In deliberate acts of personal renunciation, neither Edward VII nor George VI became King Albert, even though in both cases it was their first name. When the future King George V was christened with such a resoundingly Hanoverian name, the Queen was much put out; and when he in turn fathered his first son, he, too, braved the old Queen's wrath by not giving him Albert as his first name.[111] Most symbolically of all, Edward VII turned his back on Osborne as completely, and with as much relief, as Victoria and Albert had repudiated Brighton Pavilion. When he came to the throne, he at once resolved never to live in the 'family necropolis'. Although it had been left by the Queen to all her children equally, Edward set aside his sisters' protests, and allowed it to be used as a Royal Navy training college and convalescent home.[112] Like most members of the royal family, he had had enough of worshipping Albert: in this sense, it was more than just

109 Cannadine, 'Context, Performance and Meaning of Ritual', pp. 133–4.
110 Rhodes James, *Prince Consort*, p. 154.
111 Weintraub, *Victoria*, p. 333; Rose, *George V*, pp. 1, 37; Donaldson, *Edward VIII*, p. 6.
112 Magnus, *Edward VII*, p. 358; Wheeler-Bennett, *George VI*, p. 37; The Duke of Windsor, *A King's Story* (London, 1951), p. 13.

the Queen that died at Osborne, it was the whole notion of monarchy.

More generally, the First World War effectively ended that cosy European club in which royal personages formed a closed corporation, an international trades union. One of the most cherished beliefs of Victoria and Albert was that their immediate and distant relatives constituted a genuinely internationalist and unifying force; that it was through their crowned heads of state that nation might best speak unto nation; and that so long as this system prevailed, peace might be preserved. But the outbreak of the First World War meant that this system collapsed for ever. The German and British royal families were irrevocably split; the Garter banners of enemy sovereigns were removed from St George's Chapel; Battenburgs became Mountbattens and Tecks became Cambridges; and the royal House ceased to be Saxe-Coburg-Gotha and became Windsor instead. As one Bavarian nobleman remarked, 'the true royal tradition died on that day in 1917 when, for a mere war, King George V changed his name'. Nor was this the final casualty. For as the other great European dynasties fell, King George did not raise a finger to help them. In abandoning the Russian royal family during the war, and in withholding assistance from his Greek relatives during its aftermath, he resolutely put country before caste.[113]

The inevitable consequence has been that marriage partners have been increasingly recruited from the national aristocracy rather than foreign royalty, and that individual freedom of choice has been greatly increased as a result. In 1872, Queen Victoria had allowed her daughter Louise to wed the Marquess of Lorne, and a daughter of King Edward VII married the Earl of Fife.[114] But these were only aberrations from the norm: in the nineteenth century, as in the eighteenth, royalty still married royalty, it did not marry subjects. Once again, the great change came in 1917, when King George V and Queen Mary decided that in future 'our children would be allowed to marry into British families'.[115] It was, the King added, 'quite a historical occasion'. As a result, the way was open for the Princess Royal, the Dukes of York and of Gloucester, and the present Prince of Wales, to marry into the British aristocracy.

---

[113] Fulford, *Hanover to Windsor*, p. 173; Rose, *George V*, pp. 171–5, 208–18, 347.
[114] Weintraub, *Victoria*, p. 358; Magnus, *Edward VII*, p. 270.
[115] Rose, *George V*, p. 309.

In some cases, such as those of Princess Anne and Prince Andrew, they have actually married into the untitled upper middle classes. And some have taken this greater freedom of choice to even further lengths: the previous Prince of Wales with Mrs Simpson and thus the abdication; and Princess Margaret with the Armstrong-Jones marriage and the Snowdon divorce. Such behaviour had no place in Queen Victoria's royal world.

VII

Why, then, to return to the opening question, did contemporaries during the late nineteenth century, and have historians and biographers down to our own day, persisted in perpetuating the myth that from the very beginning of her reign, Queen Victoria broke completely and irrevocably with the immediate Hanoverian past, and that from the time of her marriage to Albert, the Victorian monarchy assumed in all its vital aspects an essentially modern and constitutional form? To be sure, there is some evidence in support of this view, which cannot and should not be ignored. But it is overwhelmingly outweighed by contradictory material. In its fundamental characteristics, much of the Victorian monarchy was more old than new; many of these pre-modern facets persisted to the end of the Queen's reign and into the twentieth century until our own time; and insofar as there was a major transformation in the Victorian monarchy, it took place more at the end of it than at the beginning. Why, then, has this myth of instant and pervasive modernity been so ubiquitous and so tenacious?

In general, the explanation lies in the need for precedent and in the desire for consolation which – in Britain as in all human societies – it seems that only the past can provide. At one level, those late nineteenth-century observers of the monarchy knew very well that the world, and the sovereign's place and purpose in it, had changed drastically since Queen Victoria had acceded to the throne. Words like 'unique', 'extraordinary', 'transformation' and 'unprecedented' occur too frequently in their descriptions for this to be in any doubt. But at another level, they sought to present this novelty as tradition, by finding reassuring and plausible precedents for something which was in fact newly happening. Just as developments in the Empire necessitated the rediscovery of Lord Durham and his Canadian report as the sacred imperial text, so it became essential to manufacture similar precedents for the novel changes associated with the late nineteenth-century monarchy.[116] And in searching for such illustrious precursors, there were only three candidates for constitutional canonization effectively available.

The first of these was of course the Queen herself, whose quite remarkable longevity gave a distortingly unifying impression to the years from 1837 to 1901. For the adjective 'Victorian' endowed both the history of England and the history of the monarchy with a monolithic identity and spurious unity which belied and denied the many changes that had actually taken place in both.[117] By the end of her reign, there was almost no one left who could remember what the country or the Queen had actually been like at the beginning. And so it became possible to depict her Jubilees, those supreme moments of apotheosis, as the natural and appropriate reward for long service and good conduct. In the golden retrospection of her sunset years, it was easy to claim that the Queen had intended to be good from the very outset, and that by force of circumstance and of personality, she had indeed succeeded.[118] The very extent of her reign thus endowed it with an arrestingly triumphant teleology, as she herself became her own most illustrious precedent, with the result that the date of her accession stood out emphatically as a new beginning for the monarchy.

But the second precedent – and in many ways the more appropriate one – was none other than King George III himself. He was, after all, Queen Victoria's grandfather, and like her again, his reign had been long and ultimately triumphant. He had from the beginning 'gloried in the name of Briton'; his private life was beyond reproach; he had worked devotedly and dutifully at being a monarch; his piety and dignity had earned him widespread middle-class support; and he had died as 'the father of his people'. Indeed, all this had been captured in those Zoffany conversation pieces, which depicted a decorous and decent home life, nearly a century before Landseer and Winterhalter. Moreover, George III was in many ways the unconscious precursor of that curious blend of domestic cosiness and public splendour which became so fully

---

[116] G. Martin, *The Durham Report: A Critical Essay* (Cambridge, 1972), pp. 3, 84–100.

[117] G. M. Young, *Victorian England: Portrait of an Age* (Oxford, 1960 edn), p. 181.

[118] For example, C. Bullock, *The Queen's Resolve: 'I Will Be Good'* (London, 1887).

established from the end of Queen Victoria's reign.[119] After fifty years on the throne, he had celebrated a Jubilee in 1809 which was cited in 1887 as the only immediate precedent. Accordingly, it would have required little tinkering with the historical record to present George III as anticipating Queen Victoria, and so to make 1760, rather than 1837, the major turning-point in the history of the modern monarchy.[120]

Nevertheless, George III would not do as the precedent for the transformed monarchy of the Queen's two Jubilees. To the late Victorians, he seemed a madman and a tyrant, who had lost the American colonies, and these were clearly crippling disqualifications. In a family where ill-health was a constant hazard, it was obviously both difficult and dangerous to idolize a man thought to have been a lunatic. In trying to project an image of a monarchy deliberately and eagerly conforming to Walter Bagehot's analysis, above the party-political battle, and doing little more than encouraging, warning and being consulted, it was impossible to resurrect a sovereign who was at that very time being damned by the pens of Lecky, Erskine May and George Otto Trevelyan as the worst ever English king.[121] And in an era characterized by international rivalry and imperial aggrandizement, and by increasing interest in Anglo-American amity, the King whose actions had apparently led to the loss of the thirteen colonies was self-evidently beyond rehabilitation.[122]

---

[119] L. Colley, 'The Apotheosis of George III: Loyalty, Royalty and the British Nation, 1760–1820', *Past and Present*, 102 (February 1984), pp. 108, 124–5; Schama, 'Domestication of Majesty', pp. 170–3; Ormond, *Face of Monarchy*, p. 31; Ormond *et al.*, *Landseer*, pp. 150–2.

[120] J. Lant, *Insubstantial Pageant: Ceremony and Confusion at Queen Victoria's Court* (London, 1979), pp. 13, 60, 161, 211. See also T. Preston, *Jubilee Jottings: The Jubilee of George the Third* (London, 1887); [Anon], *The Jubilee of George the Third* (London, 1887).

[121] H. Butterfield, *George III and the Historians* (London, 1957), pp. 151–68. The particular works in question were: E. May, *Constitutional History of England* (London, 1861); W. H. Lecky, *History of England in the Eighteenth Century*, vols. 3 and 4, *1760–84* (London, 1882); Sir George Otto Trevelyan, *Early History of Charles James Fox* (London, 1880), and *History of the American Revolution*, 6 vols (London, 1899).

[122] C. S. Campbell, *From Revolution to Rapprochement: The United States and Great Britain, 1783–1900* (London, 1974), p. 183. Here is Lord Esher (*Queen Victoria's Journals*, p. 35): 'Although she resembled in many ways her grandfather, George III, she could have been relied upon not to misunderstand the American colonists.' And here is the U.S. Secretary of State, William Evarts, in 1878: 'Had Queen Victoria been on the throne instead of George III, or if we

By default, that left Albert as the only possible retrospective architect of the new late nineteenth-century monarchy. As with George III, there were very real difficulties. For the Prince Consort had never been particularly popular during his life, and in many ways the British people had never really warmed to him. He was too German, too prim, too distant and too earnest to establish a popular public persona; and even in death, the cult of Albert was more a sign of his widow's lachrymose determination to commemorate him than of her husband's authentically wide appeal.[123] Moreover, during the thirty years after his death, a great deal of material was published which – often unwittingly – revealed the full extent of the political ambitions which Albert had entertained for the monarchy. This was not only true of the memoirs of Greville, of Stockmar and of Duke Ernest II of Saxe-Coburg; but it also emerged quite clearly from the pages of Theodore Martin's monumental life, which – ironically enough – the Queen herself had so actively promoted and influenced.[124]

Even so, it is highly significant that it is at precisely the time of her own Jubilees and apotheosis that Albert first appeared in his new role as the self-conscious creator of the post-Bagehot, late-Victorian constitutional monarchy. As Escott explained in 1897, 'the idea of monarchy actually operative among us today, whether in its constitutional, ceremonial or social attributes, is at all points stamped with the impress of one systematising and controlling

---

had postponed our rebellion until Queen Victoria reigned, it would not have been necessary.' (I am grateful to Dr M. J. Sewell for this reference.)

[123] This goes counter to the thesis advanced in E. Darby and N. Smith, *The Cult of the Prince Consort* (London, 1981). But *cf.* Weintraub, *Victoria*, p. 309: 'The cult of the Prince Consort was imposed rather than real.' Even the construction of the London monument was long delayed by lack of funds: S. Bayley, *The Albert Memorial: The Monument in its Social and Architectural Context* (London, 1981), pp. 138–45.

[124] H. Reeve, ed., *The Greville Memoirs*, 3 vols (London, 1874); for Stockmar's *Memoirs*, see note 49; *Memoirs of Ernst II, Duke of Saxe-Coburg-Gotha*, trans. Percy Andrae, 4 vols (London, 1888–90); Sir T. Martin, *Life of the Prince Consort*, 5 vols (London, 1875–80). Gladstone, in reviewing Martin's volumes, not only criticized Stockmar for the claims he advanced on behalf of the monarchy, but also noted that his life of Albert showed that the sovereign still possessed 'ample scope for the exercise of a direct and personal influence in the whole work of government'. See W. E. Gladstone, *Gleanings of Past Years, 1843–1879*, 7 vols (London, 1879), vol. 1, *The Throne and the Prince Consort, The Cabinet and the Constitution*, pp. 41, 75–85.

mind'. And that mind was Albert's.[125] Thus did he re-emerge as the inspired progenitor and venerated practitioner of a politically aloof, personally popular and ceremonially splendid crown, thereby consolidating from 1840 the changes already begun by his wife three years before. He was the pioneer; Bagehot was the theoretician; Victoria was their legatee; and those who came after merely followed in their wake.[126] And so a series of developments which Albert and Victoria would have looked upon as a failure – the frustration of so many of their ambitions for their throne and their family – became transformed by the alchemy of anachronism into an outstanding success, the starting-point of which was now precisely dated in the years 1837–40.

During the inter-war period, Victoria remained serenely and unassailably apotheosized, but Albert's name again went into the shadows, partly because of Lytton Strachey's misleadingly unattractive portrait of him in his biography of the Queen, and partly because his German sympathies were deemed excessive and unacceptable.[127] But from the 1950s onwards, with another young queen regnant, whose husband once again came from a minor foreign royal house which was overwhelmingly German in ancestry, the urge to present the Prince Consort as the precursor of Prince Philip became irresistible. Hence the early stress on their shared interests in technology, and the Duke of Edinburgh's more recent appointment as Chancellor of Cambridge University. Once more, as in the late nineteenth century, it was the Queen and the Prince Consort together who were deemed to have brought the British monarchy from the old world into the new. And so, instead of being understood as the unsuccessful and frustrated emulators of William and Mary, Victoria and Albert are still presented to this day as the triumphant and prescient forerunners of Elizabeth and Philip.

The liberties with the historical record which this interpretation took, and still takes, should by now need no stressing. Of course it is never easy, when writing about any past age, to strike the correct balance between what is new and what is old in it. And inevitably,

---

[125] T. H. S. Escott, *Social Transformations of the Victorian Age* (London, 1897), p. 276; W. W. Tulloch, *The Story of the Life of the Prince Consort* (London, 1887), pp. 144–5, 273–7.

[126] Both George V and George VI studied Bagehot as young men: Rose, *George V*, p. 35; Wheeler-Bennett, *George VI*, pp. 131–2.

[127] Rhodes James, *Prince Consort*, pp. xi–xii; E. T. S. Dugdale, introduction to Jagow, *Letters of the Prince Consort*, p. xiv.

the history of a long-lived and contemporary institution like the British monarchy is particularly prone to this kind of retrospective distortion, as it is always tempting to conclude a royal biography on a triumphant note of abiding relevance and forward-looking modernity. Only by looking at it over a long span of time, and by evaluating it analytically as well as biographically, is it possible to tease out the inner and abiding essence of being royal. For to say that there is much in the Victorian and post-Victorian monarchy which derives from the Hanoverians is simply to note that in their political views, in their social attitudes and in their emotional relationships, there are conventional royal wisdoms and practices which survive across the centuries with amazing tenacity, however much other things may change. And it is these underlying themes, as much as with the more personal and biographical details, that historians of the monarchy should concern themselves. It may be true, as Scott Fitzgerald remarked, that the rich are different from us. But the royals are even more so.

5. The gentrification of Victorian and Edwardian industrialists

RICHARD TRAINOR

During the last decade social historians of nineteenth- and early twentieth-century Britain have become increasingly interested in the aristocracy, the middle class, and relations between them.[1] Yet influential interpretations differ on how far provincial industrialists mingled with the landed elite and with the comparatively genteel mercantile and professional middle classes.[2] Were industrialists isolated from the rest of the propertied classes? Or did manufacturers experience 'gentrification' by purchasing landed estates, mixing with the aristocracy and gentry and modifying their own attitudes and behaviour accordingly?[3] For W. D. Rubinstein there was little gentrification, for M. J. Wiener much.[4] Lawrence and Jeanne Stone's study of Hertfordshire, Northamptonshire and Northumberland before 1880 supports Rubinstein up to that date

I wish to thank the editors, Professor F. M. L. Thompson and audiences at conferences sponsored by the Essex University Centre for Social History and the Glasgow University Enterprise, Public Policy and Society research group for comments on previous versions of this paper.

[1] R. H. Trainor, 'Urban Elites in Victorian Britain', *Urban History Yearbook 1985* (Leicester, 1985), pp. 1–17.

[2] For purposes of variety, 'aristocracy', 'landed elite' and 'upper class' are used interchangeably to refer to the peerage and landed gentry, as are 'industrialists' and 'manufacturers' to refer to the industrial (including mining) employers within the middle class.

[3] The gentrification of industrialists should be distinguished from the journalistic and geographical usage in which gentrification refers to the social upgrading of residential areas. See, for example, the discussion of 'the movement of middle- and upper-class groups into lower-income neighbourhoods of the city', in G. Harrison, 'Gentrification in Knoxville, Tennessee: A Study of the Fourth and Gill Neighborhood', *Urban Geography*, 4 (1983), p. 40.

[4] W. D. Rubinstein, *Men of Property: The Very Wealthy Since the Industrial Revolution* (London, 1981), and 'New Men of Wealth and the Purchase of Land in Nineteenth Century England', *Past and Present*, 42 (1981), pp. 125–47; M. J. Wiener, *English Culture and the Decline of the Industrial Spirit, 1850–1980* (Cambridge, 1981), especially chapters 2 and 7.

while suggesting an influx of manufacturers into landed society in the late nineteenth and early twentieth centuries.[5]

Despite these significant disagreements, there is much consensus among these writers concerning the economic, social and political marginality of industrialists, in comparison not only with the landed elite but also with the professional and commercial wings of the middle class.[6] These commentators draw heavily on recent reinterpretations of the occupational and regional distribution of wealth and income. The landed elite, it emerges, retained a majority of top fortunes until the later nineteenth century. Within the middle class, ealth accrued most not to industrialists but to those engaged in international trade, and in finance, commerce and the professions more generally. Thus resources were concentrated in London and the Southeast as a whole (which also held a surprisingly large amount of the nation's industry), and in commercial rather than industrial towns elsewhere. Moreover, as late as 1914 the religion, party and prestige as well as the wealth of top professional, financial and commercial men placed them closer to the still pre-eminent landed elite than were manufacturers.[7] Whether as a group snubbed by the aristocracy, or as one absorbed by the upper class on unequal terms, industrialists appear in these views as the weakest element within Britain's elites.

This line of argument is an important one, not least because it represents a major departure from the previously pervasive 'rising industrialist' view.[8] The diverse role that gentrification has played in this emerging consensus – both its presence and its absence having been used to support the argument – demands further

[5] L. Stone and J. C. F. Stone, *An Open Elite?: England 1540–1880* (Oxford, 1984), esp. pp. 204–8; L. Stone, 'Spring Back', *Albion*, 17 (1985), pp. 167–80.

[6] See, for example, Stone and Stone, *An Open Elite?*, pp. 411–12, though for the Stones the inferiority of top industrialists was at least partially overcome after 1880 (*ibid.*, pp. 208, 412, 424–6).

[7] C. H. Lee, 'The Service Sector, Regional Specialization, and Economic Growth in the Victorian Economy', *Journal of Historical Geography*, 10 (1984), pp. 139–55; Rubinstein, 'The Victorian Middle Classes: Wealth, Occupation and Geography', *Economic History Review*, 2nd series, 30 (1977), pp. 602–23, and 'Wealth, Elites and the Class Structure of Modern Britain', *Past and Present* 76 (1977), pp. 99–126.

[8] A. Briggs, 'Middle Class Consciousness in English Politics, 1780–1846', *Past and Present*, 9 (1956), pp. 65–74; H. J. Perkin, *The Origins of Modern English Society 1780–1880* (London, 1969); R. Q. Gray, 'Bourgeois Hegemony in Victorian Britain', in J. Bloomfield, ed., *Class, Hegemony and Party* (London, 1977), pp. 73–93.

scrutiny of the phenomenon. In addition, early critics of recent works on gentrification point to the need for further study, urging particular attention to the most heavily industrialized parts of Britain.[9]

Such an investigation can profit from concentrating, at the margin, on the industrial rather than the landed role in gentrification;[10] otherwise the inferiority of industrialists threatens to become a foregone conclusion. Likewise, land purchase and the acquisition of a landed lifestyle need to be located more securely than hitherto in the general context of relations between industrialists and the landed elite, thereby balancing the inherent advantages that the aristocracy possessed in landed circles and in society with the leverage enjoyed by the middle class in spheres such as business and, increasingly, politics. Focusing on a single region facilitates this comprehensive approach. Also, a study based on a provincial manufacturing area avoids the London-based viewpoint which exaggerates the predominance of landed, commercial and professional elites.

The region to be approached from these perspectives is the West Midlands, particularly the Black Country (see Figure 5.1),[11] an important industrial district where the landed elite played a significant role in political and social as well as economic affairs.[12] It

[9] F. M. L. Thompson, 'Business and Landed Elites in the Nineteenth Century', (unpublished typescript, 1986), p. 26; H. Perkin, 'An Open Elite', *Journal of British Studies*, 24 (1985), p. 501; D. Spring and E. Spring, 'The English Landed Elite, 1540–1879: A Review', *Albion*, 17 (1985), p. 150, and 'Social Mobility and the English Landed Elite', *Canadian Journal of History*, 2 (1986), p. 347.

[10] *Cf.* the distinction made *ibid.*, p. 335; however, the Springs, like the Stones, are primarily concerned with landed society itself.

[11] The West Midlands is taken to be the area which saw Birmingham as its metropolis, i.e. roughly the pre-1974 counties of Staffordshire, Warwickshire and Worcestershire. Within this broader *region*, the Black Country (often referred to in the essay as 'the district') is the complex of iron, coal and metal manufacturing towns, in pre-1974 Staffordshire and Worcestershire, approximately bounded by Wolverhampton, Walsall, Smethwick, Halesowen and Stourbridge. The Black Country did not include either Birmingham or Coventry.

[12] For previous studies of the landed elite in the West Midlands, see: D. Cannadine, *Lords and Landlords: The Aristocracy and the Towns 1774–1967* (Leicester, 1980), part 2; N. Mutton, 'The Foster Family: A Study of a Midland Industrial Dynasty 1786–1899' (unpublished Ph.D. thesis, University of London, 1974), especially pp. 65–84; T. J. Raybould, *The Economic Emergence of the Black Country: A Study of the Dudley Estate* (Newton Abbot, 1973), and 'Aristocratic Landownership and the Industrial Revolution: The Black Country Experience c. 1760–1840', *Midland History*, 11 (1984), pp. 59–86; D. Smith, *Conflict and Compromise: Class Formation in English Society 1830–1914, A Comparative*

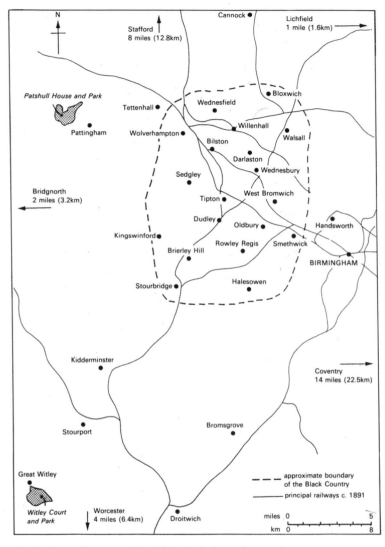

5.1 The Black Country and its vicinity in the later nineteenth century

will be argued that in the Black Country – and, with variations, in provincial Britain more generally – there was increasing co-operation between the aristocracy and industrialists. Middle-class migration to the countryside was one of a number of significant factors which fostered this harmony. Yet the limited and complex nature of gentrification did much to ensure that, while the upper class preserved some of its influence, industrialists became more powerful in their relations with aristocratic and other rival elites at the district, regional and national levels. Located in the overall pattern of landed/middle-class relations, therefore, gentrification can help to reconcile the traditional emphasis on rising industrialists with the recent stress on resilient aristocrats and on well-heeled London merchants and professionals.[13]

I

The gentrification of the middle class, and especially of industrialists, long a subject of discussion among historians,[14] has recently attracted renewed interest as anxieties about Britain's relative

Study of Birmingham and Sheffield (London, 1982), chapters 1 and 2; R. W. Sturgess, 'Landownership, Mining and Urban Development in Nineteenth Century Staffordshire', in J. T. Ward and R. G. Wilson, eds., *Land and Industry: The Landed Estate in the Industrial Revolution* (Newton Abbot, 1971) , pp. 173–204; R. H. Trainor, 'Authority and Social Structure in an Industrialized Area: A Study of Three Black Country Towns, 1840–1890 (unpublished D.Phil. thesis, University of Oxford, 1981), pp. 67–71, 88, and 'Peers on an Industrial Frontier: The Earls of Dartmouth and of Dudley in the Black Country, c. 1810–1914', in D. Cannadine, ed., *Patricians, Power and Politics in Nineteenth Century Towns* (Leicester, 1982), pp. 69–132. Although aristocratic influence was strongest in Dudley and West Bromwich where the urban Dudley and Dartmouth estates were centred, other peers had significant impact on local towns (especially the Clevelands on Wolverhampton and the Bradfords and Hathertons on Walsall). In addition, these and other upper-class families had significant contact with the district through various county and regional institutions. Moreover, there were several major country seats in the West Midlands, notably the Dartmouths' Patshull House and the Dudleys' Witley Court (see Figure 5.1).

[13] *Cf.*, among others, W. L. Arnstein, 'The Survival of the Victorian Aristocracy', in F. C. Jaher, ed., *The Rich, the Well Born and the Powerful* (New York, 1973), pp. 203–57; P. J. Cain and A. G. Hopkins, 'Gentlemanly Capitalism and British Expansion Overseas: II. New Imperialism 1850–1945', *Economic History Review*, 2nd series, 40 (1987), pp. 1–26.

[14] P. Anderson, 'Origins of the Present Crisis', *New Left Review*, 23 (1964), pp. 26–51; Perkin, *Origins*, pp. 86, 430–7; E. P. Thompson, 'The Peculiarities of the English', *The Socialist Register 1965*; F. M. L. Thompson, *English Landed Society in the Nineteenth Century* (London, 1963), pp. 116, 118–19, 122–3, 127–32, 285.

economic decline have intensified. For Wiener, 'The consolidation of a "gentrified" bourgeois culture, particularly the rooting of pseudoaristocratic attitudes and values in upper-middle class educated opinion, shaped an unfavourable context for economic endeavour.'[15] Such factors, Wiener argues, encouraged many industrialists to turn to the role of landed gentleman. This diversion of talent, he suggests, impoverished industry, whose influence on national political decisions remained weak. However, this popular[16] set of arguments takes too little account of economic historians who have argued for the vitality and rationality of late Victorian firms.[17] Also, Rubinstein has undercut the argument for the widespread rural absorption of manufacturers to which Wiener subscribes. Rubinstein shows that relatively few members of the upper middle class, in which industrialists were in any case underrepresented, bought very large parcels of land before 1914. As a result, families recently or currently in business constituted a relatively minor part of the elite which owned massive amounts of land. Rubinstein also recognizes that, especially in towns such as Birmingham and Norwich, many well-off members of the middle class clung to urban lifestyles, albeit of increasing grandeur. Thus a complete merger of the upper middle class with the landed elite did not occur, at least until after the First World War.[18]

Yet the position adopted by Rubinstein and, for the period to 1880, by the Stones, does not fully resolve the question of the place of Victorian industrialists, either within the middle class or in

---

[15] *English Culture*, p. 10 and *passim*. For previous discussion of the supposed economic harm of gentrification see, among many others: D. H. Aldcroft, 'The Entrepreneur and the British Economy, 1870–1914', *Economic History Review*, 2nd series, 17 (1964–5), pp. 128–9; D. C. Coleman, 'Gentlemen and Players', *ibid.*, 26 (1973), pp. 92–116; Coleman and C. Macleod, 'Attitudes to New Techniques: British Businessmen, 1800–1950', *ibid.*, 39 (1986), pp. 599–610; W. G. Rimmer, *Marshalls of Leeds* (Cambridge, 1960), pp. 252–3, 268–9, 290ff.

[16] R. Dahrendorf, *On Britain* (London, 1982); B. Redhead, 'A Word in Edgeways', programme on 'Industrial Decline', BBC Radio 4, 27 October 1985; P. Anderson, 'The Figures of Descent', *New Left Review*, 161 (1987), pp. 20–77.

[17] For penetrating analyses of this question and copious references, see P. L. Payne, *Entrepreneurship in Nineteenth Century Britain* (London, 1974), and 'Industrial Entrepreneurship and Management in Great Britain', in P. Mathias and M. M. Postan, eds., *The Cambridge Economic History of Europe*, 7 (Cambridge, 1978), pp. 201–11.

[18] Rubinstein, *Men of Property*, especially chapter 7 and 'New Men of Wealth', especially pp. 145–7.

relation to the aristocracy. The adoption of high cut-off points (of acreage and house size respectively)[19], below which industrial incursions into landed society are deemed unimportant, obscures significant aspects of social relations most visible near the boundaries of these classes. Thus, although Rubinstein's interpretation convincingly differs from Wiener's on the extent of industrial penetration of the peaks of landed society, their joint argument for the continued pre-eminence of the landed elite and its supposed allies in London-based finance, commerce and the professions deserves careful scrutiny. For in their effort to prove that the industrial middle class did not dominate British society – a proposition which, in its simple form, few recent historians have entertained – scholars such as Rubinstein and Wiener[20] underestimate the resources, coherence and impact of manufacturers, and of the industrial provinces as a whole. As a result, they risk making the industrial elite, long emphasized by analysts of modern British history, its most neglected element.

What is required is an effort to understand industrialists and provincial urban areas on their own terms as well as on those set by rival elites. It is necessary to escape from the proposition that entrepreneurs were dominated by landowners and merchants as well as from the alternative claim that manufacturers dominated these other types of leaders. The entrepreneurial class needs to be reintegrated into our view of modern British development in a way that recognizes its considerable political, social and economic resources while acknowledging the persisting assets of its competitors for power. Landed–industrial relations, therefore, must be seen as a wide-ranging process of give and take rather than as an interaction, consisting largely of land ownership, in which manufacturers failed to dent aristocratic dominion. By adopting this more comprehensive and more balanced approach, it may be possible to begin to re-establish a much modified form of the old argument that the Industrial Revolution boosted the influence, as well as the numbers and resources, of a middle class in which industrialists played an increasingly significant part.

[19] See Stone and Stone, *An Open Elite?*, pp. 10–11, 439–442; and note 38 below.
[20] *Cf.* also Arnstein, 'The Myth of the Triumphant Middle Class', *The Historian*, 37 (1975), pp. 205–21.

II

The Black Country is an appropriate test of these propositions because at the start of Victoria's reign it contained both a formidable landed elite and a middle class that was especially beleaguered. The district's middle-class leaders, among whom industrialists were numerous and especially influential, faced wealthy and powerful aristocrats who enjoyed local urban as well as rural resources. The towns' elites clashed with the peers on issues such as manorial rights and the selection of parliamentary candidates.[21] The Black Country's middle-class leaders also had to cope with an especially turbulent and particularly numerous working-class population, with social institutions severely strained by the area's expansion during the preceding sixty years, and with an unstable economy.[22] In short, the Black Country's middle class was of the kind which the arguments of Rubinstein as well as Wiener have conditioned us to view as especially small, poorly endowed, isolated and impotent.

Yet provincial industrialists, and the middle class generally in industrial areas, were not so few and poor as analyses based on probate and income tax statistics suggest. Concerning amounts left at death, the exclusion of leaders of consumer industries artificially depresses the industrial category. Also, manufacturers may have been especially likely to give away money to family members before they died.[23] With regard to the income tax, it seems probable that wealth generated in industrial towns was often assessed in commercial cities. In addition, many in the lower ranks of the middle class, which were relatively plentiful in the industrial provinces, would not have been assessed at all during much of the Victorian period.[24]

21 Trainor, 'Peers', pp. 70–89.
22 See Trainor, 'Authority and Social Structure', chapters 2 and 8.
23 Perkin, review of *Men of Property*, in *Social History Newsletter*, 6 (1981), pp. 13–14; M. S. Moss, 'William Todd Lithgow: Founder of a Fortune', *Scottish Historical Review*, 62 (1983), pp. 47–72; N. J. Morgan and M. S. Moss, 'Listing the Wealthy in Scotland', *Bulletin of the Institute of Historical Research*, 59 (1986), pp. 189–95.
24 *Cf.* Trainor, 'Authority', p. 48 and 'Reports of the Death of the Middle Class in Industrial Districts are Greatly Exaggerated: The Black Country 1830–1900' (unpublished paper, Urban History Group Conference, 1983); M. Jubb, 'Income, Class and the Taxman: A Note on the Distribution of Wealth in Nineteenth Century Britain', *Historical Research*, 60 (1987), pp. 117–24; C. Senior, *Hand-book of Income Tax Law & Practice ...* (London, 1863),

Even taking such sources at face value, neither the size nor the resources of even the Black Country's middle class emerges as seriously inhibiting. Admittedly the district's middle class was less numerous and less well off than its counterparts in London and some provincial commercial towns. Yet the Black Country middle class was substantial enough to exert significant influence both within local society and, at its top, on West Midland and national elites. For example, local directories suggest that at mid-century the middle class formed about a tenth (a twelfth without the humblest retailers) of the population; the proportion then rose to about a sixth (an eighth without the smallest tradesmen) by 1900.[25] Moreover, although the district's middle class was poorer than the national average, the Black Country produced the ironmaster W. O. Foster (who left nearly £2.6 million in 1899) and the steelmaster Sir Alfred Hickman (£1 million in 1910). More frequently, Blackcountrymen like the glass manufacturer J. H. Chance (£253,000 in 1900) accumulated substantial though unspectacular fortunes.[26] Thus the Black Country's middle class had a substantial 'head' as well as an unusually long 'tail'.[27]

Elites drawn from such a class could undertake successful initiatives provided that, first, modest levels of wealth as well as large fortunes were tapped for social leadership, and, second, that these leaders were able to overcome internal rifts concerning religion, political affiliation, and the grievances of the volatile lower middle class. As these conditions were increasingly fulfilled in the Black Country,[28] the industrialists who headed the district's middle-class elites were progressively better equipped to deal not only with the local working class but also with middle-class and aristocratic leaders in regional and national arenas.

In these wider contexts, Black Country industrialists were

pp. 170, 172–3, 180; G. Best, *Mid-Victorian Britain 1851–1875* (Frogmore, 1973), pp. 101, 105, 107.

[25] *Post Office (later Kelly's) Directories of Birmingham, Warwickshire, Worcestershire & Staffordshire* (London: 1850, 1864, 1868, 1876, 1888, 1900). For supporting information drawn from income tax and borough electorate figures, see Trainor, 'Authority', pp. 48–9.

[26] Rubinstein, 'British Millionaires 1809–1914', *Bulletin of the Institute of Historical Research*, 47 (1974), pp. 211, 213; 'Printed Probate Calendars', Somerset House; Trainor, 'Authority', pp. 50–7.

[27] For this terminology and the comparative context see *ibid.*, pp. 71–2, and J. Foster, 'Nineteenth Century Towns – A Class Dimension', in H. J. Dyos, ed., *The Study of Urban History* (London, 1968), pp. 283, 298.

[28] Trainor, 'Authority', chapters 3–6.

neither isolated nor impotent. At the regional level, Black Country manufacturers and coalmasters possessed increasing business, civic, family, religious and residential links with Birmingham's elite. Also, in economic terms, Black Country entrepreneurs – who had commercial and financial as well as industrial interests, and who were key figures on Birmingham's iron exchange – were not the economic inferiors of that city's merchants, bankers and lawyers. In fact, the dispersed, complex interests of leading West Midland families such as the manufacturing and banking Lloyds make it impossible to distinguish absolutely between the Black Country's upper middle class and its Birmingham counterpart.[29] Similarly, in dealing with middle-class leaders altogether outside the West Midlands, Black Country elites were decreasingly passive. For most of the nineteenth century the district's leaders absorbed various attitudes, institutions and strategies from counterparts in larger, wealthier and better-established towns. But by the end of the century the area was spreading its own innovations, such as Fair Trade and the more successful Pleasant Sunday Afternoon movement, to the Metropolis as well as to other cities.[30]

But what of Black Country businessmen's relations with the landed elite? Perhaps, if Rubinstein is correct, isolation from the aristocracy undermined the industrialists' potential for influence, especially at the regional and national levels. On the other hand, insofar as Wiener's interpretation is accurate, possibly the social potential of Black Country businessmen was neutralized as gentrification lured them away both from their firms and from the civic activities of industrial towns. It is now appropriate, therefore, to determine how far the district's top industrialists and other leading businessmen avoided this dilemma by developing interactions with the aristocracy and gentry that preserved or even enhanced middle-class leverage.

[29] *Ibid.*, chapter 3, especially p. 113; J. T. Bunce, *History of the Corporation of Birmingham*, 3 vols (Birmingham 1878–1902), vol. 1, p. 396; B. M. D. Smith, 'Arthur Chamberlain', in D. J. Jeremy and C. Shaw, eds., *Dictionary of Business Biography* (hereafter *DBB*), 5 vols (London, 1984–6), vol. 1, pp. 633–43; R. P. T. Davenport-Hines, 'Ralph Dudley Docker', *ibid.*, vol. 2, pp. 128–33; E. Jones, 'Arthur Keen', *ibid.*, vol. 3, pp. 570–3; R. A. Church, *Kenricks in Hardware: A Family Business 1791–1966* (Newton Abbot, 1969); H. Lloyd, *The Quaker Lloyds in the Industrial Revolution* (London, 1975); R. P. T. Davenport-Hines, *Dudley Docker: The Life and Times of a Trade Warrior* (Cambridge, 1984), p. 10.
[30] Trainor, 'Authority', pp. 384–8.

III

Contact between top Black Country business families and the landed elite increased significantly between Victoria's accession and the outbreak of the First World War; during the same period the relative power of the two groups altered substantially. Whereas in the early nineteenth century Black Country aristocrats dominated public affairs and had little to do with the local worthies who began to challenge their rule vigorously from the 1830s, by 1914 co-operation prevailed in a context of enhanced power and prestige for middle-class leaders.

In the interim, top Black Country businessmen penetrated even institutions centred on the landed elite such as London society and public schools. Yet for the district's business families, as for those in other regions, much social segregation persisted in these contexts. When mixing occurred, landed influence on the interaction remained much stronger than industrial.[31] The area's manufacturers secured more influence in parliamentary politics. Early and mid-nineteenth-century leverage by Black Country industrialists on mainly landed MPs had been subject to 'transmission losses'[32] on issues ranging from free trade to Irish disestablishment. Yet, by the late nineteenth century most Black Country seats were held either by local manufacturers or by professional men with extensive local business interests such as the Unionist MP for West Bromwich, the barrister and iron merchant J. Ernest Spencer. Also, from 1867 the increasing number of Black Country seats facilitated pressure on supposedly aristocratic governments, notably in bi-partisan lobbying at Westminster for concessions on transport rates and mildly progressive social legislation.[33]

Within the district, middle-class leaders secured an even better settlement with landed potentates. From the 1850s the survival of aristocratic influence in the Black Country depended upon the

---

[31] *Ibid.*, pp. 102–3; many examples of public schooling, especially at Rugby, in 'Midland Captains of Industry', *Birmingham Gazette and Express* (hereafter *BGE*), 1907–9; F. M. L. Thompson, 'Britain', in D. Spring, ed., *European Landed Elites in the Nineteenth Century* (London, 1977), pp. 33–7; L. Davidoff, *The Best Circles: Society Etiquette and the Season* (London, 1973), pp. 59–61, 63–4, 66–7; Rubinstein, 'Cultural Explanations of Britain's Economic Decline: True or False?' (unpublished paper, Enterprise, Public Policy and Society symposium, University of Glasgow, 1986).

[32] *Cf.* Perkin, *Origins*, p. 272.

[33] Trainor, 'Peers', pp. 85–9, 96–101, and 'Authority', pp. 212–22, 224–31.

peers' abandoning attempts to dominate local affairs and adopting roles as generous celebrities with diminished power. Admittedly the noblemen salvaged much from the wreck of their previously pre-eminent position. They retained a modicum of influence over elections: Lord Dartmouth's heir, for example, won West Bromwich for the Conservatives in both 1910 contests. In addition, the peers continued to draw large profits from the district, and the aristocrats' increasingly progressive social interventions discouraged urban enthusiasm for legislative limits on their mineral royalties. Nevertheless, the new aristocratic–middle class relationship which emerged after mid-century, though more favourable to the noblemen than had seemed probable during the turbulent 1840s, was at least as much on middle-class as aristocratic terms. For instance, the peers' much-diminished political leverage depended on aristocratic deference to the wishes of the businessmen and professionals who bore the brunt of organizing local election campaigns.[34] Also, in return for their reduced hostility toward aristocrats, local middle-class leaders secured resources and prestige for civic projects, directed at the largely working-class population, to which aristocrats such as Dartmouth and Dudley gave land, cash and conspicuous ceremonial presence. Moreover, while the aristocrats gained urban allies, businessmen obtained influential advocates at quarter sessions and at Westminster. For instance, the first Earl of Dudley obtained new county court facilities for the town, while his son supplied it with valuable advice on issues such as tramways and electricity supply.[35]

Thus, in marked contrast to the early nineteenth-century pattern of increasingly disputed aristocratic dominance, by the 1910s the landed–industrial relationship had become more harmonious, more balanced, and more likely to assist the propertied classes as a whole both within and beyond the district's borders. The new pattern was evident in style as well as in substance, notably in the increasingly complimentary manner in which peers and local middle-class worthies treated each other in public. As late as the 1850s Lord Hatherton was satirized at a Wolverhampton civic occasion by a city father whom he had snubbed during a meeting at the nobleman's seat.[36] Similarly, in 1857 the fifth Earl of Dart-

---

[34] Trainor, 'Authority', pp. 221–2, and 'Peers', pp. 98–100, 111–12.
[35] *Dudley Herald*, 9 May 1885; Trainor, 'Peers', pp. 103–15, especially p. 111.
[36] W. H. Jones, *The Municipal Life of Wolverhampton* (London, 1903), pp. 88–9.

mouth condemned a local government body as a 'small, noisy fidgetty busybody of the middle class'. Yet from the 1870s Lord Dartmouth showered praise on the West Bromwich iron-founder Reuben Farley, the town's most prominent civic leader. By 1898, when the sixth Earl voiced strong approval of the West Bromwich Council, and was praised in return, reciprocal congratulations had become the norm.[37] Tensions persisted, especially during elections and sectarian agitations, but the atmosphere had improved markedly.

What accounts for this local *rapprochement*? The purchase of landed estates and the adoption of a landed lifestyle by a significant minority of the district's top businessmen in the later nineteenth and early twentieth century played a significant role in this process. Rubinstein underestimates the business incursion into landed society by focusing on Bateman's 1883 list (based on the 'New Domesday' survey of the early 1870s) of those owning estates of at least 2,000 acres which yielded at least £2,000 per year. At times Rubinstein implicitly imposes even higher criteria.[38] Current or former Black Country businessmen are not numerous in Bateman. However, at least a few business families from the Black Country and nearby urban districts appear in the New Domesday as owners of significant amounts of land below the 2,000-acre threshold. For example, the Wolverhampton banker's son W. F. Fryer owned 1,182 acres, while the Burton brewer M. T. Bass had 1,001.[39] Also, subsequent to Bateman, land sales continued in the West Midlands, as they did elsewhere, probably accelerating in the years immediately preceding the First World War if not before.[40] Moreover, in the Black Country, as in other districts, whole families might buy

---

[37] *Wolverhampton Chronicle*, 23 December 1857; *Free Press* (West Bromwich), 8 June 1878; *Weekly News* (Oldbury), 30 July 1898.

[38] 'New Men of Wealth', pp. 129–38, and *Men of Property*, pp. 213–18; J. Bateman, *The Great Landowners of Great Britain and Ireland*, ed. D. Spring (New York, 1971, 4th edn; first published 1883); Spring and Spring, 'Social Mobility', pp. 336–7.

[39] *Parliamentary Papers* 1874, 72 Part II [C.1097], Staffordshire, 5, 21.

[40] *Cf.* F. M. L. Thompson, *English Landed Society*, pp. 319–20, 322, and H. Clemenson, *English Country Houses and Landed Estates* (London, 1982), p. 156. Compare Rubinstein, 'New Men of Wealth', p. 129. Of the 238 'principal seats' in Staffordshire in 1884, ninety-seven were no longer listed by 1912; of the 141 which remained, as few as seventy-four may have stayed in the same family (problems concerning surname changes and temporary occupiers prevent certainty). (Kelly & Co., *Kelly's Directory of Birmingham, Staffordshire, Warwickshire and Worcestershire* [London, 1884, 1912].)

significant amounts of land even when individual entrepreneurs did not, as the case of the iron-making Bagnalls indicates.[41] Furthermore, as a recent study of West Sussex shows, significant portions of rural areas could be bought up in comparatively small parcels.[42] More importantly, upper-middle-class individuals and the districts into which they moved might be significantly affected by land purchase even in the absence of large acreage or major country houses.[43]

Enticed by the enduring appeal of rural lifestyles, spurred by the district's increasingly dirty and dense development and encouraged by the ease of railway travel, many Black Country industrialists headed for the countryside. By the 1850s most of the important manufacturers and coalmasters of West Bromwich, for instance, lived outside the locality, and the trend accelerated thereafter. In 1872, when the ironmaster James Bagnall died at his home in the town, it was thought unusual 'for a gentleman of such princely means'.[44] A few left the West Midlands altogether, notably Lord Dudley's former chief agent, Frederick Smith, who added 'Shenstone' to his name and settled in Sussex about 1870. More frequently, West Midland businessmen moved to salubrious settings within the region. By the turn of the century rural residence by industrial families was common, as West Midland biographical directories suggest.[45] For example, in a survey of 'Midland Captains of Industry', one-third of the manufacturers with significant Black Country ties and identifiable residences had houses outside the region's towns and suburbs.[46]

This impression of significant rural penetration holds even when viewed from the perspective of the countryside itself. By the 1900s many county families had business backgrounds, mainly in industry. This was true of at least thirty-three of the sixty-nine listed by

[41] F. M. L. Thompson, 'Business and Landed Elites', *passim*; Trainor, 'John Nock Bagnall', *DBB*, vol. 1, pp. 91–6 and sources cited there.

[42] M. Beard, 'The Impact of the First World War on Agricultural Society in West Sussex' (unpublished M.Litt. thesis, University of Cambridge, 1985), chapter 1.

[43] On the latter, see F. M. L. Thompson, 'The Mighty and their Seats', *Times Literary Supplement*, 7 September 1984.

[44] 'Minutes, Lords S. C. West Bromwich Improvement Bill 1854', House of Lords RO, p. 5; *Wednesbury and West Bromwich Advertiser*, 20 January 1872.

[45] For example, E. Gaskell, *Worcestershire Leaders Social and Political* (Queenhithe, 1908), pp. 68–9; F. B. Ludlow, *County Biographies 1901: Staffordshire* (Birmingham 1901), p. 140; C. Penn, *Staffordshire and Shropshire at the Opening of the Twentieth Century* (Brighton, 1907), p. 62.

[46] Calculated from 'Midland Captains of Industry', *BGE*, 1907–9 (Birmingham Reference Library).

Walford with seats in southern Staffordshire in 1900, a strikingly high proportion even when the inclusiveness of the source is taken into account.[47] For the whole county the stricter criterion of 'principal seats' reveals a much more modest but still far from negligible proportion: at least fifteen of 170 were held by business families in 1912.[48] This picture of substantial though limited business incursion is also confirmed by the social backgrounds of the initial owners of the more distinguished West Midland country houses built between 1835 and 1914: half aristocrats and gentry, half from the middle classes.[49]

Movement to the countryside by West Midland businessmen was not restricted either to Black Country firms or to industrialists. Birmingham manufacturers and financiers also participated in this migration, as did the well-to-do Birmingham cheesemonger James Watson (later MP for Shrewsbury), and the Birmingham land surveyor Thomas Hodgetts, who became lord of the manor of Church Clent, Worcestershire and a leading figure in the religious life of the countryside.[50] In the West Midlands, industrialists, professionals, bankers and merchants seemed equally prone to gentrify; wealth levels and cultural orientation evidently were more important variables than were occupational distinctions.[51] Thus gentrification reinforced rather than weakened the links between industrialists and the region's other middle-class leaders. Also, there is little reason to suppose that either before or after their rural moves the region's industrialists found it more difficult to deal with the landed elite than did West Midland financiers, merchants and professionals.[52]

---

[47] E. Walford, *The County Families of the United Kingdom*, 40th edn (London, 1900), including all those listed as residing in the vicinity of Lichfield, Rugeley and Cannock as well as Wolverhampton and other Black Country towns.

[48] *Kelly's Directory of Birmingham . . .* (London, 1912), pp. vii–viii.

[49] Calculated from J. Franklin, *The Gentleman's Country House and its Plan 1835–1914* (London, 1981), 'Catalogue of Houses' (pp. 255–69) which understates the industrialists' representation in the study sample (Spring and Spring, 'Social Mobility', pp. 342–4).

[50] R. S. Sayers, *Lloyds Bank in the History of English Banking* (Oxford, 1957), pp. 59, 84; *BGE*, 11 June 1907; *Worcestershire Leaders*, pp. 117–18.

[51] *Cf.* Rubinstein, 'New Men of Wealth', p. 134, and *Men of Property*, p. 217; Spring and Spring, 'Social Mobility', p. 344. Compare A. C. Howe, *The Cotton Masters 1830–1860* (Oxford, 1984), p. 315.

[52] Compare Rubinstein, 'Wealth, Elites', pp. 115–16 and F. M. L. Thompson, 'English Landed Society in the Nineteenth Century', in P. Thane *et al.*, eds., *The Power of the Past: Essays for Eric Hobsbawm* (Cambridge, 1984), p. 201.

Within this rural exodus even modest estates carried significant social meaning. According to Rubinstein, such land purchases 'at best ... represented merely the respect that wealth paid to status, not an authentic transfiguration of class placement'.[53] Yet the Black Country case shows that, without bringing a total change in class identity, rural migration even to parcels of land modest by aristocratic standards enhanced the relationship between the landed elite and business families.[54] In the Victorian and Edwardian decades the line between the landed and the non-landed was blurred and complex.

The ironmaster John Nock Bagnall's retirement to less than 500 acres at Shenstone Moss near Lichfield in 1863 earned him some recognition as a 'country gentleman'. Enhanced status helped him become one of the first veterans of Black Country business to be named High Sheriff of Staffordshire. It also assisted him in his promotion of the Conservative Party and the Church of England in an area where these institutions gained many middle-class recruits in the later nineteenth century.[55] The steel giant Sir Alfred Hickman achieved greater results with even fewer acres. Having built an elaborate house at rural Wightwick, near Tettenhall, Hickman became one of the best riders in the Albrighton Hunt and made regular pilgrimages to Scottish 'shootings'. Sir Alfred's family mixed with the region's grandees at sport and church if not at table. Consequently it was plausibly suggested that Hickman displayed 'all the tastes of a country gentleman'. Hickman's success at the county level, where he was a deputy lieutenant as well as a JP, culminated a process which had begun just before mid-century with seats on the bench for a few top ironmasters, significantly often the owners of large houses in or near the countryside. Just as Hickman's move out of Wolverhampton in the mid-1890s probably contributed to his baronetcy in 1903, so his active role in the countryside helps to explain the sixth Earl of Dartmouth's presiding

---

[53] 'New Men of Wealth', p. 135.
[54] F. M. L. Thompson, 'English Landed Society', pp. 209–10. Likewise, as long as the houses on these estates were well appointed, they could be social assets without rivalling the scale or grandeur of West Midland aristocratic seats such as Dartmouth's Patshull House or Witley Court (compare Stone and Stone, *An Open Elite?*, pp. 211–25).
[55] M. Willett, *John Nock Bagnall* (London, 1885), p. 51; Trainor, 'Bagnall', pp. 91–6.

at a Tory testimonial for the industrialist and attending his funeral.[56]

Liberals as well as Tories participated in this exodus, though perhaps less frequently. Among the earliest was the ironmaster John Barker. Having acquired a seat just over the boundary in Shropshire in the 1830s, he continued to play a major role in the affairs of south Staffordshire, including close co-operation with Tory Anglicans.[57] A later counterpart was the long-serving Wolverhampton MP and Cabinet Minister Henry Hartley Fowler (subsequently Viscount Wolverhampton). A prominent local solicitor with close ties to local industrialists, Fowler built the substantial 'Woodthorne' outside the town in 1867 and lived there until his death 44 years later, having pursued a notably moderate line in politics in the interim.[58] Even Liberal migrants, then, often approached public affairs in a fashion compatible with the outlook of the landed elite.

These and other geographically mobile Black Country businessmen verified a West Bromwich doctor's 1878 comment that '[i]n the upper classes the lower grades seemed anxious to associate with those above them'.[59] Yet with the exceptions of W. O. Foster and the Staffordshire brewers ennobled in the 1880s such migrants did not seriously attempt either to become massive landed proprietors or to lead the region's landed society. Thus the business families' auxiliary role in the countryside, particularly in the first generation, does not indicate that their rural migration was socially futile.[60] Evidently tensions between old and new rural elites had less impact than did the shared appeal of the countryside's pastimes. For example, the Albrighton Hunt afforded a regular opportunity for many Black Country families to mix harmoniously with the aristoc-

---

[56] W. Pollard & Co., *The County of Stafford and Many of its Family Records* (Exeter, 1897), p. 24; Trainor, 'Sir Alfred Hickman', *DBB*, vol. 3, pp. 209–16; D. Philips, 'The Black Country Magistracy 1835–1860: A Changing Elite and the Exercise of its Power', *Midland History*, 3 (1976), pp. 161–89.

[57] F. M. L. Thompson, *English Landed Society*, p. 128; Jones, *Municipal Life*, p. 47.

[58] M. W. Greenslade, ed., *V. C. H. Staffs.*, 20, p. 5; E. H. Fowler, *The Life of Henry Hartley Fowler, First Viscount Wolverhampton G.C.S.I.* (London, 1912).

[59] *Free Press*, 14 September 1878.

[60] *Cf.* F. M. L. Thompson, 'Britain', pp. 32–3. Compare Rubinstein, 'New Men of Wealth', pp. 140–1.

racy and gentry in a sphere where businessmen such as Hickman soon played prominent roles.[61]

IV

Thus the movement of many Black Country businessmen to the countryside and their participation in rural activities encouraged co-operation between the district's upper middle class and its aristocracy. Yet gentrification was a complex process, and its intricacies do much to explain why, within this pattern of co-operation, the region's businessmen enjoyed increasing leverage in relation to the landed elite. For gentrification was neither so widespread, nor so thorough, nor so harmful to civic and industrial life nor so imbalanced as commentators such as Wiener have assumed.

By no means all members of the upper ranks of the Black Country's middle class became even small-scale country gentlemen. Despite the increasing outflow many continued to live in the towns themselves; even in the later nineteenth century the district's localities had quiet pockets available for families such as the iron-making Elwells of Wednesbury.[62] Similarly, at the turn of the century, grimy and crowded Bilston contained large houses inhabited by substantial employers such as Stephen Cole and John Harper.

Families desiring greater exclusivity and lower density could find them in nearby suburbs without moving into the countryside proper; in the West Midlands as elsewhere, suburbia catered for people desiring a semi-rural lifestyle as well as for those merely wanting a more salubrious urban life.[63] Tettenhall (just two miles from Wolverhampton town centre) was ideal for the former purpose, Birmingham's Edgbaston (only a few miles from the southern edge of the Black Country) for the latter.[64] Both offered

---

61 M. W. Greenslade and J. G. Jenkins, eds., *V. C. H. Staffs.*, 2, p. 361; 'Diary of Lady Joan Legge', in possession of Mr and Mrs J. K. Winter, Norwich, vol. 1, November 1906; J. E. Auden, *A Short History of the Albrighton Hunt* (London, 1905), pp. 38, 57, 82, 84–7, 92–3, 98–9, 110, 115, 118.

62 C. J. L. Elwell, *The Iron Elwells: A Family Social History* (Ilfracombe, 1964), p. 96.

63 *Cf.* F. M. L. Thompson, 'Introduction', in Thompson, ed., *The Rise of Suburbia* (Leicester, 1982), p. 16. Suburban, urban and rural locations were equally numerous among Black Country 'Midland Captains of Industry' (*BGE*, 1907–9).

64 *V. C. H. Staffs.*, 20, pp. 3–12, 21; Cannadine, *Lords and Landlords*, part 2.

many degrees of elegance and of seclusion: especially in the case of Tettenhall, it is difficult to determine where rural residence ended and high-class, low-density suburbia began.[65] Hickman's seat was not far from elegant houses built on only a few acres of ground. Such were the dwellings of one branch of the Manders (who built a ballroom), of the brewing Hodsons (who employed William Morris's firm as decorators), and of another Mander household (whose Wightwick Manor was so exquisitely constructed that it is now a National Trust property).[66]

If the scale of the home and its 'paraphernalia of gentility'[67] were sufficient, the urban as well as the suburban alternatives to rural migration could sustain increased public, if not social, contact with the aristocracy. For instance, Reuben Farley, who used large industrial profits to build an elaborate house in West Bromwich but refused to move farther afield, became a trusted urban collaborator of successive Earls of Dartmouth.[68] Thus, what might be called 'villa gentrification' facilitated landed/middle-class co-operation without taking upper-middle-class leaders at all far from the bulk of the population at whom their public initiatives were largely aimed.[69]

Neither rural nor suburban residence entailed a total break from the civic life of the Black Country. As new rural dwellers such as Bagnall and Hickman usually lived at most a few miles from Black Country towns, and as suburban exiles resided even closer, the role of the migrants in urban public affairs was often altered rather than ended. Continued participation was particularly easy for business-men, like the West Bromwich manufacturer and Birmingham MP Ebenezer Parkes, who retained an urban as well as a rural resi-dence.[70] Even for those industrialists with a single home outside the town in which their works was located, civic activity often remained vigorous. For instance, the Bilston pressed-metal-manufacturer J. W. Sankey, despite residing in Wolverhampton, twice served as

[65] *Cf.* T. R. Slater, 'Family, Society and the Ornamental Villa on the Fringes of English Country Towns', *Journal of Historical Geography*, 4 (1978), p. 131.
[66] On the latter see M. Girouard, *The Victorian Country House* (London, 1979 edition), pp. 375–80.
[67] *Cf.* J. A. Banks, *Prosperity and Parenthood: A Study of Family Planning among the Victorian Middle Classes* (London, 1954).
[68] Trainor, 'Reuben Farley', *DBB*, vol. 2, pp. 323–8.
[69] Compare Stone and Stone, *An Open Elite?*, pp. 403–5.
[70] Gaskill, Jones & Co., *Warwickshire Leaders Social and Political* (London, 1894), p. 116.

chairman of the former town's council and played a major role in key public improvements there.[71]

Even when various types of gentrification encouraged Black Country industrialists to drop such detailed civic involvement, their new residence and lifestyle helped them to become local philanthropic celebrities in tandem with peers and to forge useful ties to institutions at regional or national level. In a district which craved glamour, the urban leadership of top manufacturers was enhanced rather than diminished once the trappings of gentility supplemented the prestige conferred by job-generating industrial wealth. Thus in the Black Country the Kenricks, who lived in great state in Edgbaston, abandoned week-by-week municipal activity in West Bromwich, where their factory lay. Yet they became key benefactors and ceremonial presidents in many of the latter locality's civic projects and, more generally, linked that emerging town to the better-developed organizations of Birmingham itself.[72] Likewise the increasingly grand Sir Alfred Hickman, who remained loosely but prominently involved in the charities and council of Wolverhampton, coupled that town and the Black Country generally not only to Staffordshire's rural grandees but also to the West End (where he entertained liberally in his Kensington house) and to Westminster, where he tirelessly campaigned for the district's interests. Meanwhile, the more recently upwardly mobile ranks of the middle class, men like the former workman and subsequent spring-manufacturer John Brockhouse of West Bromwich, who less often lived in the countryside or even in opulent suburbs, efficiently took over week-by-week leadership in local civic organizations.[73] These various forms of continued civic involvement by the upper middle class provided a further link to such aristocrats as the second Earl of Dudley, who twice served as mayor of his titular town in the 1890s.[74]

While gentrification did not enhance business efficiency, neither did it destroy the economic effectiveness of rural migrants.[75]

---

[71] Ludlow, *Staffordshire*, p. 139; E. Jones, 'John William Sankey', *DBB*, vol. 5, pp. 61–2.

[72] *Free Press*, 16 March 1878; Church, *Kenricks*, p. 42.

[73] Trainor, 'Hickman'; C. Mackenzie, *Brockhouse: A Study in Industrial Evolution* (West Bromwich, 1945), pp. 11, 13–16.

[74] For the continued involvement of aristocrats in the municipal, philanthropic and, to a lesser extent, religious and political affairs of the Black Country, see Trainor, 'Peers', pp. 89–90.

[75] Compare J. Harris and P. Thane, 'British and European Bankers, 1880–1914: An "Aristocratic Bourgeoisie"?', in Thane *et al.*, eds., *The Power of the Past*, p. 227.

Several took leading roles in relaunching West Midland industry from the 1890s. Foremost among them was Hickman. The steel-master 'emulate[d] the Germans in the application of science to industry' and crammed business as well as hunting and politics into single weeks or even individual days. As a local newspaper com-mented, he 'combine[d] in an admirable degree the qualities of an industrial king and a country squire and would not be satisfied to relinquish active share in the sphere of either'. Of Hickman's five sons who lived to maturity, two opted for the professions, but the other three made highly successful careers, despite public school educations, in the diversifying family firms. The houses they bought were, like their father's, within easy striking distance of the Black Country.[76]

Even more thorough gentrification often took a long time to sever business ties. James Foster, the Stourbridge iron-making giant, moved to Stourton Castle in rural Kinver, five miles west of Stourbridge, in 1853. Yet, despite subsequent migrations to more extensive and more distant land purchases, the sale of the firm by Foster's great-nephew did not occur until 1919, when passive share ownership had long eclipsed landholding as well as entrepreneurship as a source of family income.[77] The Fosters' tenacity was by no means unique. In the chain-making Hingley family, second-generation Sir Benjamin's love of work and absence of genteel airs struck an obituarist as exceptional in 1905. However, the acquisition of a truly rural residence by Hingley's successor, his nephew, did not inhibit the latter's passionate involvement in business. Similarly, while Reuben Farley's sons differed from the founder in their public school education and country dwellings, they returned to the firm after military service and commuted daily from Warwickshire to the works in West Bromwich.[78] Thus at least until 1914 most gentrified Black Country families continued to draw their identity from the town and the counting-house as well as from the rural fringe and the hunting field.

Undoubtedly such persistence in business entailed costs as well as benefits. There was some justification for the view, voiced by

---

[76] *Wolverhampton Journal*, March 1905; *BGE*, 26 March 1907; Trainor, 'Hickman', pp. 211–12.

[77] *V. C. H. Staffs.*, 20 pp. 60–1; Mutton, 'Foster Family', pp. 71, 78, 80, 82–3, 210, 218, 240, and 'William Orme Foster' in *DBB*, vol. 2, p. 411.

[78] *Dudley Herald*, 20 and 27 May 1905; Trainor, 'Sir Benjamin Hingley', *DBB*, vol. 3, pp. 261–8, especially p. 262; Trainor, 'Farley', pp. 324–5.

Halesowen ironmaster Walter Somers in 1907, that Oxbridge educations had harmed many old Staffordshire firms. Yet Somers, who took his own sons into the family business after a technical education, may have been following the regional rule rather than the exception. Many Black Country business offspring supplemented public or grammar schooling either with a tour of business establishments abroad or with technically-based education in such Midland institutions as Mason's College, later the University of Birmingham.[79] Although the business enthusiasm of partially gentrified businessmen was sometimes deficient,[80] the drive of a rurally resident businessman such as Dudley Docker suggests that entrepreneurial energy often survived contact with fresh air and open spaces.[81] Perhaps such families' economic longevity blocked new entrants to the detriment of the district's prosperity. Yet there was much renewal and discrimination within families, especially to allow the dignified retirement of the old, and many altogether new recruits arrived from the 1890s as the region's economy changed significantly.[82] Often salaried managers, these newcomers were seldom rural dwellers;[83] they helped to keep the rising tide of rural migration from becoming a flood.

Thus the economic power as well as the civic influence of the Black Country's industrial elite survived the rural migration of some of its leading members. The rising power of the district's upper middle class in relation to the aristocracy was also protected by the reciprocal nature of gentrification: it affected the behaviour of the landed elite as well as the actions of the industrial migrants. Although the landed elite had the advantage in shaping interactions within rural society, country gentlemen as well as businessmen had

[79] *BGE*, 18 June 1907; M. Bache, *Salter: The Story of a Family Firm 1760–1960* (West Bromwich, 1960), p. 39. *Cf.* M. Sanderson, *The Universities and British Industry* (London, 1972), pp. 98–9, 101, and 'The English Civic Universities and the "Industrial Spirit", 1870–1914', *Historical Research*, 61 (1988), pp. 90–104, esp. p. 100. Compare the emphasis on 'gentrification' by means of public schools and Oxbridge in D. J. Jeremy, 'Anatomy of the British Business Elite 1860–1980', *Business History*, 26 (1984), pp. 9–13.

[80] For an example see Mutton, 'Foster Family', pp. 62, 70–1, 82–3, 117, 158–9.

[81] *BGE*, 11 June 1907. *Cf.* Davenport-Hines, *Dudley Docker*, especially pp. 18–19.

[82] *Cf.* L. Davidoff and C. Hall, *Family Fortunes: Men and Women of the English Middle Class 1780–1850* (London, 1987), pp. 225–6.

[83] For example, W. E. Hipkins of W. and T. Avery (*BGE*, 12 November 1907), who took over active management of the firm while the baronet who headed the family enjoyed his Thames Valley estate.

to adjust to each other's presence, notably on horseback and in the parish church. The need to co-exist in these semi-domestic settings could only further mutual adjustments in public affairs, where, for example, aristocrats like the Earls of Dudley trimmed their supposed prerogatives in estate development to suit middle-class tastes just as ironmasters like Hickman adopted 'paternalistic' attitudes in politics.[84]

Yet the increased mingling between the landed elite and the upper middle class entailed by gentrification was not so close that it stifled the identity of the migrant industrialists. Just as no Black Country aristocrat ever took his agent's place on Birmingham's 'Change, the district's businessmen rarely 'aped' the aristocracy in the extreme manner satirized by the regional novelist Francis Brett Young.[85] Even the most elaborate of the gentrified houses near Wolverhampton, Tettenhall Towers – with many domestic inventions (including an internal telegraph) as well as a theatre, a racquet court and Turkish baths – was as much the large suburban dwelling of an eccentric second-generation ironmaster as it was a mock country house.[86] Likewise, many wealthy West Midlanders, including the very well-off Alfred Baldwin, father of the future Prime Minister, took no part in rural sports. Nor did they necessarily abandon Nonconformity or the Liberal Party, both of which retained considerable business strength in the district, or drop altogether criticism of the aristocracy, merely because, like successful people in many periods and countries, they had obtained secluded large houses.[87]

---

[84] *Cf.* F. M. L. Thompson, 'English Landed Society', pp. 201, 208, 210–11; Harris and Thane, 'British and European Bankers, 1880–1914', in Thane *et al.*, eds., *The Power of the Past*, pp. 217–18, 228.

[85] *Cf.* Rubinstein, 'New Men of Wealth', p. 134. Brett Young, a doctor's son imbued with a deep love of the countryside, evidently had an axe to grind against Black Country as well as Birmingham businessmen. For a partially contrasting approach to this source see Cannadine, 'This Little World: The Value of the Novels of Francis Brett Young as a Guide to the State of Midland Society 1870–1925', (Worcestershire Historical Society Occasional Publications, 4, 1982). For a more positive fictional account of the relations between gentrifying industrialists and decaying gentry see *Fuel of Fire* (London, 1902), by H. H. Fowler's daughter Edith Thorneycroft Fowler.

[86] "The Thorneycrofts' Patents and Inventions" (Wolverhampton, 1891); *V. C. H. Staffs.*, 20, pp. 21–2.

[87] For the progressive implications of middle-class enthusiasm for traditional cultural forms, see C. Dellheim, *The Face of the Past: The Preservation of the Medieval Inheritance in Victorian England* (Cambridge, 1982), especially pp. 177–82.

Thus, even the gentrified portion of Black Country business retained some of its middle-class cultural identity and much of its self-respect,[88] while their less rurally-minded counterparts were even less likely to act as aristocratic poodles. Moreover, in a region where the aristocracy itself often paid close attention to its urban business interests, anti-industrial values were unlikely to be spread by the landed elite. Of course, it was also improbable that the aristocracy would be overwhelmed by an influx whose children only infrequently married their own,[89] and whose incursions accounted for only part of the fluidity of West Midland landed society during the half-century preceding the First World War. Nevertheless, the limited nature of gentrification allowed migrant businessmen to retain much of the leverage they were gaining in spheres removed from rural society.

A final step in obtaining a balanced view of gentrification in the Black Country, therefore, is to place it in the perspective of the many other factors influencing the relationship between the landed elite and industrialists. Some of the increased contact between the two groups owed little to the rural exodus of businessmen.[90] Also, insofar as inter-class harmony rested on aristocratic acceptance of the inevitability of increased middle-class power, industrialists displayed more influence 'on 'Change' and in urban committee rooms than in the hunting field or at quarter sessions. Moreover, movement to the countryside was a result as well as a cause of the softening of attitudes between the upper middle class and the aristocracy. H. H. Fowler, for example, effusively and publicly praised the peerage and the House of Lords five years before he built his country seat.[91]

Inter-class co-operation, then, also depended upon a number of forces other than gentrification. The diminution of sectarian

---

[88] For examples of top Black Country businessmen retaining social ties with the lesser ranks of the district's middle class see C. J. L. Elwell, ed., *A Lady of Wednesbury Forge: The Diary of Georgina Elwell 1868–1869* (Tipton, 1976), pp. 1, 7; Francis Brett Young, *My Brother Jonathan* (London, 1969; first published 1928), p. 2.

[89] Such marriages were limited to a few of the most gentrified families marrying offspring of minor landed families. For part of the national pattern of such intermarriage, see C. Erickson, *British Industrialists: Steel and Hosiery 1850–1950* (Cambridge, 1959), pp. 45–9, 118–21.

[90] Notably in business, for example the public company organized around Lord Dartmouth's most modern West Bromwich pit (Minutes, Sandwell Park Colliery Company, Staffordshire RO and West Bromwich Central Library).

[91] Fowler, *Life*, pp. 58–60.

tension in the area eased an irritant which had long poisoned relations between Anglican peers and the many Black Country manufacturers who had been raised as Nonconformists. Similarly, the considerable regional impact of the Liberal Unionist secession united many aristocrats and industrialists in a single political coalition for the first time.[92] Even more importantly, the marked interpenetration of middle-class and aristocratic economic and social interests in the district encouraged co-operation,[93] especially in the face of the Black Country's frequently imperilled prosperity and its ever more sophisticated working-class movement. Moreover, the balance of urban wealth and institutions had shifted toward the middle class, encouraging aristocratic flexibility toward its increasingly unified, active and sophisticated elites. Meanwhile, middle-class civic leaders discovered the special value, in a 'black' region, of aristocratic glamour for enhancing civic improvement projects, notably when the Duke and Duchess of York visited Wolverhampton in 1900 under the wing of the Earl and Countess of Dartmouth.[94]

Nevertheless, gentrification was related to many of these other factors promoting co-operation in a context of increased middle-class power. Even the royal visit to Wolverhampton, though it indicated the enduring importance of aristocratic rank, even more strikingly revealed the high standing of the Black Country's semi-gentrified industrial elite when the Yorks called on the Mayor, S. Theodore Mander, at Wightwick Manor.[95] While aristocratic prestige probably had particular legitimacy for most middle-class rural migrants, the effect on the upper class of finding industrialists as respected neighbours may also have been profound. In any case, rural migration discouraged sharp political and sectarian agitation even though it did not necessarily produce formal changes of affiliation. Also, shared residence almost certainly made it easier for peers and industrialists to realize the extent of their shared economic and social interests. While gentrification was not the sole or even the chief cause of inter-class co-operation, then, it helped

---

[92] Trainor, 'Authority', pp. 171–83, 193, 208–11, 229–30.
[93] Trainor, 'Peers', pp. 70–9, 95–6.
[94] 'Diary of Mary Countess of Dartmouth', in the possession of Mr and Mrs J. K. Winter, vol. 2, 21 July 1900; Jones, *Municipal Life*.
[95] G. le M. Mander, *The History of Mander Brothers 1773–1955* (Wolverhampton, 1955), p. 175.

to produce the change in relations between the landed elite and industrialists which it also symbolized.

Thus, in the Black Country extensive yet circumscribed gentrification played a significant role in a multi-faceted, though incomplete, *rapprochement* between middle-class leaders and the landed elite. Rural migration by industrialists did much to promote significant contact with the aristocracy; the complex nature of the rural exodus helped to ensure that this contact was on increasingly equal terms. Therefore, because of gentrification and a range of other factors connected with it, although the upper and upper middle classes of the Black Country had by no means merged, peers and top manufacturers were key members of an increasingly united elite which, by the end of the century, presided over an area with much better access to national power structures and a far more secure social climate than in the 1830s. Meanwhile, Black Country industrialists were also closely linked to the commercial, financial and professional leaders of the West Midlands, with whom they shared a balanced approach to gentility.

V

The Black Country, like all subjects of case studies, may be atypical in various misleading ways. Perhaps middle-class rural migration was rare elsewhere. Alternatively, conceivably the industrialists of other regions became more thoroughly and slavishly gentrified. Also, it may be that the West Midlands as a whole was unusual both in the interconnection of its various middle-class elites and in the pliability of its landed class.[96] For example, possibly the businessmen of the West Midlands suffered less from snobbery than did entrepreneurs elsewhere.[97] In addition, conceivably the combined elites of the region, as an early centre of provincial identity and of 'pressure from without', enjoyed privileged access to metropolitan power.[98]

Because the social history of Victorian elites is still a relatively new field, it is difficult to supply the comparative framework necessary to resolve these issues. Nevertheless, a few recent case

[96] On the latter, Smith, *Conflict and Compromise*, chapters 1 and 2.
[97] As suggested by Davenport-Hines, *Dudley Docker*, p. 15.
[98] *Cf.* J. Money, *Experience and Identity: Birmingham and the West Midlands, 1760–1800* (Manchester, 1977), C. Gill, *History of Birmingham* (London, 1952), vol. 1 (Manor and Borough to 1865).

studies of other industrial regions suggest that the Black Country is not the proverbial exception which proves the rule. Concerning business migration to the land, there was extensive and accelerating outward movement, with hints of corresponding changes in life-style and attitudes, in districts as varied as Clydeside, Tyneside, Humberside and the factory towns of Lancashire and the West Riding.[99] Indeed, in a sample drawn from the country as a whole manufacturers and related businessmen built a proportion of notable country houses which increased from a third to a half during the period.[100] Nevertheless, in northern areas, as in the West Midlands, the limitations to ruralization were also striking. As late as 1860 ambitious industrialists in textile Lancashire more often diversified into urban investment than into land. Likewise, until the end of the century upwardly mobile factory owners often located their large residences on the urban fringe and continued their involvements in business and local public affairs, though this was more difficult in cities than in towns.[101] In Lancashire, as in the West Midlands, grand lifestyles enhanced urban popularity.[102] Yet

[99] A. Slaven and S. G. Checkland, eds., *Dictionary of Scottish Business Biography* (Aberdeen, 1986), vol. 1; P. Joyce, *Work, Society and Politics: The Culture of the Factory in Later Victorian England* (Brighton, 1980), chapter 1; Benwell Community Project, *The Making of a Ruling Class: Two Centuries of Capital Development on Tyneside* (Newcastle, 1978), pp. 35–7; K. J. Allison, '"Hull Gent Seeks Country Residence": 1750–1850', *East Yorkshire Local History Series*, 36 (1981), p. 3; J. Reynolds, *Titus Salt and the Growth of Nineteenth-Century Bradford* (London, 1983), pp. 66, 74–5, 80, 82–3, 251. Even the figures of Anthony Howe (*The Cotton Masters*, pp. 29–32), who convincingly minimizes gentrification in Lancashire in the early part of the period, indicate that eleven per cent of the textile-manufacturers bought estates of 1,000 acres or more and that many others bought smaller parcels (*cf*. Perkin, 'An Open Elite', p. 499, and Trainor, review of Howe, in *Albion*, 18 (1986), pp. 114–15).

[100] Franklin, *The Gentleman's Country House*, p. 25, including those in 'food, drink and groceries' who arguably had more in common with industry than with banking or the professions.

[101] Howe, *Cotton Masters*, pp. 32, 252–4; Joyce, *Work*, pp. 25–8; Reynolds, *Salt*, p. 77 and chapter 4, *passim*; T. Koditschek, 'Class Formation and the Bradford Bourgeoisie' (unpublished Ph.D. thesis, Princeton University, 1981), pp. 653–4, 656–8; Trainor, 'Urban Elites', p. 5; D. A. Farnie, 'John Rylands of Manchester', *Bulletin of the John Rylands Library*, 56 (1974), pp. 93–4, 100, 107, 116, 119; N. J. Morgan, 'Perspectives on Wealth Creation and Consumption: Case Study – Sir Archibald Orr Ewing' (unpublished paper, Enterprise, Public Policy and Society Symposium, University of Glasgow, 1986); Rubinstein, 'New Men of Wealth', p. 129 n.18; *cf*. Allison, 'Hull Gent', pp. 4–8.

[102] G. N. Trodd, 'The Local Elite of Blackburn and the Response of the Working Class to its Social Control 1880–1900' (unpublished M.A. thesis, University of Lancaster, 1974), pp. 18, 35–6, 39–40, 57–8.

northern industrialists, like the provincial middle class generally, largely remained faithful to middle-class cultural patterns.[103]

Even in the late nineteenth century northern enterprise and civic life suffered less from gentrification than did the corresponding institutions of sprawling London, where the businessmen affected were more often commercial or professional than industrial. Admittedly, once the number of entrepreneurs seeking genteel living increased from the 1870s, northern towns as well as northern cities experienced more difficulties than did the Midlands in finding truly rural retreats nearby. The West Midlands was particularly fortunate in combining a regional capital with a discontinuous pattern of towns and an attractive rural fringe. Yet in Manchester too the rural exodus and its consequences for urban leadership evidently have been exaggerated. Also, as the case of Windermere shows, even after the long-standing appeal of suburbs close to northern towns faded, well-heeled emigrants could use distant second houses as staging posts for a reduction of involvement in urban business and civic life that was gradual in nature.[104]

Northern evidence also suggests that the economic stature of many West Midland industrialists, co-operation among West Midland elites, and the ability of the latter to make their combined voice heard in the Metropolis was not unique. For example, Lancashire textile masters, like their counterparts in Black Country iron and coal, generated substantial fortunes.[105] Also, the various middle-class elites of cotton Lancashire had interlocking interests which encouraged co-operation.[106] Moreover, throughout the North, as in the West Midlands, amicable relations between industrialists and the landed elite flourished without either massive

---

[103] C. Dellheim, 'Industrialism and Culture in Nineteenth-Century Britain', *Notebooks in Cultural Analysis*, 2 (1985), 227–48; Koditschek, 'Bradford Bourgeoisie', pp. 610–12.

[104] Beard, 'West Sussex', chapter 1; J. V. Beckett, *The Aristocracy in England 1660–1914* (Oxford, 1986), pp. 77–8; A. J. Kidd, 'The Middle Class in Nineteenth-Century Manchester', in Kidd and K. W. Roberts, eds., *City, Class and Culture: Studies of Social Policy and Cultural Production in Victorian Manchester* (Manchester, 1985), pp. 4, 12–13, 15; O. Westall, 'The Retreat to Arcadia: Windermere as a Select Residential Resort in the Late Nineteenth Century', in Westall, ed., *Windermere in the Nineteenth Century* (1976), pp. 42, 44–5, 50–1.

[105] Howe, *Cotton Masters*, pp. 43–6.

[106] *Ibid.*, pp. 35–7; Joyce, *Work*, p. 23. For a Sheffield contrast see Smith, *Conflict and Compromise*, chapter 2.

numbers of business migrants or their divorce from urban pursuits. Although in Lancashire the two groups had been on generally good terms even before 1860, ties between manufacturers and the aristocracy became closer in the later nineteenth century as rural migration increased. Nor did such amity imply business subservience. By the late nineteenth century Sheffield steelmasters were almost fully-fledged members of landed society yet remained active, successful industrialists. Finally, the West Midlands' influential access to Westminster does not appear exceptional, especially from the perspectives of Lancashire, with its powerful Manchester Chamber of Commerce, or of Sheffield, whose steelmasters were forces in national politics.[107]

Thus the partial gentrification of Victorian and Edwardian industrialists played a role in an accelerating shift of influence, often overlooked by recent writers, away from the aristocracy toward the middle class. At the local level the trend was most marked in the Midlands and the North, where gentrification was more limited and on more equal terms than in the Home Counties. Yet this shift of influence also prevailed in Parliament and in southern seaside resorts.[108] South as well as north of Watford, then, the upper middle class adopted a more confident approach to the landed elite. In the context of rising relative and absolute middle-class wealth, and of the increasing sophistication of middle-class elites, the limited and reciprocal convergence of lifestyle and attitudes which occurred was as much a sign of middle-class strength as of weakness. Insofar as industrialists participated, gentrification helped put manufacturers on a more equal footing with those in non-industrial middle-class occupations, who preceded manufacturers into the countryside in many regions,[109] as well as with the aristocracy. Such convergence allowed all three groups to

---

[107] Howe, *Cotton Masters*, pp. 126–32, 208–49, 262–9; Joyce, *Work*, p. 40; Smith, *Conflict and Compromise*, p. 257; A. Redford, *Manchester Merchants and Foreign Trade*, 2 vols (Manchester, 1956), vol. 2 (1850–1939).

[108] Cannadine, 'Introduction', to Cannadine, ed., *Patricians*, pp. 10–11 and *passim*. Cf. Joyce, *Work*, p. 40 and compare A. J. Mayer, *The Persistence of the Old Regime: Europe to the Great War* (London, 1981), pp. 88–94, 152–6, 162–6, 257–61. As far south as Portsmouth, businessmen displayed considerable resistance to gentility (J. Field, 'Wealth, Styles of Life and Social Tone amongst Portsmouth's Middle Class, 1800–75', in R. J. Morris, ed., *Class, Power and Social Structure in British Nineteenth-Century Towns* (Leicester, 1986), p. 99).

[109] Stone and Stone, *An Open Elite?*, p. 411.

make significant progress, in the years before 1914, toward the more fully united ruling elite which emerged after 1918.

VI

This essay has not attempted to deny that some gentrification of industrialists occurred between Victoria's accession and the First World War. It detects more of this process than does Rubinstein, though considerably less than does Wiener. Nor does it altogether reject the argument that, in combination with many factors, including some intractable structural problems, genteel lifestyle and attitudes may have made a marginal contribution to relative economic decline.[110] It would also be fruitless to dispute the argument that London-centred landed and non-industrial middle-class elites retained throughout the Industrial Revolution and beyond some of their centuries-old superiority in influence as well as wealth. Nevertheless, the essay has suggested that by 1914, in part because they were neither abject adherents nor bitter opponents of the traditional order, the incompletely gentrified manufacturing elite was not dominated by the aristocracy; nor was industry dominated by commerce, finance and the professions. It also suggests that it is wrong to posit, as Rubinstein does, an increasing or even a constant division between landowners and businessmen during the late nineteenth and early twentieth centuries.[111]

Thus, it would seem that both the maximalist and the minimalist interpretations of gentrification are recent myths rather than realities of the period preceding 1914. Industrialists, it emerges, were neither swamped by landed influence nor spurned by aloof aristocrats: manufacturers were too strong for the first outcome, the landed elite too flexible for the second. Also, at least within industrial regions, the industrialists' relationship to the landed class did not differ significantly from that of financiers and merchants. If this interpretation is accurate, it is time to begin re-writing the history of nineteenth- and early twentieth-century British elites with particular reference to the provincial entrepreneur and his fellow middle-class residents. In doing so, historians must remain conscious of gaps in resources, in prestige and in access to key

---

[110] Cf. Dellheim, 'Notes on Industrialism', pp. 236–44; B. Elbaum and W. Lazonick, eds., *The Decline of the British Economy* (Oxford, 1986).
[111] 'New Men of Wealth', pp. 143, 147.

institutions that lingered between land and trade, industry and commerce, North and South. Yet they will also need to recognize how influence passed up as well as down a social and urban hierarchy whose contours were less steep than recent interpretations have sometimes implied.

II

Power and social relations

6. *Poverty and progress in early modern England*

A. L. BEIER

Why was a system of state poor relief established in early modern England? Until recently, the reasons given would have included rising levels of poverty between *c.* 1500 and *c.* 1640 caused by the growth of population, the decline in the real value of wages, agrarian dislocation in the form of enclosure and engrossing, and increased 'subsistence migration' to towns. These developments, combined with an active state paternalism under the Tudors and early Stuarts, seemed sufficient reason for the implementation of a system of poor relief. Of late, however, this orthodoxy has come under attack, particularly in its assumption that levels of indigence were serious and growing worse in the period. Historians have re-examined the evidence and concluded that the numbers of poor have been exaggerated. The presumed causes of rising poverty have been scrutinized, and some now maintain that conditions in 'Tawney's Century' were not as bleak as previously portrayed. The country, they argue, was not overpopulated in relation to its resources and did not suffer greatly from Malthusian-type 'positive checks' to population growth; the effects of falling real wages, urbanization and harvest failures were not earth-shattering.[1] Even smallholding peasants – the period's quintessential victims accord-ing to the Tawney canon – have been rescued from enclosing and rack-renting landlords. They might have lost their lands in open-field villages, but instead of going on parish relief or becoming

I wish to thank Dr A. Grant and Mr J. E. King for their advice in preparing this essay and the editors of *History Sixth* for permission to reproduce in Section V a few lines previously published by them.
[1] D. M. Palliser, 'Tawney's Century: Brave New World or Malthusian Trap?', *Economic History Review*, 2nd series, 35 (1982), pp. 341–4, 348–51.

vagabonds, they migrated to pastoral regions, where they proliferated.[2]

But if this optimistic view were correct, would it have been
necessary to establish a system of state poor relief? None of the
historians who take the optimistic view have provided an answer to
this question. To deal with the problem, the question of the
numbers of the poor must be considered. Admittedly the danger of
debates about numbers, as Lawrence Stone warned in 1979, is that
they often generate more heat than light.[3] However, as he knows
perhaps better than most, the temperature frequently rises in
historical controversies irrespective of whether they involve quantitative issues. At any rate, the question of numbers is clearly
important, and therefore the first sections of this essay examine the
relevant evidence.

Another difficulty about quantification is that it tells us *what*
happened, but rarely *why*.[4] There are, of course, alternatives to
counting the poor to explain why England developed a system of
state relief. Traditionally, historians pointed to the institutional
shifts caused by the Reformation – the dissolution of monasteries,
religious guilds, hospitals and almshouses, and the need to replace
these facilities.[5] Another interpretation stressed the importance of
changing norms rather than numbers. The perception of poverty
among opinion-makers and magistrates was thought to have
changed with the Reformation, producing a harder line towards
mendicancy and vagrancy by the able-bodied, but encouraging
charity and official action to relieve the worthy, 'impotent' poor.
Whatever the numbers of the poor, this change of mind may have
been sufficient to bring about the institutional transformation.[6]

The origins of state relief in England do, no doubt, lie partly in
the Reformation period, but that is not the whole story, for outside
major towns and a few rural parishes, the full implementation of
parochial relief did not take place until almost a century later. This
essay's main contention is that the key period was from *c.* 1590 to

[2] R. B. Outhwaite, 'Progress and Backwardness in English Agriculture, 1500–
1650', *ibid.*, 39 (1986), pp. 8–11.
[3] L. Stone, 'The Revival of Narrative: Reflections on a New Old History', *Past and
Present*, 85 (1979), p. 12.
[4] *Ibid.*
[5] F. A. Gasquet, *Henry VIII and the English Monasteries* (London, 1906), vol. 2,
pp. 490–526; J. J. Scarisbrick, *Henry VIII* (London, 1968), pp. 511, 520–6.
[6] W. K. Jordan, *Philanthropy in England, 1480–1660* (London, 1959), pp. 254ff;
R. H. Tawney, *Religion and the Rise of Capitalism* (London, 1960), pp. 110–17.

c. 1660, and that the reason was a marked deterioration in economic and demographic conditions. That might seem obvious, since Parliament passed Acts in 1598 and 1601 making poor relief a civil responsibility of the parish, but things were not so simple. In reality, the laws were not widely enforced until after 1620, when a further downturn in the economy took place. But this was not simply the consequence of a one-off crisis; it will be argued that the establishment of state relief reflected fundamental changes in the economic and social order. Counting the poor makes a limited contribution to our understanding of these developments.

I

The most authoritative estimates for the numbers of poor in the sixteenth century are those of W. G. Hoskins. He found that that two-thirds of the inhabitants of provincial towns 'lived below or very near the poverty-line' in the early 1520s. Rural England was hardly better off: in Babergh Hundred in Suffolk nearly sixty per cent of the population 'were propertyless and must have rented what shelter they had'.[7] These figures, however, are now thought to exaggerate the numbers of poor. In towns, it is argued, Hoskins cast his net too widely: those with *nil* assessments in 1522 were not all 'total paupers'; some kept servants; others paid rents above those of the poorest cottagers. Those assessed at the lowest levels of £1 and £2 had other resources besides wage-earning – common rights, payments in kind and by-employments – which lifted them out of poverty.[8] In the countryside it has been determined that most smallholders whose lands were valued at £1 or less actually owned goods worth £3 or more. The upshot is that Hoskins's figures must be lowered: from two-thirds to a fifth in towns, and from three-fifths to one-tenth in the countryside.[9]

Similar objections are made against taking exemption from the

[7] W. G. Hoskins, 'English Provincial Towns in the Early Sixteenth Century', repr. in his book *Provincial England* (London, 1965), p. 84; W. G. Hoskins, *The Age of Plunder. The England of Henry VIII, 1500–1547* (London, 1976), p. 32.

[8] C. Phythian-Adams, *Desolation of a City. Coventry and the Urban Crisis of the Late Middle Ages* (Cambridge, 1979), p. 132; T. J. Tronrud, 'Dispelling the Gloom. The Extent of Poverty in Tudor and Early Stuart Towns: Some Kentish Evidence', *Canadian Journal of History*, 20 (1985), pp. 4–5.

[9] J. F. Pound, *Poverty and Vagrancy in Tudor England* (2nd edn London, 1986), pp. viii–xii. *Cf.* P. Slack, *Poverty and Policy in Tudor and Stuart England* (London, 1988), pp. 40–1.

Hearth Tax as a measure of poverty in the late seventeenth century. On this evidence it was assumed that between a third and a half of the population were in need in Charles II's reign; now it has been suggested that not all the exempt were actually poor. The Hearth Tax allowed exemptions on several grounds, which produced 'different and overlapping categories'. When the exempt are compared with those in the different categories and with the parish poor, it has been found that 'not all the exempt were living in poverty', and that not all the exempt were on poor relief. The inability to pay parish rates was one of the grounds for exemption, yet a significant number of those excused from the Hearth Tax actually paid rates. Another criterion for exemption was paying less than £1 a year in rent, but manorial records show some of the exempt had a few acres of land, or at least gardens, to support them.[10] In towns, it has been suggested, employment in manufacturing raised many craftsmen out of abject poverty, even though they might be exempt from tax.[11]

More specifically, when the records of parish poor relief are compared with exemptions from the Hearth Tax, it has been determined that a parish might have two-fifths of its households exempt, but that only a fifth or less appeared on the relief rolls in the same year. Finally, it has been pointed out that household size should be taken into account, because the poor usually had smaller households than the better off. When that is done, a quarter of households might have received relief, but they accounted for no more than 15 per cent of the population. Similar strictures have been levelled against Gregory King's 'Scheme' of national incomes for 1688, from which historians have deduced that 51 per cent of the population were decreasing the country's wealth. By the late seventeenth century, therefore, 'the poor in any meaningful modern sense formed only a minority of society'.[12]

Omissions are a further barrier to estimating the numbers of poor on the basis of these records. A study of Coventry in the early 1520s found that 'the "submerged" quarter of poorer households' was

[10] T. Arkell, 'The Incidence of Poverty in England in the Later Seventeenth Century', *Social History*, 12 (1987), pp. 32–3, 36.

[11] C. Husbands, 'Hearth Tax Exemption Figures and the Assessment of Poverty in the Seventeenth-Century Economy', in N. Alldridge, ed., *The Hearth Tax: Problems and Possibilities* (Humberside College of Higher Education, n.d.), p. 52.

[12] Arkell, 'Incidence of Poverty', pp. 24–9, 39–42, 45–7.

largely ignored. The assessment of 1522 alone omitted as many as 20 per cent of the city's households.[13] With lacunae on this scale is it possible accurately to determine the numbers of the needy? And the same question must be posed regarding the Hearth Taxes. A study of twenty-two counties has led one writer to conclude that nearly 40 per cent of the population were left out. Only two shires actually made returns above the 70 per cent plateau – Worcestershire and Warwickshire with 80 and 93 per cent respectively.[14] A final problem concerns the dates at which these records were compiled. The assessment of 1522 and the lay subsidies of 1524–5 antedate the period which, it is argued in this essay, experienced the greatest economic and demographic stresses, and which saw state relief being widely implemented for the first time. The Hearth Taxes, on the other hand, belong to a later period, when conditions are supposed to have improved. Neither source, then, is very helpful for testing the basic hypothesis of this essay.

Some documentation, however, does exist with which to overcome these problems. It amounts, in effect, to local censuses, which include details of people's wealth as well as their numbers. Admittedly monographic studies have obvious drawbacks, but the scarcity of the evidence rules out random sampling. Most studies to date have focused upon middling to large provincial towns, such as Ipswich, Norwich and Salisbury. This essay, in contrast, will examine seven villages (three in North Yorkshire, three in Kent and one in Norfolk), and two small to middling towns (Thirsk and Warwick). The censuses date from 1582 to 1630, and while these nine cases cannot be claimed to be typical, they are closer to the 'grass roots' than the larger towns about which most is known.[15]

Analyses of the censuses are presented in Tables 6.1 and 6.2. The gradations in wealth used derive from criteria employed by the local authorities. At Warwick, Shorne, Cawston and Thirsk four categories were distinguished: first, those able to pay poor rates; second, those unable to pay, but able to support themselves (listed as 'indifferent' at Thirsk); third, those who were poor, but were not given official relief (at Warwick described as 'ready to decay'; at Cawston, 'not so poor'); fourth, those actually granted relief or

---

[13] Phythian-Adams, *Desolation of a City*, pp. 156, 193.

[14] Husbands, 'Hearth Tax Exemption Figures', p. 46.

[15] For Cawston, see T. Wales, 'Poverty, Poor Relief and the Life-Cycle: Some Evidence from Seventeenth-Century Norfolk', in R. M. Smith, ed., *Land, Kinship and Life-Cycle* (Cambridge, 1984).

Table 6.1. *Mean household sizes*

	St Mary's, Warwick, 1582	Cawston, 1601
1 Rate-payers	(5.62)	(5.62)
2 Unable to pay, but not needing assistance	5.0	3.5
3 Poor, but not on relief	4.69	3.1
4 On relief	3.16	3.25

Sources: Warwick, T. Kemp, ed., *The Book of John Fisher, 1580–1587* (Warwick, n.d.), pp. 81–5, 87–94, 165–72; T. C. Wales, 'Poverty, Poor Relief and the Life-Cycle', in R. M. Smith, ed., *Land, Kinship and Life-Cycle* (Cambridge, 1984), pp. 390–4 (N.B. Warwick household sizes calculated from census of the poor for 1587, *ibid.*, pp. 165–72, which includes people from groups 2 and 3 in 1582; the totals for Cawston differ from Wales's because the poor granted relief, including occasional relief, are separated here).

apprenticed by the parish. At Strood, Grain, Carlton Miniott, Sand Hutton and Sowerby, the authorities lumped together the second and third groups.

In order to use this material it is necessary to calculate mean household sizes. For rate-payers (group 1, Table 6.1) a multiplier of 5.62 has been employed, based upon the mean average of Laslett's figures for gentlemen, clergy, yeomen, husbandmen, tradesmen and craftsmen. For the other groups, the multipliers have been calculated from the censuses of St Mary's, Warwick and Cawston. The figures for Cawston and Warwick are similar for group 4, but differ markedly for groups 2 and 3. This is because of the substantial numbers of lodgers in Warwick households. In a census of 1587, fifteen of the twenty-eight households in categories 2 and 3 included such 'inmates', accounting on average for two members of each household. In Cawston, the larger households were mainly families with large numbers of children.[16] Although Cawston held a market, its 700 souls hardly made it much of a town, and so its mean household sizes have been taken as the norm for rural parishes, while the Warwick results have been applied to the other town, Thirsk. There are dangers in applying mean household sizes across a number of communities, but without grasping this nettle we have

---

[16] P. Laslett, 'Mean Household Size in England Since the Sixteenth Century', in Laslett, ed., *Household and Family in Past Time* (Cambridge, 1974), p. 154; see also the list of sources in Table 6.1.

Table 6.2. Social structures and levels of need, 1582–1630 (in %)

	St Mary's Warwick 1582	Shorne 1598	Strood 1598	Grain 1598	Cawston 1601	Thirsk 1629–30	Carlton Miniott 1629	Sand Hutton 1629	Sowerby 1629
Estimated total population	n=1,828	n=354	n=723	n=63	n=768	n=1,172	n=139	n=158	n=318
1 Able to pay poor rates	30.4	66.7	69.2	61.9	57.0	64.3	64.8	81.6	77.7
2 Unable to pay, but not needing assistance	44.9	20.3	} 29.0	33.3	16.3	23.9	20.9	12.0	15.1
3 Poor, but not on relief	17.5	5.7		–	16.5	8.2	–	–	–
4 On relief	7.2	7.3	1.8	4.8	10.2	3.6	14.3	6.4	7.2

Sources: Warwick, Beier, 'Social Problems', p. 58; Shorne, E. Melling, *Kentish Sources. IV. The Poor* (Maidstone, 1964), pp. 12–17, P. Clark, *English Provincial Society from the Reformation to the Revolution* (Hassocks, 1977), pp. 239–40, Staffs., RO, D593, S/4/55/1, 10/30; Strood, Clark, *op.cit.*, Staffs. RO, S/4/55/; Cawston, Wales, *op. cit.*, pp. 369–70, 390–4; Thirsk, Carlton Miniott, Sand Hutton and Sowerby, North Yorkshire RO, ZAG 282.

no way of arriving at even an approximation of the numbers of people, as opposed to households, in the four groups.

The estimates of the total numbers in each group are presented in Table 6.2. It shows there was a substantial tax-paying element, usually accounting for between 60 and 80 per cent of the population. St Mary's, Warwick, where tax-paying households made up just 30 per cent of the total, is the exception, which may be explained by resistance there to paying rates.[17] Twenty to 30 per cent of the population were unable to pay rates, but were not themselves in need of assistance. At Strood they were described as 'the poorer sort of people, which as yet are able to work and do neither give nor take'. A third group, ranging from 6 per cent at Shorne to 16.5 per cent at Cawston, were stated to be poor, but were not given statutory outdoor relief. At Grain in Kent they were called 'the other poor', and at Shorne they were described as 'poor able labouring folk'. Fourthly, there were the poor who did receive official parish relief; their share of the population ranged from just 1.8 per cent at Strood to 14.3 per cent at Carlton Miniott.[18]

On this evidence the sceptics' criticisms appear to be justified. It would seem that nothing like half of the population was in need in the late sixteenth and early seventeenth centuries. There were gradations among the poor: a small proportion (group 4) received official assistance, but similar numbers (group 3) made do with occasional relief or none at all. And even if the two groups are taken together, no more than 10 to 20 per cent of the population was involved. Only in Cawston, with 26.7 per cent, did the figure approach one third.

II

Yet do the revised figures tell the whole story? The remainder of this essay suggests they do not. If the higher estimates of Hoskins and King were misleading, so are the revised ones. They exclude all but the very poorest, they ignore the impact of the 'life-cycle' among the poor, and they mask variations between the sexes and geographical areas. Moreover, while gradations existed among the

---

[17] A. L. Beier, 'The Social Problems of an Elizabethan Country Town: Warwick, 1580–90', in P. Clark, ed., *Country Towns in Pre-Industrial England* (Leicester, 1981), pp. 74–5; *cf.* Slack, *Poverty and Policy*, p. 178.

[18] Staffs. RO D593/5/4/55/1 (the transcription in E. Melling, *Kentish Sources. IV. The Poor* (Maidstone, 1964), p. 13, is faulty).

poor, the boundaries were more fluid and ambiguous than the groupings in Table 6.2 allow. Finally, fixed percentages take no account of change over time. Harvest failures, epidemics and trade slumps caused great short-term increases in levels of need, while the consequences of longer-term shifts in economic and demographic conditions can also be hidden by bald percentages.

In rejecting traditional estimates of the poor, the sceptics' definition of poverty is complete destitution. Coventry's poor in the 1520s have been described as 'total paupers'; the one-tenth who were needy in the countryside, and the one-fifth in towns, have been represented as living in 'absolute poverty'. Another writer has stated that the poor of the Restoration period were those experiencing 'a degree of distress that approximated to destitution'.[19] Complete destitution, however, is a dubious way of defining poverty in early modern England. It is based upon assumptions about who required or deserved relief, which often meant whoever was deemed worthy by local officials. It is not surprising, then, that the official poor sometimes formed a minority of the households exempted from the Hearth Tax.[20] But those on relief cannot be assumed to represent a complete picture of the needy. In practice the authorities means-tested the poor, separating the worthy sheep from the undeserving goats. This is demonstrated dramatically by a survey of the poor of St Mary's, Warwick, made in 1587. It showed 245 persons to be in need and/or begging. Of these, twenty-two were recent migrants who were expelled forthwith, even though one family of five had lived in the town for at least five years. Out of the remaining 223, 127 were given relief, mainly the very old and very young. Thus, had the records of the St Mary's census not survived, the 118 who were not relieved would have disappeared without a trace, and historians might have assumed that only the 127 who were relieved were 'the poor'.[21] A still more striking instance of this occurred in Thirsk in 1629–30. In October 1629 local officials listed 161 persons who were unable to support themselves, but in the following July the number given weekly

---

[19] Phythian-Adams, *Desolation of a City*, pp. 132, 156; Pound, *Poverty and Vagrancy*, p. xii; Arkell, 'Incidence of Poverty', p. 39; *cf.* Husbands, 'Hearth Tax Exemption Figures', pp. 51–2; Tronrud, 'Dispelling the Gloom', p. 2. *Cf.* Slack, *Poverty and Policy*, pp. 53–4.

[20] Wales, 'Poverty, Poor Relief and the Life-Cycle', pp. 357–8; Arkell, 'Incidence of Poverty', pp. 41–2.

[21] Beier, 'The Social Problems of an Elizabethan Country Town', p. 77.

payments was cut to forty-three, or just over one quarter of the original total. Once again, relief was limited to the 'aged, poor and impotent', and to children under seven years of age. Similarly, in the parish of St Martin's, Salisbury in 1635, 3.6 per cent of the population were in receipt of alms, but 33.3 per cent were said to be needy.[22]

It is no wonder, then, that 'the poor' in the official records were frequently widows and children, and that their numbers were considerably lower than those exempted from the Hearth Tax. These were the 'destitute' whom the parish were prepared to tax themselves to support. They were also very probably the 'paupers' listed in the censuses conducted under the Marriage Duty Act of 1694, which have formed the basis of the downward revisions of Gregory King.[23] But official surveys of the poor suggest that 'paupers' were not always *all* the poor, even in official eyes. Options other than poor relief were used in dealing with the unworthy goats. Immigrants were sent away, the young were apprenticed, the able-bodied were employed or punished. In other cases, *ad hoc* relief was supplied rather than regular doles. In yet others, as quarter sessions records abundantly testify, parish overseers refused requests for poor relief and invoked by-laws and manorial customs to deny settlements.[24] We should be sceptical, therefore, of adopting complete destitution as a definition of need. There was a substantial, barely visible element of poor who never appeared in overseers' accounts.

A corollary of defining poverty as complete destitution is the implication that the 'secondary poor' were not normally in need. The qualitative evidence cited to support this position is examined in the next section. For the moment, it is worth noticing that discrepancies in Hearth Tax exemptions cut two ways. Bidford in Warwickshire had sixty-four paupers relieved by the overseers

22 North Yorks. County RO ZAG 282, fos. 25a, 33a–38b; P. A. Slack, 'Poverty and Politics in Salisbury, 1597–1666', in Slack and P. Clark, eds., *Crisis and Order in English Towns, 1500–1700* (London, 1972), p. 176; Slack, *Poverty and Policy*, p. 17.

23 P. H. Lindert and J. G. Williamson, 'Revising England's Social Tables, 1688–1812', *Explorations in Economic History*, 19 (1982), pp. 387–91.

24 A. Fletcher, *Reform in the Provinces. The Government of Stuart England* (London, 1986), chapter 7, is the most recent treatment. For the application of settlement restrictions before 1662, the study that remains unsurpassed is P. Styles, 'The Evolution of the Law of Settlement', repr. in his *Studies in Seventeenth Century West Midlands History* (Kineton, 1978), pp. 175ff.

between 1665 and 1681, but thirty-one of them did not even appear in the Hearth Tax records. Some of the thirty-one possibly lived with relatives, while others may have been living in almshouses, which were exempt. But nine of the thirty-one had surnames which were not listed at all in the village's tax records. It was also possible to be taxed and poor at the same time. Thomas Edwards of Dunchurch was taxed because he had more than two hearths (five in 1662–5, and four thereafter), but local officials certified in 1671 that he had no goods to distrain for non-payment, and in 1673 that he was 'miserable poor'.[25]

The ages of the poor also underline the fact that not all the poor were visible in the official records. In Table 6.3, a comparison between the age-structure of the poor and that of entire populations is given. It shows a striking absence of paupers between the ages of sixteen and thirty. Adolescents and young adults in that age-group accounted for 10.6 per cent of the poor, but 26.1 per cent of the whole population. Apart from the odd example, we lack information on how the fertility and mortality rates of the poor compared with the rest of society, but a gap of 15 to 20 per cent is unlikely to be entirely explained by demographic conditions. Of course, the relative absence of adolescents and young adults is explained by their leaving home, often with official encouragement, for positions of service and apprenticeship in the households of the 'better sort'. But it would seem disingenuous to think that the departure of the young, although it relieved their parents' worries, permanently ended their own. Apprenticeship and service carried risks of their own, which resulted in vagrancy, something not normally documented by records of taxation and poor relief.[26]

Another reason for questioning a Panglossian view is the return of people to poverty from the age of thirty-one. Far from declining, the poor over thirty-one tended to surpass their share in 'normal' populations. The data in Table 6.3 suggest that old age was the critical time, because the poor over the age of sixty-one were twice as numerous as in the population generally. Ageing was certainly a serious problem, but closer examination of the data shows that forty rather than sixty was the crucial age. The group aged between

[25] P. Styles, 'Introduction' to M. Walker, ed., *Warwick County Records. Hearth Tax Returns* (Warwick, 1957), vol. 1, pp. lxxvii, lxxxiv; Slack, *Poverty and Policy*, pp. 178–9.

[26] A. L. Beier, *Masterless Men. The Vagrancy Problem in England, 1560–1640* (London, 1985), pp. 24, 217.

Table 6.3. *Age-structures in English communities, 1587–1695*

A The ages of the poor (%)

Ages	St Mary's Warwick, 1587 n=228	Ipswich, 1597 n=420	Crompton, Lancs., 1597 n=98	Bunwell, Norf., 1598 n=54	Various Kent parishes, 1598 n=208	Thirsk, 1629 n=123	Totals n=1,131
0–15	39.5	47.9	49.0	58.0	49.0	51.0	47.4
16–30	11.8	9.4	10.1	8.7	12.5	11.0	10.6
31–60	31.2	33.8	35.7	29.6	27.4	28.0	31.5
61+	17.5	8.9	5.2	3.7	11.1	10.0	10.5

B The ages of whole populations (%)

Ages	Ealing, 1599 n=423	Chilvers Coton 1684 n=777	Lichfield, 1695 n=2,861	Totals n=4,061
0–15	37.1	41.2	37.1	37.9
16–30	30.0	24.3	26.2	26.1
31–60	30.0	30.4	30.0	30.5
61+	2.9	4.1	5.7	5.5

Sources: St Mary's Warwick, T. Kemp, ed., *The Book of John Fisher*, pp. 165–72; Ipswich, J. Webb, ed., *Poor Relief in Elizabethan Ipswich*, Suffolk Record Society, 9 (1966), pp. 122–40; Bunwell, poor rate assessment, photocopy kindly supplied by Dr R. S. Schofield and the Cambridge Group for the History of Population and Social Structure; Crompton, Lancs. RO UDCr; Kent parishes (Chatham, Cliffe, Gillingham, Grain, Shorne and Strood), Staffs. RO, D.593 S/4/55/1; Thirsk, North Yorks. R.O., ZAG 282, fos. 33–7; Ealing, K. J. Allison, 'An Elizabethan Village "census"', *Bulletin of the Institute of Historical Research*, 36 (1963), pp. 96–103; Chilvers Coton, Warwicks. CRO, Newdigate Papers, C.R.136/12/fos. 64–73; Lichfield, D. V. Glass, 'Gregory King's Estimate of the Population of England and Wales, 1695', repr. in Glass and D. E. C. Eversley, eds., *Population in History*, (London, 1965), p. 212 ('King's smoothed data').
N.B. The multipliers employed in Tables 6.1 and 6.2 are not used in this table.

forty and sixty accounted for 19.4 per cent of the poor, whereas at Ealing, Chilvers Coton and Lichfield it formed only 15.4 per cent of the population. As has been seen in Warwick in 1587 and in seventeenth-century Norfolk, it was settling down and having children, and attempting to live from low wages or smallholdings, as well as being born to indigence, or becoming old and widowed, that put people at risk.

This evidence of age-structures suggests that poverty was most serious at certain points in the 'life-cycle' – in infancy and child-hood, in middle and old age. There was a respite between the ages of sixteen and thirty, when poor youngsters left home and were therefore no longer recorded among the settled poor. It seems implausible, however, to assume that none of these adolescents and young adults ever returned to the ranks of the poor. We lack life-histories of the poor in the late sixteenth and early seventeenth centuries, largely because many of those aged between sixteen and thirty appear to be absent from the records. But not even the most optimistic historian has claimed that this was a period of upward social mobility for significant numbers of the poor. When evidence is available – in settlement examinations dating from the late seventeenth century – it shows that when servants in husbandry (who generally fell into the sixteen to thirty age-group) settled down and married in later life they tended to join the ranks of the labouring poor rather than greatly to improve their lot. That is likely to have been the case also in the harsher conditions before 1650; it is hard to be sanguine about the prospects of self-better-ment in that period.[27]

If that is so – if many people aged between sixteen and thirty who were not recorded as poor sank into poverty later in their lives – then the implication is that simply counting those actually recorded as poor in a single year does not give a true picture of the *potential* poverty in a community. To overcome that problem, allowance must be made for the return to poverty, later in life, by some of those aged between sixteen and thirty. That can be done to a certain extent by calculating how many 'potential' poor need to be added to those actually recorded as poor within the sixteen–thirty

---

[27] Beier, 'Elizabethan Country Town', pp. 62–3; Wales, 'Poverty, Poor Relief and the Life-Cycle', pp. 360–7. The fate of the poorer farm servants is discussed in A. Kussmaul, *Servants in Husbandry in Early Modern England* (Cambridge, 1981), p. 83.

age-group in order to bring this up to its usual proportion within a normal population. The age-group's usual proportion within a normal population has been taken as 30 per cent, the figure yielded by the statistics from Ealing. This has been used because it is closest in time to the evidence of the ages of the poor, and because the data for Chilvers Coton and Lichfield is from a period when the birth-rate was falling and the population was older.[28]

Now, as Table 6.3 shows, the total of the poor recorded in the censuses is 1,131, of whom 120 were aged between sixteen and thirty, while 1,011 were either under sixteen or over thirty. In a normal age-structure, these 1,011 would represent 70 per cent of the whole. Thus if the poor had a normal age-structure, then the whole – the *potential* poor – would amount to 1,444 (that is, 1,011 × 100/70): some 27.7 per cent more than the total for the recorded poor in the censuses. Admittedly the whole of the increase cannot be applied, because perhaps half of the sixteen to thirty age-group would die before reaching the age of thirty. None the less, it is not unrealistic to think that 10 to 15 per cent might survive and possibly experience indigence in their middle and later years.

A further fallacy which results from attaching fixed percentages to the poor is that it masks variations between the sexes. In reality, females outnumbered males by nearly three to two, as Table 6.4 shows. The preponderance of females was considerable. Overall, females made up 58.2 per cent and males 41.8 per cent of the total of 779. Widowhood was an important cause of the imbalance, but the data in Table 6.4 shows the disparity beginning in the late teens and twenties. The preponderance of females at that stage is probably explained by girls remaining at home longer than boys, because the latter found readier entry into apprenticeship, while the former took employment in the home, knitting and spinning, and caring for disabled and elderly adults.

Overall percentages also disguise geographical variations in the incidence of poverty. The poor were not wholly absent from the central parishes of Tudor and Stuart towns, but for the most part they were concentrated in the suburbs. This resulted in some startling contrasts. The West Street of St Mary's, Warwick, was simply a suburban extension of the central High Pavement, yet

---

[28] The assumptions about mortality-rates in this and the following paragraph are based upon E. A. Wrigley and R. S. Schofield, *The Population History of England, 1541–1871. A Reconstruction* (London, 1981), pp. 710–11.

Table 6.4. *Sexes and ages of the poor, 1587–1629*

	0–15		16–30		31–60		61+	
	Males	Females	Males	Females	Males	Females	Males	Females
St Mary's, Warwick, 1587	46	27	10	12	22	39	12	23
Ipswich, 1597	1	3	6	12	41	87	17	19
Bunwell, Norf., 1597	18	9	2	1	7	9	1	1
Crompton, Lancs., 1598	27	21	2	8	15	20	6	5
Various Kent parishes, 1598	14	12	10	16	21	36	8	15
Thirsk, 1629	27	33	7	4	2	33	4	8
Totals	133	105	37	53	108	224	48	71
Percentages	55.9	44.1	41.1	58.9	32.5	67.5	40.3	59.7

Sources: As for Table 6.1
N.B. The low figures for under-sixteens in Ipswich are explained by the sexes of children not being reported in most instances.

their social complexions were as different as night and day: 44 per cent of the West Street's families were poor in 1582, as opposed to merely 3 per cent of the High Pavement's. Similar contrasts are found in Exeter, London, Salisbury and Shrewsbury.[29] It is usually the central wards and parishes with few poor that are cited to support arguments that early modern towns coped well with social problems, but the story was often different in the suburbs. These peripheral areas experienced higher rates of immigration, population growth and mortality in epidemics; had sub-standard housing (by the standards of the age), and high levels of multi-occupation; spawned exceptional numbers of vagrants; and required rates-in-aid from their better-off neighbours.[30]

The social landscape of the countryside was also a patchwork of rich and poor areas. The Hearth Tax may be a crude indicator of absolute levels of need, but this caveat does not apply to relative levels. Migration, population growth and the development of by-employments in manufacturing in the sixteenth and early seventeenth centuries produced marked differences between regions. In Warwickshire in 1670 the county-wide exemption-rate was 36 per cent, but this figure hides significant variations. In the mixed-farming southern part of the county the rate of exemption was 29 per cent, while on the plateaux between Birmingham and Nuneaton in the north it was 41 per cent. In Northamptonshire, the open-field areas had 35 per cent exempt compared with 44 per cent in forest and pastoral regions. The chief reason for the different rates of exemption was different rates of population growth. The northern plateaux of Warwickshire grew by 125 per cent between 1560 and 1670, while the felden south increased by 97 per cent (and that after a period of considerable depopulation caused by engrossing). In Northamptonshire the contrast in growth-rates was more

[29] Beier, 'Elizabethan Country Town', pp. 64ff, P. Slack, *Plague in Tudor and Stuart England* (London, 1985), p. 114; M. J. Power, 'The Social Topography of Restoration London', in Beier and R. Finlay, eds., *London, 1500–1700. The Making of the Metropolis* (London, 1986), pp. 204–6, but see also the qualifications on p. 201; Slack, 'Poverty and Politics in Salisbury', p. 179; J. Hill, 'A Study of Poverty and Poor Relief in Shropshire, 1550–1685', (unpublished M.A. thesis, University of Liverpool, 1973), p. 160.

[30] V. Pearl, 'Social Policy in Early Modern London', in H. Lloyd-Jones, V. Pearl and B. Worden, eds., *History and Imagination* (London, 1981), pp. 123–31; *cf.* Beier, *Masterless Men*, pp. 42–3, 47; Corp. London RO Repert.17/425a, ff, 446a, 32/157a–b, 41/151a–b.

striking: 43 per cent for non-forest villages between 1524 and 1670, but 126 per cent for forest villages.[31]

III

One reason given for reducing traditional estimates of the numbers of poor is that there were gradations of poor. The better-off ones – the secondary poor – kept servants, paid rents above the odds, and had substantial possessions, including smallholdings.[32] Do these signs of relative affluence mean the secondary poor were not really poor? In Coventry one in six of those rated at *nil* in the assessment of 1522 had servants living with them. Servants were symbols of wealth and status, and their numbers per household rose as one ascended the social scale. But servant-keeping was not confined to the elites in early modern society. In the 100 communities studied by Laslett nearly a third of households had resident help: nearly a quarter of traders and artisans, and one in seven (a figure very close to that for Coventry) among 'paupers, others, and not stated' had servants. Even some Elizabethan and early Stuart vagrants had servants travelling with them.[33]

The evidence concerning rents is similarly ambiguous. In Coventry some people rated at *nil* in the 1522 assessment paid rents above those of the poorest cottager. But the assumption that paying higher rents signified greater wealth is contradicted by other evidence. At Crompton in 1597 house rents among the poor were highly diverse and seemed to bear no relation to household size. Edward Wilde's family of ten were said to be 'paying no rent' at all, whereas Robert Crompton and his wife owed 13*s* 4*d* a year. The family of James Bridge, which numbered four members, paid their rent in kind by doing eight days sheep-shearing. Yet all three families were included in a list of 'all the poor in Crompton'. Elsewhere the 'fit' between poverty and low rents was possibly closer, but one example suggests that indigence was actually caused by high payments. At Knowle (Warwickshire) 'rents tended to be

---

[31] Warwicks. County RO, Q.S.11; British Library, Harl. MS 594–5; P. A. J. Pettit, *The Royal Forests of Northamptonshire. A Study in Their Economy, 1558–1714* (Gateshead, 1968), p. 142.

[32] See note 19 and the sources cited there.

[33] Phythian-Adams, *Desolation of a City*, pp. 204, 239–41; Laslett, 'Mean Household Size', p. 153. Instances of vagrants with servants: T. Kemp, ed., *The Book of John Fisher*, pp. 178–9; PRO, SP 16/314/77.

highest amongst those with the smallest holdings'.[34] These examples suggest that the payment of low rents is a poor guide to levels of need.

The possessions of the poor are also thought to show they were not all destitute. In Babergh Hundred (Suffolk) people assessed at *nil* in 1522 were later taxed on goods in the subsidies of 1524–5. Two-thirds of persons with £1 worth of land or less, which Hoskins reckoned indicated indigence, had goods worth £3 or more; the median value of their goods was between £10 and £19.[35] Using probate inventories, historians have found that the poor possessed pewter, flock beds and other goods associated with the 'consumer boom' of the Elizabethan and early Stuart periods. Where the inventories of people exempt from the Hearth Tax can be tracked down, a majority of cases (ten of seventeen in Warwickshire) surpassed the £10 threshold below which Parliament assumed people were too poor to pay.[36]

Again, the evidence bears closer examination. The key question is whether possessions are a good indicator of wealth. In some cases, at least, the answer is no. Ralph Ashe, a Chesterfield man who died in 1521, left goods valued at £13 16s 2d. In his will he distributed his clothing to kin and friends, and cash gifts to the value of 15s 4d, including 6s 8d to a maidservant. His possessions included a feather bed and nine pewter dishes: a fine early example of the 'consumer boom', it might be concluded. But another reading of the evidence is possible. Ashe's widow received the residue of his goods, but beyond the household stuff he left her nothing in his will – no house, no land, nor income – and henceforth she was presumably reliant upon kin or community. Yet Ashe's possessions suggest a measure of prosperity in the early sixteenth century; in the later seventeenth century he would have paid the Hearth Tax.[37]

[34] Phythian-Adams, *Desolation of a City*, p. 240; Lancs. RO UDCr; Arkell, 'Incidence of Poverty', p. 35; V. Skipp, *Crisis and Development. An Ecological Case Study of the Forest of Arden, 1570–1674* (Cambridge, 1978), p. 84. *Cf.* J. T. Swain, *Before the Industrial Revolution. North-East Lancashire. c. 1500–1640* (Manchester, 1986), pp. 85ff. (I owe the last reference to Dr J. Rosenheim.)

[35] Pound, *Poverty and Vagrancy*, pp. ix–x; *cf.* M. Spufford, *Constrasting Communities. English Villagers in the Sixteenth and Seventeenth Centuries* (Cambridge, 1974), p. 75.

[36] Tronrud, 'Dispelling the Gloom', pp. 19–20; Palliser, 'Brave New World', pp. 350–1; Arkell, 'Incidence of Poverty', pp. 33–5.

[37] J. M. Bestall and D. V. Fowkes, eds., *Chesterfield Wills and Inventories, 1521–1603* (Derbyshire Record Society, 1977), vol. 1, pp. 1–2.

Even the poor possessed luxury items, but these possessions give a false impression of the situation, rather like accounts in the modern press of the unemployed owning video-recorders and taking foreign holidays. Take the case of John Cotes, a pauper in Warwick in 1582, whose will and inventory were probated two years later. He owned two flock beds, a brass pan, and a lease to a cottage worth £1, suggesting a measure of affluence. But the value of his goods came to £1 13s 10d, no princely sum even before price inflation took off in the sixteenth century. The bulk of his possessions comprised basic household items: a pillow, blankets, three pair of sheets, a platter, two candlesticks, a kettle, a pot, pothooks and chain, and a few pieces of furniture.[38]

Even evidence of a substantial house and possessions may conceal a perilous degree of need. William Hurst's probate inventory, compiled in 1589, showed him living in a substantial house in Warwick. Although apparently rented, the dwelling included specialized rooms suggestive of 'the great rebuilding' – a hall, parlour, high chamber and buttery. The rooms' contents also betoken participation in a consumer boom. The hall included two decorative painted cloths, as well as four cushions for the furniture. The parlour, which was actually a bedroom, contained the inevitable flock beds (though they were noted to be 'coarse') and another painted cloth, as well as bedding and furniture. The high chamber was a second bedroom whose contents were similar to the first. The buttery contained some of the 'luxuries' noted by Hoskins's critics – six pieces of pewter and a brass pot.[39]

Yet a closer reading of Hurst's will and inventory does not suggest material ease. The total value of his goods was £1 17s 4d, and he left debts of £4 3s 4d. He had a little cash, since he bequeathed 4d each to two sons, and 1s to a daughter, but his widow's mite was almost non-existent. The residue of his goods and chattels amounted to a deficit after his debts and legacies were paid. Although Hurst was listed among those 'ready to decay' in St Mary's in 1582, his family did not appear among the parish's poor, even during the crisis of 1587. His substantial house and possessions suggest comfort, but the value of his belongings indicates a condition close to poverty.[40] Probate documents rarely exist for people

[38] St Helen's RO, Worcester, Probate Records 1584/78e.   [39] *Ibid.*, 1590/9.

[40] *Ibid.* To put Hurst's 'wealth' in perspective, those taxed in St Mary's in 1582, and who died leaving inventories, 1582–91 (eleven cases), had their goods valued at a mean average of £75 14s.

as poor as Cotes and Hurst. The lacuna is not difficult to explain: 'wealth' as meagre as theirs was hardly worth recording. Naturally the better off were better recorded, but for this reason, probate records do not represent an accurate picture of a population. It is no wonder, then, that ten out of the seventeen inventories made for people who were exempt from the Hearth Tax surpassed the £10 plateau. Indeed, the same study of thirty-two Warwickshire parishes found that just one exempt householder in ten had enough possessions to warrant the compilation of an inventory, and that only one in twenty had goods worth more than £10.[41]

The possession of a smallholding has also been thought to have provided a shield against poverty. In Norfolk and Suffolk in the 1520s some people assessed on their goods were freeholders owning or renting lands amounting to a virgate, or thirty acres. In the seventeenth century 'some of the exempt ... had up to a few acres of land or at least a large garden to help support them and their families'. Those without holdings of their own had common rights which allowed them to gather berries, nuts and seed from the common.[42] It is plausible to think that people with crofts and smallholdings were better off than those on poor relief, but the degree of comfort afforded by a few acres of land can be exaggerated. The proliferation of smallholders and squatters in the pastoral regions of forest and fen is considered to have caused economic backwardness rather than progress. One economic historian has observed that the small farmer's position 'was always precarious, a situation which made him conservative, a risk minimizer rather than a risk taker'. Partible inheritance customs, poor corn yields, diminishing herds of livestock and rising landlessness made things worse. In old age smallholders were often supported by children who took over the land, but some still required parish relief.[43]

---

[41] Arkell, 'Incidence of Poverty', pp. 33–5. In any case, to yield meaningful results, probate inventories require aggregative analysis and comparison with price levels, as in P. Clark, 'Introduction' to Clark, ed., *Country Towns*, p. 35 n.44, which shows that the value of goods of Canterbury wage-earners fell by 50 per cent in real terms in 1600–39 from 1560–99, and in Beier, 'Elizabethan Country Town', in *ibid.*, p. 53.

[42] Pound, *Poverty and Vagrancy*, pp. viii–ix; Arkell, 'Incidence of Poverty', p. 36; Husbands, 'Hearth Tax Exemption Figures', p. 51.

[43] Outhwaite, 'Progress and Backwardness', p. 15; Wales, 'Poverty, Poor Relief and the Life-Cycle', p. 385.

IV

Thus counting the poor in parish 'a' in year 'y' is of limited value. This approach also ignores change over time, which meant that the numbers of the needy rose and fell from year to year. Deficient harvests, epidemics and trade slumps were recurring events in early modern society, and they periodically increased the numbers of the poor. Recent studies of short-run fluctuations have focused upon mortality levels. They have suggested that England's experience of crisis mortality was benign compared with other parts of northern Europe, and that high death-rates were caused less and less by bad harvests. In the 1690s, when Scotland, the Low Countries and northern France suffered from high prices and heavy mortality, England was immune from its worst effects. Even before 1640 famines were on the wane, although the population was still growing: '1596–8 was the last severe starvation crisis over most of England'. Thus, it is argued, England escaped the 'Malthusian trap' of population growth outstripping food supplies.[44]

There is, however, disagreement about this interpretation. Other historians see subsistence crises continuing into the seventeenth century, and not only in the west and north of the country.[45] Whatever the case, where the poor are concerned the concentration upon short-term mortality levels is misleading. Death is one, quite terminal, form of resolving a crisis, but not the only one. Many crises stopped short of death, and yet were capable of plunging people into destitution. Mortality levels increased dramatically after some bad harvests, but most people probably experienced temporary impoverishment rather than death. Slumps in trade and manufacturing were even more liable to impoverish rather than to kill. Most illnesses, even plague, temporarily disabled more people than they carried away. Of course, the close links between widowhood and poverty were caused by mortality, but other forms of upheaval in family life also led to indigence, for example when men deserted families, and when they left wives and children because of conscription.[46]

---

[44] Palliser, 'Brave New World', p. 345.

[45] Outhwaite, 'Progress and Backwardness', p. 17; Slack, *Plague in Tudor and Stuart England*, p. 92; J. Walter, 'The Economy of Famine in Early Modern England', *Bulletin. Society for the Social History of Medicine*, 40 (1987), pp. 7–8; Slack, *Poverty and Policy*, pp. 39, 48–50.

[46] Beier, 'Elizabethan Country Town', pp. 60–1; Wales, 'Poverty, Poor Relief and the Life-Cycle', pp. 366, 376.

Local officials were aware of the vulnerability of those borderline groups who neither received relief nor paid rates. Death was one, but not the only, threat. At Strood it was observed of families who 'neither give nor take', that 'if the husband should die, [they] are likely to be a parish charge'. At Warwick those just above the poor on relief were described as 'ready to decay' into poverty. More than one parish cautioned that illness could push marginal families not receiving relief into dependence on the parish. At Grain the 'other poor' were secure only 'so long as it shall please God to send them their health'; at Shorne it was observed that the 'poor, able labouring folk ... oftentimes by any extraordinary sickness or hinderance, being visited, are commonly relieved by our alms box'.[47] We need to take account of gradations among the poor, but the implications of those finer distinctions must be examined.

Bad harvests could affect as much as one-quarter of the population who did not normally receive parish assistance. The data in Table 6.2 was taken from years of relatively good harvests, so that the extent of indigence was not exaggerated. It is interesting to compare that evidence with years when bad harvest conditions prevailed. 1586 was a particularly bad year in the Midlands, and in Warwick a census of the poor was conducted in St Mary's parish the following spring. The numbers of poor on the eve of the bad harvest are unknown, but they were probably not much greater than the 133 who required relief in 1582, since economic conditions were stable in the interim, and pauper immigration was limited. But in the survey conducted by Thomas Cartwright and local officials in 1587 the poor numbered 245, an increase of 112, or 84 per cent, over the 1582 total.[48]

Of the 112 who had newly become poor, 108 can be traced. Seventeen, or 15.7 per cent, had recently settled in the town and were expelled. But the great majority of the rest – ninety-one, or 84.3 per cent – were local people. Forty-eight were members of households listed as 'ready to decay' (group 3 in Table 6.2, above) in 1582. Another forty-three had been able to support themselves, but were unable to pay a poor rate (group 2, Table 6.2). Thus nearly one in six of the marginal population and one in twenty of the 'indifferent' were reduced to beggary after the poor harvest of 1586. In general, leaving out the immigrants who were sent away

[47] Staffs. RO, D593/5/4/55/1.
[48] Beier, 'Elizabethan Country Town', pp. 58, 76–7.

and the 133 who were already poor, 5.4 per cent of the non-paupers of the parish (ninety-one out of an estimated 1,678) found themselves in desperate straits in 1587.[49]

Elsewhere the proportion affected was higher. At Strood in north Kent in 1598 the poor numbered less than 2 per cent of the population, but after a bad harvest (probably in 1596) their share rose to 10.5 per cent (seventy-six out of 723), which meant that 8.9 per cent of non-paupers were afflicted. At Shorne near Gravesend the impact of the bad crop was still greater. Only twenty-six persons, or 7.3 per cent of the population, were granted relief in 1598, but earlier, again probably in 1596, 102 were said to have no food, which represented about 28.8 per cent of the village's population. In this instance nearly a quarter of non-paupers (23.3 per cent: seventy-six of 326) joined the ranks of the poor.[50]

It might be said that 1586 and 1596 were notoriously bad years, but the evidence indicates that poor harvests continued to occur with the same frequency and severity up to 1760. According to Hoskins, 25 per cent of wheat harvests were deficient (prices 10 per cent or more above a thirty-one-year average) between 1480 and 1619, 26 per cent between 1620 and 1759, and 29 per cent between 1760 and 1800. The numbers of really bad years (prices 25 per cent or more above the norm) also changed little until 1760, with 24 in the first period and 22 in the second. Between 1760 and 1800 there was a significant decline in the number of bad crops, but it is suspected that imports artificially depressed prices in that period.[51]

The accounts of parish overseers show that the numbers and the cost of the poor continued to be affected by harvest conditions. After a poor harvest in 1629 the numbers of poor in Southampton rose from seventy-two to ninety-eight in 1630, and expenditure jumped from £76 a year to £125. The bad years of 1648 and 1649 saw the numbers of families on relief in St Chad's parish, Shrewsbury, rise from 120 to 200.[52] Mortality crises may have been absent in the bad years of the 1690s, but bad crops and high poor-rates were evident. The Hampshire parish of Crondall saw numbers and

[49] *Ibid.*, and Table 6.2 above.
[50] Staffs. RO D593/5/4/55/1, and P. Clark, *English Provincial Society from the Reformation to the Revolution* (Hassocks, 1977), pp. 239–40.
[51] W. G. Hoskins, 'Harvest Fluctuations and English Economic History, 1620–1759', *Agricultural History Review*, 16 (1968), pp. 15–17.
[52] Southampton City RO SC10/14–15; Hill, 'Poverty and Poor Relief in Shropshire', p. 172.

costs double in just five years. The parish supported between four and eight paupers on a regular basis from 1690 to 1692 at an annual cost of £25. When harvests were bad between 1693 and 1697, the numbers on regular relief jumped to between thirteen and seventeen and the yearly cost leapt to £55. Similar rises occurred elsewhere.[53] The link between increased relief expenditure and bad harvests continued into the next century. After a poor crop in 1728 the poor-rate was doubled in Lancaster, and a workhouse was established so that the poor would be supported 'without going a begging'. Peaks in poor relief expenditure were again caused by poor harvests in southeastern England in 1796, 1801, 1813 and 1818.[54] Obviously bad years came and went, but their continuing impact upon middling and lower groups in society is further reason to question the value of establishing the percentage of poor at any one time.

Epidemics were another kind of crisis that caused increased poverty. Historians have concentrated upon mortality levels in epidemics, but morbidity probably outran mortality by two to one in the plague outbreaks that killed 750,000 people in Tudor and Stuart England.[55] Those who survived required assistance while they recovered. That was especially true of the urban poor, because the disease hit them hardest in their suburban slums. Officials and opinion-makers viewed plague as a social problem linked to 'poverty, vagrancy and suburban disorder'.[56] The countryside was also affected. From Essex in 1625 the deputy-lieutenants reported the levying of 'extraordinary taxes for the relief of the sick poor'. Outbreaks of plague also disrupted normal economic life, not least when quarantines were imposed: 'when Preston was cut off from the rest of Lancashire in 1631, it was reported that 756 out of the 887 people in the town needed relief – not because of plague, but through the secondary consequences of their isolation'. Poor-rates,

---

[53] Overseers' accounts, 1677–99, Crondall parish chest (figures calculated according to harvest year); cf. Warwicks. County RO, PR19/270–9, overseers' accounts of Astley.

[54] Quoted T. S. Ashton, *Economic Fluctuations in England, 1700–1800* (Oxford, 1959), p. 54; D. A. Baugh, 'The Cost of Poor Relief in South-East England, 1790–1834', *Economic History Review*, 2nd series, 28 (1975), p. 54. Poor crops also affected the poor on the Welsh borders in the 1790s: P. H. Goodman, 'Eighteenth-Century Poor Law Administration in the Parish of Oswestry', *Transactions of the Shropshire Archaeological Society*, 56 (1957–60), p. 339.

[55] Slack, *Plague*, pp. 174–6.   [56] *Ibid.*, p. 195.

although they were increased, were usually insufficient in such emergencies.[57]

Plague was not the only enemy. After the final visitation in 1665 the country continued to be afflicted with epidemics of fever, ague and influenza, which increased the numbers of poor and relief costs. The Warwickshire parish of Kenilworth was hit by such an epidemic in 1670; it caused poor-rates to rise from £29 to £54 within a year, and the parish had to appeal to quarter sessions for further aid. But in this instance official assistance did not obviate a mortality crisis: burials in the parish rose to fifty in 1670, or twice the mean averages of the previous and subsequent decades.[58]

Slumps in trade and manufacturing also swelled the numbers of poor. Despite Professor Supple's excellent study of early Stuart crises, and a recent monograph on the west of England, the impact of depressions upon the 'lower sort' requires examination. By all accounts the secondary poor, especially artisans in the clothing industry, were severely affected. In the depression of 1625 spinners and clothworkers in Devizes were reported to 'want work for the maintenance of themselves, their wives and children, [so] that many of them living idly do wander up and down begging both in town and country'. The Common Council accordingly set aside £150 to employ the 'many poor people of the borough'.[59] Of Devon's cloth industry Westcote wrote in 1630 that 'every rumour of war or contagious sickness (hindering the sale of those commodities), makes a multitude of the poorer sort chargeable to their neighbours, who are bound to maintain them'.[60] Wage levels improved somewhat after 1650, but trade slumps did not cease. Coventry clothworkers complained in 1674 that 'artificers are obliged, through the decay of the trade, to seek employment abroad, or to endure great poverty at home'. In the eighteenth

[57] *Ibid.*, p. 269; Essex quotation from P. Bowden, 'Agricultural Prices, Farm Profits, and Rents', in J. Thirsk, ed., *The Agrarian History of England & Wales, IV. 1500–1640* (Cambridge, 1967), p. 633.

[58] C. Creighton, *A History of Epidemics in Britain* (Cambridge, 1894), vol. 1, p. 465, vol. 2, pp. 4–26, 326–37, 455; Warwicks. County RO, DR266/44, DR0101/2; H. C. Johnson and S. C. Ratcliff, eds., *Warwick County Records. Quarter Sessions Order Books* (Warwick, 1935–9), vol. 5, pp. 139, 144–5, 152.

[59] B. E. Supple, *Commercial Crisis and Change in England, 1600–1642* (Cambridge, 1959); B. Sharp, *In Contempt of All Authority. Rural Artisans and Riot in the West of England, 1586–1660* (London, 1980); B. H. Cunnington, *Some Annals of the Borough of Devizes, 1555–1791* (Devizes, 1925), p. 181 (Book 'A').

[60] Westcote quoted in W. Cunningham, *The Growth of English Industry and Commerce in Modern Times. The Mercantile System* (Cambridge, 1907), p. 562n.

century depressions regularly followed upon the cessation of hostilities in that period's many wars.[61]

Crises were not confined to beleaguered broadcloth-producers. Coal-mining was the *wunderkind* of seventeenth-century industry, but its technical and financial teething troubles in northeast Warwickshire were serious. The mines around Bedworth expanded rapidly from Elizabethan times, but by 1619 they were unworkable because of drainage problems. In the ensuing slump the town was reported to have 500 poor colliers out of work. Another collapse occurred in the late 1650s and lasted over a decade before reinvestment revived the mines. In 1670, two years before operations were restarted, 80 per cent of Bedworth's 270 households were exempt from the Hearth Tax. If, as elsewhere in north Warwickshire, 75 per cent of them were receiving parish relief, this means that 60 per cent were in need and, allowing for variations in mean household sizes, a possible majority of the population.[62]

V

Those who take an optimistic view of the state of the poor also ignore medium- and long-term changes in their condition. Above all, they disregard the worsening of economic and demographic conditions in England between *c.* 1590 and *c.* 1660. Yet it is well known that the poor laws were first widely implemented during these seventy years. Was that a coincidence? The remainder of this essay suggests that it was not. Of course, all was not gloom and doom in these decades. There are signs of new economic activities and a new demographic regime, which in the longer term resulted in a more prosperous and stable society. But the rush to find signs of progress before 1650 – precedents, as it were, of agricultural and industrial revolutions – is as unsatisfactory as seeking the origins of the English Revolution in the economic upheavals of that time.[63]

[61] *V.C.H. Warwickshire*, vol. 2, p. 255; Ashton, *Economic Fluctuations*, pp. 74–5.

[62] *Cal. State Papers, Dom., 1622*, pp. 458–9; Johnson and Ratcliff, eds., *Quarter Sessions Order Books*, vol. 1, p. 58, vol. 4, pp. 187–8, 219, 235, vol. 7, p. 35; *V.C.H. Warwickshire*, vol. 2, pp. 220–3; J. U. Nef, *The Rise of the British Coal Industry* (London, 1932), vol. 1, pp. 360, 378. See also note 94 below.

[63] Cf. Palliser, 'Brave New World', pp. 352–3; J. Thirsk, *Economic Policy and Projects. The Development of a Consumer Society in Early Modern England* (Oxford, 1978), *passim*. Cf. Slack, *Poverty and Policy*, pp. 6, 39, 45, although he dates the economic changes somewhat differently on p. 54.

It was formerly believed that the rising food prices and sluggish wages meant hard times for wage-earners between 1500 and 1640. Real wages declined by 46 per cent for urban building-craftsmen, and 50 per cent for agricultural labourers in 140 years. For both groups of workers real wages reached their nadir in the decades between 1610 and 1630; thereafter recovery was slow, not surpassing the 50 per cent mark until after 1650.[64] Recently, however, doubts have arisen about whether these figures accurately measure the fall in wage-earners' living standards. Some building workers were self-employed craftsmen, who were not wholly dependent upon wages, and whose probate inventories suggest they were men of substance. Agricultural labourers might have worked longer hours, taken payment in kind rather than cash, bought cheaper foodstuffs, and put more family members to work. When times were hard, labourers might rely upon crofts and gardens, which many are thought to have possessed.[65]

These caveats are plausible, but not wholly convincing. There were undoubtedly prosperous builders for whom wages were of secondary importance. Further, it is possible to discover affluent craftsmen among the thousands who left probate inventories. But since inventories were mainly left by the 'better sort', it needs to be shown that prosperous artisans were not exceptional. As noted earlier, 'luxury' possessions do not invariably signify affluence. The argument that labourers responded to hardship by increasing their incomes assumes that their values and behaviour conformed to modern norms of 'economic man'. How, then, does one explain the chorus of complaints in the period about voluntary 'idleness' among workers? What, too, of servants in husbandry and domestics, a half to two-thirds of whom seem voluntarily to have changed masters each year, forsaking the security of steady employment, room, board and clothing? What, finally, of the cottar-miners of the Stanneries and the Peak District, who chose to work less rather than labour more to keep up?[66]

[64] Bowden, 'Agricultural Prices', in Thirsk, ed., *Agrarian History. IV*, p. 865.

[65] D. M. Palliser, *The Age of Elizabeth. England under the Later Tudors, 1547–1603* (London, 1983), pp. 157–9; D. Woodward, 'Wage Rates and Living Standards in Pre-Industrial England', *Past and Present*, 91 (1981), pp. 43–5; Slack, *Poverty and Policy*, pp. 46–7.

[66] Beier, *Masterless Men*, p. 24; I. Blanchard, 'Labour Productivity and Work Psychology in the English Mining Industry, 1400–1600', *Economic History Review*, 2nd series, 31 (1978), p. 14.

Censuses of the poor which record employment suggest that low wages were more important than unemployment in causing hardship. In Norwich in 1570, 76.6 per cent of the adult poor were in employment; in Ipswich in 1597 the figure was 66 per cent. Adult women in Norwich actually had higher rates of employment than men – 84.4 per cent as against 63.9 per cent – because they headed households more often than men. But the majority of adult poor were married (74.6 per cent in Norwich; 73.0 per cent in all censuses between 1570 and 1636), and both partners often worked.[67] So did many children and adolescents: 49.4 per cent of able-bodied youngsters living at home and aged five and over were employed in Norwich, 47.1 per cent in Ipswich, and 49.3 in St Edmund's parish, Salisbury, in 1635. No doubt many people were not fully employed in the modern sense. None the less, one might have expected employment levels such as these to keep people from begging and requiring poor relief. The conclusion is inescapable that they had inadequate real incomes. Low wages particularly afflicted the many Norwich women (553 out of the 683 who were in employment) who spun in the home for 'market spinners', or middleman-clothiers.[68] In two Salisbury parishes in 1635 average income per head among the poor, *including assistance from the poor rates*, was 7½d per week. It was not that these people did not work – they did, and their earnings accounted for over half of their income. Rather, they were badly paid. In comparison, apprentices and labourers in the town got 10d a day and people relieved in almshouses 1s a week.[69]

The manufacture of woollen cloth experienced a series of major depressions between 1620 and 1660. This was important for the poor because, as in Ipswich, Norwich and Salisbury, large numbers of them found employment in this industry. Indeed many schemes to employ the poor tended to treat this labour-intensive industry as

---

[67] C. Maher, 'Women and Poverty in Elizabethan Norwich', (unpublished B.A. thesis, University of Lancaster, 1987), p. 33; N. Webb, 'The Structure of Poverty in Some Elizabethan Communities Based on Censuses of the Poor' (unpublished B.A. thesis, University of Lancaster, 1980), pp. 42–3.

[68] J. F. Pound, ed., *The Norwich Census of the Poor, 1570*, Norfolk Record Society, 40 (1971), pp. 23–93; J. Webb, ed., *Poor Relief in Elizabethan Ipswich*, Suffolk Record Society, 9 (1966), pp. 122–40; P. Slack, ed., *Poverty in Early Stuart Salisbury*, Wiltshire Record Society, 31 (1975), pp. 75–8; Maher, 'Women and Poverty', pp. 33, 53, 55–6.

[69] Slack, 'Poverty and Politics', pp. 174–5; Slack, *Poverty and Policy*, pp. 65–6, 80–2.

a panacea for poverty. In some measure, the writing was on the wall in the Elizabethan years. In the 1590s bad harvests, plague and warfare abroad caused exports to fluctuate around levels dating from the third quarter of the century, which was itself depressed compared with the first half of the century. The years 1600–14 saw a short-lived recovery, but then broadcloth exports were hit by the disastrous Cockayne experiment in 1614–17, by the collapse of north European markets during the Thirty Years War, and by crises at home from 1620 to 1660 that included bad harvests, plague and civil wars. The worst years were from 1620 to 1629, after which exports fluctuated, as in the late Elizabethan years, around a stagnant level.[70]

The south of England, particularly the western shires, was probably hardest hit. But old drapery-producers in the east experienced depression in the 1620s, new draperies were in trouble in Essex in 1623 and were then hit by the war against Spain in 1625, and even the north was not wholly immune. The rising star of Leeds was temporarily eclipsed between 1625 and 1650; as late as 1662 depressed trade and large numbers of poor were still reported there.[71] There is no modern study of trade between 1642 and 1660, but Scott could find not one good year for overseas trade in the entire period. The civil wars interrupted domestic as well as foreign exchanges, so that inland shires were affected. The town of Alcester (Warwickshire) complained to quarter sessions in 1653 that it was overburdened with paupers, because a collapse in trade had thrown large numbers of knitters out of work. If a nation-wide trade slump ever occurred in pre-industrial England, the years between 1620 and 1660 are a prime candidate.[72]

England's difficulties in the first half of the seventeenth century were compounded by the continued growth of its population. Wrigley and Schofield have confirmed what historians suspected for a long time – that the English demographic recovery that began in the late fifteenth century reached its peak in the mid-seventeenth. Their figures show the population rising from 3,899,190 in 1591, to 5,058,102 in 1636, and on to 5,281,347 in 1656,

---

[70] Supple, *Commercial Crisis and Change*, chapters 1–6.
[71] *Ibid.*, pp. 57, 102–12, 130–1; W. G. Rimmer, 'The Evolution of Leeds', repr. in P. Clark, ed., *The Early Modern Town. A Reader* (London, 1976), pp. 285–6.
[72] W. Scott, *The Constitution and Finance of English, Scottish and Irish Joint-Stock Companies to 1720* (Cambridge, 1912), vol. 1, p. 466; Johnson and Ratcliff, eds., *Quarter Sessions Order Books*, vol. 3, pp. 146–7, 164, 170.

a level not surpassed until the reign of Anne.[73] This meant that the number of extra mouths was at its peak when economic conditions were worsening. The result was increased hardship, which might take the form of crises of subsistence, as in 1596 and 1622–3, but which took other forms as well.

A striking feature of the century after 1590 was the decline in the expectation of life at birth. Life-expectancy is one of the most common criteria, along with rates of infant mortality, employed by economists and demographers to measure standards of living. It has been said that 'in comparison with many traditional societies Elizabethan England was fortunate' in these departments. Expectation of life at birth 'was exceptionally high between 1566 and 1621, never falling below 37.4 years (1591) and reaching a peak of 43.7 years in 1581: these were high levels by the general standards of early modern Europe'. These conclusions are interesting, but they do not apply to later decades, or to the whole of Elizabeth I's reign.[74] Using the method of back-projection, Wrigley and Schofield found that expectation of life at birth reached a peak of 39.3 years in the twenty-five-year period surrounding the year 1576, but that decline set in thereafter, falling to 32.3 years, i.e. by 17.8 per cent, in the following 100 years. In the five-year period centring on 1681 life-expectancy at birth reached a nadir of 28.5 years, even though mortality crises were apparently not present. Reconstitution studies of twelve parishes show a less marked decline, but they are less reliable because the sample is not random. They do indicate, however, that the increased mortality affected adults as well as infants and children.[75]

The Elizabethan 'mortality regime' is thought to have been 'unusually mild by the general standards of early modern Europe', whereas the Stuart one was 'much closer to the norm'.[76] Nevertheless, the evidence suggests that Elizabethan prosperity was short-lived and was followed by a century of setbacks. In modern times both Elizabethan and Stuart rates of survival would place England in the under-developed world. Levels equivalent to Elizabethan ones were found in the Belgian Congo in 1950–2 (37.6 years for males; 40.0 for females), and to the Stuart ones in Haiti in 1950

[73] Wrigley and Schofield, *Population History*, pp. 208–9.
[74] Palliser, *Age of Elizabeth*, pp. 45–6.
[75] Wrigley and Schofield, *Population History*, pp. 236, 250, 252–3.
[76] *Ibid.*, p. 236.

(32.6 years overall). Comparisons with third-world countries might in other respects be otiose, but these help to place in perspective sixteenth- and seventeenth-century standards of living which, whatever one makes of the signs of a 'consumer boom', were still those of a pre-industrial society. Later seventeenth-century infant mortality-rates showed a gulf in living standards that is also reminiscent of the third world. At Solihull and Yardley in the West Midlands landless cottagers exempt from the Hearth Tax had 147 infant deaths per 1,000 births, while craftsmen and husbandmen taxed on one hearth had seventy-seven per 1,000, and substantial peasants and gentry assessed for two hearths or more had fifty-six per 1,000.[77]

There is growing evidence that many people had poorer, as well as shorter, lives in early Stuart England. In rural society cottagers proliferated, and subsistence migration ceased. The general pattern was the decline of middle-sized holdings in mixed-farming, lowland villages, and migration to towns, or to pastoral regions, where the poor took up smallholdings, often on wasteland. The overall result, whether in lowland or upland areas, was the proliferation of quasi-landless cottagers. In the lowland parishes of Chippenham (Cambridgeshire), Orwell (Cambridgeshire) and Terling (Essex) a growing proportion of cottagers is apparent in the early seventeenth century, caused chiefly by the elimination of middle-sized holdings and the creation of larger farms. At Chippenham and Terling these changes followed the bad harvests of 1594–7. At Chippenham the poor crops caused indebtedness among middling peasants, who were forced to sell up, and who virtually disappeared between 1598 and 1636. At Terling, the three decades after 1600 saw increasing polarization between labourers and smallholders, on the one side, and better-off craftsmen and yeomen, on the other. A similar case is that of Keevil (Wiltshire), which had a sizeable element of broadcloth-workers, and where a widening gulf opened up between the better off and the poorer sort in the early seventeenth century. When trade depression combined with bad harvests in the 1620s, the problem of poverty came to the fore in Keevil. The parish responded by shutting down in-migration, halting squatting on wasteland, and promoting out-migration by

---

[77] R. Pressat, *Demographic Analysis. Methods, Results, Applications* (London, 1972), p. 130; Skipp, *Crisis and Development*, pp. 78–9, 85.

the unemployed.[78] Lowland parishes frequently put a lid on immigration in this period. The populations of Chippenham and Orwell showed substantial natural increase between 1570 and 1650, but neither place actually grew. Substantial out-migration must have occurred, and minimal in-migration. At Terling before 1620 the parish doubled in size, chiefly because the numbers of labouring families rose, but thereafter the population stabilized because the parish began regulating immigration.[79]

Those who left the lowland parishes, or were turned away from them, often found niches in predominantly pastoral regions, or resorted to hard-pressed towns. The fenland village of Willingham (Cambridgeshire) and the five Arden parishes studied by Skipp grew substantially in the late sixteenth and early seventeenth centuries. But greener pastures were not necessarily better ones. The proliferation of cottagers and labourers, the rapid growth of these settlements, and their high rates of exemption from the Hearth Tax, suggest that many migrants were changing addresses rather than their basic condition. Willingham and the Arden parishes apparently suffered 'Malthusian crisis' between 1610 and 1620. In Arden the crisis resulted from population pressure upon the resources. That pressure came partly from in-migration from the lowland areas of south Warwickshire and north Oxfordshire, where enclosure and engrossing had sparked popular uprisings in 1596 and 1607. Of course, hardship was not inevitable. In some places, including Willingham and Arden villages, the pastoral economy was reordered in later decades to support increased populations. In others – for example, Myddle (Salop), Rowington (Warwickshire) and the Rossendale valley – the immigration of labourers continued without crises or major alterations in the local economy, because wasteland was plentiful.[80] But, however differ-

---

[78] K. Wrightson and D. Levine, *Poverty and Piety in An English Village. Terling, 1525–1700* (London, 1979), pp. 29, 175; M. Spufford, *Contrasting Communities. English Villages in the Sixteenth and Seventeenth Centuries* (Cambridge, 1974), pp. 90–1, 118; M. Ingram, 'Religion, Communities and Moral Discipline in Late Sixteenth- and Early Seventeenth-Century England: Case Studies', in K. von Greyerz, ed., *Religion and Society in Early Modern Europe, 1500–1800* (London, 1984), pp. 184–5.

[79] Wrightson and Levine, *Poverty and Piety*, pp. 80–2, 175; Spufford, *Contrasting Communities*, pp. 25–7, 61–2.

[80] Spufford, *Contrasting Communities*, pp. 136–7; Skipp, *Crisis and Development*, pp. 95–7; D. Hey, *An English Rural Community. Myddle under the Tudors and Stuarts* (Leicester, 1974), pp. 169–70; G. H. Tupling, *The Economic History of Rossendale* (Manchester, 1927), pp. 95–9, 161–5.

ent the underlying causes and the results, lowland and upland regions both saw increasing numbers of quasi-landless cottagers in the first half of the seventeenth century.

Subsistence migration increased dramatically in this period, as people were uprooted and sought new settlements. A sudy of three Midland parishes shows rising numbers of migrant paupers. They included a medley of convicted vagabonds, demobbed soldiers, gypsies and foreigners, but over three-fifths (62.3 per cent) were simply listed as 'poor travellers', who were disabled or were migrating to pastures new. The total number of these migrants will never be known, but the surviving records show startling rises in their numbers in the first half of the seventeenth century. At Pattingham (Staffordshire) the increase was from forty-eight in the decade 1611–20 to 404 in 1621–30, and to 1,152 in 1631–40. At Branston (Leicestershire) the numbers grew from 375 to 631, and to 1,025 in the same decades. At Waltham-on-the-Wold (Leicestershire) records are missing for the middle decade, but 655 passed through the parish in 1611–20, and the total by 1631–40 was 1,901. All told, these Midlands parishes witnessed nearly a four-fold increase in migrant poor between 1611 and 1640.[81]

Similar rises are evident elsewhere in the Midlands and the North. The churchwardens of Upton (Nottinghamshire) gave doles to just three migrant paupers in 1608, to thirty-two in 1631, and to 130 in 1641. At Worfield (Salop), a mean average of nine migrants received relief each year in the 1590s, in 1620 the number was twelve, in 1630 it was thirty, and in the 1640s, sixty. The town of Doncaster saw the numbers rise sharply in the 1620s, from 373 in 1621–2 to 597 in 1627–8.[82] The reasons for the rising tide of transients were not, Professor Kent states, that procedures changed, or that constables became more diligent. The numbers were swollen by three groups – foreigners (particularly Irish), families and women. Whether there was a similar increase in southern England remains to be seen, but the rise in the proportion of families also occurred among vagrants arrested in Essex, Hertfordshire, London and Wiltshire in the period. The influx from

---

[81] J. Kent, 'Population Mobility and Alms: Poor Migrants in the Midlands during the Early Seventeenth Century', *Local Population Studies*, no. 27 (1981), pp. 36–8.

[82] Beier, *Masterless Men*, p. 111 and sources cited there; Hill, 'Poverty and Poor Relief in Shropshire', p. 146.

Ireland was triggered by famine there in 1628–9.[83] The increased numbers of English transients were more gradual, no doubt reflecting the deterioration of economic and demographic conditions that began in the 1590s, and accelerated from 1620.

The widespread implementation of the Elizabethan poor laws from the 1590s is another sign of increased hardship among the 'lower sort'. We have no direct evidence of changing levels of indigence for the whole country, but local evidence supports the view that conditions took a turn for the worse from the last decade of Elizabeth I's reign. Before 1590 official action to relieve the poor was sporadic, and largely confined to the larger towns and a few rural parishes. But from the mid-1590s the evidence of more widespread action is impressive. In a few instances growing numbers of paupers can be pinpointed as the cause. The town of Shrewsbury introduced poor-rates in the 1570s, but until the 1590s the poor were allowed to beg. Between 1590 and 1650 there was a sharp rise in the proportion of the population in need: in 1590 one in eight received parish relief; by the early 1620s it was one in five; and during the civil wars, one in three. Thereafter the proportion fell to one in six in 1670, and to one in seven in 1700. In Ludlow the poor on relief accounted for one in twenty of the population in 1560, by the 1640s the figure was one in three, and then it fell to one in five after 1660. In the Gloucester parish of St Aldate's the numbers receiving relief trebled from the 1570s to the 1630s; 'in the crisis years of the 1620s nearly 40 per cent of the parish was probably destitute'.[84]

Salisbury and Winchester, both traditional textile centres, were hard hit by trade depression from the early 1620s, and took sustained action to relieve the poor, including increased poor-rates.[85] In early seventeenth-century Lincolnshire, middling towns like Gainsborough and Grantham were besieged with poor migrants, who built shacks on wastelands and risked swelling the

---

[83] Kent, 'Population Mobility', pp. 36, 42–3; Beier, *Masterless Men*, pp. 56–7, 216.

[84] Hill, 'Poverty and Poor Relief', pp. 162, 206; P. Clark, ' "The Ramoth-Gilead of the Good": Urban Change and Political Radicalism at Gloucester, 1540–1640', in P. Clark, A. G. R. Smith and N. Tyacke, eds., *The English Commonwealth, 1547–1640* (Leicester, 1979), p. 174. See also the useful discussion in Slack, *Poverty and Policy*, pp. 11, 169–178.

[85] Slack, 'Politics and Poverty', pp. 173ff; A. Rosen, 'Winchester in Transition, 1580–1700', in Clark, ed., *Country Towns in Pre-Industrial England*, pp. 157–9.

poor-rates. To the south, Great Yarmouth complained of rising numbers of poor in 1631 after a bad harvest, and rates were increased to £481 from the £330 normally laid out. The problem did not subsequently abate, despite improved harvest conditions: in 1634 the town was spending £602 a year on the poor. In the Shropshire town of Whitchurch the decline of the cloth industry at the end of the interregnum was crucial: the numbers of pensioners rose from twenty-eight in 1658 to sixty in 1665.[86]

Studies of county government show poor relief being widely enforced from the end of Elizabeth's reign, but especially after 1620 when the numbers of poor began to rise again. In Kent, despite 'widespread respectable opposition', poor-rates became ubiquitous from the late 1590s. By the time the government issued a new Book of Orders in 1630, local officials in many places had developed a sophisticated system for dealing with the poor. Kentish justices complained of increased numbers of poor in 1623, and the cost of poor relief rose sharply in the decade 1618–28: by 50 per cent in Cranbrook and three-fold at Cowden.[87] In neighbouring Sussex rising pauperism from 1600 to 1630 meant that 'parish after parish was forced to fall back on taxation for the aid of its poor'. By the 1620s and 1630s most parishes were levying poor-rates, and by the civil wars 'the poor rate had become a fact of life'. In seventeenth-century Lincolnshire, magistrates were apparently galvanized into action by the Book of Orders of 1630, and thereafter the poor laws became the heaviest burden in their administrative work.[88] But elsewhere, as in Kent and Sussex, implementation of the laws pre-dated the Caroline programme. Lancashire's quarter sessions rolls survive from the 1590s, and from the 1620s 'the poor law administration was already functioning in a substantial number of parishes'. In Shropshire rural parishes began to administer poor relief from the 1590s, and in the mid-seventeenth century relief expenditure more than doubled because of rising numbers of poor. Somerset justices increased their enforcement of the laws in the

---

[86] C. Holmes, *Seventeenth-Century Lincolnshire*, *History of Lincolnshire*, vol. 7 (Lincoln, 1980), pp. 31, 33, 37; PRO SP 16/188/80, 271/101; Hill, 'Poverty and Poor Relief', pp. 128, 144–5.

[87] Clark, *English Provincial Society*, pp. 241, 245, 321, 351.

[88] A. Fletcher, *Sussex, 1600–1660. A County Community in Peace and War* (London, 1975), p. 156; Holmes, *Seventeenth-Century Lincolnshire*, pp. 79, 111.

1620s, but the bench was already receiving increased numbers of petitions requesting poor relief in the 1620s.[89]

Of course, there was not unhindered, universal application of the poor laws of 1598 and 1601. After the crises of the 1590s a period of comparative prosperity ensued in many places, and the legislation was barely enforced. The Act of 1601 lapsed when the Addled Parliament of 1614 was dissolved, and the next Parliament in 1621 failed to renew the legislation, as commentators, aware of deteriorating conditions, anxiously noted.[90] In addition, there was opposition to poor-rates, which offended people's notions about charity as well as hitting their purses. The growing numbers of settlement disputes and the many hundreds of petitions by the poor to the benches – for example in Derbyshire, Lancashire, Somerset and Warwickshire – attest to the unwillingness of many parish elites to shoulder the burden. The old forms of neighbourly charity died slowly in many places, and were probably never wholly supplanted. Some communities adapted the laws to their circumstances, combining some statutory action with traditional customs.[91] Pastoral communities with extensive wastelands such as Myddle, or with expanding mining operations such as Bedworth, and Madely and Brosely in Shropshire, continued to accept subsistence migrants. In the case of Myddle, as in much of neighbouring Wales, the poor were not much of a problem until the end of the century.[92]

VI

Despite the reservations and exceptions, it seems that the years from 1590 to 1660, and particularly from 1620 to 1660, were the

[89] A. Fessler, 'The Official Attitude Towards the Sick Poor in Seventeenth-Century Lancashire', *Transactions of the Historic Society of Lancashire and Cheshire*, 102 (1951), p. 106; Hill, 'Poverty and Poor Relief', pp. 113, 148; T. G. Barnes, *Somerset, 1625–40* (Cambridge, Mass., 1961), chapter 7; also Quarter Sessions Rolls, Somers. RO.

[90] G. W. Prothero, ed., *Select Statutes and Other Constitutional Documents* (4th edn, London, 1954), p. 105; G. Roberts, ed., *The Diary of Walter Yonge*, Camden Society, 1st series, 41 (1848), pp. 51–2; M. S., *Grievous Groans for the Poor* (1622), cited in F. M. Eden, *The State of the Poor* (London, 1797), vol. 1, pp. 154–5; Fletcher, *Reform in the Provinces*, p. 184.

[91] Hill, 'Poverty and Poor Relief', pp. 133, 193–5, 197; Fletcher, *Reform in the Provinces*, pp. 183–9; A. H. Dodd, *Studies in Stuart Wales* (Cardiff, 1952), p. 18. For petitions and settlement cases, see the records of quarter sessions in the counties cited.

[92] Hey, *An English Rural Community*, p. 178; Hill, 'Poverty and Poor Relief', p. 136; Dodd, *Studies in Stuart Wales*, pp. 17–18.

decisive ones for the implementation of the poor laws in early modern England. Quantitative methods make a limited contribution to our understanding of this development. Much of the evidence – of trade depressions, declining life-expectancy, the erosion of the middling peasantry, increased subsistence migration and rising poor-rates – provides indirect or localized measures of living conditions. Indeed, the chief obstacle to counting the poor is incomplete evidence. The best records of taxation relate to the early 1520s and the 1660s and 1670s, but these cannot be applied to the period from 1590 to 1660. Hoskins may have exaggerated the numbers of the early Tudor poor, but recent downward revisions of his figures should be treated with caution. It appears that many of the poorest were possibly omitted from Henry VIII's assessments and lay subsidies, and from the Restoration Hearth Taxes. The accounts of parish overseers are also suspect, because means-testing excluded significant numbers from relief payments – usually the 'better-off' poor thought able to work. Problems arise, too, with the rare censuses from which mean household sizes can be calculated. This is because of the impact of the life-cycle, which meant that the proportion of society who experienced need in the course of their lives was probably significantly greater than the proportion counted as poor at any one juncture. Above all, the virtual disappearance from the ranks of the poor of those aged between sixteen and thirty, and their re-entry into poverty after the age of thirty, must be considered. Finally, overall percentiles gloss over the fact that poverty varied greatly in its impact depending upon gender and geography.

All told, it appears that a strictly quantitative approach is not the best way to understand the problem of the poor in early modern England. Admittedly there are risks in adopting a more impressionistic approach. As noted above, instances can be discovered of the poor keeping servants, paying high rents and owning pewter; of affluent building-craftsmen in an age of falling real wages; and of new industries springing up when old ones were depressed. Of course there were gradations among the poor, and the economic outlook was not without some silver linings. But whether such examples are representative has still to be demonstrated. Similar issues of typicality arise with many official and literary sources, which tended to use hyperbole and stereotypes in describing the poor. Nevertheless, contemporary opinion deserves greater attention. In a hierarchical society, if those in positions of authority thought that levels of deprivation were unacceptably dangerous, then the precise numbers of the poor may be of secondary importance. There is also a wealth of literary evidence to support the view that early modern England retained many features of a pre-industrial economy, including serious underemployment.[93]

The reasons for the implementation of the poor laws in early modern England included, as we have seen, a deterioration in demographic and economic conditions between 1590 and 1660. But the underlying causes were longer term changes in the English economy and social order. The first of these was the decline of the traditional woollen broadcloth industry, which from the mid-fourteenth to the mid-sixteenth century was the country's leading export industry. The eclipse of the industry was not universal – it hung on in parts of the West Country, the West Riding and Lancashire until the age of cotton – but it affected many traditional centres such as Ludlow, Salisbury, Whitchurch and Winchester. Judging by the case of Keevil, even some villages, where the industry is often assumed to have relocated, were involved in the shut-down. After 1660 England's foreign trade and manufactures were diversified and increasingly centred upon colonial and re-export trades. But the interim period was a painful one for many centres, which implemented measures to control and relieve their poor.

The second structural change was the growth of the landless, or near-landless, cottager/labourer element in society. Again, the impact of this development varied, and no doubt precedents can be found in the Middle Ages. But the seventeenth-century evidence seems sufficiently compelling to suggest reopening the enquiry into what Marx saw as a key development in the growth of capitalism in England. The decline of middle-sized peasant holdings is evident in Chippenham, Orwell and Terling in the early seventeenth century. The corollaries were out-migration, or at least the discouragement of in-migration, which must have augmented subsistence movements generally. Another consequence was the polarization between the 'better sort' and the poor, with the first group attempting to 'discipline' the second, often using the poor laws, as in Keevil and Terling. Even where the middling elements held their own, as in Keevil, the poor proliferated,

---

[93] D. C. Coleman, 'Labour in the English Economy of the Seventeenth Century', *Economic History Review*, 2nd series, 8 (1956), *passim*.

demanding housing and doles, and posing a problem of order because of immigration and trade depressions.

There was more room for migrants in some towns, fenland and wood/pasture regions, but in their new surroundings many occupied exiguous smallholdings and took up vulnerable by-employments. As their numbers grew, their resources frequently diminished. The poor were a problem even where extraordinary kinds of economic adaptation took place. The transformation of the Warwickshire village of Bedworth into a coal-mining town, subject to boom and bust, was an extreme, but not wholly untypical, case. Many of Bedworth's Arden neighbours experienced similar processes of adaptation and growth, and from the mid-seventeenth century they began to administer poor relief. When those who 'receive weekly collection and live upon the common and in town houses [*sic*]' were listed in the Hearth Tax for Hemingford Hundred in the early 1670s, they formed between 56.3 and 81.5 per cent of the exemptions. Literally, the poor had come to stay, even on the seventeenth century's new frontier.[94] Thus progress and poverty were not a matter of either/or. The enforcement of the poor laws presupposed a body of tax-payers, who were the beneficiaries of progress, but also considerable numbers of paupers, who were its casualties.

[94] Skipp, *Crisis and Development*, pp. 73–4; Styles, *Hearth Tax Records*, pp. lxxvii–lxxviii.

7. Ambiguity and contradiction in 'the rise of professionalism': the English clergy, 1570–1730

MICHAEL HAWKINS

Much of Lawrence Stone's work, with its deft marriage of the historically contingent with social theory and political analysis, has successfully attacked Whiggish and Marxist variants of historicism. The latter derive part of their ancestry from the modernization theory of the Enlightenment. In this essay another application of modernization theory, that dealing with the learned professions, will be discussed. An effort will be made, in a minor way, to apply to it some of Lawrence Stone's scepticism. It will be argued that early modern historians are in danger of not learning from the difficulties sociologists have encountered in defining both 'professions' and 'professionalization', and that the problems are more serious than sociologists have generally recognized. It is probably necessary to live with the term 'profession', however loosely defined, but it is better to distinguish the 'rise of the professions' from professionalization. To illustrate these points the clergy ordained as deacons in the diocese of Peterborough between 1570 and 1730 will be used as a case study.

I

The sociology of the professions has long had a strong historical element. 'Professionalization' has been regarded as a recognizable process with a marked breakthrough at industrialization. Theories of professionalization descend indirectly from ideas about the process of rationalization held by Weber to be characteristic of modern Western society. The descent is indirect because Weber himself, in so far as he dealt with professions at all, drew sharp distinctions between them and modern capitalism and bureaucracy: motivation, education and the degree of hierarchical authority differed. Nevertheless, the seeds of a common approach were always present: from Durkheim and Spencer modern professions, businesses and bureaucracies were all seen as demonstrating an advanced stage of the division of labour, with the division of knowledge itself being seen as especially apposite to the professions. The sense of common development was heightened by a greater awareness of structural similarities between twentieth-century professions, bureaucracies and businesses: modern businesses were seen as more bureaucratized and as applying impersonal standards. Such standards, specified functions and an hierarchical structure could be seen as common features in a process of rationalization which applied to a variety of institutions including both old and new professions.[1]

In such discussions a familiar cluster of traits has generally been used to identify professions and professionals. These traits are often seen as mutually dependent. They include, first, the offering of skills, primarily non-manual, which are not available in such a developed form elsewhere. Such skills represent the application of a generalized body of theoretical or abstract knowledge requiring lengthy periods of education and training. Secondly, there is usually a formal point of, and procedure for, entry to the profession, with access and performance regulated by senior members of the profession itself. A profession insists on high standards of behaviour towards clients: this is usually reinforced by internal discipline, including powers of expulsion from professional practice. This self-regulation is necessary because of the esoteric content of the profession's knowledge, which is often of especial significance to society. In the case of the 'ancient' professions of law, medicine and divinity, it concerns crime, disease and sin, or, more positively, social order, health and salvation. Such knowledge is more than mere skill and justifies high rewards. Entry and

---

[1] For extended discussion of these issues necessarily raised only briefly here, see M. Weber, *The Theory of Social and Economic Organisation* (London, 1964), especially pp. 329–40; T. Parsons, *The Structure of Social Action* (New York, 1968); R. Dingwall and P. Lewis, eds., *The Sociology of the Professions* (London, 1983), pp. 2–4, 7, 11–12, 41, 47, 57, 81–3, 86, 94, 102–3, 177–8, 180–3, 185, 191–3, 198, 213–4, 219–20; P. Elliott, *The Sociology of the Professions* (London, 1972), pp. 2, 5, 7–10, 12, 14, 51; P. A. Jackson, *Professions and Professionalization* (Cambridge, 1970), pp. 3–4, 13, 19–22; M. L. Cogan, 'Towards a Definition of Profession', *Harvard Educational Review*, 23 (1953), pp. 36–8, 41, 48–9. For an argument denying the descent, see G. Harries-Jenkins, 'Professionals in Organisations', in Jackson, *Professions and Professionalization*, pp. 51–107.

promotion are in principle on merit, and there is usually a graded hierarchy. Professions are institutionally organized, this being usually necessary to secure control over access, and their services are open to all comers, dependent only on ability to pay for them. Often a system of fees from clients is ardently defended as a criterion of professional status, dependence on a salary being seen as leading to its loss. Connected with these characteristics is a range of less precisely definable qualities, such as a developed *esprit de corps* and a high regard by outsiders, some writers stressing a public 'mandate' to perform certain functions.[2]

Such traits are very well known, but old criticisms of them have been revived and new ones added in the last twenty years. The list of characteristics has been attacked as either too imprecise to distinguish professions from other occupations (especially given the convergence towards other forms of organization mentioned above), or because it implies a functionalist view which emphasizes the professions' role in social equilibrium and integration: the professions' own evaluation of themselves is being accepted at face value. Instead two connected alternative approaches have been stressed: professions should be placed within a general typology of occupations and their self esteem should be punctured by reviving Schumpeter's view of them as monopoly providers of services or by seeing them as 'conceptive ideologists' for the bourgeoisie. The emphasis is on their place in the structure of power and on the commercial element in their relationships with their clients. They are seen, as they were by the Webbs or indeed by the Levellers, as conspiring against the public and stressing their arcane knowledge as a way of improving their worth in the market.[3]

---

[2] A. M. Carr-Saunders and P. A. Wilson, *The Professions* (London, 1933); T. H. Marshall, 'The Recent History of Professionalism in Relation to Social Structure and Social Policy', *Canadian Journal of Economics and Social Science*, 5 (1939), pp. 325–40; E. C. Hughes, *Men and their Work* (Glencoe, Illinois, 1958); B. Barker, 'Some Problems in the Sociology of Professions', *Daedalus*, 92 (1963), pp. 669–88; J. Ben-David, 'Professions in the Class System of Present-Day Societies', *Current Sociology*, 12 (1963–4), pp. 247–330; W. J. Goode, 'The Theoretical Limits of Professionalization', in A. Ezioni, ed., *The Semi-Professions and their Organization* (New York 1969), pp. 266–313; *ibid.*, 'Encroachment, Charlatanism and the Emerging Professions', *American Sociological Review*, 25 (1960), pp. 902–14; Dingwall, *Sociology of the Professions*, pp. 4–5, 7, 23–5, 52, 54, 56, 90, 94, 135–6, 197–8, 224–5; Elliot, *Sociology of the Professions*, pp. 12, 57, 64; Jackson, *Professions*, pp. 5–8, 24–32, 37; Cogan, 'Towards a Definition of Profession', pp. 34–49.

[3] J. A. Schumpeter, *Imperialism and Social Classes* (Oxford, 1951); T. J. Johnson, *Professions and Power* (London, 1972); I. Illich, *Disabling Professions* (London,

Some writers have tried to avoid the problem of definition by reviving an historical approach, arguing that professionalism should not be seen as a 'timeless constant'. It is not for an historian to criticize the view that professionalism may mean different things at different times, but such an approach does not obviate the need for definition: expert knowledge may be 'historically variable', but it remains expert knowledge and presumably definable.[4] The main danger of an historical approach is not one of definition but the assumption of a process. Historians may accept for definitional purposes a Weberian 'ideal-type' of profession, characterized by the above traits, which no actual profession realizes, but the Weberian model is dangerous for historians in its easily accepted implication that there is a process of 'professionalization' in history by which professions come nearer the ideal.

The temptation to assume a developmental sequence which unhappily combines teleology and functionalism and allows theory to dominate, or even exclude, the need for evidence is a common one.[5] In the case of the professions the difficulties are worse: within the definition or list of characteristics above there are several potential contradictions at least as significant as the degree to which they are mutually reinforcing. This confronts historians with a particular problem since it is change over time that is likely to

1977); H. S. Becker, 'The Nature of a Profession', in his *Sociological Work* (Chicago, 1970); E. Freidson, *Profession of Medicine: a Study of the Sociology of Applied Knowledge* (New York, 1970), and *Professional Dominance: The Structure of Medical Care* (Chicago, 1970); Goode, 'Theoretical Limits' and 'Encroachment, Charlatanism', also 'Community Within a Community', *American Sociological Review*, 22, (1957), pp. 194–200; Cogan, 'Towards a Definition of Profession', pp. 35–9, 41, 43; Elliott, *Sociology of the Professions*, pp. 2–14, 92; Dingwall, *Sociology of the Professions*, pp. 3–4, 7, 12, 19–37, 39, 41–52, 54, 56–7, 85–9, 106–20, 136–7, 149, 182, 197, 224–7; Jackson, *Professions*, pp. 6–7, 10–14, 19–26, 29, 33–7.

[4] T. Parsons, 'Professions', *International Encyclopedia of the Social Sciences*, 12 (New York, 1968), pp. 536–47; M. Cain, 'The General Practice Lawyer and the Client: Towards a Radical Conception', in Dingwall, *Sociology of the Professions*, pp. 106–30; Elliott, *Sociology of the Professions*, pp. 2–5, 11, 40; Jackson, *Professions*, pp. 3–5, 25; Dingwall, *Sociology of the Professions*, pp. 21–3, 31–5, 55, 85–6, 136–7, 196–7.

[5] Carr-Saunders and Wilson, *Professions*; E. Freidson, 'The Theory of the Professions: State of the Art', in Dingwall, *Sociology of the Professions*, pp. 19–37; Jackson, *Professions*, p. 23; Cogan, 'Towards a Definition of Profession', pp. 34, 40. This development is, however, often seen as confined to Anglo-American society, where, because of the supposedly limited role of the state, professional autonomy was more pronounced (Freidson, 'Theory of the Professions', pp. 21–6, 32–5, and Dingwall, *Sociology of the Professions*, pp. 46–7).

sharpen the contradictions and make them apparent. In a pioneering article Charlton mentioned two of them, saying that 'professional lawyers, for example, owe a duty to both client and
community' and that 'a professional man can often find himself in
conflict over his fees and his professional ethic or code of
conduct'. But more can be added; a professional man's loyalty to
his profession (Goode's 'community within a community') may
conflict with his responsibilities to society at large. There is
potential conflict between restricted entry, which benefits the
income of existing members, and wider entry, of benefit to
society and to the general influence of the professions as a whole.
There is also potential conflict between the hierarchical organization of a profession and promotion on merit, since the former
may emphasize mere seniority. The principle of entry on merit
does not square easily with a profession's desire to perpetuate
itself and take advantage of its high status. Historically the latter
has often meant that sons of existing members follow their
fathers' careers.

Above all, there is potential conflict between self-regulation and
the maintenance of the highest standards, the latter depending on
the elimination of personal influence. These are independent of
possible tensions between education, training and techniques
within professional practice: the relationship between jurisprudence and advising clients, between medicine and treating the
sick or between theology and saving souls is not always clear or
comparable across professions. Equally the degree of autonomy of
professional knowledge may vary: lawyers are not solely responsible for writing statutes, nor, in early modern Europe, did the
clergy solely determine theology or ecclesiastical practice.[6]

To discuss the historical development of professions is therefore
to enter a minefield. If a profession is said to rise, does this mean
more or fewer members? Either could mean more social prestige,
more political weight or higher standards of behaviour, or one of

[6] K. Charlton, 'The Professions in Sixteenth-Century England', *University of
Birmingham Historical Journal*, 12 (1969), pp. 20–41, especially p. 22. Some but
by no means all of these points are touched on in Elliott, *Sociology of the
Professions*, pp. 41, 61, 79–80; Dingwall, *Sociology of the Professions*, pp. 35, 42,
45, 56, 137, 180–1, 199–200, 206, 223; Jackson, *Professions*, pp. 4–7, 26–32;
Freidson, *Profession of Medicine* and 'Theory of the Professions'; Johnson,
Professions; Goode, 'Theoretical Limits' and 'Encroachment, Charlatanism'; *cf.*
the reference in Dingwall, pp. 199–200, to the 'Janus-like character of the
professions'.

these without the others. Generally fewer members may mean higher quality, but this can be offset by the greater impersonality in assessing entry or promotion which may follow from larger numbers.[7] These difficulties are inbuilt in the common notions of professionalism. But it may help to distinguish between the 'rise (or fall) of the professions or professionals' and that of 'professionalism or professionalization'. Under the former may be placed changes which increase or decrease the influence and power of a particular professional group: numbers, income, attractiveness to entrants, access to social or political influence are obvious ways of assessing these. On the other hand, 'professionalism' or 'professionalization' can be used when discussing quality of performance and the effectiveness of the structures designed to achieve it. These twð ways of looking at the same data may not produce the same answer when deciding whether a particular professional group 'rose': they may be compatible (in certain circumstances higher standards of behaviour may lead to greater influence in society) but equally they may not (more corruption may accompany or even lead to greater influence). These problems are particularly acute given the role of patronage in early modern society.

II

Until fairly recently, however, early modern historians have been happily able to ignore these problems. The vexed relationships of the professions to business and the state were seen as essentially problems of modern society. Carr-Saunders and Wilson's standard history concentrated above all on the establishment, often in the nineteenth and early twentieth centuries, of institutional bodies within professions to regulate entry, promotion and conduct. Reference to apparently similar bodies in earlier periods, such as the Inns of Court, colleges at the universities and the Royal College of Physicians, was met by doubts about how effectively they regulated standards and their independence from outside pressures. More generally, early modern professions were seen (too simplistically) as high-status groups more concerned with a life

[7] Cf. G. E. Aylmer, *The State's Servants: the Civil Service of the English Republic, 1649–1660* (London, 1973), for an argument that the expanded bureaucracy of the interregnum was, to an extent, accompanied by a more professional approach to the notion of government service.

of gentlemanly privilege than with their responsibilities to the public. The shift from 'status' or 'estate' to 'occupational' professions came with the Industrial Revolution.[8]

More recently, there has been a tendency to look at the early modern period as at least an important formative one. In 1969 Charlton tentatively made two general points about sixteenth-century professions. First, he detected a growing division of labour with the greater diversification of existing professions and the development of new ones. This was connected with the growth of esoteric fields of knowledge. Secondly, he saw a general secularization of the professions, which freed themselves from regulation by the church. This was part of the spread of self-regulation.[9] Eight years later this caution became the bold statement, 'The growth of professionalism in the seventeenth century', with which Orpen began an article on schoolmastering.[10] O'Day has expanded this, saying that 'the emergence [in early modern England] of large professional groups having a common academic, institutionalized training; an accepted internal hierarchy, rules, regulations and codes of conduct; and similar interests, ambitions and lifestyles, made a great impact on society'.[11] The tendency exists to antedate Weberian modernization: already the biological or evolutionary imagery of the historicist approach is evident in the titles of recent books: *The Rise of the Barristers*;[12] *The English Clergy: the Emergence and Consolidation of a Profession, 1558–1642*.

[8] *Cf.* Carr-Saunders and Wilson, *Professions*, and many of the references in note 1 above. For example, Elliot, pp. 14–15, says that 'the professional occupations in pre-industrial and post-industrial Britain differ sharply in their characteristics'.

[9] 'The Professions', p. 41.

[10] P. K. Orpen, 'Schoolmastering as a Profession in the Seventeenth Century: The Career Patterns of the Grammar Schoolmaster', *History of Education*, 6 (1977), p. 183.

[11] R. O'Day, *The English Clergy: The Emergence and Consolidation of a Profession, 1558–1642* (Leicester, 1979), p. 1.

[12] W. R. Prest, *The Rise of the Barristers: A Social History of the English Bar, 1590–1640* (Oxford, 1986). I have received W. Prest, ed., *The Professions in Early Modern England* (London, 1987), which includes (pp. 25–63) an essay by R. O'Day, 'The Anatomy of a Profession: The Clergy of the Church of England', too late to consider its conclusions in the text of this article. Many of them do, however, appear to agree with points made here (e.g., the limits on the church's autonomy, the early indiscriminate mass ordination by the bishops, the church's difficulties with patronage and rewards, the doubts about academic qualifications and the career-structure in the church), but a stadial approach is still evident in the section on 'estate to profession' (pp. 28–33), professionalization is still seen as a 'continuum' (p. 50) and 'structural change ... was more or less completed by 1662' (p. 27). The biological imagery is even more explicit in references to

At first sight it would be surprising if the clerical profession rose in early Protestant society either in the sense of increasing its influence in society or by becoming more professionalized. In some ways it can be argued that the appearance of distinctive professions in sixteenth- and seventeenth-century England was made possible by the break-up of the near monopoly of professional work held by the clergy for much of the Middle Ages. Protestant theology was a handmaid of the continuing laicization of society and has often been said to have contributed to the demystifying of the clergy. In terms of professionalism this meant undermining, or even denying any claim that the clergy had special skills. This was accompanied by attacks on clerical numbers – through the abolition of minor and regular orders – and on clerical wealth. Those things which survived the Reformation can hardly be said to have facilitated the development of professionalism. The church's control over recruitment and promotion at best remained partial and to an extent declined. Assessment of fitness to enter the surviving orders of deacon and priest remained within the purview of the diocesan authorities, but lay influence grew over actual appointment to vicarages and rectories and to the lesser clerical posts, such as the various types of curacies, readerships and lectureships, and over promotion within the church. The clerical profession could still discipline its own members through the ecclesiastical courts, but this was nothing new.

Certainly the clergy were given new functions, but many of them were of a rather mundane nature – keeping the poor box or parish registers – and performance of them was often variable. Anyway, such functions do not constitute professionalism: they are the tasks which members of a profession delegate to others, and it may be that the growing role of the parish clerk should be noted here. More important was the new emphasis on pastoral rather than priestly functions, requiring, it is argued, a knowledge of scripture and an ability to expound it in sermons and catechizing. The first stage was the abolition of the unlearned clerical 'proletariat', especially in the reign of Edward VI. Visitation articles formed the basis of inquiry by the clerical hierarchy into the standards of their subordinates.

In particular, a substantial improvement has been claimed when the number of graduates entering the profession is measured. It is

'metamorphosis', 'chrysalis' and the emergence of 'the butterfly' (pp. 28, 50). See my forthcoming review in *History of Education*.

unquestionable (and further evidence is presented below) that the clergy had become a largely graduate profession by 1640. The change began in London and near the universities and gradually spread. But it is an open question as to how far an unspecialized arts degree, not primarily oriented towards theology, could fit a man to meet the new aspirations for the clergy, even when that degree was carried to master's level. Bishop Burnet held that ordinands 'came from [universities] less knowing than when they went to them'. In modern times a period of specialized postgraduate training is often necessary to prepare someone for professional work after a non-vocational degree. Those professions, such as the civil service, which do not have specialized entry requirements, are often the subject of most controversy about standards and performance. Protestant England, despite the setting up of 'puritan' colleges, especially at Cambridge, did not offer the specialized seminary training received by certain recruits to the Catholic clergy. It is not clear that a B.A. or M.A. degree obtained via Emmanuel differed in substance from one acquired at Peterhouse. It will be seen that, in so far as the universities, in the bachelor and doctor of divinity degrees, did offer specialized theological training, this tended to be for those destined for, or already embarked upon, careers at the top of the clerical or educational hierarchy. Such careers never exposed them to, or soon removed them from, parochial responsibilities.

However, it is intended not to deny the improvements in clerical education, but to stress ambiguities and contradictions in the notion of the development of a profession. Learning may have helped to make the clergy an estate more distinct from unlettered parishioners, but another view is possible. Lay learning rose faster (from a lower base) than that of the clergy, and clerical learning was itself partly a response to rising lay expectations, especially among the elite. Lay assessment of the clergy seems to have become more pronounced. The early enthusiasm among the upper clergy itself for a learned, preaching ministry became more muted, and the hierarchy became more concerned to differentiate the clerical order from lay society by re-emphasizing its sacramental functions. If the clergy were given an expanded and specialized role it was only at the cost of sustained and increased interference from outside, from both the Crown and radical critics: this culminated in the abolition of its upper ranks and an even more substantial disruption of its lower ones than had occurred in the mid-sixteenth century. It is difficult to speak of the 'consolidation of a profession' in the days of Root and Branch. The existence of 'mechanick preachers' was a direct affront to the claim to status and employment based on possession of a university degree.

There were similar ambiguities in two other fields: clerical wealth and clerical marriage. Generally the sixteenth-century attack on clerical wealth must be seen as an attack on the profession in the first sense (that of its power and influence in society), but there were limits. Heal and O'Day have stressed the wealth and income remaining in the English church at various levels;[13] attacks on long leases and attempts to buy impropriations represent efforts by the pre-Civil War hierarchy to extend the church's control of that wealth. Equally, despite the decline in bequests for ecclesiastical purposes documented by Professor Jordan,[14] there were endowments of, for example, lectureships intended to provide a professional income for approved clergymen. Thus the new demands on the clergy were not wholly without financial backing, and there is even clearer evidence of rising income after the Restoration.[15] But little progress was made towards providing an hierarchy of income paralleling professional advancement. Clerical income depended too much on the vagaries of the relationship between inflation and tithe (whether commuted or not) and estate income for there to be any real progress towards professionalism in this field. Too many clergy, at diocesan or parochial level, had to show the skills of an estate manager or litigant. The income of incumbents was a lottery rather than a rational distribution of rewards based on status and achievement: therefore pluralism and nonresidence persisted with the consequence of diminished professional performance in the second sense referred to above. Even the efforts of interregnum governments to increase the income of poor livings were *ad hoc* rather than systematic and were undertaken when the structure of the established church was thoroughly disrupted. It was not until the very end of our period that the Commissioners of Queen Anne's Bounty attempted something a little more rational.

[13] Elliot, *op. cit.*, p. 29. R. O'Day and F. Heal, eds. *Princes and Paupers in the English Church, 1500–1800* (Totowa, New Jersey, 1981).

[14] W. K. Jordan, *Philanthropy in England, 1480–1660: A Study of the Changing Patterns of English Social Aspirations* (London, 1959).

[15] J. Pruett, *Parish Clergy under the Later Stuarts* (Urbana, Illinois, 1978).

Clerical marriage is another example of the problems inherent in the development of professionalism. It can be argued that it facilitated the rise of a professional class by offering the opportunity to create dynasties of clergymen, who perpetuated a professional outlook setting them apart from the rest of society. But equally it may be that marriage made the clergy more, not less, like the rest of society in their outlook and preoccupations, while, perhaps more significantly, it hardly helped the competitive open access to posts and promotions characteristic of rational professionalism.

In short, the combination of ancient institutional forms and new expectations facing the church in the Reformation world hardly facilitated the development of professionalization. The church's claim to arcane knowledge, while still strong, was questioned; entry and promotion were only partly on merit or under the church's control; aspects of the clergy's lifestyle became if anything even more like that of the laity; and rewards were largely independent of services to clients. A more ambiguous picture appears if the clergy's *esprit de corps* and public repute are considered. Before 1640 a high level of lay expectation was met, it is said, by more and better qualified recruits, but that can be seen as a mixed blessing. Without doubt many newly educated laymen wished for a clerical career, but neither the training they received nor its application in parochial work prevented the church from being severely disrupted in the mid-seventeenth century. The pre-Civil War concern over the church made it both more attractive and more vulnerable: professional autonomy was hardly to be looked for. It took upper-class reaction to the perceived excesses of the 1640s and 1650s to reduce the church's vulnerability. This was, however, at the cost of losing a substantial minority of its clientele to Nonconformity and thus in practice abandoning its claimed monopoly of arcane knowledge. It will be seen that there are other ways in which the position of the post-Restoration church was only questionably more professionalized, however attractive it may have been as a form of employment to certain social groups.

III

These general reflections need to be tested against more specific evidence. O'Day says, 'it is rarely possible to obtain detailed and equivalent information about the careers of a substantial group of clergy during this period'.[16] The fullest attempt is Longden's monumental study of the clergy of the diocese of Peterborough,[17] and the rest of this essay is devoted to an analysis of it. The Longden studied two overlapping, but not coterminous, groups: those recorded as holding any sort of clerical employment in the newly created diocese, and those ordained in the diocese (or by the bishop elsewhere), even if, as was often the case, they had no subsequent employment in it. The following analysis is based on those ordained deacon in the diocese, either by the bishop or by other authority, from the start of systematic record-keeping in the 1570s.[18]

Most analyses of the clergy focus on those holding livings: they are valuable in assessing the church's impact on parishioners,[19] but omit those who entered the profession without making discoverable progress in it. Since entry to the diaconate was controlled by the church itself, it offers a better gauge of the clergy as a profession than do benefice-holders, whose appointment was so often subject to lay influence. Deacons rather than priests have been chosen because entering the diaconate was the first defined step in a professional clerical career in the Protestant church. In Table 7.1 every year has been calculated, but otherwise the central five years of each decade (for example 1573–7 inclusive) have been taken as a large sample: where reference is made to the 1570s cohort it is those ordained deacon in those years who are meant. The data has been checked against the Peterborough Ordination Books when available.[20] Seven decades before the Civil War (1570s–1630s) and seven after the Restoration (1660s–1720s) have been analysed, both to put the Civil War in perspective and to try to assess the effects of the disruption of the interregnum.[21]

The moving averages shown in Figure 7.1 illustrate longer trends

[16] pp. 7–8.
[17] H. Isham Longden, *Northampton and Rutland Clergy from 1500*, 15 vols (Northampton, 1939–52).
[18] The relatively few ordained by the Bishop of Peterborough in London and elsewhere outside the diocese have been excluded.
[19] For recent examples see O'Day; W. J. Sheils, 'The Puritans in the Diocese of Peterborough, 1558–1610', *Northamptonshire Record Society Publications*, 30, (1979), chapter 6; M. Steig, *Laud's Laboratory: The Diocese of Bath and Wells in the Early Seventeenth Century* (London, 1982), chapter 3; P. R. Jenkins, 'The Rise of A Graduate Clergy in Early Seventeenth-Century Sussex', *Sussex Archaeological Collections*, 120 (1982), pp. 161–9.
[20] Northants. RO, X959, 961, 956; ML732, 724, 733.
[21] Very few ordinations are recorded in the 1640s and naturally none in the 1650s.

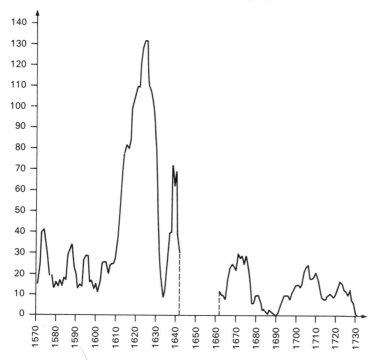

Figure 7.1 Numbers of ordinations of deacons in the Diocese of Peterborough, 1570s to 1720s (three-year moving averages)
These figures differ in some respects from those in O'Day (p. 19); doubtful cases are omitted.

and reduce the distortion possibly introduced by the, usually brief, vacancies in the see. They do not hide the extreme fluctuations in the numbers presenting themselves and accepted for ordination in this diocese. These must not be taken as necessarily indicating national trends: O'Day has given evidence of a partly compensating rise in ordinations at Oxford in the 1630s,[22] but it is clear, as she states, that there were real changes in the level of demand for ordination. It is also inconceivable that changes of this size could follow from diocesan control over the qualifications of applicants. Neither Longden's work nor the Ordination Books allow us to discover how many applicants were rejected, as can occasionally be

[22] p. 18.

Table 7.1. *Educational qualifications of ordinands to the diaconate in the diocese of Peterborough, 1570s to 1720s*

Cohort	Number of deacons	Known to have attended university	Attended university but no evidence of degree	B.A. before or in year of ordination[a]	B.A. after ordination[a]	'Literate'·b	of whom no evidence of university	of whom university but no evidence of degree	Degree after ordination	M.A. before or in year of ordination	M.A. after ordination	B.D. before or in year of ordination	B.D. after ordination	D.D. (all after ordination)
1570s	175/181+	72/89	14/22	59/63	3/4	7	5	2	0	25/26	16	0	14	3/4
1580s	117	106/107	6/7	99/100	0	8	7	0/1	0	55/56	21/22	0	16	4
1590s	125/127	119/121	8	101/110	2/3	13	6	5/6	1	62/65	21/22	0	23/24	7
Total: Elizabethan Period	417/425	297/317	28/37	259/273	5/7	28	18	7/9	1	142/147	58/60	0	52/53	14/15
1600s	117	93	7/8	83	3	31	22	7/8	1	32	28	0	12	6
1610s	395	351/352	27/28	315/317	7	60	40	14/15	5	141	111	2	36	15
1620s	593/594	565/567	25/26	512/517	27	63/64	24/25	23/24	14	214	197	3	44	14/15
1630s	106	102	1	99	2	3	2	0	1	46	31/32	0	3	5
Total: early 17th century	1,211/1,212	1,111/1,114	60/63	1,009/1,016	39	157/158	88/89	44/47	21	433	367/368	5	95	40/41
Total: pre-Civil War Period	1,628/1,637	1,408/1,431	88/100	1,268/1,289	44/46	185/186	106/107	51/56	22	575/580	425/428	5	148/149	54/56

Period													
1660s	67	61	4	53	4	26	3	1	14	5	0	4	1
1670s	119/121	119/121	0	114/116	5	59	0	0	24/26	0	0	2	0
1680s	13	13	1	12	0	3	0	0	4	0	0	0	1
Total: 1660s–1680s	199/201	193/195	5	179/181	9	88	3	1	42/44	5	0	6	2
1690s	48	39/42	0	38/41	1	12/13	0	0	10	0	0	0	2
1700s	109	109	1	106	2	47	0	0	12	0	0	3	3
1710s	49	49	1	46	2	21	0	0	6	0	0	6	7
1720s	61	57	2	55	0	15	2	0	15	2	0	2	2
Total: after 1688	267	254/257	4	245/248	5	95/96	2	0	43	2	0	11	14
Total: after Restoration	466/468	447/452	9	424/429	14	183/184	5	1	85/87	17	0	17	16

a Including the very occasional B.C.L. or Ll.B degrees when obtained instead of B.A.s. Such degrees obtained after a B.A. and the very few M.D., M.L., D.Med. or Ll.D. degrees are omitted: the omissions total five before the Civil War and five after 1660.

b If a candidate for ordination had not already obtained a first degree (or was at the point of receiving it), the diocesan authorities sometimes certified him as 'literate', either on the basis of their own examination or on that of testimonial letters, or both. This was never done if a degree had been obtained, but often was when a candidate was already at university or even, for a small number especially in the 1620s and 1630s, when a degree was obtained later. The practice was almost discontinued after the Restoration except briefly in the 1660s, when an apparently relatively low number of graduate candidates presumably reflects the educational and political uncertainties of the immediate past. There were also, oddly, a couple of cases in the 1720s. Following Longden, the term 'literate' is used, but perhaps 'lettered', implying proficiency in the ancient tongues, would be more accurate in modern usage.

+ Such double entries in this and the following tables show the range of possible or probable cases: that is, 175 were certainly ordained deacon in the 1570s cohort, with another six possible or probable.

done elsewhere,[23] but there is no reason to believe the number suddenly rose in the 1630s on the scale implied by the fall in ordinations. Much more likely is that the demand for ordination in this diocese reflected, but in a grossly exaggerated way, the trends in the output of graduates which Lawrence Stone has notably illustrated.[24] But the main point here is not the level of demand, which cannot be conclusively shown from one diocese, but the position of the ecclesiastical authorities. Whatever compensations may have occurred for these changes in other dioceses, such fluctuations confronted any individual bishop with an almost impossible task in relating entry to job opportunities, a necessary aspect of the development of professionalism if the overstaffing of the 'unprofessional' medieval church was not to be repeated. How far the evidence allows us to assess whether such overstaffing was avoided will be discussed below, but here it is claimed that, if it was, it was due more to the rough workings of the labour market than to any professional regulation by the diocesan authorities.

The same point can be made about standards of entry. Tables 7.1 and 7.2 present evidence on the educational careers of the ordained deacons. A first degree or 'literate' status are the recorded signs that the church was satisfied with a candidate, even if it had perforce to ordain others. Table 7.2 converts the relevant totals in Table 7.1 into percentages of the total number of deacons (both tables show the range of uncertainty).

It is unsurprising that Peterborough, one of the two main ordaining centres, catering especially for Cambridge University,[25] saw early the well-known transition to a largely graduate clergy. It is clear that the most dramatic change occurred between the 1570s and 1580s. The level of over 90 per cent recorded in the last column of Table 7.2 was maintained thereafter except in the 1690s, when the dip was probably an aberration due more to the small numbers than to the difficulties of the church after 1688. However, there is an interesting decline in the 1600s in the percentages of both university men and graduates, and a connected switch from grad-

---

23 *Ibid.*, pp. 61–5. I have discovered one example at Peterborough: an ordination in 1573 after the candidate had been rejected in 1570.
24 'The Educational Revolution in England, 1560–1640', *Past and Present*, 28 (1964), pp. 41–80.
25 O'Day, *English Clergy*, p. 20. Usually between four and eight times as many Cambridge as Oxford men were ordained at Peterborough in any decade, though in the 1720s the numbers were almost equal.

Table 7.2. *Educational qualifications of deacons in the diocese of Peterborough, 1570s to 1720s*

Cohort	(Percentages of total numbers ordained)				
	Known to have attended university	Known to have attended university but without evidence of degree	Having obtained B.A. before or in year of ordination	Of literate status	Total of two previous columns
1570s	41/49	8/11	34/35	4	38/39
1580s	91	5/6	85	7	92
1590s	95	6	81/87	10	91/97
Total: Eliza-bethan period	71/75	7/9	62/64	7	69/71
1600s	79	6/7	71	26	97
1610s	89	7	80	15	95
1620s	95	4	86/87	11	97/98
1630s	96	1	93	3	96
Total: early 17th century	92	5	83/84	13	96/97
Total: pre-Civil War	86/87	5/6	78/79	11	89/90
1660s	91	6	79	7	86
1670s	100	0	96	0	96
1680s	100	8	92	0	92
Total: 1660s–1680s	97	2/3	90	2/3	92/93
1690s	81/89	0	79/85	0	79/85
1700s	100	1	97	0	97
1710s	100	2	94	0	94
1720s	93	3	90	3	93
Total: after 1688	95/96	1	92/93	1	93/94
Total: after Restoration	96/97	2	91/92	1/2	92/94

uate to 'literate' status. It may be that candidates then felt able to present themselves earlier in their academic career. Only in the 1620s did the percentages rise again to the level of the 1590s. Other criteria will be considered below to try to see whether this means that the clerical job market in the 1600s was again moving in favour of the applicant after twenty years in which it had been necessary to offer higher qualifications. If so, it did not last: in the 1610s and 1620s the surge in numbers of ordinands was paralleled by one in qualifications, especially in the number of graduates. It is clear that in this period 'more' did not mean 'worse'. But equally the rise in qualifications continued when numbers declined in the 1630s.

In these circumstances it is difficult to see the rise of an over-whelmingly graduate clergy as an exercise in quality control by the diocesan authorities. No attempt seems to have been made to offset the marked fluctuations in demand for ordination and quality of applicant which the authorities of this diocese faced. It could be further argued that, as the possession of a degree became accepted as the main requisite for ordination, diocesan authorities generally were becoming more, not less, remote from the training and assessment procedures in the profession. Again, the rise in the quality of the market – assuming a first arts degree really meant such a rise – should be seen more as a response (and not necessarily an informed one) to the clerical labour market than as a step towards the institutionalization of professionalism. These data may show that the clerical profession became at certain times more popular, and generally better qualified, but those were not necess-arily sustainable processes and they could be at odds with another aspect of professionalization, control by the hierarchy.

Other aspects of the known careers of these ordinands sharpen these points. The rise in quality at the B.A. level before 1640 was paralleled quite closely at the Master's, again independently of the numbers coming forward. There was the same downturn in the 1600s and revival later, but Table 7.3 shows interesting deviations.

The revival in the last three decades before 1640 in the numbers of those with Masters' degrees at ordination did not raise the level to that of the 1580s and 1590s: in this sense the early seventeenth-century ordinands at Peterborough were less well educated than their predecessors. Also the improvement at this level was not sustained after the Restoration. Overall the proportion of ordi-nands with Masters' degrees declined from about half in the 1580s

Table 7.3. *Percentages of deacons obtaining masters' degrees in the diocese of Peterborough, 1570s to 1720s*

Cohort	During life	Before ordination
1570s	23	14
1580s	65/67	47/48
1590s	67/68	50/51
Total: Elizabethan period	48/49	34/35
1600s	51	27
1610s	64	36
1620s	69	36
1630s	73/74	43
Total: early 17th century	66	36
Total: pre-Civil War	61	35
1660s	60	21
1670s	69/70	20/21
1680s	54	31
Total: 1660s–1680s	65/66	21/22
1690s	46/48	21
1700s	54	11
1710s	55	12
1720s	49	25
Total: after 1688	52	16
Total: after Restoration	57/58	18/19

and 1590s to a quarter or below after 1688. It is necessary to qualify Holmes's statement that 'most Augustan clergymen were Masters of Arts',[26] by stressing that most achieved this status only after ordination.

Furthermore, as Table 7.4 shows, changes in demand did not eliminate the practice of ordaining below the canonical age of twenty-three. Ages are sparsely available so certain periods have been conflated to give meaningful totals.

Despite some improvement in the 1620s and 1630s, a situation in which from the 1610s to the 1720s between one-fifth and one-third of the candidates were accepted below age does not imply a clear-minded search for professional standards by the authorities. It may be argued that this was not necessary, because numbers and

---

[26] G. Holmes, *Augustan England, Professions, State and Society, 1680–1730* (London, 1982), p. 4.

Table 7.4. *Ages of ordinands in the diocese of Peterborough,
1570s to 1720s*

Cohort	Numbers of ordinands whose ages are known	Percentage of these aged 22 or less[a]
1570s–1600s	77	12
1610s	56	32
1620s	117	29
1630s	48	21
Total: pre-Civil War period	298	24
1660s–1690s	120	25
1690s–1720s	209	20
Total: post-Restoration	329	22

[a] These are minima: many doubtful cases in which the age could be twenty-two or twenty-three have been omitted.

standards of applicants were rising at least from the 1620s. But it is precisely in this situation that a profession would take advantage of its better bargaining position to change some of the practices which led to complaints. One improvement was attempted but with limited, and in some respects negative, results. From the 1580s to the 1620s inclusive it was very common for men to be ordained deacon and priest on consecutive days, certainly in a large majority of cases without the full year which was expected to elapse. Table 7.5 shows the pattern of further ordinations in the Peterborough diocese.

O'Day says, 'the number of men ordained deacon and priest on the same day (by licence) dropped dramatically after 1604 – there was no slackening off in the attempt to restrict the practice in later years, rather the reverse'.[27] In fact, in the diocese of Peterborough 1604 was followed by a quarter of a century in which ordination to the priesthood very often occurred the *following* day. Between 1630 and 1631 this practice was suddenly almost completely stopped, a change apparently due to the arrival of William Piers as bishop in October 1630 and consistent with the more elevated status which Laudians ascribed to the priesthood. But the con-

[27] *Ibid.*, p 19.

Table 7.5. *Ordinations as priests of deacons ordained at Peterborough, 1570s to 1720s[a]*

Cohort	Numbers of deacons [b]	Percentage remaining as deacons	Percentage ordained priest in same calendar year	Percentage ordained priest in next calendar year	Percentage ordained priest in two or more calendar years
1570s	175	35	46	13	6
1580s	117	14	62	20	5
1590s	125	4	90	32	3
Total: Elizabethan period	417	20	64	12	4
1600s	117	9	61	15	15
1610s	395	13	60	13	14
1620s	593	11	71	9	9
1630s	106	38	7	31	24
Total: early 17th century	1211	14	60	13	13
Total: pre-Civil War period	1628	15	61	13	11
1660s	67	33	22	18	25
1670s	119	43	8	19	30
1680s	13	69	15	15	0
Total: 1660s–1680s	199	41	14	19	26
1690s	48	29	6	31	33
1700s	109	27	3	23	48
1710s	49	14	6	18	61
1720s	61	34	16	11	38
Total: after 1688	267	26	7	21	45
Total: after Restoration	466	33	10	20	37

[a] This table includes priests ordained in dioceses other than Peterborough.
[b] This excludes doubtful cases of ordination because the doubt is usually whether the individual was ordained deacon or priest.

Table 7.6. *Geographical origins of ordinands to the diaconate in the diocese of Peterborough, 1570s to 1720s*

Cohort	Total of known geographical origin	Origin within diocese of Peterborough	Origin outside diocese of Peterborough
1570s–1590s	111	28	83
1600s–1630s	459	107	352
Total: pre-Civil War	570	135	435
1660s–1680s	170	56	114
1690s–1720s	247	72	175
Total: after Restoration	417	128	289

sequences of reform are often unexpected and unwelcome: in this case there was a marked increase in the proportion of men who never became priests at all. The change may have contributed to the decline of Peterborough as an ordination centre from the 1630s. Only in the 1690s did the proportion of those proceeding to the priesthood at least two calendar years after the diaconate exceed, for the first time since the 1610s, those remaining deacons.

The preceding discussion illustrates some of the ambiguities and contradictions in the different criteria for professionalization noted in section I: development of professionalization in one sphere was at odds with it in another. The variations in numbers are much more satisfactorily explained by fluctuating demand, itself dependent on 'outside' political and social factors, than by postulating a process of professionalization. This view is supported by the fact that the diocesan authorities remained remote from the careers of those they ordained. Table 7.6 shows that those from outside the diocese were always a large majority of those ordained.

Table 7.7 shows that, in so far as evidence of clerical employment exists, most of those ordained during the boom years were to work wholly outside the diocese. It was only with the reduced demand from the 1630s that the balance began to be redressed, and only after 1688 that the diocesan authorities were to have any further responsibility for the employment of the majority of those they ordained.

Table 7.7. *Location of clerical employment of Peterborough ordinands, 1570s to 1720s*

Cohort	Number known to have had clerical employment	Of whom: wholly outside diocese of Peterborough	Wholly inside diocese of Peterborough	Both inside and outside diocese
1570s	69	51	17	1
1580s	68	48	16	4
1590s	70	56	10	4
Total: Elizabethan period	207	155	43	9
1600s	50	24	22	4
1610s	171	142	20	9
1620s	295	252	36	7
1630s	45	25	17	3
Total: early 17th century	561	443	95	23
Total: pre-Civil War period	768	598	138	32
1660s	42	23	16	3
1670s	61	33	19	9
1680s	7	5	2	0
Total: 1660s-1680s	110	61	37	12
1690s	33	12	9	12
1700s	89	25	35	29
1710s	46	4	24	18
1720s	46	15	12	19
Total: after 1688	214	56	80	78
Total: after Restoration	324	117	117	90

Before the Civil War less than 1 per cent of candidates for ordination came armed with a testimonial from another bishop requesting ordination to a particular cure in the latter's diocese: the overwhelming majority were admitted deacon without any evident concern for their future employment. Incidentally, this lack of concern with either the earlier or the later careers of deacons may help to explain why, during the episcopate of the 'Arminian',

Table 7.8. *Career patterns of Peterborough deacons, 1570s to 1720s*

Cohort	Percentage of deacons known to have been employed	Percentage known to have been employed in church	Percentage employed elsewhere[a]	Mean period before first employment in church (years)	Percentage of first known posts in church as:					Percentage of highest known posts in church as:				
					Curate	Vicar[d]	Rector[d]	Higher[b]	Other[c]	Curate	Vicar[d]	Rector[d]	Higher[b]	Other[c]
1570s–1590s	58/61	51/56	5	5.1	7/9	36/40	47	2	2/3	4	27/28	60	8/9	1
1600s–1630s	51/59	47/54	4	6.7	12/14	35/36	43	2	4	9	29/30	50/52	7/8	3
Total: pre-Civil War	52/59	48/55	4	6.3	11/12	36/37	44/45	2	4	7/8	28/29	53/54	8/9	3
1660s–1680s	58/67	55/62	3/5	5.3	20/21	29/31	44	3	3/4	6	27	52	12	2
1690s–1720s	85/86	81/83	3	1.7	73/74	10	13/14	1	1/2	28	25	36	9	1/2
Total: after Restoration	73/78	70/73	3/4	2.9	54/56	17	24	2	2	20	26	41/42	10	2

[a] Usually as college fellows or schoolmasters.
[b] Includes cathedral clergy (above minor canons) and chaplains to members of the royal family, aristocracy or bishops.
[c] Includes, for example, minor canons, lecturers, 'preachers', ministers, etc.
[d] Rectors have been counted as higher than vicars, though the latter could sometimes receive more income; this merely illustrates the difficulties of discovering the 'professional' career-structure of the clergy.

Thomas Dove (1601–30), ordinations at Peterborough of men from the 'puritan' colleges, Emmanuel, Christ's and Sidney Sussex, were at a peak as a proportion of those from Cambridge as a whole.

This lack of concern seems to be confirmed by what was evidently an unsatisfactory job market. Table 7.8 summarizes what can be said about three of its features: the percentage known to have obtained clerical employment; how long they had to wait for it; and the pattern of promotion.

Only tentative conclusions can be drawn from Table 7.8, particularly because there is only sporadic reference before the 1690s to the licensing of curates. But that lack may itself be symptomatic of the unprofessional approach to the organization of the clergy. After 1688 such licensing usually occurred at ordination and was not paralleled in extent earlier. The fact that it did occasionally occur then shows there was no objection in principle to it. If it had occurred on the same scale in the 1620s, it would probably only have meant a large group of unbeneficed jobbing clerics, reviving memories of the unreformed church. Such licensing means that the post-1688 period presents much clearer evidence than any earlier one of a 'professional' career-structure: a higher level of employment in the church; a much shorter period on average between ordination and employment; and a greater difference in status between first and highest posts held.

Being tentative, the evidence of Table 7.8 can be no more than a contribution to the debate around Curtis's 'alienated intellectuals' thesis, which relates disaffection in the ministry to over-production of graduates before 1640.[28] But it may be noted that generally the early seventeenth century seems to have had a marginally lower level of employment than the Elizabethan period and that the decade of the greatest number of ordinations (the 1620s) also saw the longest gap (7.3 years) between ordination and known employment. Also, with reference to the comment above that the end of the sixteenth century may have seen an easing of the job market allowing lower qualifications to be presented, it is of interest that this gap fell from 5.6 to 5.1 years between the 1580s and the 1590s. Furthermore, both these decades recorded the highest levels of general and clerical employment before the Civil War (1580s: 69/75 per cent general and 58/66 per cent clerical; 1590s: 60/68 per cent and 58/65

[28] M. Curtis, 'The Alienated Intellectuals of Early Stuart England', *Past and Present*, 23 (1962), pp. 25–43.

per cent). Nevertheless, of the four early seventeenth-century decades employment levels were highest in the 1620s (54/61 per cent and 50/58 per cent). The inflated intake of the 1620s may have had to wait longer for a job, but they were more likely to find one than their immediate predecessors and successors, although this is probably due partly to the disruptive effects of the 1640s on the careers of the 1630s cohort. Generally, as is to be expected, the evidence for the forcible interruption of careers for political and/or religious reasons is much greater before 1640; between ninety and ninety-seven of the deacons ordained then lost or gave up a post permanently or temporarily for such reasons, compared with only six or seven of the post-1660 ordinands.

While the post-1688 period saw the clearest evidence of an hierarchical career-structure, still over a quarter of those employed in the church are not recorded as rising higher than a curacy. Many of those included earlier among the unemployed now stayed on the bottom rung. Furthermore, problems at the top remained throughout the period: those aiming at the highest clerical posts (archdeacon, royal chaplain or above) needed almost always to have been elected to a college fellowship when young. Rectories or vicarages might come their way, very often on presentation by their college, but, if they embarked on parochial work at or as soon as possible after ordination, they in effect debarred themselves from such promotion. If there was an hierarchical career-structure, it had two tiers: a parochial route for the vast majority, stopping at a rectory at best; a collegiate route, usually associated with a B.D. and D.D. degree later in life, for the future elite.

IV

As far as this evidence will go, it shows that the post-Restoration period, especially after 1688, saw a more integrated and 'professional' career-structure for these deacons than is apparent before 1640. Ordination at Peterborough appears to have become much more closely associated with employment in the diocese itself within a reasonably brief period, with more marked progress from low- to high-status posts, and with much less 'political' disruption of careers. Of course, it may be said that the pre-Civil War situation is similar to that in many modern professions: very often assessment of qualifications for entry is separate from the search for employ-

Table 7.9. *Known social origins of Peterborough deacons, 1570s to 1720s** *(percentages of total number of deacons in parentheses)*

Cohort	Ordinands with lay gentry fathers	Ordinands with lay non-gentry fathers	Ordinands with clerical fathers	Ordinands holding post in same parish as clerical father	Ordinands with sons or sons-in-law in orders	Sons or sons-in-law holding post in same parish as father
1570s–1610s	19/20(2)	40/42(4/5)	42/47(4/5)	6(1)	37/38(4)	9(1)
1620s–1630s	41/45(6)	64/65(9)	63/69(9/10)	15/16(2)	33/36(5)	6(1)
Total: pre-Civil War	60/65(3/4)	104/107(6/7)	105/116(6/7)	21/22(1)	70/74(4/5)	15(1)
1660s–1680s	10(5)	31/32(15/16)	46/49(23/25)	11(5/6)	14(7)	5(2/3)
1690s–1720s	40/41(15)	55/57(21)	76(28)	25/26(9/10)	22(8)	9(3)
Total: post-Restoration	50/51(11)	86/89(18/19)	122/125(26/27)	36/37(8)	36(8)	14(3)

* This table omits other evidence for clerical dynasties e.g. fathers-in-law, brothers, brothers-in-law and nephews of clerical status.

ment and the former does not guarantee the latter. But the gap must not become too great if the status of a profession is to be maintained: too large an entry and either associated unemployment or rapid expansion may be a recipe for declining repute, as the modern teaching profession, at school or university level, may witness. As historians have noted, similar disruptive influences may have been at work on the pre-Civil War clergy.

One final set of data derivable from Longden's work drives home the paradoxes inherent in seeing this period as one of professionalization. There is not space here to discuss fully the tensions between the 'parson's freehold' and professionalism, but Table 7.9 presents evidence of the spread of clerical dynasties and of the interest of the upper classes in a clerical career for their sons.

Again the patchiness of the evidence makes conclusions tentative, but, in the best-documented group, there were proportionate increases in the sons of clergymen generally and in those who were employed in their father's parish. Many of these sons began work as curates in their father's parish before succeeding to his rectory. They exemplify both 'professionalism' in following a career with more clearly defined promotion, and 'anti-professionalism' in owing that career to patrimony. Equally, in another relatively well-documented field may be noted the relatively increased interest of the gentry, both when the church was attracting more entrants before the Civil War and when it seemed to offer an improved career-structure and prospects after 1688. In the aftermath of the interregnum, the gentry may have hesitated before recommending a clerical career to their sons: certainly the growth of their interest was halted. After 1660 as a whole the sons of clergy and gentry provided 37/38 per cent of all deacons ordained and 66/67 per cent of those whose social origin is known. It may be that here is another aspect of that drawing back from the erstwhile 'openness' of English society to which Lawrence Stone has drawn attention,[29] and a further example of the complex interaction between politics and social change on which he has so often worked. It seems to have required the 'growth of political stability' for the church to strengthen its tendencies towards social exclusiveness and patrimony: no doubt such developments in turn fed that stability.

In general, men responded to circumstances as they experienced them more strongly than they were prepared to bet on the future.

[29] 'Educational Revolution', especially pp. 68–9, 73–5.

This means marked fluctuations in the demand for clerical posts, and it seems possible that the social elite and the clergy themselves were quickest off the mark when circumstances seemed promising. But they were no more omniscient than anyone else: they appear to have been too eager in the 1620s, helping to produce a decline in demand in the 1630s and the disruption of the 1640s and 1650s. The revival of confidence in the 'Augustan Age' may have meant that the 'profession' of the clergy rose socially and became more cohesive, just as the 1610s and 1620s had seen it rise more simply in terms of its attractiveness as a possible career for first-generation graduates. But to see this as a 'process' of professionalization is much more difficult. The very popularity of a career in the church did not prevent, and may have increased, its vulnerability to attack, while, after 1688, the human desire of those already inside to pull up the ladder behind them and their families reduced the possibilities of competitive entry and promotion. The improvements in the educational standards of the ordinands was not sustained; the church remained open to the abuses of pluralism, non-residence and ordination below canonical age; its authorities exercised only a limited influence over numbers and careers, while specific reforms like that carried out by Piers seem to have been counter-productive; the system of rewards remained chaotic; and the structure of promotion still distinguished sharply between the fate of the elite and that of the clerical mass. It seems apparent that the appearance or strengthening of one of the 'traits' of professionalism was achieved only at the cost of undermining others. Perhaps historians need to be as suspicious of 'process' as most of them have long since learnt to be of 'progress'.

8. *Bourgeois revolution and transition to capitalism*

ROBERT BRENNER

Lawrence Stone has played a central role in what might be seen as two successive phases in the historiography of Tudor–Stuart England. During the 1940s and 1950s, he was instrumental, along with R. H. Tawney and Christopher Hill, in establishing a variant of the classical theory of the bourgeois revolution as the dominant interpretation of the causes of the English Civil War.[1] The general thrust of this interpretation was to link long-term transformations in the nature and wealth of the landed classes – themselves interpreted as the product of the epochal transition from feudalism to capitalism in the countryside – to the outbreak of the mid-seventeenth-century conflicts. Then, during the 1960s and 1970s, especially with his monumental work *The Crisis of the Aristocracy* (Oxford, 1965), Stone helped largely to demolish the reigning version of the bourgeois revolution interpretation. At the same time, by providing a new and multi-dimensional account of the changing economic, social and political character of the greater landed classes over the period roughly from 1500 to 1640, he established the potential foundations for an alternative paradigm. The fact remains that, in the quarter-century since the publication of *The Crisis of the Aristocracy*, no new interpretation of the English Civil War has succeeded in establishing itself as the

[1] The fundamental statements of this position are Christopher Hill, *The Revolution of 1640* (London, 1940); R. H. Tawney, 'The Rise of the Gentry', *Economic History Review*, 11 (1941); R. H. Tawney, 'Harrington's Interpretation of his Age', *Proceedings of the British Academy* 27 (Oxford, 1941); Lawrence Stone, 'The Anatomy of the Elizabethan Aristocracy', *Economic History Review*, 18 (1948). For the famous controversy which ensued, see what amounts to an extended bibliography in the end notes to Lawrence Stone, 'The Social Origins of the English Revolution', in *The Causes of the English Revolution 1529–1642* (New York, 1972), pp. 41–3. See also R. C. Richardson, *The Debate on the English Revolution* (London, 1977).

emerging orthodoxy. Even more striking, no alternative social interpretation linking socio-economic change, and specifically changes in the nature of the landed class, to the mid-seventeenth-century conflicts has even been advanced to challenge for intellectual hegemony. This is perhaps especially surprising in view of the fact that much of the recent historiography has only further confirmed and developed the view that the Tudor–Stuart period was, indeed, a period of far-reaching social and economic change in a capitalist direction.[2] It is thus the aim of this essay to take a small, first step toward constructing an alternative social interpretation of the political conflicts of the seventeenth century. I hope to accomplish this by investigating the theoretical foundations of the traditional social interpretation, and in particular by demonstrating that certain fundamental problems of the traditional social interpretation resulted from the ways it was linked to, and depended upon, a more general theory of the transition from feudalism to capitalism.

I shall try to show, then, that the traditional social interpretation of the English revolution and the most powerful critique of that interpretation are based upon, or follow the lines of, two differing and incompatible theories of transition, each of which, paradoxically, derives from the work of Karl Marx. The first of these theories of transition was presented in Marx's earlier work from the *German Ideology* to the *Poverty of Philosophy*, and was powerfully sketched in the *Communist Manifesto*. Nevertheless, its real originator was Adam Smith, upon whom Marx was profoundly dependent for his own formulation, and it bears all the characteristic marks of Smith's theory of history. The central explanatory notion at the core of this theory is the self-developing division of labour. The division of labour directly expresses the level of the development of the productive forces; it evolves in response to the expanding market; and it determines, in its turn, the social relations of class and property. The theory's basic image of transition from feudalism to capitalism encompasses the maturation of the developing bourgeois society, nourished by constantly-growing world trade, within the womb of the old feudal society.

The second of these theories was presented in *Grundrisse*, *Capital*, and other later works of Marx's, but was never fully worked out by him. Its master principle is the mode of production,

---

[2] For an overview, see C. G. A. Clay, *Economic Expansion and Social Change in England 1500–1700*, 2 vols (Cambridge, 1984).

conceived as a system of social–property relations which make possible, and thereby structure, societal reproduction – in particular, the maintenance of society's individual families and constituent social classes. The model of transition from feudalism to capitalism arising on the basis of this mode of production idea starts from the *conflictual* reproduction, on the one hand, of a class of peasant producers who individually possess (have direct, non-market access to) their means of subsistence, and, on the other hand, a class of lordly rulers and exploiters, who reproduce themselves by means of extracting a surplus from the peasant producers through extra-economic compulsion. The model's ultimate objective is to explain 'the so-called primitive accumulation' which, from this standpoint, refers not to an initial amassing of investment funds, as in Adam Smith, but to the series of social processes by which the fundamental social–property relations that constituted the feudal mode of production were broken up and transformed through the action of feudal society itself – in particular, the social processes by which the lords lost their capacity to take a rent by extra-economic compulsion and the peasants were separated from their possession of the means of subsistence.

I shall thus begin by arguing that the first of these models of transition to capitalism, focused on the growth of the division of labour, leads naturally to understanding the English Civil War as a bourgeois revolution. Moreover, as is well understood, the traditional social interpretation of the mid-seventeenth-century conflicts was, indeed, patterned after it. Nevertheless, because this first model ultimately *assumes* the transition to capitalism in order to explain it – seeing the self-development of bourgeois society *and* the dissolution of feudalism as directly determined by the rise of trade and the growth of the productive forces – it ends up depriving the associated account of revolution of much meaning or point.

I shall argue next that the second of these models, focused on the transformation of social–property relations, offers a powerful point of departure both for laying bare the conceptual weaknesses of the first model and for grasping the distinctive character of the transition to capitalism in England; that is, the assertion of landlord property as constituting a fundamental social condition for the establishment of, as well as a framework for, the development of agrarian capitalism. Moreover, as I shall try to show, the most powerful contributions to the contemporary historiography of

Tudor–Stuart England, highlighted by Lawrence Stone's *The Crisis of the Aristocracy*, effectively confirm the second, counter-model of transition to capitalism, while buttressing a critique of the traditional social interpretation inspired by this second model. In so doing, however, they make it difficult to understand the English revolution along the lines envisioned by the traditional bourgeois revolution interpretation.

I shall thus conclude that, in order successfully to confront the task of interpreting the English Civil War, it will be necessary to reassess the manner in which capitalist development actually conditioned the course of political evolution in early modern England. The latter can best be accomplished, I shall argue, by taking as our point of departure capitalism's development *within the framework of – and not in contradiction to –* aristocratic landlordism.

I

Marx's classic statement of the bourgeois revolution idea, in the *Communist Manifesto*, depends on a very specific understanding of the transition from feudalism to capitalism. Marx interpreted feudalism itself as having resulted from the barbarian invasions of Europe. These invasions had the effect of radically disrupting the commercialized economy bequeathed by ancient society. Above all, they dealt a near-fatal blow to its highly developed forms of trade and industry. On the other hand, the conquests partially preserved the agriculture that ancient society had spread far and wide throughout the empire, although they left the rural settlements separated and scattered. In Marx's famous phrase, 'If antiquity started out from the *town* and its small territory, the Middle Ages started out from the *country*.' Finally, Marx emphasized that the invaders superimposed their communities of invading warriors on the older, scattered peasant agricultural communities. In this way, they established and reproduced the fundamental lord–serf relationship which constituted feudalism.[3]

Marx understands the transition from feudalism to capitalism as taking place through a very definite mechanism, expressing what might be seen as Marx's initial conception of historical materialism,

---

[3] K. Marx, *The German Ideology*, in *Collected Works* (New York, 1976), vol. 5, pp. 33–4.

specified in *The German Ideology* and other works of the 1840s. Thus, according to the Marx of the 1840s, the way people produce their means of subsistence – their *mode of subsistence* – determines what they are. In turn, it is the growth of the division of labour which lies behind the ongoing transformation of the way in which people produce their means of subsistence. As a consequence, the key to the stage-by-stage evolution of society is to be found in the growth of the productive forces. This is because 'each new productive force, in so far as it is not merely a quantitative extension of productive forces already known . . . causes a further development of the division of labour'.[4]

For Marx the division of labour has two aspects. The first is specialization, by which tasks previously combined in a single unit or branch of production are divided off to be carried on in separate units or branches. This process takes place because more specialized activities are more efficient, more productive. The second aspect of the division of labour involves the direct organization of production internal to the unit, the labour process or form of co-operation in so far as it is not mediated by exchange and the market. This, too, is technically determined by the development of the productive forces.[5]

Secondly, just as the development of the productive forces brings about the development of the division of labour by determining at once growing specialization by units and branches and the evolution of the labour process, the division of labour determines the evolution of classes and property relations through determining the developing division between mental and manual labour. Each form of co-operation or labour process, by constituting the structure of interdependent roles through which production is carried out, thus brings with it a particular form of the division between mental and manual labour, between conception and execution, and the reigning form of division between mental and manual labour directly gives rise to the prevailing form of property relations, of relations between dominant and dominated classes. In Marx's words, 'The relative position of these individual groups [in co-operation] is determined by the way work is organized.' In turn, this 'division of labour implies the possibility, nay the fact, that intellectual and material activity, enjoyment and labour, production and consumption, devolve on different individuals'. It is therefore understand-

[4] *Ibid.*, pp.31–2.   [5] *Ibid.*, pp. 31–2, 43.

able that 'the various stages of the division of labour are just so many different forms of property, i.e., the existing stage of the division of labour determines also the relations of individuals to one another with reference to the material, instrument, and product of labour'.[6]

Finally, with each stage in the development of the division of labour, there emerges a corresponding form of politics and state. The form of state expresses the level of development of the productive forces and functions to protect the dominant class and the existing property forms and, in particular, the monopolies on which, in Marx's view, these depend.[7]

Schematically speaking, then, we get the following theory: the development of the productive forces determines the successive stages in the evolution of the mode of subsistence, in accord with the following causal chain: development of the productive forces → development of the division of labour (specialization and co-operation) → form of division between mental and manual labour → nature of class and property relations (distribution of material, instrument and product of labour) → form of state.

Marx's account of the rise of capitalism rigorously follows the foregoing schema. Thus, feudalism transformed itself into capitalism by way of the evolution of the division of labour. The first and fundamental step was the flight of the serfs from the countryside so as to found towns, leading to the separation of craft from agricultural production, and the triumph, in competition, of specialized craft production in the towns over the merged craft–agricultural production of the rural households. In the towns, production was originally organized by owner–operators, but with the growth of production there very quickly emerged a fully-fledged division of labour. The form of specialization between units was rudimentary: the organization of production into separate branches composed of single, integrated complex crafts. The mode of co-operation was also simple: master craftsmen carried on the full range of skilled tasks required to produce the goods, helped out by relatively untutored journeymen. On the basis of this organization of production, this mental/manual division of labour, the masters were

---

[6] Ibid., pp. 32, 43, 66–74 (see especially p. 73).

[7] On the political forms which corresponded to each property form and level of development of the productive forces, see, especially, K. Marx, 'Moralizing Criticism and Critical Morality' (1847), in Collected Works (New York, 1976), vol. 6.

able to dominate and exploit the journeymen. The masters bolstered their proprietary position through their corporate guilds, which sought to monopolize both the product and labour markets. In turn, the leading townsmen joined together to constitute urban communal governments in order to maintain their property and their guild monopolies.[8]

Finally, the consolidation of this first and fundamental division of labour, the separation of town from country, depended, for Marx, on the freeing of the burghers' economic development from the control and the depredations of the feudalists. 'In the Middle Ages the citizens of each town were compelled to unite against the landed nobility to save their skins.' 'These towns were true "unions", called forth by the direct need of providing for protection of property, and of multiplying the means of production and defences of the separate members.' It was the creation and reproduction of the urban commune, and its successful revolt against the feudal lords, which made possible the subsequent evolution of bourgeois society, freeing it, to a great extent, from the fetters on the growth of production constituted by lordly pillaging and political parasitism.[9]

Following the stage of craft production based on town–country specialization and the dominance of the masters in the labour process, the separation of commercial from industrial functions constituted, for Marx, the next major stage in the division of labour. The merchants brought about a profound broadening of commerce and market, and this resulted in intensified competition between the hitherto protected crafts of the different towns. Competition ultimately forced the break-up of the complex, unified crafts into their simplified component parts. The rise of manufacture on the ruins of the crafts thus brought a new form of specialization, constituted by separated units carrying out simplified 'detail' production, and a new mode of co-operation, based on the manufactory in which merchants controlled the semi-skilled labour processes. Founding itself on the new division of labour between mental and manual labour, which was derived from the new mode of co-operation, a new class of merchant–manufacturers arose to exploit a new class of semi-skilled workers. The merchant–manufacturers bolstered their proprietary position by using the newly emerging national states – the absolutist state in some places,

8 *German Ideology*, pp. 34–5, 64–5.   9 *Ibid.*, pp. 65, 76.

the city-state in others – for defence against the nascent working class, for the protection of their monopoly of national industry against foreign competition, and for warfare for trade routes and colonies.[10]

Finally, with the maturation of the world market and the consequent intensification of competition among manufacturers in the same nation and, ultimately, different nations, production characterized by the application of machinery superseded the hitherto dominant manufacturing stage. Specialization among units now took place on the basis of separate factories, and co-operation within units (factories) was structured by the requirements of the machines. Industrial capitalist managers now directed and exploited completely de-skilled factory proletarians, and these two great classes came to constitute society. In particular, the English industrial capitalists emerged as the first great industrial capitalist class; they did so by winning an initial monopoly of the world market which they exploited on the basis of their productiveness and free trade policies.[11]

Meanwhile, economic developments in the countryside paralleled those in the city. Also in response to the rise of trade, the feudal aristocracy dismissed its retainers, freed its serfs, installed commercial tenants, and kicked the remainder of the peasants off the land into the ranks of the industrial proletariat. Thus, in response to the presence of commerce: (1) feudal property gave way to the absolute capitalist property of the landlords; (2) the feudal lords acted in a capitalistic fashion to transform their estate economies; and, in the process, (3) feudal social relations were transformed into capitalist ones. Capitalism was thereby established on the land.[12]

Finally, in the *Communist Manifesto* and other works of the later 1840s, following lines initially laid out by liberal French historians of the early part of the nineteenth century – in particular, François Mignet, Augustin Thierry and François Guizot – Marx completed the foregoing schema with his notion of the bourgeois revolution *per se*. Thus, Marx has the bourgeoisie and absolute monarchy entering into alliance in the early modern period in order to destroy their common enemy, the parasitic feudal nobility. Then, as the

---

[10] *Ibid.*, pp. 66–70.   [11] *Ibid.*, pp. 71–4.
[12] *Ibid.*, pp. 68–9. *Cf. The Poverty of Philosophy*, in *Collected Works* (New York, 1976), vol. 6, p. 185.

bourgeoisie grew in strength, the absolute monarchy gravitated back toward the old nobility. But, by this point, there was little remaining of the feudal nobility. The majority of landlords no longer possessed either their military retainers or serfs; they had transformed their estates so as to take advantage of the market. What remained of feudalism was now effectively constituted by the absolutist state itself. The taxes and monopolies by which this state nourished itself went to support what was left of the tottering feudal class, whose members depended for their maintenance largely on court office. The state's absolutist levies constituted a fetter upon the bourgeoisie's free enjoyment of its property and its development of the productive forces.[13] The bourgeois revolution thus functioned to break these external political–parasitic barriers and to facilitate the continuation of the ongoing economic evolution.

As a theory of *transition* the foregoing account appears rather peculiar, for in neither town nor country is anything amounting to a transformation from one type of society to another actually envisaged. As for the urban economy, it is, from its origin, entirely bourgeois. Even the serfs who resist and flee from the feudal lords' domination do so with the intention of setting themselves up as bourgeois craftsmen or traders (not merely as free peasant producers for subsistence). Of course, the medieval town is, from the start, dominated by bourgeois classes with bourgeois forms of production. Moreover, each successive stage in its development represents the maturation – economically, socially and politically – of an already existing bourgeois form of society. Most significant of all, the mechanisms which drive the process forward – above all the growth of exchange and competition – are quintessentially bourgeois mechanisms. As to rural development, feudalism – the feudal mode of production – has no positive role. It constitutes a fetter on

[13] As Marx put it in an essay of 1847,

born from the defeat of the feudal estates, and having the most active share in their destruction, [the absolute monarchy] now seeks to retain at least the semblance of feudal distinctions. Formerly encouraging trade and industry and thereby at the same time the rise of the bourgeois class, as necessary conditions both for the national power and for its own glory, absolute monarchy now everywhere hampers trade and industry, which have become increasingly dangerous weapons in the hands of an already powerful bourgeoisie. From the *town*, the birthplace of its rise to power, it turns its alarmed and by now dull glance to the *countryside*, which is fertile with the corpses of its old, powerful opponents ... Taxes are the existence of [this] state expressed in economic terms.   'Moralizing Criticism and Critical Morality', p. 328

the development of the productive forces, but is subject to dissolution under the economic impact of growing trade. Indeed, the feudal lords reveal themselves as essentially bourgeois in attitude and action just as soon as they come into contact with commercial opportunities. Finally – and perhaps most problematic for the bourgeois revolution idea – the bourgeoisie's rise to power is quasi-automatic. Because the growth of trade and competition both drives forward bourgeois economy in the town and causes feudalism to disintegrate in the countryside, it is only a matter of time until the bourgeoisie is able to assert its hegemony.

The paradoxical character of this theory is thus immediately evident: a theory of revolution based on a mechanically-deterministic theory of transition, it renders revolution unnecessary in a double sense. First, there really is no *transition* to accomplish: since the model starts with bourgeois society in the towns, foresees its evolution as taking place via bourgeois mechanisms, and has feudalism transcend itself in consequence of its exposure to trade, the problem of how one type of society is transformed into another is simply assumed away and never posed. Second, since bourgeois society self-develops and dissolves feudalism, the bourgeois revolution can hardly claim a necessary role.

II

The manifestly self-defeating character of Marx's initial theory of transition and revolution becomes less puzzling when we specify its intellectual roots: these are to be found in the mechanical materialism, the economic determinism, of the eighteenth-century Enlightenment, and above all in the work of Adam Smith. Marx was profoundly dependent upon Smith, not only for his general approach but also for the actual historical process he laid out. Smith presented his general theory, of course, in Book I of *The Wealth of Nations*.[14] In this account, the pursuit of their rational self-interest leads individual producers to try to make use of the specialized productive capacities of other producers in order to reap the benefits from reduced costs of production, and thus cheaper goods. They do this, Smith believed, by specializing themselves and by offering their output for exchange to their prospective trading partners, who can then be expected to do the same. Individual

[14] *The Wealth of Nations*, ed. E. Cannan (New York, 1937), pp. 3–12.

rational self-interest thus leads, in the aggregate, to specialized production for exchange, bringing increased returns to the trading parties – the gains from trade – and increased efficiency to the economy as a whole. Economic development takes place more or less naturally through the growth of self-interested exchange, leading to the growth of the division of labour.

Smith actually applied the foregoing theory of the invisible hand to historical evolution as a whole. He was one of the first exponents of the so-called four-stages theory of history, which, like Marx's first theory outlined above, had historical evolution taking place through changes in the 'mode of subsistence' – from hunting and gathering to pastoralism to settled agriculture to commercial society. In Smith's view, commercial society first established itself in the ancient world of the Mediterranean.[15] However, in archetypically Smithian fashion, he also understood the natural progress of commercial society in the ancient world as having been interrupted by an artificial, external intrusion – the barbarian invasions. The ensuing disruption of trade led to the imposition of feudalism and a reversion back from commercial to subsistence economy, natural economy.[16] The rise of feudalism and its negative effect on development thus exemplified for Smith the general fetter, or parasitism, of the political on the economic which Smith saw as perhaps the main threat to economic development.

In any event, following the establishment of feudalism, human nature reasserted itself. Order was restored, trade developed, and one witnessed the rise of the towns. Interestingly, at this historical juncture Smith discovers a bourgeois revolution of his own. The towns and the monarchy ally together against the feudal barons and, as a result, the towns win their freedom from feudal controls and levies. Once these fetters are removed, commercial society can and does resume its natural progression.[17] Meanwhile, in the countryside, the feudal lords are driven to dismiss their retainers in order to free funds to enjoy the increased consumption that the rise of exchange has now made possible. At the same time, they turn some of their customary tenants into commercial farmers on competitive leases and dismiss the others to go to the towns. In short, the rise of trade allows the hitherto feudal lords to shed their

---

[15] Ronald Meek, *Social Science and the Ignoble Savage* (Cambridge, 1976), especially chapters 3 and 4.
[16] *Wealth of Nations*, p. 361.   [17] *Ibid.*, pp. 374–7, 379.

feudal garb, transform their tenants, assert their implicitly absolute property in the land, and install capitalist property forms under their own auspices.[18]

Just how closely Marx's first theory of transition from feudalism to capitalism follows the lines of Smith's should be evident. Like Smith's, Marx's was a theory of the evolution of the mode of subsistence. As did Smith, Marx saw historical evolution as taking place via the growth of the division of labour, economically determined by the growth of trade and competition. Marx, of course, rejected in theory Smith's working conception of the human being as *homo economicus*; nevertheless, he followed Smith, in practice, in seeing an initial rise of – or at least movement toward – capitalism in the ancient commercial society of the Mediterranean, as well as in viewing the rise of feudalism as a consequence of the barbarian invasions and the resulting interruption by outside forces of the self-developing commercial dynamic of the ancient world. Both Smith and Marx saw bourgeois commercial and industrial classes as the bearers of progress over and against (at least initially) feudal agrarian classes who stood for the parasitism of the political on the economic; moreover, they both viewed economic development as taking place under the auspices of the bourgeoisie by means of the beating out of less efficient production in the presence of commerce and under the pressure of competition. Correlatively, in the rural sector, both saw the rise of trade inducing the hitherto feudal landed class to transform itself and rural socio-economic relations in a capitalist direction. In sum, in his earlier works, Marx ended up following Smith in failing to attribute to distinct forms of society distinctive forms of economic activity and developmental patterns; correlatively, like Smith, he attributed to the growth of trade and the development of technique a universal capacity to determine a pattern of growth along

---

[18] *Ibid.*, pp. 391–2:

> A revolution of the greatest importance to the public happiness was in this manner brought about by two different orders of people, who had not the least intention to serve the public. To gratify the most childish vanity was the sole motive of the great proprietors. The merchants and artificers, much less ridiculous, acted merely from a view to their own interest, and in pursuit of their own pedlar principle of turning a penny wherever a penny was to be got. Neither of them had either knowledge or foresight of that great revolution which the folly of the one and the industry of the other was gradually bringing about . . .

capitalistic lines, whatever the prevailing, historically developed societal form.

Smith preceded Marx in putting forward a primitive version of the bourgeois revolution theory that plays a role in Smith's conception of historical development much like that which Marx's plays in his conception – i.e. that of overthrowing the political, specifically feudal, extra-economic fetters on the development of the productive forces via trade and competition. It is true, of course, that Smith's bourgeois revolution via the alliance of the urban classes and the King against the nobility takes place in the medieval period, at the very start of the process of economic development, whereas Marx's classical bourgeois revolutions take place in the seventeenth and eighteenth centuries to facilitate that process's completion. Nevertheless, in view of its theoretical function, there is a real logic in expecting the bourgeois revolution to occur very early in the process of development, for some sort of revolution against the feudalists appears to be necessary to provide the essential conditions for the further development of urban industry. Moreover, as noted, in his works of the 1840s and early 1850s, Marx himself was drawn to emphasize, theoretically and historically, the importance of the medieval communal revolution for the consolidation of bourgeois society and for engendering the ensuing long-term evolution.[19] It should be pointed out, in addition, that Smith's contemporary Hume, to whom Smith was much indebted for his conception of the rise of capitalism, did actually put forward some essential elements for the interpretation of the English revolution as an early modern bourgeois revolution. Indeed, Hume's materials appear to have provided a key source for the French liberal historiography that was the main inspiration for Marx's own bourgeois revolution idea.[20]

[19] See, especially, 'Marx to Engels, 27 July 1854', in *Collected Works* (New York, 1983), vol. 39, pp. 473–6. For a discussion, see George Lichtheim, 'Bourgeois Society', in *Marxism* (New York, 1962).

[20] Thus, in language which is reminiscent of Smith's, and upon which Smith may well have directly depended, Hume wrote:

The habits of luxury dissipated the immense fortunes of the ancient barons . . . the landed proprietors also, having a greater demand for money than for men, endeavoured to turn their lands to best account with regard to profit; and either enclosing their fields or joining many small farms into a few large ones, dismissed those useless hands which formerly were always at their call in every attempt to subvert the government or oppose a neighbouring baron. By all these means the cities increased; the middle rank of men began to be rich and powerful; the prince, who in effect was the same with the law, was implicitly obeyed; and

It might appear that, despite all of these similarities, Marx's theory actually differs fundamentally from Smith's, in that it focuses, at each stage, on class and property relations, and especially the connection between these relations and the process of development. It is, after all, in the supposed contradiction between the development of the productive forces and feudal socio-political relationships that Marx finds the mechanism behind the bourgeois revolution. Nevertheless, it may be doubted if Marx's first theory of transition and revolution does much more than extend Smith's basic paradigm, and wondered if this, in turn, does not greatly vitiate his theory of the bourgeois revolution.

The crucial point, in this respect, is that Marx's understanding of the place of class and property relationships is, in these earlier works of his, explicitly *techno-functionalist*. Thus, the structure of roles within the labour process (co-operation within the unit) is technically determined by the nature of the productive process; in turn, the structure of roles within the labour process (co-operation within the unit), by virtue of its determining the division between mental and manual labour, itself constitutes the structure of class relations; as a result, the individuals who constitute classes do so by virtue of their occupation of technically-constituted roles within the labour process. The evolution of class and property relations is thus determined by the evolution of the productive forces via the latter's determination of the evolution of the labour process (co-operation within the unit). In consequence, despite appearances, class relations and class struggles occupy a passive and determined position, rather than an active and determining role, within Marx's early

though the further progress of the same causes begat a new plan of liberty, founded on the privileges of the Commons, yet in the interval between the fall of the nobles and the rise of this order the sovereign took advantage of the present situation, and assumed an authority almost absolute.
He added that
The spirit and judgement of the House of Commons appeared, not only in defence of their own privileges, but also in their endeavour, though at this time in vain, to free trade from those shackles which the high exerted prerogative of Elizabeth had imposed upon it. While the Commons were those attempting to give liberty to the trading part of the nation, they also endeavoured to free the landed property from the burden of wardships, and to remove those remains of the feudal tenures under which the nation still laboured.
David Hume, *The History of England* (London, 1840), pp. 496, 810.
Quoted in George C. Comninel, *Rethinking the French Revolution* (London, 1987), p. 62. this appears to be Marx's bourgeois revolution *avant la lettre*.

conception of historical evolution. Marx was, of course, at pains to bring out the nature of the class struggles which mark each stage of his evolutionary schema. But, in the end, these struggles are merely effects of the essential and inexorable development of the division of labour via the progress of the productive forces. For it is the development of the productive forces which, by virtue of its determining the growth of the division of labour, determines the evolution of class and property relations. By making class and property relations mere appendages of the division of labour, Marx ends up elaborating, rather than breaking from, Smith's historical materialism.

In the light of Marx's first, Smithian theory of transition from feudalism to capitalism the bourgeois revolution can take its place only on highly uncertain foundations. It is true that, from the standpoint of that theory, one can view the revolution as removing the last remaining fetters upon capitalist development, these being constituted by the absolutist state as the ultimate bulwark of the feudal class. But, in view of the fact that Marx's first theory of transition has the development of the productive forces, in the context of the rise of trade and competition, both transform agrarian feudalism and determine the successive socio-economic phases in the evolution of bourgeois urban-industrial society, and thereby effectively dissolve the problem of transition, the bourgeois revolution can, at best, hurry along an inexorable process in which class conflict is merely epiphenomenal.

III

By the end of the 1850s, Marx had significantly transformed his conception of historical materialism, precisely by transforming his understanding of the relationship between class and property relations and the development of the productive forces. The result was a radical reformulation of the problem of transition from feudalism to capitalism which had critical consequences for the conceptualization of the classical revolutions, notably the English revolution of 1640.

In *Grundrisse* and *Capital*, Marx defines property relations as, in the first instance, the relationships of the direct producers to the means of production and to one another *which allow them to reproduce themselves as they were*. By this account, what distinguishes pre-capitalist property relations – asiatic, antique, feudal – is that they provided the direct producers with the full means of reproduction. What made it possible, in turn, for the pre-capitalist cultivators, the peasants, to enjoy this full possession of their means of subsistence was the existence of, and their membership in, *communities* of cultivators devoted to constituting and maintaining this possession.

The object of all these communities is preservation, i.e., the production of the individuals which constitute them as proprietors, i.e. in the same objective mode of existence, which also forms the relationship of the members to each other, and therefore forms the community itself.[21]

In turn, precisely because the pre-capitalist producers enjoyed full access to their means of subsistence and did not, in consequence, have to rent land or seek waged employment to survive, pre-capitalist ruling classes were incapable of maintaining themselves merely through the ownership of (other) property. They could maintain themselves as rulers and exploiters only by taking a surplus by extra-economic compulsion. The latter was made possible only by the lords' establishing and reproducing their own communities to accomplish this very purpose.[22]

Marx's new conceptualization of property relations brought with it a transformed idea of the nature of economic development and of the transition from pre-capitalist societies to capitalism. Above all, Marx now relinquished his former, techno-determinist view whereby the productive forces, by determining the division of labour within the work process and thereby the structure of productive roles, determined the division between mental and manual labour and thereby the distribution of property and class relations. Instead, Marx now argued that, far from determining the structure of property relations, the character of production is itself conditioned by the established structure of property relations. In pre-capitalist systems, the established structures of property relations were constituted and maintained by the communities of cultivators and of lords. These formed, as it were, an historically-given starting-point or framework for the development of pro-

21 K. Marx, *Pre-Capitalist Economic Formations*, ed. E. J. Hobsbawm (New York, 1969), p. 92.
22 K. Marx, 'The Genesis of Capitalist Ground Rent', in *Capital* (New York, 1972), vol. 3, chapter 47, pp. 793–4. *Cf.* Maurice Dobb, *Studies in the Development of Capitalism* (New York, 1947).

duction. Thus, in all pre-capitalist forms, whether the cultivators' possession was mediated through the tribe (asiatic), the city-state (antique), or the assembly of cultivators (Germanic/feudal),

a man appears from the start as something more than the abstraction of the 'working individual', but has an *objective mode of existence* in his ownership of the earth, which is *antecedent* to his [labouring] activity and does not appear as its mere consequence ... What immediately mediates this attitude [to the land] is the more or less naturally evolved, more or less historically evolved and modified, existence of the individual as a *member of the community.*[23]

Starting from this new understanding of pre-capitalist property relations as reproduced by communities of rulers and cultivators which made possible the economic reproduction of their individual members, Marx went on to reformulate his conception of economic activity in pre-capitalist and capitalist societies and, on that basis, provided a powerful critique of his earlier, Smithian view. Just as the productive forces could no longer determine, by determining the structure of productive roles in the division of labour (cooperation), the nature of classes and property, similarly, the development of the productive forces under the pressures of trade and competition could no longer determine the evolution of classes and property. On the contrary, the structure of property, reproduced by the community, constituted a fundamental constraint under which the economic actors chose their economic goals and, in turn, decided just how they would respond to the emerging opportunities for exchange that had played such a determining role in the first, Smithian version of Marx's historical materialism.

In the first place, then, because they possessed the means of subsistence, the peasants could now find an economic basis, and an economic rationale, for choosing as the fundamental goal of their production the securing of subsistence. In Marx's words,

The individual is placed in such condition of gaining his life as to make not the acquiring of wealth his object, but self-subsistence, his own reproduction as a member of the community; the reproduction of himself as a proprietor of the parcel of ground and, in that quality, as a member of the community.[24]

From the premise that peasant possessors would take as their

---

[23] Marx, *Pre-Capitalist Economic Formations*, p. 81 (italics are Marx's).
[24] *Ibid.*, p. 74.

goal production for subsistence – thus diversifying in order directly to produce their needs and marketing only physical surpluses – Marx arrived at a conclusion of fundamental importance in shaping his revised understanding of the transition from feudalism to capitalism. In view of the relationship to the means of production enjoyed by pre-capitalist producers, although often engaging in trade, they would not trade to the extent of involving themselves in 'production for exchange'; that is, they would not, normally, freely *choose* to make themselves *dependent* upon exchange for their reproduction. Rather,

> The purpose of [their] labour is not the creation of [exchange] value although they may perform surplus labour in order to exchange it for *foreign* labour, i.e., for surplus products. Its purpose is the maintenance of the owner and his family as well as of the communal body as a whole. The establishment of the individual as *worker*, stripped of all qualities except this one, is itself a product of *history*.[25]

That this point of departure leads to results entirely incompatible with, and destructive of, Marx's first, Smithian theory of transition can easily be seen. In consequence of the prevailing system of property relations, both lords and peasants could, and very likely would, fail to respond to the opportunity to trade by fully specializing so as to maximize exchange value, allowing themselves to become market dependent, as in Smith's model. Exchange could not therefore be assumed to bring with it the developmental dynamic taken for granted by Smith, as well as by Marx in his first theory of transition to capitalism. On the contrary, where pre-capitalist property relations prevailed, the rise of trade, far from bringing development and transition, could easily co-exist with patterns of individual economic activity that both were subversive of overall economic growth and entirely compatible with the maintenance of the old order. How was this?[26]

First, and perhaps ultimately most critically, in allowing both exploiters and producers direct access to their means of reproduction, pre-capitalist property forms freed both exploiters and producers from the necessity to buy on the market what they needed to

[25] *Ibid.*, p. 68 (italics in original).

[26] The following six paragraphs are not taken directly from Marx; they represent one possible construction of an argument from Marx's premises, given above, to his conclusions, given below, designed to bring out the general character of his newly-revised historical materialist approach.

maintain themselves, and thus of the necessity to produce for exchange, of the resulting necessity to sell competitively on the market their output, and of the consequent necessity to maximize the price/cost ratio of their output. In consequence, both producers and exploiters were relieved of the necessity to cut costs so as to maintain themselves, and so of the necessity constantly to improve production through specialization and/or accumulation and/or innovation. The property relations, in themselves, even in the presence of trade, thus failed to impose that relentless pressure on the individual economic actors to improve in order to compete, which is the indispensable condition for economic development.

Without the necessity to maximize exchange values, the direct producers, as individuals and as members of communities of cultivators, tended to find it most sensible to deploy their resources so as to ensure their maintenance by producing directly the full range of their necessities (i.e. to produce for subsistence). Given the low level of agricultural productivity which perforce prevailed, harvests and therefore food supplies were highly uncertain. Since food constituted so large a part of total consumption, the uncertainty of the food market brought with it highly uncertain markets for other commercial crops. It was therefore sensible for the peasants to avoid dependence upon the market – above all dependence upon purchases of subsistence goods, but also dependence upon sale of commercial crops. To avoid this dependence, the peasants had to diversify, so as to produce directly all they needed. This does not mean that they failed to use the market, but simply that they tended to market only physical surpluses. Indeed, it does not seem unreasonable to assert that, under pre-capitalist conditions, peasants would likely have sought to avoid specialization and dependence on exchange, not only in order to avoid the specific risk of market failure in necessities, but, more generally, in order to avoid becoming entirely subjected, in what they would produce and where they would produce it, to the dictates of the market, and the whole transformation of life that subjection to the market would have entailed. The resulting tendency to production for subsistence naturally constituted a powerful barrier to commercial specialization and ultimately the transformation of production.

Nor, given the prevalence of pre-capitalist property relations, were the exploiting lords much better situated than were the peasants to pursue a pattern of economic action supportive of development and socio-economic transformation, even in the presence of trading opportunities. As noted, the lords' possession of the requirements for their reproduction as lords freed them from the necessity of increasing their income for the purpose of increasing their productive capacity. But even if the lords wished, for other reasons, to increase their income, they were by and large prevented from doing this by means of improving the productiveness of their men and land. To the extent that pre-capitalist property relations prevailed, if lords wished to organize production themselves, they had to depend on labourers who were peasants and thus possessed their means of subsistence. This being the case, the lords could get their workers to labour only by directly coercing them, and careful labour would require high costs of supervision. Similarly, the lords could not 'fire' their peasant labourers for shoddy work, and they thereby were deprived of perhaps the most effective means yet discovered to impose labour discipline in a class-divided society.

It needs, in this context, to be emphasized that individual lords did not have the option of moving to increase their incomes by expropriating their peasants and bringing in commercial tenants and wage labourers. Because, in the economy as a whole, the direct producers possessed their means of reproduction, the lords had no class of producers devoid of the means of subsistence to turn to in order to rent out or directly farm their land. In other words, there was no developed market in tenants and wage workers.[27] The lords could not, then, as individuals, rationally move to get rid of their peasants in order to install capitalist property relations to take advantage of the opportunities to exchange.

In view of the difficulty, in the presence of pre-capitalist property relations, of raising returns from their estates via either capital investment or the transformation of property relations, the lords found that, if they wished to increase their income, they had little choice but to do so by redistributing wealth and income away from their peasants or from other members of the exploiting class. This meant that, far from having to specialize, accumulate and innovate in production, the lords were obliged to deploy their

---

[27] This is not, of course, to maintain that wage labourers and commercial tenants were absent from the medieval European economy, and any full historical account would have to explain their origins, functioning and effects within that economy. Abstraction is made here from these important phenomena – and also below in the brief reference to merchants, guilds and the urban economy – for purposes of exposition.

surpluses toward building up their means of coercion by investment in military men and equipment. This was the opposite of improving the level of the productive forces and carrying through social transformation.

Given the prevalence of pre-capitalist property relations and the modes of economic activity which it tended to impose on lords and peasants, the merchant class – which, in Smith's theory, played the pivotal role in providing the stimulus for and actually organizing the growth of the division of labour – was unable to find it in its interest to function in an economically progressive manner. Facing the same difficulties as did the lords and peasants in improving production on the land, as well as the barriers posed by the guild-based communities of artisans to developing production in the towns, merchants could best profit through pursuing trade. Merchants thus tended to assume the task of insuring the trade of the artisan-produced luxury and military goods required by the lords in exchange for the peasant-produced food and raw materials required by the artisans for their economic subsistence. In this way, merchants played a central role in maintaining the entire socio-economic system.

However, dependent as they were on profits from pure exchange, merchants had to be able to buy cheap and sell dear. Yet, within the pre-capitalist context, the only way merchants could insure their continuing capacity to do this – i.e. to prevent overtrading and the reduction or elimination of profit that this would bring – was by securing the ability to control entry to their markets. Such monopoly control could only be secured via political assistance from, thus by means of alliance with, the monarchy and/or the lordly class. Far from transforming the old system economically or subverting it politically, the merchant class thus tended to live off the old socio-economic order and to constitute one of its main bulwarks.

As Marx concluded, 'commerce imparts to production a character directed more and more toward exchange value'; nevertheless, 'its development [and that of merchant's capital] ... is incapable by itself of promoting and explaining the transition from one mode of production to another'. Indeed, 'wherever merchant's capital still predominates, we find backward conditions'. Thus:

> Commerce ... has a more or less dissolving influence everywhere on the producing organization ... whose different forms are

mainly carried on with a view to use value. To what extent it brings about a dissolution of the old mode of production depends on [the old mode's] solidity and internal structure. And whither the process will lead ... what new mode of production will replace the old, does not depend on commerce, but on the character of the old mode of production itself.[28]

The results of Marx's new analysis were far-reaching: essentially, they were to turn his first approach to transition upside down. In the presence of pre-capitalist property relations, the economic actors – lords, peasants, merchants – could hardly be assumed to find it rational or possible to act in a capitalist manner or transform the old system, even given the rise of trade. On the contrary, given the prevalence of pre-capitalist property systems, one could expect individual lords and peasants to adopt economic strategies for maintaining and improving their condition that were in no way capitalist and therefore, society-wide patterns of economic evolution that did not lead to economic development. Thus, in contrast with Smith and early Marx, the later Marx attributed to distinct forms of society – ancient, feudal, capitalist, and so on – their own distinctive forms of economic functioning, their own characteristic 'laws of motion'. Correlatively, Marx explicitly affirmed that, in order to create the conditions for sustained economic development, it was necessary to break up the extant pre-capitalist property system: first, to separate the direct producers from possession of the means of subsistence and, secondly, to deprive the lords of the capacity to reproduce themselves by extra-economic coercion.[29] Only if the direct producers were rendered *market dependent*, thus *subject to competition*, and thus *required* to maximize their productive effectiveness in order to survive on the market, could the direct producers be counted upon to attempt, systematically, to cut costs by specialization, accumulation and innovation. Only if the direct producers were freed to combine

[28] 'Facts about Merchant's Capital', in *Capital*, vol. 3, chapter 20, pp. 326, 327, 331–2.

[29] *Pre-Capitalist Economic Formations*, pp. 97–108. The subsequent literature on the transition from feudalism to capitalism is, of course, immense. For some recent views, see *The Brenner Debate. Agrarian Class Structure and Economic Development in Preindustrial Europe*, ed. T. Aston and C. H. E. Philpin (Cambridge 1985); J. E. Martin, *Feudalism to Capitalism: Peasant and Landlord in English Agrarian Development* (London, 1983); R. J. Holton, *The Transition from Feudalism to Capitalism* (London, 1985); Alan Macfarlane, *The Origins of English Individualism* (Oxford, 1978).

factors and move themselves in accord with the dictates of profitability, could the potential for efficiency and creativity inherent in an economy composed of market-dependent, competitive economic actors be realized. It therefore followed that the problem of explaining the transition from feudalism to capitalism could be clearly posed: it was the problem of accounting for the transformation of pre-capitalist property relations into capitalist property relations via the action of pre-capitalist society itself.

Marx never went much beyond the foregoing posing of the problem of the transition from feudalism to capitalism. He did not systematically analyse the operation of pre-capitalist systems, as he did that of capitalism; nor did he explain how their own functioning could bring about a transition to capitalism. Nevertheless, he did give a descriptive account of how capitalist property relations emerged in the English countryside that exemplified his general approach to the problem of transition. In Marx's opinion, bourgeois historians had told only one side of the story of the assemblage of the socio-political conditions for ongoing economic development: this was to be found in these historians' accounts of the direct producers' emancipation from the political controls of serfdom and of the guilds. To provide a full analysis, Marx asserted, it remained to narrate the manner in which the direct producers were separated from their means of subsistence (particularly their possession of the land) and from their means of production, for these were, of course, the preconditions for the full emergence of capitalist property relations. To accomplish this task was the object of Marx's famous chapters in *Capital* on 'the so-called primitive accumulation'.[30]

Marx thus argued that 'The expropriation of the agricultural producer, of the peasant, from the soil, is the basis of the whole process.' He stressed that this expropriation took place in different ways in different times and different places, and that 'in England

---

[30] *Capital*, vol. 1, part 8, pp. 713–16. Marx speaks of the *so-called* primitive accumulation in order to distinguish his discussion from that of Adam Smith in two ways. First, he wishes to disavow the just-so story of frugality, diligence and intelligence by which Smith explained the original accumulation of investment funds. More to the point, he mainly wishes to argue that mere commerce and the simple accumulation of hoards of wealth (in whatever form), though important preconditions for economic development, cannot in themselves determine economic development, for the latter depends upon certain fundamental transformations in the system of property relations.

alone, which we take as our example, has it the classic form'.[31] For Marx, this classic form involved a series of processes by which the English lords used coercion, law and taxation to reduce the former peasant possessors to market dependence; by which a class of capitalist tenant farmers emerged to take up the lords' commercial farms on economic leases; and by which, through force and the market, a proletariat devoid of the means of subsistence and production arose to hire themselves out to the capitalist farmers as agricultural labourers.[32]

Marx's account of the so-called primitive accumulation in England helps to clarify further his revised view of the transition from feudalism to capitalism; however, precisely in so doing it appears definitively to undermine his old conception of the bourgeois revolution. Marx was much clearer about the character and consequences than about the causes of the process of transition in England that he described. He did not explain exactly why the English landlords did not desire or lacked the capacity to maintain or reconstruct serfdom (as did their counterparts in East Elbian Europe). Nor did he make clear what made it possible for the English lords to succeed in expropriating the peasants from possession of their means of subsistence and in reducing them to commercial farmers and wage labourers, when their counterparts in France could not accomplish this. Questions such as these about the deep roots of the transition from feudalism to capitalism in England remained unanswered by Marx. Nevertheless, what he did bring out very clearly was that, in the classic case of England, the peasants had, indeed, succeeded, during the later Middle Ages, in dissolving serfdom. Equally crucially, the lords had, during the early modern period, largely succeeded in clearing their estates of the possessing peasants and constructing, under their auspices, the famous tripartite structure of capitalist agriculture, constituted by landlords, capitalist tenant farmers and wage labourers. In England, then, the rise of capitalism took place within a landlord shell.

Nevertheless, from these premises a question immediately posed itself: if, having been unable to prevent the dissolution of serfdom, the English lords, by virtue of their power and their landlordship,

---

[31] *Ibid.*, p. 716.
[32] See 'The Expropriation of the Agricultural Population from the Land', in *Capital*, vol. 1, chapter 27.

had carried through the so-called primitive accumulation and, in so doing, had created the necessary conditions for capitalist development – in accord with Marx's conception of the transition from feudalism to capitalism – what function remained for the bourgeois revolution? If the transformation of the English lords, in the wake of the collapse of serfdom and the separation of the peasants from their land, had brought the end of feudalism, there could remain no significant feudal class, fettering production, to be overthrown. Marx's idea of the so-called primitive accumulation, the characteristic conceptual product of his new approach to transition – especially as this was exemplified in the economic history of late medieval and early modern England – appeared to undermine the historical and theoretical foundations of the theory of bourgeois revolution.

IV

As is widely recognized, the traditional social interpretation of the English revolution, developed by Christopher Hill, R. H. Tawney and Lawrence Stone during the 1940s and 1950s, follows very closely the (early) Marxian(–Smithian) theory of the bourgeois revolution. In the conception of these authors, the rise of trade provided the original motor of development in England. But commercialization had an impact on the nascent bourgeois elements quite different from its impact on the old feudal classes. A new urban and, in particular, a new rural bourgeoisie seized the opportunities provided by commercialization to grow increasingly rich and powerful. However, the old feudal class was unable to respond to the new economic conditions for a series of reasons. The old aristocracy, it was argued, maintained itself via its military–feudal following; this necessitated retaining paternalistic relations with tenants, who were often also political clients. But paternalism was, of course, the opposite of what was required to take the maximum commercial benefit from the land. To make matters worse, the price revolution of the sixteenth century especially penalized those landlords unable or unwilling to raise rents, while it benefited tenants and aggressive rack-renters. Finally, leading sections of the aristocracy were hurt by their high requirements of consumption. Bastard feudal magnates had to live like lords to maintain their standing with their followers. Court nobles had to assume heavy diplomatic costs, while also keeping up conspicuous consumption for prestige purposes. In sum, bastard feudal, passive and court-connected aristocrats suffered in the new economic environment, while non-feudal, active and country gentry profited. By the late sixteenth century, the aristocrats' immobilism had left them in financial crisis, while the gentry grew from strength to strength. To compensate for their economic difficulties the aristocracy sought political remedies and was obliged to turn to the monarchy for support. The monarchy provided succour to the crisis-bound aristocracy through the creation of court offices, and it financed these sinecures by granting commercial and industrial monopolies and by levying taxes on the newly-developing bourgeois economy, seriously fettering the growth of production. In response, the bourgeoisie, notably the gentry, was obliged in its own material interests, to fight for commercial freedom and parliamentary liberties, and ultimately precipitated revolution.[33]

The weaknesses of the traditional social interpretation reflect the weaknesses of the Smithian–early Marxian theory on which it was based, especially the inability of that theory adequately to conceptualize the problem of transition from feudalism to capitalism. If England was, in fact, essentially a feudal society – if, in particular, its rural economy was constituted by peasants who possessed the land and by lords who took their surpluses by extra-economic coercion – it was necessary to explain why the rise of trade should have led to capitalist development rather than the reproduction of the old feudal order. Why, in particular, should there have emerged in the countryside a bourgeois landlord class, a rising gentry? On the other hand, if English feudalism was on its way to dissolution – and if, in particular, rural lords could no longer take their surpluses by extra-economic compulsion, but could rely on commercial rents from free tenants – rural society was already well on its way toward capitalism, and it was necessary to explain why its landlords were anything but capitalist. Why, in particular, should an aristocracy that had subjected its peasants to economic rents have been unable to adjust to commercial pressures and opportunities, at least in the medium term?

In fact, the bourgeois revolution thesis ultimately collapsed in consequence of the inability of its adherents to demonstrate that English agrarian society was reproducing both a feudal and a

[33] For the previous two paragraphs, see references in footnote 1.

capitalist landed class in the seventeenth century, let alone that these classes took opposing sides in the political conflicts of that era. This failure was manifested in the incapacity of the proponents of the 'rise of the gentry/crisis of the aristocracy' thesis systematically to distinguish within the population of English landowners two different classes, reproducing themselves in two systematically different ways, let alone two different classes which, respectively, profited by and suffered from the economic changes, and particularly the agrarian progress, of the Tudor–Stuart period. It is reasonably clear today that, while many of socio-economic phenomena observed by the proponents of the bourgeois revolution idea were very real, these cannot be systematically associated with separate classes, let alone classes which opposed one another politically.[34]

It is, in fact, possible to read Lawrence Stone's *Crisis of the Aristocracy* not only as a systematic critique of the various planks which constituted the rise of the gentry theory, but also as a powerful demonstration of an alternative hypothesis – that the dominant trend of the period from the close of the Middle Ages down to the mid-seventeenth-century conflict is less the crisis of the aristocracy than its transformation, both economically and politically. Thus, the series of developments that the early Stone saw as causing problems for the aristocracy, the later Stone treats as not only creating aristocratic problems, but also as leading to aristocratic solutions.

Stone's results, now a quarter of a century old, seem only to have been vindicated by subsequent research. With the death of serfdom in the later medieval period, the English lords could no longer take their incomes in the form of feudal rents, i.e. by extra-economic compulsion based on the control and coercion of unfree peasants. The customary, formerly villein tenants had obtained their freedom and had gained access to the King's courts. As a result, if the lords were to continue to secure significant incomes from their

---

[34] The *locus classicus* for the series of arguments showing that the adherents of the 'rise of the gentry/crisis of the aristocracy' thesis fail to demonstrate the existence of distinct rural social classes corresponding to 'gentry' and 'aristocracy' is J. H. Hexter, 'Storm Over the Gentry', in *Reappraisals in History* (New York, 1961). In his critique, Hexter builds on H. R. Trevor-Roper, 'The Elizabethan Aristocracy: An Anatomy Anatomised', *Economic History Review*, 2nd series, 4 (1952); H. R. Trevor-Roper, 'The Gentry, 1540–1640', *Economic History Review*, Supplement 1 (1953); J. P. Cooper, 'The Counting of Manors', *Economic History Review*, 2nd series, 8 (1956).

customary lands – rather than see customary rents fixed and eroded by inflation – they had no choice but to attempt to subject these lands to economic rents, which could be varied in accord with supply and demand.

In his classic work on *The Agrarian Problem in the Sixteenth Century* (1912), Tawney described a process in which rural landlords did, over the course of the sixteenth century, succeed in overcoming the difficulties that initially had confronted them as a result of the prevalence of copyhold tenures, as well as of long leases, in the context of rising prices. Over time, of course, even long leases fell in. Furthermore, Tawney argued, although the courts tended to support manorial customs, landlords could, in a majority of cases, sooner or later subject customary holdings to economic rents because relatively few tenants enjoyed tenures for which manorial custom dictated the right to inherit with inheritance fines fixed. Lords could achieve economic rents on non-heritable copyholds simply by assuming control of the plots when the term of years or lives had expired. On plots held 'by inheritance' where tenants could prove no custom of fixed inheritance fines, lords could simply substitute such fines, levied at whatever rate the market would bear, for market rents – or, at least, they could do so until the late sixteenth and early seventeenth centuries, when the courts began to support a doctrine of 'reasonableness' for fines on plots held by inheritance.[35]

Tawney's most powerful critic, Eric Kerridge, sharply attacked his illustrious predecessor, but, ironically, reached conclusions not all that different from those of Tawney himself.[36] But this is not

[35] *The Agrarian Problem of the Sixteenth Century*, pp. 296–310, especially p. 296, footnote 2.

[36] Like Tawney, Kerridge provides evidence that, over much of the country, copyholders held for years or lives and subject to arbitrary fines. This is to say that their landlords could ultimately charge them economic rents – in the case of the copyholders for years or lives, by introducing a terminable lease when the specified years or lives had expired, and in the case of copyholders with arbitrary fines, by charging fines in accord with what the market would bear at the times tenures changed hands. It is true that Kerridge does seem to differ with Tawney, to some degree, in his understanding of those cases where copyholders held by inheritance subject to arbitrary fines, stating that, in such instances, the landlord could only charge 'reasonable fines'. Yet, he seems also to say, as did Tawney, that the courts actually began to support a doctrine of reasonableness only in the late sixteenth and early seventeenth centuries. Eric Kerridge, *Agrarian Problems in the Sixteenth Century and After* (London, 1969), pp. 38–40. Compare Kerridge, p. 39 with Tawney, p. 296, note 2. Kerridge's dispute with Tawney seems to be largely verbal, over the term 'security'. Kerridge contends

really surprising, for had customary tenants succeeded in preventing the landlords from setting rents in accord with market forces, especially in the context of the sixteenth-century price rise, landlords in general could hardly have avoided deep and sustained financial difficulties. But there is no evidence of generalized, let alone long-term, landlord economic problems. Over the course of the early modern period, customary peasants were reduced to market-dependent commercial tenants, losing the full possession of the land that formerly, to a significant degree, had shielded them from the necessity to compete productively on the market in order to hold on to their land. The emergent class of commercial tenant farmers, subjected to competition both in the market for leases and in the market for their output, had little choice but to maximize their profits by specializing to the greatest extent possible, reinvesting their surpluses, and applying improved agricultural methods. Capitalist property relations thus brought increased productivity and increased rural differentiation. Landlords could hardly help but benefit from the higher rents that resulted from intensified competition for their land among increasingly well-off and efficient capitalist farmers, as well as from the general rise in population.

Indeed, in his chapter on estate management in *The Crisis of the Aristocracy*, Lawrence Stone directly refutes the idea that either tenant right or long leases posed insuperable problems for aristocratic incomes, and traces instead an extended process by which the aristocracy rationalized its estates. Stone demonstrates, in line with the conclusions of Tawney and Kerridge, that landlords could adjust to copyholds held 'by inheritance' through substituting entry

that 'Security of tenure can only mean the legal security of the tenant against wrongful eviction or ouster, not against all the hazards of this fleshly world. One thing security of tenure cannot mean by any stretch of the imagination is a perpetual and inalienable right to possess a certain property' (p. 54). The fact remains that Tawney used the term security of tenure precisely with reference to what he called the 'question of tenant right'. This was not, for Tawney, the question of whether or not customary tenants could have their rights, whatever they happened actually to be, protected in the courts (Tawney, like Kerridge, thought that they generally could); it was the question of whether or not those rights gave them security of inheritance and from the landlords' raising their rents in accord with market forces. It was the question, for Tawney, of whether or not the tenant could be subjected, sooner or later, to economic, uncertain, market-determined rents, or whether they held with fixed payments and by inheritance, whether customary land was ultimately theirs or the landlords'. *Cf.* P. Croot and D. Parker, 'Agrarian Class Structure and The Development of Capitalism: France and Britain Compared', in *The Brenner Debate*, pp. 82–3.

fines at the market rates for economic rents. Stone explains, as well, how landlords, bit by bit, substituted more rational and market-sensitive instruments for less, ultimately turning to rack rent pure and simple.[37] With demand for land continuing to rise throughout the early modern period, only very unlucky or extremely incompetent landlords could, in Stone's view, have failed, in the end, to do well. Stone thinks that rents actually doubled between 1590 and 1640, a period in which prices rose by only one-third. As he concludes, 'The disadvantages in estate management under which the aristocracy laboured in the late sixteenth century were only temporary and were caused by features peculiar to the age. When times changed in the seventeenth century and when they set their minds to the problem of more efficient management, the many who still owned thousands of acres of under-exploited land were able to make a striking recovery. The evidence of their success is writ large in the family archives of the early seventeenth century . . .'[38]

In his brilliant chapter on power in *The Crisis of the Aristocracy*, Stone provides an account of the localized forms of magnate power inherited from the Middle Ages and explains how the efforts of some nobles to continue to maintain these forms led them, at various points during the sixteenth century, into serious and some-times fatal financial difficulties. Nevertheless, Stone's central theme here is less of crisis than of adjustment. First, since, with the end of serfdom, lords could no longer extract rents through exploiting their tenants' unfreedom, access to force was of much less direct economic use. Secondly, as the Tudor state grew in strength – and received the backing of broad sections of a landlord class fed up and exhausted from civil war – magnate gangs had decreasing scope for marauding, banditry and the overawing of the courts. Thirdly, with the growing possibility, during the course of the sixteenth century, of deriving increasing incomes from com-mercial rents in a context of growing demand for land, lords had growing incentive to make maximum use of all opportunities from their estates.

Faced with these trends, the magnates had decreasing reason to

[37] Stone, *Crisis of the Aristocracy*, pp. 307–10, 314–22 and ff.
[38] Stone, *Crisis of the Aristocracy*, pp. 327–8, 334. For the long-term recovery following the short-term crisis, see also J. H. Hexter, 'The English Aristocracy, its Crises and the English Revolution, 1558–1660', *Journal of British Studies*, 8 (November 1968), pp. 22–78.

maintain their military followings, and Stone describes the complex processes by which they reduced their entourages and clientages, profited from the resulting reductions in the costs of hospitality and patronage, and found it increasingly possible and rational to regard their tenants as sources of rent, rather than of military support. Certainly, in the course of the sixteenth century, a number of individual magnates went under as a result of their unwillingness or inability to adjust, broken politically by the monarchy or destroyed economically through financial ineptitude. But, as Stone demonstrates, by the early seventeenth century almost the entirety of the greater landed class had relinquished the magnate mode of lordly reproduction and had, as a direct consequence, vastly improved its overall economic outlook.[39]

Even as early as 'The Anatomy of the Aristocracy', his initial statement of the thesis of aristocratic crisis, Stone had attributed the aristocracy's economic difficulties less to its long-term problems of adjustment to incipient capitalism than to conjunctural pressures stemming from the demands of war finance during the late sixteenth-century conflict with Spain and from Elizabeth I's stinginess in handing out gifts during the same period. In *Crisis*, Stone reaffirms the hypothesis of noble financial difficulties during the latter part of the sixteenth century and further clarifies its short-term character. He goes on, moreover, to provide ample evidence that, overall, the aristocracy recouped its losses when James I came to the throne and more than compensated through his generosity for his predecessor's parsimony.[40]

At the same time, Stone demonstrates just how small, in relative terms, was the English court and how limited its capacity to provide economic support for more than a very restricted section of the aristocracy. Had the English aristocracy been in crisis, the court could not have bailed it out. Of course, as Stone concludes in *Crisis*, the aristocracy was not, by the early seventeenth century, suffering financial crisis. In consequence, few of its members needed the court to maintain themselves, which is not, of course, to say that

[39] Stone, *Crisis of the Aristocracy*, pp. 199–272. For these processes, see also the parallel series of studies by M. E. James: *Change and Continuity in the Tudor North*, Borthwick Papers, no. 27 (York, 1965); *A Tudor Magnate and the Tudor State*, Borthwick Papers, no. 30 (York, 1966); 'The First Earl of Cumberland and the Decline of Northern Feudalism', *Northern History*, 1 (1966); 'The Concept of Order and the Northern Rising, 1569', *Past and Present*, 60 (August 1973).

[40] Stone, *Crisis of the Aristocracy*, pp. 473–5.

they did not wish to profit from court offices. On the other hand, the cost of the English court was, in European terms, exceedingly small, and probably actually decreased quite a bit during the 1630s. In view of the court's minimal and declining costs, it is hard to see how court *parasitism* could have provoked the rebellion (and had it done so, rebellion should have occurred in the later 1620s, rather than in 1640).[41]

The conclusions of Lawrence Stone's *The Crisis of the Aristocracy* thus have a paradoxical thrust. On the one hand, by showing the way in which the English greater landed classes gradually gave up the magnate form of politico-military organization, commercialized their relationships with their tenants, rationalized their estates, and made use of – but avoided dependence upon – the court, Stone tended to confirm the traditional view that agrarian capitalism in England arose within the framework of landlordism. This was a result which fitted very well with the Marxist account of the so-called primitive accumulation. On the other hand, precisely by laying out a process in which the greater landed classes ended up transforming themselves so as to take advantage, economically and politically, of the new capitalist agrarian order and the unified national state, he ended up helping to destroy the traditional social interpretation of the mid-seventeenth-century conflict as a revolt by a new bourgeoisie, growing up within the interstices of the feudal order, against a still heavily feudal ruling aristocracy.

To sum up: the Smithian–early Marxian theory of the transition from feudalism to capitalism, built upon Smith's and the early Marx's mechanical materialism, underpinned Marx's bourgeois revolution theory (itself probably derived from Smith and Hume via liberal French historians) and provided the model for the social interpretation of the English revolution. In turn, Marx's revised approach to the transition from feudalism to capitalism, rooted in his revised version of historical materialism and exemplified in his notion of the so-called primitive accumulation, provided an alternative model both for criticizing the Smithian/early Marxian approach to transition and to bourgeois revolution and for interpreting the rise of capitalism in early modern England in terms of its emergence within the framework of commercial landlordism.

[41] Stone, *Crisis of the Aristocracy*, pp. 464–70, 475–6, 503–4; and his 'Trevor-Roper's General Crisis', *Past and Present*, 18 (November 1960).

Finally, modern scholarship, notably Lawrence Stone's *Crisis of the Aristocracy*, tends to confirm the idea of capitalist development within a landlord shell implied by the idea of the so-called primitive accumulation and thereby to undermine the traditional social interpretation of the English revolution, itself rooted in the Smithian–early Marxian understandings of the transition from feudalism to capitalism and of bourgeois revolution.

V

Are we to conclude, then, that social interpretations of the English revolution are bound to fail, that there is no connection between the rise of agrarian capitalism within an aristocratic and landlord shell and the mid-seventeenth-century conflicts? In my opinion, such a conclusion would be premature, to say the least.

Over the length of the early modern period, England experienced what was, in the European context, a virtually unique political evolution: the precocious, and exceedingly thorough, development of a unified national state via the elimination of bastard feudal regionally-based magnates and the monopolization of the legitimate use of force by the government; the short-circuiting of all tendencies toward the growth of absolutism, of the tax/office state; the establishment of parliamentary rule; and, ultimately, by the eighteenth century, the erection of an extraordinarily powerful centralized state, with higher levels of taxation and more advanced forms of bureaucratic administration than could be found perhaps anywhere else in Europe. Nevertheless, this unique series of political outcomes was, in my view, only made possible as a consequence of the parallel emergence of a similarly unique aristocracy. This aristocracy no longer relied for its income on coerced levies from the peasantry, and was accruing vast and growing incomes through rationalizing its estates and renting its lands on commercial competitive leases to improving farmers. Yet it shared a significant range of economic and political interests with both commercial tenants and owner-operating farmers. This aristocracy did not, in consequence, require a tax/office state to support it economically through court favours and national and local offices, yet it was vitally interested in and supportive of a powerful centralized state – via its involvement in Parliament, trade, and colonies. It was, I believe, the development of capitalism within an aristocratic landlord framework that both provides the key to the specific path of long-term political evolution in early modern England and helps to explain why this evolution did not take place without profound conflicts – conflicts that revolved around a far from capitalist monarchical state and that involved the powerful intervention of social forces outside the landed class. But actually to make the case for this connection must be the task of another study.

9. Crowds, carnival and the state in English executions, 1604–1868

THOMAS W. LAQUEUR

In late winter of 1984, James David Autry, convicted for the murder of a Port Arthur convenience store clerk, asked the federal district and appeals courts to compel the Texas Board of Corrections to allow his execution by lethal injection to be televised. Don Kobos, a reporter for Houston's Channel 13, joined in the suit. The Texas Attorney General did not, in principle, object and a heated public debate ensued. On the one hand there were those who argued that if capital punishment was meant to be a deterrent then more publicity could only enhance its effect. Also, since executions were by their nature 'public' and theatrical, i.e. formal acts of the state which were more or less widely witnessed and reported, television journalists had as much right to use the tools of their trade as did their colleagues of the press. If audiences had the right to read about dramatic judicial killings they also had the right to see them 'live'. On the other hand, there were those who objected that 'there is simply no way in the world that televising the death of a human being ... can be anything but sensationalized'. The nature of the event, heightened by the special qualities of television, guaranteed it. Allowing an execution to be broadcast, they argued, would trivialize human life, reduce state action to the level of a sitcom, and elevate the criminal to the status of hero.[1]

I have presented shorter versions of this paper at the Humanities Center of Wesleyan University and to the history department at Harvard and am grateful to my audiences there for their comments and suggestions. I owe a great debt to Stephen Greenblatt, Randall McGowen, Robert Post, Randolph Starn, Reginald Zelnik and to the editors of this volume for their tough and constructive criticisms of an earlier draft of this piece. I want also to thank my research assistant Shery Kroen for all her help.

[1] See the *San Antonio Light*, 1 March 1984; the *Bryan College Station Eagle*, 28 February 1984; the *Houston Post*, 14 March 1984; the *Houston Chronicle*, 11

Opponents of Autry's request invoked history as well to make their case. Televising his death would be an unwelcome return, said one commentator, to 14 August 1936, when Rainey Bethea was hanged before a crowd of 10,000 in Owensboro, Kentucky, one of the last occasions on which the American public was permitted to watch an execution. People gathered during the night in anticipation of the main event; they drank and attended 'hanging parties'. Throughout the early morning hours hawkers worked the crowd selling popcorn and hot dogs; spectators climbed telephone poles and trees to be assured of a good view. By 5.00 a.m. the festive, cheering crowd began to cry 'Let's go, bring him out!' Bethea appeared at 5.20 a.m., visibly engorged with an enormous dinner of chicken, pork chops and watermelon, and was pushed through the crowd. At 5.28 a.m. there was a swish and a snap; the body dangled dead beneath the scaffold. Now the crowd started clawing at the black death-hood he wore and a lucky few went away with swaths of cloth as souvenirs of the morning.[2]

This history of festivity, which extends back centuries, is not what historians generally remember in their discussions of old regime punishment. Executions, they argue instead, are 'ceremonies by which power is manifested'; they are 'imposing demonstration[s]' of the state's might and authority played out at the grass roots level.[3] Recall Michel Foucault's deliciously detailed account of the public dismemberment of the would-be regicide Damien, or, for the English case, J. A. Sharpe's description of last dying speeches and, most recently, Randall McGowen's analysis of the role of the body in eighteenth-century punishment, which all evoke images of solemn state theatre. The condemned confessed, if not to the specific crime for which he or she was about to be hanged, then at least to a lifetime of sin and sabbath-breaking. Those about to die acknowledged the justice of their sentence, asked forgiveness, and warned members of the audience, which 'stood in hushed expectation', to change their evil ways. Finally the body, 'launched into eternity', provided, as McGowan puts it, 'a condensed image that was meant to convey a message to society': that the consequences

---

March 1984. I am grateful to William Bennet Turner, Esq., of the San Francisco firm Turner and Brorby for giving me a copy of his file on this subject.

[2] Ellen Goodman, 'Commentary', *The Courier-Journal*, 20 March 1984, A5.

[3] Michel Foucault, *Discipline and Punish*, trans. Alan Sheridan (New York, 1977); J. A. Sharpe, ' "Last Dying Speeches": Religion, Ideology and Public Execution in Seventeenth-Century England', *Past and Present*, 107 (1985), p. 166.

of disorder, represented by the criminal, were death to the social body.[4]

Douglas Hay has offered the most comprehensive version of what has become the dominant account of English judicial dramaturgy. A great long list of capital statutes intermittently enforced, complex rituals of sentencing, sermons to the condemned, an elaborate system of patronage invoked to procure pardons, and finally the terror of the gallows, he argues, all served to confirm the majesty, power, and legitimacy of the law and of the state. Before pronouncing his awful decision, for example, the scarlet-robed figure on the raised bench would put on a black cap of death; he would then lecture the criminals standing below and before him on the righteousness of the law, the wickedness of their acts and the justness of their particular horrible fates.[5] Judges were likened to God, deriving their authority not just from the state but from still higher sources, a view reinforced by sermons which proclaimed that earthly justice stood in metonymic relationship to the divine Throne of Last Judgement: the sentence of death, said one clergyman, was 'the gospel in epitome'.[6]

Of course Hay and others who subscribe to this reading of executions do not deny interpretative slippage. Earthly justice is, after all, but an imperfect representation of its heavenly counterpart. On occasion, if the sentence seemed unjust or if the rights of the condemned seemed to have been violated, either the victim or the crowd could turn a controlled hanging into a public disputation

---

[4] Sharpe, *ibid.*; Randall McGowen, 'The Body and Punishment', *Journal of Modern History* 59.4 (1987), pp. 651, 665–6. I agree with much of McGowen's reading but will argue that it works only because executions were not the sort of events that he takes them to be.

[5] Douglas Hay, 'Property, Authority and the Criminal Law', in Hay, Peter Linebaugh *et al.*, *Albion's Fatal Tree. Crime and Society in Eighteenth-Century England* (New York, 1975), pp. 17–64.

[6] Samuel Rossell, *The Prisoner's Director* (London, 1729), p. 63; David Edwards, *Sermons to the Condemned* (London, 1775), p. 2, quoted in Randall McGowen, 'The Changing Face of God's Justice: The Religious Dimension of the Debate over the Criminal Law', unpublished MS which argues that religion, and particularly doctrines of judgement and of hell, underlay the criminal law of the eighteenth century and that changes in religious beliefs help account for the criminal law reforms of the early nineteenth century. I do not quarrel with this view but want only to point out that the ritual at the gallows itself does not reproduce, or even seek to reproduce – unless one assumes monumental incompetence – the theories of judgement and punishment in which earthly events mirror those of the Last Days.

of the state's justice and authority.[7] Riots over possession of the bodies of criminals who had been sentenced to the extra ignominy of dissection regularly disrupted the smooth workings of state theatre.[8] Indeed, the executions of the old regime were distinguished from the panoptical penitentiary, Foucault argues, precisely by their relative openness.

Moreover, as Hay points out, terror did not exist primarily as an efficient deterrent to crime, i.e. it did not have to work according to the rational standards of another age. Rather, the gallows were but an element in a complex negotiation in which the powerful bartered mercy for deference. All that was required was that in some cases, selected more or less by chance, the death of an offender should provide a thunderous reaffirmation of the state's might and authority. Thus the evidence adduced by criminal law reformers to show that the bloody code was random in its application and a hindrance to the effective prosecution of crimes was irrelevant.[9] A huge number of capital statutes remained on the books, Hay argues, because of their part in the dramaturgy of power. Finally, of course, the penitentiary did replace the gallows as the cornerstone of criminal justice just as the realistic novel replaced the romance.[10] A new sort of determinancy, a new assault on the mind and not the body of the criminal, came to dominate punishment.

But of course the old way did not die. Public executions, though smaller in number – dramatically so after 1838 – became ever grander in scale until their final abolition in 1868. Railways, better publicity and public hunger born of rarity made nineteenth-century hangings far larger and more boisterous occasions than their earlier counterparts. As Leon Radzinowic muses, public executions lived on long after their justification had been discredited.[11]

---

[7] See Michael Ignatieff, *A Just Measure of Pain: The Penitentiary in the Industrial Revolution, 1750–1850* (New York, 1978), pp. 22–3.

[8] Peter Linebaugh, 'The Tyburn Riot Against the Surgeons', in Hay *et al.*, *Albion's Fatal Tree*, pp. 65–118. Riots for possession of the body occurred not only in London but in Oxford and indeed wherever there was a medical teaching establishment to which the law consigned the corpse of the condemned.

[9] The chances of a criminal's being executed for some capital offence other than murder were proportionately less than the chances of a coal-miner dying a violent death in the course of his work. *Second Report from His Majesty's Commissioners on Criminal Law* 1836 (343) xxxvi, 19–20.

[10] See John Bender's brilliant account of the shared epistemological assumptions of the novel and the prison. *Imagining the Penitentiary: Fiction and the Architecture of Mind in Eighteenth-Century England* (Chicago, 1987), especially chapter 1.

[11] Leon Radzinowicz, *A History of English Criminal Law and its Administration from 1750*, 4 vols (London, 1948–68), vol. 4, pp. 352–3.

The reason for this, and indeed for the continued existence, in the face of mounting criticism, of the 'bloody code' until the middle of the nineteenth century lies outside the dominant interpretation of juridical theatre which I have outlined. This interpretation of public executions regards the state – wrongly, in my view – as the writer and director of a drama in which it appropriates to itself the active, authorial role while the people and the condemned are assigned subsidiary parts as compliant actors and appreciative viewers who understand the semiotics of state power to which they are being treated. Hay, and Foucault too, regard executions as semiotically stable and relatively closed. Things may go wrong – Damien's arm may fail to come off his torso properly – but the lineaments of the text and its meaning are clear and distinct.

I want to argue, on the contrary, that a wide range of evidence undermines this dramaturgical solidity and supports instead a theatre of far greater fluidity. The crowd, and particularly the carnivalesque crowd, was the central actor in English executions. Public carnivalesque executions, though not executions as carnival, ceased, for reasons fully articulated only in the debate over their abolition, only when the crowd came to have a new relationship to the power of the state.

I

The hangings and beheadings of seventeenth-, eighteenth- and nineteenth-century England were unpromising vehicles for the ceremonial display of power, if by this is meant the sovereign power of the state. They were more risible than solemn as they lurched chaotically between death and laughter. As often as not, executions were, and were known to be, utter disasters as 'imposing demonstrations' of authority, religious or secular. They were held in unprepossessing locations, with little attention to dramatic detail and many opportunities for generic slippage. Executions were the most aleatory of occasions and those responsible did very little to make them otherwise, to insure the triumph of a prescribed interpretation. The state seemed to show a perverse lack of interest in the solemnity of hangings and in making its presence decently manifest. On the contrary, it perpetrated the shabbiest of rituals with the minimum of authorial control. Considerable evidence suggests too that those who watched the deaths of criminals and

Figure 9.1   William Capon (1757–1827), pencil and wash drawing, 'View of Tyburn towards Hyde Park', 1785. On the right is a viewing stand, 'the property of Mr Mitchel who let out the Gallery on the day of Executions'. (Reproduced by courtesy of the Trustees of the British Museum.)

traitors understood the bodies of the condemned in very different ways from what the state might have intended. The script, the staging and the public's response were thus all wrong if the point of executions was to put on 'an imposing demonstration of the state's might and authority played out at the grass roots level'. Some, or indeed even the majority, might have skirted dramatic disaster, but any such success was due more to accident than to authorial competence.

Tyburn itself, where the great proportion of London executions took place, was the unlikeliest of venues for displaying the power of the state.[12] The gallows from which a world power launched its criminals into eternity was just outside a barnyard (see Figure 9.1). William Capon (1757–1827), a Norwich-born scene-painter working for Kemble at his Drury Lane theatre, went out to sketch the old hanging grounds in 1785, two years after executions moved to the front of Newgate prison. Looking toward Tyburn from the last house on Upper Seymour Street he drew the bucolic scene and commented on the back that the structure on the right, one of three from which people could watch executions, 'was the property of Mr Mitchel who let out the Gallery on the day of Executions'. Twenty-five years later Capon produced a watercolour painting from his earlier sketch (Figure 9.2). Tyburn, where thousands met their death, has been transformed completely into a lovely country park scene. Only the shadow of the gallery now plays across the Edgeware Road and only the artist's note tells us that it is the shadow of Mr Mitchel's gallery from which executions were viewed. The eastern end of Connaught Circle where the hanging tree stood, Capon writes, is 'now built on the very spot of ground then occupied by a low barn and Dust and Cinder heaps'.[13]

---

[12] It is impossible to extract figures from the 1819 report which would allow one to determine the ratio between London and provincial executions since data are not given for all judicial circuits. In the years 1805 to 1818, between 1 in 8 (5 out of 39 in 1809) and 1 in 3.5 (21 out of 70 in 1815) of those executed in England and Wales met their death in London or Middlesex. *Report from the Select Committee on Criminal Law Relating to Capital Punishment* 1819 (585) viii. By the 1830s the ratios were as few as two out of thirty-three people executed in 1833. See *Capital Crimes in 1830, for which the Punishment of Death has been Abolished, showing the number of persons committed and executed for various years. . . .* 1846 (21) xxxiv.

[13] Capon's comments, presumably contemporaneous, are written in pencil on the back of the 1785 sketch, British Library, Crace Collection xxx/2 and on a separate sheet with the final wash drawing, Crace xxx/1. Biographical information on Capon, who, in addition to his work in the theatre, exhibited architectural and

Figure 9.2   William Capon, watercolour done from the sketch in Figure 9.1 of Tyburn looking toward Hyde Park 'from one pair of Stair's window, at the last House at the end of Upper Seymour Street, Edgeware Road . . . The Eastern end of Connaught Place is now built on the very spot of ground then occupied by a low barn and Dust and Cinder Heaps' (1810). All that might distinguish this picture of the site where scores of people were executed each year from an ordinary rural scene is the shadow on the right, which, Capon informs us, 'is produced by one of the three Galleries which were standing in 1785 . . .'. (Reproduced by courtesy of the Trustees of the British Museum.)

No systematic survey of execution sites outside London or of alternative sites within the metropolis exists. But there was certainly no systematic effort to hang offenders near architectural reminders of state power or even near the scene of their crimes. Thirty-seven citizens of Aylesbury who lived 'near and opposite the county hall' petitioned the Grand Jury assembled for the Lenten assizes in 1809 to complain about its decision to move executions to the front of the County Hall. Under the old procedures it had taken ten minutes, they wrote, to move the condemned out of town

landscape drawings from time to time, is from Lawrence Binyon's catalogue, available in the Prints and Drawings Room of the British Library.

to be hanged and no resident was inconvenienced 'by the melancholy procession' for more than 'one fourth part of that time'. But the new procedure 'will exhibit before our doors and windows, for upwards of an hour, a Spectacle, at which Human Nature must shudder, whilst we lament that it is necessary such Punishments should be inflicted'. If the state wanted a more centrally located and portentous venue for its juridical drama, an important segment of its audience was far more interested in maintaining the peace and quiet of the neighbourhoods.[14] (Homeowners near Newgate complained bitterly but to no avail when executions were moved to there from Tyburn in 1783.)

Moreover, the icons used frequently by printers to illustrate their broadsheets for provincial executions evoke memories of quiet rural gatherings (Figure 9.3), not of the majesty of the law. Nothing in this image commemorates the power of the state except the anticipated, though not actually shown, hanging itself.

While the courtroom and the chapel were redolent with the signs of state power and the majesty of the law, these were conspicuously absent from the scene of punishment itself. 'If we consider', writes Bernard Mandeville in 1725, 'the mean Equipages of the Sheriff's Officers, and the scrubby horses that compose the Cavalcade [to Tyburn], the Irregularity of the March, and the Want of Order among the Attendents,' it becomes clear that the occasion is 'devoid of that decent Solemnity that would be required to make [it] awful.'[15] A German visitor in 1739 noted that executions in England are performed without the 'terrible Apparatus' employed in other countries. 'There is not that Number of Halbardiers, nor all that Gravity, which sometimes strikes a greater Awe than the execution itself.'[16] Another German visitor, who like many foreign visitors took in the strange sight of an English execution, noted in

---

14 Petition is Q/Uncat/H in the Buckinghamshire Record Office, Aylesbury. Under the old system the condemned went by dung-cart to a spot two furlongs, i.e. a quarter of a mile, outside town, along 'Gallows Road'. See Robert Gibbs, *A History of Aylesbury with its Borough and Hundred* (Aylesbury, 1885), p. 542. Lawrence Stone tells me that Oxford executions were not held in St Giles near the residence of the assize court judges nor in front of the Castle, but on the London road well out of town. Students and friends of the condemned fought regularly over bodies designated for dissection, the former trying to bring them into town, the latter trying to keep possession themselves.

15 Bernard Mandeville, *An Enquiry into the Causes of the Frequent Hangings at Tyburn* (London, 1725), p. 24.

16 Carl Ludwig von Poellnitz, *Mémoires de C. L. Baron de Poellnitz* (London, 1739), vol. 2, pp. 458–9.

Figure 9.3 Catnach print of a quiet rural execution from the broadsheet 'An Interesting and Heartrending Account of a Dreadful and Unnatural Murder Committed by Jessy Dalton Upon the Body of Her Mother', early nineteenth century. (Reproduced by courtesy of the St Bride Printing Library.)

1761 that it should 'in reality be performed by the sheriff, a respectable citizen appointed for that purpose', but that he 'generally pays somebody well to do it for him'.[17] All the evidence suggests a remarkable lack of care in the production of would-be state ceremonial. 'If the only defect were the want of ceremony,' noted critics of Tyburn in their campaign to move executions to Newgate, 'the mind of beholders might be supposed to be left at least in a state of Indifference ... But' – and here they echo Mandeville –

> when they view the Meanness of the Apparatus, a dirty cart and ragged harness, surrounded by a sordid Assemblage of the lowest among the vulgar, their sentiments are more inclined to ridicule than Duty. The whole Progress is attended with the same effect.[18]

Moving executions away from Tyburn did not help. In 1785, the ageing executioner, now working at Newgate, was given a new robe by the sheriff which he promptly sold to a fortune-teller named Old Cain.[19]

Neither soldiers nor indeed any other functionaries of the state are portrayed in prints of most nineteenth-century London or provincial executions; if they were present they were not represented to the imagination of the public. The imposing facade of Newgate itself, which John Bender argues was meant to ensure that 'any view of a hanged criminal had to include the consideration of state authority present in this backdrop', was also studiously ignored in most popular prints.[20] Even in Rowlandson's famous 'An Execution Outside Newgate Prison', (Figure 9.4), where the prison does serve as the backdrop to the hanging, it is relegated to the wings of the image and is more lightly drawn than the building bursting with people on the left. The great majority of nineteenth-century execution prints, despite the fact that the prison was intended by the authorities to be the setting of the absorbing juridical tableau, continues to place St Sepulchre's Church at the

[17] Frederich Kielmansegge, *Diary of a Journey to England in the Year 1761–1762*, trans. Philippa Kielmansegge (London, 1902), p. 159.
[18] Barnard Turner and Thomas Skinner, *Account of the Alterations and Amendments in the ... Office of Sheriff ...* (London, 1784), p. 23, quoted in Ignatieff, *A Just Measure of Pain*, p. 89.
[19] Horace Bleackley, *The Hangmen of England* (Montclair, N.J., 1929, 1977 reprint), pp. 131–2.
[20] Bender, *Imagining the Penitentiary*, p. 246.

Figure 9.4   Thomas Rowlandson, 'An Execution outside Newgate Prison', 1790s. The backdrop of this scene is, of course, not the prison at all but the Church of St Sepulchre. The crowd seems to swell up from ground level and flow over the building on the left, which, because it is in the shadows, is more darkly drawn than Newgate. The crowd itself is represented very much like Hogarth's in Figure 9.7 below.

centre of the image and merely to suggest the presence of Newgate on the right,[21] (see Figures 9.5 and 9.6 for example).

The English state was moreover remarkably reluctant to manage the behaviour of the condemned, to force them to play a specified role. It is, of course, not easy to exercise control over one about to die even in the most brutal of circumstances.[22] But the authorities in other countries of early modern Europe, unlike those in England, did at least try. Montaigne, for example, reports that in Rome monks or members of a special brotherhood continually held a picture of Christ before the face of the criminal on the way to the place of execution, forcing him to kiss it incessantly, so that the crowd en route could not even see his face. At the gallows they 'still kept this picture against his face until he is launched'.[23] Spectators on the Dam could watch the condemned enter the chamber reserved for capital sentencing through Quellien's great bronze doors depicting the fall of man and the sword of divine judgement. They could see the various officials sitting beneath the Eye of God and various other representations of justice. Finally, a magistrate accompanied the victim out onto the scaffold as the rest of the magistrates watched from a balcony. Everything, in short, was done to ensure that the state's version of judicial theatre was that which was produced.[24]

The English, on the other hand, allowed those about to die very considerable licence and did almost nothing to ensure a proper demeanour. It is testimony to the cultural power of the normative role, to its capacity to take over the condemned's psyche, that, in the absence of coercion, so many died as the Ordinary and the

---

[21] See below for a discussion of the pictures on broadsheets. Executions of notorious or political prisoners – Dr Dodds, Lord Ferrer, the Cato Street conspirators – constitute an exception. But even here artists seem to have conflicting views about representing troops, as the wide variation in the scenes on Ferrer broadsheets suggest.

[22] See, for example, Primo Levi, *The Drowned and the Saved*, trans. Raymond Rosenthal, (New York, 1988), pp. 155–6.

[23] Michel de Montaigne, *Travel Journal*, trans. with an introduction by Donald M. Frame (San Francisco, 1983), p. 77. For a discussion of the 'pictures of redemption' produced in the late sixteenth, seventeenth and eighteenth centuries and used in various Italian cities, see Samuel Y. Edgerton, Jr, *Pictures and Punishment: Art and Criminal Prosecution during the Florentine Renaissance* (Ithaca and London, 1985), chapter 5.

[24] Katharine Fremantle, *Focus on Sculpture: Quellien's Art in the Palace on the Dam* (Amsterdam, 1979), pp. 22–9. I am grateful to Jan De Vries and Simon Schama for advice on this matter.

Figure 9.5, 9.6   Two versions of a standard early-nineteenth-century execution scene, the lower third of which is filled with a socially diverse crowd. In the centre, under the image of a scaffold, a father in a top hat holds up one of his children while his other child asks to be lifted up as well. Next to them are two working men in Billingsgate Porters' hats. The frame was filled as the occasion required. Thus, in the top print, 'The particulars of the execution of Those Unfortunate Young Men, that Suffered this Morning at the Old Bailey', 1823, the figure on the right, the reprieved George Wyeth, has been rubbed out. Three weeks later Wyeth's reprieve ran out and he came to occupy a frame of his own (bottom print).

secular authorities might have wished. But a great many did not. 'Generally speaking,' as Nietzsche points out in his genealogy of the 'bad conscience', 'punishment makes men hard and cold . . . it sharpens the feeling of alienation, it strengthens the power of resistance'.[25] Through laughter, outrageous clothes, misplaced sentimentality and silence some prisoners subverted the roles assigned to them. Others were too weak, scared or oblivious to act as they should and others still found themselves caught in stage disasters – grisly, generically comic foul-ups beyond their control in the technology of death. Whatever the proportion of disastrous to decorous executions, there was enough variation within any one 'hanging fair', enough laughter and comic chaos, to make them unsuitable for the imaginative realm of sublime terror, just reward, or tragedy.

Theatre depends on both believing and not believing that actors mean what they say; and when, as is generically the case in executions, stage action is 'real', the meaning of performances becomes still more hopelessly and poignantly ambiguous. Neither contemporaries nor historians know whether the condemned meant what they said, however they chose to die. In a scene described by a nineteenth-century observer as 'like a stage play altogether', the criteria for distinguishing between the studied resistance of a cunning murderer and the bumblings of a pathetic, mentally defective creature are simply absent. Samuel Sewell, hanged in 1830, made his appearance before the crowd gathered in front of the Buckinghamshire County Hall, and 'continued that silly, half-idiotic conduct he had maintained all through, which, whether assumed or real, could only be known to those well acquainted with his antecedents'.[26] Maybe they would know; but, in general, executions were immensely difficult to read.

Silences too were opaque. There was overt resistance with the apparent intention of offering a deviant and defiant performance. Edward Bird in 1718 remained immune to the best efforts of three clergymen who took turns exhorting him in the cart from which he was to be 'launched'. He refused to make a public devotion and he refused to ask the crowd to pray for him or take warning. Instead, he asked for a glass of wine and when told that was not available

[25] Friedrich Nietzsche, *On the Genealogy of Morals*, trans. Walter Kaufmann and R. J. Hollingdale, (New York, 1969), p. 81, 2.14.
[26] Gibbs, *Aylesbury*, p. 519.

used snuff to toast several nearby gentlemen. His death was no nicer: 'he bled very much at the Mouth and nose, or both'.[27] Before the famous pirate Captain Kidd left Newgate he promised the Ordinary that he would make a full confession and die properly. But, once at the scene, 'contrary to my expectations,' the Ordinary laments, 'he was unwilling to own the justice of his condemnation, or even so much as the providence of God'.[28] Thomas Munn had nothing whatsoever to say at the execution site because 'he had written it all out', and only insisted that Mr Vender 'take care that his Life should be published'.[29]

The Ordinary's accounts bear witness to the near impossibility of producing the canonical show. Francis Robinson refused to address the crowd when admonished to do so because, he said, his speech 'would signify nothing'; year after year people make last dying speeches but to no effect. Robinson died 'neither shedding a tear or appearing much dejected'. His companion at Tyburn, John Gowan, refused for an hour and a half to confess and pray despite the Ordinary's most strenuous efforts, the sheriff's objections to the long delay, and demands from the spectators that he should confess whether he had murdered his wife or not so that the hanging could proceed.[30] And even if one criminal died as he

27 [Paul Lorraine, Ordinary of Newgate], 'The Behaviour and Last Dying Words of Edward Bird, Gent . . .', executed 23 February 1718/19, BL 515 1. 2. 224.

28 'A Full account of . . . Captain Kidd and other pirates that were executed on the execution dock in Wapping, 27 May 1701', BL 515 1. 2. 193. This hanging, like most, was a mixed affair: of those hanged with Kidd, one cheerfully submitted to the judgement against him and two remained silent. Lorraine did finally extract repentance from Kidd under the extraordinary circumstance outlined below.

29 'The Life of Thomas Munn, alias the gentleman bricklayer, alias Tom the Smuggler, who was executed with John Hall on Friday 6 April 1750 at Chelmsford and hung in Chains near Rumford . . . A full Account of his behaviour during a great number of years as a notorious smuggler, gamester and . . . together with the many pranks he played . . .', BL 1417 e. 56, p. 21. So much of this pamphlet is in the exaggerated style of the criminal as romantic hero that one might want to discount its veracity on the subject of Munn's last words. But Hall's death is given quite straightforwardly and Munn's resistance is, as this paragraph suggests, by no means unusual.

30 'A True Account of the Prisoners executed at Tyburn on Friday 23 May, 1684', BL 515. 1. 2. 81. Newspaper accounts of inappropriate behaviour by the condemned are briefer than the Ordinary's accounts but frequently make clear that a performance did not follow the normative script; Ann Williams, burnt at the stake in Gloucester on 14 April 1753, for poisoning her husband, is a telling illustration because her punishment was an especially humiliating and – if the prisoner was not first choked into unconsciousness – painful one reserved for persons who had most egregiously offended against the public order. On an occasion when the state seemed to be pulling out its biggest semiotic guns the

should his companions might not. John Cooper, a burglar executed on 24 May 1700, 'was not in a capacity to give any Account of himself', because he was 'seized with jayl fever, which is a violent fever, attended with delirious light headedness'. One of his companions died aggressively silent, a third brazenly cheerful playing the role of carnival king and a fourth suitably contrite.[31]

Accounts of executions, like that of a late seventeenth-century French traveller, all remark on the internal inconsistencies of the execution drama. He waxes lyrical about the light, jesting quality of the English execution, about the criminal's making sure that he was well shaved 'and handsomely drest, either in Mourning or in the Dress of a bridegroom', about flowers being strewn in his path and drink offered to him on the way to the gallows. But 'to represent things as they really are, I must own', this observer concludes, 'there are many who go [to the gallows] slovenly enough, and with very dismal Phizzes'.[32] The historical record is full of such 'phizzes'. Of eight people executed at Tyburn on 18 September 1691 one arrived in style by private coach and departed properly with a confession and penitent speech. 'As for the rest,' those too poor to hire a coach who arrived by cart, 'they had but little to say.' Three desired prayers, the remaining four 'were not much concerned'. One especially seemed to have 'little sense of his misery', paying no attention to the Ordinary and casting his eyes ostentatiously upon the crowd.[33]

Only two of the five men whom the novelist Samuel Richardson saw executed on one occasion were 'suitably sad', and presumably followed the normative script in other ways as well. The other three grew 'most shamefully daring and wanton', laughing, talking obscenely, swearing, and generally behaving 'in a manner that would have been ridiculous in men in any Circumstances whatever'.[34] Performances were no more consistent a century later. When a father and son, for example, shared the scaffold on 31

victim was free to refuse to acknowledge her crime and to die 'with a Behaviour quite unbecoming her melancholy departure'. *Felix Farley's Bristol Journal*, 21 April 1753.

[31] 'A Full account of the . . . condemned criminals that were executed 24 May 1700', BL 515 1. 2. 185.

[32] Misson H. de Valbourg, *M. Misson's Memoires and Observations in his Travels over England*, trans. Mr Ozell (London, 1719), article on 'hanging', pp. 123–5.

[33] [Ordinary of Newgate], 'The True Account . . . of the eight criminals executed at Tyburn 18 Sept. 1691', BL 515 1. 2.142.

[34] Samuel Richardson, *Familiar Letters on Important Occasions* (London, 1928, first published 1741), letter 160, pp. 217–20.

March 1828 in front of York Castle, the older man kept trying to pass notes to the younger telling him to keep silent, to not play his assigned part. While the son looked pale and distressed, the father 'cast a careless look into the crowd', surveying the audience even while the Ordinary prayed. In the end, the son did confess his crime and repeat the Lord's Prayer while the father remained resolutely free of 'parental feeling, contrition, or remorse'. Ten thousand people watched this ragged show and until the end of public hangings in England the performances of the condemned were no more predictable.[35] It is impossible to read such complex scenes as coherent state theatre.

The laughter of derision and the chaos of comedy were also regularly brought to bear against the state's effort to re-establish order. Far from resigning themselves to their fate and to the legitimacy of the state's action against them – as Hobbes points out it is unreasonable to expect traitors to consent to their deaths in this fashion – the condemned have laughed over the centuries at fate and authority.[36] It was a complex laughter intimately tied to carnival, as I will discuss below, to the *hilaritas* of the martyr which would have been so familiar to English audiences in Fox's *Book of Martyrs*,[37] to the tradition of *galgenhumor*, to the deeply serious play of life and death. It seemed that the more important the occasion, the more egregious the comic lapses. Several of the Cato Street conspirators – caught trying to blow up the Cabinet in 1819 – came up upon the scaffold before an enormous crowd in great good cheer and with an air of gaiety. They offered cheers, which the crowd returned and, after they were decapitated, the hapless assistant executioner – his boss had fled the stage earlier – was met with loud booing and hissing as he held up the heads one by one and announced, 'Behold the head of a traitor'.[38] Similarly, the only one

---

35 'Report of the Trial of William and John Dyon, for the Willful Murder of Mr. John Dyon of Bancroft, York Castle, March 31, 1828' (by H. Deighton), in the local history collection of the York Reference Library.

36 *Leviathan* (New York, 1976) chapter 28, para. 13, p. 224.

37 Kerby, for example, was 'as one that should be married with new garments, nothing changed in cheer or countenance', when he was brought to the stake.

38 *Manchester Observer*, 6 May 1820; *Times*, 2 May 1820. It was widely known, publicly and privately, that the conspirators 'were unbelievers in *that Saviour!* who alone c.' and 'died impenitent'. The immense space for self-fashioning which Stephen Greenblatt identifies in the heroic scaffold scene of Sir Walter Raleigh remained characteristic of English state executions. It was the traitor's and not the state's version of death that prevailed. See S. Greenblatt, *Sir Walter Raleigh* (London, 1973), pp. 119–20, 169–70.

of the Spa Field rioters to be executed in 1817 'exhibited much
levity', waved to the crowd and joined them in their groans and
hisses.[39]

But even if the condemned or the crowd did not laugh, boo or
hiss in the face of authority, executions great and small were
susceptible to ludicrous and macabre mishaps of various sorts.
Captain Kidd's execution, for example, was marred not only by his
surprise failure to confess but by the rope breaking, leaving the
dazed pirate shaken but alive on the ground.[40] From an immense
crowd in nineteenth-century London came 'crys of utmost horror'
renewed again and again, as Charles Thomas White managed to
kick one of his feet on to the edge of the scaffold as the drop fell and
as the executioner struggled amidst the chaos to complete his
work.[41] At what was supposed to be a great showcase hanging – the
only execution of a peer for a criminal act in the eighteenth century
– Earl Ferrers ruined everything by mistakenly giving a five-guinea
token of forgiveness to the assistant rather than to the executioner
himself. An 'unseasonable Dispute ensued between these unthink-
ing Wretches' to which the sheriff had to put a stop before the main
event could proceed.[42] Even very special occasions somehow took
unexpected turns.

II

The historical record of English executions thus abounds with one
disaster – madcap and melancholy – after another. Moreover,
considerable evidence suggests that, from the audience's perspective, executions were a species of festive comedy or light entertainment. A young man in nineteenth-century London might visit a
coffee house for breakfast on a Sunday morning, walk to the Old
Bailey to see how preparations for an execution were proceeding,

---

[39] Camden Pelham (pseud.), ed., *The Chronicles of Crime; or, The Newgate
Calendar* (London, 1886), vol. 2.

[40] Robert C. Ritchie, *Captain Kidd and the War against the Pirates* (Cambridge,
Mass., 1986), pp. 226–7.

[41] BL 1888 c. 3. 108. No date is given but the broadsheet is bound with others from
the late 1820s and early 1830s. The crowd's displeasure with botched executions is
a common theme. See for example Macaulay's description of 'the state of high
fury' to which the crowd was raised by the mess made of the Duke of Monmouth's
beheading: *History of England* (London, 1849), pp. 626–8.

[42] 'An account of the Execution of the Late Lawrence Shirley, Earl Ferrers,
Viscount of Tamworth . . . published by Authority of the Sheriffs' (1760), BL 515
1. 10 (8), 6–7.

have dinner, and then pick up his mistress for a walk over to Horsemonger Lane to check on how the construction of a scaffold for another hanging was coming along. The next day he might get up early to catch both events, commenting on how well the condemned behaved, remarking that he had never seen a woman hanged before, and that this was, as far as he could remember, the only occasion on which two people were hanged on the same day. A witness before the parliamentary committee hearing evidence on capital punishment reports interviewing a viewer of a public hanging. At the first appearance of the criminal this respondent claims to have been a bit discomfited, but 'the actual execution was rather pleasant and satisfactory than otherwise and he went away satisfied'. The semiotic significance of capital punishment seems to have escaped these viewers.[43]

The theatricality of executions was parodied by their opponents. 'Grand Moral Spectacle', proclaims a broadsheet laid out as a playbill: 'A Young Girl, 17, to be PUBLICLY STRANGLED in front of the County Jail, Bury St. Edmunds . . . This Exhibition (the Admission is free) is provided by A Christian Legislature . . . '[44] The square before Newgate became theatre. Those content 'to mingle with the mob below' could 'witness the horrible exhibition gratis . . . the pit [i.e. ground level] lay dark and crowded below, and there the audience at free entrance.' But others bargained for better viewing spots with hawkers who cried out, 'Comfortable room! Excellent Situation! Beautiful Prospect! Splendid View!'[45] Henry Angelo's account of his successful bargaining for a window seat to watch the execution of Thistlewaite and the other Cato Street conspirators makes the judicial drama seem decidedly secondary to avoiding excess charges: 'What! to see four men have their heads cut off? [the asking price was 1 guinea] I'll give you half a crown a head.'[46]

43 'MS Diary of Nathaniel Bryceson', 5 and 6 January 1846, City of Westminster Archives Department, Victoria Library, 730/1. Before the criminal law reform of the late 1830s it would not have been rare to see two people executed in one day, either in London or in large provincial cities. Report of the Capital Punishment Commission 1866 [3590] xii, Q. 849.

44 Broadsheet in BL 1888 c. 3 (18), printed in London by C. Gilpin, 1847.

45 Thomas Miller, Picturesque Sketches, Past and Present, of London (London, 1851), pp. 183 and 183–9 passim. Miller, evidently an opponent of capital punishment, places executions in the context of the Lord Mayor's Show and Royal Processions.

46 The Reminiscences of Henry Angelo (London, 1904), pp. 2, 139. Angelo got in for the price he offered.

Last-minute or too-late pardons, even if they were, as Douglas Hay has argued, part of an elaborate system of patronage and control, also poised every execution on the brink of comedy.[47] The condemned might show up on the scaffold looking foolishly unprepared because he had expected a pardon. The audience was constantly titillated by the possibility of sudden reversal. One broadsheet, for example, comments on 'the long suspense in which the whole of the capital convicts are kept', as of course was the public, until the very end. The failure of the expected pardon to arrive on this occasion presumably contributed to making the parting of friends especially melodramatic, 'a scene we can not describe'.[48] Completed executions in the ballad literature became the penalty more for some silly slip-up than for a crime: 'the Sadler of Bantry', as the saying goes, 'was hanged for leaving his liquor. Had he stopt, as usual', the old saw continues, his reprieve, which was actually on the road, would have arrived in time and saved him.[49]

The audience's preferred ending clearly depended on the nature of the crime being punished. Macheath's stage execution in the *Beggar's Opera* is declared to be a manifestly wrong 'catastrophe', because operas – and dashing highwaymens' lives – should end happily. The 'rabble' is directed to call out that a reprieve has arrived and that the hero is to rejoin his wives. Everyone expected a reprieve for the famous Dr Dodd and was disappointed when none came. But at the execution of Dr Henneset for treason in 1758, at which seats went for 2s and even 2s 6d per person, a riot broke out when he was reprieved and many of the seats were destroyed by patrons who presumably did not get their money back.[50]

Pardons may well have been a way of reminding the people of the King's power, but at the same time they also spoke of his vulnerability and of the delicate negotiation between the state and the

[47] See Hay's introduction to Douglas Hay *et al.*, *Albion's Fatal Tree*.
[48] 'Trials and Executions of John French for Horse-stealing and John Williams for House breaking', n.d. but early nineteenth-century, Museum of the History of London, Box 173B, 2212.
[49] British Museum, Department of Prints and Drawings, Pennant Collection, Box vii, 38.
[50] J. Timbs, *Curiosities of London* (London, 1868, 2nd edn), p. 809. The riot, in this interpretation, is of the theatre riot genre – outbreaks occasioned by higher prices, a change of play or actor, or some other affront to the audience by the producer.

crowd that constituted the execution scene. The King is 'as one set on a stage, whose smallest actions and gestures, all the people gazingly do behold', said James I in the second edition of the *Basilikon Doron*. He is 'as one set on a *skaffold*' in the first edition.[51] Far from being safe at the centre of a neo-Platonic masque, the King – like the sacrificial carnival king – is immensely vulnerable: to eyes 'bent to look and pry', to the mockery and laughter of theatrical companies and to the chopping-block itself. Theatre, as Steven Orgel points out, is 'too anarchic' to be confined by the explicit intentions of its patrons. And so too is the theatre of the scaffold, where the antic is an intimate of the throne.[52]

On 27 November 1603 Sir Dudley Carlton wrote to his friend John Chamberlain of the 'tragical proceedings' that ensued when two plots – the so-called 'bye' or 'priests' ' plot to seize the King and the 'main' plot to put Arabella Stuart on the throne in his stead – were discovered. 'I may as well leap in . . . and proceed in an order by narration', Carlton said in his next letter, since the events he

---

[51] The first quotation is from the 1616 edition of the *Basilikon Doron*, James I's book of advice on kingship addressed to his son Prince Henry; it follows the text of the second 1603 edition, which was the basis for all subsequent ones. See *The Political Works of James I*, edited with an introduction by Charles Howard McIlwain (Cambridge, Mass., 1918), p. 43. The second quotation is from James I, *Basilikon Doron* (Edinburgh, 1599, reprint of the first edition, privately printed for the Roxburgh Club by Westheimer, Lea, and Co: London, 1887), edited by Charles Edmonds, which gives variations between editions at the conclusion of the text. I am grateful to Stephen Orgel for pointing out this remarkable change. Of course, the word 'scaffold', in seventeenth-century usage, could mean any platform on which a person, action, theatrical event or spectators to any of these were placed, and not exclusively the platform upon which a criminal was executed, although it did have that specific use as well. Perhaps the textual periphrasis from 'scaffold' to 'throne' from the 1599 to all subsequent editions is James's effort to excise the platform upon which the King sits from the linguistic field in which it is so close a neighbour to the platform upon which his mother died and his son was to be beheaded. 'Throne', as James intimates, is not much safer.

[52] The Children of the Revels, for example, acted as if the protection of the crown bestowed the freedom to attack and mock it. See Stephen Orgel, 'The Spectacles of State', in Richard C. Trexler, ed., *Persons in Groups: Social Behavior as Identity Formation in Medieval and Renaissance Europe*, Medieval and Renaissance Texts and Studies, vol. 36, (Binghamton, N.Y., 1985), pp. 119 and 101–21 *passim*. James used the stage image in the introduction of the second and subsequent editions as well as in the place cited above, but here the peoples' gaze is more aggressive, i.e. prying. The King is as one upon 'a publike stage, in the sight of all the people; where all the beholders eyes were attentively bent to look and pry'. *Basilikon Doron*, p. 5.

would recount there 'were part of the same play and . . . other acts came in betwixt to make up a tragical comedy'.[53]

Between late November and 11 December, in other words, the political drama changed genre. While the drawing, hanging, quartering and beheading of two priests and the beheading of a third conspirator might just have sustained tragedy, the executions of Henry, Lord Cobham, Sir Griffin Markham and Lord Grey of Wilton took a decidedly comic turn.

The two priests died with some degree of aesthetic propriety, though even they did not exit without subverting the prescribed ritual. The one who was supposed to have had the more merciful death died the hardest and vice versa; both 'died boldly' and neither was repentant. Still, things could have gone worse and did. George Brooke's beheading slipped a bit further from the ideal. 'At the holding up of Brooke's head, when the executioner began the same cry ['God save the King!'], he was not seconded by the voice of any one man but the sheriff.' The audience failed to applaud the death of a traitor and greeted the display of the King's justice with ostentatious silence.[54]

But there was worse to come. Without its brilliant comic catastrophe the 'executions' of Cobham, Markham and Grey would have been complete failures. 'A fouler day could hardly have been picked out.' Markham, who was first upon the scaffold, was full of complaints and manifestly unprepared for his end because he had been led to believe that he would, at the last minute, be pardoned. He had no speech ready, though he did manage to regain his composure enough to declare that he did not blush to face death. But just before the axe was to fall on this uneven performance the sheriff stopped the show. Because Markham was so unprepared he was to have two hours' respite which he would spend in the great hall of Winchester castle, where King Arthur's round table was

---

[53] I want to consider this seventeenth-century comedy of pardons in some detail, in part because it illustrates the relationship between comedy and the semiotic instability of executions which I am trying to develop here, in part because it seems inappropriate to honour Lawrence Stone without invoking, however ritualistically, his century, and because there is a confusion of order and transgression in this Jacobean scene – and in the carnival of execution – which draws me to the story and to my subject generally. *Dudley Carlton to John Chamberlain: Jacobean Letters*, edited with an introduction by Maurice Lee, Jr (New Brunswick, N.J., 1972), letters of 27 November 1603, pp. 38–47, and 11 December, pp. 47–53.

[54] *Ibid.*, pp. 47–8, 51.

stored. Lord Grey, who was next to be beheaded, acted less appropriately still. He approached death in the midst of friends and young courtiers 'with such cheer in his countenance that he seemed a dapper young bridegroom'. (This was a common role for the condemned in eighteenth-century processions to the gallows.) He said that he did not deserve to die and kept the crowd waiting in the rain for half an hour as he prayed on and on for the King's health. When he seemed to finish, or in any case paused, the sheriff broke in with an unexpected intervention. Grey too was to have a temporary respite, presumably in another part of the hall. Finally Cobham, 'who was now to play his part', threatened an even more unsatisfactory performance. 'His former actions', Carlton says, 'promised nothing but *matière pour rire*.'[55]

For the third time, the sheriff intervened. The execution, he said, would be momentarily halted so that Cobham could be confronted with other, unspecified prisoners who turned out to be none other than Grey and Markham brought back from the wings. They all looked 'strange one upon the other, like men beheaded and met again in the other world', since they had no idea of what had happened. They, and the audience, were equally in the dark as to what would happen next. 'All the actors being together on stage', it was time for the surprise dénouement. The King, proclaimed the sheriff, had pardoned Grey, Cobham and Markham.[56] No one had to 'beg a plaudit of the audience', with such a closing scene. In sharp contrast to Brooke's execution, which really happened, when no one seconded the cry of 'God save the King!', the scaffold drama with the unexpected comic end – the execution *manqué* – brought 'hues and crys' from the assembled multitude which echoed from the castle to the town and back again. Back in London applause began with those near the King and made its way around the court when James announced his pardon.[57]

In many ways the theatre of royal power could hardly have worked better. James created immense anxiety in several of his more powerful and troublesome subjects which he alone could

[55] *Ibid.*, pp. 49–50.
[56] *Ibid.*, p. 51. Sir Walter Raleigh, who, watching the scene and thinking of his turn upon the scaffold scheduled for the following Monday, must have 'had hammers working in his head to beat out the meaning of this stratagem', Carlton speculates.
[57] *Ibid.*, pp. 51–2.

assuage with his gratuitous gift of life.[58] Like God on the throne of judgement, James from his earthly throne tempered justice with mercy. The masses, moreover, responded warmly to James's pardon, as did the court. Royal power and beneficence shone all about.

On the other hand, the play's success with its audiences seems too precarious and unpredictable for it to carry the symbolic freight supposedly borne by the theatre of punishment. The real executions failed to elicit confessions, dying speeches or appropriate audience behaviour, while those which were about to happen but were halted promised to be even less satisfactory had they actually been allowed to proceed. It is also quite possible that James I, in giving a pardon, had responded to, and had been seen as responding to, a political drama not of his own making or choosing and very much out of his control. As Stephen Greenblatt points out, Sir Walter Raleigh managed during the course of his trial for complicity in the 'main plot' to turn himself from a universally hated figure into 'a symbol of the lives of all men threatened by an overwhelmingly powerful system', a powerful representation of 'the radical alienation of the individual from the state'.[59] It might well appear that James simply caved in to the outcry over Raleigh's and his co-conspirators' trial and condemnation. In any case, the state clearly did not enjoy a monopoly on the writing of scripts for its own juridical playhouse.

Instead of recalling its divine counterpart, James's act of mercy bordered on farce. 'But one thing had like to have marred the play', writes Carlton. James forgot to sign his letter to the sheriff before he sent it off by messenger on Thursday noon. Fortunately for the condemned, 'the king remembered himself and called him [the messenger] back again'. Once in Winchester 'there was another cross adventure'. The poor messenger, now bearing the properly autographed pardon could not get through the crowd to the scaffold so as to deliver it to the sheriff. He was 'thrust out amongst the boys and was fain to call out to Sir James Hay, or else Markham might have lost his neck'.[60]

---

[58] On the creation of anxiety by this episode and as a tool of Tudor and early Stuart rule, see Stephen J. Greenblatt, *Shakespearean Negotiations* (Berkeley and Los Angeles, University of California Press, 1988), chapter 5.

[59] Greenblatt, *Sir Walter Raleigh*, pp. 119–20 and chapter 4, *passim*.

[60] Dudley Carlton, *Letters . . .* , p. 52.

These sorts of dramatic inconsistencies, rife in the executions of the seventeenth, eighteenth, and nineteenth centuries, were of course not hidden to contemporaries. Samuel Richardson, who as author of *Pamela; or Virtue Rewarded* and *Clarissa* knew a great deal about manipulating emotion through art, was deeply disturbed by the generic dissonance of Tyburn: 'the face of everyone spoke a kind of mirth, as if the spectacle they had beheld had afforded Pleasure instead of pain, which I am wholly unable to account for'.[61]

Henry Fielding, a successful playwright and theatre manager before he became a novelist and magistrate, saw the aesthetic problem more clearly. The theatrical and hence public failure of executions, he says, can be explained by 'recourse to the poets', who if asked could tell the politicians that it is not so easy to evoke terror. Admiration and pity 'are very apt to attend whatever is the object of terror in the human mind'; the natural tendency of every right-thinking person will be to have compassion for the criminal who seems to be dying 'to make a holiday for, and to entertain, the mob'. Therefore, the state must strive to inspire countervailing feelings if terror is indeed one of the prime objects of public hangings. Secondly, the state should not hold executions in public. Again, politicians must learn from poets, society's masters of the emotions. 'A murder behind the scenes, if the poet knows how to manage it, will affect the audience with greater terror than if it was acted before their eyes.' Garrick's offstage murder of the King in Macbeth, for example, makes the viewer's hair stand on end much more effectively than if blood had been spilt in full view. As a general principle, an object is 'lessened by being looked upon', because the mind is much more capable of 'magnifying' than the eye, from which it follows that executions like stage murders had best be performed out of sight. And finally, the state should strive to make executions solemn, like those in Holland. It is not the essence of the thing itself, i.e. the execution, but the 'dress and

---

[61] Samuel Richardson, *Letters Written to and for Particular Friends* ... (London, 1741). This was, and to a large extent remains, the stereotypical middle-class reaction to execution crowds. Charles Dickens, more than a century later, wrote that he saw 'no emotion suitable to the occasion', 'No sorrow, no salutary terror, no abhorrence, no seriousness, nothing but ribaldry, debauchery, levity, drunkenness ...' Never, he said, had he found his fellow man more odious. 'A Letter to the Daily News', 28 February 1846, reprinted in David D. Cooper, *The Lessons of the Scaffold* (Athens, Ohio, 1974), p. 80.

apparatus' of it, which count with the public. To have any chance of political success, Fielding suggests, capital punishment must be appropriately staged, which in his view it was not.[62] The theologian William Paley, often cited by contemporaries as one of the great defenders of the bloody code's reliance on terror, recognized both the dramaturgical failure of executions as then performed and the political barriers to effective staging. What was required was a way to 'augment horror without offending or impairing the public sensibility'. He seems almost wistful about the fact that an obviously ironic recent proposal to cast murderers 'into a den of wild beasts, where they would perish in a manner dreadful to the imagination, yet concealed from view', would not pass political muster. It would clearly solve the aesthetic problems of capital punishment.[63] (Proponents of private execution in the 1860s argued too that 'the mystery and indefiniteness attending the punishment serves only to increase its terrors'.[64])

Edmund Burke makes the same sort of critical arguments from a different aesthetic position. On the principle that the nearer something 'approaches the reality, and the further it removes us from all idea of fiction, the more perfect its power', Burke assumes that an execution would be more compelling to an audience than the most sublime tragedy. The theatre would empty if 'a state criminal of high rank is to be executed in the adjoining square'. But the power of executions is realized only under proper theatrical circumstances, and Burke has little faith in the directorial powers of judicial authorities to make these obtain. He wrote a number of letters and an essay advising the Lord Chancellor and others responsible for such matters on how to punish those found guilty of capital offences during the Gordon riots. Some of his advice is primarily political – who should be singled out for hanging, how many should be executed given the death toll of the riot's suppression and the importance of appearing just and merciful, for example – but much is theatrical. The executions must be solemn; the bodies must not be given to friends, as was customary, because otherwise they become the object of compassion, even veneration; only one person should be executed at a time in any one place – he

---

[62] Henry Fielding, *An Enquiry into the Causes of the Late Increase of Robbers . . .* (London, 1751), sect xi, pp. 449–53.
[63] William Paley, *The Principles of Moral and Political Philosophy*, in *The Works of William Paley, D.D.* (London, 1847), Book 6, chapter 9, p. 230.
[64] *Hansard*, 5 March 1868, col. 1130.

recommends that six of the fittest examples be chosen in all – because this 'fixes the attention and excites awe', while 'the execution of multitudes dissipates and weakens the effect'.[65] Richardson, Fielding, Paley and Burke thus agree that, however appropriate capital punishment might be, its political aesthetics in the eighteenth century left much to be desired. Very little changed to make their views obsolete before 1868 when public executions ceased.

III

The most telling evidence against the prevailing account of juridical dramaturgy comes, however, from the relevation of its central actor. At the heart of the British execution is not the state, nor even the condemned, but 'the people' themselves, gathered in a carnivalesque moment of political generativity. From Mandeville to Dickens, accounts of the procession to Tyburn or of the crowds before Newgate and other venues portray, in breathless prose, a festive, buoyant, holiday crowd wholly unconcerned with serious state theatre and unaffected by its efforts. The condemned leaves prison, where inmates are 'either drinking madly, or uttering the vilest Ribaldry'; the route to the gallows 'is one continued Fair, for whores and Rogues of the meaner Sort'; there is pushing and shoving, brawling, throwing dirt, and lots of 'jeneva' (gin). The 'scene of confusion' grows worse as one nears the hanging tree, with more noise, ribaldry and drink, so that 'the best dispos'd Spectator seldom can pick out anything that is edifying or moving'.[66] At the heart of the canonical image of the execution is the crowd: boisterous women, men, and children of all ages and classes engaged in festival.

Visual representations of executions, from Hogarth's 'The Idle 'Prentice Executed at Tyburn' (Figure 9.7) to late nineteenth-century prints, make this apparent. Hogarth's image, like Rowlandson's of an execution before Newgate (Figure 9.4), and other, later, prints depict a genuinely communal festival. Rich and poor

---

65 Edmund Burke, *On the Sublime and Beautiful*, sect I, pt xv, vol. 1, p. 35, *Letters with Reflections on the Executions of the Rioters in 1780*, vol. 2, pp. 416–19, in *The Works of the Right Honourable Edmund Burke*, 2 vols (London, 1834).

66 Mandeville, *Enquiry*, pp. 19–25. There was of course no procession after 1783, and drinking in prison by the nineteenth century was severely curbed. But as I argue below, pp. 349–52, nineteenth-century accounts, in their tone and in the mood they describe, are substantially the same as Mandeville's.

Figure 9.7 William Hogarth, 'The Idle 'Prentice Executed at Tyburn', from 'Industry and Idleness', plate 11, 1747. This print, in which the crowd and its various carnivalesque characters are the focus of visual interest, became the source of many subsequent execution images.

Figure 9.8 'The Life, Trial, and Execution of R. Cooper', 1862. In this print of an execution in front of Newgate, looking south rather than east toward St Sepulchre's, the condemned on the scaffold is an artistic afterthought, crudely added in the space cut out from the image of the prison at the left. The rooftops and windows are filled with people who have paid for the privilege of gaining a better view. The social diversity of the crowd is again represented by the wide variety of hats. The boys and dogs quarrelling repeat similar themes from Hogarth. (Reproduced by courtesy of the Guildhall Library.)

Figure 9.9 'The Sorrowful and Weeping Lamentation of Four Lovely Orphans Left by J. Newton'. This is a reversed image of part of Hogarth's 'The Idle 'Prentice Executed' (Figure 9.7), staged in front of Newgate rather than at Tyburn. The vendor of broadsheets and the man tossing a dog have been shifted from centre right to centre left. The woman beating up a man has moved to the right of the vendor, and the woman smashing fruit into a man's face has moved from far right to far left.

Figure 9.10 'Hanging in Chains of Francis Fearn, on Loxley Common, Near Sheffield'

are joined either at the same level as in Figures 9.5 and 9.6, or, as they would be in the theatre, with the rabble below and the more prosperous in the bleachers, or on rooftops and in windows overlooking the scaffold (Figure 9.8). A common drama unites them. Top hats and the broad-brimmed hats of the fish-porter from Billingsgate (the market that gave its name to various forms of slang, vulgar language and low humour), fashionable bonnets and not so fashionable bonnets are side by side as everyone gathers to participate by witnessing the sacrifice.[67]

It is clear, moreover, that the subject of these pictures is the holiday crowd itself, for which the death of the condemned seems to provide only the occasion. The state is almost totally unrepresented, but so is death – the gallows and the criminal. In Hogarth, Rowlandson and other 'execution prints the crowded, action-filled foreground catches the eye well before one's gaze focuses on the nominal subject, the hanging itself. The 'last dying speeches' vendor, not the gallows or the doomed apprentice in his cart, forms the apex, nearest the viewer, of the triangle formed in Hogarth's picture by these centres of interest. In later reworkings of Hogarth's image (Figure 9.9) the vendor is still more prominent, commanding, like her source, the central space of a more circumscribed composition. It is as if the representation of the hangings – the broadsheets – are of greater import than the hanging itself, just as the crowd watching the event seems to matter more than what they are watching. '

Similarly, the commanding figure of the ballad-seller facing out of the plane of Rowlandson's picture (Figure 9.4, lower left), and ignoring the event her wares speak about, is more captivating, engages the viewer more actively, than the slightly-worked figures hanging from the cross beam. In Figure 9.10, 'Hanging in Chains of Francis Fearn', the light of the rising sun shines on the spectators in the foreground and on the upturned faces of the crowd generally while the backlit body of the condemned, suspended between two circus tents, is in darkness and indistinctly rendered. One has to look very hard to find the body at all in Figure 9.8, 'The

---

[67] See also, for a further example, BL Pennant viii/50: 'The new gallows at the Old Bayley'. Eight or so people are on the stage; behind and in front of a fence there are a few hapless soldiers; but the real subject is the crowd. A fat wigged gentleman looks through a monocle, a caricature Jew occupies the bottom right; tri-cornered and various other sorts of hats and many different kinds of bonnets represent the truly communal nature of the execution crowd.

Figure 9.11 'Preparing for an Execution'. The crowd, with well-delineated execution types, is the subject of this image, while a scaffold is just barely discernible far in the back on the right.

Life, Trial, and Execution of R. Cooper'; it is almost totally absorbed amidst a sea of humanity in an 1884 illustration (Figure 9.11) for a history of the bygone public execution.

But even in Figures 9.5 and 9.6, where the hanging body is prominently displayed in a central frame, the men, women and children who look out of the plane of the picture mediate between the viewer and the enactment of sacrifice. They, and the crowd generally, fill almost half the picture. It is their scene, and week after week, as the plate is reused, they remain while bodies come and go to fit the specific story of the broadsheet. So, for example, the hanging figure – the effigy of George Wyeth – was rubbed out at the last minute in Figure 9.5 when a reprieve was announced, but was easily reinserted in Figure 9.6 when Wyeth was finally hanged some weeks later.[68] Indeed the crowd was used on

---

[68] Actually, the printer used exactly the same text as well and changed only the number of figures. A separate plate for the inserts was apparently made out of soft metal, which made it easy to add or subtract figures as the occasion required. Each printer had a separate basic crowd.

Figure 9.12 'The Trial and Sentences of All the Prisoners . . . Old Bailey, September 1822'. The crowd remains even when there is no criminal.

broadsheets even when no one was executed, for example in Figure 9.12, 'The Trial and Sentences [but not yet executions] of All the Prisoners . . .', as if themselves to bear witness to the processes of justice.

The crowd at British executions was specifically a carnival crowd. It was so generically because executions bore a quite specific structural resemblance to carnival as the Lenten feast in which Christ's triumph over death is prefigured by the election: feasting accompanied with much ribaldry, trial and sacrifice of a carnival king in whose disorderly demise the ultimate chaos of death is contained. (This form was of course generalized to other early modern European festivals.) The wildness, inversion and feasting of the carnival finally gives way, and the proper world order is restored.

British executions were carnivalesque too in a more generalized sense, described by Mikhail Bakhtin:

> Carnival celebrates temporary liberation from the prevailing truth of the established order; it marks the suspension of all hierarchical rank, privilege, norms, and prohibitions. Carnival was the true feast of time, the feast of becoming, change and renewal.

Carnivalesque laughter in Bakhtin's account is 'the laughter of the people'. Carnival is a time in which the 'grotesque body' of the people is made manifest. It is an overflowing, fecund body, 'not in a private, egotistic form, severed from the other spheres of life, but as something universal, representing all the people'.[69]

Stallybrass and White transpose this sense of carnival to a more general level and treat it as 'an instance of a wider phenomenon of transgression'. As such, it is not just a popular festival which may or may not be politically conservative. (In the British case it almost always, though not in January 1649, reinforced established order.) Rather, carnival is part of the process through which social classification takes place. It becomes the boundary between 'the classical/classificatory body and its negations ... what it excludes to create its identity as such'. Executions on this account are just such a classificatory and socially constitutive ritual, defining the boundaries between state and society, between the propertied and the propertyless, between high and low.[70]

In all of these senses the natural genre of execution is carnival and it is only remarkable that it is ever anything else. As Nietzsche put it, 'without cruelty there is no festival ... and in punishment, there is so much that is *festive!*' There is the exquisite pleasure of venting power on the powerless, 'the voluptuous pleasure "*de faire le mal le plaisir de la faire*"'. In watching punishment the lowly could participate, if only for the moment, in the 'right of the masters'.[71]

Executions are of course a sacrifice – 'sacrificed to the laws of his country', as the broadsheets describe a malefactor's death – and as such are a repulsive instance of the 'generative unanimity', to use René Girard's term, that is born of ritual, communal killing. The 'spontaneous' lynch mob, but also the institutionalized, legalized procedures of capital punishment, carry with them the seeds of their origins in the sacrifice of the surrogate victim in antiquity. Capital punishment in Girard's account is 'a direct extension of

---

[69] M. M. Bakhtin, *Rabelais and his World*, trans. H. Iswolsky (Cambridge, Mass., 1968), pp. 11–12, 19, 109.

[70] Peter Stallybrass and Allon White, *The Politics and Poetics of Transgression* (Ithaca, 1986), p. 26 and 'Introduction' *passim*.

[71] Nietzsche, *Genealogy*, p. 67, 2.6, p. 65, 2.5. 'The entire mankind of antiquity is full of tender regard for "The spectator", as an essentially public, essentially visible world which cannot imagine happiness apart from spectacles and festivals – and, as aforesaid, even in great *punishment* there is so much that is festive!' p. 69, 2.7.

generative violence', of the sacral expulsion of pollution from the community. Nothing could be more festive.[72] There are, moreover, specific iconographic associations of execution with carnival. Its founding moment – Christ's crucifixion – is represented as a festival of inversion and sacrifice. Great crowds in the street cry for Jesus and jeer the victim who claims to be King but is crowned not with gold but with thorns, soldiers play dice and gamble for his clothes and vinegar takes the place of water. These motives are eerily recapitulated in eighteenth-century England. John Smith is said to have been taken 'off the cross' when his reprieve arrived five minutes after he had been 'cut off'.[73] A struggle between friends and executioner for the victim's clothes is a common theme of the English literature, and Hogarth's 'The Idle 'Prentice Executed at Tyburn' (Figure 9.7), the major visual source of all subsequent English execution scenes, is in turn based on Breughel's 'Christ Carrying the Cross' (Figure 9.13).[74] In both, games and festivity all but hide the death in their midst. (The 'Hanging in Chains of Francis Fearn', Figure 9.10, seems also to transform a moor near Sheffield into Golgotha.) Fielding writes of the 'apotheosis' of the famous thief-catcher Jonathan Wild.

The secular imagery of execution is also explicitly carnivalesque. Famous executed criminals were represented as harlequin, the mischievous character of Italian comedy who in his English incarnation is the clown in pantomime who carries a bat as a magic wand and is supposed to be invisible to the others. Thus Jack Sheppard, famed for his miraculous prison escapes, i.e. for his 'tricks', becomes 'Harlequin Sheppard', in a play by John Thurmond, within twelve days of his death in 1724 (Figure 9.14). A broadsheet of Jonathan Wild's execution (Figure 9.15) shows harlequin characters parading around with bones and meat-cleavers, and the frontispiece to Swift's *A Tale of a Tub* (Figure 9.16) shows, through the window of the room where a preacher is holding forth, a mountebank, assisted by a fool, performing his tricks on stage right next to a hanging.[75]

---

72 René Girard, *Violence and the Sacred*, trans. Patrick Gregory (Baltimore, 1977), pp. 297–9 and *passim*.

73 BM Crace Collection xxx/7, engraved for the *Malefactors Register*. The specific illusion is to the cross beam from which Smith was hanged. This configuration is unusual in English execution scenes.

74 Ronald Paulson, *Hogarth's Graphic Works*, 2 vols (New Haven, 1971), vol. 1, plate 176.

75 The print dates from 1696 but I have taken it from the 6th edition of 1724.

Figure 9.13 Breughel's 'Christ Carrying the Cross', the source of Hogarth's 'The Idle 'Prentice Executed'. One has to look carefully to find Christ amidst the general gaming and merrymaking.

Figure 9.14   Jack Sheppard as Harlequin Jack Sheppard, from the frontispiece to John Thurmond, *Harlequin Sheppard*, first performed at Drury Lane Theatre, 28 November 1724.

Figure 9.15   'The Funeral Procession of the Celebrated Mr Jonathan Wild Thief Taker General of Great Britain and Ireland'. Across the top are traditional carnival figures – harlequins, devils, butchers making 'music' with meat-cleavers and bones. In the oval at the lower left the criminal is being crowned King of the Gypsies.

Figure 9.16 'The Tub Preacher and the Mountebank', an illustration from Jonathan Swift's *A Tale of a Tub* (6th edn, 1724; print dates from 1696). Note the scene visible through the window of the room in which the tub preacher is expounding: a man about to be executed is praying, or pretending to pray, on the ladder, while next to him a mountebank is performing on stage.

The intimate iconographic connection of execution and carnival is not an exclusively British phenomenon. Italian carnival festivals began in some instances with the hanging in effigy of a criminal dressed as a harlequin.[76] Large festive holiday execution crowds are common in all European countries, but by all accounts the British state was, as I have argued above, so hapless as to appear unconcerned with resisting the carnivalesque. Indeed it permitted, and even encouraged, conditions under which carnival and the representation of capital punishment as carnival flourished, under which the 'natural genre' of execution could express itself freely.

Thus, members of the crowd were allowed to rush up and touch the magic body of the condemned. Boswell notes that he and a number of Italian noblemen witnessed 'a superstition as weak as any in their own country – no less than four diseased persons had themselves rubbed with the sweaty hands of malefactors in the agonies of death, and believed this would cure them'. The criminal as carnival king partakes here of thaumaturgic kingship, which in turn derives from the special relationship of kings to Christ. The authorities also permitted the crowd in York which feared the 'resurrection' of the highwayman Dick Turpin – i.e. his dissection by the surgeons – to take the body and parade it triumphantly through town on a bier – much as the effigy of Elizabeth I might have been borne through the streets of London – and finally to bury the body themselves so that it would be unavailable to the authorities.

Similarly the authorities did little to prevent executions from becoming drunken feasts. A ballad tells of the last days of a man named Summers, executed in Aylesbury in 1693, who sold his body for 8s to the surgeons in advance of his death so that he could die drunk.

> No sooner was the money paid,
> and put in Summers hands,
> But strait he drank it out in wine
> until he could not stand . . . [77]

All accounts of criminal heroes like Dick Turpin stress the drunken revelry in jail and en route to the gallows, as do all those who comment on eighteenth-century executions. By the nineteenth

---

[76] E. Rodocanachi, 'Les Courses en Italie aux vieux temps', *Revue des études historiques*, 66 (1900), p. 249, note 3. See also M. Boiteux in *Annales ESC* 32.2 (1977), p. 365. I am grateful to Richard Trexler for these references.

[77] 'Summer's frolic', no. 437 of *The Pepys Ballads*, ed. Hyder Edward Rollins (Cambridge, Mass., 1931) vii, 42.

century drinking in jail was restricted, but there is no suggestion that the crowd or other prisoners were any more sober or serious. Inmates of Newgate played ball or marbles and generally behaved in 'a most indecent manner' within hours or even during an execution, the Ordinary told a parliamentary committee in 1819.[78] Up to the abolition of public executions, crowds seemed to behave in the same raucous manner as their forbears. They went to executions as if to a prize fight, said Police Inspector Kittle; people continued to drink; they would knock off the hats of fellow spectators and roar as these were bounced back through the crowd; they might even bounce along a spectator, with his legs in the air and his head down.[79] Twelve people died, according to a Home Office report, in 1844 at an execution in Nottingham (not counting the murderer William Saville) when 'a confusion excited by mischievous persons throwing hats, shoes' excited 'the general desire to escape from the overpowering pressure'.[80]

Ribald sexuality, male potency and death – intimately bound together in the carnivalesque – are also ubiquitously associated in the imagery of eighteenth-century executions and in the constant association of prostitutes with hanging crowds. James Boswell makes this more explicit than most other commentators in his emotional cascade, from a passionate plea for 'the supreme happiness', addressed to a Countess, to an execution, to a splendidly lit altar ('raging love – gloomy horror – grand devotion'),[81] but the theme is ubiquitous. In the first place, a heroic few, when en route to execution, 'make themselves as fine as if they were going to a wedding'.[82] 'One would take 'em for bridegrooms going to espouse their Old Mrs. Tyburn', says another description of an eighteenth-century execution, which goes on to argue that the powdered wig, Holland shirt, gloves and nosegay 'sometimes meliorate the terrible Thoughts of the meagre Tyrant Death'. In any case, to go dressed in a slovenly fashion would be to aid the hangman, to die of shame for being in so deplorable a condition.[83]

---

78 *Select Committee on Criminal Laws* . . . 1819 (585) viii, p. 63.
79 *Report of Capital Punishment Commission* 1866 [3590] xxi, pp. 877, 886, 961.
80 HO 45, 05861, quoted in David Cooper, *The Lesson of the Scaffold* (Athens, Ohio, 1974), pp. 20–1 and 105.
81 James Boswell, *Boswell on the Grand Tour 1765–1766*, ed. Frank Brady and Frederick A. Pottle (New York, 1955), pp. 40–1.
82 Mission de Valbourg, *Memoirs of England*, p. 108.
83 *Memoirs of the Right Villainous John Hall, the late famous and notorious robber* (London, 4th edn, 1714), p. 26. BL 1418 b. 31.

The great majority of course did go 'dressed slovenly', and certainly by the nineteenth century the dress of criminals was somewhat more controlled. But the images of crime, death and sexual attraction live on in criminal romances and ballads. Duval is memorialized as 'the Ladies' joy';[84] Macheath, in Gay's *Beggar's Opera*, is reprieved in order to go back to his 'wives', and in the last song of the opera compares himself to 'the Turk with his doxies around'. Daniel Defoe goes so far as to argue, with some irony, that one reason for the increase in the number of 'town thieves' is the sexual glory with which prominent criminals are executed.

They go to Execution as neat and trim as if they were going to a Wedding. G—d D—mn, says one Rogue to another, *Jack* Such-a-one made a clever Figure when he went to *Tyburn* the other Day, and died brave, hard, like a Cock.[85]

Commercial sex, moreover, pervaded what feeble attempts were made to portray executions as dignified occasions of confession and repentance. Not only were prostitutes said to be regular attendants among the execution crowd, but advertisements for new editions of *Onania, Dr. Drakes and Several Physicians Opinions of Hermaphrodites*, or for patent medicines to cure clap or impotency fill the back of even the Ordinary of Newgate's most pious accounts.[86] Even contrite speech shared the page with a burgeoning new pornography.

All of these execution scenes are also carnivalesque in their emphasis on inversion and on the grotesque individual and social body. They depict an overflowing vibrant, alive, noisy, fat, body/body politics overturning itself in all directions. In the Hogarth print (Figure 9.7) a maelstrom of energy surrounds and almost hides the nominally central figure of the doomed apprentice. At the lower right corner, a woman is beating up a man – presumably for upsetting her cart – by smashing an orange into his face, while another woman, right in the centre of the picture, stands triumphantly over a fellow whose hat she has knocked off. Variations on these images, in turn, are reproduced in subsequent

84 From Claude Duval's epitaph, quoted in S. M. Ellis's Epilogue, 'Jack Sheppard in Literature and Drama', to Horace Bleackley, *Jack Sheppard* (London, 1933), p. 65.

85 [Daniel Defoe], *Street Robberies Considered* (London, n.d.), p. 52. BL h. 13. 4.

86 See the working-class radical Francis Place's complaints on this score in his papers: BL Add. MS 27826 fos.81–82; on the back of BL 515. 1. 2. 131 there is an advertisement for 'an antidote against lust in a discourse on uncleanness'.

execution pictures (Figure 9.9). Worlds upon worlds turned upside down! But even without such reversals, Figures 9.4, 9.8 and 9.11, for example, speak of disorder – fights of various sorts, bashing with sticks, tossing dogs, quarrelling dogs, women struggling with men and fat-rumped women hoisted up by men to get a better view – all somehow safely contained by the death of one or a few members of the community.

'The Idle 'Prentice Executed' is, moreover, rich with specifically carnivalesque figures that are variously borrowed in the execution prints of the next century and a half. The figure on top of the scaffold, for example, may be a helper, but his ludicrously relaxed pose and smoking pipe suggest that he is 'Funny Joe', a half-wit who regularly attended executions at the time this print was made. (Crazy-looking, toothless hags are equivalent figures in some prints.[87]) The fat woman tippling on the cart is Mother Douglas, the Bawd from Covent Garden, who also appears, drinking again, in Hogarth's 'The March to Finley' and 'Enthusiasm Delineated'. Tiddy Doll the ballad-singer is the most characteristic of carnival figures. 'King of itinerant tradesmen', he is dressed as a gentleman with a ruffled shirt and plumed hat; his shirt suggests still another inversion.[88]

Even those opposed to public capital punishment, like the novelists Thackeray and Dickens, are caught up in the great surge of humanity that accompanied a major execution, in the carnivalesque breaking of boundaries and expression of a grotesque body politic. The accounts of Sykes's 'hanging' and Fagin's execution in *Oliver Twist* stand out not only for their urgent, hurried, exuberant prose but as the two moments in the novel when a society fragmented by class and urban spaces is reunited. The seething unbounded body politic is described as it constitutes itself from individual bounded bodies.

Sykes has made his way to the top of a building on Jacob's Island, which, as Tyburn had been, was construed as a kind of no-man's-land outside the bounds of civilization – 'the most extraordinary of

---

[87] See for example 'The Arrival of Sam Shepard at Tyburn' (Printed by F. Glover, Fleet Street, W. Clerk, litho). BL Crace Collection xxx/11. xxx/10 shows Shepard en route, sitting good-naturedly on his coffin smoking a pipe; a fat, aproned, laughing innkeeper and his pretty daughter look on; a soldier raises a pint in his honour and a girl waves her handkerchief.

[88] On these characters see Paulson, *William Hogarth's Graphic Works*, no. 178.

the many localities that are hidden in London, wholly unknown, even by name, to the great mass of its inhabitants'.

Of all the terrible yells that ever fell on mortal ears, none could exceed the cry of the infuriated throng . . . The crowd had been hushed during these few moments, watching his motions and doubtful of his purpose, but the instant they perceived it and knew it was defeated, they raised a triumphant execration to which all their previous shouting had been whispers. Again and again it rose . . . it echoed and re-echoed; it seemed as though *the whole city had poured its population out to curse him.*

On pressed the people from the front – on, on, on, in a strong struggling current of angry faces . . . The houses on the opposite side of the ditch had been entered by the mob; sashes were thrown up, or torn bodily out; there were tiers and tiers of faces in every window; cluster upon cluster of people clinging to every house-top.

At this moment of social unity Sykes emerges and puts a rope around his body with which he intends to lower himself to the ground. He loses his balance. He slips. The noose tightens around his neck. He falls.

There was a sudden jerk, a terrific convulsion of the limbs; and there he hung . . . The murderer swung lifeless against the wall; and the boy, thrusting aside the dangling body which obscured his view, called to the people to come and take him out, for God's sake.[89]

Sykes's dog leaps from the same window as his master had used to exit from, falls into the ditch and dashes out his brains. Having expelled evil from its midst, the grotesque social body dissolves, the classical ordered body is restored.

'The whole city', the *civitas*, the animate mass of individuals become, indeed are, the state in these passages. Or conversely, the abstract inanimate state is turned, in a characteristically Dickensian move, into the people. In the carnival of execution the fleshly nature of the 'social contract' is made manifest.

Fagin's execution similarly provides Dickens with the occasion to wax lyrical about the festive, generative powers of sacrifice. 'A peal of joy from the populace outside' greets the news of Fagin's sentence. The building rings 'with a tremendous shout, and another and another, and then it echoed loud groans, then gathered

89 Charles Dickens, *Oliver Twist*, chapter 50, my emphasis.

strength as they swelled out, like angry thunder'. The people 'swelling out' is the Dickensian version of Rabelaisian carnival, of the grotesque social body, described by Bahktin. At Fagin's execution itself, Dickens writes of 'the great multitude' smoking and playing cards, pushing, quarrelling, joking, once again 'swelling out' in its social generativity; 'everything told of life and animation'.[90]
The killing of Fagin, the carnival king, makes this social joy possible. It takes little imagination to read it as the most primitive of sacrifices, the offering up of a victim for the sake of the community.[91] There is the 'dark cluster of objects in the centre of all – the black stage, the cross beam, the robe and all the hideous apparatus of death'. The holiday crowd gives 'cry upon cry that penetrated even those massive walls' until Fagin is killed. Dickens in his more sober moments might have found public hangings embarrassing and repulsive, but he was enthralled by them in his fiction and beholden to their power.

William Makepeace Thackeray, who was part of the crowd at the execution of François Courvoisier, the Swiss butler who had murdered his master Lord William Russell, is caught in a similar bind. On the one hand he is contemptuous of the execution crowd and its base emotions; on the other, he is acutely sensitive to the carnivalesque and socially binding qualities of the occasion. The crowd is festive, 'jokes bandying from here and there'. The mob 'is extra-ordinarily gentle and good humoured'. The gin shops open early. Here is a face that might have served Cruickshank as a model for his image of Nancy in *Oliver Twist*; there is Lord—; in the windows are mustachioed dandies and on the front lines of the crowd ruffians and blackguards. And for all the electrifying horror of the scaffold itself, the *populus* in all its ragged glory has manifested itself at the execution scene and in the polity at large.[92] In 1840, the year between the first and the second great Chartist petitions, it is as if only carnival could establish, even for the moment, a deeper community out of a society riven by class division. Almost despite himself, Thackeray, like Dickens, is

90 *Oliver Twist*, chapter 52.
91 In addition to Girard, *Rites of Violence*, see M. Detienne, 'Between Beasts and Gods', in R. L. Gordon and R. G. A. Buxton, eds., *Myth, Religion and Society* (Cambridge, 1981), pp. 215–28.
92 W. M. Thackeray, 'Going to See a Man Hanged', *Fraser's Magazine*, 20 (July 1840), pp. 150–8.

caught up in the blood ritual. 'It seems', he says, 'that I have been abetting an act of frightful wickedness and violence performed by a set of men against one of their fellows.'

Indeed he and the mass of humanity of which he was a part were *the* central political actors in the violence of the British execution. The people are the state in the ritual sacrifice of criminals. Indeed the cleansing power of executions inheres in their being not august state rituals but carnival instead.

Until the drop was introduced, 'the people' were in intimate physical, not just semiotic, contact with the scaffold and the body of the condemned. In the days of the 'hanging tree', the 'L' or 'T' structure on which the condemned were left hanging, they literally helped to kill the victim. The body in those days was not so much 'launched into eternity' as left to strangle when the cart upon which it had stood was pulled away. 'I am told', said the German observer, 'that his Friends or Neighbours pull him by the Feet, in order to dispatch him the sooner'; his 'best friends at once held him down by the feet', noted another foreign visitor, 'and kept holding him there, so that from the first moment nobody noticed the slightest movement'. Ann Green, hanged in Oxfordshire, seems to have revived in her coffin despite her friends having tried to insure her quick death by tugging on her suspended body.[93]

Moreover, the sheer physical imbalance of forces between the state and the crowd at public executions, right up to their abolition – crowds became bigger over the course of the nineteenth century as executions became rarer and railway travel made getting there easier – meant that any hanging could take place only with the tacit consent of the crowd. 'It must appear very wonderful', wrote 'Philonomos', 'that no attempt has ever been made to rescue any of the prisoners, than which, in the circumstances, nothing certainly could have been made more easy.'[94] *The Times*, arguing almost a century later for the retention of public executions, makes the political point more explicit. 'The people,' it says, reign in England through Queen, Lords, and Commons. They 'inflict the last penalty

[93] Pollnitz, *Memoirs* vol. 2, p. 459; see also Kielmansegge, *Diary*, pp. 157–8; J. B. Winslow, *The Uncertainty of the Signs of Death* (Dublin, 1748), p. 64.
[94] Philonomos, 'The Right Method of Maintaining Security in Person and Property', quoted in Leon Radzinowicz, *A History of English Criminal Law*, pp. 1, 172.

of the law in this country and the publicity of the process is significant.'[95]

The whole final debate about the abolition of public execution turns on this claim.[96] Those opposing its abolition argued that only through the sort of theatre I have been describing could the true relationship between state and society be represented. 'It had long been the wise practice of this country for centuries to make people feel that the law was an expression of their own judgment and will', argued one member of the Commons. Withdrawing executions from public view would make them seem 'an act of the executive itself'.[97] 'The principle of our law was, that the execution of a person was the act of the whole nation', said another.[98] 'The poor man', said a third, 'had the right to be hanged in public.'[99] (One is reminded of the perhaps apocryphal remark of Lord Eldon that Peel's new police would violate the Englishman's right to riot.) Executions on this account were part of the delicate negotiations and displays through which plebs and patricians asserted their respective claims.[100]

Public execution allowed the people to confirm the 'neutrality' of the law. Their presence ensured that rich malefactors would not be treated differently from poor ones, that they would not be allowed to escape or to be more gently killed. And similarly, the poor would not be treated with greater harshness. The people thus appeared to sacrifice the offender and to guarantee the sacrifice's propriety.

IV

For centuries, the enormous and unchallenged power of aristocratic oligarchy had been purchased at the cost of public disorder. Riot was allowed as the representation of a delicate balance between

[95] *Times*, 17 July 1856, p. 8, quoted in Cooper, *Lessons of the Scaffold*, p. 80.
[96] This is not of course the only issue. As in earlier and later inquests, including the *Royal Commission on Capital Punishment*, which met from 1949 to 1953, the question of whether capital punishment deterred crime was inconclusively debated. But deterrence is itself a function of the nature of juridical theatricality, as I will argue.
[97] Knatchbull-Hugessen, *Hansard*, 5 March 1868, 1138.
[98] Mr Darby Griffith, *Hansard*, 21 April 1868, 1056.
[99] Mr Sarjeant Gaselee, *Hansard*, 5 March 1868, 1132.
[100] See E. P. Thompson's 'Patrician Society, Plebeian Culture', *Journal of Social History*, 7 (1974), pp. 382–405.

governors and governed. The carnival of spirited death and mockery, the overwhelming presence of the crowd and the absence of restraint, the drink, sex and ribaldry inscribed again and again the notion that in England the law, liberty and the state were grounded in community. Carnival and the penalties of the law that were enacted through it became expressive of what at least for the moment seemed community values.[101]

But this was not so in the world of the 1867 Reform Act, which gave most of the urban working class the vote, of the Secret Ballot Act and the reform of elections in 1872. Election riots, common in the nineteenth century, ceased to be legitimate expressions of popular sentiment as the rational, private exercise of the vote came to define the relationship between subject and government. Private executions, Lord Cranworth testified to the parliamentary commission in 1866, were better suited 'to the modern state of the world'.[102] But executions were not to be private in the literal sense; they were to take place in the 'presence of proper representatives of the public', by which was meant doctors, the press and select witnesses.[103] A coroner's report would verify the death to which the crowd had attested in former times. Dickens's plan for private executions sought to recreate a representative public by calling a special twenty-four-member 'witness jury', one third of which would be summoned on a low, one third on a middle, and one third on a high qualification.

In this new world, carnivalesque executions were not simply an embarrassment as they had been to many observers before; they had become irrelevant. In 1868 the public carnival of execution was finally stopped and the condemned thereafter met their fate indoors, watched by various officials and medical men. The state which for centuries had absented itself from the moment when its power was most manifest reasserted itself behind closed doors.

But the truth remains that the infliction of death upon the body has an unexpressible power, quite independently of whether it

---

[101] On law as expressive, see Robert Post, 'Cultural Heterogeneity and the Law: Pornography, Blasphemy, and the First Amendment', *California Law Review*, 76 (1988), pp. 297–335.

[102] *Capital Punishment Commission*, 1866 [3590] 1866, Q82.

[103] Mr Neate, *Hansard*, 21 April 1868, 1058. He calls elsewhere for 'recourse to modern science' to make executions less painful. He proposes using gas, which would remove the 'painful necessity' of having the hangman's hands actually touch the condemned. *Ibid.*, 1071.

deters further offences, is the cheapest way of ridding society of dangerous criminals, or even whether it satisfies a social or individual desire for revenge. Capital punishment, like death in war, is the gold standard of community expression. But, as Justice Frankfurter testified to the Royal Commission on Capital Punishment, there appears to be no appropriate way for a liberal democracy under the rule of law to exercise this option.[104] As execution becomes ever more private and untheatrical it becomes ever more irrelevant. As it becomes public – if not on television then through the printed media – it becomes carnival which does not fit well with the culturally dominant view of the body politic.

In 1927 a *Daily News* photographer managed to smuggle a camera, strapped to his ankle, into the death chamber where Ruth Snyder was about to die for conspiring with her lover to kill her husband. The photographer succeeded in snapping a picture just as the current surged through Snyder's body. The photo sold half a million extra copies of the *News*.[105] More recently, Gary Gilmour, who offered to wear a 'Timex' watch as he faced the firing squad in the hope that film footage showing a still functioning watch on the dead wrist might make a nice commercial, fashioned himself into what was merely the latest in a long line of great carnival clowns. When Texas resumed capital punishment in 1983, boys wearing hats displaying the hindquarters of a pig – the most carnivalesque of images – partied away the night awaiting the fatal injection.[106] Plebeian camp, of course. And the natural genre of execution again reasserting itself.

104 Minutes of Evidence, 21 July 1950, p. 580.
105 This anecdote comes from Simon Michael Bessie, *Jazz Journalism: The Story of the Tabloid Newspapers* (New York, 1938). I am grateful to Richard Ohmann for this reference.
106 *Amnesty International USA Matchbook* (February 1983), p. 10.

10. *Interpersonal conflict and social tension: civil litigation in England, 1640–1830*

C. W. BROOKS

Over the past fifteen years or so, there has been a lively debate about the role of law in the seventeenth and eighteenth centuries. Work by Douglas Hay, E. P. Thompson, J. A. Sharpe, J. M. Beattie and many others has been full of important insights which have extended the horizons of social and political as well as legal history.[1] However, one curious fact about the vast majority of these studies is that they have focused almost exclusively on the criminal law. With the notable exception of some perceptive comments by Lawrence Stone,[2] an historian who has always had time for the litigious, the civil law, or the rules and legal processes by which people made and enforced agreements about property rights, contracts and debts, or sued for remedies in actions of slander or negligence, has been largely ignored. Yet it is arguable that the civil law is even more important than the criminal law in maintaining the social and economic relationships in any society. It is certainly the case that many more people of all ranks of society in early modern England came into contact with the legal system through the civil rather than the criminal courts. To take but one example, in 1776

I would like to thank David Lemmings, Henry Horwitz and Joanna Innes for their helpful comments on an earlier draft of this essay.

[1] For example, Douglas Hay, Peter Linebaugh *et al., Albion's Fatal Tree. Crime and Society in Eighteenth-Century England* (London, 1975); J. A. Sharpe, *Crime in Early Modern England 1550–1750* (London, 1984); J. M. Beattie, *Crime and the Courts in England, 1660–1800* (Oxford, 1986).

[2] Lawrence Stone, *The Crisis of the Aristocracy, 1558–1641* (Oxford, 1965), pp. 240–2, and 'Interpersonal Violence in English Society: 1300–1980', *Past and Present*, 101 (1983), pp. 22–3. J. A. Sharpe, 'Debate: The History of Violence in England: Some Observations', *Ibid.*, 108 (1985), pp. 206–15. Lawrence Stone, 'A Rejoinder', *Ibid.*, pp. 216–24.

more than half of the prison population of England and Wales was composed of insolvent debtors rather than criminals.[3]

Lawsuits are, therefore, an important part of the story of the administration of justice, and this paper undertakes a preliminary investigation of the subject by reconstructing the volume and nature of civil litigation in the main royal courts at Westminster in the period between 1640 and 1830, from the English Civil War to the point at which major law reforms began to transform the old common law system. The study is based partly on data collected by parliamentary inquiries in the 1820s, but mostly on figures obtained from the records of the courts of King's Bench, Chancery, and Common Pleas.

Quantifiable information about litigation can be extracted from certain groups of records which were generated within the courts for the purposes of providing easier access to the main series, collecting fees, or complying with technical formalities. First, alphabetical indexes of all of the bills filed in the court of Chancery, which survive from 1673 to 1859, are an excellent guide to the numbers of causes commenced in the court, although they tell little about the litigants or their troubles.[4] Second, the docket rolls and docket books of the King's Bench and Common Pleas were formalized notes, compiled in the offices of the prothonotaries, which provide a key to the contents of the plea rolls of the two courts. The entries in them have been counted in order to obtain figures on the number of cases which had reached 'advanced stages'; that is, the point at which the defendant had come to court in order to answer the plea of the plaintiff and either put himself on the country or confessed the action.[5] Third, in order to be sure of collecting their fees, the prothonotaries of the Common Pleas made notes of the number of *nisi prius* records, or cases being sent to trial in the country, which they issued each term. These provide easily

[3] John Howard, *The State of Prisons* (first published 1777; London, 1929), p. 17. 2,437 debtors out of a total population of 4,084.

[4] They are classified in the P[ublic] R[ecord] O[ffice] IND series.

[5] For a description of the docket rolls for the period up to 1640, see C. W. Brooks, *Pettyfoggers and Vipers of the Commonwealth: The 'Lower Branch' of the Legal Profession in Early Modern England* (Cambridge, 1986), pp. 48–51. The docket rolls (PRO IND) of the King's Bench survive in a continuous series up to 1702, when they were converted to docket books (PRO IND). This coincided with the creation of the judgement rolls (PRO KB 122) as the formal record of civil pleas. Before 1702 both criminal and civil pleas had been enrolled on the *coram rege* rolls (PRO KB 27), but even before 1702 the docket rolls referred to civil cases only.

collectable material on the number of lawsuits in the court which had surpassed the procedural stages and were about to be argued before a jury.[6] Fourth, the Rolls of Warrants of Attorney, which survive for the entire period in Common Pleas, but not in King's Bench, were an enrolment of the certificates which verified the appointment by litigants of their lawyers. They give brief details about the social status of the litigants and their business, both of which have been subjected to quantitative analysis.[7]

The statistical profile of court usage which these sources reveal is hardly perfect. The different types of document tell us different things about each court, and the data are incomplete. For example, it would ideally be desirable to compare the number of causes started in each court at as many dates as possible across the entire period, but, until commissions of inquiry appointed by Parliament went to work in the 1820s, the relevant statistics are available only for Chancery.[8] This is a difficulty because, as we shall see, the use of arrest as the leading process in cases of debt in the common law courts may have significantly reduced the ratio of cases which reached advanced stages as the period progressed. At the same time, none of the figures permits a proper appreciation of the differences between cases which were of general significance, or involved large outlays of financial and emotional capital, and those which were of much less consequence. For instance, a cause in Chancery might arise from a dispute over manorial customs between tenants and their landlord. On the other hand, many 'cases' in the King's Bench involved little more than the enrolment of a record on the plea rolls in order to back up a business transaction.[9] Court business did not invariably involve contention.

Nevertheless, the statistics are interesting because, as Part I of this essay shows, they point, first, to a massive decline, and, then, to unusually low levels of litigation in the central courts during the

---

[6] PRO CP 36.

[7] See Brooks, *Pettyfoggers and Vipers of the Commonwealth* , pp. 57–71. After the creation of the King's Bench judgement rolls in 1702, the warrants of attorney for cases in that court were recorded in the plea rolls on the same piece of parchment as the full record of the case and no longer compiled into a roll of their own.

[8] On the differences between causes commenced and causes in advanced stages, see Brooks, *Pettyfoggers and Vipers of the Commonwealth*, pp. 49, 75–7.

[9] For example, in 1750, a significant number of King's Bench defendants confessed judgements against themselves on a date prior to that on which they were due to repay sums of money. This practice enabled the lender to take uncontested legal action in case of default. PRO KB 122/242 and 243, rot's. 108, 403, 640.

course of the eighteenth century. The remainder of the essay goes on to explain the causes of these phenomena and to investigate their implications. Since it involves an interpretation of alterations in mass behaviour over nearly two centuries, the resulting picture is inevitably complex. Broad social and economic changes are discussed in conjunction with legal developments such as the establishment of urban small-debt jurisdictions known as courts of requests, and within a context of public dissatisfaction with the common law system. Next, an analysis of social composition of litigants and the nature of their lawsuits considers the significance of changes in levels of contentiousness and in the behaviour of different social groups with regard to the keeping of promises. The conclusion briefly compares the history of the civil law with that of the criminal law during the period.

I

The late sixteenth and, to a lesser extent, the early seventeenth centuries witnessed an expansion in central court litigation unprecedented in English history. In 1640 there was probably more litigation per head of population going through the central courts at Westminster than at any time before or since.[10] But one hundred years later in 1750, the common law hit what appears to have been a spectacular all-time low. There was subsequently a modest recovery of business between 1750 and 1830, but at the latter date, after the population of England had more than quadrupled, the number of cases entertained by the major central courts of the realm was no more than half as great as it had been in 1640.

The general trends over the 190 years break down into five distinct phases.

1. Although the courts were inevitably disrupted by the civil wars of the 1640s (see Table 10.1), the 1650s, 1660s and 1670s were decades in which the increase in litigation characteristic of the post-Reformation period continued, although at a very modest pace. The total number of cases in advanced stages in King's Bench and Common Pleas (Figure 10.1) rose slightly from 28,734 in 1640 to 29,371 in 1669–70. Equally, the first reliable figures for litigation in Chancery (Table 10.2), those for 1673/4, show 4,717 causes commenced, a level which is almost certainly higher than that

[10] Brooks, *Pettyfoggers and Vipers of the Commonwealth*, pp. 77–8.

Table 10.1. *Common Pleas: number of cases sent for trial at Assizes in the office of a single prothonotary, 1645–62*

1645–6	17
1646–7	218
1647–8	409
1650–1	698
1655–6	1,115
1661–2	1,348

Source: PRO CP 36/1.

Table 10.2. *Number of bills entered in the Court of Chancery, 1673–1809*

1673–4	4,717
1700–01	5,707
1720–1	3,453
1745[a]	1,836
1746[a]	2,032
1750	1,827
1752[a]	1,023
1800–9[a]	1,500 (average)

Sources: PRO IND 1/2136; 14,421; 14,451.
[a] *Parliamentary Papers: The Report of the Committee Appointed to Enquire into the Causes that Retard Decisions in the High Court of Chancery* (1811), vol. 2, p. 507.

reached at any stage before the Civil War. However, against these moderate increases in the work of the three most important central courts of the realm, we must set the fact that two very active pre-Civil War jurisdictions, the court of Star Chamber and the Council of the North had been abolished during the Civil War era, and were not replaced after the Restoration.[11]

2. By contrast, between 1680 and 1700, King's Bench and Common Pleas entered their first period of decline. The counts of records sent for trial at assizes by Common Pleas (Figure 10.2) fell by 19 per cent between 1682 and 1692, and then another 18 per cent between 1692 and 1703. Similarly, the number of cases in advanced stages in the Common Pleas dropped by 40 per cent between 1670 and 1700. In King's Bench, the flight of litigants was even more

---

[11] *Ibid.*, pp. 55–6. J. H. Baker, *An Introduction to English Legal History* (2nd edn, London, 1979), pp. 106, 184.

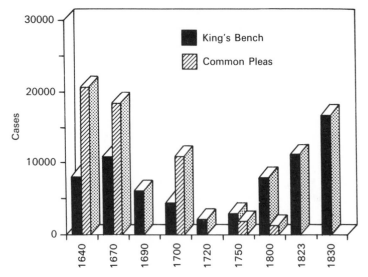

Figure 10.1   Cases in advanced stages in King's Bench and Common Pleas, 1640–1830
Sources: King's Bench: PRO IND 1/1369–70, 6054–5, 6076, 6092–3, 6132, 6194–5, 6293–4, 6339–40, 6353–5. Common Pleas: PRO IND 1/353–8, 572–580, 779–786, 997, 999, 1002–1007, 1133

dramatic. There were 40 per cent fewer cases in advanced stages in 1690 than there had been in 1670, and there was a further drop of 30 per cent in the 1690s. Overall, by 1700, the number of cases in advanced stages in the two courts was 15,306, barely half of the level of 1670.

3. Between 1700 and 1720, litigation in King's Bench continued to decline quite sharply,[12] but in Common Pleas the change appears to have been less dramatic (see Figures 10.1 and 10.2). The number of Common Pleas trials dropped off almost imperceptibly between 1702 and 1720. Thus it is hardly surprising that in response to a question put to him in Parliament, Sir George Cooke, chief prothonotary of the Common Pleas and an official of twenty years'

---

[12] In the year 1719–20, the docket books of the King's Bench record 2,258 cases in advanced stages (PRO IND 6132–3). In 1728, John Croft, deputy to the Master of the Bill of Middlesex office told the House of Commons that his records showed that the King's Bench issued about 3,000 writs a year to commence actions. This may have been an underestimate, but it confirms the general trend in Figure 10.1. T. Vardon and T. E. May, *Journals of the House of Commons* (London, 1803), vol. 21, p. 267.

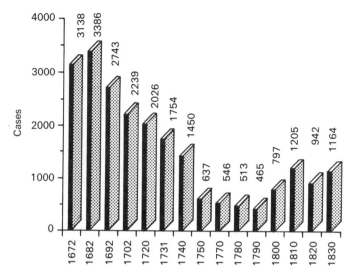

Figure 10.2   Number of cases sent for trial at Assizes, Common Pleas, 1672–1830
Sources: PRO CP 36/2–4, 6–9, 11–12, 14, 15–18, 21

standing, said that he believed there was more business in the court
in 1728 than there had been 'formerly'. This statement has always
been taken at face value by historians,[13] and from the point of view
of Cooke it may well have been true. Common Pleas business
which reached advanced stages was divided between the offices of
the three prothonotaries of the court, and the number of *nisi prius*
records enrolled in Cooke's own office had risen slightly since the
early years of the eighteenth century while that of the court as a
whole more or less held steady.[14] The real significance of this
episode lies not in Cooke's claim, but in the fact that he was forced
to answer a question about the amount of business in his court in
the first place.

   4. In any case, what Cooke was unable to foresee in 1728 was that
during the 1730s, and especially the 1740s, both Chancery and
Common Pleas would lose business at a truly spectacular rate. In
1750, only 1,827 bills were filed in Chancery, just over half as many

[13] *Ibid*. See, for example, Brooks, *Pettyfoggers and Vipers of the Commonwealth*,
    p. 75 and G. Holmes, *Augustan England: Professions, State and Society, 1680–
    1730* (London, 1982), p. 130.
[14] PRO CP 36/3.

as in 1720. The number of cases sent for trial by the Common Pleas fell only slightly in the 1730s, but they were halved in the 1740s. Although its business contracted by more than 25 per cent between 1700 and 1750, the King's Bench made something of a recovery after 1720 and sustained its position in the mid-eighteenth century much better than the other two courts. It is from this period that it finally achieved domination over the Common Pleas.[15] Nevertheless, the law as administered at Westminster was clearly at a nadir in 1750. Together King's Bench and Common Pleas heard only 4,891 cases in advanced stages in that year, only one-third as many as in 1700, about a sixth of the number in 1670.

5. Nor did the position improve significantly until the end of the eighteenth century. Cases in advanced stages in King's Bench grew by more than five times between 1750 and 1830, but most of this increase came after 1790 and especially in the 1810s and 1820s. The statistics compiled by the parliamentary inquiries make the latter decade the first for which absolutely sound evidence is available on the number of actions commenced, and these show an increase by one-third in the space of the years 1823–7. Equally, in Common Pleas, the number of cases sent for trial remained fairly constant between 1750 and 1800, but then rose sharply between 1800 and 1830, a trend which is also reflected in the figures for suits commenced which were collected by the House of Commons. Much the same was true of Chancery and the Exchequer of Pleas.[16]

The fluctuations in the volume of litigation across the period are surprisingly large, but most of the available evidence refers to causes in advanced stages rather than causes commenced. Hence there is an immediate question as to whether the decline observed

---

[15] The decline of the Common Pleas seems likely to have been caused in part by a decline in the professional reputation of the serjeants at law, the lawyers who had a monopoly right of audience there. J. H. Baker, *The Order of Serjeants at Law. A Chronicle of Creations with Related Texts and a Historical Introduction* (Selden Society Supplementary Series, vol. 5, London, 1984), pp. 111–15. [Edward Wynne], *A Miscellany Containing Several Law Tracts* (n.p., 1765), pp. 382–4, noted that 'at present, the number [nine] of Serjeants is more than the business of the court'.

[16] *Parliamentary Papers: First Report Made to His Majesty by the Commissioners Appointed to Inquire into the Practice and Proceedings of the Superior Courts of Common Law* (London, 1829), pp. 146–202. For the equity side of the Exchequer, a jurisdiction which has not been considered at length here, but in which litigation fluctuated in much the same pattern between 1640 and 1830 as has been outlined above, see W. H. Bryson, *The Equity Side of the Exchequer* (Cambridge, 1975), p. 168.

may not be in part an optical illusion created by changes in court procedure which altered the proportion of the cases started which eventually reached advanced stages, and to a limited extent this does appear to have been true.

The most important development in this respect was the increased use of the practice of arresting and holding to bail defendants in actions of debt before any pleadings had been entered in court (arrest on *mesne* process). This mode of procedure had been available from the King's Bench since the early sixteenth century, but it only became a regular feature of Common Pleas practice after the introduction of new writs by Chief Justice Francis North in the 1670s.[17] The effect on the number of cases which reached advanced stages was twofold. First, arrest on *mesne* process replaced traditional methods which were more expensive and which allowed the plaintiff to arrest defendants only after the time-consuming and expensive business of issuing them with several summonses. Therefore, the new procedures may have made it easier for plaintiffs to force out of court settlements on their opponents before a case ever reached advanced stages.[18] Equally important, impecunious debtors who were unable to raise bail could be left to languish in prison for a considerable period of time without further action being taken against them. For example, very few of the debtors in the Wiltshire gaol at Fisherton Anger in the late 1760s, many of whom had been imprisoned for well over a year, appear in the records of cases in advanced stages in King's Bench and Common Pleas.[19]

However, an eighteenth-century legislative attempt to modify the impact of arrest on *mesne* process introduced complications which also need to be taken into consideration. A statute passed by

[17] Roger North, *The Lives of the Right Hon. Francis North, Baron Guilford; The Hon. Sir Dudley North; and the Hon. and Rev. Dr. John North . . . Together with The Autobiography of the Author*, ed. Augustus Jessopp, 3 vols (London, 1890), vol. 1, pp. 128–9. Another development which might have reduced litigation, the use of commissions of bankruptcy to settle the affairs of insolvent debtors, seems unlikely to have had a significant effect. B[ritish] L[ibrary] Add. MS 36, 118 (Lord Hardwicke's Legal Papers), fo. 151, an account of the number of commissions of bankruptcy issued between 1714 and 1748, shows that the rate remained constant at between 200 and 300 each year, except for the years 1725–8, when there were between 400 and 500.

[18] Attorneys claimed that this was the effect of an earlier attempt to use similar procedures in the Common Pleas in the 1620s. Brooks, *Pettyfoggers and Vipers of the Commonwealth*, pp. 127–9.

[19] Wiltshire County RO, Trowbridge, A2/3/4. Petitions of insolvent debtors.

Parliament in 1725 restricted such arrests to cases where the amount in dispute was more than £10, thereby depriving creditors of the cheapest means of coercing payment of small sums of money. In these circumstances, the creditor could not have his defendant arrested until he had pursued his case through to a verdict. This required the outlay of additional sums of money, although these could in theory be recovered as costs from the defendant once the court's decision had been reached.[20]

According to the legal writer Richard Boote, the impact of this statute on litigation was rather paradoxical. On the one hand, he claimed that creditors attempting to recover less than £10 were reluctant to go to law at all because they rightly feared the additional costs, and, although the 1725 act is hardly ever mentioned specifically, it no doubt contributed to the persistent claims, which will be examined below, that the common law courts were ineffectual for the purposes of collecting small debts. On the other hand, in Boote's opinion the act actually added to the difficulty of debtors as well as creditors. If the plaintiff did proceed with legal action in such circumstances, his 'Revenge is sharpened by reason of his Costs, and the same Costs in an Addition to the Defendant's Debt' made it all the more unlikely that the defendant would be released from prison or his creditor satisfied.[21]

The 1725 act obviously did little to diminish the hostility associated with arrest on *mesne* process, and it is also unclear how far it had an impact on the number of lawsuits in either initial or advanced stages. Imperfect evidence from the early eighteenth century suggests that most common law business at that date involved considerably more than £10, but by the 1790s a great deal of business from the London area concerned sums less than £20.[22]

---

20   12 George I, c. 29, 'An act to prevent frivolous and vexatious arrests'. [Robert Richardson], *The Attorney's Practice in the Court of Common Pleas or An Introduction to the Knowledge and Practice of that Court*, 3rd edn, 2 vols (London, 1758), vol. 1, pp. 83–9.

21   R. Boote, *An Historical Treatise of An Action or Suit at Law: And of the Proceedings used in the King's Bench and Common Pleas* ... (London, 1766), pp. 36, 59–63.

22   A sample from the 'D' section of the King's Bench docket roll for 1700 (PRO IND 1/6093), which includes only cases in advanced stages, gives the following values for debts: £600, £280, £60, £120, £1,000, £5, £5 5s, £68, £60, £500, £480, £150, £170, £100, £30, £100, £27, £60, £60, £90, £3,000, £74, £450, £10, £30, £40, £500, £32. In 1792 a parliamentary committee found that of 9,500 bailable writs issued by the King's Bench in Middlesex (exclusive of London), 7,000 were for

It is impossible to say exactly how many creditors simply did not bother to sue if the sum sank below £10. More significantly, and for the present purposes more to the point, there is little reason to doubt that there was an overall increase in the use of arrest on *mesne* process during the period from 1670 to the end of the eighteenth century, and it was probably responsible for changes in the ratio of causes commenced to causes in advanced stages. In the period up to 1640, it is likely that twice as many suits were commenced as ever reached advanced stages, but the much more accurate figures available for the 1820s indicate that by then the ratio had risen to four to one.[23] The degree of distortion which this factor creates in the picture of rates of litigation at any point before the 1820s can only be estimated. It cannot have been the primary cause of the measured decline in the volume of court business in any of the five phases because King's Bench business declined even though the court used the procedure over the entire period. Moreover, litigation in all of the jurisdictions fell after 1700, long after the new technique had been introduced in Common Pleas. Most importantly, we can still say with confidence that whereas in 1640 some 1,149 causes were started in the central courts per 100,000 of total population, in 1830 there were only 653.[24] If the ratio of causes commenced to cases in advanced stages in 1750 is taken to be two to one, then the number per 100,000 could at that date have been as low as 175. Even if we use the factor of four to one, the total of causes commenced per 100,000 still comes to only 350.

II

What happened to the common law in the Age of Reason? The answer lies in a complex combination of demographic, economic, social, legal and behavioural characteristics of English society. Population stagnated at just below or above five million throughout the second half of the seventeenth century, only gradually reached

sums under £50 and half were for less than £20. *Commons Journals*, vol. 47, p. 645.

[23] Brooks, *Pettyfoggers and Vipers of the Commonwealth*, pp. 75–6. *Parliamentary Papers: First Report of His Majesty's Commissioners (on the) Common Law* (London, 1829), p. 11.

[24] Brooks, *Pettyfoggers and Vipers of the Commonwealth*, pp. 77–8, for the figures and the methods of calculation.

5.7 million in 1750, and then doubled between 1760 and 1830. Late eighteenth and early nineteenth-century population growth may therefore account partly for the renewed vitality of the common law in the 1790s and early 1800s. On the other hand, since population increased only marginally between 1640 and 1750, it is not surprising that central court litigation did not expand over those years. But there was nothing in this demographic regime which accounts for the massive decline in business up to 1750.[25]

The significance for court usage of long-term trends in the economy is more problematic. It is easy to see a connection between the increase in litigation after 1790 and the late eighteenth-century take-off in agricultural and manufacturing productivity known as the 'Industrial Revolution', although both the scale of the increase and the total volume of litigation in 1830 are a surprisingly pale reflection of a conjunction of demographic and economic conditions which should have led to a massive increase in the number of economic transactions and consequently to more disputes at law. The economic state of the realm between 1660 and the mid-eighteenth century is still shrouded in obscurity, but there were several economic and social changes during these years which may explain, at least in part, the fall in the amount of court business.[26]

The 1690s, the years in which the decline in litigation first became evident, were characterized by economic dislocation caused first by a shortage of specie and then by the recoinage of money in 1695–6 in an attempt to repair the problem.[27] Furthermore, quite apart from unprecedentedly high levels of taxation, the War of the Grand Alliance (1689–97) led to a revolution in finance, including the establishment of the Bank of England, which enabled the English state to borrow money at interest from the population at large in order to pay for government expenditure generally, but especially for the large outlays connected with war. Subsequently, during the first half of the eighteenth century, England was involved in three lengthy periods of war (1702–13, 1739–48, 1756–63), and there is evidence that, during each of them, people in southeastern

[25] E. A. Wrigley and R. S. Schofield, *The Population History of England 1541–1871* (London, 1981), Table 7.8
[26] D. C. Coleman, *The Economy of England 1450–1750* (Oxford, 1977), chapter 9. See also D. Little, *Deceleration in the Eighteenth-Century British Economy* (London, 1976).
[27] J. R. Jones, *Country and Court. England 1658–1714* (London, 1978), p. 271.

England with cash to invest transferred their money from the private market in loans to government stocks.[28] Since much of the business of the central courts involved credit transactions between individuals (see Table 10.6, p. 388 below), the creation of a major alternative to private lending may well have contributed to some contraction in the legal business which arose from it.

No less importantly, as studies of crime suggest, war may have helped to alleviate underemployment and low incomes amongst smaller artisans and wage-labourers, particularly in the first half of the eighteenth century when stagnant population and increased agricultural output resulted in generally high real wages.[29] Even in major royal courts such as King's Bench and Common Pleas, a large percentage of lawsuits involved relatively small sums of money amounting to less than £20, and the number of cases heard by the courts must have depended significantly on the availability of credit and the ability of shopkeepers, tradesmen and wage-labourers to pay on time.[30]

However, the same conjunction of limited population growth and generally high productivity of foodstuffs which made conditions more comfortable for those involved in non-agricultural occupations had a much more deleterious effect on farmers and brought a significant decline in the number of smallholders.[31] Since nearly 30 per cent of all defendants in the Common Pleas in both 1640 and 1750 were described as yeomen or husbandman farmers (see Table 10.5, p. 384 below), this change in their position had a direct impact on the overall volume of litigation. Both of the periods in which litigation dropped most dramatically, the 1690s and the 1730s and 1740s, were associated with severe bouts of agricultural depression in which many of them were forced to sell up.[32] An important sector of the traditional maket for legal services was withering away.

---

[28] D. M. Joslin, 'London Bankers in Wartime 1739–84', in L. S. Pressnell, ed., *Studies in the Industrial Revolution Presented to T. S. Ashton* (London, 1960), pp. 156–76.

[29] Beattie, *Crime and the Courts*, pp. 220ff.　　[30] See above, note 22.

[31] K. Wrightson, *English Society 1580–1680* (London, 1982), pp. 132, 142–5. J. Thirsk, ed., *The Agrarian History of England and Wales, Vol. 5, 1640–1750, II. Agrarian Change* (Cambridge, 1985), pp. 64, 75, 172, 241.

[32] *Ibid.*, p. 81. G. E. Mingay, 'The Agricultural Depression 1730–1750', *Economic History Review*, 2nd series, 3 (1956), pp. 323–38. A. H. John, 'The Course of Agricultural Change 1660–1760', in Pressnell, ed., *Studies in the Industrial Revolution*, pp. 134, 150.

Table 10.3. *Geographical distribution of litigation in King's Bench and Common Pleas, 1606–1750 (percentages by assize circuit)*

	Common Pleas			King's Bench	
	1606[a]	1640[a]	1750[b]	1606[a]	1750[c]
Home (Kent, Essex, Sussex, Herts., Surrey)	16	15	8	12	11
Midland (Derby, Lincs., Notts., Rutland, Northants., Warw., Leics.)	13	13	12	11	3
Norfolk (Norfolk, Suffolk, Cambs., Hunts., Beds., Bucks.)	19	18	11	13	3
Northern (Yorks., Northumb., Westmorl., Cumb.)	5	4	23	2	10
Oxford (Oxon., Berks., Glous., Mon., Heref., Worcs., Shrops., Staffs.)	13	12	12	14	12
Western (Hants., Wilts., Soms., Dors., Devon, Cornwall)	12	15	14	25	26
London and Middlesex	16	22	19	21	32
Lancs., Cheshire, Durham	4	1	.3		3
Illegible	2			2	
Total	100	100	100	100	100

[a] Brooks, *Pettyfoggers and Vipers of the Commonwealth*, p. 64.
[b] PRO CP 40/3575.
[c] PRO IND 1/6194.

Changes in agricultural society are also the best explanation for the changes in the regional distribution of litigation which are displayed in Table 10.3. For example, in the late sixteenth and early seventeenth centuries, much of the prodigious boom in litigation, particularly in Common Pleas, came from East Anglia, a region noted for its large number of contentious freehold farmers and for its famous lawyers with names like Spelman and Coke.[33] But by 1750, the cloth industry in Norwich was sagging in the face of competition from other areas, and the region as a whole was becoming a regional backwater.[34] Common Pleas work from the

[33] Brooks, *Pettyfoggers and Vipers of the Commonwealth*, pp. 63–5.
[34] P. J. Corfield, 'The Social and Economic History of Norwich, 1650–1850: A Study in Urban Growth' (unpublished Ph.D. thesis, University of London, 1976), pp. 115, 207, 671. A. Young, *A Farmer's Tour Through the East of England* (London, 1771).

Norfolk assize circuit shrank to less than the average for the nation as a whole, and in King's Bench the decline was even greater. On the other hand, the relative success of King's Bench in the mid-eighteenth century may owe something to the fact that it was evidently more successful in attracting business from the economic centre of gravity, London. Furthermore, both courts, but especially Common Pleas, saw a significant increase in the percentage of cases from northern England. In part this was a result of the abolition of the Council of the North in 1660 as a major tribunal for hearing causes which arose north of the Trent, but it is also an indication of the extent to which some parts of Yorkshire, Northumberland, Cumberland and Westmorland had finally been integrated into the national economy.[35]

Another major social change which contributed to the decline in litigation was a steady growth in the proportion of the English population which lived in towns. Between 1670 and 1700, urban population as a percentage of total population increased from 13.5 per cent to 17 per cent. By 1750 the figure had risen to 21 per cent, and by 1800 to 27.5 per cent.[36] Many of the new town dwellers were prosperous, self-employed merchants and tradesmen, but as urbanization progressed, a larger proportion of them were men and women who came to towns in order to work for others and who were therefore dependent on wages.[37] The rise of this urban proletariat is directly connected with trends in litigation. They were

---

[35] Thirsk, ed., *Agrarian History of England and Wales*, p. 82. J. V. Beckett, 'The Decline of the Small Landowner in Eighteenth- and Nineteenth-Century England: Some Regional Considerations', *Agricultural History Review*, 30.2 (1982), pp. 97–111. Similarly, the increase in central court litigation from northeastern England which was noticed by E. Hughes, *North Country Life in the Eighteenth Century. The North-East 1700–1750* (Oxford, 1952), pp. 77ff., is attributable to both the increased affluence brought to the area by the development of the coal industry and the concurrent decline of the palatinate courts at Durham, as inhabitants of the area increasingly sought legal redress from the royal courts in London; see K. Emsley and C. M. Fraser, *The Courts of the County Palatine of Durham* (Durham County Local History Society, 1984), pp. 38–9, 45, 76, 82–4. See also J. and G. Spearman, *An Enquiry into the Ancient and Present State of the County Palatine of Durham* ([Edinburgh], 1729).

[36] E. A. Wrigley, 'Urban Growth and Agricultural Change: England and the Continent in the Early Modern Period', *Journal of Interdisciplinary History*, 15 (1985), p. 688.

[37] P. J. Corfield, *The Impact of English Towns 1700–1800* (Oxford, 1982), chapters 8 and 9. No less important, the eighteenth century also saw a great deal of 'industrial' expansion in the countryside. J. Rule, *The Experience of Labour in Eighteenth Century Industry* (London, 1981), pp. 18, 30.

too poor, and their economic interests too trivial, to bring them very often before the central courts at Westminster, but at the same time it is clear that they constituted the majority of defendants in new types of legal institutions which were peculiarly characteristic of the eighteenth century, the provincial courts of requests (also known in some places as courts of conscience). These were small-debt jurisdictions established by statute at the petition of local communities, usually towns. The powers and administrative details of the courts varied significantly from place to place, but the petitions and statutes calling for their foundation invariably stressed the existence of a large labouring population which was frequently in need of credit, and therefore ran up debts, especially in times of sickness or unemployment.[38]

The chronology of the foundation of courts of requests reflects the course of urbanization in England during the late seventeenth and eighteenth centuries. The first was set up in London during the reign of Henry VIII, but pressure for the foundation of new ones did not arise again until the end of the seventeenth century. In 1673, Parliament received unsuccessful petitions from Southwark and Tower Hamlets, two suburbs of London, which was, of course, the fastest-growing metropolitan area in Europe. In the early 1690s, several major urban centres petitioned for courts, and grants were made to Gloucester, Norwich, Bristol and Newcastle, the last three being the largest towns in the realm apart from London.[39]

However, no new courts were established during the first fifty years of the eighteenth century.[40] Indeed, a good series of court records from Newcastle indicates that the course of litigation in

---

38 W. H. D. Winder, 'The Courts of Requests', *Law Quarterly Review*, 52 (1936), pp. 369–94. See, for example, J. Brand, *The History and Antiquities of the Town and County of the Town of Newcastle upon Tyne*, 2 vols (London, 1789), vol. 2, pp. 644–7. *Commons Journals*, vol. 26, pp. 368–9. H. W. Arthurs, '"Without the Law": Courts of Local and Special Jurisdiction in Nineteenth Century England', in A. Kiralfy, Michele Slatter and Roger Virgoe, eds., *Custom, Courts and Counsel. Selected Papers of the 6th British Legal History Conference Norwich 1983* (London, 1985), pp. 130–3, shows that most of the business of the courts in Bristol and Sheffield in the early nineteenth century involved shopkeepers who were suing their less well-off customers for goods sold and delivered.
39 *Commons Journals*, vol. 9, pp. 312, 371; vol. 10, pp. 77, 85, 277, 545.
40 *Parliamentary Papers: Second Part of the Appendix to the Fourth Report of the Common Law Commission* (London, 1832), Appendix (I) V: 'Returns of All Process Issued From Borough Courts, County Courts, Liberty Courts, Hundred Courts, Manor Courts and Courts of Requests. Between the 12 February 1830 and 12 February 1831'.

Table 10.4. *Actions in the Newcastle town courts, 1665–1830*

	Court of Conscience[a]	Sheriff's Court[b]	Mayor's Court[c]	Sheriff's and Mayor's Court[d]
1665–6		1,471		
1679–80			836	
1689–90			616	
1691–2		1,578		
1696–7		1,175		
1697–8	1,826			
1703–4			241	
1706–7		1,016		
1711–12	1,789			
1729–30		418	170	
1743–4	923			
1744–5		313		
1745–6			111	
1752–3		398		
1772–3	544			
1804–5	378			
1808–9				255
1809–10	1,044			
1829–30	3,921			576

The spread of dates has been determined by the availability of evidence.
[a] T[yne] and W[ear] A[rchives] D[epartment], Newcastle, NCX/CT5/1, 3–6. *Parliamentary Papers*, 'Returns of All Process Issued From Borough Courts, County Courts [etc.]'.
[b] TWAD NCX/CT2/2/2–4, 7, 15, 20–1.
[c] TWAD NCX/CT1/2/1, 3–4, 6, 10.
[d] This jurisdiction was in effect created in the second half of the eighteenth century, when the records of the Sheriff's Court and Mayor's Court were joined together, TWAD NCX/CT3/3/2, 13.

local jurisdictions during this half-century generally mirrored that at Westminster, a fact which must be taken as a strong indication that the relatively high real wages of this period kept the level of indebtedness low. As Table 10.4 shows, legal business in the town probably reached a peak a decade or so after the introduction in 1690 of a court of requests to supplement two older jurisdictions, the Sheriff's Court and Mayor's Court. Subsequently, litigation in all the courts, but especially in the Mayor's and Sheriff's Courts, dropped off to reach low levels throughout the remainder of the eighteenth century. Significant increases came only in the 1800s.

Newcastle was a traditional provincial capital which shared in the urban growth of the years 1650–1750. After 1750, however, its population rose only slightly;[41] from this date newer urban centres such as Birmingham, Liverpool and Manchester rapidly took over the leading places in the urban league table after London. As they did so, new courts of requests quickly followed. Petitions from Birmingham and Liverpool, which stressed their recent growth and commercial success, were received by the House of Commons in 1750. There were bursts of acts enabling a variety of towns to create the new jurisdictions between 1760–5, 1775–85, and, especially, 1805–10.[42]

All told, between 1690 and 1830 there were well over 100 acts of Parliament establishing courts of requests. Although the total volume of litigation in all jurisdictions in 1830, at 2,767 suits per 100,000 of the population, was significantly lower than in the early seventeenth century (4,638 cases per 100,000 in 1606), the courts of requests clearly absorbed some of the legal business which departed from the central courts in the eighteenth century. In the 1820s, parliamentary inquiries found that older communal jurisdictions such as those of the manor or the borough had long been moribund, but the courts of requests were hearing some 200,000 cases each year, or about 2.5 times the number entertained by the central courts in London.[43]

Furthermore, while social change – a contraction in the population of smaller landowners and an expansion in urban wage-labour – was a fundamental cause of this development, the rise of the courts of requests was also accompanied by a notable degree of mutual recrimination between those who advocated them and the common law establishment on both the national and local levels.

[41] From 29,000 in 1750 to 33,000 in 1801. Wrigley, 'Urban Growth and Agricultural Change', p. 686. B. R. Mitchell and P. Deane, *Abstract of British Historical Statistics* (Cambridge, 1962), pp. 24–7.

[42] *Commons Journals*, vol. 26, pp. 368–9, 415, 421, 426, 555, 584; vol 29, pp. 433–4, 707; vol. 34, p. 72; vol. 36, p. 671; vol. 41, pp. 623, 855.

[43] *Parliamentary Papers*: 'Returns of All Process issued From Borough Courts, County Courts [etc.]'. Although it is a subject which warrants further study, and although there were particular exceptions, it is extremely unlikely that manorial courts or borough courts ever recovered much of the litigious business they lost during the course of the late sixteenth and seventeenth centuries. Brooks. *Pettyfoggers and Vipers of the Commonwealth*, pp. 76–7, 96–101. S. Webb and B. Webb, *English Local Government from the Revolution to the Municipal Corporations Act: The Manor and the Borough* (London, 1924).

The preamble to the Newcastle Act of 1690 stressed that the costs of prosecuting small debts in the courts at Westminster frequently amounted to more than the cause of action itself, thereby leading to the ruin of the debtors, their wives and children, and to 'great charges to the corporation for their support and maintenance'.[44] Most petitions of the eighteenth century pointed out that costs and delays in both the royal courts and borough courts meant that creditors were unwilling to risk bringing actions for small debts, a circumstance which, it was feared, led many debtors to think that they could get away without paying.[45]

On the other hand, many lawyers were equally hostile towards the courts of requests. A number of attempts to set up the new jurisdictions were opposed, or completely frustrated, by officials in established urban small-debt courts.[46] Theirs were the voices of narrow self-interest, but the courts of requests also offended legal sensibilities more generally because they bypassed formalities and limited the role of professionals. The cost of writs, documents and other procedural steps were kept to a minimum, and the use of lawyers other than local attorneys was discouraged.[47] Most import-antly, the courts of requests dispensed with that 'ancient and valuable barrier of British liberty, the *trial by jury*'. The decision-making members of the tribunals were commissioners selected by town authorities or parish vestries from amongst local merchants and tradesmen, usually on the basis of a property qualification. Since there were no juries and no requirement that strict legal rules be followed, the commissioners had a very large degree of latitude in arriving at their judgements, a point which was latched on to by lawyers such as William Blackstone, whose *Commentaries on the Laws of England* (1765–9) attacked the 'petty tyrannies' exercised by jurisdictions where amateur judges exercised unlimited auton-omy of action.[48]

Although based on the perennial suspicion of lawyers for

---

[44] Brand, *History and Antiquities of the Town and County of the Town of Newcastle upon Tyne*, vol. 2, pp. 644–7.

[45] See for example the petition of Liverpool, *Commons Journals*, vol. 26, pp. 368–9.

[46] *Ibid.*, vol. 25, p. 984; vol. 36, p. 738; vol. 40, p. 435.

[47] Winder, 'The Courts of Requests'.

[48] W. Hutton, *A Dissertation on Juries: with a Description of the Hundred Court: As an Appendix to the Court of Requests* (Birmingham, 1789), p. 2. William Blackstone, *Commentaries on the Laws of England*, 4 vols (Oxford, 1767), vol. 3, p. 82. See also Winder, 'Courts of Requests', pp. 370, 376–8.

informal means of resolving disputes,[49] such doubts about the courts of requests were not entirely without foundation. Nor did they come exclusively from the legal profession.[50] Some of the courts may have been based on earlier urban jurisdictions,[51] but the fact that commissioners were drawn from local elites, and uncontrolled by juries, meant that the customary law they administered was largely that of the better-off inhabitants of towns and that their powers were subject to abuse. The possibility of oppression of the poor was frequently referred to in petitions against new statutes. Although many courts of requests developed a tradition of encouraging debtors to make repayments of a few pence a week, their procedures for summonsing defendants, and those for executing judgements, were enforced by the sanction of imprisonment.[52] In 1780, a parliamentary bill designed to restrict this power was inspired by fears that there were too few limits on its abuse.[53] In 1792 the sheriff of the county of Lancaster petitioned the House of Commons with allegations of misconduct against the commissioners in the local court of request, 'whereby the lower Class of People and the labouring Poor within the said County are grievously harrassed and oppressed'.[54]

Even the most articulate advocate of courts of requests, the self-made Birmingham bookseller William Hutton, admitted that before his own appointment as a commissioner in 1762, the Birmingham court had been dominated by a dipsomaniacal local

---

49 A point developed but seriously overstressed in H. W. Arthurs, 'Without the Law'. Administrative Justice and Legal Pluralism in Nineteenth-Century England (Toronto, 1985).

50 See, for example, A Letter to the Manufacturers and Inhabitants of the Parishes of Stoke, Burslem and Wolstanton, in the County of Stafford, on Courts of Request, Occasioned By the Bill intended to be brought into Parliament this Sessions, for the Establishment of that Jurisdiction in the Potteries: by a Manufacturer [? James Caldwell] (n.p., 1794).

51 Michele Slatter, 'The Norwich Court of Requests – a Tradition Continued', in Kiralfy, Slatter and Virgoe, eds., Custom, Courts and Counsel, pp. 97–107.

52 The extent of the use of imprisonment probably varied from place to place and over time. Parliamentary Papers: 'Returns of All Process Issued From Borough Courts, County Courts [etc.]'. The instalment system was certainly in use in Newcastle and Lincoln. Tyne and Wear Archive Department, Newcastle, NCX/CT5/1. Court of Conscience Records, 1697–1700. Lincolnshire Archives Office, Lincoln. Lincoln City Archives, L1/2/2–3, Court of Request Minute Books, 1797–1806. See also Commons Journals, vol. 37, pp. 692–3, 766.

53 Commons Journals, vol. 37, pp. 692, 759, 762–3, 766, 774, 783, 786–7, 792. A large number of urban communities sent in petitions opposing the measure. It was never reported to the House.

54 Ibid., vol. 47, p. 383.

attorney who acted as the court clerk. Moreover, 'The Commissioners, who attended business without studying it, sometimes forgot to treat the suitors as brethren whom they were bound to assist, but brow-beat them as little men, in little office, are apt . . .'[55] Nevertheless, Hutton was convinced that the courts of requests were necessary largely because of the even greater failings of the common law. A vituperative hatred of lawyers was a constant theme of his writings. He suggested that Blackstone's praise of the common law was nothing more than the praise of a certain kind of business activity by a man who had made a lot of money out of it. He thought that local attorneys were broken-down drunkards who stirred up unnecessary suits in order to fleece their clients with exorbitant fees. Legal process itself was long, unintelligible, and costly. In sum, he thought that

> There is a striking resemblance between the law and the schoolmaster; in *both* schools we expect to find instruction and protection, but instead of these, we find the rod. *Both* were designed for common benefit; they begin with mildness, they become burdensome, and at last, end in tyranny. Their institution was excellent, their reform is necessary.[56]

III

William Hutton's doubts about the quality of the legal services offered by the Westminster courts were widely shared. Fears about the high cost and increasing complexity of litigation go some way towards explaining the low levels of central court business during the eighteenth century.

Public concern about abuses in the law courts was expressed both inside and outside Parliament at regular intervals throughout the late seventeenth, eighteenth and early nineteenth centuries,[57] but the parliamentary agitation for law reform in the 1720s, just before

[55] W. Hutton, *Courts of Requests: Their Nature, Utility, and Power Described, with A Variety of Cases Determined in That of Birmingham* (Birmingham, 1787), p. 374.

[56] *Ibid.*, pp. 7, 10, 36. Hutton. *A Dissertation on Juries*, pp. 9–11, 31.

[57] For investigations of the legal system by the House of Commons in the later seventeenth century, especially the 1690s, see H[istorical] M[anuscripts] C[ommission], *The Manuscripts of the House of Lords 1689–90*, 12th Report, App. Part VI (1889), p. 313. *Ibid.*, 13th Report, App. Part V (1892), pp. 17, 19, 23, 128–9. *Ibid.*, vol. 2, new series (1905), pp. 69–70, 71–2, 81–2. *Ibid.*, vol. 4, new series (1908), pp. 62–3, 279. *Commons Journals*, vol. 14, p. 12.

the most catastrophic drops in central court litigation, is particularly instructive. At that time, MPs focused on a range of issues from the regulation of attorneys, solicitors and court officials to the illogicality of the fact that court proceedings were written in Latin.[58] However, the single general theme which lay behind most of the particular calls for reform was the claim that going to law had become excessively difficult and expensive. For example, in 1728 the House of Commons received a number of petitions from justices of the peace and other gentlemen assembled at various meetings of quarter sessions in Yorkshire and the West Country which complained about the impossibility of using the royal courts to recover small debts. Like others, that from the West Riding of Yorkshire, a cloth-manufacturing region, explained that 'there is in ... [this] Part of the Kingdom a great Number of Manufacturers, and other laborious People, who are often entitled to receive Small sums from Persons they deal with, which sometimes they cannot procure without considerable Expenses of Suit, whereby they are rendered less able to support their Families'. It then went on to suggest as a remedy that JPs be granted summary jurisdiction to hear and determine small debts.[59] These petitions were almost certainly associated with disputes in the clothing districts over the payment of weavers' wages,[60] but subsequent parliamentary activity went well beyond this particular issue. The House of Commons investigated court officials, obtained the appointment of a royal commission on fees from the King, and considered several

---

[58] *Commons Journals*, vol. 21, pp. 267, 274–7, 297, 313, 622–3, 640, 676, 741, 892–3; vol. 22, pp. 23, 243, 258. For extra-parliamentary views, see, for example, [Anon.], *A Bill For the More Easy and Speedy Recovery of Small Debts* (London, 1730). *A Letter to A Member of Parliament With some few Remarks on the Act made for the better Regulation of Attornies and Solicitors ... Together with Animadversions on the Grievances the Subjects of England, especially the Poor, labour under, with regard to the great Fees paid by them when prosecuting for their Debts and Dues ... By a Gentleman of Wilt[shire]* (London, 1730). *Gentleman's Magazine*, vol. 1, pp. 19 (January 1731), 100 (March 1731), 106 (March 1731), 213 (May 1731); vol. 2, pp. 899–900 (August 1732), 1015 (October 1732), 1045 (November 1732). [Anon.], *A Discourse on Fees of Office in Courts of Justice* (London, 1736).

[59] *Commons Journals*, vol. 21, pp. 274, 236–7, 313, 622–3. Petitions were also received from the other Yorkshire Ridings and from Wiltshire and Devon.

[60] J. De L. Mann, 'Clothiers and Weavers in Wiltshire during the Eighteenth Century', in Pressnell, ed., *Studies in the Industrial Revolution*, pp. 69–71. Political conflicts between Whigs and Tories, which have not been investigated here, may also have been significant.

bills for the establishment of small-debt courts based on the commissions of the peace. As far as the crucial question of legal costs is concerned, there is every reason to believe that contemporary suspicions were justified. A proliferation in the number of court officials, increases in the amounts they charged for their services, the practice of making litigants pay for numerous copies of case paperwork, and, from 1695, the application of government stamp duties to legal work all contributed to the rising costs of lawsuits. Parliamentary investigations of fees in the 1690s suggest that there had by then already been significant increases. A comparison of published lists of court fees in 1654 and 1695 with those produced in response to parliamentary investigations in 1730 show both a multiplication in the number of officials and an uneven but clearly detectable increase in some court fees.[61] In addition, the fees of barristers, which accounted for a significant proportion of the costs of any suit which went to trial, and especially those in the court of Chancery, had been increasing steadily throughout the course of the seventeenth century. During the reign of James I, the accepted normal fee was 10*s* for appearances or the signing of bills and pleadings. By 1700, however, young counsel could expect a guinea (21*s*) for the same services, and important lawyers involved in major causes took up to four or five times that amount.[62]

No less importantly, the decline in litigation itself appears to have had a profound impact on the structure and fee-taking conventions of the lower branch of the legal profession, the attorneys and solicitors who were usually the practitioners most often in contact with potential litigants. The account books of the King's Bench attorney Henry Travers, and of the Cambridgeshire practitioner Ambrose Benning, show that the decline in the general levels of litigation from the 1690s onwards was reflected in the

---

[61] E. Hughes, 'The English Stamp Duties, 1664–1764', *English Historical Review*, 56 (1941), pp. 234–44. *The Practick Part of the Law, Shewing the Office of a Complete Attorney* (London, 1654 and 1696 edns). *Lists, Accounts and Tables of Fees of the Officers and Servants belonging to the Judges of the several Courts in Westminster Hall, and the Circuits, the Associates and Clerks of Assize Presented to the House of Commons Persuant to their Order of the 23rd Day of March 1729* (London, 1730).

[62] W. R. Prest, 'Counsellors' Fees in the Age of Coke', in J. H. Baker, ed., *Legal Records and the Historian* (London, 1978), pp. 168, 182; D. F. Lemmings, 'The Inns of Court and the English Bar, 1680–1730' (unpublished D. Phil. thesis, University of Oxford, 1985), pp. 232–8.

private practices of individuals.[63] Furthermore, as the amount of business they handled in London melted away, so the typical seventeenth-century pattern of practice which saw attorneys making regular termly trips to the capital began to be abandoned.[64] Admissions to the inns of chancery in London, the term-time residences of such practitioners, fell significantly in the first half of the eighteenth century, and the lower branch as a whole gradually became much more oriented towards purely provincial work, most of which was non-litigious, than it had been before 1690.[65] In 1730, William Heron of Harbury in Yorkshire found it extremely irksome to have to go to London at all; by that date most country attorneys were regularly conducting their business in the Westminster courts through London agents.[66]

This development compounded the decline in litigation in two ways. Rather than charging clients a flat rate of 3s 4d per term for litigious work, as had previously been the practice, attorneys in the eighteenth century began to add on fees for the time they spent consulting with clients, writing letters for them, and travelling to London or assizes. For instance, in the fee book which he began in 1681, Ambrose Benning made his first charges for travelling to London in 1701.[67] Over the course of the century, these additional fees became commonplace and thereby contributed significantly to the cost of litigation.[68]

However, the new provincial orientation of the profession was also damaging to the central courts because it discouraged some practitioners from advising people to go to law at all. As the perceptive legal writer Richard Boote pointed out in 1766,

[63] BL Harleian MS 569. Travers recorded cases he entered on the plea rolls between 1653 and 1699. Cambridge County Record Office, 423/B1 (a), 'This book belongs to Ambrose Beninge Liber C of Triplow in Cambridgsheire Or of Bernards Inn in Holborne London, gent.'
[64] Brooks, *Pettyfoggers and Vipers of the Commonwealth*, pp. 31–4, 146–9.
[65] Gray's Inn Library, London. The Admissions Registers of Barnard's Inn, 1622–1753 [fos. 30–53]. M. Miles, ' "Eminent Practitioners": The New Visage of Country Attorneys c. 1750–1800', in G. R. Rubin and D. Sugarman, eds., *Law, Economy and Society, 1750–1914: Essays in the History of English Law* (Abingdon, 1984), p. 491.
[66] Leeds City Archive Department, Acc. 1361. Letter book of William Heron, 1728–33. Letters of 20 April, 17 and 31 October 1730.
[67] Account book of Ambrose Benning, fo. 69. He charged £2 for travel to London and four days' work there.
[68] Calderdale District Archives, Halifax, HAS 759. Bill book of John Howarth of Ripponden 1748–53.

attorneys received only a modest proportion of the money clients laid out for the procedural steps which accompanied any lawsuit.[69] In fact, the fee-structure by then worked in such a way that they could make just as much money out of a dispute by encouraging a settlement through arbitration, which might or might not be undertaken in connection with the purchase of London writs. Late eighteenth-century critics of the profession, who wrote mainly from London, continued to attack pettyfogging practitioners who stirred up lawsuits, but the letters of the Bath solicitor John Jeffreys suggest that by the 1780s he frequently found his income from litigious work scarcely worth the trouble it caused him.[70] Furthermore, a recent study of the Bradford attorney John Eagle shows that he in fact handled more arbitrations than cases which went the course through the courts.[71] The full extent of this practice is virtually impossible to measure, but it could clearly have had a powerful influence on the volume of central court litigation.

These changes in the structure of the legal profession attracted little attention from the law reformers. Nor was very much achieved in correcting those abuses which they did notice. Despite the complaints and parliamentary agitation of the years around 1730, virtually nothing was done to tackle the problem of high legal costs in general or about the particular issue of the excessive expense involved in bringing actions to recover small debts. Statutes were passed to regulate the training of attorneys and solicitors, and to translate legal proceedings into English, but bills for the establishment of small-debt courts floundered on the vested interests of office-holders.[72] The royal commission appointed in 1732 to investigate fees was wound up in 1746 with little to show for its efforts apart from a bill for the clerk's salary.[73]

As a result of the unchecked increases in fees, the overall cost of

[69] Boote, *An Historical Treatise*, pp. xi, xiv.

[70] A. Grant, *The Progress and Practice of A Modern Attorney: Exhibiting the Conduct of Thousands towards Millions* . . . (London, n.d. [1790s]; Somerset RO, Taunton, DD/WLM, Box 1. Letter books of John Jeffreys, Solicitor of Bath, 1773–c.1800. Vol. 1, 11 October 1774, 13 February 1775, 13 October 1777; vol. 2, 11 January 1784.

[71] Miles ' "Eminent Practitioners" ', pp. 495–6.

[72] 2 George II, c. 23 and 4 George II, c. 26. *Commons Journals*, vol. 23, pp. 234, 287, 298, 699, 636, 653.

[73] BL Add. MS 36,118, fo. 575. The commission completed its investigation of the court of Chancery in 1740, but had not sat since then. Lord Chancellor Hardwicke, who was responsible for the activities of the commission, evidently did little to encourage it.

litigation in the central courts doubled between 1680 and 1750. In the 1660s and 1670s, the overwhelming majority of the clients of the Hertfordshire attorney George Draper paid less than £10 for their suits at common law.[74] Between 1750 and 1830, figures of between £20 and £30 for the same kind of work appear constantly in the fee books of attorneys, literature calling for reform, and the reports of parliamentary inquiries.[75] It became an eighteenth-century commonplace that most people would rather lose their rights than risk their money in going to law. Richard Boote linked the decline in litigation at Westminster with the effects of high clerical fees and the stamp duties.[76] Another legal observer pointed out that high office fees also accounted for the fact that by 1730 attorneys were no longer extending credit to less well-off litigants, thereby identifying the decline of a practice which had been important in fuelling the late Elizabethan and early Stuart boom in litigation.[77] As we have seen, eighteenth-century petitions for the establishment of courts of requests constantly complained about the difficulties of suing for small debts, and in 1823 a parliamentary committee collected evidence from tradesmen who unanimously agreed that no prudent businessman would risk going to law for a debt of less than £15. In their view, the difficulty this imposed on collecting for goods sold on credit meant that they had to charge all customers more than would have been the case if there had been a reliable means for forcing payment.[78]

Some people, most notably Sir William Blackstone, continued to

74 Brooks, *Pettyfoggers and Vipers of the Commonwealth*, p. 105.
75 Calderdale District Archives, Bill book of John Howarth. [A. Grant], *The Public Monitor; Or A Plan For the More Speedy Recovery of Small Debts; Wherein the expediencey of Erecting County Courts and of enlarging the Powers of the Courts of Request is Pointed Out* ... (London, 1789), pp. vi–viii. Hutton, *Courts of Requests*, p. 81. *Parliamentary Papers* (London, 1829), Appendix (M.) no. 1: 'Bills of Costs', pp. 687–716; C. W. Francis, 'Practice, Strategy, and Institution: Debt Collection in the English Common-Law Courts, 1740–1840', *Northwestern University Law Review*, 80.4 (1986), p. 858.
76 *A Letter to A Member of Parliament With some few Remarks on the Act made for the better Regulation of Attornies and Sollicitors*, pp. 2–3. *Commons Journals*, vol. 21, p. 640. Boote, *An Historical Treatise*, p. x.
77 *A Letter to A Member of Parliament With some few Remarks on the Act made for the better Regulation of Attornies and Sollicitors*, p. 9. Brooks, *Pettyfoggers and Vipers of the Commonwealth*, pp. 105–6.
78 *Parliamentary Papers. Report from the Select Committee on the Recovery of Small Debts in England and Wales* (London, 1823), pp. 3, 13–15.

defend the common law system. Many others paid lip-service to the notion that in substance the English enjoyed the best of all possible laws.[79] But the periodical literature of the eighteenth century reveals a very articulate body of public opinion which saw excessive fees as only one aspect of an 'oppressive' system of justice which was also subject to delay and unreasonable complexity. A writer in *The Universal Spectator* (1731) explained that the law began as customs which were well suited to the needs of the people, but as circumstances changed, new forms of practice were introduced until the legal system was precipitated into a miserable state of intricacy, expense and confusion.[80] In 1750, *The Gentleman's Magazine* approvingly outlined law reforms recently undertaken by the King of Prussia and compared them favourably with the 'engine of oppression' which English law had become.[81] Writing in 1792, Jeremy Bentham mockingly sparred with a speech in praise of the law which had been delivered by Sir William Ashurst to the Middlesex Grand Jury. In response to Ashhurst's claim that 'No man is so low as not to be within the law's protection', Bentham wrote:

Ninety-nine men out of a hundred are thus low. Every man is, who has not from five-and-twenty pounds, to five-and-twenty times five-and-twenty pounds, to sport with, in order to take his chance for justice.[82]

At about the same time, another critic complained about the difficulty of using the law to recover property, as well as about the injustices, particularly the practice of arrest on *mesne* process, which had grown up on the fringes of the legal system so that an essentially litigious society could carry on its business. 'Either John Bull must be a contentious wicked fellow, or else there must be some strange and unaccountable defect in the Laws by which he is governed.' There was little that was new in the conclusion of the parliamentary investigators in 1830 that excessive costs and defects

---

[79] See also Daines Barrington, *Observations on the Statutes, Chiefly The More Ancient, from Magna Charta to the Twenty-first of James the First* (London, 1766), pp. iv, 337–8.

[80] Reprinted in *The Gentleman's Magazine*, vol. 1, p. 100 (March 1731).

[81] *Ibid.*, vol. 20, pp. 215–17 (May 1750).

[82] 'Truth versus Ashurst; or, Law as It Is, contrasted With What It Is Said To Be', in *The Works of Jeremy Bentham, Published Under the Superintendence of his Executor, John Bowring*, 11 vols (Edinburgh, 1843), vol. 4, p. 233.

Table 10.5. *Social status of litigants in Common Pleas, 1640 and 1750* (percentages, numbers in round brackets)

	1640[a]			1750[b]		
	Plaint.	Def.	Total	Plaint.	Def.	Total
Gent and above	25(271)	39(561)	33(832)	11(114)	16(171)	14(285)
Yeomen	–	22(314)	13(314)	–	25(265)	13(265)
Husbandmen ('farmer')	–	6(88)	4(88)	–	4(38)	2(38)
Total landed	25(271)	67(963)	50(1234)	11(114)	45(474)	29(588)
Commercial/Artisan	.5(5)	18(255)	10(260)	1(13)	25(269)	13(282)
Clergy	1(15)	3(43)	2(58)	2(16)	.5(8)	1(24)
Attorneys	.7(7)	3(37)	2(44)	4(41)	2(26)	3(67)
Widows	6(60)	2(23)	3(83)	3(29)	3(35)	3(64)
Miscellaneous	.2(2)	6(92)	4(94)	.7(8)	6(65)	3(73)
Not given	66(706)	1(13)	29(719)	79(815)	19(203)	48(1,018)
GRAND TOTAL	100(1,066)	100(1,426)	100(2,492)	100(1,036)	100(1,080)	100(2,116)

[a] Brooks, *Pettyfoggers and Vipers of the Commonwealth*, p. 283.
[b] PRO CP 40/3575. In connection with this table, and Table 10.6, there is no reason to think that the dates 1640 and 1750 were atypical from the point of view of litigation. Since inaccuracies in the style given to defendants were a ground for non-suiting plaintiffs, it is likely that most of the defendants for whom no style is given were of non-armigerous status.

in legal administration amounted to a 'denial of justice' in the face of greater demands for justice which had by then been created by the increased population, wealth and commerce of the nation.[83]

IV

Thus, by the 1730s, social change, alterations in the legal profession and increased fees were putting the great 'Law Shops' at Westminster Hall beyond the reach of many potential litigants. Nevertheless, these factors do not necessarily rule out the possibility that the decline in litigation was also a consequence of a general change in attitudes and behaviour which led to a decline in contentiousness between 1640 and 1750. This is an hypothesis which has been stressed by Lawrence Stone. Along with an apparent fall in the rate of homicide, it is in his view further support for the broader claim

[83] Grant, *The Progress and Practice of a Modern Attorney*, p. 54. *Parliamentary Papers. Fourth Report of the Commissioners on the Practice and Proceedings of the Superior Courts of Common Law With a Supplement and Appendix [Part I]* (London, 1831–2), pp. 5–54.

that the social tension which characterized English society before 1650 gradually gave way to an eighteenth-century world of less violence and less contention.[84] The issue raises questions of almost unlimited scope, but an analysis of those litigants and disputes which did come before the central courts is a logical first step in dissecting them.

Changes in court record-keeping, a decline in the accuracy and regularity with which men attached styles to their surnames, and the need for further study all dictate caution in jumping to conclusions about the nature of litigants in the main Westminster courts in the mid-eighteenth century. Even so, a glance at Table 10.5, which compares the social status of Common Pleas litigants in 1640 and 1750, reveals a very significant decline in the percentage of both plaintiffs and defendants who were styled as gentlemen, esquires, knights or one of the ranks of the peerage. The trend is further corroborated by the dramatic drop in the levels of business in Chancery, a court which was particularly concerned with the affairs of the gentry. In addition, it can be illustrated more concretely through the accounts of the legal work handled by the attorney John Donne for the wealthy Somerset family, the Pauletts. Between 1729 and 1773, the Pauletts ran up legal costs totalling some £953 (an average of about £22 per annum). However, apart from the relentless prosecution of a man who had aided a gaol-break and invaded the family garden at Hinton St George, two Chancery suits, and a couple of ejectments against tenants, most of Donne's work over the course of forty-four years involved miscellaneous errands and the drawing of instruments such as deeds, wills and warrants for gamekeepers.[85]

A more stable land market, the development of mortgages as a way of raising capital, and the effectiveness of the strict settlement as a means of reducing inter-familial conflict over property may well account for a large part of this decline in gentry litigation.[86] So, too, may the reputation of the law. Some parts of the gentry

[84] Stone, 'A Rejoinder', pp. 216–24.

[85] Somerset RO, Taunton, DD/MR 101. Fee book of John Donne, fos. 52–73v. It took over two years and the staggering sum of £321 14*s* 6*d* to get Thomas Burridge transported for seven years in 1735. Two other prosecutions for theft, one involving a silver spoon, were brought for less than £10. By comparison, one Chancery case which ran for four years cost £107 18*s* 5*d*; the other, which lasted three years, came to a minimum of £62 11*s* 2*d*.

[86] For the strict settlement, see L. Stone and J. C. F. Stone, *An Open Elite? England 1540–1880* (Oxford, 1984), p. 74.

community must have been aware of the criticisms of the law which were circulated in the press and sometimes debated in Parliament.

All squires would have recoiled in anger from an account published in the 1730s, which described how the masters in Chancery exploited estates which had been put into their hands in connection with litigation over mortgages.[87] At the same time, some gentlemen may have thought that it besmirched their honour to have their affairs discussed publicly in court or press reports.[88]

On the other hand, the decline in gentry litigants may reflect little more than the fact that it was hard to get the elite to pay their debts. For instance, at the time of his death the attorney John Donne had received only £41 18s of the £953 due to him from Lord Paulett for legal services; if his case is typical then the legal profession obviously had a vested interest in keeping the aristocracy out of court.[89] More generally, tradesmen frequently complained that it was difficult to get gentlemen to settle their accounts. Peers of the realm could not be arrested for debt. Given the high cost of litigation, richer gentlemen may have been protected from the law by their potential ability to out-purse creditors who were thinking of taking legal action against them.[90] Although army and navy officers, most of whom were the offspring of the lesser gentry, appear sometimes to have ended up in debtors' prison, Alexander Grant must have been largely correct in claiming that the richer part of the nation had little experience which would enable them to imagine the horrors of the Fleet or the King's Bench prison.[91]

The decline in the percentage of Common Pleas business which involved landed society suggests that the work of the courts was being concentrated increasingly on the affairs of merchants, tradesmen and artisans, and this is in fact quite consistent with an overall drop in litigation. We have seen already how these groups benefited

---

87 *The Gentleman's Magazine*, vol. 3, p. 467 (September 1733).
88 [Anon.], *The Locusts: Or, Chancery Painted to the Life, and the Laws of England Tryed in Forma Pauperis. A Poem* (London, 1704), Preface.
89 Somerset RO, Fee book of John Donne, fo. 73v.
90 Grant, *The Progress and Practice of a Modern Attorney*, pp. 73–5. J. Brewer, 'Commercialization and Politics', in N. McKendrick, J. Brewer, and J. H. Plumb, *The Birth of a Consumer Society. The Commercialization of Eighteenth Century England* (London, 1982), pp. 198–9.
91 *The Most Humble Petition of the Several Persons in the Fleet-Prison in Behalf of Themselves and several Thousand imprison'd Debtors in the King's-Bench, and the Several Gaols of this Kingdom* (London, n.d., but *c*. 1727). [Grant], *The Public Monitor*, p. 28.

from early eighteenth-century economic trends. In addition, from the later Middle Ages, if not long before, the culture of urban communities stressed fair dealing and probity in business transactions. Towns maintained their own institutions, such as guilds, which were essentially hostile to the adversarial nature of deciding disputes at common law.[92] Commercial opinion is well reflected in John Marius's famous remark that 'The right dealing merchant doth not care how little he hath to do in the Common Law.'[93] Tradesmen like William Stout and Thomas Turner were probably not atypical in their extreme reluctance to use the law against those who owed them money.[94] By 1750, the older institutional fabric in which these values had grown was in decline, but the customs of merchants continued to colour transactions, and newer social organizations, such as the ubiquitous tradesmen's clubs of the eighteenth century, promoted the virtues of honesty and fair dealing, including the payment of debts on time.[95] Furthermore, between 1650 and 1750, a number of changes were introduced into the common law which helped to accommodate it better to commercial needs, and which may also have contributed to the reduction in the number of lawsuits.

As Table 10.6 shows, in 1640, actions of debt made up the vast majority of cases in King's Bench and Common Pleas. In turn, most of these lawsuits involved written obligations under seal which were associated with loans or other financial arrangements. Moreover, in the sixteenth and seventeenth centuries the action was frequently called upon in connection with a legal instrument known as the conditional bond, which was widely used to enforce agreements to perform certain actions or pay off debts. The form of the bond was usually that a debt should be paid or an action undertaken by a specified date. If there was a default, then the defaulter was obliged to pay a penal sum of money which had been agreed beforehand by both parties. Bonds were a relatively secure way of carrying out business which left both the details of the agreement and the degree

---

[92] S. Thrupp, *The Merchant Class of Medieval London* (Chicago, 1948), p. 21. Brooks, *Pettyfoggers and Vipers of the Commonwealth*, p. 35.

[93] Quoted in J. Milnes Holden, *The History of Negotiable Instruments in English Law* (London, 1955), p. 42.

[94] *The Autobiography of William Stout of Lancaster 1665–1752*, ed. J. D. Marshall, Chetham Society, 3rd series, no. 14 (1967), pp. 119–20. Thomas Turner, *The Diary of a Georgian Shopkeeper*, ed. R. W. Blencowe and M. A. Lower, 2nd edn (Oxford, 1979), p. 26.

[95] Brewer, 'Commercialization and Politics', pp. 200, 214, 217, 229.

Table 10.6. *Forms of action at common law, 1640–1750 (percentages)*

	Common Pleas		King's Bench	
	1640[a]	1750[b]	1640[a]	1750[c]
Debt	88	32	80	32
Actions on the case	5	37	13	42
Ejectment	1	16	2	13
Trespass	3	13	5	10
Miscellaneous	3	2	–	3
Total	100	100	100	100

[a] Brooks, *Pettyfoggers and Vipers of the Commonwealth*, p. 69.
[b] PRO CP 40/3575.
[c] PRO IND 1/6194.

of the penalty to be exacted for non-compliance largely up to the parties themselves.[96] Moreover, bonds and other written obligations were enforced quite rigorously by the courts; if the writing could be produced in court, there was little the defendant could do to prevent a judgement being given against him. On the other hand, one disadvantage of such instruments was that they had to be written out and sealed. Another was that debts created in this way were not assignable. That is, a debt owed to a designated creditor could not be used by the creditor to pay his own debts. By the early seventeenth century, this was a source of constant complaint from the merchant community because it limited the fluidity of credit and was contrary to common business practices which English merchants found elsewhere in Europe.[97]

However, by the later seventeenth century the rigours of the common law of contract were being relaxed in favour of the generally more forgiving customs of merchants. The court of Chancery led the way by providing debtors with relief from the stringent penalties of the conditional bond if it appeared that they had been defrauded or had some genuine reason for failing to carry out the conditions.[98] The common law courts followed suit. By

[96] Brooks, *Pettyfoggers and Vipers of the Commonwealth*, pp. 67–8.
[97] Holden, *The History of Negotiable Instruments in English Law*, pp. 66–8.
[98] A. W. B. Simpson, *The History of the Common Law of Contract. The Rise of the Action of Assumpsit* (Oxford, 1975), pp. 118–24.

1750 they were regularly using mechanisms which eased the rules that obligations had to be performed on a certain day and which forced creditors to accept partial payments of debts. Although the exact chronology is somewhat obscure, during the course of the eighteenth century the superior courts, like the courts of requests, were facilitating the repayment of debts by weekly or monthly instalments.[99] In addition, after 1640, there were two important changes associated with litigation which came into the common law courts under a broad category of legal remedies known as actions on the case. Actions on the case for *assumpsit* were used more and more widely to enforce informal written or verbal contracts of all kinds. What is no less important, by 1704 the courts were allowing actions on the case to be used to enforce the honouring of bills of exchange and promissory notes, both of which were negotiable instruments of credit.[100]

The rise between 1640 and 1750 in the percentage of actions on the case sued in both King's Bench and Common Pleas (see Table 10.6) is largely the result of these changes in the way men did business. Moreover, it is possible that the development of negotiable promissory notes helped to cut down the number of lawsuits. Because of the ubiquity of small-scale borrowing and lending, most landowners and businessmen were simultaneously creditors and debtors. When the conditional bond was the primary means of arranging loans, creditors could not be lenient with their debtors because they themselves might need cash in order to pay debts of their own which were due under the strict terms of the bond. Hence one reason for the large number of lawsuits in the period from 1560 to 1640.[101] By contrast, since promissory notes enabled debts to be transferred, they helped to take some of the urgency, and hence some of the hostility, out of the debtor–creditor relationship. So, too, did the practice of encouraging partial payments or payments by instalments.

However, although they may have contributed to a general drop

99 PRO KB 125/151. King's Bench rule book, 1750. William Bohun, *Institutio Legalis: Or An Introduction to the Study and Practice of the Laws of England As Now Regulated and Amended by several late Statutes*, 3rd edn (London, 1724), p. 4; Francis, 'Practice, Strategy, and Institution', p. 827.

100 Holden, *The History of Negotiable Instruments*, pp. 30, 32, 36, 52, 66, 79, 99–100.

101 Thomas Wilson, *A Discourse Upon Usury*, ed. R. H. Tawney (London, 1925), p. 235.

in the amount of litigation, the growth in the number of actions on the case for debt also meant an increase in the percentage of all suits at Westminster which eventually ended up going for a trial before a jury. Since a defendant who had signed his name to a written agreement usually had little to gain by putting his case to a jury, relatively few cases of 'debt on specialty', as they were known, entered the records of suits sent for trial at assize. But actions on the case, where the promises to be kept were sometimes complicated or ill defined, and the penalties had not been prescribed by the litigants, were potentially much more likely to involve both fraud and contention. Over 50 per cent of all actions on the case which reached advanced stages in the King's Bench in 1750 went for trial at *nisi prius*.[102] Therefore, as the total number of actions on the case increased, so too did the percentage of all cases which were heard by a jury. In the Common Pleas in the 1680s and 1690s, between 20 and 25 per cent of all cases in advanced stages went to trial. In the King's Bench in 1750, 40 per cent did so.[103]

Litigation about debts and contracts was important because it was so frequent; the history of civil litigation between 1640 and 1750 is primarily the history of how English society made and enforced promises. Nevertheless, other types of legal business entered the court records, and Table 10.6, which displays the relative frequency of each of the forms of action at common law, provides a means of tracing its profile.[104]

We have seen already that many actions on the case involved debts or contracts, but although it is impossible to break it down statistically, this category also includes other important types of case including slander (malicious words), malfeasance (the inadequate performance of a task or obligation) and negligence. On the other hand, actions of ejectment were made up of a large number of collusive actions to establish titles to land as well as cases in which landlords were suing for rent or evicting tenants. Finally, trespass was another broad category which housed a wide range of disputes. It included allegations of assault resulting in personal injury as well as actions of false imprisonment. At the same time, trespass

---

[102] PRO IND 1/6194.
[103] PRO CP 36/11, which contains a contemporary analysis of the number of cases sent for trial versus those ('common judgements') which were not. PRO IND 1/6194.
[104] For more detail on the forms of action see Brooks, *Pettyfoggers and Vipers of the Commonwealth*, pp. 66–71.

frequently involved mishaps or disagreements associated with agricultural life such as the destruction of crops or the damaging of sheep by dogs, and the action was sometimes associated with cases which hinged on a disputed title to land. It was also used by husbands to sue men who had committed adultery with their wives. For example, in 1750 an inhabitant of Oxfordshire asked for £1,000 damages against a victualler of Wallington whom he accused of having carnally known his wife.[105]

Thanks to the notes which the judge Sir Dudley Ryder made of civil cases tried before him at the Middlesex assizes between 1754 and 1756, it is possible to penetrate more deeply into the complex issues which some of these civil actions actually involved. Predictably, actions on conditional bonds were settled with relatively little controversy once the existence of the bond had been proven. But a suit over a promissory note which was given in connection with the sale of 'slops', or civilian clothing, to a regiment of marines had to be put out to arbitration by three people who were familiar with the exact functions of military quartermasters.[106] In general, the striking feature of what can be described as the commercial cases is both the extent to which legal process was allowed to intervene in business affairs and the wide discretion left to juries. For example, a case in which the plaintiff accused an organ-maker of overcharging for an incompetent repair job raised questions about whether the work was done properly, whether the price was fair, and whether the organ-maker had taken too much profit from the work of his employees. Similarly, a suit for wages which Ann Byers brought against her employer, Sarah Mackay, led to a series of witnesses discussing the levels of pay due for various kinds of work in the mantua-maker's trade.[107]

Actions of assault, slander and unlawful imprisonment were also quite common. As in the seventeenth century, these appear frequently to have arisen out of the processes by which criminal accusations were brought during the early modern period. Since there was no professional police force, people who thought that crimes had been committed against them had to be active personally in getting constables to make arrests and in presenting

[105] PRO CP 40/3574, rot's. 567, 594. In 1750, 6 per cent of all Common Pleas, and 3 per cent of King's Bench cases involved the action of trespass and assault.

[106] Lincoln's Inn Library, London. Transcript of Dudley Ryder's Law Notes by K. L. Perrin: Doc. 12, p. 12; Doc. 16, p. 16.

[107] Ryder Law Notes: Doc. 12, p. 12; Doc. 13, p. 17.

accusations to JPs or judges. Hence actions for damages as a result of unlawful imprisonment, or for slander for words which implied that the plaintiff had committed a crime, constituted a method of countering unjust prosecutions or malicious rumours.[108] Equally, some people sought compensation for assaults through the civil rather than the criminal court system. A Dutchman who had been impressed on an English East Indiaman won both a moral case and £10 damages from the Middlesex jurors by bringing an action of assault against the ship's mate for immoderately punishing him. More surprisingly, a young distillery-worker successfully sued a squire for threatening him with a gun, tearing his clothing and keeping him prisoner for several hours.[109]

However, other actions of assault or slander seem to have originated from relatively more trivial petty quarrels. In many suits for assault tempers had flared suddenly, sometimes in conjunction with provocative words. In one such, a defence lawyer commented that 'this sort of action ought to be discouraged'. In several of the others, Ryder was understandably uncertain as to how to direct the jury, and the derisory damages of a shilling or so awarded by the jurors suggest that they found the task of assessing blame virtually impossible or hardly worth the effort.[110] It was much the same with many cases of slander, some of which involved business rivals making unkind remarks about each other, while many others seem the product of little more than personal hostility.[111] Nor was mid-eighteenth-century London short of litigious souls. A glazier who had slandered his local churchwarden at one point in their quarrel boasted that he 'liked a little law now and then'.[112]

Although they refer only to cases from metropolitan London, Ryder's notes suggest that much petty contention existed alongside

108 Brooks, *Pettyfoggers and Vipers of the Commonwealth*, pp. 107–11, 279. J. Kent, *The English Village Constable 1580–1642. A Social and Administrative Study* (Oxford, 1986), pp. 246, 261. R. H. Helmholz, 'Civil Trials and the Limits of Responsible Speech', in Helmholz and T. A. Green, *Juries, Libel, and Justice: The Role of English Juries in Seventeenth- and Eighteenth-Century Trials for Libel and Slander* (Los Angeles, 1984), pp. 3–36. Interestingly, John Jeffreys of Bath told Lord Camden that many men refused to become JPs because of the 'Great applica[tio]n necessary to avoid being entangled in Vexatious, harassing Law Suits, even for a slip, an Error, not a premeditated wrong'. Somerset RO, Letter Books of John Jeffreys, vol. 2, 10 August 1783.
109 Ryder Law Notes: Doc. 12, pp. 1, 8, 30; Doc. 13, p. 26; Doc. 16, pp. 34, 54.
110 Ryder Law Notes: Doc. 12, pp. 1, 11, 24, 59.
111 Ryder Law Notes: Doc. 12, pp. 15, 37, 50, 59; Doc. 16, pp. 19, 50.
112 Ryder Law Notes: Doc. 12, pp. 22–3.

more serious disputes, and this is a conclusion which also emerges from the more general picture found in Table 10.6. The significant increase between 1640 and 1750 in the percentages of trespass, ejectment and actions on the case is a warning against assuming that the mid-eighteenth century was much more tranquil than the mid-seventeenth. If we make the admittedly risky calculation of the number of cases involving actions of trespass or ejectment in 1640, as opposed to 1750, there appears to have been a decline of only 20 per cent compared with a much greater decrease in the overall volume of litigation. Unfortunately it is impossible to discover how many actions on the case involved slander as opposed to debt or other kinds of commercial case, but the great increase in the percentage of such suits raises doubts about whether there was in fact any significant drop in disputes over contentious words.

The most clear-cut changes in the nature of litigation between 1640 and 1750 appear, therefore, to have occurred in the field of interpersonal promises. Although bound up inextricably with technical legal developments, these changes reflect alterations in behaviour and attitudes among the urban middling sort and gentry which may have contributed to the decline of litigation. Much depends on the significance attached to the fact that the widespread use of sealed written agreements before 1640 gave way by 1750 to the informal written agreement or verbal promise as the primary means through which business transactions were conducted.

The conditional bond, the most common legal device of the period before 1640, presupposed the importance of having an agreement written down on parchment or paper and sealed with wax, presumably because one's neighbours, or potential jurors, could not otherwise be trusted. It was associated with a social world of contentious gentry and smallholders, and the psychological context in which it flourished is reflected in the writings of political and social observers. Thomas Hobbes's obsession with the problem of how people could be made to keep their promises was typical of English legal thinking from the 1520s up until the time he wrote in the middle of the seventeenth century.[113] The quip of the Chancery

---

[113] 'The Replication of a Serjeant At The Laws Of England', in J. A. Guy, ed., *Christopher St German On Chancery And Statute*, Selden Society, Supplementary Series, 6 (London, 1985), pp. 99–105. [Anon.], *A Petition to the Kings most excellent Maiestie, the Lords Spirituall and Temporall, and Commons of the Parliament now assembled, Wherein is declared the mischiefes and inconueniences, arising to the King and Commonwealth, by the Imprisonment of mens*

official George Norburie in the 1620s that a man's word without his signature on a bond was worthless is characteristic of his age.[114]

By contrast, the radically divergent viewpoint suggested by the phrase 'a man's word is his bond' seems to have arisen in the eighteenth century, and is consistent with the ways in which contracts were made at that date, at least amongst the urban middle classes.[115] It also corresponds with the observations of the eighteenth-century economist Adam Smith. In his lectures on jurisprudence, Smith postulated that peoples with highly developed commercial habits were more likely to keep their promises than those living in less civilized times and places. In this respect he thought the Dutch were ideal, but he also believed that by the second half of the eighteenth century the British were catching up.[116] Furthermore, there is evidence that such values were shared even in professional legal circles. The papers of the solicitor and town clerk of Bath, John Jeffreys, which include letters to the sometime Whig Chancellor Lord Camden, reveal a man who was tediously proud of his elevated sensibilities, who believed that 'Natural Justice . . . obliges every man . . . to render unto every Man what is substantially just and right', and who expressed revulsion at the contentiousness he found in some of the people with whom he had to deal.

Nevertheless, it is noteworthy that Jeffreys's patience could only be stretched so far. In 1778, he warned a man who owed him money that he was 'resolved . . . to be trifled with no longer, for I will use the means that the Law has given me for recovering money, let the consequences be what it will'.[117] More generally, there are three serious flaws in any explanation of the decline in litigation which concentrates exclusively on the emergence during the eighteenth century of more urbane views such as his.

First, many legal authorities were convinced that the replacement of the bond by verbal promises made fraud en-

bodies for Debt (London, 1622), p. 16. Thomas Hobbes, Leviathan (London, 1914 edn), pp. 66, 68, 70–1, 75–6.

114 G. Norburie, 'The Abuses and Remedies of Chancery', in F. Hargrave, ed., A Collection of Tracts Relative to the Laws of England (London, 1787), p. 433.

115 Brewer, 'Commercialization and Politics', p. 214.

116 Adam Smith, Lectures on Justice, Police, Revenue and Arms Delivered In The University of Glasgow . . . Reported by a Student in 1763, ed. E. Cannan [1896] (New York, 1964), pp. 253–9.

117 Somerset RO, Letter books of John Jeffreys, vol. 1, 12 October 1775, 21 December 1776, 19 December 1778, 24 September 1779. Vol. 2, 1 April 1783.

demic.[118] Second, the great trough in litigation was relatively short-lived. Central court business increased from the 1790s onwards. From 1700, and particularly after 1750, the erection of more and more courts of requests was accompanied by an overall increase in the number of lawsuits,[119] and brought growing numbers of the urban poor within the ambit of a very strict discipline which taught the necessity of honouring obligations. For instance, William Hutton claimed that he was deeply moved by the predicament of the great number of indebted families where the husband was both an apprentice and under age, but he was clear that the Birmingham court of requests seldom accepted a plea of minority in favour of a defendant, because that would teach him a 'wicked argument' against paying his just debts.[120]

Third, in the eighteenth century, as in the seventeenth, the sanction of imprisonment stood behind every business deal, behind the implicit bargain which took place every time a shopkeeper extended credit to an urban wage-labourer. In the common law courts, and in the courts of requests, every stage in a lawsuit, from the first writ of summons to that which called for a settlement at the conclusion, was backed up by the threat of imprisonment.[121] In fact, many courts of requests laid down schedules which specified the number of days in gaol which were necessary in order to purge a debt of so many tens of shillings.[122]

Despite the decline in litigation, it is unlikely that there was a proportionate decline in the number of prisoners, and in particular the number imprisoned for relatively small debts. A list of 359 debtors in the King's Bench prison in 1654 shows that most of them were there because they owed considerable sums of money (an average of £2,439 each).[123] In the early eighteenth century statutes

---

[118] Simpson, *Common Law of Contract*, pp. 592, 603
[119] Brooks, *Pettyfoggers and Vipers of the Commonwealth*, pp. 77–8.
[120] Hutton, *Courts of Requests*, pp. 25, 53.
[121] For a good outline of the procedure in the central courts, see J. Innes, 'The King's Bench Prison in the Later Eighteenth Century: Law, Authority and Order in a London Debtor's Prison', in J. Brewer and J. Styles, eds., *An Ungovernable People* (London, 1980), p. 252.
[122] *Parliamentary Papers. Appendix [Part II] To the Fourth Report . . . 1831–2*, Appendix (I), V: 'Returns of All Process Issued From Borough Courts, County Courts, Liberty Courts, Hundred Courts, and Courts of Requests'.
[123] *A List of all The Prisoners In the Upper Bench Prison, remaining in Custody the third of May, 1653 Delivered in by Sir John Lenthall to the Committee appointed by the Councell of State, for examining of the state of the said prison, with the times of their first Commitment . . .* (London, 1654).

for the relief of insolvent debtors frequently set the upper limit on the amount to be relieved at £100, which suggests that large numbers of people were imprisoned for less than that relatively small sum. In the 1720s, petitions for the relief of imprisoned debtors came not just from London, but from the provinces as well.[124] Samuel Johnson was only one of many people in the mid-eighteenth century who thought that more men died as a result of imprisonment for debt than in war.[125] In the 1780s, the population of the King's Bench prison fluctuated at between 400 and 500 debtors each year, and a survey of 1789 suggested that no less than 165 of them owed less than £20. Arrest on *mesne* process out of the Westminster courts had become a fearful scourge, which, it was claimed, ruined thousands.[126] With the introduction of additional courts of requests many more poorer people than ever before were involved. Alexander Grant calculated the total number of prisoners for debt in 1789 at 16,409. Not surprisingly, this period also saw the establishment of charitable foundations to relieve their plight.[127]

V

In conclusion, since it was a period of very low overall levels of litigation, there was in one sense certainly less contention in the eighteenth century than there had been before or there was to be afterwards. However, what we do not know is how many people were prevented from using the law because of its inaccessibility, and who therefore turned to arbitration to settle their disputes, or who suffered the frustration of having to lose what they considered their just causes. The numbers are impossible to measure, but the volume of complaint was loud. Whereas much pre-1640 criticism of

---

[124] 2 George II, c. 22. Petitions in 1728 were received from Bristol, Lincoln and Coventry. *Commons Journals*, vol. 21, pp. 228, 236. A report on the Fleet prison in London suggests that as many as 520 were incarcerated there. *Ibid.*, pp. 275–6.

[125] P. Haagen, 'Eighteenth-Century English Society and the Debt Law', in S. Cohen and A. Scull, eds., *Social Control and the State* (Oxford, 1983), p. 224.

[126] Innes, 'The King's Bench Prison', p. 263. [Grant], *The Public Monitor*, p. vii. Grant underestimated the total population of the King's Bench prison at about 300 persons. Grant, *The Progress and Practice of A Modern Attorney*, pp. 62–73.

[127] [Grant], *The Public Monitor*, p. 19. J. Neild, *An Account of the Rise, Progress, And Present State of the Society for the Discharge and Relief of Persons Imprisoned for Small Debts Throughout England and Wales* (London, 1802).

the legal system stressed the disruptive social consequences of ready access to the law amongst the lower orders,[128] after 1700 the reiteration of the difficulty of finding justice in the English legal system is too persistent to be ignored. Moreover, while it is certainly true that recourse to law became less frequent during the eighteenth century in rural areas, imprisonment for debt and payment through the instalment plan as promoted by the courts of requests emerged as major features of urban life.

As we have seen, there is some evidence from the gentry and middle ranks of society to support Lawrence Stone's view that the drop in litigation was associated with a spread of urban values which led to a decline in contentiousness, and, perhaps, a growing willingness to honour obligations, but it is hard to disentangle this conclusively from the consequences of social and legal change, or the unsavoury reputation of the law. The middling orders in particular found the common law itself a constant source of irritation and injustice. Meanwhile, the courts of requests and imprisonment for debt subjected the urban poor to arbitrary control over their personal liberty by their creditors and local worthies which hardly contributed to a relaxation of social tension. William Hutton of Birmingham never forgot the night in 1791 when a group of rioters manhandled him and set fire to his house. The mob shouted 'Down with the Court of Conscience!'; significantly, their rage appears to have been associated with the way in which the court dealt with tallies run up in ale-houses.[129]

Changes in the patterns of litigation in eighteenth-century England are best explained by social and economic change in both urban and rural society, and by the further ossification of the 'ancient regime' bureaucratic practices of the common law courts. Furthermore, there are a number of striking similarities and interconnections between the administration of the criminal and the civil law during the period.[130] In both fields, urban growth and the process of proletarianization were the most important stimulants to change. If, by 1750, concern about rising levels of crime and the emergence of alternatives to the death sentence were associated

---

[128] Brooks, *Pettyfoggers and Vipers of the Commonwealth*, pp. 133–6.

[129] William Hutton, *The Life of William Hutton, F.A.S.S., including A Particular Account of the Riots at Birmingham in 1791. Written By Himself* (London, 1816), pp. 180–5.

[130] The view of the criminal law discussed here is taken largely from Beattie, *Crime and the Courts in England*, especially chapter 11.

largely with questions about how to deal with the crimes of the urban poor and the reform of their behaviour, the debates over the establishment of the courts of requests hinged on the necessity of exercising financial discipline and moral regulation over the same groups of people. Just as transportation to the colonies and terms of imprisonment were developed as 'secondary' punishments to the death sentence, so, too, the growing use of repayment of debts by weekly instalments was an alternative to the hopelessness of imprisoning poor people for debt. The plight of imprisoned debtors had been, since the later sixteenth century, the subject of an endless dialectic in which humanistic concern, and despair over the illogical economic consequences of the practice, contested with a fear of deceit and the dangers of allowing people to get away without honouring their obligations. But the injustice of a system which was frequently perceived as one in which unfortunate people were punished as if they were criminals became even more obvious in the later eighteenth century, when men were thinking increasingly that punishments should be proportionate to crimes and imprisonment was being adopted as an alternative to hanging for the punishment of more serious offences.[131] At the same time, the growing involvement of the legal profession in criminal trials for felonies fits so well into the chronology of the early eighteenth-century decline in litigation that it is impossible not to suspect that lawyers sought a share in criminal business at least in part to make up for the difficulty of earning a living in the civil courts.

Interestingly, the greatest differences between the administration of the civil and the criminal law appear to lie in the attitude of the public towards each. After 1750, there is evidence that people who felt themselves to be victims of crime, like those who were owed bad debts, were put off from using the law because of high costs. But according to Professor Beattie, before the mid-century, and outside London afterwards, there was very little hostility to the existing system of criminal law. By comparison, the civil law was subject to a constant stream of criticism which reached particularly acute levels in the 1690s, the later 1720s, the 1790s, and the 1820s and 1830s. In this respect, the crucial differences between

---

[131] Arrest on *mesne* process was abolished in 1838, but aspects of the system continued into the twentieth century. G. R. Rubin, 'Law, Poverty and Imprisonment for Debt, 1869–1914' in Rubin and Sugarman, eds., *Law, Economy, and Society*, p. 241.

the two systems lay in the role played by bureaucracy and the legal profession. Eighteenth-century criminal law was still largely a local and non-professional process. Judges from Westminster delivered the gaols all over the country, but in rural areas all of the steps leading to a trial took place in the neighbourhood where the alleged offence occurred, and the most important officials involved, the constables and JPs, were largely unpaid members of the local elite. On the other hand, a civil lawsuit which went to Westminster could not proceed without paying off sinecurists in London for largely incomprehensible steps which were necessary if the case was to progress, and lawyers, never the most popular of social groups in England, were usually seen as being busy manipulating the system for largely unscrupulous ends.

Thanks to the high profile of the court officials in London, and to the fact that in matters of civil law a squire paid as much as a pleb, some gentry MPs in the years around 1730 actively led demands for law reform. However, the middling sort, particularly the urban middle classes, were the main forces calling for substantial change in the civil side of the common law in the eighteenth century. Always an important source of litigants, they became increasingly the primary customers of the courts as the eighteenth century progressed. This is not to say that the landed gentry had no interest in the law and the legal system, but by 1750 their economic and social pre-eminence was evidently sufficiently secure to render recourse to law less frequent than it had been before, a point which is particularly evident in the decline of Chancery litigation. By contrast, it was the urban middling orders who were responsible for parliamentary legislation which enlarged the use of promissory notes, petitioned for the establishment of courts of requests, and gave hostile evidence to parliamentary inquiries into the common law in the 1820s. Much of eighteenth-century substantive law must have been shaped to a very significant extent by these same social groups, albeit with the intervention of lawyers. It is clearly no longer tenable to think of English law in the eighteenth century as simply a matter of gentry hegemony over the rest of the population.

11. *Church and state allied: the failure of parliamentary reform of the universities, 1688–1800*

JOHN GASCOIGNE

There is a moral for historians in Sherlock Holmes's success in solving one of his mysteries by reflecting on the implications of the fact that a dog did *not* bark in the night – for the absence of change can be as important a problem as change itself. The hostility to reform which was so marked a feature of the 'long eighteenth century' – 1688 to 1832 – is as important for understanding the nature of that society as the progress of reform is for evaluating the Victorian period. Among the possible avenues for explaining why reform was resisted for so long and so successfully in the period between the Glorious Revolution and the Great Reform Bill is an analysis of the relations between church and state.[1] The Glorious Revolution was, after all, a settlement that affected both church and state, and throughout the eighteenth century attempts to change the ecclesiastical order were resisted as potential threats to the constitution more generally. Indeed, when widespread political reform was finally achieved in the 1830s it was preceded by a breakdown in the traditional alliance between church and state, with the abolition in 1828 of civil penalties for Protestant dissenters and, more momentous still, the passage in 1829 of the Catholic Emancipation Bill – a measure which Cannon describes as 'the battering ram that broke down the old unreformed system'.[2]

This alliance between church and state, which underlay the foundations of the English old regime, was reflected in miniature in unreformed Oxford and Cambridge – not least in the fact that the universities emerged from the eighteenth century with no funda-

[1] On the importance of the church in the unreformed constitution see the recent work by J. C. D. Clark, *English Society 1688–1832* (Cambridge, 1985); also J. Gascoigne, 'Anglican Latitudinarianism and Political Radicalism in the late Eighteenth Century', *History*, 71 (1986), pp. 22–38.

[2] J. Cannon, *Parliamentary Reform 1640–1832* (Cambridge, 1973), p. 191.

mental changes to their constitution. The close association between the universities and the defence of the established church was of long standing. Appropriately, those interregnum radicals opposed to a state church had directed considerable criticism at the universities as a 'fountain of ministers'.[3] When the union of crown and altar was restored after 1660, the new regime devoted particular attention to ensuring that the universities were purged of Nonconformists and harnessed to the task of re-establishing the Church of England after its time of troubles. The fact that dissenters were excluded from taking degrees until 1854 at Oxford and 1856 at Cambridge, and from holding fellowships at either university until 1871, further underscored the long and close association between the universities and the established church. Throughout the eighteenth century, Oxford and Cambridge, despite their often troubled relations with the state, continued to act as an integral part of the larger social order – for it was the universities which trained the clergy of the established church and which were chiefly responsible for the ideological defence of the church and the traditional patterns of social deference and order with which the ecclesiastical system was so closely intertwined.

The strongly clerical character of the universities is evident in the fact that at Oxford at the turn of the eighteenth century, 70 per cent of graduates entered the church, while at mid-eighteenth-century Cambridge this figure rose to 76 per cent.[4] As Bennett writes of the eighteenth-century universities: 'Oxford and Cambridge were the key institutions in the national religious establishment',[5] or, as a would-be university reformer pungently put it in 1717: 'There is the centre of good or evil, as it is to be found in the clergy, there are the roots from whence they spring; the schools from whence they come forth, finished either for God or the devil.'[6]

On the other hand, although Oxford and Cambridge saw their primary function as the education of the clergy, they also continued

[3] C. Hill, 'The Radical Critics of Oxford and Cambridge in the 1650s', in his *Change and Continuity in Seventeenth-Century England* (London, 1974), p. 146.

[4] G. V. Bennett, 'University, Society and Church', in L. S. Sutherland and L. G. Mitchell, eds., *History of the University of Oxford. The Eighteenth Century* (Oxford, 1986), p. 393, and C. A. Anderson and M. Schnaper, *School and Society in England: Social Background of Oxford and Cambridge Students* (Washington, 1952), p. 8.

[5] Bennett, 'University, Society and Church', p. 360.

[6] Anon, *Reasons for Visiting the Universities* . . . (London, 1717), p. 28.

to provide many of the leisured laity with some measure of educational polish. True, as Stone has pointed out,[7] the post-Restoration universities were less popular with the landed classes than with their pre-Civil War counterparts – perhaps because of the greater indifference on the part of the eighteenth-century laity to the concerns of the clergy. None the less, a sizeable and influential portion of eighteenth-century England's politicians passed through Oxford and Cambridge. All of the eighteenth-century Prime Ministers (if one takes Walpole as the first of that line), apart from the Duke of Devonshire and the Earl of Bute, spent some time at one of the universities, as did approximately one-half of all MPs.[8] This remarkable concentration of the elite in two educational institutions – a situation which had few parallels elsewhere in Europe – helps explain the cohesion of the English establishment, since a considerable proportion of it was linked by a common education and, in many cases, first-hand acquaintance. Moreover, the commingling of the sons of the governing classes with the trainee clergy of the established church was a further illustration of the way in which the universities reflected in microcosm the alliance between church and state. Both churchman and parliamentarian had in many cases received the same basic education and were therefore likely to share common intellectual presuppositions. Significantly, specialist clerical seminaries were not established until after the traditional alliance between church and state had been fundamentally altered in the nineteenth century.

Since Oxford and Cambridge were so central to the alliance of church and state, an examination of the attempts to reform them should help cast light not only on the nature of the universities themselves but also on the character of the unreformed constitution, both political and ecclesiastical, before it was remoulded in the course of the nineteenth century. With these questions in mind this study focuses on attempts at reform which were initiated by Parliament (or by those associated with it) rather than on movements for reform from within the universities themselves, since the

---

[7] Lawrence Stone, 'The Size and Composition of the Oxford Student Body 1580–1910', in Stone, ed., *The University in Society*, 2 vols (Princeton, 1974), vol. 1, pp. 46–57.

[8] In general elections between 1734 and 1761 the proportion of MPs with an Oxbridge education was *c.* 45 per cent, rising to *c.* 50 per cent in the period 1768–1812. G. P. Judd, *Members of Parliament, 1734–1832* (New Haven, 1955), p. 42.

actions (or, at times, inaction) of government bring the issues of church–state relations into clearer view.

The essay begins by examining the way in which the strained relations between church and state produced by the Glorious Revolution and the Hanoverian succession helped to produce the most serious of eighteenth-century proposals for reform of the universities, culminating in an abortive bill in 1719. The failure of this bill was a testimony to the growing realization, even on the part of some anti-clerical Whigs, of the dangers of further alienating the church. The decline in anti-clericalism by the mid-eighteenth century can be seen in the lack of success of proposals for university reform prompted by continued manifestations of Oxford Jacobitism in the wake of the 1745 uprising. In the late eighteenth century the bonds between church and state strengthened still more, which, it will be argued, helps to account for the further waning of any movement for reform of the universities.

I

In the recitation of the misdeeds of James II and his 'evil Counsellors', which William of Orange issued on 30 September 1688 to justify his forthcoming invasion of England, the behaviour towards Oxford and Cambridge of the King and his ministers received specific mention. James had undermined those 'laws enacted for the preservation of those [traditional] rights and liberties, and of the Protestant Religion', among other ways, by appointing papists to university offices and, in particular, by permitting his Commissioners for Ecclesiastical Causes to

> have turned out a President chosen by the Fellows of Magdalen College [Oxford], and afterwards all the fellows of that college, without so much as citing them before any court that could take legal cognisance of that affair, or obtaining any sentence against them by a competent judge ... and now those evil counsellors have put the said College wholly into the hands of the Papists.[9]

These were accusations which were long remembered, both as instances of the importance of the universities in the defence of the established church and as illustrations of the dangers posed by

---

9 E. N. Williams, *The Eighteenth Century Constitution* (Cambridge, 1960), pp. 11–12.

outside interference in their affairs – or, indeed, in those of any private corporation.

Although James II had clashed so spectacularly with both universities in his attempt to open these Anglican preserves to his Roman Catholic co-religionaries, James's deposition involved for many dons too drastic a reappraisal of the doctrine of passive obedience which had been central to the Restoration church. Thus the universities, like the church more generally, responded to the Glorious Revolution with faint enthusiasm and even some outright opposition. Despite Oxford's reputation as the 'home of lost causes', the number of non-jurors was greater at Cambridge: at the former it was twenty-six and at the latter forty-one.[10] Moreover, although the great majority of fellows outwardly conformed to the new regime, many of them remained inwardly ambivalent. As the Cambridge don William Whiston later wrote in his autobiography:

Yet do I well remember, that the far greatest part of those of the university and clergy that then took the oaths to the government, seemed to me to take them with a doubtful conscience, if not against its dictates. Nor considering the doctrines of passive obedience and non-resistance, they had generally been brought up in, and generally signed before, was it to be otherwise expected.[11]

This reluctant response to the Glorious Revolution on the part of the clergy in general, and Oxford and Cambridge in particular, focused public attention on the universities and raised the question of how far they should remain dominated by the clerical estate. Faint echoes of this debate can be heard in the proposal made in the House of Commons in February 1691 to add a clause to the 'Act for Conforming the Charters of the Universities' which would permit colleges to allow any number of fellows to profess law or medicine.[12] Such a move would have meant a major change in the character of the universities, where the great majority of fellowships (87 per cent at Cambridge)[13] were reserved for those taking orders. William III, however, wished to avoid a confrontation with the clergy, and his attitude helps account for the failure

---

[10] C. Wordsworth, *Social Life at the English Universities in the Eighteenth Century* (Cambridge, 1874), pp. 603–5.

[11] W. Whiston, *Memoirs of the Life and Writings of . . .* (London, 1753), pp. 27–8.

[12] C. H. Cooper, *Annals of Cambridge*, 5 vols (Cambridge, 1842–1908), vol. 4, pp. 16–18.

[13] Figure derived from Cambridge University Library, MS Mm.1.48, fo. 455.

of this proposal as well as for the rejection of Lord Somers's suggestion that there be a royal visitation of the universities.[14] Relations between church and state continued to be strained by clerical hostility to the conception of the nature of the monarchy and the church which, the Whigs claimed, was basic to the revolutionary settlement, and there was further agitation to reduce the clerical character of the universities. The hostility of anti-clerical sections of the Whig party to the clergy, and in particular to their traditional bastions, the universities, was so great that in 1708 Jonathan Swift was moved to write in his *Sentiments of a Church of England Man* ... :

> It seems clear to me that the whigs might easily have procured and maintained a majority among the clergy and perhaps in the universities, if they had not too much encouraged or connived at this intemperance of speech and virulence of pen in the worst and most prostitute of their party; among whom there has been ... such scandalous reflections on universities for infecting the youth of the nation with arbitrary and Jacobite principles that it was natural for those who had the care of religion and education, to apprehend some general design of altering the constitution of both.[15]

In 1709, the year after the publication of Swift's pamphlet, there was another abortive attempt in Parliament to relieve fellows of the obligation to take orders – a proposal that was prompted partly by the attempt of the warden of All Souls to insist that a number of Whig lawyer–fellows, notably including the deist Matthew Tindal, take orders.[16] Churchmen of all political persuasions saw this proposal as an attack on their order. Though a Whig, Archbishop Tenison rallied the bishops to oppose the bill,[17] while Bishop Trelawny, another staunch defender of the Glorious Revolution, attacked the bill with characteristic pugnacity as calculated to turn the colleges into 'nurseries of lawyers and attorneys' and to expose them to litigation 'in Westminster Hall, where atheism, socinianism and a proper detestation of the principles and government of the universities is allowed and justified'.[18] Like Trelawny, Swift regarded the bill as indicative of a campaign by the Whigs to break

14 W. R. Ward, *Georgian Oxford* (Oxford, 1958), p. 23.
15 Cited in N. Sykes, 'Archbishop Wake and the Whig Party: 1716–23. A Study in Incompatibility of Temperament', *Cambridge Historical Journal*, 8 (1945), p. 93.
16 Bennett, 'University, Society and Church', p. 391.   17 *Ibid.*
18 Ward, *Georgian Oxford*, p. 34.

the universities' traditionally close association with the church and 'to remove the care of educating youth out of the hands of the clergy, who are apt to infuse into their pupils too great a regard for the church and monarchy'.[19]

II

Swift's comments underline the close association between the Whig party and university reform in the early eighteenth century. This became still more evident after the accession of the Hanoverians in 1714 provided the Whigs with the opportunity to settle old scores with the Tories and their clerical supporters. In the last years of Queen Anne's reign, the Tories had sought to undo some of the effects of the Act of Toleration of 1689 and, thereby, to shore up the position of the established church by passing the Occasional Conformity Act of 1711 and the Schism Act of 1714. This latter act, if properly enforced, would have eliminated Oxford and Cambridge's main competitors, the dissenting academies. But this programme of consolidating Anglican privilege – and, with it, Tory power – fell to the ground with the death of Queen Anne, and the Tories made themselves even more vulnerable to Whig revenge through their disastrous mishandling of the succession issue. Along with the repeal of the Occasional Conformity and Schism Acts in 1719, another measure which the Whigs sought as part of their programme to break Tory power and more effectively to subordinate the clergy to a Whig-dominated state was a reform of the universities – for it was these institutions which would form the minds of the next generation of clergy and help to reinforce in them a continued hostility to many of the changes in church and state wrought by the Glorious Revolution.

In contemplating government action against Oxford and Cambridge, the Whig ministry was spurred on by a rather heterogeneous coalition of forces. On the one hand, there were members of the clergy concerned to improve church–state relations and to strengthen the universities as places of sound clerical education; on the other, there were the 'true Whigs' or 'commonwealthmen', who were influenced by deistic views which made them suspicious of the claims of revealed religion and hostile to the power of an estab-

[19] Cited in J. A. W. Rembert, 'Swift and the Dialectical Tradition' (unpublished Ph.D. thesis, University of Cambridge, 1975), p. 124.

lished church. The clerically-dominated universities provided an obvious target for such commonwealthmen, who believed that human reason was the true source of all knowledge and that education should therefore be removed from the grasp of a clerical caste claiming to be the custodians of revealed truth. The universities made themselves even more vulnerable to such an assault by their behaviour during the 1715 Jacobite uprising: Cambridge had been relatively faithful to the Hanoverian regime (although even there undergraduate demonstrations occurred in favour of the Pretender),[20] but Oxford's loyalty had been so doubtful that it was necessary to send troops to garrison the city. The officers of this force conveyed evidence of widespread Jacobite sympathy within the university, which further alarmed the government.[21] Such behaviour was grist to the mill of those anti-clerical commonwealthmen who hoped to achieve some reduction in clerical control of the universities and, with it, a decline in ecclesiastical influence in society more generally.

In 1717, the commonwealthman Robert Molesworth renewed his assault on the universities in his *Count Patkul*, an assault which he had earlier outlined in his influential *Account of Denmark* (1694). In the preface to the *Account* he had combined an attack on the principle of passive obedience and on clerical power with the assertion that 'The constitution of our universities, as to learning, seems as unfortunately regulated as it is to politics', since their statutes had been framed by those 'who had a quite different notion and taste of learning from what the world had at present . . . '[22] Nor could Molesworth be dismissed as a powerless crank: in 1714 he was elected an MP and thereafter he received various marks of royal favour. In 1714 he was made privy councillor for Ireland and a commissioner for trade and the plantations, and in 1719 the King elevated him to the baronetage. His influence also helped to promote the work of a number of his deistic associates, of whom the best known was John Toland.

Like Molesworth, Toland also urged the government to take action against the universities to reduce their dependence on the

[20] B. Lenman, *The Jacobite Risings in Britain 1689–1746* (London, 1980), p. 116.
[21] P. Langford, 'Tories and Jacobites 1714–1751', in Sutherland and Mitchell, *Eighteenth-Century Oxford*, p. 106.
[22] C. Robbins, *The Eighteenth-Century Commonwealthman* . . . (Cambridge, Mass., 1959), p. 101; R. Molesworth, *An Account of Denmark* . . . (London, 1694), p. 28.

church. In his *Memorial presented to a Minister of State, soon after his Majesty King George's Accession to the Crown*, Toland argued that the clergy were 'made equally proud and insolent at the universities'. To diminish the clerical character of the universities, he proposed that the requirement that most fellows should take orders ought to be abolished and that the Crown should encourage the universities to cultivate such secular professions as agriculture, navigation and mining.[23] Like Molesworth, too, Toland renewed his attack in 1717, when reform on the universities was high on the political agenda, and in his *State Anatomy* (1717) he asked: 'Why may not Oxford, for example, be reformed or purged by a royal visitation tomorrow, as Aberdeen was the other day, or as Oxford itself was at the Reformation?' Predictably, Toland envisaged that such a visitation would reduce the clerical character of the university and so change its intellectual life. He was hostile to the type of scholarship pursued at Oxford, which was known for its study of the historical bases of Anglican belief,[24] and he expressed the hope 'that instead of the bare editors of old books, they [Oxford dons] become the authors of new ones'. To spur the Whigs to action, he harped on the theme that the university actively propagated views opposed 'to those revolution-principles upon which the present succession is grounded'.[25]

Commonwealthmen such as Molesworth or Toland represented one extreme of the spectrum of the universities' critics, but there was also agitation for a visitation of Oxford and Cambridge from a very different group of critics: members of the clergy who, unlike many of their brethren, thought it essential for the welfare of the established church to improve its relations with the Whigs and who consequently wished to intervene to prevent the universities from continuing to act as centres of clerical defiance. Motives such as these had prompted Bishop Patrick of Ely to propose in the House of Lords, after rowdy high-church demonstrations at Cambridge in the course of the 1705 elections, 'that the judges may consider how far a royal visitation may be necessary to reclaim these disorders'.[26]

23 J. Toland, *A Collection of Several Pieces*, 2 vols (London, 1726), vol. 2, pp. 240, 241, 248.
24 Bennett, 'University, Society and Church', p. 359, and M. Hunter, 'The Origins of the Oxford University Press', *The Book Collector*, 24 (1975), pp. 511–34.
25 J. Toland, *State Anatomy*, 3rd edn (London, [1717]), pp. 71, 72, 74.
26 C. Jones, 'Debates in the House of Lords on "The Church in Danger", 1705 and on Dr Sacheverell's Impeachment, 1710', *Historical Journal*, 19 (1976), p. 767.

Some clergy, too, felt that Oxford and Cambridge were not properly fulfilling their basic function of training the clergy and forming both lay and clerical students in proper habits of morality and sobriety. For such critics of the universities, the increasing interest of the Whigs in the cause of university reform provided an opportunity to see their proposals put into practice.

Among the most active of the clerical critics of the universities was the learned Humphrey Prideaux, dean of Norwich. Prideaux's objections to the standard of discipline at the universities were of long standing: in 1692, when asked by his brother-in-law to recommend a college for his son, Prideaux replied, 'I think that Cambridge method of education preferable to that of Oxford, though as to the discipline, it is too loose for this age in both of them.'[27]. The growing interest of the Whigs in the possibility of a royal visitation of the universities provided Prideaux with the opportunity to see some of his long-contemplated reforms implemented. Although a strong supporter of the Hanoverian succession, Prideaux himself was not closely identified with either of the two warring political parties,[28] but naturally it was to the Whigs that he turned in his search for political allies. Thus in 1715, following discussions with the Secretary of State, Lord Townshend,[29] he drew up his 'Articles of Reformation for the Two Universities',[30] a document which he hoped would provide a blueprint for government action.

In his 'Articles' Prideaux offered minute prescriptions about such predictable disciplinary matters as the time of college prayers, the hour of locking the gates, the prevention of members of the university from resorting to taverns and the expulsion of 'lewd women'. However, he also revealed his concern that the universities were wanting not only in their standard of discipline but also in their standard of theological instruction.[31] Prideaux's motive for instituting a visitation of the universities was directly opposed to that of the commonwealthmen: where they hoped to see the universities

[27] Historical Manuscripts Commission, 5th report, Pine-Coffin MSS, p. 374.
[28] Anon, *Life of Prideaux* (London, 1748), p. 150.
[29] Oxford, Christ Church, Wake MS 20, fo. 30.
[30] Oxford, Bodleian Library, MS Top. Oxon, e.125. Printed (with a few additions) in *Life of Prideaux*, pp. 199–237.
[31] Similar criticisms of the universities were made by the Cambridge cleric Dr John Edwards, in an unpublished MS that dates from the same period. *Cambridge Antiquarian Society Communications*, no. 8 (1866–7), pp. 126–34.

secularized both in their personnel and their curriculum, Prideaux wished to see the universities' clerical function reinforced and strengthened through a reform of both their discipline and their standard of theological teaching and writing. Prideaux was concerned to make the universities act as a more effective bulwark against the threats to the established church posed by such writers as Molesworth, Toland and a host of other adversaries. 'Atheists, Deists, Socinians, Arians, Presbyterians, Independents, Anabaptists, and other adversaries and sectaries', he wrote, 'surround us on every side, and are set as in battle array against us: and if we do not come armed and provided with equal knowledge and learning to the conflict, how shall we be able to support our cause against them?'[32] To meet such threats Prideaux proposed in his 'Articles' that the universities demand from their undergraduates a knowledge of the biblical languages and that no student should be permitted to graduate until 'he shall have undergone an Examination of his knowledge of the Christian religion and be able to give a good account thereof as taught and professed in the Church of England'.

In the eyes of the Whig ministry, such proposals to advance the universities' good order and sound religion were of far less interest than the mechanism for government intervention which Prideaux suggested might be used to achieve these ends. Prideaux proposed that an act of Parliament establish a standing committee of twenty-one (six from the Commons, six from the Lords and six nominated by the King, together with the two archbishops and the Lord Chancellor or Lord Keeper) with power 'to visit the said universities and to reform and correct all excesses and defects so that these places of public education may be made in the best manner to answer the end of their institution'. Such a committee would allow the ministry to crush university Jacobitism by ensuring that senior posts were given to those with sound pro-Hanoverian credentials, and the presence of the two archbishops would help to lessen clerical outrage.

While the Whig ministry did not give legislative form to any of Prideaux's specific proposals, his document none the less helped to focus government attention on the practical details of university reform. It was also an indication that a visitation of the universities might not necessarily lead to a full-scale confrontation with all

[32] A. D. Godley, *Oxford in the Eighteenth Century* (London, 1908), p. 201.

sections of the clergy, particularly since Prideaux was to be active in recruiting episcopal support for such a move. Thus on 10 February 1716 Prideaux sent a copy of his 'Articles' to William Wake, the newly-consecrated Archbishop of Canterbury, urging him to use his influence to initiate a visitation of Oxford and Cambridge as a means of bringing about basic reforms within the church. 'What at this time seems most necessary to be done', wrote Prideaux to the archbishop, 'for the redeeming of this Church out of its present dangers and distractions is to reform the two universities and regulate the matter of ordinations and the latter can scarce be effected without the other.'[33]

When Wake replied by pointing out some of the difficulties which stood in the way of such a visitation, Prideaux responded in a letter written on the 23 February 1716 suggesting that he obtain suitable legislation if necessary:

> for if the two fountains of learning must still remain in their dirt nothing but dirty streams can be sent out from them all over the nation to the corrupting of all orders of men among us and we have already found too much of it especially among the clergy scarce one in five of them being what they should be.

Moreover, added Prideaux, there was no time more appropriate than the present to achieve such a reform of the universities 'considering the provocations which both of them have at present given the government'. Perhaps in order to sting the reluctant Wake into action, Prideaux combined his remarks on the need to reform the universities with an exhortation to Wake to check the behaviour of those unruly high-churchmen who had challenged the power of the bishops (and that of the government) in Convocation. In his less than tactful manner, Prideaux urged Wake and his fellow bishops 'to resume their authority (which hath been too much dropped of late) and so far exert it as to make the clergy know that they are their superiors, which too many of them of late have forgot'.[34]

Prideaux's linking of the cause of university reform with the need for the episcopate to re-establish its authority over the lower clergy and to ensure their obedience to established authority in church and state was a sound tactical move. Wake and other members of the episcopate were greatly concerned at the damage that had been done, and that was still being done, to the relations between church

[33] Wake MS 20, fo. 30.   [34] *Ibid.*, fo. 35.

and state by the claim made by the high-church leaders of the lower house of Convocation that Convocation was independent of royal control. The concern of the bishops was further heightened by the frequent refusal of the lesser clergy in the lower house to comply with the wishes of the bishops in the upper house. The Convocation crisis dated from the publication of *Letter of a Convocation Man* in 1697 by Francis Atterbury of Christ Church, who, along with other Oxford high-churchmen, did much to foment and lengthen the controversy[35] – once again emphasizing the need for a visitation of that university. It was the need to restore better relations between church and state, and the bishops' determination to assert their authority over the lower clergy, which explain why Archbishop Wake was eventually to follow Prideaux's suggestion and join with the Whig ministry in planning a visitation of the universities – even though such a project was also associated with such notorious anti-clericals as Molesworth and Toland.

III

In 1717, Wake was closely consulted by Lord Chief Justice Parker (after 1721, Earl of Macclesfield) when he, along with Lord Chancellor Cowper, came to draw up a 'Bill for the Reformation of the two Universities'.[36] An experienced politician, Parker was no doubt well aware of the importance of involving the Anglican hierarchy in a move which was so closely linked with the interests of the church. Among Parker's papers is an undated manuscript entitled 'A Memorial Relating to the Universities'[37] which indicates his close interest in the subject of university reform – an interest that may well have been stimulated by Parker's active involvement in the prosecution of Sacheverell in 1710, a trial which made apparent the danger that high-church principles posed to the Whig party. Parker's 'Memorial' reflects this hostility to clerical power: in it he proposed that the universities should be prevented from purchasing further livings (which would have given them greater independence from secular patrons), and he also suggested that clerical restrictions on college fellowships be lifted, opening

[35] G. V. Bennett, 'Against the Tide: Oxford under William III', in Sutherland and Mitchell, *Eighteenth-Century Oxford*, p. 57.

[36] *Cf.* two undated letters of Parker to Wake asking him to comment on drafts of the bill. Wake MS 15 (not folioed).

[37] B[ritish] L[ibrary] MS Stowe 799, fos. 1–13.

half of them to laymen in order to provide 'greater encouragement to law and physic'. He also advocated the teaching of more secular disciplines within the universities, in particular 'the law of nature and nations', chemistry, mathematics and experimental natural philosophy, although he was concerned, too, that the teaching of divinity be reformed and made more systematic. His determination to ensure that only the politically acceptable should hold senior office in the universities is apparent in his proposal that the heads of colleges should be appointed by the great officers of state 'and such of the archbishops and bishops as shall be thought proper'.

In the 'Bill for the Reformation of the two Universities' Parker and his Whig colleagues went much further than the measures suggested for political control of the universities in his 'Memorial'. Not only were the headships of colleges placed in the gift of the crown but also virtually all other university posts down to those of undergraduate scholars and exhibitioners. Unlike the 'Memorial', the bill was entirely concerned with the political significance of the universities and had nothing to say on academic matters. The political motives for the bill were evident from its preamble, which spoke of 'the wild attempts of men of turbulent and fanatical spirits to make schisms and divisions in the church and to overthrow the supremacy of the crown'.[38]

Like most bills it was no doubt the product of compromise – in this case of parties which could agree on little more than that Oxford and Cambridge ought to be made more politically accept- able to the Hanoverian regime and its ministers. Whig politicians such as Parker had little interest in the religious goals of such would-be clerical reformers as Prideaux or Wake and were mindful of the pressures from the anti-clerical Whigs who moved in circles which were influenced by the commonwealthmen. On the other hand, the politicians knew that the passage of the bill would be greatly eased if it were seen to have the support of churchmen such as Wake, who would naturally be opposed to the attempts by 'true Whigs' like Molesworth and Toland and, to a lesser extent, those of more mainstream Whigs like Parker, to lessen the clerical character of the universities. Thus the goals of the two main sources of support for the reform of the universities – Whig anti-clericalism and clerical concern at the universities' failings as effective sem-

[38] B. Williams, *Stanhope. A Study in Eighteenth-Century War and Diplomacy* (Oxford, 1932), p. 456.

inaries loyal to the established order in church and state – virtually cancelled themselves out. The result, then, was a bill which was concerned solely with the political mechanism for subduing the universities rather than with any reappraisal of the aims or methods of Oxford and Cambridge.

By contrast, what appears to have been an earlier draft of the bill in the papers of the third Earl of Sunderland (Lord Privy Seal, 1715–18; first Lord of the Treasury, 1718–21)[39] included the provisions outlined in the bill for state control of university posts but also reflected the demands of the Whig anti-clericals by referring to the need for the elimination of 'popish' college statutes which 'are become obsolete, useless and inconsistent with our present Protestant establishment under his most sacred majesty King George'. This draft also appears to have envisaged some measure of reform based on academic as well as simply political criteria, since it proposed 'that all decrees enjoining the reading of particular books . . . and prohibiting the reading of others may be totally repealed and declared void'. But the elimination of such provisions, one suspects, was the price that the Whig ministry was prepared to pay for the support of Archbishop Wake and other sections of the clergy.

Although the bill was drafted in 1717, it was deferred in favour of an abortive attempt in that year to repeal the Occasional Conformity Act, the ministry deciding that it would be unwise to tackle two measures which raised so many sensitive problems for church–state relations at the same time.[40] In the event the bill for the reform of the universities did not finally come before Parliament until late 1719, after the repeal earlier that year of those symbols of Tory-based clerical power, the Occasional Conformity and Schism Acts. But the fortunes of the university bill were tied to an even more important measure for destroying Tory power, Sunderland's peerage bill, which would have had the effect of ensuring a permanent majority for the Whigs in the House of Lords, and with the defeat of the peerage bill by 269 votes to 177[41] the bill for the reform of the universities also lapsed into political oblivion.

Even if it had passed, the different, and even conflicting aims of

[39] BL Add. MS 61,495, fos. 93–4.
[40] N. Sykes, *William Wake, Archbishop of Canterbury*, 2 vols (Cambridge, 1957), vol. 2, p. 134.
[41] Williams, *Stanhope*, p. 416.

the bill's sponsors might have made its operations difficult to implement. It is doubtful, too, whether Wake could have sufficiently contained clerical, and even episcopal, outrage at its proposed measures for it to be regarded as other than a major assault on the church. Even Bishop Fleetwood of Ely – a staunch Whig in and out of season – had expressed his dismay to Wake in December 1715 at finding that their tentative discussions about the possible reform of the universities had been interpreted as support for government control of university appointments. He warned Wake, too, that if the parliamentary visitation were regarded as the result of episcopal initiative, 'whatever odium (as indeed much may) arise on this occasion, it must all be laid upon us'.[42] Fleetwood's fears were not exaggerated – a mere sample of the clerical outrage that the bill was likely to cause is a letter to Wake of 18 March 1717 from John Baron, the vice-chancellor of Oxford. Baron called on the archbishop to oppose the attempt to institute a royal visitation of the universities just as he had shown 'zealous and successful opposition . . . to a bill, which was prejudicial to the interest of the church, with which those of the two universities have always been judged to be closely united'[43] – presumably a reference to Wake's opposition to Whig attempts to remove from the clergy their traditional control over charity funds.[44]

Baron's linking of the defence of the universities with the defence of the church showed considerable tactical insight. Wake was increasingly concerned at the vehemence of Whig anti-clericalism and, in same month as the vice-chancellor's letter, had learnt with alarm of ministerial plans to repeal not only the Occasional Conformity and Schism Acts but also the Test Act, the cornerstone of the constitutionally privileged position of the established church.[45] While Wake and some of his fellow clerical Whigs may have been prepared to countenance a measure of university reform, the possible association of this reform with a full-scale assault on the church's privileges made their co-operation in such a scheme increasingly problematical. But when it came to the point, the Whigs drew back from repealing the Test Act, since to do so would have risked cutting those bonds between church and state

[42] Wake MS 15 n.f.   [43] *Ibid.*
[44] G. V. Bennett, *The Tory Crisis in Church and State 1688–1730* (Oxford, 1975), p. 214.
[45] *Ibid.*

which were still fundamental to the existing order. Such considerations help to explain why the Whigs also drew back from a parliamentary visitation of Oxford and Cambridge. Although sections of the clergy might be politically recalcitrant, the church as a whole was too important a part of the constitution and of the social fabric to be alienated by an assault on the universities, to which so many of the clergy were attached by ties of sentiment and tradition.

IV

The 1719 bill was the nearest any eighteenth-century government came to such a reform of Oxford and Cambridge, for thereafter the increasing (though at times still uneasy) rapprochement between church and state made the prospect of reform less and less politically realistic. Like the issue of the repeal of the Test and Corporation Acts, that of university reform continued to be raised by anti-clerical Whigs in the Walpole years, but with little effect. In 1721 the *Independent Whig* (edited by the commonwealthmen Thomas Gordon and John Trenchard) spoke of would-be clergy being sent to the universities where they learned not 'to find out what is truth, but to defend the received system, and to maintain those doctrines which are to maintain them' (p. 30). Even a more politically powerful 'true Whig' like Arthur Onslow (speaker of the House of Commons, 1728–61) voiced similar opposition to the clerical character of the universities. In 1733, he wrote to Conyers Middleton, a heterodox fellow of Trinity College, Cambridge, that a university should be concerned not with the defence of orthodoxy but rather with 'the search of knowledge, which can only be had by the freedom of debate, and without which an university would contradict its nature and shall I say its name'.[46] But, as his opposition to the repeal of the Test and Corporation Acts suggests, Sir Robert Walpole was too conscious of the need to maintain good relations with the church to give his support to university reform, an issue about which he reportedly said 'he never could or would attempt any thing of that kind; that he had work enough upon his hands, of a different nature ... '[47] The nearest the anti-clerical Whigs came to affecting the universities was through the passage of the Mortmain Act of 1736, an earlier version of which had been

[46] BL Add. MS 32,457, fo. 85v.
[47] Anon, *A Blow at the Root* ... (London, 1749), p. 32.

vainly proposed by Speaker Onslow in 1725.[48] The 1736 bill limited the right of clerical institutions to purchase further advowsons, since it was claimed this 'would render the clergy independent on the laity' and thereby increase the 'power in the Church'.[49] The universities, however, with Walpole's support, succeeded in gaining significant exemptions to the measures proposed[50] – an indication of their improving relations with the governing classes and hence of the decreasing likelihood of a parliamentary visitation.

The prospect of such a visitation briefly surfaced in the wake of the 1745 Jacobite uprising, which, like that of 1715, prompted the state again to confront the problem of the universities' (and, in particular, Oxford's) doubtful loyalty to the House of Hanover. But this time the proposals for university reform did not even get to the point of a draft bill as in 1719, and the episode served to emphasize the increasing security of the universities and, conversely, the waning strength of Whig anti-clericalism. In contrast to the Jacobite uprising of 1715, there was no need in 1745 to station troops in Oxford, and the defeat of the Young Pretender was greeted by Oxford with official rejoicing – an indication of the university's improved relations with the Hanoverian regime. However, at the end of 1748 there were undergraduate demonstrations of Jacobite sympathy which appeared to be condoned by the university's authorities. When these were followed by an inflammatory speech which hinted at Jacobite sympathies, by William King (principal of St Mary's Hall) at the opening of the Radcliffe Camera in April 1749,[51] members of the Whig ministry – notably Lord Hardwicke, the Duke of Bedford and Lord Gower[52] – once more proposed a royal visitation of Oxford and Cambridge.

As in the early years of George I's reign, these proposals had some support from sections of the clergy. Like Prideaux, Richard Newton (principal of Hart Hall, Oxford, 1710–53) urged the need

[48] G. Best, *Temporal Pillars: Queen Anne's Bounty, the Ecclesiastical Commissioners, and the Church of England* (Cambridge, 1964), p. 104.
[49] Historical Manuscripts Commission, Egmont MSS, Diary of First Earl of, vol. 2, p. 256.
[50] T. F. J. Kendrick, 'Sir Robert Walpole, The Old Whigs and the Bishops, 1733–1736: A Study in Eighteenth-Century Parliamentary Politics', *Historical Journal*, 11 (1986), p. 439.
[51] P. Langford, 'Tories and Jacobites 1714–51', pp. 121–2 and Lenman, *Jacobite Risings*, p. 204.
[52] Ward, *Georgian Oxford*, p. 175.

for reform of the universities in order that they might better perform their role as places of moral and theological formation. In articles in the *General Evening Post* between January 1750 and July 1751, Newton argued that since 'the ancient discipline [of Oxford] is lost' and since 'it cannot reform itself, the assistance then of the legislature is *necessary* to its reformation'.[53] Like Archbishop Wake, the influential Thomas Sherlock, Bishop of London, supported university reform[54] – presumably because he, too, wished to improve the relations between church and state. But by the middle of the century, there was no longer that widespread anti-clericalism within the Whig party which in 1715–19 had given political momentum to the cause of university reform. As a consequence, the proposals for university reform did not, as in the early eighteenth century, extend to a possible diminution in the clerical role of the universities. This, along with the more tentative nature of the moves for a visitation in 1749, helps to explain why they prompted much less clerical outrage than did the proposed reforms in the first two decades of the century. Thanks to the use of Whig patronage, the church (or at least its upper echelons) had largely been tamed and was now sufficiently subservient to the state for the issue of clerical power no longer to be a major political concern. Whereas in the early years of George I's reign leading Whig politicians like Stanhope and Sunderland made no secret of their hostility to the privileges of the church and the universities, by the mid-century the Whig party was dominated by the Pelhams, firm Erastians but none the less loyal sons of the Church of England. The ambivalent attitude of Thomas Pelham, Duke of Newcastle, Secretary of State and *de facto* minister for church affairs, to the issue of university reform is apparent in his reply on 21 January, 1749, to Bishop Sherlock's letter urging the need for such government action. Newcastle conceded that 'the late, & notorious conduct of the University of Oxford' might make such a visitation necessary, but his chief concern appears to have been to protect Cambridge (of which he was chancellor), 'whose behaviour is as meritorious, as the other is justly to be censured'.[55] Despite such criticisms, by 1749 even Oxford had sufficiently made its peace with the Hanoverian

---

[53] [R. Newton], *A Series of Papers on Subjects the Most Interesting to the Nation in General and Oxford in Particular* ... (London, 1750), p. 16.
[54] T. Sherlock to Newcastle, 20 January 1748/9. BL Add. MS 32,718, fo. 29.
[55] *Ibid.*, fo. 31.

regime to muster influential allies, of whom the most conspicuous was Frederick, Prince of Wales, who gathered around him a group of Tories made up of thirteen peers and 103 MPs pledged to defend the university.[56]

Moreover, in contrast to the tense early years of George I's reign, the more settled conditions of the middle of the century, when the Hanoverian dynasty was securely lodged on the throne, led the Whigs to take a more reflective view of the wider implications of any parliamentary visitation of the universities. While Whigs might favour the subjection of the clergy to the state, they, like their Tory opponents, were also hostile to state intervention in established institutions. After all, the Glorious Revolution had been largely prompted by James II's attack on the ancient privileges of corporations (including the universities) – a parallel emphasized by Horace Walpole in his *Delenda est Oxonia*, a pamphlet prompted by the proposed visitation of 1749. Although Walpole himself described Oxford as 'the sanctuary of disaffection',[57] he regarded this defence of its privileges as in intention 'very whig' since it set out 'to show that the scheme of the ministry, was parallel to the behaviour of King James II, which had given rise to the Revolution'. In the pamphlet Walpole emphasized the dangerous precedent that government intervention in the affairs of the university would pose:

> If the election of their Chancellor is to be taken from the University of Oxford, because two or three boys have huzzahed for the Pretender, there can be no reason why any corporation in the kingdom may not be divested of the right of choosing their chief magistrates on similar pretences ... It is dangerous to let the crown into any new privilege: wherever royalty is permitted to taste, it cannot rest till it swallows the whole.[58]

Walpole's pamphlet was seized at the printers under government orders, so it had no direct influence, though the arguments advanced would have been familiar to a governing class well-acquainted with the role of Oxford and Cambridge in the events that led to the Glorious Revolution. Considerations such as those raised by Walpole probably prompted Speaker Onslow to denounce

56 Langford, 'Tories and Jacobites 1714–51', p. 124.
57 R. Sedgwick, ed., *The History of Parliament: The House of Commons, 1715–54*, 2 vols (London, 1970), vol. 1, p. 75.
58 P. Toynbee, 'Horace Walpole's *Delenda est Oxonia*', *English Historical Review*, 42 (1927), pp. 95, 105.

the proposed visitation as tyrannical,[59] even though Onslow was one of the Whigs' fiercest opponents of the privileges of the clergy and the universities. Faced by such opposition within their own ranks and by the rather lukewarm attitude of Newcastle, the ministerial supporters of university reform abandoned the issue without even drafting a bill; by 15 April 1750 Lord Hardwicke, one of the main advocates of a parliamentary visitation, commented to Newcastle that 'as all further thoughts about the universities seem to be laid aside, it seems to be the only thing left to give some encouragement and spirit to the well-affected there . . . '[60] Thus the complete failure of the parliamentary visitation of 1749 was an indication of the increasing security of the universities' position – a security which reflected a more fundamental improvement in the relations between church and state.

V

In the late eighteenth century the degree of public support for any externally-imposed reforms ebbed further as the governing classes' aversion to change was strengthened by the American and, *a fortiori*, the French Revolutions. Even a critic of Oxford and Cambridge such as Vicesimus Knox could write in 1781 that those 'who wish to destroy or totally alter their [the universities'] constitution, are of that description of men . . . who, from an unfortunate mode of thinking, endeavour to overturn all the ancient establishments, civil and ecclesiastical'.[61] As late as 1817, when the English old regime still appeared fragile, despite the recent victory over Napoleon, a seemingly trivial proposal for Oxford to redesignate its doctorate of laws as a doctorate of civil laws prompted one correspondent to the *Gentleman's Magazine* to observe: 'As innovations, either in church or state, are extremely dangerous, I cannot see, without great concern, the confusion which is likely to follow upon a change of no great importance in itself . . . '[62] The exasperated comment of a pamphleteer who in 1798 vainly proposed the abolition of the requirement that fellows of colleges remain celibate provides an apt summary of the fate of reform movements more generally in the late eighteenth century:

[59] Ward, *Georgian Oxford*, p. 180.   [60] *Ibid.*, p. 185.
[61] V. Knox, *Liberal Education* . . . (Dublin, 1781), p. 242.
[62] *Gentleman's Magazine*, 87 (1817), vol. 2, p. 200.

In these times ... innovation is viewed with such suspicion, that in order to accomplish an alteration in any long-established institution, it is not merely sufficient to prove its utility in a general way, but absolutely necessary to obviate every trifling objection which can be brought against it.[63]

In 1783, Parliament did pass an act correcting a minor anomaly affecting the universities, whereby some heads of Oxford halls and colleges could not marry whereas those at Cambridge could.[64] This prompted further discussion of the possibility of relaxing the requirement that a fellowship must be vacated at marriage – an issue that had been briefly and inconclusively raised at both universities in 1765–6.[65] But such a change represented too marked a departure from established custom to be taken seriously. Those who bothered to refute the proposal argued (as a correspondent of the *Gentleman's Magazine* did in 1783) that the removal of compulsory celibacy would have the effect of 'retarding the succession [of fellows] in colleges'.[66]

Celibacy, with its associations with monasticism and popery, was perhaps the feature of Oxford and Cambridge colleges which most emphasized the clerical character of these institutions, and so the issue did raise questions about the extent to which the university ought to be distinct from the wider society. The lack of any broad support within the parliamentary classes for abolition of celibacy was an indication of their reluctance to alter the fundamentally clerical character of the university. Indeed, in an age when church and state were under attack from political and religious radicals, the clerical character of the universities increasingly came to be seen by members of the Anglican political establishment as a source of strength rather than as a matter of criticism. In 1781 a Cambridge preacher in a commencement sermon entitled *The Important Station of an English University* could claim that Oxford and Cambridge should do more to emphasize their clerical identity – what he called 'their ancient cast and complexion' – and do more to keep themselves 'distinct from the world'. This, he continued, was what society expected from them: 'Whatever language may be held

63 Anon, *Reflections on the Caelibacy of Fellows of Colleges* (Cambridge, 1798), p. 20.
64 Cooper, *Annals of Cambridge*, vol. 4, p. 407.
65 D. Winstanley, *Unreformed Cambridge* (Cambridge, 1935), pp. 300–1; BL Add. MSS 32,628, fo. 41 and 32, 973, fo. 285.
66 *Gentleman's Magazine*, 53 (1783), p. 129.

by a few fantastic men, the greatest and best part of the world will blame us for abandoning our character, and applaud us for adhering to it.' The role of a don, he insisted, was to serve 'sound, temperate, established religion, such as our engagements to the public require of us', particularly since 'a spirit of irreligion is everywhere gaining ground'.[67]

This view that the governing classes wished to see the universities stand fast in their ancient and clerical ways was later to be echoed in a rather more influential work, Edmund Burke's *Reflections on the Revolution in France* (1790). Burke maintained that a clerically-controlled system of education helped shore up those bonds between church and state which were fundamental to a stable social order:

> Church and state are ideas inseparable in their [the majority of the people of England's] minds, and scarcely is the one ever mentioned without mentioning the other. Our education is so formed as to confirm and fix this impression in the hands of ecclesiastics, and in all ages from infancy to manhood.

Burke went on to argue for the benefits of the fact that in England there had been no fundamental reform of ecclesiastical institutions in general and Oxford and Cambridge in particular:

> So tenacious are we of the old ecclesiastical modes and fashions of institutions, that very little alteration has been made in them since the fourteenth or fifteenth century: adhering in this particular, as in all things else, to our old settled maxim, never entirely nor at once to depart from antiquity. We found those old institutions, on the whole, favourable to morality and discipline; and we thought they were susceptible of amendment, without altering the ground ... And after all, with this Gothic and monkish education (for such it is in the groundwork) we may put in our claim to as ample and as early a share in all the improvements in science, in arts, and in literature, which have illuminated and adorned the modern world, as any other nation in Europe ... [68]

Burke, then, was taking the opposite position to the commonwealthmen and anti-clerical Whigs of the early eighteenth century who had regarded Oxford and Cambridge not as a source of

[67] W. Arnald, *The Important Station of an English University. A Sermon preached at Cambridge, Commencement-Sunday, 1781* (London, 1803), pp. 8–9, 12, 18.

[68] E. Burke, *Reflections on the Revolution in France* (London, 1967), pp. 96–7.

strength and stability for the existing political and religious order
(as Burke did) but rather as a potential fifth column in its midst.
Criticisms of the universities like those raised by the earlier
anti-clerical Whigs could still be heard in the late eighteenth
century, but by then they could no longer be portrayed as a means
of defending the existing order. On the contrary, by the late
eighteenth century (and particularly in the age of the French
Revolution) anti-clerical attacks on Oxford and Cambridge were
associated with political and religious radicals who made no secret
of their desire to change not only the universities but also the
existing constitution in church and state – a conjunction of aims
which still further strengthened the universities' standing with the
governing classes as bastions of order in a troubled age.

One of the more notable of such would-be university reformers
was the Unitarian William Frend, who in 1793 was expelled from
the University of Cambridge (though not from his Jesus College
fellowship) following his publication of a pamphlet entitled *Peace
and Unity Recommended to the Associated Bodies of Republicans
and Anti-Republicans* (1793) – a work which made apparent his
sympathy for many of the aims of the revolutionaries and his
strong commitment to a programme of thorough-going reform in
church and state. After his expulsion, Frend appealed to the
House of Commons to institute a reform of the universities,
describing Oxford and Cambridge in very much the same terms as
the early eighteenth-century commonwealthmen. Thus he urged
the Commons to act lest

> the places, in which our young men are to be trained up to the
> love of their country, and the knowledge of every useful science,
> are not to be degraded by the pitiful resentment of monks ...
> that by a timely interference on your part, an abominable spirit
> of bigotry and fanaticism may be crushed in our seminaries of
> learning...

As these comments suggest, Frend envisaged the reform of the
universities as being linked with their declericalization: 'Let it not
then be required of a man of letters', he wrote, 'to go into orders for
academical preferment, but make the rise of an individual depend
solely on his progress in literature.'[69] Predictably, Frend's proposals received no support from Parliament, and his attempt to use

[69] W. Frend, *An Account of the Proceedings in the University of Cambridge against
William Frend* (Cambridge, 1793), pp. i, vi.

the civil courts to have his expulsion from Cambridge reversed was equally fruitless.

In the early eighteenth century such anti-clerical views had gained significant support from within a governing class afraid of the political power of a clerical estate many of whose members were hostile or at best lukewarm towards the revolutionary settlement in church and state. By contrast, however, by the late eighteenth century, when the English old regime was under threat from the movements associated with the American and the French Revolutions, the established church and its clergy were now regarded as useful allies of a social order under seige. Gentlemen who had once regarded their clerical neighbours with suspicion were, by the late eighteenth century, increasingly inclined to encourage them to join their lay counterparts on the commissions of the peace,[70] and a growing number of the sons of the well born began to make their way into the church as it once again came to be regarded as a career fit for a gentleman.[71] The rise in enrolments at both late eighteenth-century Oxford and Cambridge[72] also suggests an increasing convergence between the values and outlook of the clergy and the laity after a long period of anti-clericalism which derived from the Glorious Revolution and its aftermath.

VI

Oxford and Cambridge, then, survived the eighteenth century without any significant changes to their basic constitution – changes which would have required parliamentary assent, unlike the internally-prompted changes in curriculum and examination methods which indicate that the unreformed universities were not as devoid of life as commonly believed. For in the late seventeenth and early eighteenth centuries, Cambridge almost totally aban-

---

[70] Best, *Temporal Pillars*, pp. 70–1.

[71] N. Ravitch, *Sword and Mitre: Government and Episcopate in France and England in the Age of Aristocracy* (The Hague, 1966), pp. 120–1.

[72] The annual average number of admissions at Oxford went from 182 in 1750–9 to 254 in 1780–9 and 245 in 1790–9. At Cambridge the equivalent figures were 149, 171 and 162. Lawrence Stone, 'The Size and Composition of the Oxford Student Body 1580–1909', in Stone, *University and Society*, vol. 1, pp. 91–2. On the significance of the increasing enrolments at traditional educational institutions in the late eighteenth century, see P. Lucas, 'A Collective Biography of Students and Barristers of Lincoln's Inn, 1680–1804: A Study in the "Aristocratic Resurgence" of the Eighteenth Century', *Journal of Modern History*, 46 (1974), pp. 227–61.

doned the scholastic curriculum which had had its origin in the high Middle Ages and adopted in its place a course of studies in which the mathematical achievements of Newton took pride of place. Closely related to this was the development over the course of the eighteenth century of the Cambridge Mathematical Tripos, an examination system which was to serve as the model for competitive examinations more generally when, in the nineteenth century, pressure mounted for civil service appointments to be made on the basis of publicly-attested merit rather than through patronage.[73] At Oxford the changes were less pronounced, but there too mathematical and scientific studies advanced more than the university's critics have allowed, and the syllabus proved sufficiently flexible to incorporate such novel developments as the work of Locke and the study of common law. Moreover, with the introduction of the New Examination Statute in 1801, Oxford followed Cambridge's lead in requiring its graduates to compete publicly for academic honours.[74]

During the first half of the eighteenth century Oxford, and, to a lesser extent, Cambridge, had been viewed with suspicion by significant sections of the governing classes. Apart from the subtle workings of patronage, they had none the less been left unchanged by Parliament, since their reform would have endangered the already fragile relations between church and state and would have provided a precedent for state intervention in the affairs of an independent corporation, which was foreign to post-1688 ideology. The failure of the attempts in 1717–19 and in 1749 to institute parliamentary reform of Oxford and Cambridge underlines the considerable autonomy that universities have frequently enjoyed and the disjunction that can exist between the values and political outlook transmitted by a university and those held by the dominant groups in the larger society. As Stone remarks, the university has

---

[73] On developments at Cambridge, see J. Gascoigne, 'Politics, Patronage and Newtonianism: The Cambridge Example', *Historical Journal*, 27 (1984), pp. 1–24, and 'Mathematics and Meritocracy: The Emergence of the Cambridge Mathematical Tripos', *Social Studies of Science*, 14 (1984), pp. 547–84. (Before 1824 the Mathematical Tripos was officially known as the Senate House Examination.)

[74] On changes in the Oxford curriculum, see Sutherland and Mitchell, *Eighteenth-Century Oxford*, pp. 481, 586, 659–81. On the introduction of the New Examinations Statute, see *ibid.*, pp. 623–37, and S. Rothblatt, 'Student Sub-culture and the Examination System', in Stone, *The University in Society*, vol. 1, pp. 280–303.

not been 'a Marxist superstructure, automatically providing the ideological props for the group which currently controls the means of production'.

None the less, even in the first half of the eighteenth century, when many within the governing class viewed Oxford and Cambridge as dangers to the revolutionary settlement in church and state, the universities continued to reflect, through the often distorting mirror of their own institutional idiosyncrasies, many of the characteristics of the larger society of which, inevitably, they formed a part. To cite Stone's discussion of the nature of the university once more:

> And yet, in the long run, no institution can survive indefinitely in glorious isolation, and the interaction between the university's own built-in conservatism and the pressures upon it to adapt to new external conditions is one of the most potentially illuminating, but most practically obscure, aspects of the process of historical change.[75]

In what ways, then, can the unreformed universities of the eighteenth century be said to have adapted to at least some of the needs of the larger society?

In the first place, even Oxford's defiant Toryism, though very much a product of its own traditions, provided it with a niche in early eighteenth-century society, which long remained divided on party lines. Oxford was the natural haven for a significant – if, after 1714, largely powerless – section of the elite, particularly those drawn from the lesser gentry and the lower clergy, who remained loyal to Tory conceptions of the role of church and state. Cambridge, by contrast, which after about 1730 was increasingly under Whig dominance, provided an alternative political milieu for other sections of the elite. Thus 269 of the 617 Tory MPs who entered Parliament between 1715 and 1760 were from Oxford alumni as against seventy-six from Cambridge.[76]

Secondly, and more obviously, the universities continued to act as one of the main supports of the established church, which, even when Whig anti-clericalism was at its height in the early eighteenth century, proved to be too closely intertwined with the existing

---

[75] Stone, Introduction, *University and Society*, vol. 1, pp. iv, v.
[76] L. Colley, *In Defiance of Oligarchy. The Tory Party 1714–60* (Cambridge, 1982), p. 85.

political and social order to be fundamentally disturbed. Such bonds between church and state were to become even stronger as the English old regime came under challenge in the late eighteenth century from both political and religious radicals. As a consequence, effective parliamentary reform of the universities could not take place until the state was no longer so dependent on the church. It was not until the repeal of the Test and Corporation Acts in 1828 and the Catholic Emancipation Act of 1829 largely removed the church's constitutionally privileged position that such reform was politically feasible. Reform of Oxford and Cambridge, then, was inseparably linked with reform of the church, and in a period such as the eighteenth century, when church and state were, as Burke put it, 'one and the same thing, being different integral parts of the same whole',[77] ecclesiastical reform could not be insulated from political reform. The unreformed nature of the universities reflected the attitudes of a society that remembered with horror the upheavals of the interregnum and was wary of reforming any of its institutions lest change in one portion of its constitution should contaminate the whole.[78] Even Gibbon, no admirer of the church and still less of the universities, reflected this reluctance to initiate any major change – a reluctance that does much to explain the failure of any parliamentary reform of the universities to eventuate. 'If you begin to improve the constitution,' he wrote under the shadow of the French Revolution that had further strengthened the governing classes' suspicion of reform, 'you may be driven step by step from the disenfranchisement of Old Sarum to the king in Newgate, the lords voted useless, the bishops abolished.'[79]

Moreover, the unreformed universities also reflected that strong emphasis on the independence of corporations and private institutions which the eighteenth century regarded as one of the finest fruits of the Glorious Revolution. But, as the following century was to show, the universities, like the larger society of which they formed a part, were sufficiently adaptable to change in the wake of the momentous changes unleashed by the French and Industrial

---

[77] Williams, *The Eighteenth-Century Constitution*, p. 325.
[78] *Cf.* Lawrence Stone, 'The Results of the English Revolutions of the Seventeenth Century', in J. G. A. Pocock, *Three British Revolutions: 1641, 1688, 1776* (Princeton, 1980), p. 59.
[79] Cited in N. Hampson, *The Enlightenment* (Harmondsworth, 1968), p. 273.

Revolutions. Just as Oxford and Cambridge in the eighteenth century reflected the conservatism and cautiousness of the age, so, too, in the nineteenth century they were to reflect the widespread preoccupation with reform and change[80] – a further testimony to the resilience and flexibility of that long-lived institution, the university.

[80] D. A. Winstanley, *Early Victorian Cambridge* (Cambridge, 1940), p. 157.

III

Urban society and social change

12. *Resistance to change: the political elites of provincial towns during the English Revolution*

ROGER HOWELL, Jr

'The condition and attitude of the entrenched elite' is, as Lawrence Stone has observed,[1] one of the vital elements in creating a revolutionary situation. The municipal office-holders of seventeenth-century England were, by definition, a power elite. They were also, in many cases, a local economic elite. The pressures to create closed corporations had come predominantly from the most powerful and prosperous economic elements in the urban community, and they were the ones who monopolized the self-perpetuating power-structures that were created by restrictive charters. In addition, the sharply rising levels of civic expenditure, triggered by heavier administrative responsibilities accompanied by inflationary pressures, meant that towns, from the sixteenth century on, had to rely heavily on short-term loans from their civic leaders and on the meeting of small-scale expenditure by out of pocket payments by town officials. Conditions tended to force a merging of the elites of power and wealth. 'Insistence on wealthy office holders was not only a matter of upper class choice but of civic necessity.'[2]

Whether the governing elite also constituted a social elite was rather more variable. In larger boroughs, such as Bristol, Newcastle and York, which could maintain their independence from surrounding county forces, the town elite combined political power, economic dominance and social status. The gentry of the surrounding countryside, however, often dominated smaller towns, certainly in a social sense, and at times in economic and political aspects, notably parliamentary representation, as well.

[1] Lawrence Stone, *The Causes of the English Revolution, 1529–1642* (London, 1972), p. 9.
[2] P. Clark and P. Slack, *English Towns in Transition 1500–1700* (Oxford, 1976), p. 130.

But in the last analysis, the core of the political elite's position, its dominance of municipal office-holding, tended to remain inviolate, protected by a formidable array of chartered privileges.

To assert that 'within the limits set forth in its charter the town authority was an independent unit with practically the power of a sovereign state'[3] is rather an exaggeration, but the local political elites clearly did aspire to something akin to such a position. By the first three decades of the seventeenth century these aspirations were facing substantial and varied forces of opposition. The 'continuous growth of oligarchic magistracy' may have been the most notable feature of English urban history during the century and a half that preceded the Revolution,[4] but it was a process that had been frequently accompanied by a vigorous, if unsuccessful, anti-oligarchical agitation in towns as various as Newcastle, Maldon, High Wycombe, Woodstock, Nottingham, Norwich and Colchester.[5]

Such opposition was not necessarily united. Those within the local community who most closely resembled the incumbent political elite in economic and social status wanted a modest extension of the scope of the elite to include themselves but at the same time desired the retention of oligarchical and self-perpetuating control. Those more removed from the economic and social position of the political elite but still within the general body of freemen frequently desired a genuine broadening of the political base of the local community. As for the aspirations of those beyond the general body of freemen, the surviving records are, for the most part, silent. There are isolated instances of alliances being formed between discontented freemen and the unprivileged members of the community; the 1633 disturbances at Newcastle may be such a case.[6] But the fear of popular anarchy made such alliances exceptional.

Protests about the nature of civic government, its exclusivity and corruption, could often become entwined with other forms of

---

3 J. H. Thomas, *Town Government in the Sixteenth Century* (London, 1933), p. 26.
4 P. Clark and P. Slack, eds., *Crisis and Order in English Towns 1500–1700* (Toronto, 1972), p. 25. See also Clark and Slack, *English Towns in Transition*, chapter 9.
5 For Newcastle, see R. Howell, *Newcastle upon Tyne and the Puritan Revolution* (Oxford, 1967), pp. 39–42. For Maldon, High Wycombe, Woodstock, Nottingham, Norwich and Colchester, see Clark and Slack, *English Towns*, p. 133.
6 Howell, *Newcastle and the Puritan Revolution*, pp. 53–62.

protest, such as puritan opposition to the Laudian church or the agitation over monopolies. But no single or simple model of the convergence of different strands of opposition can be constructed. Entrenched elites, as, for example, that of Gloucester, could be firmly within the puritan fold.[7] Opposition could stem from men whose economic and political ideals were close to those of the incumbent elite. Or the convergence of different strands could be only partial, as at Newcastle where some of the opposition were clearly puritans but where there was no direct or unique connection between civic discord and puritanism.[8]

As England drifted into the beginnings of its Revolution, municipal political elites were in an exposed position. Popular pressure threatened them from below, while in the years immediately prior to the Revolution there was growing suspicion about their political and religious outlooks from the Crown above. It would seem logical to expect that the turbulent events of the next twenty years would have provided a context within which existing discontents about oligarchical management could become focused and achieve the success which hitherto had proved elusive, yet in the main this did not happen. Whatever the aspirations and loyalties of the 'middling sort' in provincial towns were, they do not appear to have had much in the way of sustained success in ousting the entrenched elites. To assert, as some have done, that 'the rebelliousness of the middle sort of men . . . converted riot into revolution'[9] may have some

---

[7] P. Clark, ' "The Ramoth-Gilead of the Good": Urban Change and Political Radicalism at Gloucester 1540–1640', in P. Clark, A. G. R. Smith and N. Tyacke, eds., *The English Commonwealth 1547–1640: Essays in Politics and Society Presented to Joel Hurstfield* (Leicester, 1979), pp. 167–87.

[8] Howell, *Newcastle and the Puritan Revolution*, pp. 115–17.

[9] B. Manning, *The English People and the English Revolution* (London, 1976), p. 238. A similar point of view has been consistently argued by Christopher Hill. See C. Hill, 'A Bourgeois Revolution?', *Collected Essays of Christopher Hill*, 3 vols (Brighton, 1985–6), vol. 3, pp. 94–124. It should be stressed that the point I am making here is not whether the Revolution should be described in overall terms as bourgeois in nature, but rather that in one particular political aspect, the control of provincial towns by traditional political elites, continuity is more characteristic than change.

London has not been considered along with the provincial boroughs, despite its importance in the Revolution. In terms of physical size, scale and complexity of economic life, and intensity and sophistication of political expression, it is simply not comparable to the provincial towns. On London see V. Pearl, *London and the Outbreak of the Puritan Revolution* (Oxford, 1961); R. Ashton, *The City and the Court 1603–1643* (Cambridge, 1979); R. Brenner, 'The Civil War Politics of London's Merchant Community', *Past and Present*, 58 (1973), pp. 53–107.

validity with respect to the choosing of sides in the conflict, but at a fundamental level it is not an adequate description of what actually transpired during the course of the Revolution in most provincial towns. The level in question is that of control of the political machinery of the towns. Traditional oligarchs, though threatened and shaken, obstinately retained their privileged positions.

What lies behind the resilience of the political elite in provincial towns? Examination of that question should provide insight both into the strategies of elite survival and into what was and was not revolutionary in the English Revolution. Part I of this chapter considers the reality of the intrusions and threats faced by the political elites of provincial towns. Part II considers the evidence for survival, despite those intrusions and threats, while Part III considers the means that made survival possible.

I

The threat to existing conditions that was present during the Revolution was very real. War, by its very nature, was potentially disruptive to the smooth continuance of normal practices. That was the point most emphatically stressed by the author of a speech prepared for the Mayor of Shrewsbury to welcome Charles I in 1642: hardly the sort of partisan speech the occasion demanded, it was primarily concerned about possible loss of town liberties and the difficulty of normal administration under such circumstances.[10] Such generalized fears took concrete form as the Revolution unfolded. The intrusion of external authorities into the affairs of towns complicated and compromised the position of the political elite. Confronted with conflicting and fiscally onerous demands from the two warring sides, many town magistrates found themselves in a perplexing situation. It is little wonder that, in such circumstances, so many towns attempted to maintain a neutral stance. Reactions in Bristol to the impending crisis were typical; members of the council argued that the city should not be allowed to become a parliamentary garrison since this would only incite the royalist forces. Even in towns where there appears to have been a

---

10 W. A. Leighton, 'The Mayor of Shrewsbury's Intended Speech 1642', *Transactions of the Shropshire Archaeological and Natural History Society*, 1st series, 2 (1879), pp. 398–9.

sizeable partisan feeling for one side or the other, there was evident rejection of the intrusion of that side's authority into what were seen as areas of local concern, as witnessed by royalist Worcester and puritan Barnstaple.[11]

Most towns, in the end, were forced to submit to intrusions; Worcester admitted a garrison and in Barnstaple construction of fortifications went ahead. But the problem of the intrusion of external authority hardly ended there. The repeated story of nearly every garrison town was conflict between the garrison commander and the town authorities. Nottingham provides a clear case in point.[12] Sharp differences of opinion existed between the governor and the corporation over what exactly the garrison was to defend. The decision of the governor, Colonel Hutchinson, to restrict the defensive work to the castle only led to open protest by the townsmen, who threatened to pull the castle down if they could not have 'their ordnance again upon their works'. Conflict intensified when the governor seized alderman Drury and fourteen other principal inhabitants, who had opposed removal of the cannons from the town works, and sent them as prisoners to Derby. In December 1643 the parliamentary committees resident at Nottingham Castle moved the town to create a committee of its own to lessen misunderstanding, and this was duly done five days later. The move did not, however, quell the controversy, but in some ways simply provided an additional vehicle for expressing it. In November 1644 the inhabitants of Nottingham petitioned the committee of both kingdoms about 'their unhappy differences and dissensions' between the governor and the town. Civic pride and position were, to their minds, very much at stake. The whole situation was, in their words, 'a great abuse and scandal to ourselves and the whole Corporation'. Even if the town a year later made Hutchinson a burgess, remitting his £10 fee for the privilege, the relationship had clearly been a stormy one.

It was not just the presence of military governors that aroused

---

11 For Bristol, see J. Latimer, *The Annals of Bristol in the Seventeenth Century*, reprint edn (Bath, 1970), pp. 154–65; Bristol Common Council Book 1627–42, Bristol RO, fos. 119 and 122; Common Council Book 1642–9, pp. 5, 6, 13, 21; for Worcester, *The Diary of Henry Townshend*, ed. J. W. Willis-Bund, Worcestershire Historical Society, 2 vols (Worcester 1915–20), vol. 2, p. 84; for Barnstaple, see Oxford, Bodleian Library, Tanner MSS 62, fos. 218 ff.

12 L. Hutchinson, *Memoirs of the Life of Colonel Hutchinson*, 7th edn (London, 1848), p. 157; *Records of the Borough of Nottingham*, ed. W. H. Stevenson *et al.*, 7 vols (London 1882–), vol. 5, pp. 221–2, 228–32, 239.

concerns for the safety of existing political structures. Hull, which had already in 1643 complained to the speaker of the House of Commons about the 'tyrannical' government of Sir John Hotham, 'whose will was the rule of all his actions and by whose power all the liberties of this poor Corporation were trampled under foot', in 1645 resisted association with the northern counties on the grounds that it would destroy the liberties and freedoms of Hull, and that the 'civil government will be trampled upon', Hull itself being reduced to a 'parcel' of the East Riding.[13]

If there was an element of paranoia in the fears of Hull, the reality of interference was none the less present. Both sides purged municipal governments in order to remove contrary voices from town corporations. Such an action, in turn, had several consequences potentially damaging to elite control of municipal affairs. It introduced an element of instability into town government. It presented the possibility of the forced intrusion into the elite sanctum of non-elite elements against the wishes of the oligarchs, and, by removing wealthy office-holders, it could narrow the economic base of the governing corporation, making the spreading of the special levies occasioned by wartime expenditure all the more difficult for those who remained. Royalist Worcester, for example, was reluctant to remove or accept the resignation of any member of the governing body, even if he was a known parliamentarian; such reluctance would appear to be equally the product of a general desire to uphold the chartered rights of the town against royalist interference in office-holding and a desire to retain wealthy members of the common council so that financial pressures of war-related levies could be spread more evenly.[14] Worcester likewise provides a clear case of the sort of instability which political purges produced. When Parliament briefly controlled the city, its forces displaced three aldermen and put in three of its own men. When the royalists gained control, they purged the parliamentary appointees and reinstated the three royalists.[15]

Certain circumstances made town corporations especially vulnerable to external pressure. Obviously moments of shifting in political allegiances, either of the town itself or in more general,

[13] The Hull Letters, ed. T. T. Wildridge (Hull, 1888), pp. 37–8, 70, 74.
[14] P. Styles, Studies in Seventeenth Century West Midlands History (Kineton, 1978), p. 231.
[15] The Chamber Order Book of Worcester 1602–50, ed. S. Bond, Worcestershire Historical Society, new series, no. 8 (Worcester, 1974), pp. 358, 364–5.

national terms, were unsettling. The capture of a town during hostilities was almost invariably followed by some reshuffling of the rulers of the town. The victory of Parliament over the King led to an ordinance of Parliament on 4 October 1647 banning from office all who had been in arms against Parliament or who had aided and abetted the royalist cause; that ordinance was eventually to lead to the ouster of fifteen members of the aldermen and common council of Weymouth and Melcombe Regis.[16] The Rump showed an active concern about borough charters. Following the Restoration there was to be even more extensive remodelling of municipal governments by the commissioners appointed under the Corporation Act. In Reading, Gloucester, Newcastle-under-Lyme, Leicester and Shrewsbury more than half of the members of the governing body were removed.[17]

The period of Cromwell's experiment with the major-generals provided a particularly tense moment for municipal elites. Cromwell had issued a proclamation in September 1655, of dubious (if any) legality, which extended the life of the Rump's expiring statute against royalists serving on municipal corporations; to it, he added a new condition that magistrates be godly. Desborough in the west appears to have taken the injunction particularly to heart. At Tewkesbury, he forced nine members of the corporation to resign, at Tiverton five, at Gloucester four and at Bristol three. Desborough realized that such overt interference was a delicate matter; as he reported to Thurloe, 'I adjudged it my duty to declare against such, wheresoever I find them, but resolved to do it with as little noise as I could.'[18] Others expressed even stronger doubts, but then proceeded to the task. Whalley wrote, after displacing the Mayor at Lincoln, 'I was forced at Lincoln . . . to assume a little more power than (I think) belonged to me.'[19]

His doubts were more than echoed by the town itself when he quashed both elections to the disputed position of town clerk and forced the council to elect his own nominee, threatening to confiscate the town charter if they refused to comply; he acted, the town minutes bluntly recorded, 'by a usurped, illegal, pretended

---

16 *Weymouth and Melcombe Regis Minute Book 1625 to 1660*, ed. M. Weinstock, Dorset Record Society (Dorchester, 1964), p. 76.
17 Clark and Slack, *English Towns*, p. 138.
18 *A Collection of the State Papers of John Thurloe*, ed. T. Birch, 7 vols (London, 1742), vol. 4, p. 396.
19 *Ibid.*, vol. 4, p. 197.

power'.[20] Towns which resisted such interference were met not only with threats but also with force, reaching an extreme at Hythe, where soldiers surrounded the town hall.[21]

Political interference by outside forces was not the only way in which the Revolution affected the position of the elite. Elite political power usually went hand in hand with economic dominance, and this too was threatened. The high cost of holding municipal offices, already a problem before the civil wars, was greatly exacerbated by them, and for some this imposed the uncomfortable dilemma of holding on to political power or resigning or refusing it for financial reasons. The reality of the problem is shown by two prominent members of the Worcester elite during the Revolution, Henry Foord and Francis Frank; they continued to hold office at great personal cost, and when they left the council both required special payments because of their reduced financial position.[22] Refusal by members of the elite to hold expensive offices created similar problems, though they could be coerced into compliance as William Evett of Worcester was; elected sheriff in August 1644, he refused to accept the office until he was threatened with a £100 fine in October, at which point he took the oath and the fine was remitted.[23]

There were even more pressing economic concerns of a general nature. The disruption of war dislocated trade and manufacturing in many instances and had a negative influence on the economic position of many town magistrates. Numerous towns found their economic control challenged by foreigners who had arrived in the town in the confusion of the wars and by interlopers who ignored or evaded their tightly-held privileges.

The presence of external threats was particularly upsetting when the internal opposition to the political elite sought to use them as a lever to gain power. Given the progressive contraction of town government in most places into the hands of a highly restricted, self-perpetuating and often inter-married elite, there existed in most localities a counter-elite made up of persons not noticeably different in wealth or social class from those who held the reins of power. Tension and jealousy between the two groups tended to be

[20] J. W. F. Hill, *Tudor and Stuart Lincoln* (Cambridge, 1956), p. 165.
[21] D. Hirst, *Authority and Conflict: England 1603–1658* (Cambridge, Mass., 1986), p. 339.
[22] Styles, *Studies in Seventeenth Century West Midlands History*, pp. 255–6.
[23] Bond, *Chamber Order Book of Worcester*, p. 387.

marked, both before the war and during it; as Thomas Povey observed in 1643, 'scarce any city or corporation is so unanimous, but they have division enough to undo themselves'.[24] The observation was correct, and as the country divided into opposed camps in the early 1640s the implications of the situation were not lost on those vying for control in the towns. If the dominant oligarchy was tied to the court or court supporters, it was both easy and natural for the local opposition to seize the issue close to hand, hostility to the court, and use that against the incumbents. For example, in Hastings in 1640 what seems at first to be a militant body of freemen provoked to action by national issues turns out on closer examination to be a group using those issues but primarily concerned with the municipal position of the oligarchy.[25] The extent to which deteriorating national conditions provided an opportunity for the local counter-elite to make a bid for power is underlined by the example of those towns where the controlling oligarchy was leaning towards the side of the national opposition, as in Maidstone and Northampton; here the internal opposition tended to make a more pro-court stand.[26]

In political and economic aims, the counter-elite had little intention of ending oligarchical rule; it simply aimed at securing a share of the spoils itself. While this might lead to some broadening of the political elite, it clearly did not mean its destruction. On the other hand, there were also present forces whose aspirations might well encompass the elimination of both the elite itself and elite privileges. There was always concern about what the generality of freemen or the unprivileged residents might do, particularly if they could find support from some external source which had no stake in preserving the existing structure and conceivably an interest in dismantling it. Newcastle provides a clear example. Members of the counter-elite did force themselves into the inner ring of government in the wake of the parliamentary victory. To their consternation, they were almost at once faced by a challenge to their position from the unprivileged sector of the community supported by outside interests.[27]

[24] T. Povey, *The Moderator* (London, 1643), p. 11.

[25] D. Hirst, *The Representative of the People? Voters and Voting in England under the Early Stuarts* (Cambridge, 1975), p. 135.

[26] *Ibid.*

[27] For a detailed discussion of these points see Howell, *Newcastle and the Puritan Revolution*, chapters 5 and 7.

II

There can be little doubt, then, that elite control in towns was faced with severe challenges in the years of the Revolution. It is equally clear, on the other hand, that elite elements displayed a considerable capacity for survival under that pressure, both in the physical sense of the continuity of personnel and in their attitudes, as shown through the continuity of behaviour patterns and opinions about the rightness and suitability of elite rule. Admittedly, few towns escaped totally unscathed from the experience of those years. Even the small borough of Calne, substantially untouched by the fighting in the war, felt its impact on local finances; in 1644 the constables' accounts showed a total amount expended of £65 13s, compared with £1 12s 5d in 1651 and £3 3s 5d in 1655.[28] But despite the pressures which such extraordinary expenditure must have placed on town officers, it appears that continuity of political control in the town was maintained. The normal pattern of the offices of guild stewards being held by the burgesses in turn, with individuals frequently serving several times in their lifetime, appears to have remained the order of the day.[29] William Jeffrey, who had already served in the post in 1636, served four more times between 1643 and 1657, and his son held the post in 1660. Robert Forman, who had been in the office five times between 1619 and 1635, held it three more times during the Revolution (1642, 1652 and 1659), while Arthur Estmead, who had served in 1631 and 1637, reappeared in the post in 1644, 1650 and 1657. In like fashion, people who had not served before 1640 entered the rotation in a perfectly normal pattern. Although there appears to have been some concern about the security of the governors, as witnessed by disbursements for the renewing of the charter in 1655,[30] the evidence overwhelmingly suggests that the political elite continued to function smoothly and in familiar patterns.

That a relative backwater such as Calne was not profoundly shaken in these years is not all that surprising. Rather more startling is the evidence for continuity in towns where partisan

---

[28] *Guild Stewards' Book of the Borough of Calne 1561–1688*, ed. A. W. Mabbs, Wiltshire Archaeological and Natural History Society Records Branch, no. 7 (Devizes, 1953), pp. 61, 65, 68.

[29] The following is derived from the list of guild stewards printed *ibid.*, pp. xxii–xxiii.

[30] *Ibid.*, p. 67.

loyalties apparently ran high or where there was major fighting. At Barnstaple, a steady element of continuity was present in the common council.[31] Of those who were serving in 1642, just under 40 per cent (six out of sixteen) were still serving in 1650; exactly the same number of carry-overs from 1650 remained in office in 1658 and three of these were survivors from 1642. The pattern was not dissimilar to more peaceful times. The same sense of continuity is conveyed by the succession of mayors.[32] Of the mayors between 1642 and 1649, only one was not already a member of the common council in 1642. After 1650 more new men appeared, but there remained a noticeable element of continuity; of the mayors holding office from 1650 to 1662, three had been on the common council as early as 1642 and were each serving a second term as mayor, while an additional four were already common councillors by 1650. Given such circumstances, it is difficult to disagree with the judgement that by the 1650s the affairs of the corporation had resumed their customary course and that the government of the town was being conducted on familiar lines and by familiar hands.[33]

A similar pattern of continuity is revealed in Reading and in Shrewsbury. Reading clearly experienced some dislocation in its municipal government; for example, on 13 August 1645 two aldermen were dismissed for absence and neglect, and on 24 January 1646 a petition was presented calling for the removal of eight aldermen and assistants, which culminated a month later in the displacing of seven of the eight.[34] Since the remaining member of the group does not appear in subsequent lists of the corporation, he too was presumably removed. Despite such disruptions, elite control of the magistracy remained firm, as a comparison of the aldermanic benches of 1642, 1645, 1648 and 1654 suggests.[35] The mayor, two justices and the aldermen formed a group of thirteen, while the steward and assistants who completed the corporation

---

[31] The following is drawn from the lists printed in J. B. Gribble, *Memorials of Barnstaple* (Barnstaple, 1830), pp. 444, 463–4.

[32] *Ibid.*, pp. 202–3, for the list of mayors.

[33] R. W. Cotton, *Barnstaple and the Northern Parts of Devonshire during the Great Civil War* (London, 1889), p. 542.

[34] *Reading Records: Diary of the Corporation*, ed. J. M. Guilding, 4 vols (London, 1892–6), vol. 4, pp. 159, 181–3, 185.

[35] *Ibid.*, vol. 4, pp. 55–6, 167, 306, 314, 544. For the changes in 1645, *cf.* the list of the corporation in October 1646, *ibid.*, vol. 4, pp. 214–15, with the purges as indicated in note 34 and the list of the corporation in October 1645, *ibid.*, vol. 4, p. 167.

numbered twelve. In 1645, eleven of the thirteen members of the higher branch had already been members of the corporation in 1642. In 1648, all thirteen had been members of the corporation in 1645 and eight survived from 1642. In 1654, all thirteen had been members of the corporation in both 1645 and 1648 and again eight had been part of it as early as 1642. Although there had been considerable turnover at the top (only four of the higher branch in 1654 had been in that place in 1642), the political elite had clearly succeeded in filling vacancies caused by removal or death by recruitment from its own ranks. The recruitment was by familiar patterns and apparently of familiar types on the basis of seniority. For example, after the purge of 1646, there were three aldermanic vacancies; they were filled by the three senior assistants.

The succession of mayors at Shrewsbury tells much the same tale.[36] In 1638 Shrewsbury had received a new charter, in which the chief change had been the reduction of the two bailiffs to a single mayor; in customary fashion, the initial office-holders (twenty-four aldermen and forty-eight assistants) were named. This, then, was a political elite which had consolidated its chartered hold on its privileges on the very eve of the Revolution. Its capacity to retain that grip, at least at the top in the office of mayor, is striking. No one who was not an original alderman held the office of mayor until 1652, when Richard Cheshire, one of the original assistants, was elected. Out of twenty-seven holders of the office between 1638 and 1662, only five, all occurring after 1653 and three of them falling in the years 1660, 1661 and 1662, were not named members of the original corporation of 1638.

The strength of continuity that is shown at Barnstaple, Reading and Shrewsbury appears to have been very widespread in corporate towns. A modest broadening of the elite in Newcastle sufficed to produce political order.[37] In Norwich, the elevation of new men to office did little to change the character of the political elite.[38] In York, the machinery of government continued to function much as it had in the past.[39] Scarborough suffered considerably during the

---

[36] H. Owen and J. B. Blakeway, *A History of Shrewsbury*, 2 vols (London, 1825), vol. 1, p. 534 (list of mayors), pp. 407–9 (list of corporation appointed under charter of Charles I).

[37] Howell, *Newcastle and the Puritan Revolution*, chapter 5.

[38] J. T. Evans, *Seventeenth Century Norwich: Politics, Religion, and Government 1620–1690* (Oxford, 1979), p. 139.

[39] *VCH Yorkshire, The City of York*, ed. P. M. Tillott (London, 1961), p. 183.

fighting. Its strategic location, strong castle and harbour made it an important target; it changed hands no less than seven times in seven years. But for all that, there was never any serious breakdown of either town government or order.[40] At Boston, the corporation took the precaution in February 1653 of forwarding their charters to London in order to confirm their validity under the Commonwealth, but this appears to have been purely a formality 'for a study of the Corporation minutes over the whole of the Interregnum period reveals no change in the Corporation's composition, its administrative machinery, nor business proceedings'.[41] Even alterations that are described by contemporaries as being breaches in continuity need to be examined in critical fashion. Two of the aldermen deposed at Hull following the Restoration and described as being 'brought in by the usurper' turn out to be rather different.[42] John Rogers had been a chamberlain in 1636, was sheriff in 1641 and mayor in 1652; despite his removal at the Restoration, he was again to serve as mayor in 1673. Francis Dewick was a member of the Merchant Adventurers and had likewise served as chamberlain before the Revolution (1637) and then as sheriff (1646) and mayor (1650). The tensions in Rye, which has been described as a borough violently divided, are as much evidence of the survival of traditional forms and attitudes as they are of their collapse, for what was happening was not a confrontation between citizens but a determined attempt at preservation on the part of town officials of long-standing forms and practices that seemed threatened by the military garrison.[43]

The determination of the Mayor and jurats of Rye to preserve those forms is typical of the way in which there was continuity of attitudes at work as well as continuity of persons. John Ashe, reporting to Speaker Lenthall in November 1645 about elections at Weymouth and Melcombe Regis, reflected on the firm hold that local tradition had on electoral behaviour. 'For three vacant places there stood seven men; and so many speeches made against strangers and

40 J. Binns, 'Scarborough and the Civil Wars 1642–1651', *Northern History*, 22 (1986), pp. 120–2.
41 A. A. Garner, *Boston: Politics and the Sea 1652–1674* (Boston, 1975), p. 14.
42 E. Gillett and K. A. MacMahon, *A History of Hull* (Oxford, 1980), p. 181; Wildridge, *Hull Letters*, biographical notes, s.v. Dewick, Francis and Rogers, John.
43 F. A. Inderwick, 'Rye under the Commonwealth', *Sussex Archaeological Collections*, 39 (1894), pp. 1–15; *Historical Manuscripts Commission, Corporation of Rye* (London, 1892), especially pp. 216–37.

unknown persons that if three townsmen had stood they had carried it against all that interposed; for they rejected four able men and chose a poor simple townsman.'[44] Nothing was more likely to bring continuity of attitudes to the fore than a threat to the economic foundations of elite control, a point vividly illustrated by the prolonged clash between Newcastle corporation and Ralph Gardner. It is indicative of the tenacity with which the new men defended elite privilege that Gardner was ultimately more critical of them than of their predecessors. It was of Bonner and Dawson that Gardner bitterly commented that they understood 'their offices no more than a company of geese only they can carry a white staff and sit where other knowing mayors hath done'.[45] The point, of course, was exactly the opposite. They understood their officers all too well; realizing the implications of Gardner's escalation of his personal grievances about not being able to trade in defiance of Newcastle's monopolies to a general assault on the validity of chartered privileges, they entered on a battle they could not afford to lose with every weapon at their disposal.

The reaction of corporations to the major-generals and of the major-generals to corporations provides further evidence for the continuity of attitudes and behavioural patterns even among governing bodies that had been 'reformed' in the process of Revolution. The thoroughly negative attitude expressed at Lincoln towards Whalley's handling of the case of the town clerk, mentioned earlier, can probably be taken as typical of the reaction of towns to the manipulation or attempted manipulation of town officials by the major-generals. That is not to say that everything they did met with opposition. Lilburne's active support of the proposed college at Durham doubtless commended itself to the Newcastle authorities, since they too had a lively interest in the matter, but in other areas there was clearly tension, and members of the Newcastle magistracy appear to have worked actively against Lilburne in the 1656 parliamentary elections.[46] A recurring theme

---

[44] Quoted in A. R. Bayley, *The Great Civil War in Dorset 1642–1660* (Taunton, 1910), p. 294.

[45] *Monopoly on the Tyne 1650–58: Papers relating to Ralph Gardner*, ed. R. Howell, Society of Antiquaries of Newcastle upon Tyne, Record Series no. 2, (Newcastle, 1978), p. 122. The introduction to this volume contains a full account of the Gardner case.

[46] R. Howell, *Puritans and Radicals in North England: Essays on the English Revolution* (Lanham, 1984), pp. 191–4.

in the correspondence of the major-generals is the refractory nature of the corporations with which they had to deal. Given their instruction to ensure a godly magistracy, the major-generals had particular reasons to express concern about corporations, but it is none the less striking to find Whalley commenting about Coventry 'that wicked magistrates, by reason of their numbers, over-power the godly magistrates'.[47] Coventry, after all, was a town whose incumbent mayor Robert Beake saw himself as a stern guardian of public morality and who recorded in his diary how he spent his Sunday by going to the park to observe 'who idly walked there'.[48] Desborough thought that it was 'a disease predominating in most corporations' that they retained 'old malignant principles, discountenancing the godly and upholding the loose and prophane'.[49]

III

The capacity to resist and the ability to maintain elite political control under what was, at times, extreme pressure cannot be explained by any single cause, nor is there an explanatory model that will satisfactorily cover every individual case. Numerous variables affected the political life of towns and in turn influenced the entrenched nature of the elite. Factors ranging from the level of literacy to the volume of circulation of polemical tract literature, from the status of the local economy to the relation of the urban elite to the surrounding county power-structure, all play a part. But certain general explanations can be offered which, taken in conjunction with the specific local circumstances, will help to explain what transpired in any given town.

It is reasonably clear that many towns were not zealous partisans in the Revolution: most desired neutrality and business as usual, and they tended to choose sides reluctantly and under duress. This important strand of neutralism and its accompanying willingness to make an accommodation with whatever was the winning side constitutes one significant reason for the survival of traditional town governors. Nearly every corporation had a solid core of

[47] *Thurloe State Papers*, vol. 4, p. 273.
[48] 'Diary of Robert Beake, Mayor of Coventry 1655–1656', ed. L. Fox, in R. Bearman, ed., *Miscellany I*, Publications of the Dugdale Society, no. 31 (Oxford, 1977), p. 136. Whalley did feel that Beake was one of the godly magistrates.
[49] *Thurloe State Papers*, vol. 4, p. 396.

office-holders who managed to work with every regime of the period from the personal rule of Charles I to the protectorate of Cromwell to the restored monarchy of Charles II. While it is tempting to see such office-holders as time-servers, secular counterparts of the Vicar of Bray, such a view can be misleading. While personal considerations certainly played a role in their behaviour, they were also people with a sense of corporate responsibility, who put the welfare of the town as they understood it above personal ideological inclinations. Without the presence of such men in town government, the periodic purges would have had a much more destabilizing effect as governing elite and counter-elite vied for control.

The presence of a core of municipal office-holders capable of adjusting to each change of regime cannot, however, by itself suffice to explain the enduring quality of elite political control. In their own defence, the magistrates could adopt various strategies that enhanced their chance of survival. One such method, obviously, was to reach some sort of pragmatic accommodation with the counter-elite. In normal times this usually meant no more than allowing a trickle of new men into major political office and following a policy that would not unduly provoke those outside the inner circle. In the period of the Revolution, purges meant that the rate of the trickle increased, and this forced the elite to adopt rather more vigorous means to ensure that the process led only to a reshuffling of the elite rather than a wholesale replacement. The capacity of the surviving core to work with the new men was crucial, and, at times, it extended to co-operating in the removal of established members of the political elite. It is suggestive that at Newcastle, for example, the only removals of aldermen after the Dawson clique assumed its place were of men who were outspoken opponents of the new men, and, in both cases it would appear that the core of survivors went along willingly.[50]

The political elite also employed a further strategy which could be termed pre-emptive purging, that is anticipating and forestalling outside interference by making changes themselves before the external authorities could act. Newcastle again appears to provide a clear example of this. The evidence suggests that the parliamentary ordinance for settling the government of Newcastle confirmed an existing situation rather than created a new one; in the period

50 On these cases see Howell, *Puritans and Radicals*, pp. 24–6.

between the reduction of the town and the parliamentary ordinance, the key new figures Henry Dawson and Thomas Bonner had both entered into aldermanic office, while one of the aldermen named in the parliamentary ordinance never appears to have taken office at all, his place being taken by a relative of Henry Dawson.[51]

Equally suggestive of pre-emptive action on the part of the elite to secure its position is the behaviour of a number of corporations in the 1650s at a time when the Cromwellian government was showing a keen interest in calling in and revising town charters. The town authorities of Salisbury, for example, took the lead in securing its new charter, with the corporation's desire to secure confirmation of its recent acquisitions of the dean and chapter lands being one of its most evident motives.[52] The case of Leeds seems similar.[53] At Leominster, the controlling elite sought to exploit the opportunity to reduce the size of the governing body, while the inhabitants of Aylesbury were careful in requesting a new charter to specify precisely what immunities and alterations they wished.[54]

Against some of the threats to their power, the town governors could and did resort to force. As the case of the unfortunate shipwright Thomas Cliffe reveals, this could at times be physical force; he and his men were assaulted by authorities from Newcastle and in the course of the fracas, his wife received blows that led to her death and another onlooker had her arm broken.[55] The force employed was more likely to be that of the law, as the lengthy and vigorous legal harassment of both Cliffe and Ralph Gardner by the Newcastle corporation attests. Such tactics, while they might well suffice against local foes with no extensive power base of their own, were hardly suitable for fending off the potentially much more dangerous force of central authority. Admittedly, the threat from

---

[51] Dawson and Bonner were among the signatories of a letter to Lenthall a month before the first official notice of their appointment. *House of Commons Journals*, vol. 3, p. 714. Henry Lawson was named in the parliamentary ordinance but in the earliest list of the revised corporation his place had been taken by William Dawson. *Extracts from the Newcastle upon Tyne Council Minute Book 1639–1646*, ed. M. H. Dodds (Newcastle, 1920), p. 21; Newcastle Chamberlains' Accounts 1642–5, Tyne and Wear County Archives, fo. 167.

[52] 'The Commonwealth Charter of the City of Salisbury', ed. H. Hall, in *The Camden Miscellany vol. xi*, Camden Society, 3rd series, no. 13 (London, 1907), pp. 161–98. See also *Calendar of State Papers Domestic 1655–6*, pp. 41, 195, 330.

[53] *Calendar of State Papers Domestic 1656–7*, p. 181.

[54] *Ibid.*, pp. 220 (Leominster), 330 (Aylesbury).

[55] Howell, *Puritans and Radicals*, chapter 5, gives a full account of the Cliffe case.

the centre was more potential than actual in many instances. In fact, a major explanation of the survival of the urban political elites lies in the inability and unwillingness of the central authority to do very much about them. The limits of central authority are nowhere indicated more clearly than by the capacity of town corporations to disregard or frustrate dictates, if not permanently, at least for considerable stretches of time. The slowness with which Weymouth and Melombe Regis responded to directives to purge the corporation is illustrative.[56] The purge of January 1649 had its origins in a parliamentary ordinance of 4 October 1647. If foot-dragging in this case was ultimately unsuccessful, other boroughs were able to do much the same sort of thing more successfully. In October 1642, the King addressed a letter to the corporation of Shrewsbury containing a list of members of the governing body whom he wanted removed from office, but a month later, when action was finally taken, only three of the thirteen persons on the list were displaced. All three seem to have been non-resident, and no further measures appear to have been taken against any of the others.[57] At Nottingham, where the town clerk was not only loyal to the King's cause but indeed an active supporter of it, the corporation did not vote him unfit to hold his office until August 1644 and did not actually remove him from office for another year.[58] Worcester, on more than one occasion, frustrated the desires of central authority simply by ignoring it. After failing to evade royal intervention in the election of the mayor in 1643 by a bewildering series of moves that ended up with the same man, Thomas Hacket, being chosen both mayor and sheriff, the following year the corporation ignored a royal injunction not to elect Hacket mayor; the common council calmly informed the court that no objection has been raised against Hacket in the chamber, and the matter was dropped.[59] Worcester likewise resisted parliamentary pressures: two of the most prominent royalists on the corporation, William Evetts and Sir Daniel Tyas did not leave office until 1649, and in fine disregard of the spirit of parliamentary intentions, the corporation retained Tyas

[56] Weinstock, *Weymouth & Melcombe Regis Minute Book*, pp. 73–4, 76.
[57] Owen and Blakeway, *History of Shrewsbury*, vol. 1, pp. 430–1.
[58] Stevenson, *Records of the Borough of Nottingham*, vol. 5, pp. xv, 223–4, 237.
[59] Bond, *Chamber Order Book of Worcester*, pp. 370, 373–4, 383–4.

and another dismissed royalist Edward Solley as trustees of the city lands throughout the interregnum.[60]

The period of the major generals would, on the surface, appear to be a time when central authority was in a position to over-ride such tactics, but in practice this proved not to be the case. Recent work has raised doubts about whether the system of major-generals represents the high point of early modern centralization; overall, success in reforming local government was minimal.[61] But there was more involved than just an incapacity to translate zealous endeavours into lasting reforms. There was also a question of intent, and here circumstances favoured town magistrates in their efforts to retain power. While there is no doubt that Cromwell desired godly magistrates and was willing to use pressure at times to see them placed in office, it is also the case that he respected chartered rights. Even more to the point, so did William Sheppard, who was responsible for drafting the municipal charters in this active phase of interference with the boroughs. Sheppard's charters reflect considerable respect for existing conventions through their confirmations of former privileges, and, with their acompanying tendency to narrow the franchise, they posed little threat to oligarchical control, though they could pose problems of dispossession for individual members of the political elite. Sheppard's attitude was underlined in 1659 in his book *Of Corporations, Fraternities and Guilds*. In it, he showed considerable sensitivity to the balance of power between local corporations and the central authority that granted them that incorporation; 'Sheppard's book, written at the threshold of the modern era in charter-making, remains a period piece marking the highest development of medieval charters.'[62] And his practice tended to coincide with his theory.

The unfolding of the long, bitter and complex struggle within the corporation at Colchester shows how charter revision at the hands of the Cromwellian government did not unduly threaten elite

[60] *Ibid.*, pp. 447–8; Styles, *Studies in Seventeenth Century West Midlands History*, p. 241.

[61] Hirst, *Authority and Conflict*, p. 338; A. Fletcher, 'Oliver Cromwell and the Localities: The Problem of Consent', in C. Jones, M. Newitt and S. Roberts, eds., *Politics and People in Revolutionary England* (Oxford, 1986), pp. 187–204.

[62] N. L. Matthews, *William Sheppard, Cromwell's Law Reformer* (Cambridge, 1984), p. 140. There is a good discussion of Sheppard's work on pp. 49–58 and of his book *Of Corporations* on pp. 133–42.

political control.[63] Two factions within the governing body had been struggling with each other since the Civil War. This was clearly a struggle within the existing political elite, rather than a struggle between it and wider forces. Henry Barrington, who led one of the factions, had served as bailiff of the town before Colchester even had a mayor; under the 1635 charter of Charles I he had twice (1637 and 1641) served as mayor before hostilities broke out. Thomas Reynolds, who led the other faction, was a major clothier and his followers included many of the substantial men in the town. By 1654 the two factions had become evenly balanced within the corporation, a particularly destabilizing factor, since balance invited an appeal to outside forces to break the deadlock. The Reynolds faction appealed to all the free burgesses to oust the Barrington faction; the latter, in turn, appealed to the courts and to the Protector for restitution. Cromwell's handling of the problem was cautious. The Barrington faction was more supportive of him than the Reynolds group, yet the Reynolds group obviously had considerable support in influential sectors of the town. On the other hand, its appeal to the general body of burgesses threatened tight elite control. In nominating a new corporation, Cromwell responded to the Barrington appeal for a charter which would correct the defective constitution of the borough by which 'in many particulars too great a power is given to the people to slight the Magistracy of the ... Town and render them useless in their places'.[64] The new charter effectively excluded the burgesses from the corporation and guaranteed a majority for the Barrington faction, but, very importantly, it also preserved some place for the Reynolds group. Cromwell's actions had not only tightened oligarchical control; they had secured a place for representation of both factions of a divided political elite.

The cases of boroughs that followed a different course from the prevailing pattern of retention of elite political control are themselves revealing as to the reasons why the incumbent magistrates tended to survive. Bedford and High Wycombe have been frequently cited as towns in which concessions were made to popular sentiment and a 'drift to the left' occurred. But why did the

---

63 S. R. Gardiner, *History of the Commonwealth and Protectorate 1649–1656*, reprint edn, 4 vols (New York, 1965), vol. 4, pp. 55–76 gives a full discussion of the Colchester case; see also J. H. Round, 'Colchester during the Commonwealth', *English Historical Review*, 15 (1900), pp. 641–64.

64 Round, 'Colchester during the Commonwealth', pp. 656–7.

magistrates lose their grip? In the case of Bedford[65] it appears that a major reason was that the incumbent elite not only failed to follow one of the key strategies for survival, pragmatic accommodation with the counter-elite, but went to the other extreme of deliberately adopting measures that would antagonize it. In December 1647, it had restricted admission to burgessdom in the town and at the same time it took on itself the election to the common council of the thirteen 'representative' freemen. Reaction to such provocative restrictions was inevitable and resulted in the so-called Levelling Act of 1650 which abolished the distinction between freemen and burgesses, putting them on an equal basis with regard to the composition of the governing body. It was a substantial, if fleeting, victory for the popular party, but it sprang from a confrontation that might well have been avoided by more pragmatic and adaptable governors.

In High Wycombe, there was, as at Colchester, a split in the governing ranks.[66] The faction led by Nicholas Bradshaw displayed at best a limited talent for accommodation, as shown by their attempt to exclude a rival, Steven Bates, from the mayoralty in 1650. Besides having grievances, the rival faction had two weapons to hand: a long-standing local quarrel going back to at least the 1620s over the use by the corporation for municipal purposes of money intended for relief of the poor, and the ability to appeal to central authority, charging the incumbents with misgovernment and royalist sympathies. The combination of an emotive local issue with the government's concern about royalist conspiracy proved too challenging a set of hurdles for an entrenched but not very flexible political elite to clear.

IV

The cases of Colchester, Bedford and High Wycombe all suggest the dangers to elite control of internal divisions. Given the right set

[65] Material on Bedford is drawn from *The Minute Book of Bedford Corporation 1647–1664*, ed. C. G. Parsloe, Bedfordshire Historical Society, no. 24 (Streatley, 1949), and C. G. Parsloe, 'The Corporation of Bedford 1647–1664', *Transactions of the Royal Historical Society*, 4th series, 29 (1947) pp. 151–65.

[66] Material on High Wycombe derived from *The First Ledger Book of High Wycombe*, ed. R. W. Greaves (Buckinghamshire Record Society, 1956), pp. 132 ff; L. J. Ashford, *The History of the Borough of High Wycombe* (London, 1960), pp. 126–43; W. H. Summers, 'Cromwell's Charter, High Wycombe', *Records of Buckinghamshire*, no. 7 (1897), pp. 511–28.

of circumstances – lack of political skill or accommodation on the part of the entrenched office-holders, long-standing and divisive local issues, some particular reason for central government concern – such a situation could lead to a weakening of control. Ironically, however, the general experience of towns in the period would suggest that the very tendency to internal division, at one level a weakness of considerable danger, was at another level a fundamental reason for survival of traditional government. The discontented element almost invariably had to appeal for additional support to achieve its ends. And the implications of that additional support, whether it was sought through broadening the political base of the town or through appeal to central authority, always entailed at least the possibility of diminution of elite political control. If the dominant group could be sufficiently accommodating and flexible, it could always call on that argument to disarm its opponents, many of whom were, after all, as interested in elite forms of government as the incumbents. In the end, it was in the interest of both elite magistrates and their opponents not to allow their rivalry to be the cause of the intrusion into town affairs of forces which neither of them wished to encourage. The realization that pushing disagreements to prolonged confrontation might lead to just that undesired end was probably as important as any other factor in the survival of urban political elites during the revolutionary years.

But survival of the oligarchical political elites was not solely dependent on the unwillingness of the general body of freemen to divide against itself or on the fears raised by the allies which were needed to make such division effective. The inability of the central government to force its wishes on the local community in any consistent fashion stands out as an equally significant factor in the situation. Foot-dragging is not normally the best defence for elites; indeed, if the opposition is strong and willing enough, such a posture is more likely to lead to catastrophe than it is to salvation. But in the context of revolutionary England, it was a successful strategy, especially when it was combined with adequate doses of pragmatic accommodation to events. In the process of accommodation the core of survivors who faithfully served under successive regimes was crucial. In themselves, they provided an important element of continuity; in addition, their willingness to work with the new men who did intrude, even to the extent of co-operating in the removal of the most intransigent of the old men, eased the pressure from below, while their ability to accept and perhaps help engineer pre-emptive rearrangements of the local power elite worked against the exertion of effective pressure from above.

The use of forcible repression appears to have been the least-employed strategy for survival, unless one considers the closing of the ranks of the privileged against the spectre of the many-headed monster an expression of force. Repression was successfully resorted to on occasion, and doubtless the threat of it was a recurring factor, but town magistrates at best could only employ it against those below them, not against the more threatening forces of the central government. In turn, the central government had a limited capacity to coerce the towns. Moreover, when it was in its strongest position to exert such coercion, at the time of the major-generals, it was, in important ways, inclined not to do so. The traditional outlook of William Sheppard with respect to chartered rights deeply influenced the policy of the Protectorate towards towns; what a central government less encumbered by such traditional conceptions could do to town oligarchies was left to the later Stuarts to demonstrate.

Urban political elites, though shaken, survived the English Revolution. Their own actions facilitated that survival but the broader revolutionary context was equally if not more important. Though there was ample discontent from below, it was rarely able to coalesce into a unified revolutionary movement against the entrenched oligarchs, and, when it did, as at Bedford, it achieved that status as the result of provocative and politically inept actions on the part of the governing elite itself. From above, the state was no Leviathan; neither was it, with regard to continued control of boroughs by self-perpetuating oligarchies, all that revolutionary. In short, urban political elites survived in part on their own wits, in part as a result of the failure of a coherent revolutionary movement to develop below them, and in part through the unwillingness or inability of the various revolutionary regimes above to act vigorously against them.

13. *The London Whigs and the Exclusion Crisis reconsidered*

GARY S. DE KREY

> I have indeed wondered often that, among the many books, of
> one sort or other, that have come out ... none have offered at
> a clear relation of these city doings; although the importance of
> them to the public, was great ... For the transactions, however
> limited within the liberties of the City ... improved to a grand
> crisis of state, and hinged about the whole machine of King
> Charles II's government...
>
> Roger North, *Examen* (1740), p. 595

The Exclusion Crisis cannot be viewed apart from current historical
debates about the meaning of seventeenth-century political, social
and religious experiences. The Crisis has not perhaps received as
striking recent attention as the politics of the 1620s' Parliaments, or
the mid-century breakdown and replacement of the Stuart regime,
or the institutional restructurings that followed the events of 1688.[1]
Nevertheless, the revisionist school of historians that gained
momentum in the 1970s and that has claimed orthodoxy in the
1980s has provided as unmistakable and 'unwhiggish' a view of this
crisis as of the others. In the work of J. R. Jones, J. P. Kenyon and
John Miller, in particular, an interpretation of the Exclusion Crisis
may be found that is focused upon Parliament and personalities and
that, while noting the importance of the localities, treats them
primarily as epicentres of the principal storm.[2] Finding little

---

[1] J. R. Jones, *The First Whigs: The Politics of the Exclusion Crisis, 1678–1683*
(London, 1961) remains the standard historical monograph, but it has been
extensively supplemented by K. H. D. Haley, *The First Earl of Shaftesbury*
(Oxford, 1968) and more recently by Richard Ashcraft, *Revolutionary Politics and
Locke's Two Treatises of Government* (Princeton, N.J., 1986).

[2] Jones, *First Whigs*; Jones, *Charles II: Royal Politician* (London, 1987); J. P.
Kenyon, *The Popish Plot* (Harmondsworth, 1974); Kenyon, *Stuart England*
(Harmondsworth, 1978), pp. 213–17; John Miller, *James II: A Study in Kingship*

parliamentary extremism, save for that of Shaftesbury and his immediate associates, these historians argue that the constitution was more a force of unity than of division.[3] Cautious in their treatment of party, they tend to see the first Whigs as an opposition fashioned and directed from Westminster by politicians seeking to advance the single cause of Exclusion.[4] To political ideas they devote selective attention, dismissing 'radical' or 'revolutionary' ideas in particular as without influence, or as without sincere proponents, or as epiphenomena arising from the anachronistic semantics of certain historians.[5]

Revisionist demythologizing leaves the first Whigs somewhat less cerebral than the first Tories, who were firm in their ideals of hereditary succession, divine right, and obedience in church and state. It also leaves the Whigs less motivated by religious scruples.[6] According to Jones, even at the height of the Exclusion Crisis, few dissenters were to be found among Whig leaders in Parliament or in the boroughs.[7] This absence is explained on several grounds. The dissenters are said to have 'turned their backs on the political

(Hove, 1978); Miller, 'Charles II and his Parliaments', *Transactions of the Royal Historical Society*, 5th series, 32 (1982), pp. 1–23. Jones has called attention to the importance of the localities and has done significant work on them for the reign of James II: *The Revolution of 1688 in England* (London, 1972), pp. 11, 14–16, 138ff. Nevertheless, these historians have done little with the local dimensions of Exclusion. As Miller acknowledges, his study of 'The Crown and the Borough Charters in the Reign of Charles II' is only incidentally about the internal politics of the boroughs: *English Historical Review*, 100 (1985), pp. 53–84.

[3] Jones, *First Whigs*, pp. 213–15; Jones, 'Parties and Parliament', in Jones, ed., *The Restored Monarchy, 1660–1688* (London, 1979), pp. 60–2; Miller, 'The Later Stuart Monarchy', in Jones, ed., *Restored Monarchy*, pp. 41–3; Miller, 'Charles II and his Parliaments', pp. 22–3; Miller, 'The Potential for "Absolutism" in Later Stuart England', *History*, 119 (1984), pp. 197, 205; Miller, *Restoration England: The Reign of Charles II* (London, 1985), pp. 53–6.

[4] Jones, *First Whigs*, pp. 7, 117–26, 211; Jones, *Revolution of 1688*, pp. 38–9; Jones, *Court and Country: England, 1658–1714* (Cambridge, Mass., 1978), pp. 197–8; Jones, 'Parties and Parliament', pp. 48–9, 59–60; Kenyon, *Stuart England*, p. 271; Miller, *Popery and Politics in England, 1660–88* (Cambridge, 1973), pp. 170, 187–8; Miller, 'Charles II and his Parliaments', p. 17.

[5] Jones, *First Whigs*, pp. 15–16, 213–15; Miller, *James II*, pp. 92–6; Miller, 'Charles II and his Parliaments', pp. 20–1; Miller, *The Glorious Revolution* (London, 1983), pp. 26–7; Miller, *Restoration England*, pp. vii, 65, 76. Kenyon's general views may be found in *Stuart England*, pp. 12, 195, 257, 271.

[6] Jones, *First Whigs*, pp. 10–12; Jones, 'Parties and Parliament', pp. 66–7; Kenyon, *Stuart England*, p. 219; Miller, 'Charles II and his Parliaments', p. 21; Miller, *Glorious Revolution*, pp. 30–1; Miller, *Restoration England*, p. 64. Kenyon's study of political ideas after the Revolution also bears upon these questions: *Revolution Principles: The Politics of Party 1689–1720* (Cambridge, 1977).

[7] Jones, 'Parties and Parliament', pp. 64, 211 n. 33.

activism of their Puritan fathers and grandfathers'.[8] They are said to have constituted a '*very* low proportion of the population'.[9] And they are said to have been effectively excluded from public office-holding and political life by the Corporation Act of 1661 and the Restoration oaths of allegiance and supremacy.[10]

No simple summary of the extensive work of these historians can reflect the many ways in which, individually, they have enriched and enlivened discussion of late seventeenth-century English political history. Nevertheless, whether their interpretations do justice to the events and issues that made Exclusion a 'critical' affair is a question worth considering. The Crisis of 1678–83 was, after all, a multi-dimensional crisis.[11] It involved constitutional disputes between the two Houses of Parliament. It involved disputes over the army[12] and over the organization of English trade.[13] It involved disputes over foreign policy and over judicial independence. It involved the passage of the Habeas Corpus Act, an end to press licensing, upheavals in many boroughs,[14] an effort to revise the Religious Settlement,[15] a Scottish rebellion – and last, but not least, a move to exclude the Duke of York from the succession. Features such as these were, no doubt, among those that inclined Lawrence Stone to characterize the Crisis as the first of three post-1660 'tremblors' or aftershocks of the mid-century earthquake that he defines as England's 'Great Revolution'. More so than the revisionist historians, he sees both the social conjuncture of religious dissent with trading wealth and the ideological disjuncture of rival

---

[8] Kenyon, *Stuart England*, p. 237; Jones, *Court and Country*, pp. 85, 139.

[9] Kenyon, *Stuart England*, p. 185 (my italics); Miller, *Restoration England*, pp. 71–2.

[10] Kenyon, *Stuart England*, pp. 182–3. Miller acknowledges the political importance of dissent in some boroughs: 'Crown and Charters', p. 70.

[11] I follow Jones's *First Whigs* in using the broad dates 1678–83 for a crisis deriving its name from the Exclusion Bills of 1679–81.

[12] See especially Lois G. Schwoerer, *'No Standing Armies!': The Antiarmy Ideology in Seventeenth-Century England* (Baltimore, 1974), pp. 95–136.

[13] P. Loughead, 'The East India Company in English Domestic Politics, 1657–88' (unpublished D. Phil. thesis, University of Oxford, 1981) pp. 163–74; William R. Scott, *The Constitution and Finance of English, Scottish and Irish Joint-Stock Companies to 1720*, 3 vols (Cambridge, 1910), vol. 2, pp. 139–49.

[14] These may be surveyed through the constituency studies in Basil Duke Henning, *The House of Commons, 1660–1690*, in *The History of Parliament*, 3 vols (London 1983), vol. 1.

[15] Henry Horwitz, 'Protestant Reconciliation in the Exclusion Crisis', *Journal of Ecclesiastical History*, 15 (1964), pp. 201–17.

political belief systems as formative in the Crises of 1678–83, 1688–9 and 1712–15.[16]

The present essay, an exploratory reinterpretation of London Whiggism in the first of these related crises, focuses upon the importance both of religious dissent and of radical political ideas.[17] The arguments will be made that the London Whig leadership was tightly interlocked with a London dissenting leadership of noteworthy social calibre, and that the visibility of religious dissenters in corporation politics antedated the Exclusion Crisis by a decade.[18] Further arguments will be made that the first London Whigs were imbued with radical ideas and that those ideas probably reflected the dissenting and puritan heritage of so many of their leaders. To argue in this way is also to raise rather delicate questions of political taxonomy.

All historians who write about seventeenth-century political radicalism are greatly indebted to J. C. D. Clark for his recent recital of the methodological problems inherent in their work.[19] Clark's strictures surely require a more systematic response than can be provided here, but the evidence from exclusionist London does point to a body of opinion and a body of people for whom an epithet such as 'radical' seems appropriate. To be specific, the London proponents of Exclusion advanced an ideological rationale for their political actions which challenged the Restoration order in city, state and church. This challenge arose from the London Whigs' popular understanding of civic government and electoral

---

16 Lawrence Stone, 'The Results of the English Revolutions of the Seventeenth Century', in J. G. A. Pocock, ed., *Three British Revolutions: 1641, 1688, 1776* (Princeton, N.J., 1980), pp. 24, 28, 30–1, 33ff.

17 Important work about London and the Exclusion Crisis includes: Tim Harris, *London Crowds in the Reign of Charles II* (Cambridge, 1987); David F. Allen, 'The Crown and the Corporation of London in the Exclusion Crisis, 1678–81' (unpublished Ph.D. thesis, University of Cambridge, 1977); Arthur G. Smith, 'London and the Crown, 1681–85' (unpublished Ph.D. thesis, University of Cambridge, 1967); Haley, *The First Earl of Shaftesbury*, especially chapter 29, pp. 684–704.

18 Evidence about Nonconformist office-holding in London during the Exclusion Crisis is entirely compatible with the recent demonstration that 25 per cent of Commons' members in the Exclusion Parliaments were from dissenting backgrounds. Henning, *The House of Commons*, vol. 1, pp. 13, 52–3. See also Richard Davis, 'The "Presbyterian" Opposition and the Emergence of Party in the House of Lords in the Reign of Charles II', in Clyve Jones, ed., *Party and Management in Parliament, 1660–1784* (London, 1984), pp. 1–35.

19 J. C. D. Clark, *Revolution and Rebellion: State and Society in England in the Seventeenth and Eighteenth Centuries* (Cambridge, 1986), pp. 97–103.

processes. City Whigs based these understandings upon right rather than upon prescription, and they derived the institutions and the processes of London government from custom rather than from the crown. Furthermore, both in their words and in their deeds, London exclusionists sanctioned resistance to magistrates whose actions showed disagreement with these premises. A designation of persons holding such views as radical, despite their unfamiliarity with the modern meaning of the term, may be somewhat anachronistic and historicist. Nevertheless, use of the term seems much less dangerous than the alternate and antiquarian danger of transposing seventeenth-century terminology like 'fanatic' or 'Oliverian' into contemporary analytical categories.[20] The approach to radicalism adopted here, then, is similar to that of Richard Ashcraft, who recently has not only portrayed the Exclusion movement as radical but has also rediscovered its chief philosopher and radical ideologue in John Locke.[21]

I

Londoners figured prominently in the events of the Exclusion Crisis, and the corporation of London is well known to have been an institutional centre of Whiggism. In the city, the struggle between exclusionist Whigs and loyalist Tories reached its apogee in the controversial election of sheriffs for London and Middlesex in 1682 and in the crown's ensuing *quo warranto* campaign against the corporation's charter in 1683. These events captured the attention of an anxious nation. They were both widely celebrated and widely lamented in contemporary verse, drama, broadsides, prints and playing cards. Indeed, the editors of the Yale edition of *Poems on Affairs of State* accord more space to poetry about the 1682 London shrieval election and the loss of the London charter than to poetry about any other theme or episode between 1660 and 1710, the Glorious Revolution included.[22] Why, then, we may ask,

[20] This point has also been made by J. C. Davis, 'Radicalism in a Traditional Society: The Evaluation of Radical Thought in the English Commonwealth 1649–1660', *History of Political Thought*, 3 (1982), pp. 202–4, and by Richard L. Greaves, *Deliver Us from Evil: The Radical Underground in Britain, 1660–1663* (New York, 1986), pp. 4–5.

[21] Ashcraft, *Revolutionary Politics*.

[22] George de F. Lord, Elias F. Mengel, Jr and Howard H. Schless, eds., *Poems on Affairs of State, 1660–1714* (hereafter *POAS*), vols 1–3 (London, 1963–8), vol. 3, pp. 207 ff., 421 ff.

did London politics so arouse the interest and the imaginations of the late-Caroline reading audience? What was it about the London Whigs in particular that so alarmed the crown and loyalist propagandists?

How urban Whiggism was perceived by its opponents is most strikingly revealed in the satirical verse of the late 1670s and the early 1680s. Two themes recur in anti-Whig verse polemics. The first is that the Whigs were really surreptitious puritans embarked upon a renewed crusade to refashion the Church of England. Inspired by Calvin and Knox, the London Whigs (or 'saints' or 'fanatics') were pictured as yearning for 'those blest reformation days' that ended with the return of Charles II.[23] The second anti-Whig theme is that the Exclusionists really intended to alter radically or even to overthrow the Restoration constitution. Decried as king-killers and commonwealthmen, the Whig leaders were damned with the deeds of 1641 and 1649; and they were associated with John Pym and John Hampden, with Hugh Peter and Old Noll, and with rebels as various as Absalom, Cataline and the Duke of Guise.[24] According to John Dryden, the London Whigs sought first to establish their commonwealth in the city, to 'make London independent of the crown: A realm apart, the Kingdom of the Town'.[25] Were these charges true?

The evidence about Whiggism and dissent, to be considered first, suggests that loyalist poetic propaganda does not exaggerate the Nonconformist texture of the city Exclusion movement. Identification of many hundreds of wealthy or politically active London dissenters of the Restoration allows some quantitative assessments of Nonconformist political strength in the corporation. The number of dissenters among the common councilmen is revealing. In 1681, the climactic year of Whig influence on the court of Common Council, at least sixty dissenters were elected to that body. They accounted for over 50 per cent of the Whig common councilmen of that year and for over one-quarter of the entire court.[26]

---

[23] *Ibid.*, pp. 224, 233, 264–5, 269, 272, 275, 366–71.

[24] *Ibid.*, pp. 232, 265, 359–60, and BL, Luttrell Collection of Ballads, nos. 15, 30 and 59 may be cited as examples.

[25] John Dryden, 'Prologue to *The Duke of Guise*', in *POAS*, vol. 3, p. 277. For an extended treatment of Tory propaganda and satire during the Exclusion Crisis, see Tim Harris, *London Crowds in the Reign of Charles II* (Cambridge, 1987), chapter 6, pp. 130–55.

[26] Smith, p. 24 n. 25, gives the number of Whig common councilmen for 1681 as 109. The total number of common councilmen was 234.

The presence of Nonconformists among the Whig aldermen of 1680–3 is even more notable. Seven of nine Whigs on the court of aldermen during those years were dissenters. They included both old Commonwealth civic leaders like Sir Thomas Alleyn and Sir John Frederick and younger men like Sir Patience Ward and Henry Cornish, the subsequent Rye House Plot martyr. The London dissenters' political spokesmen also included three of the city's four MPs in the Exclusion Parliaments – Alderman Thomas Pilkington, Chamberlain Sir Thomas Player[27] and the former alderman William Love. The 'old enthusiastic breed', who had so infiltrated the magisterial and legislative agencies of urban government, also confronted the judges on juries empanelled by Whig sheriffs; and they required purging from commanding positions within the London militia and lieutenancy. At least two-thirds of the London grand jurors empanelled in November 1681, for instance, can be identified as dissenters.[28]

Nonconformist office-holding and civic participation on this scale require an explanation, especially because the Restoration oaths and religious statutes were intended to prevent it. When, why, and how had London dissenters overcome these political obstacles? If the annual return of Nonconformists among common councilmen may be taken as a barometer of dissenting pressure in the corporation, a civic puritan revival clearly coincided with the expiration of the first Conventicle Act in 1668 (see Table 13.1).[29] During the act's operation, known dissenters on Common Council had been too few to affect urban governance; but in 1669 and again in 1671, forty identifiable dissenters served on the court. Among these dissenting common councilmen were perhaps a score of Commonwealth

[27] Evidence for Sir Thomas Player's religious views is difficult to interpret, but I am inclined to regard him as a dissenting spokesman. See Henning, *The House of Commons*, vol. 3, pp. 250–2.

[28] John Dryden, 'Absalom and Achitophel', (1681), 11. 529–30, in *POAS*, vol. 2, p. 475; PRO SP 29/417 (pt. 2), fos. 112–14; HMC *Ormonde*, new series, vol. 6, pp. 193, 197–9, 208. 39 per cent (88 of 225) of all London jurors empanelled by Whig sheriffs in 1681–2 have so far been identified as Nonconformists. I am indebted to Professor Smith for sharing his lists of Exclusion era London juries.

[29] Most of the sources employed in making these identifications of dissenting common councilmen and other dissenting office-holders are listed in Gary S. De Krey, *A Fractured Society: The Politics of London in the First Age of Party* (Oxford, 1985), pp. 74–85, 272–5. I here use the concepts of 'dissent' and 'nonconformity' in the same sense that I used the phrase 'dissenting interest' in *A Fractured Society*.

Table 13.1. *Nonconformist common councilmen in London,*
1664–83

1664:	21	1669:	40	1674:	35	1679:	38
1665:	16	1670:	33	1675:	50	1680:	54
1666:	19	1671:	40	1676:	50	1681:	60
1667:	26	1672:	36	1677:	45	1682:	51
1668:	22	1673:	32	1678:	36	1683:	44

veterans resuming places they had relinquished in the early 1660s,
but more notable were the emerging dissenting spokesmen of a new
generation, such as Thomas Pilkington and Samuel Swynoke.
Prophetically, Alderman Sir John Robinson, the court's staunchest
city ally, warned in 1671 of the danger from a 'gang' of 'factious
men' on Common Council.[30] By 1674–6, the King's city friends
were even more concerned about disaffected common councilmen;
and an accompanying upsurge of dissenters on the court, to fifty,
occurred then.[31]

The Nonconformist common councilmen of 1680–2, then, drew
strength both from their numbers and from a long-term renewal of
dissenting civic experience. Aldermanic selections between 1667 and
1681 tell a similar story of long-term puritan resurgence culminating
in the Exclusion Crisis. Between those dates, dissenters accounted
for 43 per cent of all individuals nominated from the wards for
vacancies on that court.[32] Those same fifteen years saw an extraordinarily high number of vetoes of aldermanic nominees by the full
court of aldermen. The principal explanation for these vetoes is
surely the fact that three-fifths of the rejected nominees can be
identified as separatists from the established church.[33]

This chronological survey provides an answer to the question of
when London dissenters returned to politics, but the why and how
of their return are more complicated questions. A complete expla-

---

[30] *CSPD 1671–72*, p. 40
[31] See, for instance, Sir R. Viner to H. Coventry, BL M/863/11: MS Coventry 16,
fos. 21–2. I hope to examine the role of dissent in corporation politics from the
Restoration to the Exclusion Crisis elsewhere.
[32] Names of aldermanic nominees may be found in the ward sections of Alfred B.
Beaven, *The Aldermen of the City of London temp. Henry III–1908*, 2 vols
(1908–13), vol. 1, *passim*.
[33] Thirty-two aldermanic nominees, of whom nineteen have so far been identified as
dissenters, were rejected by the court of aldermen between 1667 and 1681.
Beaven, *Aldermen*, vol. 1, pp. 247–8.

nation would require consideration of the encouragement received from clerical leaders, of the effects of haphazard enforcement of changeable religious policies, of the seeming stimulus of sharp if short-term persecution, and of the sheer force of Nonconformist numbers. What will be emphasized here is the additional and instrumental factor of a dissenting political leadership extending to the highest reaches of commercial society.

Historians of mid-seventeenth-century trade, especially Robert Brenner, have argued for an association between pronounced religious dissent and unregulated overseas trade and interloping activities.[34] However, dissenters were also prominent, after 1660, among the magnates of regulated, monopoly companies. The Levant Company, the East India Company and the Royal African Company all benefited from the favour of the state; and the two joint-stocks among them are sometimes pictured as 'Restoration' companies with leaderships tied to the court. Nevertheless, at least 35 per cent of their directors, from 1660–88, may be identified as dissenters.[35] Among these captains of dissenting capital were such civic exclusionists as Sir John Frederick, William Love, Thomas Papillon and Thomas Pilkington, all of whom served on the aldermanic bench at one time or another. Similarly, 31 per cent of those East India investors whose large stock holdings made them eligible in 1682 for election to the company's directing body can be tied to dissent.[36] And the adherence to dissent of about one-third of the London merchants active at the time of the Crisis again points to trading wealth as the marrow of dissenting political respectability.[37]

Clearly, London Nonconformists were able to challenge the Restoration polity because so many of their spokesmen possessed the wealth, status and civic esteem that commanded office and

[34] Robert Brenner, 'The Civil War Politics of London's Merchant Community', *Past and Present*, 58 (1973), pp. 53–107.

[35] 35 per cent (90 of 257) of the Restoration (1660–88) directors of the East India Company, Royal African Company and Levant Company have so far been identified as Nonconformists.

[36] Fifty-seven of 181 East India Company investors of April 1682 with £1,000 stock or more can be identified as probable or definite dissenters. PRO SP 29/418, fo. 174.

[37] Seventy-three of 225 importers (32 per cent) paying £30 duty or more in the London port books for December 1680 to April 1681 may be identified as dissenters, a sample sufficiently large to establish the figure. I am indebted to Professor Smith for sharing his transcripts of Exclusion era port books and stock lists.

influence. If historians are to repeat the contemporary association of Nonconformity with the 'trading interest', they need to be mindful of the social complexities which this language encodes. The trading interest of London, from which its dissenting interest arose, extended from the city's middling sort to its merchant princes. Behind these civic dissenting eminences stood the serried ranks of numerous urban dissenting congregations, distinguishable by persuasion and social calibre.

That the 'faction' and the 'fanatics' were interchangeable terms in the London loyalists' political lexicon should, therefore, occasion little surprise.[38] Both the number of Nonconformist office-holders and the social resources of the dissenting community were essential to the Whigs' political strength in the city. And in the corporation, the loyalist perception that Whig success spelled both a church and a crown in danger not only preceded the Revolution of 1688–9 but also informed the first London Tories. Although London and Westminster churchmen worried about popish designs, they were still more worried about the designs of 'a malicious fanatic party' intent on driving the Crisis to an 'end as fatal to the crown as formerly'.[39]

II

So generic an identification of London Whiggism with dissent also raises questions about the ideology of the London Whigs. Much work has been done on the relationship between religious and political radicalism in the mid-seventeenth century, and Richard Ashcraft makes a case for a radical Exclusion movement intimately associated with Nonconformity. If the London Exclusion movement was so strongly a dissenting movement, can it also have been a politically radical movement? Or, as Sir Roger L'Estrange repeatedly charged, were the first London Whigs driven forward by fiery spirits attached to the 'Good Old Cause'?

This question is not a new one, but the quest for elusive city radicals has so far proved disappointing. Three misconceptions have clouded the issue. First, political radicals have been sought more on the peripheries of the Whig following than in the party's

---

[38] HMC *Seventh Report*, Appendix, p. 475; HMC *Ormonde*, new series, vol. 5, p. 345, and vol. 6, p. 154.
[39] HMC *Ormonde*, new series, vol. 4, p. 496.

centre. Radicalism has been associated with Whiggish artisans and tradesmen almost to the exclusion of the thriving retailers and overseas merchants who provided the London Whig leadership. Secondly, radicalism and republicanism have been confused and need to be distinguished.[40] To be sure, the radical city Whigs included both nostalgic republican intellectuals like Sheriff Slingsby Bethel or John Wildman and diehard republican plotters like those who frequented the Baptist club at the Salutation tavern, Lombard Street.[41] For the most part, however, city radicalism was a more pragmatic populism. It emerged more from widespread reflection upon the corporation's history and purposes than from the philosophical niceties of any school of republicanism.

Thirdly, the study of London radicalism has been retarded by the acceptance of models of radical ideology and behaviour drawn from parliamentary affairs. Approaches to political radicalism in seventeenth-century England have frequently suffered from the assumption that radical ideas were inherently related to dramatic parliamentary confrontations over constitutional issues of national importance. Such approaches run the risk of overlooking the local circumstances in communities represented at Westminster that strongly influenced the political development of radical attitudes. London radicals, as a case in point, need to be understood intellectually within the context of the city corporation, a constitutional environment that was more immediate to them than the related but broader one found in the geographically adjacent national seat of power. In times of crisis, London citizens were as likely to view the politics of Westminster and Whitehall from the perspective of the politics of Guildhall and the livery companies as vice versa. In the Exclusion Crisis, the political language with which London radicals approached the struggle for power between the court and the opposition was fundamentally fashioned within the city's own collective structures of government.

The argument to be presented here, then, is that a radical, but not consciously republican, ideology inspired and motivated the first London Whigs. That ideology arose within the political environment of the corporation, although it was certainly sharpened, redirected and refined in its application to national affairs. If

---

[40] Tim Harris makes the same point in an unpublished essay about the Green Ribbon Club. I am grateful to him for sharing this essay with me.
[41] *Calendar of State Papers Domestic 1682* (hereafter *CSPD*) pp. 357–8, 493–7.

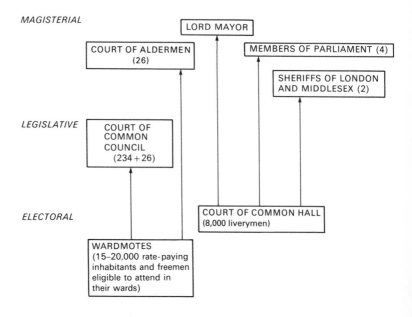

MAGISTERIAL

LORD MAYOR

COURT OF ALDERMEN
(26)

MEMBERS OF PARLIAMENT (4)

SHERIFFS OF LONDON
AND MIDDLESEX (2)

LEGISLATIVE

COURT OF
COMMON
COUNCIL
(234 + 26)

ELECTORAL

COURT OF COMMON HALL
(8,000 liverymen)

WARDMOTES
(15–20,000 rate-paying
inhabitants and freemen
eligible to attend in
their wards)

Figure 13.1   Institutions and personnel of Corporation of London Governance
The major electoral processes within the corporation are indicated by arrows.
Common Councilmen were directly chosen by the wardmotes, and MPs were
directly chosen by Common Hall. Elections of aldermen and of the Lord Mayor
were indirect, with the Court of Aldermen choosing from nominees forwarded,
respectively, by a wardmote or by Common Hall. Whether shrieval elections were
direct or indirect was a major constitutional issue in the Corporation, as is
explained in the text. The twenty-six aldermen also sat as a separate and distinct
body in the Court of Common Council.

the London Whigs of the Exclusion Crisis are to be properly
understood, therefore, they need to be examined not only with
reference to the critical issues of the political macrocosm, such as
the succession, the church, the army and foreign policy, but also

with reference to the political circumstances of the civic microcosm. Several historians have examined London Whiggism of the early 1680s using the first of these methods; but the relatively unfamiliar details of the corporation's constitution have made more difficult a comprehension of London radicalism in its local political environment. Attention to the largely neglected corporation controversia of 1680–3 suggests that the London Whigs advanced as radical and populist an understanding of civic government as had been offered by the Levellers and city radicals of the previous generation.

III

The 'heats' within the corporation that accompanied the Exclusion Crisis involved deep-seated constitutional disagreements between the first London Tories and the first London Whigs. The fundamental issue in dispute was whether political authority in the city resided primarily with the Lord Mayor and Court of Aldermen or with the Common Council, the electoral Common Hall, and the freemen and liverymen (see Figure 13.1).[42] The Tories argued for the first and traditional alternative; the Whigs insisted that the second arrangement ought to prevail. Clashes occurred in May 1681, for example, when Thomas Papillon and other leading Whigs pushed through Common Council a petition to the crown for a successor to the Oxford Parliament.[43] In doing so, the Whig Common Council majority ignored the customary veto that the predominantly Tory Court of Aldermen had expected to exercise. In this assertion of the legislative independence of Common Council from magisterial direction, the Whig city leaders also denied the Lord Mayor the presiding authority in that court which was claimed

---

[42] The best short account of the city's seventeenth-century constitution is Valerie Pearl, *London and the Puritan Revolution* (Oxford, 1961), pp. 45–68.

[43] Journals of the Court of Common Council (hereafter Journal) 49, fo. 205; Repertories of the Court of Aldermen, Corporation of London RO (hereafter Repertory) 86, fo. 128. H3429 (first references to seventeenth-century pamphlet titles are given in short form as catalogued in the Wing *Short-Title Catalogue . . . 1641–1700*, 3 vols (New York, 1945–51), and they are preceded by their Wing numbers): *The Humble Petition and Address of the Right Honourable the Lord Mayor . . . of London* (London, 1681); L2882: *A Brief Account of What Pass'd at the Common Council . . . 13th. day of May. 1681* (1681); *True Protestant Mercury*, no. 37, 11–14 May 1681.

for him by the Tories. As one Whig author wrote in 1682, the Common Councilmen had full authority to determine disputed elections, to arrange their own agenda, to consider petitions, and to elect appropriate corporation officers free from the influence or interference of the Lord Mayor and the aldermen.[44] This was so because the common councilmen were 'the representatives of the people',[45] deriving their powers from the anterior and superior authority of the liverymen and the freemen, 'the people' who made up the city's two-tier electorate.

Although the radicalism of the first London Whigs included an elevation of the powers of Common Council in relation to those of the aldermen and the Lord Mayor, their arguments really centred upon the authority and the electoral integrity of the 8,000 liverymen when assembled in Common Hall. The annual meetings of that body on Midsummer's Day and on 29 September, for the respective elections of the sheriffs of London and Middlesex and of the Lord Mayor, became ideological forums during the Exclusion Crisis. Whigs like Alderman Thomas Pilkington and Recorder Sir George Treby publicly contended, in the strongest possible language, that Common Hall was 'the supreme authority in London' and 'the greatest of all lawful Assemblies in the Kingdom'.[46] And, if this was true, as the argument was enlarged upon by Whig pamphleteers, then the will of the Common Hall majority could be restrained neither by the magistrates nor by Common Council.

The disputed 1682 shrieval election, the climax of London's Exclusion Crisis and the occasion for the crown's 'riot' charge against leading city Whigs, saw the fullest articulation of the Whigs' popular understanding of electoral supremacy in the corporation.[47] The Tory Lord Mayor, Sir John Moore, sought to make binding upon the liverymen his use of the traditional mayoral

---

[44] Journal 49, fos. 277–8; N9: D. N., *A Letter from an Old Common-Council-Man to one of the New Common-Council* [1682]; *True Protestant Mercury*, no. 99, 14–17 Dec. 1681.

[45] W1687: James Whiston, *Serious Advice, Presented to the Common Council* (London, 1681), p. 5.

[46] S4469A: *Some Account of the proceedings at Guildhall . . . 24th of June* (London 1682); *CSPD 1682*, p. 417.

[47] Contemporary accounts include A356: *An Account of the proceedings at Guild-Hall on the 19th. Instant, 1682* (London, 1682); *Some Account of the Proceedings*; and Luttrell, *A Brief Historical Relation of State Affairs*, 6 vols (Oxford, 1859), vol. 1, pp. 196ff. Also see successive issues of the *Observator* and *True Protestant Mercury*.

nomination of one sheriff. The first of several Common Halls required to complete the election was disrupted when a majority of the liverymen refused to recognize both Moore's designation of Dudley North as one sheriff and his power to dissolve the unruly Hall. Responding to the dissident electors, the incumbent Whig sheriffs proceeded with a poll after Moore's departure; and they declared the election of Thomas Papillon and his fellow Whig merchant, John Dubois. With the assistance of the crown, and despite strenuous opposition, Moore and the Tory aldermen succeeded, in subsequent reconventions of the Hall, in overturning this popular choice and in declaring the election of loyalist sheriffs. They could not, however, silence the expression of radical Whig sentiment.

During this episode, the Whigs maintained that the sheriffs, and not the Lord Mayor, were the proper officers for conducting and managing Common Hall business.[48] The Lord Mayor ordinarily was expected to summon the liverymen. According to the Whigs, however, he could not dissolve Common Hall, and his presence was not required to legitimate Common Hall actions.[49] If he participated in the affairs of Common Hall – and Whig writers were divided as to whether he should – he participated in his capacity as elector and not in any presiding capacity, 'being there only in the quality of a *concivis*, or fellow-citizen'.[50] Needless to say, the Lord Mayor could make no claim of a prescriptive right of nomination in shrieval elections.[51] In fact, his authority as principal officer of the corporation was entirely derived from popular consent: 'What power the mayor has is but delegated from the citizens.'[52] The sheriffs, too, were subordinate to the Common Hall, acting as

---

[48] E3578: *An Exact Account of the Proceedings at Guildhall* (London, 1682); N244: *The Nature of a Common-Hall Briefly Stated* (London, 1682); S3235: *The Sheriffs of London for the Time Being, are the Proper Managers* (London, 1682).

[49] R1516: *The Rights of the City Farther Unfolded* (London, 1682), pp. 2–3.

[50] *Sheriffs of London for the Time Being.* Also see: C857: *The Case between the L.d Mayor & Commons of London concerning the Election of Sheriffs* (London, 1682), p. 6; M1304: *The Matters of Fact in the Present Election of Sheriffs* (London, 1682), p. 2; R1504: *The Right of Electing Sheriffs* (London, 1682), p. 4. An alternate radical view is found in L3049: *The Lord Mayor of London's Vindication* (London, 1682), pp. 3–4.

[51] See, for instance: I76: *An Impartial Account of the Proceedings of the Common-Hall of the City of London . . . June the 24th, 1682* (London, 1682); P3533: *The Priviledg and Right of the Free-men of London* (London, 1682), pp. 4–5; *Sheriffs of London for the Time Being.*

[52] *Case between the L.d Mayor & Commons*, p. 7.

'servants' of the liverymen, who might 'remove them when they will'.[53] Finally, as the 'supreme authority' in London, the liverymen could meet on their own initiative: 'In case he [the Lord Mayor] should fail in convocating them at due times and seasons, and for the necessary affairs and occasions of the Corporation, they may come together of their own accord.'[54]

Despite the infrequency of its meetings, Common Hall was, in the Whigs' popular conception, clearly the directing body of civic governance, an electoral institution that operated entirely according to consensual processes. Common Hall owed its supremacy to two facts: it was the largest assembly of citizens in the corporation, and its liveried members spoke not just for themselves but for all those free of the corporation, many of whom might yet don the liveries of their companies. Common Hall was as much a 'representative' body as Common Council because, in one court as in the other, a group of citizens acted on behalf of all the citizens, who vicariously or 'congruously' participated in the actions of their representatives.[55] In other words, the 'people' of the corporation, its 15–20,000 rate-paying freemen, were the ultimate source of legitimacy in the city. Radical Whig writers did not use the phrase 'popular sovereignty', but their conception of civic government was not so different from what subsequent writers and historians have meant by that phrase. The Whigs' popular understanding of civic government and electoral processes made the corporation a real democracy of sovereign freemen.

IV

How could such a radical understanding of London government be justified? What legitimated popular rule on the very threshold of the King's court? Whig writers developed answers in which civic governance and electoral processes were based upon right rather than upon prescription and were derived from custom rather than from the crown. In doing so, they again departed from assumptions about the civic order that had prevailed before the Revolution and that had been operational since the Restoration.

The most philosophical of these justifications of popular rights in

---

[53] C4341A: *The Citizens of London, by their Charter* [1680].
[54] *Rights of the City Farther Unfolded*, p. 3.
[55] *Priviledg and Right*, p. 6.

the corporation is found in Thomas Hunt's *Defence of the Charter, and Municipal Rights of the City of London*. Writing in 1683, Hunt was specifically concerned to combat court pressure upon Common Council, then firmly in Tory hands, to surrender the corporation charter and thereby to spare the crown the reproach of having it declared legally forfeit. He maintained that Common Council could not deprive the London citizens of their electoral rights and that Common Council decisions could be overturned by Common Hall acting on behalf of the citizenry.[56] This was so, according to Hunt, because Common Council was a historically recent creation of the more ancient Common Hall, which had given it limited and delegated powers. Moreover, just as it was the 'business and trust' of Common Council 'to manage and defend, govern and protect . . . the Rights of the City', so also Common Hall could not surrender the rights of individual citizens. Because surrendering the charter implied a dissolution of the corporation and a loss of rights, such a surrender could take place only by action of the corporation's members, the citizens and freemen, the source of political authority in the city. As a 'body politic', the corporation had originated before its first charter in the unanimous resolve of its founders to leave the state of nature together; and it could be freely dissolved, with an accompanying loss of rights, only by the unanimous agreement of its present members.[57]

Hunt's *Defence* more faithfully reflects the radical character of city Whig argument than the corporation's more circumspect counsel in the *quo warranto* case.[58] However, Whig pamphleteers of the city's Exclusion Crisis generally centred their arguments on civic rights derived from custom rather than on natural rights protected by contract. Their avoidance of the abstract language of nature and contract is not surprising. The political discourse of London citizens was fashioned within a tangible framework of written charters and by-laws that largely obviated recourse to hypothetical contracts. City Whig argument needed to appeal to an active but philosophically unsophisticated citizenry reared in the petty schools of ward and parish duty and in the grander schools of guild regulation, chartered trade and civic ritual. In each of these

---

[56] H3750: Thomas Hunt, *A Defence of the Charter* (London, 1683), p. 35.

[57] *Ibid.*, p. 41.

[58] T. B. Howell, ed., *A Complete Collection of State Trials*, 33 vols (London, 1816–26; hereafter *ST*), vol. 8, 1039ff.; Jennifer Levin, *The Charter Controversy in the City of London, 1660–1688, and its Consequences* (1969), pp. 34ff.

spheres, according to the Whigs, London freemen exercised fundamental rights – or 'radical liberties'[59] – that could not be infringed
without a collapse of the entire civic order. These rights were a
'possession'[60] guaranteed by the corporation's successive charters,
but they originated neither in royal prescription nor in parliamentary regulation. Their origins were located rather in immemorial custom; and in explaining how this was so, Whig spokesmen
utilized the well-studied common law theory of an 'ancient constitution'.[61]

The argument for civic rights grounded in ancient custom was
again most fully developed with reference to the free election of
sheriffs by Common Hall, and it was again developed in a distinctly
popular manner. As one anonymous pamphleteer wrote, 'The
privilege of choosing sheriffs ... did anciently belong to the
freeholders, ... and that right they long enjoyed without the
authority of any act of parliament or statute, merely by virtue of the
common law of the land, upon the foundation of immemorial
usage.'[62] Another pamphleteer wrote, 'The barons of London,
which were the freemen, chose sheriffs by the name of portreeves,
long before a mayor was in London, as may be seen by the ancient
records', adding that 'our Court of Common Hall is in nature of the
old folkmoot'.[63] To the radical mind, these assertions negated any
by-laws supporting a mayoral claim of nomination in shrieval
elections; and they also destroyed the loyalist argument that the
freemen's liberties rested upon the royal grants of successive city
charters.[64] The charter granted by William I, for example, merely
confirmed that the 'freemen shall continue a city and county', by
pledging 'that he should not by his power break in upon the rights of
the county of the city of London'.[65] Moreover, both this charter
and those that followed were granted 'with the consent and

---

[59] C1164: *The Case of the Sheriffs for the Year 1682* (London, 1682), pp. 14–16.
Although radical writers also referred to the 'privileges', 'franchises' and 'liberties' of the citizens, they used these terms largely as synonyms for 'rights' or as
rhetorical reinforcements of the meaning of right.

[60] T2377: *A True Account of the Irregular Proceedings at Guild-Hall* [London,
1682], p. 3.

[61] J. G. A. Pocock, *The Ancient Constitution and the Feudal Law: English
Historical Thought in the Seventeenth Century* (Cambridge, 1957).

[62] *Priviledg and Right*, p. 2.

[63] *Lord Mayor of London's Vindication*, pp. 2, 5.

[64] *Ibid.*, p. 2. Also see *Right of Electing Sheriffs*, pp. 1–3.

[65] Hunt, *Defence of the Charter*, p. 39. Hunt's arguments from nature were
supplemented by arguments from custom.

authoritate parliamenti.[66] In other words, because such fundamental rights as choosing sheriffs belonged to the London electors 'by appointment of the common law', they could be altered only by Parliament in its role as guardian of the ancient constitution.[67]

The theory of an ancient constitution was, of course, neither inherently radical nor necessarily republican, and it could easily be put to conservative use. In fact, the London pamphleteers who utilized the ancient constitution during the Exclusion Crisis thereby deprived themselves of the Leveller concept of a 'Norman Yoke', which lent itself so well to a systematic reconstruction of institutions. Nevertheless, the city Whigs' employment of common law ideas in their constitutional arguments was a radical employment that served to legitimate a democratic civic order. Incorporating a folk myth of the immemorial past as popular as the royalist myth of Filmer was patriarchal, these ideas also served to stiffen widespread resistance to magistrates and ministers upholding the Restoration order in city and state.

V

The involvement, alleged or actual, of leading city Whigs such as Henry Cornish, Sir Patience Ward, Thomas Papillon and Slingsby Bethel in armed resistance or conspiracy, beginning in 1683, has long been noted in the historical literature. However, these leaders have been treated as individuals; and their actions have not been well related to the intellectual and strategic evolution of London's civic opposition towards ever greater extremism and desperation. The critical questions in evaluating this evolution (as in evaluating that of the parliamentary Whigs) are whether, when, and to what extent opposition transcended the corporation's ordinary constitutional procedures to become extra-constitutional resistance. The shrieval election of 1682 again seemingly marked a transition from the occasional Whig resort to rhetorical violence and physical force to the rationalization and legitimization of such behaviour as instruments in Whig party warfare. This protracted election clearly became the *pièce de résistance* of radical obstacles to the restoration of magisterial and royal authority in London.

Lacking potential support from a sitting House of Commons, the London Whigs saw their efforts in the summer of 1682 as an

[66] *Priviledg and Right*, p. 2.   [67] Hunt, *Defence of the Charter*, p. 39.

essential defensive manoeuvre against that 'cankerworm' or 'Tarantula', the Duke of York, who had returned from Scotland 'to cut the citizens' throats', as Thomas Pilkington reportedly stated.[68] The reasoned language of Whig argument increasingly gave way to angry words and angry deeds in the series of Common Hall meetings that began in June. To adopt the court and Tory perspective, Whig actions became so threatening as to require the prosecution of city Whig leaders for riot to prevent activities more dangerous still.

In his determination to overturn the original selection of Whig shrieval candidates by Common Hall, Lord Mayor Sir John Moore was confronted and impeded time and again by the chants of massed Whig liverymen: 'No pensioner, no bribed magistrate!'; 'No new election!'[69] To the Whigs, these refrains were the 'sacred sound'[70] of popular authority combating magisterial misdeeds. The Whigs reminded the lord mayor and the Tory aldermen that Common Hall was styled a court because of its ability to sit in judgement over corporation officers.[71] If the liverymen represented the entire body of citizens, as the Whigs also argued, then they were entrusted with a popular right to check the behaviour of their magistrates. Should the aldermen accept shrieval candidates favoured by the court but not favoured by the majority of the electors, 'the Common Hall may vote them out, and choose others in their room'.[72]

The popular arsenal of punishments and reprisals placed in readiness for the Lord Mayor and loyalist aldermen also included lawsuits, indictments and disfranchisements. Some seventy-five Whig citizens, with financial backing from their leaders, initiated King's Bench suits against the Lord Mayor for all manner of evil, including treason.[73] The Whigs further directed the Lord Mayor's

---

[68] Library of Congress, MS Sydserf Newsletters (B), 21 March 1682; *ST*, ix, 299ff.; Luttrell, *Brief Historical Relation*, vol. 1, p. 240. I am grateful to Professor Smith for sharing his transcripts of the Sydserf newsletters.

[69] MS Sydserf (B), 24 June 1682; A356: *Account of the Proceedings at Guild-Hall on the 19th. Instant, 1682* (London, 1682).

[70] Whiston, *Serious Advice*, p. 5.

[71] *Matters of Fact*, p. 1; *The Rights of the City Farther Unfolded*, p. 2.

[72] *Matters of Fact*, p. 4.

[73] MS Sydserf (B), 29 July, 1 and 3 August 1682; M2368: *A Modest Enquiry Concerning the Election of the Sheriffs* (London, 1682), p. 43; *Nature of a Common-Hall; Case between the Ld Mayor & Commons*, p. 5; *Right of Electing Sheriffs*, p. 4; *The Rights of the City Farther Unfolded*, p. 2; *Priviledg and Right*, p. 7.

attention to the parliamentary impeachment of Sir Richard Gurney in 1642 for having betrayed his trust as Lord Mayor in supporting 'arbitrary government'.[74] They cited as timely the example of Sir Nicholas Brembre, the Lord Mayor executed in 1388 'for neglecting the duty of his place, and acting according to the dictates of Court ministers'.[75]

It is perfectly true that these responses involved actions or envisaged actions initiated through the judicial and political systems of the state or the corporation; but the language employed is that of intimidation rather than that of counsel. All these actions were extraordinary and controversial remedies designed to reverse an implied breakdown of the city's ordinary constitutional order. What the Whigs were really engaged in was extreme action to preserve their understanding of the corporation against its enemies in high places. Their example of the trial and execution of a Lord Mayor was, against the background of 1649, also an example of the constitutional and legal ambiguity of their reprisals. The Whigs were, in fact, proceeding in an extra-constitutional manner, both in their rhetoric and in reality. Their remedies found ultimate sanction not in the employment of judicial forms but in the articulation of a popular right of resistance which many citizens were prepared to exercise.

Accordingly, the hustings displayed memorable scenes of Whig sheriffs and Whig aldermen publicly defying mayoral order and royal writ and claiming popular instruction in their support. On two occasions, opposing magistrates proceeded with opposing polls for opposing candidates as if the city had opposing governments. The Common Hall of 5 July 1682 was reportedly attended by 'many people ... armed as if they had been going to a battle'; and a delegation of Whigs who subsequently attended the court of aldermen to remonstrate with the Lord Mayor also included 'an incredible number of people well armed'.[76] After the Common Hall of 14 July, the Lord Mayor was confronted by dissidents threatening 'to pull him from the chair'; and two months later, he required armed rescue from 'the people' outside his barricaded chamber at Guildhall.[77] Moore's increasing reliance upon the

---

[74] *Modest Enquiry*, p. 27; Pearl, pp. 155–8.   [75] *Matters of Fact*, p. 4.

[76] MS Sydserf (B), 6 and 8 July 1682. The information against the city rioters reiterates that they acted 'with force and arms', language that was seemingly employed for more than form's sake. *ST*, ix, 219–26.

[77] MS Sydserf (B), 27 July and 21 September 1682.

trained bands and royal guards to police Common Hall, and to protect himself, only stimulated further resistance to 'military power'.[78] Although Tory sheriffs and a new Tory lord mayor secured their offices in the face of such resistance, the Whigs disrupted civil authority anew in April 1683, when Thomas Papillon and John Dubois, the disappointed Whig shrieval candidates, prompted the brief arrest of the new Lord Mayor and the Tory aldermen on a mandamus for the offices they still claimed.[79] If popular resistance was not yet rebellion, the seeds of rebellion had been well planted in the city by the radical Whigs.

VI

The city Whigs' radical understanding of London government and electoral processes was, therefore, advanced through unequivocal words and deeds. They based their arguments upon both right and custom, and they countenanced popular resistance to the Restoration order in the corporation. The radicals' understanding of the civic constitution was that of neither the London Tories nor the court, who believed that, since 1660, the government of the corporation had been resumed on the basis of royal grant and magisterial prerogative. As the Whigs offered their popular understanding of the constitution, London and court loyalists insisted that the corporation was 'a body politic, consisting of a head and members . . . in which . . . the mayor is not only an integral part; but the most eminent and principal, as the head to the body; and nothing can be done by the Corporation without him'.[80] If the radical assertion of Common Hall authority prevailed, then, claimed the Tories, 'the law of the land, the charter, and constitution of the city [would be] overthrown at a dash; and an absolute, arbitrary, and unaccountable power, lodged in the multitude'.[81] Success for the Whigs' campaign of popular resistance was all that was required for 'the introducing of a democracy, and making

[78] *Ibid.*, 19 and 28 September 1682; Luttrell, *Brief Historical Relation*, vol. 1, 224; *True Account of the Irregular Proceedings*, pp. 1–2.
[79] Repertory 88, fo. 128; *Observator*, no. 329, 28 April 1683; Luttrell, *Brief Historical Relation*, vol. 1, p. 256; *ST*, x, 319 ff.
[80] L3051: *The Lord Mayor's Right of Electing a Sheriff Asserted* (London, 1682), p. 6.
[81] *Observator*, no. 176, 24 July 1682.

London a theatre of violence and disorder, as much as Rome or Florence was'.[82]

The political disorders in the civic microcosm that stemmed from the London Whigs' ideology threatened, moreover, to infect the macrocosm of the Restoration state as well. No matter how firmly the city opposition renounced republicanism in favour of the forms and principles of 'English monarchy',[83] it was a somewhat different form of monarchy that Cavalier parliamentarians thought they had restored twenty years earlier. Civic loyalists, therefore, saw the philosophy of their opponents as entirely destructive of the political and social ideals of the Stuart regime: 'And if you can but once top the Lord Mayor and Court of Aldermen with a Common Hall, it is but one step more ... to the binding of your kings in chains and your nobles in links of iron.'[84] Because the London Whigs' leadership and electoral support was drawn so heavily from dissenting ranks, civic Tories concluded also that the challenge from the Whigs raised fundamental religious issues that had not been so decisively settled in the early 1660s after all. How else were they to interpret Whig and dissenting casuistry about the taking of oaths and sacraments or the explicit city Whig goal of eliminating statutory impediments to Nonconformist worship?[85]

These shocked and incredulous Tory responses better reflect the nature of London Whig ideology than the perspectives of some historians who have professed so much difficulty in finding radical ideas after 1660. Tory writers indulged in rhetorical inflation, to be sure, as did their Whig counterparts; but no doubt can exist in this case that the rhetoric embellished real constitutional and ideological conflicts. Although Tories were too prone to construe London Whig arguments in republican categories, they were not amiss in pointing out how radically and fundamentally these arguments differed from traditional political assumptions. Moreover, the city Whigs' critics appropriately pointed to the corporation rather than to Westminster as the constitutional arena in which

---

[82] *Lord Mayor's Right*, p. 2.
[83] Journal 49, fo. 206; *Humble Petition and Address*.
[84] *Observator*, no. 163, 1 July 1682. Also see S2205: *A Seasonable Address to the Right Honourable, the Lord Mayor* [London, 1680], pp. 1–2.
[85] *Observator*, no. 66, 29 October 1681; *Case of the Sheriffs*, pp. 14–16, 20, 26, 32; S3234: *The Sheriffs Case Whether* (London, 1681); T2809: *A True Narrative of the Proceedings at Guild-Hall, London, the Fourth of ... February* (London, 1681).

the Whigs' radicalism found its original idiom and was most continuously displayed.

An exhaustive interpretation of the radicalism of the first London Whigs would require a reassessment of their participation in strategies to bind Charles II in the parliamentary chains of a Protestant succession, a Protestant foreign policy, a less restrictive religious policy and a more restrictive military settlement. This task will not be attempted here. Enough has been said to reveal the radicalism of the original London Whigs in their formative constitutional environment. Enough has also been said to raise doubts about whether the revisionist belittlement of Whig radicalism is the best corrective to the errors of those 'whiggish' historians too prone to assimilate seventeenth-century radicalism to nineteenth-century categories. The London Whigs of the Exclusion Crisis, considered as an example of seventeenth-century radicalism, may not have offered the programmatic radicalism that inspired some British radicals after the French Revolution. They none the less articulated a radically libertarian philosophy of civic government. That they did not generally intend to replace one set of political institutions with another, either in the city corporation or in the English state, is really no argument against their radicalism. Full implementation of their proposed reversal of the chain of command between the electorate and the chief magistrate would have effected a radical redistribution of power within the corporation.

Similarly, that the London Whigs of the early 1680s were, for the most part, not philosophical republicans is no argument against their radicalism. In their case, as in the case of the radical John Locke, the true measures of radicalism are not to be found in republican institutional blueprints but rather in advocacy of a wide and free electorate, accountable government, and individual rights secured through appropriate actions, including resistance.[86] Finally, although the London Whigs were pragmatic radicals, they cannot be dismissed as opportunistic or insincere in their profession of popular principles.[87] The London Whigs of the Exclusion Crisis were not a wealthy clique of political fortune-hunters buying their way to power through popular appeasement; they were rather a broad-based party, or 'faction', whose ideology reflected the beliefs

[86] For these reasons I find too schematic the definition of 'effective radicalism' in J. C. Davis's otherwise helpful 'Radicalism in a Traditional Society'.
[87] Miller review in *Journal of Ecclesiastical History*, 38 (1987), p. 157.

and motivations of electors drawn from many social orders. Only because this was true did they pose so acute a challenge to Restoration government in city and state.

The interpretation of the first London Whigs provided here should stimulate renewed discussion of their religious and ideological character. Such further attention to the early city Whigs will also need to focus upon a number of implications and ramifications of the arguments of this essay. First, the revisionist views of the Exclusion Crisis do not seem to capture adequately either the ideological richness or the constitutional and social complexity of the affair. In addition, the early history of London Whiggism points to the weaknesses of what we now call the Restoration Settlement, a patchwork of measures that failed to eliminate the causes of Stuart political and religious conflict, that settled somewhat less than was at first thought, and that entirely satisfied few.[88] The case of these city radicals also suggests that historians of seventeenth-century political ideas may need not only to clarify their conception of radicalism but also, perhaps, to recognize the existence of a variety of radicalisms. Moreover, although the city of London was no doubt an exceptional political community, the radical appropriation of local customs, traditions and rights in London contrasts with the frequent assertion that such local appropriations were, in the seventeenth century, generally conservative and inward-looking. Beyond this, the militant political *élan* of the Restoration London Nonconformists is of particular importance to the study of Nonconformity elsewhere in England because of the frequency with which dissenters in many boroughs and counties looked to London for guidance and inspiration. Finally, the radicalism of the first London Whigs is instructive in interpreting both the actual remodelling of corporation government along popular lines after 1649 and the expression of radical ideas in London after the Revolution of 1688.[89] Just as the interregnum experiment in civic democracy retained its normative character in the minds and recollections of many guildsmen, so also post-1688 civic radicalism was no sudden or fleeting phenomenon. Further study of the

[88] See Ronald Hutton, *The Restoration: A Political and Religious History of England and Wales, 1658–1667* (Oxford, 1985).

[89] James Farnell, 'The Politics of the City of London (1649–1657)' (unpublished Ph.D. thesis, University of Chicago, 1963); De Krey, *A Fractured Society*, pp. 48–51; De Krey, 'Political Radicalism in London after the Glorious Revolution', *Journal of Modern History*, 55 (1983), pp. 585–617.

personnel of Restoration radicalism and of the pre-history of the first Whigs in London and other localities may well justify or refine assertions such as these.[90]

In conclusion, in London, the Exclusion Crisis was indeed a very considerable 'tremblor' after England's great mid-century Revolution. A party of constitutional opposition was largely commanded by men outside the political nation as it was defined by Restoration civil and religious statute. Many of these dissenting Whig leaders moved within the most enterprising commercial circles in an era of unprecedented trade expansion and capital accumulation. The circumstances of public life, however, drew both socially substantial Whig-dissenting leaders and their followers towards a radical ideology that turned civic debate into ideological and religious polarization. The 'good old cause' was very much alive in the corporation in the 1680s, provided that the political desiderata of Restoration puritanism be understood as radically libertarian rather than as dogmatically republican. This conclusion may seem a bit 'old hat', but then, occasionally, when an old hat is a good fit, it is a pleasure to wear it still.

[90] I am currently investigating the personnel of Exclusion era radicalism in London and hope to publish my findings elsewhere. Recent studies of Restoration boroughs offer little about ideology, but they do suggest that the same 1670s revival of political puritanism occurred elsewhere. Judith J. Hurwich, ' "A Fanatick Town": The Political Influence of Dissenters in Coventry, 1660–1720', *Midland History*, 4 (1977), pp. 15–57; John T. Evans, *Seventeenth-Century Norwich: Politics, Religion, and Government* (Oxford, 1979); Michael Mullet, ' "Deprived of our former Place": The Internal Politics of Bedford 1660 to 1688', *Publications of the Bedfordshire Historical Records Society*, 59 (1980), pp. 1–42; M. A. Mullett, 'Conflict, Politics and Elections in Lancaster, 1660–1688', *Northern History*, 19 (1983), pp. 61–86.

14. *Cultural life in the provinces: Leeds and York, 1720–1820*

J. JEFFERSON LOONEY

During the century ending in 1760 leisure is said to have changed from a rare commodity enjoyed primarily by the rich to a growth industry geared to meeting expanding middle-class demand for the pleasures and social benefits conferred by a wide range of leisure activities. During this transforming 'commercialization of leisure' a variety of activities moved out of the drawing-rooms of the wealthy and into commercially or corporately operated facilities which were open or semi-open to the paying public, often at prices that a large segment of the middle class could afford. This broadening of accessibility and increased commercialization has been described as occurring in almost every conceivable leisure activity by 1760. Instances cited in a path-breaking lecture by J. H. Plumb include a growing print trade, expansion in theatrical and musical performances, and professionalization and standardization of rules in horse-racing, boxing and cricket. The underlying cause was the numerical growth and increasing wealth of the 'middling sort' and the opportunities many leisure activities afforded for pleasure, self-improvement and social emulation and advancement. But equally important was the speed and zest with which a large group of brilliant entrepreneurs – men like Robert Walker for newspapers, John Walsh for published music, William Hogarth and Arthur Pond for engravings, Philip Astley for the circus, John Spilsbury for the jigsaw puzzle, above all John Newbery for medicines and children's books – perceived a potential market and exploited it fully.[1]

[1] J. H. Plumb, *The Commercialisation of Leisure in Eighteenth-Century England* (Reading, 1974). For Newbery and Spilsbury, see J. H. Plumb, 'The New World of Children in Eighteenth-Century England', *Past and Present*, 67 (1975), pp. 64–95. For Pond, see Louise Lippincott, *Selling Art in Georgian London: The Rise of Arthur Pond* (New Haven, 1983). For a good case study of a successful

This portrayal of an innovative leisure industry in early Georgian England seemed to herald the beginning of serious research on a new, important, and particularly interesting, even entertaining field of study. Unfortunately, despite initial enthusiasm little advance has been made in understanding eighteenth-century leisure.[2] Local case studies are badly needed.[3] The tendency has been to stake out a position by culling relevant data from a multitude of towns and then generalizing in national terms,[4] an approach which can obscure as much as it illuminates. Recent work on science represents the most fruitful attempt to understand provincial culture as something other than one national monolith. Efforts to explain the growing strength of popular science as closely linked to industrialization or dissent or utilitarianism no longer seem to hold up. Sometimes in specific towns where science should have flourished under such theories it did, but just as often it did not. Comparisons of the experience of one town to another and between types of activity are crucial if progress is to be made,[5] and this is equally true in moving beyond science to leisure and cultural activity as a whole. Through a case study of two towns, York and Leeds, this essay examines the timing and nature of English commercialization of leisure. It suggests that it came later than has been argued and that new industrial centres experienced it differently and more tardily than traditional gentry gathering-places.

A better understanding of how and when leisure activities became commercialized has broad implications and is particularly significant to the history of the English provincial town. During the

printer of the second rank, see C. Y. Ferdinand, 'Benjamin Collins, Salisbury Printer', in M. Crump and M. Harris, eds., *Searching the Eighteenth Century* (London, 1983), pp. 74–92.

2 Unlike the Victorian period. See for example Hugh Cunningham, *Leisure in the Industrial Revolution c. 1780–c. 1880* (London, 1980); Peter Bailey, *Leisure and Class in Victorian England: Rational Recreation and the Contest for Control 1830–1885* (London, 1978); James Walvin, *Leisure and Society 1830–1950* (London, 1978); John K. Walton and James Walvin, eds., *Leisure in Britain 1780–1939* (Manchester, 1983).

3 One good example is John Money, *Experience and Identity: Birmingham and the West Midlands, 1760–1800* (Manchester, 1977). For a useful, though more specialized, study, see Trevor Fawcett, *Music in Eighteenth-Century Norwich and Norfolk* (Norwich, 1979).

4 For a particularly unsatisfying example, albeit one which just predates Plumb, see R. M. Wiles, 'Provincial Culture in Early Georgian England', in Paul S. Fritz and David Williams, eds., *The Triumph of Culture* (Toronto, 1972), pp. 49–68.

5 R. S. Porter, 'Science, Provincial Culture and Public Opinion in Enlightenment England', *British Journal for Eighteenth-Century Studies*, 3 (1980), pp. 20–46.

eighteenth century English towns other than London more than doubled their share of the population[6] and reorganized themselves economically. The wholesaling of goods moved increasingly from open markets to private rooms in great urban inns, fixed-site shops accounted for a growing share of sales of retail goods, and seasonal fairs began to decline. Competition between towns and their hinterlands gave way to integration, as townspeople specialized in executing high-quality work and finding markets for cruder wares which flowed in from outlying villages and rural areas.[7] Social change kept pace. Peter Borsay perceives an 'urban renaissance' in the eighty years ending in 1760, marked by better town planning, the provision of public amenities, construction of leisure facilities, and growing numbers and specialization of townspeople employed in selling luxury goods and servicing fashionable leisure activity. The towns of this period became both armouries and battlefields in struggles over social status. Fine arts and fine clothes were tools equally seized upon by a newly prosperous and numerous class of civil servants, army and navy officers, lawyers and clergymen, even shopkeepers and craftsmen, all anxious to carve out and defend an appropriately respectable niche in the social pecking order.[8] The appeal of science has also been explained in these terms. Much of the audience for scientific lectures and books consisted of gentry and those aspiring to gentility. Such an audience took a course of

[6] Excepting London, towns with more than 2,500 people accounted for 8 per cent of the population of England and Wales in 1700 and for 20 per cent in 1801. P. J. Corfield, *The Impact of English Towns 1700–1800* (Oxford, 1982), p. 9.

[7] Peter Clark, 'Introduction' to Clark, ed., *The Transformation of English Provincial Towns, 1600–1800* (London, 1984), pp. 13–61; Peter Clark, 'Introduction: English Country Towns 1500–1800', in Clark, ed., *Country Towns in Pre-Industrial England* (New York, 1981), pp. 2–43; Angus McInnes, *The English Town 1660–1760* (London, 1980); Alan Everitt, 'Urban Growth, 1570–1770', *Local Historian*, 8 (1968), pp. 118–25; Corfield, *Impact of English Towns*. For changes in marketing patterns see Alan Everitt, 'The Marketing of Agricultural Produce', in Joan Thirsk, ed., *Agrarian History of England and Wales Volume IV 1500–1640* (Cambridge, 1967), pp. 466–592; Alan Everitt, 'The English Urban Inn, 1560–1760', in Everitt, ed., *Perspectives in English Urban History* (London, 1973), pp. 91–137, 256–60; Ian Mitchell, 'The Development of Urban Retailing 1700–1815', in Clark, *Transformation*, pp. 259–83.

[8] Peter Borsay, 'The English Urban Renaissance: The Development of Provincial Urban Culture *c.* 1680–*c.* 1760', *Social History*, 5 (1977), pp. 581–603. See also his 'Culture, Status, and the English Urban Landscape', *History*, 67 (1982), pp. 1–12; and his ' "All the town's a stage": Urban Ritual and Ceremony 1660–1800', in Clark, *Transformation*, pp. 228–58. For the emergence of a class of urban 'pseudo-gentry' after 1660, see Alan Everitt, 'Social Mobility in Early Modern England', *Past and Present*, 33 (1966), pp. 56–73, especially 70–3.

lectures as it would attend a concert series: with the goal of developing taste, smoothing away rustic clownishness and becoming men and women of refinement, sensibility and information. Those who went beyond this desire for superficial polish to form literary and philosophical societies or conduct serious research were often motivated either by an inadequate supply of civilizing institutions in their towns or by being frozen out of the strata of society to which they aspired.[9]

In sharp contrast to Borsay's depiction of urban life and Roy Porter's of English society, J. C. D. Clark has argued that by relying on selective, impressionistic evidence, recent historiography has grossly overstated the trend towards commercialization and individualism in the eighteenth century. Primary stress should rather be placed on religion and politics, hierarchy and aristocracy, deference and paternalism, in English society up until 1832. Exceptions to this largely static picture are regarded as unusual or unimportant.[10] This study will suggest that the pace of commercialization in English towns may well have been overstated and that the involvement of new groups led some who were already participating in certain forms of commercialized activity to withdraw. None the less, the conclusion that England was experiencing increasingly pronounced social change as the nineteenth century began seems inescapable.

I

Advertising and news coverage of leisure activities in the newspapers of York and Leeds are here summarized during four sample years chosen at approximate twenty-year intervals between 1720 and 1807.[11] Newspapers are emphasized for practical reasons.

---

[9] Porter, 'Science, Provincial Culture and Public Opinion'. In Bath and Manchester the serious scientists tended to be those who used their hobby either to break into the upper crust or to console themselves for failing in the attempt. See also Roy Porter, *English Society in the Eighteenth Century* (London, 1982).

[10] J. C. D. Clark, *English Society, 1688–1832* (Cambridge, 1985); J. C. D. Clark, 'Review Article: Eighteenth-Century Social History', *Historical Journal*, 27 (1984), pp. 773–88.

[11] The sample years are 1741, 1760, 1784 and 1807. The newspapers of 1720 were also examined, but unfortunately in that year the newspapers still carried very little advertising, less than one advertisement a week, including nothing relevant to this study.

From their advent outside London in the early eighteenth century[12] they are the only source which offers some semblance of comprehensive coverage of a wide variety of activities over a wide range of years. The government tax on newspaper advertisements, which rose from one to three shillings between 1712 and 1789, made them expensive when compared with handbills and street cries,[13] which would make a study of the latter forms of advertising particularly useful as a control. Unfortunately, handbills and good evidence on verbal advertising rarely survive. Frequently newspapers contain the only extant information on clubs and fraternal orders, dancing, music, theatre, sports, travelling shows, and circulating libraries. Ultimately any finding based on newspapers alone will have to be confirmed and tempered using material scattered through a broad and unlikely spectrum of material, from letters and diaries to subscription lists and account books to tickets, handbills and other ephemera. But newspaper advertising and reporting are the obvious starting-points.

Newspapers began publishing in Leeds in 1718 and York in 1719, and neither town was without at least one thereafter. Leeds supported a second newspaper starting in 1767, and after several false starts York became a two-paper town in 1772 and harboured yet a third as of 1790. The longest-lasting papers in Leeds were the stridently Tory *Leeds Intelligencer* and the Whig *Leeds Mercury*. For much of the century the generally neutral *York Courant* was the most widely circulated newspaper in York and indeed in Yorkshire, but it came to be challenged by the Tory *York Chronicle* and the Whig *York Herald*, a great sporting paper. Evidence on the circulation of these papers is almost non-existent, but one can speculate that in 1760 the *York Courant* was distributing 3,000 copies a week while the *Leeds Intelligencer* sold a third of that figure. By 1807 both Leeds papers and the *York Herald* may have had runs of 2,000 copies, with the other two York papers distributing rather less.[14]

---

12 For more on this development see G. A. Cranfield, *The Development of the Provincial Newspaper, 1700–1760* (Oxford, 1962); R. M. Wiles, *Freshest Advices: Early Provincial Newspapers in England* (Columbus, Ohio, 1965); and J. J. Looney, 'Advertising and Society in England, 1720–1820: A Statistical Analysis of Yorkshire Newspaper Advertisements' (unpublished Ph. D. thesis, Princeton University, 1983).

13 For the finances of advertising see Looney, 'Advertising and Society', pp. 36, 87–114.

14 Looney, 'Advertising and Society', pp. 30–33, 97–105. Except for the *Leeds Intelligencer* the political stance of these papers was often not very pronounced.

York and Leeds were chosen for this study because, although situated close enough together to minimize regional variation, they varied economically in potentially interesting ways. York had no large-scale industry. By 1700 its merchants had been supplanted as exporters of cloth and dealt mainly in the agricultural produce of its hinterland.[15] The city's craftsmen and shopkeepers serviced not only local farmers but travellers on the Great North Road and gentry hailing from all over Yorkshire, attracted by York's status as a legal, administrative and religious capital and social centre. During its semi-annual assizes, horse-races and parliamentary elections, York was crowded with visiting gentlemen and those anxious to make money from them. Even apart from these special occasions, York succeeded in developing a fashionable season lasting much of the winter. In 1742 Samuel Richardson commented that 'the present support of the city is chiefly owing to the gentry, who make it their winter residence ... And as the inhabitants abound with the conveniencies of life, they likewise partake of its diversions, there being plays, assemblies, music-meetings, or some entertainments, every night in the week.'[16]

Thanks to its status as gateway to the West Riding textile industry, Leeds grew much more rapidly than York. The latter's population grew from around 12,000 in 1700 to almost 17,000 in 1801. In the same period that of Leeds expanded from 7,000 to some 30,000.[17] Broad woollen cloths, both white and coloured, were produced in Leeds's immediate hinterland and sold to its merchants, who began finishing (i.e., cutting, dyeing and packing) the cloth themselves by 1750. In addition, until well past 1800 the worsteds of Bradford and Halifax and the kerseymeres of Huddersfield were marketed primarily by the merchants of Leeds, who alone in the West Riding had developed the foreign contacts, sent out the factors and acquired the know-how necessary to engage in

---

[15] *Victoria County History: City of York* (London, 1961; cited henceforth as *VCH: City of York*), p. 219.

[16] Daniel Defoe, *Tour Thro' the Whole Island of Great Britain*, 3rd edn, 4 vols (1975 New York photofacsimile of 1742 London edn revised and expanded by Samuel Richardson), vol. 3, p. 151. In the first edition Defoe wrote that York had 'no trade indeed, except such as depends upon the confluence of the gentry'. Daniel Defoe, *Tour Through the Whole Island of Great Britain*, ed. Pat Rogers (London, 1971), p. 523. See also Francis Drake, *Eboracum: or the History and Antiquities of the City of York* (London, 1736), pp. 239–41.

[17] *VCH: City of York*, pp. 212, 254; R. G. Wilson, *Gentlemen Merchants: The Merchant Community in Leeds: 1700–1830* (London, 1971), pp. 197, 202.

international trade directly. In the 1770s, 30 per cent of England's cloth exports passed through Leeds. The application of steam power was rapidly altering the face of the textile industry by 1800, but most of the structural changes it entailed were still some years off. Throughout the eighteenth century Leeds's merchants dominated its elite. With a few exceptions, the numerous cloth-manufacturers were small-scale operators of comparatively limited means.[18]

In describing the towns which participated in the urban renaissance, Borsay distinguishes between commercial or industrial centres such as Bristol, Manchester or Birmingham, which created wealth, and social centres, which attracted wealth. Towns of the latter type include new spas and seaside resorts like Bath and Scarborough, shire towns like Shrewsbury, which were traditional gathering places for local gentry, and transport towns like Stamford, which stood on the main roads and flourished by serving the prosperous folk passing along the newly-graded turnpikes. One wonders whether these different kinds of towns experienced their rebirth differently. York and Leeds will serve as a test case since, in Borsay's terms, York attracted wealth while Leeds created it. York's population of gentry and professional men, artisans and shopkeepers who catered to them, and small merchants and craftsmen supporting agriculture contrast sharply with that of Leeds, a cloth town with an elite of large-scale merchants and a large middling group of cloth-makers, but comparatively few resident or visiting gentry and professional men. The difference in the towns is reflected in their differing audience for and experience of leisure.

For purposes of analysis, leisure is here divided into three categories loosely based on audience. Freaks and shows, museums and scientific lecturers, singers and performing animals are examined first. Such short-term promotions, which tended to aim at a wide audience, were imported from outside the town and often timed to arrive when the town was packed because of a fair, assize or race meeting. Next, evidence is given relating to amateur activities organized from within, such as the meetings of clubs and fraternal orders. The example of the thriving club culture among artisans and small masters in Birmingham[19] might suggest that such

---

[18] Wilson, *Gentlemen Merchants*, pp. 44, 54–60, 111–35, and *passim*.
[19] See Money, *Experience and Identity*, cited above.

activities appealed to a middling element. Finally, leisure activities of the resident elite, including concerts, theatre and assemblies, are discussed. The boundaries of all of these divisions are blurred: theatre increasingly attracted a popular audience, and those who listened to scientific lectures were usually quite well off. None the less some interesting hypotheses emerge when leisure activities are grouped in this way.

II

Freaks, magicians and managers of trained or exotic animals had travelled a circuit of fairs, races and any other gathering likely to attract a crowd long before the beginning of the period under study. The advent of the peripatetic scientific lecturer was a more recent and in some ways more significant development.[20] Drawing a firm boundary line between educational and entertaining acts would be anachronistic, however, since the distinction in the eighteenth century was blurred. The major discernible difference in the sample is less between town and town than between year and year. After 1760 a big increase can be observed in the volume of advertising for 'travelling leisure', shows which frequently were linked to times when a town would be packed, such as the assizes or races in York, or the fairs in Leeds. More such acts may have been on the road, and more of the acts which did travel were better organized, more likely to stay in town long enough to place an advertisement or settled enough in schedule to place an advertisement in the next town on their route before leaving the current stop, and better able to afford the investment represented by advertising. In a word, they were more commercialized. Around 1800, large travelling shows, such as circuses, zoos and menageries, began to travel and compete for custom with traditional one-caravan shows or one-act routines. For most of the eighteenth century little difference in what was offered the patrons of York and Leeds is apparent; many showmen visited both towns. A difference does emerge with the biggest shows of 1807. Four of five

---

[20] For a discussion of the importance of itinerant scientific lecturers to the technological changes associated with the Industrial Revolution, see A. E. Musson and E. Robinson, 'Science and Industry in the Late Eighteenth Century', *Economic History Review*, 2nd series, 13 (1960–1), pp. 230–4, and the expansion of this argument in Musson and Robinson, *Science and Technology in the Industrial Revolution* (Manchester, 1969), pp. 101–11.

circuses, zoos and museums which passed through that year stopped in Leeds rather than York. The one which did stop in York was the smallest in scale; where Leodonians were shown lions and a stuffed rhinoceros, residents of York had to make do with a seal and a tarantula. York still held its own as a lure to smaller shows and expensive entertainers, but despite its central position on the Great North Road it was not populous enough to encourage the newer, titanic shows to stop.

In 1741 two scientific lecturers advertised in York. F. Midon gave a series of seven lectures on pneumatics. The series was apparently well attended, for he repeated the lectures twice that year. Robert Sowerby, 'teacher of the mathematics in York', eventually competed with a set of ten lectures on various sciences, promising to avoid technical terms and thus 'render the whole intelligible to the lowest capacity'. 'The FAMOUS AFRICAN', a Hottentot fresh from a thirteen-month run in London, went on display during York's race week, and John Parry gave concerts on the treble harp in both York and Leeds.[21] In 1760 Mr Johnson, 'the most surprizing man in Europe', brought his trick-riding act to both York and Leeds during their respective race weeks. One of his more spectacular feats was riding 'two horses with one foot in each inside stirrup; and whilst the horses are in full gallop, he leaps from the stirrups, one foot upon each saddle, and, in that posture, continues tossing his cap and smacking his whip, while the horses are in full career'.[22]

---

[21] Midon: *York Courant* (cited henceforth as *YCo*), 2 June, 10 and 17 November and 15 December 1741. Sowerby: *YCo*, 24 November 1741. African: *YCo*, 28 July and 4 August 1741. Parry: *YCo*, 20 January 1741; *Leeds Mercury* (cited henceforth as *LM*), 24 February 1741. Parry was a blind Welshman who popularized both the Welsh harp and traditional Welsh music. Stanley Sadie, ed., *New Grove Dictionary of Music and Musicians*, 20 vols (London, 1980), vol. 14, p. 245.

[22] *YCo*, 12 August 1760; *Leeds Intelligencer* (cited henceforth as *LI*), 16 September 1760. The horse-races themselves were an 'imported' leisure activity, in which York led the region until overtaken by the fixture at Doncaster early in the nineteenth century. York's August Races were supplemented in 1763 by a May meeting which survived but lacked the popularity of its elder. The Leeds race meeting was short-lived, appearing only in the 1760 sample and altogether escaping the notice of the historian of Yorkshire racing. Cockfights were invariably scheduled to coincide with races. J. Fairfax-Blakeborough, *Northern Turf History. III: York and Doncaster Races* (York, 1950); Drake, *Eboracum*, p. 241; Tate Wilkinson, *Memoirs of His Own Life* (1966 Louisville, Kentucky microcard reprint of four-vol. 1790 York edn), vol. 3, p. 144; *LI*, 26 February and 29 April 1760 (Leeds races and cockfighting); *YCo*, 27 April, 20 and 27 July 1784; 24 August 1807; *York Herald* (hereafter *YH*), 17 January and 8 August 1807 (York cockfighting).

Leeds races were visited by a dromedary and a Bactrian camel, and S. Dellany delivered 'A Monody on his late Majesty' shortly after the death of George II.[23]

The pace had quickened considerably by 1784. In both York and Leeds, Mr Weavor delivered a course of twelve lectures in 'natural and experimental philosophy', and Adam Walker displayed his 'Eidouranion; or large transparent orrery'. Mr Long, from London, read 'an experimental lecture' on electricity in York in October. Two magicians, the Sieur Hermon Boaz and Mr Lowe, performed in Leeds. Lowe's three-part lecture included sleight-of-hand, mind-reading, causing 'an egg to fly round the room', display of a clockwork automaton and some 'beautiful paintings', and lectures which included 'the comic representations of Nobody! – Somebody! – Anybody! – A Busybody! – and Everybody!'[24] The recently-invented balloon always drew a crowd, and showmen were quick to capitalize on it. Both York and Leeds hosted balloon launches and displays of tethered balloons, including one whose proprietor made the spurious claim that his balloon had been manufactured by the Montgolfiers and was exhibited with their consent.[25] Signior Petro put on an elaborate fireworks display in Briggate, Leeds, in December, relying for his profit on a collection made during an intermission in the performance. 1784 was also a good year for freaks and animals. Rival 'Irish Giants' visited York-shire, with one claiming to be over eight feet tall. A seventeen-month old 'SURPRISING FEMALE CHILD' with breasts exceed-ing 'those of the most of women' and other peculiar measurements was exhibited at a York coffee-house.[26] Last but far from least, the

[23] Dromedary: *LI*, 3 June 1760. Dellany: *LI*, 28 October 1760. Dellany charged six pence admission.

[24] Weavor: *York Chronicle* (cited henceforth as *YCh*), 23 January 1784; *LI*, 13, 20 and 27 April 1784. Walker: *YCo*, 2 November 1784; *LI*, 16 November 1784. Long: *YCo*, 26 October 1784. Boaz: *LI*, 9 and 16 March 1784. Lowe: *LI*, 28 December 1784. For more on Walker, see Richard D. Altick, *The Shows of London* (Cambridge, Mass., 1978), pp. 364–6.

[25] Balloon launches: *YCo*, 16 March 1784; *LI*, 30 March 1784. Tethered balloons: *YCo*, 3 February 1784; *YCh*, 27 August 1784; *LI*, 16 March 1784. For the 'Montgolfier' balloon, see *YCh*, 12 March 1784. Balloons were also incorporated into scientific lectures, and the theatre displayed both real balloons during intermissions and fake balloons to transport Harlequin during pantomimes. Lectures: *YCo*, 9 March and 26 October 1784. Theatre: *LI*, 22 June and 25 May 1784; *YCo*, 27 April 1784.

[26] Petro: *LI*, 30 November 1784. Giants: *YCo*, 29 June and 17 August 1784; *LI*, 20 April 1784. Female child: *YCo*, 3 November and 14 December 1784.

Learned Pig visited both York and Leeds during the year. He was trained by John Nicholson, whose impressive record already included 'having taught a turtle to fetch and carry . . . perfecting six turkey-cocks in a regular country dance . . . [and teaching] three cats to strike out several tunes on the dulcimer with their paws, and to imitate the Italian manner of singing'. The Pig, who could spell, count and keep time, went on to London in 1785, and achieved great renown. Boswell, Wollstonecraft, Parson Woodforde, Mrs Trimmer, Wordsworth, Coleridge and Thomas Jefferson all saw or alluded to him.[27]

By 1807 the scale of the productions being displayed had increased dramatically. Where a single animal or exhibit had sufficed hitherto, now whole museums and zoos were on the road. 'Mr. Sand's Museum of Natural and Artificial Curiosities' visited York exhibiting a collection which included a crocodile, a Mediterranean seal, a centipede and a tarantula. Mr Kite brought his circus, which featured equestrian performances, acrobatics, and bird imitations by 'The English Rosignol' to Leeds during that town's July fair. The same fair was visited by Signor Belzoni, a strongman whose entertainments also featured a waxwork depiction of Nelson's funeral, a slide show using Chinese shadows, a waterworks display, and a ten-piece band. Visitors to the Leeds autumn fair could enjoy Polito's Menagerie, with six large caravans transporting more than fifty quadrupeds, among them lions, tigers, kangaroos, a beaver, an opossum, and an ursine sloth from Bengal, as well as two emus, an ostrich, pelicans and vultures. In December 'the Liverpool Museum' reached Leeds. Its 4,000 curiosities ranged from stuffed animals, including a rhinoceros, through an ethnography section with some of Captain Cook's specimens to a collection of antique British arms and armour and a mélange of works of art.[28]

---

[27] *YCo*, 13 July and 10 August 1784; *LI*, 21 September 1784. G. E. Bentley, Jr, 'The Freaks of Learning: Learned Pigs, Musical Hares and the Romantics', *Colby Library Quarterly*, 18 (1982), pp. 87–104; MS account book of Thomas Jefferson, 1783–90, entry dated 21 March 1786, Massachusetts Historical Society. See also Altick, *Shows of London*, pp. 40–2.

[28] Sand: YH, 27 December 1806, 3 and 10 January 1807. Kite: *LI*, 6 July 1807. Belzoni: *LI*, 6 July 1807. Polito: *LI* 26 October 1807. Liverpool Museum: *LI*, 23 November and 21 December 1807. For Belzoni's subsequent career as an Egyptologist, see Altick, *Shows of London*, pp. 243–6. The Liverpool Museum was owned by William Bullock, who subsequently moved it to London and became the greatest showman of his day. See Altick, *Shows of London*, pp. 235–52.

Such stupendous shows failed to crowd out smaller operators. R. Dalton delivered nine lectures on 'pneumatic chemistry, electricity and galvanism' in both York and Leeds, and in York Mr de Philipsthal put on 'mechanical and optical performances', which included sending a balloon to the ceiling and then detaching from it a small 'parachute, with figures'. At the theatre in Leeds Mrs Rosoman Mountain from the London Theatre Royal performed a number of songs embedded in a dramatic monologue called 'The Travellers, or the Unexpected Meeting'.[29] A month later the opera singer Madame Catalani gave three concerts in York and one in Leeds during her wildly successful national tour. Even at a top ticket price of fifteen shillings, Catalani's two scheduled concerts in York were so well attended that a third was added at the last minute.[30] A young lady lacking arms and legs demonstrated her ability to sew, write, draw and paint miniatures in both towns, which were also visited by the Naval Panorama, a 4,000-square-foot painting of the Battle of Trafalgar and death of Nelson. The showman's year in York concluded in November with a display of fireworks, which boasted as its grand finale 'a fixed piece of Lord Nelson's naval pillar' with the 'Royal Victory' on top, followed by 'a GRAND SALUTE OF 21 ROUNDS'.[31]

III

While learned pigs and patriotic fireworks drew large crowds, anniversary banquets and the activities of clubs presumably attracted a smaller, more middling element. Convivial activities tended to be run from within and intended only to break even, and thus

29   Dalton: *YH*, 4 and 11 April 1807; *LI*, 5 January 1807. De Philipsthal: *YCo*, 29 December 1806; *YCh*, 1 January 1807. Mountain: *LI*, 7 September 1807. Dalton showed his gratitude for his hospitable reception in Leeds by launching a balloon there to benefit the Leeds General Infirmary. *LI*, 20 and 27 July 1807. For Mountain see *DNB*.

30   *YH*, 3 and 10 October 1807; *YCo*, 19 October 1807; *LI*, 19 October 1807. A set of hair combs was even named 'the Catalani' in her honour (advertisement of the perfumer Mr Pretious, *LI*, 30 March 1807). For more on Catalani see *New Grove Dictionary*, vol. 4, pp. 4–5. Decades later Elizabeth Gaskell alluded to her in chapter 5 of *Mary Barton*.

31   Young lady: *YH*, 15 August 1807; *LI*, 6 July 1807. Panorama: *YH*, 4, 11 and 25 July 1807; *LI*, 18 and 25 May 1807. Fireworks: *YCo*, 23 November 1807. During its visit to York the naval painting was displayed inside York Minster, a venue presumably sanctioned because of its patriotic theme.

had little reason to advertise or publicize their existence. Advertisements and news items do mention a number of clubs, which often are otherwise unknown. Collecting all such allusions permits the hazarding of generalizations about the ebb and flow of such activity. However the demonstrable insufficiency of the source for this category is at least equally significant. Jumbling together all club meetings and festive dinners mentioned in a given year certainly compares many apples with oranges, but doing so points to two hypotheses about clubs and societies. First, the preponderance of relevant advertisements comes after 1760. New societies were forming and ongoing activities were beginning to be advertised. Second, for every sample year Leeds lags well behind York in the number of advertisements in this category.[32] Given the overall tendency of Leeds advertisers to be not less but more willing to publicize their activities,[33] apparently more activity of this kind went on in York than Leeds. Perhaps the greater incidence of this sort of activity in York is explained by the greater preponderance of professional men in that city. Its status as a legal and religious centre gave it disproportionate numbers of attorneys and clergymen living there year-round, and these were eminently 'clubbable' men, as the limited evidence on the membership of book clubs suggests.[34]

Advertising and reporting together account for two organizations meeting in York in 1741 and three in 1760. In the former year 'the Royal Society of Gardeners and Lovers of a Garden, within the City and County of York' met in York, inviting those attending to bring 'such rarities as the season affords', with a gold ring awarded to the one who produced the best carnation. A news item reported that 'the concert held by a number of gentlemen, at the George in Coney-street, York, every Wednesday evening, will be held October the 7th, and not September the 31st, [sic] as was expected'.[35] A political group, the Rockingham Club, advertised

---

[32] With the exception of advertisements for benefit society feasts, which are a special case, being as much invitations to non-members to join the society as calls to revelry for the members.

[33] See the discussion of 'rite-of-passage' advertisements in Looney, pp. 206–13.

[34] Paul Kaufman, 'English Book Clubs and Their Role in Social History', *Libri*, 14 (1964), p. 24. Two of the three stewards for an old boys' feast held in York in 1784 for alumni of Trinity College were clerics. *YCo*, 10 February 1784.

[35] Gardeners: *YCo*, 28 July 1741. Concert: *YCo*, 29 September 1741.

quarterly meetings in York in 1760. Old boys of St John's College, Cambridge, held a reunion in the city, as did alumni of York's charity schools.[36] More activity is discernible by 1784. Flower-fanciers held four shows awarding prizes to the best hyacinths, tulips, ranunculuses and carnations, and a 'shew of canary birds' judged the best yellow and yellow-mottled birds. Alumni of Trinity College, Cambridge, held a reunion and the Apollo Lodge of Free and Accepted Masons gave a St John's Day banquet.[37] Four banquets combining political with festive elements were publicized. The anniversary of the battle of Culloden and the second Lord Rockingham's birthday were commemorated. More topically, after the 1784 general election dinners were given for supporters of the winning and losing slates to represent York in Parliament.[38] In 1807 the Society of York Florists remained active, sponsoring shows of tulips in May, ranunculuses in June, pinks in July, and carnations and gooseberries in August. The York Agricultural Society met and awarded premiums twice, during fairs in March and August.[39] The masonic Provincial Grand Lodge of the Province of York met at the Grand Lodge Room in Blake Street, York. The Yorkshire Law Society met in York on 10 March, during assize week.[40] The friends of three candidates held banquets after

[36] Rockingham: *YCo*, 1 January 1760. St John's: *YCo*, 29 April 1760. St John's alumni seem to have pioneered the tradition of holding convivial reunions. See *YCo*, 7 April 1741, for an earlier example, in Pontefract. Charity schools: *YCo*, 26 February 1760. Though the charity schools meeting was not advertised beforehand, £44 in contributions for these institutions were collected.

[37] Flower fanciers: *YCo*, 4 May, 1 and 22 June and 17 August 1784. Only the first meeting was advertised. The flower-lovers customarily met at the Sandhill Inn in Colliergate. Bird show: *YCo*, 19 October 1784 (news item). Trinity alumni: *YCo*, 10 February 1784. Masonic banquet: *YCo*, 21 December 1784.

[38] *YCo*, 20 April (Culloden), 1 June (Rockingham), 10 August (Lord Galway and Richard S. Milnes, the winners) and 9 November 1784 (Lord John Cavendish and Sir William M. Milner, the losers). The latter banquet was not advertised.

[39] Florists: *YH*, 30 May, 27 June and 11 July 1807; *YCh*, 13 August 1807. Agricultural society: *YH*, 21 March and 8 August 1807; *YCh*, 19 March and 20 August 1807. The Society of Florists continued to meet at the Sandhill Inn in Colliergate. None of the four shows was advertised. The July list of prizewinners shows that fanciers named their plants, often using topical themes including the names of some of the various candidates in the recent election. For more on agricultural societies and flower fanciers, see J. H. Plumb, 'The Acceptance of Modernity', in Neil McKendrick, ed., *The Birth of a Consumer Society: The Commercialization of Eighteenth-Century England* (Bloomington, Indiana, 1982), pp. 316–34.

[40] Masonic lodge: *YH*, 24 October 1807. Law society: *YH*, 28 February 1807. The society was founded in 1786. Its minute book for the period 1786 to 1834 survives,

the election.[41] Finally, the annual feasts of six benefit societies were advertised or reported on.[42]

Leeds by contrast seems to have been much less 'clubbable'. The only advertisement for, or newspaper account of, a social meeting or banquet in 1741 or 1760 in Leeds was a meeting and dinner of the Gentlemen Cricket Players on 26 May 1760. The only relevant advertisements in 1784 were those publicizing the annual meetings and dinners of five benefit societies.[43] In 1807 advertisements appeared for a reunion of St John's College alumni and two celebration banquets for the supporters of Lord Milton, the victorious Yorkshire MP. The results of the annual gooseberry show were reported in the news columns, and four benefit societies advertised their annual dinners.[44]

York's apparently greater share than Leeds of convivial activity needs to be tempered by the limitations of the source. The difference may in fact be something of an illusion. Most advertised gatherings were irregular or annual meetings timed to coincide with the races or an assize week. Virtually no club, broadly defined, routinely advertised its meetings in either town. Passing references to the existence of cricket clubs, of flower and bird fanciers, and of masonic lodges are tantalizing but very far from being inclusive. The York Musical Society met every other week during the season from 1767 until beyond the period under study but did not advertise its meetings. Neither did an unnamed scientific society which was

and is discussed in Robert Robson, *The Attorney in Eighteenth-Century England* (Cambridge, 1959), pp. 36, 38–43.

[41] *YH*, 15 and 22 August (William M. Milner), 5 September (Henry Lascelles) and 17 October 1807 (Mark M. Sykes). Only Milner's banquet was advertised beforehand.

[42] *YH*, 27 December 1806 – the Female Benefit Club; *YCh*, 29 October 1807 – Old Union Benefit Society; *YH*, 26 September 1807 – Lord Hawke's Brotherly Benefit Society; *YH*, 10 October 1807 – The New Union Benefit Society, and the Farmer's Union Society; *YH*, 24 October 1807 – the Amicable Society. Only the first two of these feasts were advertised.

[43] Cricket: *LI*, 20 May 1760. Benefit societies: *LI*, 31 August 1784 – the New Union, or Benevolent Society; *LM*, 29 June 1784 – the Brotherly Posterior Society; *LM*, 27 July 1784 – the Leeds Union Society, and the Prince of Wales Society; and *LM*, 28 September 1784 – the Leeds Benevolent Society. Despite the odd name, the advertisement makes it clear that the Brotherly Posterior Society was a benefit society. The 'Wager-Club' of Wakefield also met: *LI*, 27 January 1784.

[44] St John's alumni: *LI*, 4 May 1807. Milton: *LI*, 15 and 22 June 1807. Gooseberry show: *LM*, 22 August 1807. Benefit societies: *LI*, 8 June 1807 – The Brotherly Posterior Society; *LI*, 27 July 1807 – the Old Union Society; *LM*, 20 June 1807 – the Hunslet Humane Society; and *LM*, 27 June 1807 – the Benevolent Society.

active in Leeds in 1784 and a literary club meeting in York at the same time.[45] The Gentlemen Cricket Players of Leeds advertised a meeting and dinner in 1760 and sponsored a play in 1784, but their matches earned no notice at all. Packs of hounds were kept in the vicinity of both York and Leeds, but neither advertised and only in the 1807 sample did one newspaper, the horsy *York Herald*, give their schedules.[46] Presumably a large but indeterminate share of the cultural activities in which the upper and middling element participated, as well as virtually everything run by and for the poor,[47] were still organized by the participants, not carried on for profit, and not 'commercialized'.

IV

During the eighteenth century, most large English towns developed a round of fashionable entertainment which mimicked as closely as possible the various features of the London season. Theatres, assembly rooms, promenades, bowling greens, racecourse grandstands and pleasure gardens were constructed, often by public subscription.[48] Such facilities gave those with pretensions to gentility a chance to mingle, to see and be seen, to make matches and snub upstarts. Provincial towns became an increasingly popular site for battles over status. Hitherto such competition may more commonly have focused either on one's home estate or on London, which was a centre of fashion and conspicuous consumption from at least the sixteenth century.[49] That is, status had

[45] Reginald Rose, *History of the York Musical Society and the York Choral Society* (York, 1948). The Musical Society's minute books for 1767–72 and 1786–1800 exist and would repay further study. Joseph Priestley may have belonged to the Leeds society, which existed from 1783 until at least 1786. E. Kitson Clark, *The History of 100 Years of Life of the Leeds Philosophical and Literary Society* (Leeds, 1924), pp. 1–2. The York Literary Club was founded in 1771 and lasted for almost twenty years. The members, who were mostly clergymen, physicians and lawyers, took turns hosting the meetings. Robert Davies, *A Memoir of the York Press* (London, 1868), p. 297.

[46] Cricket: *LI*, 20 May 1760 and 22 June 1784. The Leeds hunt began around 1740 (Wilson, *Gentlemen Merchants*, p. 232).

[47] Throwing at the cock in York was suppressed only in 1751 (*VCH: City of York*, p. 246), but the sport was certainly not advertised before that. See Cunningham, *Leisure in the Industrial Revolution*, for a good discussion of developments in popular leisure after 1780.

[48] C. W. Chalklin, 'Capital Expenditure on Building for Cultural Purposes in Provincial England, 1730–1830', *Business History*, 22 (1980), pp. 51–70.

[49] F. J. Fisher, 'The Development of London as a Centre of Conspicuous Consumption in the Sixteenth and Seventeenth Centuries', *Transactions of the Royal Historical Society*, 4th series, 30 (1948), pp. 37–50.

been acquired and defended either at the metropolis or in the country. In the eighteenth century the provincial town apparently became an intermediate locus which could accommodate both players with landed and those with newer, monied forms of wealth.[50] For much of the century a cosmopolitan urban culture grew and flourished, but well before George III's death definite signs of decay can be seen in the established pattern of elite entertainment.

York's status as social capital of the north for much of the century is confirmed by the strength of its assemblies and concerts. As early as 1713, when regular Monday and Thursday assemblies were a recent invention, Mary Pierrepont attended one and observed that if men seeking wives 'don't regard worldly muck, there's extraordinary good choice indeed. I believe last Monday there were two hundred pieces of woman's flesh (fat and lean).'[51] Defoe believed that the institution originated at York. The elegant York Assembly Rooms, built in Blake Street by Lord Burlington between 1730 and 1732, were among the first in the country to be erected to serve that specific purpose. In 1736 the rooms sheltered dancing and card-playing on Mondays and music concerts on Fridays.[52]

Newspaper advertising columns flesh out the picture painted by Drake. In 1741 the Friday concert series began in the middle of October and lasted until the beginning of March, when the last of four benefit concerts for the various members of the orchestra was given. The orchestra then travelled elsewhere before returning to York in the autumn. The orchestra's presence in York from mid-October to early March in the early 1740s implies that their subscription concert series comprised around twenty nights.[53] Certainly this was the case in 1760, when the 'Music Assembly' at

---

[50] Quarter sessions and assizes, hitherto ill-attended, began to be regarded as a kind of shire parliament and to attract substantial gentry attendance around 1600. Clark, *Country Towns*, p. 8. Still, the great age of the town as a social centre attracting outlying gentry seems to have begun in the late seventeenth century. For the case of York see D. M. Palliser, 'A Crisis in English Towns? The Case of York, 1460–1640', *Northern History*, 14 (1978), pp. 108–125, especially p. 120.

[51] The year given is approximate, since the letter is undated. *Letters and Works of Lady Mary (Pierrepont) Wortley Montagu*, eds. Lord Wharncliffe and W. Moy Thomas, 2 vols (London, 1887), vol. 1, pp. 83–4. According to Drake the York assemblies were founded around 1716. Drake, *Eboracum*, pp. 240–1.

[52] Defoe, *Tour*, p. 520. Drake states that the music assembly was founded around 1733. Drake, *Eboracum*, pp. 240–1. *VCH: City of York*, pp. 245–7.

[53] *YCo*, 24 February and 6 October 1741. Most members of the orchestra performed in a concert at the Hull Assembly Rooms in September. *YCo*, 15 September 1741.

the Assembly Rooms consisting of twenty concerts on Friday nights opened 17 October and ran until March. Every morning during race week in August concerts were also given. In 1784 the York concert series still comprised around twenty concerts spread over four and a half months. By that year the York card assemblies, which were also held at the Assembly Rooms, were being advertised in the York newspapers. They opened on 1 November and were held each Monday 'so long as the company shall think fit to continue them', which apparently meant until the beginning of May. Drake mentioned the card assemblies in 1736, when they were also being held on Mondays.[54]

By 1807 significant evidence that the season at York was in decline begins to appear. The Friday subscription series at the Assembly-Rooms now consisted of only six concerts, held fortnightly between 9 January and 10 April. Benefits for the individual performers held in the intervening weeks plus two concerts given during Lent assizes boosted the total to twelve, which was little more than half the figure for 1784. The card assemblies began more than a month later than in the preceding sample year, on 7 December.[55]

Leeds had a very different pattern. Neither in 1741 nor in 1760 was a concert series advertised. In both years scattered references to an 'Assembly Room' appear. Its location is not given, but it was probably the great room of an inn. No hint that a regular season of concerts or assemblies existed is to be found. A concert followed by a ball was advertised in April 1741, but this apparently was the graduation exercise of Mr Graves's dancing school, not part of an otherwise unadvertised concert series. The 'Musick-Meeting' was held on 23 October, according to an enigmatic advertisement which merely informed subscribers that the meeting would be held 'at the usual place' at 6 p.m. The only musical event advertised in 1760 was a concert followed by a ball held at the Assembly Room on

---

[54] Concerts: *YCo*, 11 March, 19 August and 14 October 1760. Although they went unadvertised, concerts very likely also were given during race week in 1741. The 1784 concerts ran from 10 December to the end of April rather than mid-October to early March. The subscription series had dropped to fourteen concerts, but benefit concerts brought the total to around twenty. *YCo*, 16 November 1784, and *YCh*, 30 April 1784. Card assemblies: *YCo*, 26 October 1784; Drake, *Eboracum*, pp. 240–1.

[55] Subscription series: *YH*, 3 January 1807. Benefits: *YH*, 31 January, 21 February, 21 March and 4 April 1807. Cards: *YH*, 21 November 1807.

December 11.[56] More activity than the advertisements alone describe may well have been occurring, but throughout 1760 nothing like the organized round of activity prevailing in York appears to have existed in Leeds.

By 1784 Leeds boasted a 'Gentlemen's Subscription Concert' at the great room of the Rose and Crown Inn given on fourteen successive Mondays beginning on 13 September, with 'miscellaneous music' and oratorios alternating. No benefits for individual performers were advertised, however. The Rose and Crown Inn also hosted 'The Leeds New Assembly', which opened Thursday 7 October, and continued every three weeks 'throughout the winter'. Perhaps the opening of this New Assembly at some point between 1760 and 1784 heralded a shift from employment of rooms only for sporadic balls and concerts on special occasions to their use for an organized season of music and assemblies. The Leeds Music Meeting reappeared in the advertising columns in 1784. By this time the function was apparently the social event of the year, taking place on three days in late November and attracting a sufficiently large crowd that advertisements were placed requesting ladies not to wear hoop skirts and advising those who came in carriages to follow certain specified routes.[57] The Leeds concerts had declined as rapidly as those at York by 1807. The subscription series dropped from fourteen to four concerts, held monthly from January to April at the 'Music-Hall' in Albion Street, and unlike York, supplemental benefits for the performers were not advertised. The Music Meeting was not held this year. The dances at the Assembly Rooms held their own, however, with a series of fourteen subscription balls scheduled more or less fortnightly from early November to late April.[58]

The theatre in York operated on a schedule similar to that of its

[56] Mr Graves's school: *LM*, 10 February 1741. 'Musick-Meeting': *LM*, 13 October 1741. Concert: *LI*, 2 December 1760.

[57] Gentlemen's subscription: *LI*, 7 September 1784. New Assembly: *LI*, 21 September 1784. The music meeting had a programme of Handel oratorios at St Paul's Church in the morning and miscellaneous concerts followed by assemblies and in one case a 'mask ball' in the evenings. *LI*, 26 October, 2, 16 and 23 November 1784.

[58] Subscription concerts: *LI*, 5 and 26 January, 16 and 30 March 1807. The series was in benefit of the Leeds General Infirmary. The music meeting may have been held at regular intervals less frequently than annually. A two-day Handel festival was given at Leeds in 1769. Fawcett, *Music in Eighteenth-Century Norwich and Norfolk*, p. 62. Dances: *LI*, 2 February and 2 November 1807.

assemblies. In Leeds it did not, partly because the same troupe operated in both towns. Thomas Keregan's troupe of actors had been performing regularly in York since 1715, and in a theatre of their own since 1734. The theatre was open twice a week in 1736, when Drake thought that York had 'the best strollers in the kingdom'. In 1744, Keregan's widow built a new theatre on the site of the present Theatre Royal. She died the same year and was succeeded by Joseph Baker. Baker ran the theatre until his death in 1770, but was manager in name only from 1766, when effective control passed to the imposing figure of Tate Wilkinson. Wilkinson built up a circuit which came to include theatres at York, Leeds, Hull, Pontefract, Wakefield and Doncaster. Since he owned the freehold or long-term leases for and kept scenery at each of these theatres, he was able to open in one town a day or two after closing in another. He was succeeded at his death in 1803 by his son John.[59]

The Wilkinsons spent several months of each year in York, Hull and, from 1771, Leeds. Wilkinson asserted that until then Leeds 'never had a decent Theatre, but had been harrassed out with plays by a set of bad conducted players, void of merit as performers', who wore out their welcome by staying at Leeds for seven or eight months a year. Leeds had in fact had occasional visits from Keregan and Baker as well as the company of James Whitely, but a durable foothold in that town seems not to have been established previously.[60] In 1760 the theatre in York was open from 5 January to 14 May.[61] 1784 saw little change. The theatre operated from 22 January to 15 May and from 21 August to 3 September. The schedule changed in 1807, with the theatre open from 3 March to 5 June, 13 to 18 July, and 24 to 31 August. In Leeds no adver-

[59] For Yorkshire and its theatres see Wilkinson, *Memoirs*; Tate Wilkinson, *The Wandering Patentee; or, A History of the Yorkshire Theatres, from 1770 to the Present Time*, 4 vols in two (1973 London photofacsimile of 1795 York edn); Linda Fitzsimmons, 'The Theatre Royal, York', *York History*, no. 4 (n.d.), pp. 169–92; Drake, *Eboracum*, pp. 240–1. For examples of playing in two towns one and two days apart see Wilkinson, *Wandering Patentee*, vol. 2, pp. 131, 169–70.

[60] Wilkinson, *Wandering Patentee*, vol. 1, pp. 75–6; vol. 3, pp. 63–4; Sybil Rosenfeld, *Strolling Players & Drama in the Provinces 1660–1765* (Cambridge, 1939), pp. 111, 113, 131–2, 138, 139, 141–2. Wilkinson began bringing his company to Leeds after competition crowded him out of Newcastle. Wilkinson, *Wandering Patentee*, vol. 1, pp. 73–4, 100–1.

[61] The newspaper does not give this information in 1741. Although no advertisements appeared, the troupe very likely also appeared for a week-long stint during the July assizes and/or the August race week.

tisements appeared in 1741 or 1760, probably because players came there only briefly or not at all. Wilkinson's company played in Leeds from 19 May to 20 August 1784 and in 1807 from 8 June to 21 August, broken by the week in July spent in York. Evidently theatrical activity peaked in York and Leeds around 1784. The theatre did business in York for some four and a half months in that year (and probably in 1760 as well) and for three months in Leeds. By 1807, York's theatre was open for three and a half months while that of Leeds was active for two and a quarter months. The company had expanded its circuit, playing more one-week stands in towns during a race week or fair and shortening its longer runs.

Two conclusions emerge from this material on music, assemblies, and theatres. First, York had a well-developed season beginning quite early in the eighteenth century, while Leeds did not. In York theatre, subscription concerts and card assemblies tended to overlap each other for at least a couple of months in the winter (or, by 1807, spring). During the period of peak activity one could attend a concert, a card assembly or the playhouse on every weeknight. Leeds acquired these trappings of elite culture more slowly. The city did not possess a theatre and an annually-returning troupe until 1771, and apparently an organized round of concerts and assemblies also began between 1760 and 1784. Thereafter such attractions were spread out over the year. The theatre was open in the summer while balls and concerts were given during the other three seasons. The interval between balls and concerts was greater than in York, monthly when York's were fortnightly and every third week when York's were weekly. The impression is that York's social year revolved around visitors who came together for a month or two to enjoy each other's company and the pleasures that the city had to offer. Leeds on the other hand attracted few rural gentry to its fleshpots. Its home-grown elite accordingly savoured cultural activities by patronizing them year-round.

Second, in both York and Leeds, the amount of theatrical and dramatic activity dropped markedly between 1784 and 1807. The theatre was open a month less in York and three weeks less in Leeds, while the concert season became less than half as long in both places. Other evidence confirms that patronage of such events by the urban elite and well-heeled visitors was falling off. Wilkinson felt that theatre in Yorkshire peaked in 1771, complaining in

1794 that 'Bath and London is [now] the word'.[62] By 1811 an actor could write home boasting of having had good receipts at York even though 'You know York is a bad theatrical town.'[63]

Rosy memories of past successes and gloomy comparisons by actors are suspect, but other evidence from the later years of the management of Wilkinson and his son points to a changing audience profile accompanied by deteriorating finances. In the 1790s unruly audiences rioted unless actors gave encores of songs and prologues as and when asked. Wilkinson complains of nights when those seated in the (cheaper) gallery seats talked all through the featured play and then gave their undivided attention to the lighter fare comprising the afterpiece, and alleges that by the 1780s subscriptions to his series of plays in York, Hull and Leeds, once filled by respectable families, were being purchased by laundresses and artisans who scalped the tickets on good nights and attended themselves on poor ones. On Shrove Tuesday a particularly plebeian and rowdy crowd was wont to attend the theatre.[64] Wilkinson ended the subscription system and raised his prices for performances on Shrove Tuesday but found no answer for his greater problem, the need to restore a profitable balance in his clientele between elegant and less exalted patrons.

Indirect evidence also suggests that Wilkinson's audience was changing. He prided himself on having promoted respectable theatre, and to this end he banned various undignified customs prevalent in most troupes, such as thanking the audience from the stage at the conclusion of benefits and soliciting custom for them beforehand. He also bought a royal patent in 1769 for his York and Hull theatres, partly for the added cachet, and emphasized drama over spectacle.[65] Gradually he found he had to lower his standards and respond to audience demand for lavish spectacles involving

---

[62] Wilkinson, *Wandering Patentee*, vol. 1, pp. 80–1, 242; vol. 3, pp. 132–3; vol. 4, p. 229.

[63] Anne Jackson Mathews, *Memoirs of Charles Mathews, Comedian*, 2nd edn, 4 vols (London, 1839), vol. 2, pp. 150–1.

[64] Wilkinson, *Memoirs*, vol. 4, pp. 4–5; Wilkinson, *Wandering Patentee*, vol. 2, pp. 216–27; vol. 3, pp. 218–27 (for Wilkinson's account of his worst riot, which occurred at York on 12 May 1791); vol. 4, pp. 40, 209–16.

[65] Thanks and solicitation by actors: Wilkinson, *Memoirs*, vol. 3, pp. 127–9; vol. 4, pp. 65–7. The patent cost almost £500. Wilkinson, *Memoirs*, vol. 4, pp. 68–9, 98; Wilkinson, *Wandering Patentee*, vol. 1, pp. 71–3. Wilkinson ended the prevalent practice of fleshing out performances with preludes, interludes and afterludes on actors' benefit nights. Wilkinson, *Memoirs*, vol. 4, p. 128; Wilkinson, *Wandering Patentee*, vol. 2, pp. 103–4.

elaborate machinery and sets. A 1784 production included 'a new comic dance call'd The Clown in the Coal Pit: or, The Colliers in an Uproar' which featured views of 'the inside of a coal pit', 'an illuminated pastoral temple', and 'a glass-house, which changes into a dye-house, and Harlequin takes a leap into the furnace'. 'The Magic Oak', an 1807 pantomime, had as its 'principal scenes . . . the Cave of Merlin, with the Magic Oak withered – a beautiful grotto of shell work – a wonderful deception with a magical chest – a wind mill – the Magic Oak in full leaf – a superb golden equestrian statue of Marcus Aurelius in the Capitol at Rome – a ludicrous metamorphose from the change of a table – a prison. A beautiful bower, in the centre a golden fountain in motion, with figures spouting water, &c. &c.' Wilkinson commented in his autobiography that a good farce was preferable to a pantomime as an afterpiece because the increased take at the box-office generated by the latter seldom offset the vast cost of preparing it, but he had to rely to an ever greater extent on such entertainments.[66]

The Wilkinsons tried every expedient to balance their books, from hiring 'Signior Scaglioni and his Dancing Dogs' and performers on the glass harmonica to having an actor 'fly' with the assistance of wires. Increasingly they relied on guest appearances by popular London stars, such as 'the Little Devil' and his team of acrobats in 1784 and Sarah Siddons and Charles Kemble in 1807. Nothing worked. Glittering spectacles and guest stars were quick fixes with tremendous overheads and hidden costs. They paid their expenses but failed to bail out a theatre in decline, as the later history of the Yorkshire company demonstrates. John Wilkinson went bankrupt in 1813, and from then until 1864 twenty-five individuals managed the York Theatre Royal, with none lasting more than eight years. Terms of one or two years became the rule.[67]

[66] *LI*, 8 June 1784; *YH*, 28 March 1807; Wilkinson, *Wandering Patentee*, vol. 4, p. 71.

[67] Wilkinson, *Wandering Patentee*, vol. 2, pp. 178 (flying actor), 182, 228–9 (Scaglioni), 193 (harmonica); vol. 3, p. 20 (for a troupe of Italian tumblers). Little Devil: *LI*, 13 July 1784. Siddons: *YH*, 4 July 1807; *LI*, 6 July 1807; Kemble: *YH*, 15 and 22 August 1807; *LI*, 17 August 1807. Fitzsimmons, 'The Theatre Royal, York', pp. 180, 189. Reliance on stars lowered morale in the resident troupe and reduced respect for their efforts by the audience. Wilkinson found that Siddons's profitable seventeen-night stint in 1786 'absolutely killed the whole succeeding year', by causing audiences to make invidious comparisons with his regular performers. *Wandering Patentee*, vol. 3, pp. 5–7, 89.

Apparently the gentry and other members of the urban elite were abandoning the theatre. Perhaps they were driven out by the attendance of a rough element, but arrival of the latter may have been as much an effect as a cause. Avoiding contamination from laundresses and artisans was presumably less of a problem at the concerts and assemblies, yet decay is observable there as well. One cause of the decline is probably improved turnpikes and a better coaching network. In 1796 travel between London and York by coach took thirty-one hours, which was two to three times faster than in 1761.[68] A gentleman could more easily take his family to London or Bath, and, if he chose to stay on his estate, a short visit to York rather than wintering there was beginning to be practical. Second, competition from a new set of rivals had begun undercutting both York and Leeds by 1807. Even in 1784 concerts in Wakefield and Halifax and assemblies in Doncaster were advertised. By 1807 theatres in Halifax and Huddersfield, balls in Ripon and Skipton, subscription concerts in Halifax, and oratorio performances in Bingley, Illingworth, Hull and Scarborough were publicized.[69] Gentry were less likely to visit York and Leeds because an adequate range of activities was being offered closer to home.

Most speculatively, perhaps the evidence points to elite withdrawal from certain organized types of leisure as a more private, domestic culture began to emerge. Growing evangelical antipathy towards gaming, dancing and theatre could have played a part.[70] Parallel developments can be observed in the architecture of Bath, where a pattern of living close together in terraces and crescents and spending most of the day promenading, relaxing and recuperating in unison began to be replaced by a more reclusive lifestyle based on villas in the early nineteenth century. Changes in the architecture of country houses also point to increased elite attention to and desire for privacy, and by 1800 many families were entering a more reclusive era which celebrated the joys of dom-

[68] VCH: City of York, p. 477.
[69] LI, 5 October (Halifax), 23 November (Wakefield) and 21 December 1784 (Doncaster). LI, 19 January and 8 June (Halifax concerts), 2 February (Halifax theatre), 9 February (Skipton) and 28 September 1807 (Bingley); LM, 31 January and 28 February (Huddersfield), 25 July (Illingworth), and 26 September 1807 (Hull); YCo, 9 February and 13 April 1807 (Ripon); YH, 1, 8 and 15 August 1807 (Scarborough).
[70] Wilkinson devotes a great deal of space in his memoirs to his run-ins with the Methodists. See Wilkinson, Wandering Patentee, passim.

esticity and paternal authority.[71] Perhaps the very success of commercializers of leisure in reaching new audiences prompted some elite groups to withdraw into their homes. The unified upper-class culture of the eighteenth century may have begun to break down, and as new challengers for status emerged, established groups found that the best response was a dignified refusal to compete.

V

Collectively York and Leeds point to new hypotheses about Hanoverian leisure and society. The evidence suggests that traditional gentry gathering-spots like York were much quicker to mimic London trends than commercial and industrial centres like Leeds. By the accession of George III, York had been attracting a large body of gentry to its winter season of plays, concerts, card-playing, billiards, dancing and parties for a half-century. York attracted a theatrical troupe, built an assembly room and laid out a promenade much more quickly than Leeds.[72] The latter town did not develop a compact season at all, and its biggest social event, the music festival, aped a provincial model.[73] Probably a difference in audience explains this divergence. Leeds lacked a numerous group of visiting and resident gentry. Members of its merchant elite were slower to patronize commercialized leisure activity, and when they did so they had no need to confine such pleasures to the winter and spread them out accordingly.

The nature of the audience may also explain two other perceived differences between York and Leeds. Membership in clubs and feasting at convivial banquets represent a form of leisure which may have appealed most strongly to a town's middling element. In so far

---

71 Mark Girouard, 'Society on Parade – Aspects of Eighteenth-Century Bath', lecture to York Georgian Society, York, 24 November 1979; Lawrence Stone and Jeanne C. Fawtier Stone, *An Open Elite? England 1540–1880* (Oxford, 1984), pp. 326–8, 344–9 (taste in country house architecture changed gradually, but the century after 1750 would appear to be the time when earlier innovations in this regard achieved wide acceptance); Lawrence Stone, *The Family, Sex and Marriage in England 1500–1800* (London and New York, 1977), pp. 666–80.

72 For billiards see *YCo*, 13 January 1741 and 23 and 30 March 1784. The corporation constructed the New Walk along the river Ouse, starting in 1732. *VCH: City of York*, p. 207.

73 Starting around 1713 the Three Choirs Festival brought the cathedral choirs of Hereford, Gloucester, and Worcester together annually. Plumb, *Commercialisation of Leisure*, p. 15.

as this activity can be gauged from the newspapers, it increased markedly after 1760, and it seems to have been stronger in York than Leeds, perhaps because of York's large contingent of clergy, lawyers and physicians. Organized by its participants and without a profit motive, however, such activity remained largely invisible in the press and removed from any shift towards commercialization. Showmen, lecturers and virtuosi passed through both towns in every year sampled. While individual acts were aimed at specific parts of the market, collectively they tended to appeal to a broad audience.[74] The big increase in advertisements for this imported, travelling leisure between 1760 and 1784 and the increased size of the acts which took to the road after 1784 suggests that at least in Yorkshire this form of entertainment became commercialized only in the fifty years after 1760.[75] The one apparent difference between York and Leeds came around 1807, when the largest shows were visiting Leeds and skipping York. The sizeable and increasing advantage of Leeds in overall population became more and more decisive to the attraction of the biggest acts with correspondingly high overheads.

Towns which created wealth did experience leisure differently from those which attracted it. In the former leisure was slower to develop in a commercialized form, likelier to develop in ways somewhat more distinct from the influence of the metropolis and to be pitched at a wider audience. The differences in the way leisure changed from group to group, town to town and region to region need to be studied much more thoroughly and will doubtless yield

---

[74] The standard admission price for most curiosities in 1784 was one shilling. The manager of the 'Surprising Female Child' charged ladies and gentlemen one shilling, 'tradesmen' sixpence, and 'servants and children' threepence. The latter two prices were announced after the act had been in town for some time and interest was, presumably, on the wane. *YCo*, 30 November and 14 December 1784. Weavor's scientific lectures cost half a crown each. *YCo*, 9 March 1784.

[75] A study which analyses such advertisements over several decades is needed to confirm these findings, which are based on the fairly small numbers of acts passing through given towns in possibly unrepresentative years. Such a study could also come to grips with questions which my research thus far has enabled me to formulate but not answer. Did a recognized 'circuit' exist among showmen and lecturers, which dictated the towns in which to stop and, perhaps, the order in which to travel among them? Showmen tended to stop at certain inns; was there further specialization in this respect? Did one book at an inn well in advance, and were the inns conduits of information preventing, say, two Irish giants from visiting a town too close together?

surprises. None the less a broad hypothesis about the chronology of eighteenth-century leisure can be advanced. Plumb argues that by 1760 reasonably modern, professional and commercialized approaches had replaced older forms in the marketing of a very wide range of leisure activities. This development was fuelled by and in turn stimulated expenditure on leisure by an ever increasing proportion of the middle stratum of society. The underlying assumption seems to be that commercialized leisure and cultivation of a middle-class market were necessarily linked.

In Yorkshire only the elite season in York seems to match this hypothesis of cultural transformation by 1760. A preferable alternative is that while commercialization had overtaken many forms of leisure activity by that year, the process tended to begin with the capture of a comparatively small, well to do, somewhat London-oriented clientele. The use of these techniques to extend the market to a broader swathe of the middle class and more securely into the provinces often did not occur until the 1790s and beyond. Ironically, even as a wider market for many leisure activities was born, the concurrent decline of theatre and sub-scription concerts in Yorkshire suggests that the audience for which commercialized leisure was originally developed was abandoning it. Other evidence bolsters this formulation. Children's books on science are a good example. In 1761 Newbery sensed a market and published *The Newtonian System* by 'Tom Telescope'. The book sold well and was reprinted six times between then and 1787. It encountered virtually no competition until the 1790s, when a flood of juvenile scientific works began to appear on the market. In addition to being numerous, such books increasingly were aimed at a specialized market niche: some were designed as school texts and others were devoted to a specific scientific field.[76] Similarly, a study of Suffolk imprints shows that the spread of printing to smaller towns and a threefold increase in the number of items printed in larger towns both occurred in the 1790s. Late in the century the number of towns with their own newspapers, and of towns which had already had at least one and acquired a second or third, similarly expanded. The number, variety, and scope of provincial

---

[76] James A. Secord, 'Newton in the Nursery: Tom Telescope and the Philosophy of Tops and Balls, 1761–1838', *History of Science*, 23 (1985), pp. 127–51, especially 140–1.

libraries, reading clubs and learned societies seems also to have grown rapidly around this time.[77]

The example of leisure may point to wider conclusions about the commercialization of English social and economic life. The pace of change has perhaps been overstated. Borsay's urban renaissance might profitably be regarded as extending into the early 1800s, a time scale which would make it coincide with structural economic change and continuing population growth in the towns. None the less, the conclusion that eighteenth-century England's society was a commercializing one seems inescapable. From the perspective of the provincial town Clark's vision of a static, aristocratic, deferential society seems as skewed as that of the histories he decries. The great need is for a framework which gives due weight to both elements in English life rather than dismissing either as atypical, beneath notice, or unreal.

[77] Alan Sterenberg, 'The Spread of Printing in Suffolk in the Eighteenth Century', in M. Crump and M. Harris, eds., *Searching the Eighteenth Century* (London, 1983), pp. 28–42. In 1782, fifty English provincial newspapers were being published. By 1808 the number exceeded 100 and it was over 150 in 1830. Donald Read, *Press and People, 1790–1850* (Westport, Conn., 1975 repr. of 1961 edn), p. 59. Although some of the dates are firmer than others, two-thirds of the book clubs for which founding dates are given in Kaufman's census were founded after 1780. Kaufman, 'English Book Clubs', pp. 4–8. A figure of around 60 per cent founded or first mentioned after 1780 can also be inferred from his data on subscription and circulating libraries. Kaufman, 'The Community Library: A Chapter in English Social History', *Transactions of the American Philosophical Society*, new series, 57, part 7, pp. 50–4.

15. The dynamics of class formation in nineteenth-century Bradford

THEODORE KODITSCHEK

In 1965, Lawrence Stone lamented that 'the map of English social history is full of huge blank spaces, more often than not labelled "here be the rich".'[1] Since then, he and others have begun to fill these spaces, and we now know far more, not only about the aristocracy and upper gentry, on whom Stone concentrates, but also about urban merchants, landlords, professionals, and even the parish gentry in the countryside.[2] Nevertheless, in this renaissance of elite social history, one group, the nineteenth-century industrial bourgeoisie, has been curiously overlooked. This contemporary neglect of the early industrial capitalists is all the more remarkable since, until quite recently, they had been regarded as a social group of indisputable world historical significance – an absolutely central agent in the making of the modern world. Indeed, this devaluation of the nineteenth-century industrial bourgeoisie's historical significance constitutes the dominant tone of scholarship among historians of every stripe and tendency, from conservatives who

---

I would like to thank David Cannadine and LeeAnn Whites for their suggestions for improving the manuscript and James Rosenheim for his careful editorial work.

[1] Lawrence Stone, *The Crisis of the Aristocracy*, (Oxford, 1965), p. 1.
[2] For the most notable examples, see Lawrence Stone, *The Family, Sex and Marriage in England: 1500–1800* (London and New York, 1977); with Jeanne Fawtier Stone, *An Open Elite? England 1540–1880* (Oxford, 1984); J. T. Cliffe, *The Yorkshire Gentry from the Reformation to the Civil War*, (London, 1969); Philip Jenkins, *The Making of a Ruling Class: The Glamorgan Gentry, 1640–1790* (Cambridge, 1983); G. E. Mingay, *English Landed Society in the Eighteenth Century*, (London, 1963); F. M. L. Thompson, *English Landed Society in the Nineteenth Century*, (London, 1963); R. G. Wilson, *Gentlemen Merchants: The Merchant Community in Leeds, 1700–1830*, (New York, 1971); David Cannadine, *Lords and Landlords: The Aristocracy and the Towns, 1774–1976*, (Leicester, 1980); W. J. Reader, *Professional Men: The Rise of the Professional Classes in Nineteenth Century England*, (London, 1966); M. Jeanne Peterson, *The Medical Profession in Mid-Victorian London* (Berkeley, 1978).

emphasize continuities with the pre-industrial era to Marxists who, in confronting the urban industrial transformation, are more preoccupied with the agency of the capitalist working class.[3]

Seeking to debunk the 'rags to riches' myth, most recent work on the social origins of nineteenth-century industrialists has emphasized their essentially middle-class backgrounds, while the research of W. D. Rubenstein into the social composition of the wealthy has revealed how far they continued to be overshadowed by merchants, financiers and landowners throughout this period, even after their entrepreneurial ascent.[4] Simultaneously shorn of his vaunted pedigree of poverty and denied the full measure of his destination of success, the nineteenth-century industrial entrepreneur now cuts a far less heroic figure than he did in his own day.

Of course, consciousness of the inadequacies of Britain's present economic performance has indisputably contributed to enhancing our awareness of the limits of entrepreneurship in the past. Even more decisive than the devaluation of the nineteenth-century entrepreneur's economic significance, however, has been the demotion within most recent historiography of his once presumed hegemonic cultural and political role. In so far as nineteenth-century industrial capitalists gained any entry into Britain's ruling cultural or political elite, they are now presumed to have done so either by becoming landlords or, at least, by aping genteel conservative values and by refurbishing within an urban context the paternalist style of social dominance which agrarian aristocrats had originally forged.[5] Indeed, drawing on these recent trends in historiography, Martin Wiener has gone so far as to deny that Britain ever had 'a straightforwardly bourgeois or industrial elite'. While power was eventually yielded by the landed aristocracy, this only occurred after 'the acceptance of many aristocratic values by members of the new elite'.[6]

[3] For two examples from the opposite extreme, see E. P. Thompson, *The Making of the English Working Class* (New York, 1963), and W. L. Burn, *The Age of Equipoise* (New York, 1965).

[4] W. D. Rubenstein, 'Wealth, Elites, and the Class Structure of Modern Britain', *Past and Present*, 76 (1977), pp. 99–126; *Men of Property: The Very Wealthy in Britain since the Industrial Revolution* (New Brunswick, 1981).

[5] D. Cannadine, 'The Present and the Past in the English Industrial Revolution, 1880–1980', *Past and Present*, 103, (1984), pp. 131–72; D. Roberts, *Paternalism in Victorian England*, (New Brunswick, 1979); Patrick Joyce, *Work, Society, and Politics: The Culture of the Factory in Later Victorian England*, (New Brunswick, 1980).

[6] M. Wiener, *English Culture and the Decline of the Industrial Spirit, 1850–1980* (Cambridge, 1981), pp. 8, 12.

While this insistence upon the limits of bourgeois hegemony constitutes a useful corrective to the uncritical generalizations which once prevailed, it tends to sanction scholarly neglect of the industrial entrepreneurs of the period, who did, after all, constitute an ascendant, if never entirely dominant, social group. Indeed, so much recent scholarship has been devoted to demonstrating all the things that the nineteenth-century industrial bourgeoisie was not, that we now know even less about what it was than when Stone originally wrote. As part of an effort to redress the balance this essay will examine the experience of a new generation of entrepreneurial capitalists within a single industrial town. As the most dynamic of Britain's new cities, early nineteenth-century Bradford was, of course, an unusual social environment where the dominating presence of ascendant industrial capitalists can scarcely be ignored. Nevertheless, for this very reason it offers a unique opportunity to explore locally a kind of bourgeois hegemony which, at the national level, remained more obscure and incomplete.[7]

I

Before 1825, Bradford was a modest, regional market town in the West Riding highlands, one of the centres of a thriving worsted handicraft industry and trade. Although spinning was largely mechanized during the first quarter of the nineteenth century, the other processes of worsted manufacture remained essentially proto-industrial, even as their volume substantially increased. Organized by relatively large-scale capitalist clothiers into a far-flung network of rural cottage handicrafts, this proto-industry was worked by villagers scattered throughout the countryside who were increasingly dependent on wage labour because of their inability to eke out a living from infertile and increasingly sub-divided land.

[7] See Theodore Koditschek, *Class Formation and Urban Industrial Society, Bradford, 1750–1850*, (Cambridge, forthcoming) for a fuller account on which this article frequently draws. In recent years, a handful of other social historians have begun to focus on nineteenth-century industrial capitalists and urban entrepreneurs, particularly in Lancashire. See especially Geoffrey Howe, *The Cotton Masters* (Oxford, 1985); R. J. Morris, 'The Middle Classes and British Towns and Cities of the Industrial Revolution, 1780–1870', in D. Fraser and A. Sutcliffe, eds., *The Pursuit of Urban History* (London, 1983), pp. 286–306; and J. Seed, 'Unitarianism, Political Economy, and the Antinomies of Liberal Culture in Manchester, 1830–50', *Social History*, 7.1 (1982), pp. 1–25.

Yet, although social relations in Bradford, even during the eighteenth century, were already deeply affected by capitalist class divisions, before 1825 these underlying social fissures remained embedded in an essentially rural and domestic environment governed by traditional cultural values, modes of living and methods of work.[8]

This legacy of traditionalism can be seen even in the behaviour of the local capitalist elite. Dominated by the old-style putting-out masters, from whom most of the early spinning mill-owners were drawn, this group formed an increasingly tightly-knit establishment, composed almost entirely of Anglicans or of Quakers or Presbyterians, who had grown increasingly conservative in cultural and political terms by the early nineteenth century. Cultivating an ever more oligarchical sense of their place within the community and an ever more protectionist attitude towards industry and trade, these men did, in many ways, conform to the now dominant image of the nineteenth-century industrialist: tending to avoid risky innovations, aping aristocratic lifestyles, and increasingly turning themselves into *rentiers* – most often by buying up urban property and becoming landlords in the town.[9]

After 1825, however, all this was dramatically altered, with the rise of a new generation of entrepreneurially-minded industrialists who presided, during the next half-century, over a full-scale industrial revolution which transformed the worsted industry into a mechanized system of centralized factory production whose products were marketed in large volume over the entire world. Concentrated in Bradford, this industrial revolution went hand in hand with an urban environmental metamorphosis which transformed what was in 1821 a market town of 26,000 into what was three decades later a city of over 100,000, then probably the fastest-growing urban centre anywhere in the world.[10]

This massive urban industrial revolution was accompanied by a displacement of Bradford's capitalist elite. Of the 293 worsted firms listed in the 1850 *Directory*, only 6 per cent had been in business two decades before. By contrast, of the forty-nine listed in the 1830 *Directory*, only 32 per cent remained in business at mid-century. Notwithstanding this rapid entrepreneurial turnover and the

---

[8] Koditschek, *Class Formation*, chapter 2.   [9] *Ibid.*, chapter 5.
[10] *Ibid.* chapter 3; B. R. Mitchell, *Abstract of British Historical Statistics* (Cambridge, 1962), pp. 24–6.

emergence of a new generation of businessmen, the period was also one of industrial concentration, in which those who successfully surmounted its challenges emerged decisively as an economic elite. Thus, in contrast to the period before 1825, when a mass of medium-sized, relatively marginal proto-industrial producers co-existed with a tiny mercantile elite, by 1850, 76 per cent of the town's 32,856 worsted workers were now concentrated in the 129 largest factory firms.[11]

Consequently, the second quarter of the nineteenth century maked a sharp departure from the economic environment of the pre-1825 period. Competition became increasingly cut-throat amidst a volatile trade cycle in which great opportunities existed alongside enormous risks. Those who succeeded tended to do so spectacularly, while those who failed found themselves either reduced to the status of paid employees, or relegated to the burgeoning ranks of the urban lower middle class.[12] Not surprisingly, then, the new generation of industrialists who emerged by mid-century were different, in almost every respect, from the oligarchy of conservative traditionalists who had preceded them as a local elite. Generally young immigrants who were overwhelmingly Nonconformist (predominantly identified with the newer Baptist, Congregationalist and Methodist sects), these new men were both the products and creators of Bradford's new market-dominated world. With some justice they could regard their own intensely entrepreneurial personality type as the one most naturally suited to the urban industrial milieu.[13]

Examination of the social backgrounds and life trajectories of these rising capitalists shows that much in their actual experiences affirmed the utility of competitive individualism, and confirmed their liberal values of self-reliance and self-help. While few of these parvenus actually began in rags, and some attained only modest riches, nearly all who successfully negotiated the treacherous economic currents of the 1830s and 1840s were elevated above the circumstances into which they had been born. Thus, although few of the new entrepreneurs came from genuinely proletarian backgrounds, most of those who rose most dramatically, like the

[11] C. Richardson, *A Geography of Bradford* (Bradford, 1976), p. 64; *Pigot's Directory* (London, 1828); *Ibbetson's Bradford Directory* (Bradford, 1850); *Parliamentary Papers* (hereafter *P.P.*), (1852–3, LXXXVIII), 722–4.
[12] Koditschek, *Class Formation*, chapter 7.
[13] Koditschek, *Class Formation*, chapter 6.

manufacturers Isaac Holden and Titus Salt, or the stuff merchant Robert Milligan, came from small-scale yeoman farming families in Scotland or the Yorkshire hinterland. Others, like the German-born merchants Jacob Behrens and Charles Semon were the children of travelling pedlars, while John Priestman and Benjamin Berry came from families of small shopkeepers in other provincial towns.[14] Of course, some of the new capitalists, like Henry Forbes, William Fison or W. E. Forster, came from more substantial middle-class families, while a significant minority, such as Henry Ripley, Daniel Illingworth, Christopher Waud, William Rouse, Swithin Anderton, James and Richard Garnett, or John and William Rand, inherited relatively small, largely proto-industrial worsted businesses which they transformed into large, fully industrial firms.[15] Nevertheless, it is significant that the largest of the proto- and early industrial capitalist dynasties such as the Fawcetts, the Hustlers and the Peckovers did not survive the urban industrial revolution and only one of the new manufacturers, Samuel Cunliffe Lister (later Lord Masham), actually came from gentry stock. His experience of upward mobility was, in any case, perhaps the most spectacular, as he accumulated through entrepreneurship a vast fortune (worth £648,588 in non-landed assets alone in 1906 when he died), that far exceeded the modest competence which he had originally inherited as a younger son.[16]

While most of these men obtained some material assistance from their families, such benefits were entirely inadequate to the needs of entrepreneurship in an era when the minimum scale of operation was beginning substantially to increase. Most had to rely on credit to finance their operations, especially during their firms' critical early years.[17] Independent entrepreneurship often became possible

14 *Bradford Observer*, 3 July 1862; 23 January 1868; 18 October 1870; 22 December 1891; J. Behrens, *Memoir of Jacob Behrens*, (London, 1925); Anon., *The Face of Worstedopolis*, (Bradford, n.d.), p. 27; Anon., *Fortunes Made in Business* (London, 1864), vol. 1, pp. 7–9; Alice Priestman, *Recollections of Henry Brady Priestman* (Bradford, 1918), pp. 1–10.
15 *Bradford Observer*, 18 February, 20 October 1868; 5 April 1869; *Bradford Observer Budget*, 3 February, 19 May 1906; 5 June 1907; T. W. Reid, *Life of Rt. Hon. W. E. Forster* (London, 1884), pp. 75–9; W. Cudworth, *Historical Notes on the Bradford Corporation* (Bradford, 1881), p. 164; *Histories of Bolton and Bowling* (Bradford, 1891), pp. 244–9; *The Century's Progress: Yorkshire Industry and Commerce* (London, 1893), p. 65.
16 *Fortunes Made in Business*, vol. 1, pp. 47–86.
17 Koditschek, *Class Formation*, chapter 7.

only after several years of salaried employment, when capital might be accumulated and experience could be obtained. Even then, circumstances usually necessitated a period of abstinence, long working hours and delayed marriage while the business was set on a solid footing and profits ploughed back into the firm.[18]

The ability and willingness of these young parvenus to commit themselves to so self-denying a lifestyle suggest that what their families had not bequeathed to them in material resources was compensated by a psychological legacy of ambition and abstemious industry that raised the competitive threshold of performance for Bradford's worsted industry as a whole. Biographical evidence attests to the impact of early religious influence on these individuals, from tightly-knit lower-middle-class families of origin in which maternal roles and authority were potent and visible, even when paternal prestige and resources were comparatively weak.[19]

The impetus towards achievement which such an upbringing facilitated can be seen in the commitment to self-culture and education which most of these men exhibited. In most cases, inadequate parental resources brought an end to formal schooling between the ages of ten and sixteen by the need to earn a living and find remunerative work. Nevertheless, transforming this necessity into a virtue, most of them began to articulate a distinctive pedagogic vision in which learning was conceived as a lifelong mission which pervaded the whole personality, informing action and behaviour in every sphere. 'The great rough world', declared the editor of the *Bradford Observer*, 'is the best schoolhouse', in which 'the mind is educated and the character is formed.'[20]

Hence the necessity of finding a career that could also become a calling – that could provide some higher sense of purpose in a fluid environment like that of early industrial Bradford, where a collection of rootless immigrants without the guidance of predetermined patrimonies sought to forge viable personal lives and identities with their individual characters as their most valuable assets. In this

[18] *Ibid.*, chapter 8. So powerful and pervasive were these imperatives that the new men tended to reduce personal and household expenditure to a minimum even after marriage. An examination of servant-holding from the 1851 census manuscripts shows that even then they remained, as a group, considerably more frugal than local elites who were older and/or less entrepreneurially inclined.

[19] *Ibid.*, chapter 7.

[20] *Bradford Observer*, 4 March 1847; *The Bradfordian*, 1 January 1862, p. 18; F. G. Byles, *William Byles* (Weymouth, 1932), chapter 1.

context, their impulse to seek self-justification and direction found a natural outlet in the radically egocentric, salvation-centred theology which pervaded the domestic and congregational culture of their families' Calvinist or neo-Calvinist sects.[21]

Of course, the link between the entrepreneurial spirit of capitalism and the Protestant, predestinarian creed was long ago powerfully drawn by Max Weber.[22] In Bradford, men like Holden, his brother-in-law Jonas Sugden, Milligan, Ripley, Salt, and even Lister, very closely embodied the psychology of worldly asceticism which Weber imagined such existential preoccupations with religious justification was likely to induce. Nevertheless, although these men convinced themselves that capitalist entrepreneurship would be the most effective vehicle for expressing their worldly ascetic impulses, the connection between the two was, by no means, self-evident from the start. Indeed, many of Bradford's most successful industrialists, including Salt, Holden, W. E. Forster and J. V. Godwin, had not originally planned to be entrepreneurs at all. When other opportunities fell through, however, and circumstances pushed them in this way they all began to perceive entrepreneurship as a providential destiny through which they might not only seek personal fulfilment, but also demonstrate their status as visible agents of divine will.[23]

According to his biographer, 'The rise of Mr Sugden was not the effect of chance':

It was the result of deep thought, a settled plan and invincible determination. He saw that in the free constitution of this country, the recent improvements in machinery, the enterprise of the age, and the openings for trade that are appearing in every part of the world, an opportunity was presented to the manufacturers of Britain without an equal at any other period.[24]

Of course, Sugden's subsequent success amply demonstrated from hindsight the correctness of his entrepreneurial choice. For him, as for other local capitalists, worldly prosperity might be taken as evidence of divine favour – proof that God had elected them to read His providential signs aright. However, doing God's work

---

[21] Koditschek, *Class Formation*, chapter 7.

[22] Max Weber, *The Protestant Ethic and the Spirit of Capitalism* (New York, 1958).

[23] R. Balgarnie, *Sir Titus Salt* (London, 1877), pp. 28–31; Reid, *Forster*, vol. 1, pp. 36–8, B. Godwin, 'Autobiography' (MSS, Bradford Central Library), fos. 164, 528–9; E. Miall, *The British Churches in Relation to the British People*, pp. 294–7.

[24] G. S. Hardy, *Commerce and Christianity* (London, 1857), p. 57.

entailed pursuing a course which benefited not only oneself but others. Thus, Sugden's biographer hastened to insist, 'The vision before him was not that of mansion, equipage, and rank: but of prosperous brothers and happy sisters ... of a whole neighbourhood through every one of its classes and constituents, moral in character, comfortable in its homes, and hallowed in its religious principles.'[25]

While it would be easy to dismiss this as empty self-promotion, there were certain features in the new worsted entrepreneurship of the post-1825 period that facilitated a sense of higher mission and sanctioned the belief that in pursuing private profits, the entrepreneur would also be promoting the public good. The intensification of competition, the extension of markets, and the spread of mechanization to all parts of the production process which characterized the worsted industry during the decades after 1825, all seemed to be forcing entrepreneurs to become more innovative, to introduce new products and manufacturing techniques in their own self-interest that would substantially increase the productivity of labour and create a new wealth of products and jobs.[26]

Fundamentally, however, the relationship between entrepreneurial self-interest and the public interest would depend less on the incremental benefits which capitalism brought to world-wide consumers than on the effects that it had on local producers whose livelihoods depended on textile work. Yet, here it was far more problematic to claim an inherent commonality of interest between workers in the stuff industry and the capitalists who organized their labour and appropriated the finished goods. Moreover, during the critical 1825–50 period, the changes that were transforming the worsted industry and were bringing a new generation of industrialists to wealth and power had a generally devastating impact on the class of labourers that they employed.

II

The 1825–50 period was one of trauma and suffering for worsted workers for the same reason that it was a period of great danger and opportunity for the new entrepreneurial elites. The same logic that

[25] *Ibid.*

[26] Koditschek, *Class Formation*, chapter 9; Balgarnie, *Salt*, pp. 61–78; E. M. Sigsworth, *Black Dyke Mills* (Liverpool, 1958), pp. 43–55; *Bradford Observer*, 10 April 1845; J. James, *History of the Worsted Manufactures in England* (London, 1857), pp. 70–9; Sigsworth, *Black Dyke*, pp. 62–8.

drove capitalists to respond to a volatile and increasingly competitive economic climate by introducing more marketable products also compelled them to embark upon a sustained strategy of industrial reorganization to reduce radically their labour costs. Of course, labour cost reduction had long been an essential part of successful worsted entrepreneurship and the early spinning machinery had afforded a comparatively painless method of dramatically increasing output while reducing unit cost.[27] After 1825, however, as this windfall was exhausted, it became evident that continued progress in reducing labour costs would require not only greater entrepreneurial creativity, but a more intrusive penetration into the traditionally male, cottage-based labour processes of weaving and combing, ultimately leading to their mechanization and reconstitution in urban factories where they could be tended by more compliant and lower-paid female and adolescent operatives in town. The first stage of this process involved the mechanization of weaving, which, between the 1820s and 1850, replaced tens of thousands of rural male handloom weavers with 17,642 automatic looms. Thus, families were forced to emigrate to Bradford where at least wives and children could obtain factory jobs. By the early 1830s, the machine had already pushed wages so far downward that a rural weaving family, according to one account, had been reduced to a weekly income of 12 s.[28] During the depressed 1837–42 period, when weaving wages further collapsed, the move to the city became almost inescapable for most of those who still remained in the hinterland.

Since Bradford worsteds, unlike Lancashire cottons, provided relatively few well-paid adult male factory jobs, it was the wives and daughters of these ex-weavers who replaced them in manufacturing, while the men crowded into the preparatory process of combing which remained the last bastion of the artisan. Yet, as their numbers swelled to 10–15,000 in the mid 1840s, this occupation also became badly overstocked. Consequently, here too, working conditions rapidly deteriorated and wages, which had been 14–18s. per week in the 1830s, dropped precipitously to

---

[27] Koditschek, *Class Formation*, chapter 3.
[28] W. Cudworth, *Condition of the Industrious Classes in Bradford* (Bradford, 1887), p. 45; *Report and Resolution of a Meeting of Deputies from the Handloom Worsted Weavers* (Bradford, 1835), p. 8; E. M. Sigsworth, 'An Episode in Woolcombing', *Bradford Antiquary*, new series, 45 (1971), pp. 113–16.

7–9s.[29] In the late 1840s, the development of a viable mechanical wool comb by Isaac Holden and S. C. Lister completed the feminization and total proletarianization of the worsted workforce, by knocking out the hapless hand wool-comber.[30]

This long-term structural process of proletarianization was made more threatening because it occurred within the cyclical framework of conjunctural crisis that generated bouts of wholesale depression every few years. The periods 1824–6, 1837–43 and 1846–9 not only marked milestones in the progressive degradation of the textile handicraftsmen, but also drew factory operatives, skilled artisans and lower-middle-class shopkeepers at least temporarily into the vortex of destitution. In 1842, as 25 per cent of Bradford Township's factory horsepower lay idle and only 61 per cent of the mills ran full-time, two-fifths of the entire worsted workforce was reported to be unemployed. Even among skilled machinists, wages dropped 15–50 per cent as a third of their numbers were laid off. In 1848, the situation was reported to be even worse.[31] During such depressions, capitalists found their profits shrinking, or were driven to heroic gestures of competitive prowess to ensure that they would remain among the fit who survived. Workers, however, found themselves utterly destitute and increasingly dependent on the meagre earnings of their wives or children, who during the worst periods might themselves be unable to find remunerative work.

These differentials in economic resources and work experiences were further exacerbated by the experience of urban living itself. Bradford's extraordinarily rapid urban development, entirely through the mechanism of the free market, provided no social services and amenities, however essential, for those who could not afford to pay. The result, was that the underpaid and often unemployed workers who had been forced to migrate into the town were obliged to live in an environment of squalor, pollution and

---

[29] James, *Worsted Manufactures*, p. 441; A. L. Bowley, 'Statistics of Wages in the United Kingdom', *Journal of the Royal Statistical Society*, 65 (1902), pp. 104–6; Cudworth, *Industrial Classes*, pp. 45–6; Sigsworth, 'Episode in Woolcombing'.

[30] Koditschek, *Class Formation*, chapters 3, 13.

[31] *Bradford Courier*, 24 November 1825; 30 March, 6 April, 18, 23 May, 29 June, 6, 13 July 1826; *Bradford Observer*, 1, 8 , 15 June, 20, 27 July 1837; 19 September, 12, 19 December 1839; 2, 9, 16, 23, 30 January, 13 February, 23 April 1840; 10 November 1842; 19, 26 March, 2, 9, 16, 23, 31 April, 14 May, 28 June, 11, 18, 25 July 1846; 21, 28 January, 4, 11, 18, 25 February, 11, 18, 25 March, 8 April, 27 May, 3 June, 18, 25 November, 16, 30 December 1847; 6 January, 27 April, 25 May, 1 June, 6 July 1848.

almost unbelievable overcrowding, from which their employers were largely able to escape.[32]

How, under these inescapable circumstances, in which the suffering of proletarianization was compounded by the curse of urban blight, would it ever be possible to reassert the notion that workers and capitalists shared a common interest, or to depict the latter as individuals whose pursuit of their own self-interest automatically made them into agents of the common good? One way was to focus on the direct contribution made by the entrepreneurial capitalist to the world of work. Critical here was the role of the entrepreneurial innovator as industrial inventor or engineer. In particular, Lister and Holden's successful construction of a cost effective power wool comb which replicated the delicate motions and sequences of the artisan's hand was, by all accounts, a triumph of hard work and technical ingenuity. Hence, the profits which these men ultimately reaped in consequence could be portrayed not simply as incidents of capitalist property ownership, but as a special kind of earned remuneration for the performance of a rare and uniquely skilled kind of work.[33]

By thus transforming the entrepreneur into a particularly heroic kind of labourer, it was possible to portray him as the natural aristocrat of the entire productive world, the man who, in the words of Samuel Smiles, 'rose to celebrity', not by intrigue or accident, but 'by their habits of observation, their powers of discrimination, their constant self-improvement and their patient industry'.[34] In contrast to traditional hereditary aristocrats, these entrepreneurial aristocrats of the new urban industrial world displayed a nobility not of birth, but of merit, and took their places as leaders of the community of producers only by virtue of the laws of the marketplace in which their competitive superiority was proved. Their triumph was much more than a personal victory – it was, according to Smiles, the triumph of a new conception of elite legitimacy grounded no longer in the cultivation of erudition or valour within a

---

[32] Perhaps nothing illustrated these environmental differences more dramatically than the 1841 mortality statistics, which revealed that workers' life expectancies were less than half that of members of the bourgeoisie, Koditschek, *Class Formation*, chapter 4; *Bradford Observer*, 25 September 1845.

[33] S. C. Lister, *Lord Masham's Inventions* (Bradford, 1905), pp. 8–46; *Fortunes Made in Business*, vol. 1, pp. 3–86; S. Smiles, *Lives of the Engineers* (London, 1874), vol. 1, p. xvii.

[34] S. Smiles, *Self Help* (London, 1925), p. 34.

privileged minority but in the success of exceptional 'genius and labour' in increasing the fund of material 'necessaries, comforts, and luxuries' enjoyed by the entire population, whose general level of civilization might thereby permanently be advanced.[35]

The 'work' of the entrepreneurial labourer might set him temporarily in opposition to the wage labourer, as he performed his tasks within the production process by regimenting, reorganizing and ultimately superseding those that traditionally had been their own. Nevertheless, in the long run, this transformation would redound to the benefit of future generations, whose labour would be less arduous within a modernized work process that would lay the foundations for a sounder, more productive economic base.[36] By feeding the cornucopia of industrial expansion upon which mid-Victorian Bradford's prosperity would eventually be based, mechanization, the reduction of labour costs and even the creation of a factory proletariat in town would, it was argued, ultimately benefit the workers, even if these benefits actually accrued only to wives, dependants and future descendants of the dispossessed artisans who found themselves stripped of their traditional independence and earning power.[37]

However regrettable, such temporary dislocations were deemed unavoidable and the momentary divergences of class interest and outlook which they engendered had to be subordinated to the underlying verity that workers and entrepreneurs were both producers and that the latter constituted the former's highest form. 'The distinction of labourer and capitalist', claimed the *Bradford Observer*.

> is a natural and not an artificial one . . . it arises spontaneously by the natural working of the social elements, and is not consequent on arbitrary and one-sided class legislation. Every day men are passing from the class of labourers to that of capitalists, by the mere force of industry and integrity, or of mechanical skill and commercial tact. There are no laws of 'caste' as in India which fix a man's lot to a particular occupation forever, as by an irreversible decree of fate.[38]

Of course, it would be folly to deny the reality of class antagonisms,

[35] *Ibid.*   [36] K. Marx, *Capital*, (Moscow, 1954), vol. 1, pp. 312–15.

[37] M. Berg, *The Machinery Question and the Making of Political Economy* (Cambridge, 1980).

[38] *Bradford Observer*, 28 May 1840.

but in insisting that the interests of capital and labour were fundamentally the same, entrepreneurial ideology located the central line of societal fissure not in a mere functional distinction between economic groupings, but in what it portrayed as a deeply-rooted and ultimately irreconcilable political opposition between the body of citizens who created the wealth of society and the clique of parasitic drones who were empowered by illegitimate privileges to live off the producers' work.

Here was a far more powerful approach to confronting the deep and painful class contradictions which the dialectic of capitalist development had thrown up. For if the diagnosis of urban industrial dysfunction could somehow deflect responsibility away from the internal dynamic which the logic of capitalist development had disclosed, perhaps it could be displaced on to an external class of parasitic depredators who, in hindering the course of economic expansion, could be made targets to bring capital and labour together in a struggle against a common enemy. In this underlying conflict between parasites and producers, entrepreneurial capitalists could be portrayed as natural leaders of an insurgent 'people' whose realization of their progressive potential largely depended on their readiness to follow the entrepreneurial lead.[39]

By dissipating the scarce resources of society away from productive employment, the illegitimate reign of aristocratic parasitism was seen as diminishing not only the profits of the capitalist but the wages and opportunities of the labourer, who, it was contended, depended even more urgently on the freedom of capital to augment social wealth. Seen in this light, working-class misery might be blamed not on the profits of the industrial capitalist but on the greed of an idle landed class.[40] In particular, it was argued by entrepreneurial ideologues that the government policy of agricultural protectionism, which diminished the capitalists' profits, took an even heavier toll of the hapless worker, whose position in the labour market was subverted by the ensuing diminution in the pool of available jobs. Indeed, the artificial inflation of the landlord's rent rolls at the expense of the manufacturing sector, whose productivity British agriculture could not match, distorted the distributive workings of the market and therefore impeded the

---

[39] Koditschek, *Class Formation*, chapter 9.
[40] J. A. Hobson, ed., *Richard Cobden: International Man* (London, 1918).

overall course of social progress.[41] Since the Corn Laws were a self-inflicted wound on society which benefited a small clique of monopolists at the expense of everyone else, their existence pointed to the entrenched system of political privilege by which aristocratic economic monopoly was sustained. In the end, both progress and prosperity would remain elusive until the 'people' rose up to demand parliamentary representation and to empower those entrepreneurial agents of economic liberty who were uniquely placed to advance the cause of liberty as a whole.[42]

Yet, as modern historical research has demonstrated, this dethronement of aristocratic political dominance took place in a slow, ultimately attenuated fashion, and even the triumph of market freedom as an animating principle of government occurred without a concomitant degree of political ascendancy for the entrepreneurial bourgeoisie.[43] Nevertheless, as our analysis of nineteenth-century entrepreneurial ideology should indicate, bourgeois hegemony was conceived as a double-edged process, in which the assault on aristocratic privilege was envisioned only in the context of a broad-based alliance of all producers which would provide the germ of a future social consensus around which a new regime of urban industrial capitalism might take shape. The entrepreneurial bourgeoisie's success in accomplishing this positive mission of social reconstruction within its own competitive, urban industrial world took precedence over unseating within the halls of Westminster, a traditional oligarchy whose power base was shrinking and which was increasingly prepared to govern in their name. Hence, for Bradford's rising generation of entrepreneurial insurgents, throughout the course of the early urban industrial age, the impulse to elevate a new clique of rulers was overshadowed by the compelling need to create a viable urban industrial society for them to rule over.

Here, the liberal entrepreneurial instinct to fall back on the economic mechanism of market equilibration in its broader search for means of social and cultural integration into the structure of urban industrial life posed a profound and ultimately intractable obstacle, that could not be papered over with anti-aristocratic

---

[41] T. Perronet Thompson, *Exercises, Political and Other* (London, 1842), vol. 4, pp. 498, 508.
[42] Thompson, *Exercises*, vol. 1, p. 223.
[43] N. Gash, *Politics in the Age of Peel* (New York, 1953).

rhetoric. In part this was because there were some goods and values which simply could not be provided by the exchange mechanism, but more significantly, it was because behind the apparent equality of individual competitors in Bradford's market-place stood the underlying reality of a capitalist society composed of unequal participants in a mode of production that structured their access to exchangeable resources along class lines.

Faced with the need to create a liberal capitalist community that could incorporate inherently non-entrepreneurial social groups into an essentially entrepreneurial culture, the new capitalist elites had to find new values, and institutions that could cast them in more universal terms. Somehow, the principles of competitive individualism on which entrepreneurial authority was ultimately based had to be made accessible to precisely those elements within the population that had most suffered from the alienation unleashed by the triumph of competitive capitalist life. To provide individuals with a collective identity and protection from the perils of competitive excess, without obstructing their ability to pursue their own aims – this was the central challenge of an urban industrial capitalist order which sought not only to be a mode of producing commodities, but to become a system of human organization which found stability in progress rather than in stagnation or retreat.

III

Fortunately, in the format of the voluntary association, Bradford's rising entrepreneurial capitalists found what seemed an almost flawless instrument for combining their need for social integration and self-advancement with the larger social project of extending their class values to other non-entrepreneurial social groups. Of course, voluntary associations were not new in nineteenth-century Bradford, having long played an important role in the town's religious and secular life. In the past, however, they had been viewed as supplementary agencies, augmenting the primary integrative institutions of the established church, community and state.[44]

By contrast, during the first half of the nineteenth century, voluntary associations began to proliferate, first in the religious,

---

[44] *Bradford Observer*, 5 October 1868; M. Weber, *Economy and Society* (Los Angeles, 1978), 24, 29–30, 63–74, 82–6.

then in the secular sphere. Not merely supplementing but now supplanting established institutions of collective identity, voluntarism itself became the organizing principle of a society which increasingly resembled a free market in competing associational agencies – a society whose inner structure was revealed by an apparently anarchic array of associational agencies, each providing its own recipe for urban industrial integration, among which every individual had the right and responsibility to choose.[45]

This triumph of voluntarism as a principle of social organization can be seen most clearly in the dramatic expansion of Nonconformist congregations, particularly within the Baptist, Congregationalist and Methodist denominations. From an insignificant religious minority they grew during the first half of the century to a dynamic and wealthy majority encompassing 11,500 worshippers in almost forty different chapels, or almost two and a half times as many as those who appeared in Bradford's churches.[46]

To the men and women who freely chose to worship in this constellation of chapels, the officially established Anglican state church appeared as a self-serving set of 'political arrangements' whereby 'the religion of love [is] upheld by the sword, and the maintenance of its institutions enforced by a palpable violation of its weightiest precepts'.[47] By contrast, their own Nonconformist congregations, where, according to Reverend Godwin, 'every separate church was an independent community ... a little republic, a pure democracy, in which every individual had equal rank and equal power', seemed to represent a more attractive framework for social identity, more compatible with the principles of liberal individualism and more appropriate to the dynamism of the urban industrial milieu.[48]

Particularly for the aspiring entrepreneurial parvenu, this 'little republic' of the independent congregation provided a perfect environment, not only to facilitate impulses towards personal piety and self-improvement, but also to promote that capacity for command and self-government, so necessary for men who aspired to elite roles. Indeed, congregational work and governance, which absorbed enormous quantities of energy, money and time, were

[45] *P.P.*, (LXXXIX, 1852–3), cclii-cclxxii.
[46] Miall, *British Churches*, pp. 88, 361.
[47] B. Godwin, 'Autobiography' (MSS, Bradford Central Library), fo. 622.
[48] *Ibid.*, A. D. Gilbert, *Religion and Society in Industrial England* (London, 1976); W. R. Ward, *Religion and Society in England* (New York, 1973).

eagerly undertaken by even the busiest and most abstemious entrepreneurs, who would have been entirely unwilling to make similar commitments in other spheres outside remunerative work.[49]

Although the pragmatic importance of chapel membership should not be underestimated – an importance that was enhanced in the case of recent immigrants who lacked family connections and local commercial ties – for many of the new entrepreneurs, active involvement in the life of the chapel was more than an obligatory gesture of respectability. It became a unique opportunity for developing a social practice to prepare them for larger cultural and political roles. The 1851 religious census figures showed that through open competition with the church and with one another, the new Nonconformist denominations had built a broad social base in the capitalist city, nurturing its distinctive values of competitive individualism within the framework of a democratic associational culture, particularly well suited to the fluid and dynamic character of Bradford's urban industrial milieu.[50]

Nevertheless, the attendance figures revealed that only a quarter of Bradford's population attended any religious service, demonstrating that the liberal bourgeois culture of Nonconformity had failed to penetrate all but a tiny minority of the urban working class. Research into the social composition of chapel membership shows that most of the workers who did participate were concentrated among the predominantly lower-middle-class Methodists.[51] Among the more rigorously predestinarian Baptists and Congregationalists who embodied most completely the principles of liberal voluntarism and boasted the largest concentrations of rising entrepreneurial elites, working-class participation was rapidly diminishing by the 1830s. The very features which made the dissenters' associational culture so attractive to the new bourgeoisie, also

---

[49] Anon., *Horton Lane Chapel Centenary Memorial* (Bradford, 1883), p. 44.

[50] W. Cudworth, *Horton Lane Chapel, Old Time Reminiscences* (Bradford, 1893); *The Centenary, A History of the First Baptist Church in Bradford* (London, 1853); *The Century Souvenir: Sion Baptist Chapel* (Bradford, 1924), *P.P.*, (LXXXIX, 1852–3), cclii–cclxxii.

[51] *Bradford Observer*, 24 March 1853; 'Horton Lane Gravesites' (MSS, Bradford Archives); W. W. Stamp, *Historical Notes on Wesleyan Methodism in Bradford* (Bradford, 1841); J. N. Dickons and R. Poole, *Kirkgate Chapel, Bradford*, (Bradford, 1911); *Eastbrook Chapel, 1825: Centenary Souvenir* (Bradford, 1925); *One Hundred Years of Primitive Methodism in Great Horton* (Bradford, 1924).

rendered it increasingly ill-suited to a programme of evangelical outreach through which bourgeois approaches to self-help and salvation could be extended to the propertyless working class.[52]

Not surprisingly, bourgeois hopes of forging a voluntary alliance with the workers, having failed in the transcendent religious sphere, shifted to a more prosaic level of secular activity where the search for common values of independence, opportunity and self-reliance could be reopened in a more pragmatic way. The first and most successful of these new secular self-help organizations was the Bradford Temperance Society. Inaugurated in 1830, the Temperance Society never drew more than a small working-class minority; nevertheless, with about 6 per cent of Bradford's adults enrolled in 1840, it had grown larger than any one of the Nonconformist denominations.[53]

As Brian Harrison has persuasively argued, temperance was a kind of secular religion, and the temperance diagnosis of urban industrial capitalism does reveal a number of striking parallels with the liberal, Nonconformist religious world view. Like Nonconformity, temperance implied a moral rather than a materialist critique that focused not on the inequities of wage labour or the anarchy of competitive individualism, but on the personal inadequacies of the individual who could not successfully operate within these social forms. To visualize the evils of industrial capitalism through the lens of temperance was to see a pattern of moral degeneration and barbarism, whose proper antidote was not class militancy or state intervention, but precisely the enlightened, purposive, individualist mentality which the entrepreneurial society both rewarded and required.[54]

Yet, far more than religious Nonconformity, temperance, with its overtly secular orientation, generated a series of cultural counter-attractions to provide teetotallers with a viable and, in many ways, a superior alternative to the dominant working-class culture of drink. From the start, the Society sponsored a constant round of teas, anniversaries, fairs and festivities at Whitsun and Easter, to serve as antidotes to the beer-shop and the traditional

[52] Koditschek, *Class Formation*, chapter 10.

[53] G. Field, *Historical Survey of the Bradford Temperance Society* (Bradford, 1897), pp. 4–5; *Bradford Observer*, 24 December 1835; 13 March 1837; Bradford Temperance Society, *Annual Report* (Bradford, 1832).

[54] B. Harrison, *Drink and the Victorians*, (London, 1971), pp. 179–95, 354–9; Koditschek, *Class Formation*, chapter 11.

rural wake. However, the most impressive achievement of the movement was the erection in 1837, at a cost of £1,400, of a Temperance Hall, which became the first large meeting hall and public building in town.[55] By providing an infrastructure of collective reinforcement for the values of competitive individualism and self-help, temperance counter-culture offered a vehicle for the translation of the liberal entrepreneurial personality-structure into terms that would be appropriate for those who were unable to construct it on their own.

As an assault on working-class demoralization and debility, temperance constituted no more than the foundation stone on which a larger edifice of self-improvement could be built. Since it never encompassed more than a small minority of workers under its aegis, its real purpose was the preparatory work of clearing the cultural territory on which a positive programme of working-class self-culture and self-education could grow. Here, bourgeois liberals encountered enormous difficulty in fabricating a self-help culture for the workers that would advance their ideological agenda and remain firmly under their leadership and control. The agency which came closest to meeting these requirements was the Bradford Mechanics Institute, formed in 1832 by a group of *petit bourgeois* businessmen who found themselves 'greatly hampered in their individual attempts to improve their minds'.[56] Taken in hand by the leading Nonconformist entrepreneurs and clergymen who contributed time and money to keeping it afloat, the Institute quickly developed into a major focus for urban public life. Within a few years, a substantial circulating library had been assembled, a semi-popular lecture series was set up, and a regular class in writing and arithmetic was organized. By the end of the decade, more advanced classes were projected, and after £3,000 was collected, an imposing downtown headquarters was built.[57]

Although its commitment to so expensive a programme ensured the preponderance of bourgeois management, the Institute was

55 Ibbetson, *Directory of Bradford*; P. Raistrick, 'The Bradford Temperance Movement' (typescript, Bradford Central Library), fo. 28; Field, *Bradford Temperance Society; Bradford Observer*, 23 April 1835: 21 April 1836; 1 December 1844.

56 C. Federer, 'The Bradford Mechanics Institute', in L. A. Fraser, ed., *Memoirs of Daniel Fraser* (London, 1905); J. Farrar, *Autobiography* (Bradford, 1889), pp. 44–61.

57 Bradford Mechanics Institute, *Annual Reports* (Bradford, 1833–5); Federer, 'Mechanics Institute', pp. 233–45.

intended primarily as a vehicle for the education and assimilation of the urban working class. 'Who can tell,' Reverend Ackworth, its first president prophesied, 'but that some happy thought, suggesting itself to the mind of some hitherto obscure member of a Mechanics Institute, may pave the way to results, far surpassing in splendour and usefulness, those which the genius of a Watt, a Bolton, or an Arkwright has achieved.'[58] Sceptical as to whether it could ever be 'the great means of regenerating the world, and of raising all operatives & mechanics, & labourers to the intellectual elevation of philosophers and scholars', Reverend Scott was sure that it would foster material progress and facilitate the emergence of a moral and intellectual consensus around the principles of open competition and disciplined work. Indeed, this bourgeois-inspired Mechanics Institute was founded in the wake of an abortive venture undertaken by radical artisans and tradesmen and was deliberately designed to ensure the creation of an adult education infrastructure that would eschew controversial subjects and strengthen 'the bonds by which society is united'.[59]

Nevertheless, such ambitions were doomed to failure because the Mechanics Institute, like Bradford's other bourgeois-inspired voluntary associations, failed to touch the mainstream of urban industrial working-class life. During the 1840s, membership peaked at 937, about one-third that of the Temperance Society, and a study of the social composition of the 1842 writing and arithmetic class indicated that its primary constituency was not mechanics, but warehousemen and clerks.[60] Confronted with such facts, many entrepreneurial capitalists could not help but question the efficacy of liberal voluntarism as a socially integrative ideal. Proletarianized workers were apparently less likely to become junior partners in progress than alienated, unassimilable impediments to the materialization of a viable urban industrial world. Such doubts can only have been reinforced when they were echoed by cries of despair from the ranks of the workers themselves. 'When we leave off work,' one group of wool-combers lamented, 'we are fit only for sleep or sensual indulgence, the only alternations our leisure knows.' 'We are sunken, debilitated, depressed,' they continued,

[58] J. Ackworth, *Speech at Inauguration as President of Bradford Mechanics Institute* (Bradford, 1837), p. 20.

[59] Ackworth, *Speech as President*, pp. 8–9, 24–5.

[60] J. V. Godwin, 'The Bradford Mechanics Institute', in the National Association for the Promotion of Social Science, *Transactions, 1859* (London, 1860), p. 342.

'unnerved for effort; incapable of virtue, unfit for anything which is calculated to be of any benefit to us at present or any future period.' With 'no power to rise above our circumstances or better our condition . . . no time to be wise, no leisure to be good', how could the bourgeois-inspired religious congregations, temperance societies or mechanics' institutes meet the needs of men and women who were not, in fact, autonomous individuals, but wage-labourers bound by increasing material dependence to a capitalist system which often scarcely provided them with the means to live?[61]

The behaviour of Bradford's workers during the second quarter of the nineteenth century shows that in so far as they were not hopelessly 'sunken', it was largely because they were able, in the face of bourgeois opposition, to adapt the liberal framework of associational voluntarism to their own very different class values and ends. Indeed, there was no inherent reason why workers could not form their own independent associations that would eschew the bourgeois programme of individual self-help and salvation, and draw on indigenous plebeian traditions of mutuality to advance their distinctive interests as a class. By definition, voluntary associations were instruments of collective action, vehicles of social co-operation towards some mutually desired end. Taken up by pro-letarianized workers, they were easily turned against the entre-preneurial programme of competitive individualism and employed as vehicles through which natural impulses towards solidarity could be translated into self-conscious forms of class organization that could operate in Bradford's urban industrial world. In fact, it was the workers' very commitment to progressive ideals of self-improvement that seemed to oblige them to repudiate the ego-centric core of competitive individualism which stood at the heart of the liberal entrepreneurial creed. For Bradford's proletarianized workers, self-help was not something that could be achieved by individuals; it was something which had to be won collectively for their class.[62]

The first, and always the largest, of these working-class voluntary associations were the friendly societies, in which a group of individuals pooled weekly contributions to insure their families against accident, illness and death. Although precursors can be

[61] Quoted in J. Burnley, *The History of Wool and Woolcombing* (London, 1889), pp. 177–8.
[62] Koditschek, *Class Formation*, chapter 16.

traced to the late eighteenth century, it was the rise, during the 1830s and 1840s, of the great affiliated national orders, the Oddfellows, the Ancient Forresters, and Druids, that brought the friendly society movement to maturity.[63] By 1871, Bradford had 133 district lodges with a total of 10,016 members, as well as, 3,805 trade unionists with friendly society benefits. Together they constituted 37 per cent of the town's adult men.[64]

When bourgeois observers contemplated this profusion of friendly societies, their reactions were mixed. In one sense, the phenomenon seemed to represent an incontrovertible triumph for liberal voluntarism, providing a genuinely mass-based mechanism for workers to achieve self-reliance without dependence on charity or intervention by the state. Yet, unlike the mainstream Nonconformist denominations, temperance societies or mechanics institutes, the friendly societies were not bourgeois-run institutions of evangelical outreach but spontaneous creations of the workers themselves. Their imperviousness to elite influence and authority and their frequent immersion in an indigenous plebeian culture of drink elicited considerable bourgeois unease.[65]

Perhaps most alarming, however, were the friendly societies' secret meetings and rituals, which, it was feared, could easily become covers for conspiracies of class revolt. Such fears were, in fact, greatly exaggerated, for the friendly societies were generally careful to steer clear of active political affiliation and studiously refrained from asserting the considerable economic muscle that they potentially possessed. Nevertheless, they did become important models for more aggressive collective associations of workers like trade unions and co-operatives, which openly sought to defend their members position in the labour market and ultimately to circumvent the capitalist wage–labour relationship itself.[66]

To be sure, trade unions, in themselves, posed no fundamental threat to the capitalist system, especially when they were confined to the largely traditional skilled craft occupations that the process

[63] J. James, *History and Topography of Bradford* (Bradford, 1866), p. 265; H. J. Maltby, 'Early Bradford Friendly Societies', *Bradford Antiquary*, new series, 8 (1933).

[64] *P. P.*, (1854, VIII), 41–2; (1874, XXIII), II, 206.

[65] *Bradford Observer*, 8 November 1842.

[66] J. T. Illingworth, *The Progress of Oddfellowship in Yorkshire* (Huddersfield, 1867); *Bradford Observer*, 18 February, 7 July 1836; 9 February, 9 November 1837; 3 January 1839; 2, 23 April 1840; 6 September 1842; 27 March, 15 May 1845; 12 April 1849.

of proletarianization had not yet undermined. However, when the movement spread to the mass of endangered textile handicraftsmen a more ominous pattern began to emerge. Organizing out of the artisanal traditions with which they identified, but acting according to the logic of the proletarians which they had now become, these workers were driven deeper into industrial militancy as what had originally been intended as a defence of customary privileges was transformed by the new reality of unrestrained market competition into a challenge to the capitalist–property relationship itself.[67]

In 1825, this new challenge openly errupted into a bitter half-year-long strike by 20,000 unionized combers and handloom weavers who were determined to arrest falling wages and deteriorating working conditions. Although the workers' demands were initially quite modest, the strike was transformed into a full-scale class struggle when the employers took the offensive with an industry-wide lock-out and blacklist that sought to destroy the union.[68] Not surprisingly, the employers' decisive victory in this confrontation sent the textile workers' unions underground. However, with the return of prosperity in the early 1830s, another wave of mass unionism gathered steam. Moreover, the workers began to look beyond the limits of trade unionism, as they were exposed to Ricardian socialist and syndicalist propaganda, attempted to organize embryonic producers' co-operatives, agitated against the New Poor Law, and involved themselves in the campaign for factory reform.[69] By the end of the decade, when the return of depression had raised the temperature of social antagonism and vitiated the efficacy of the older trade union forms, the

[67] J. Reynolds, *The Letterpress Printers of Bradford* (Bradford, 1970); *United Kingdom Trades Directory* (London, 1861); *Bradford Observer*, 14 April 1836; 23 July 1840; 2, 9, 16 April 1846; I. Prothero, *Artisans and Politics* (Folkestone, 1979); R. G. Kirby and A. E. Musson, *The Voice of the People: John Doherty, 1798–1854* (Manchester, 1975).

[68] John Tester, 'A History of the Bradford Contest' (MSS, Bradford Archives); W. Scruton, 'The Great Strike of 1825', *Bradford Antiquary*, old series, 1 (1888), pp. 67–73; J. Smith, 'The Strike of 1825', in D. G. Wright and J. A. Jowitt, eds., *Victorian Bradford: Essays in Honour of Jack Reynolds* (Bradford, 1982), pp. 63–79.

[69] E. C. Tufnell, *The Character, Objects and Effects of Trades Unions* (London, 1834), p. 30; J. Sanders, 'Working Class Movements in the West Riding Textile District, 1829 to 1839, with Emphasis on Local Leadership and Organization' (unpublished Ph.D. thesis, University of Manchester, 1984); R. C. N. Thornes, 'The Early Development of the Co-operative Movement in West Yorkshire, 1827–63' (unpublished D.Phil. thesis, University of Sussex, 1984).

workers organized explicitly political associations that soon joined forces with the Chartist campaign for universal suffrage.[70]

In Chartism, Bradford's organized workers mounted a populist challenge that flung the abstract principles of liberalism back in the bourgeois liberals' faces. Here the workers themselves employed the language of liberty not only to repudiate entrepreneurial leadership but also to advance a set of claims on the political process that could only set workers and capitalists further at odds. Through their increasingly vocal threats of violence and their openly social democratic policy aims the Chartists were perceived as posing what amounted to a revolutionary danger by all sectors of the local elite.[71]

Thus, at the very moment when competitive success in the market-place was making them wealthy and powerful men, Bradford's new generation of entrepreneurial liberals found the ideological paradigm which legitimized their social dominance collapsing into contradiction and disarray. Unable to attract workers into a voluntary consensus through their associations of religious salvation and secular self-help, they had to question whether capitalist social relations could really be reduced unproblematically to free market terms. To incorporate proletarianized workers into urban industrial society seemed to necessitate providing them with goods and services that the competitive market simply could not supply. Indeed, to allow them free access to voluntary association was not to reconcile them to bourgeois values, but to open the way for angry challenges on the hustings and in the work-place which cast the inviolability of private property and competitive capitalism into doubt. Obliged to confront the harsh reality that their dreams of social progress and liberty might be incompatible with the imperatives of political order which their economic enterprise required, many of Bradford's rising entrepreneurial liberals were forced to re-examine their creed.

IV

The entrepreneurial parvenus' dilemma was made more troubling when they found themselves faced not only with hostility from the

[70] A. J. Peacock, *Bradford Chartism, 1838–40* (York, 1969); D. G. Wright, 'Politics and Opinion in Nineteenth-Century Bradford' (unpublished Ph.D. thesis, University of Leeds, 1966), pp. 188–307.

[71] *Bradford Observer*, 8 November 1838; 14 February 1839.

workers, but with scorn from a group of older, more established Anglican Tory capitalists like John Wood, Matthew Thompson or the Rand brothers, who had been hostile towards liberalism from the outset. Longing for a return to a more stable and hierarchical, if less dynamic and competitive, socio-economic order, these men believed that what the industrial worker really needed was not the voluntarist programme of self-help individualism, but the kind of protection from destabilizing economic forces that only employer paternalism could provide.[72] As the contradictions of ideological liberalism became evident during the early 1830s, such sentiments were framed into a new kind of radical Toryism by men like Richard Oastler, who saw an opening for conservatism as a counter-ideological antidote to 'The absurd notion that every individual in seeking his own aggrandizement must necessarily pursue the course which will benefit society'. Fired by Oastler's stirring rhetoric, the leading Tory capitalists began to experiment with building model cottages for a proportion of their workers, endowing churches in the vicinity of their mills, unilaterally reducing the length of their working day, and providing factory schools for the child labourers whom they employed.[73]

Of course, this conservative vision of voluntary industrial paternalism was even less viable as a mode of capitalist social organization than associational liberalism had been. In practice, few other mill-owners followed the example of Wood or Oastler, and those who did soon discovered that in so far as it involved more than symbolic gestures, paternalism was simply too expensive for employers who had to compete with others who paid it no heed.[74]

[72] *Bradford Observer*, 15, 22 May 1845; *Bradford Observer Budget*, 21 April 1906, *P.P.*, (1833, XXI), 22; C. Driver, *Tory Radical. The Life of Richard Oastler* (New York, 1946), pp. 3–35; J. C. Gill, *The Ten Hours Parson* (London, 1959); *Parson Bull of Byerley* (London, 1973).

[73] Driver, *Tory Radical*, p. 52: Gill, *Ten Hours Parson*, p. 191; J. T. Ward, 'Old and New Bradfordians in the Nineteenth Century', *Journal of Bradford Textile Society*, (1964–5), pp. 17–32. John Clark, 'History and Annals of Bradford, or Family Book of Reference' (typescript in Bradford Reference Library), vol. 2, fos. 29, 35. R. Oastler, 'Address to Meeting of Trades Delegates' (MSS, Bradford Archives); W. Walker, *Free Trade, its Principles and Results* (London, 1858); W. Scoresby, *American Factories and their Female Operatives* (London, 1845).

[74] Those, like Wood, who could not stomach the prevailing standard of exploitation and who were able to accumulate sufficient means, usually abandoned the industrial city as soon as they were able, transferring their paternalist impulses to the more propitious environment of the agrarian countryside. For discussions of industrial paternalism, see P. Joyce, *Work, Society and Politics. The Culture of the Factory in Later Victorian England* (New Brunswick, 1980); D. Roberts,

Nevertheless, if Tory paternalism as a serious social ideology was fundamentally doomed from the start, political conservatism, with its emphasis on order and hierarchy, began to find an increasingly receptive audience among successful entrepreneurs for whom the necessity of protecting property was taking precedence over the desire for further social change. More importantly, with the failure of voluntary employer paternalism, Wood and Oastler insisted that what the capitalist could not accomplish as an individual ought to be legally enforced by a regulatory state.[75] Here again, Oastler's militantly Anglican, almost theocratic, vision of a hierarchical corporate state could be easily dismissed as a reactionary fantasy. However, by placing the cause of factory reform on the legislative agenda, he not only stimulated the workers' ten hours movement, but also compelled the incumbent Whig ministry to devise its own Benthamite alternatives in the 1833 Factory Act and 1834 Poor Law.[76]

The significance of these developments was, initially, lost on Bradford's liberals, who simply tried to ignore them as long as they could. Local liberals, with their penchant for seeking consensus through an anti-aristocratic critique, were initially inclined to approach the entire realm of politics essentially in negative, underdog terms. This tactic had worked well during the Reform Bill struggle, when, under the aegis of the Bradford Political Union, both 'employers and the employed caught the mighty excitement', and joined together to demand a 'broad representation of the people'.[77] However, after 1832, the new borough's £10 franchise tended to divide the ranks of the reformers as the local party machinery gravitated away from the radical politics of mass mobilization and towards the routine work of canvassing voters and pandering to the concerns of a narrow propertied electorate.[78]

Paternalism in Early Victorian England (New Brunswick, 1979); and Koditschek, *Class Formation*, chapter 15.

[75] Driver, *Tory Radical*, pp. 237–50; J. T. Ward, 'Slavery in Yorkshire', and 'Two Pioneers of Industrial Reform', *Journal of Bradford Textile Society*, (1961–3), pp. 35–51; W. Walker and W. Rand, *A Letter Addressed to Sir James Graham on the Ten Hours Question* (Bradford, 1841).

[76] Driver, *Tory Radical*; D. Fraser ed., *The New Poor Law in the Nineteenth Century* (New York, 1976); S. E. Finer, *The Life and Times of Edwin Chadwick*, (London, 1952).

[77] Godwin, 'Autobiography', fos. 491–525.

[78] Wright, 'Politics and Opinion', pp. 108–10, 289–307; *Bradford Observer*, 4, 11 April 1835; 29 June 1837.

By the late 1830s, when this complacency was compounded by the growing conservatism of beleaguered entrepreneurs, Bradford liberalism began to founder, distancing itself from the radical reform agenda after 1837 and, in 1841, actually losing to the Tories in one (almost both) of the local parliamentary seats.[79] Clearly, the prevailing climate of economic crisis and class conflict was not conducive to the success of liberalism even within the capitalist elite. For liberalism was nothing if not a consensual doctrine of progress, and if it could not find a way of becoming a philosophy for the workers, how long could it remain the philosophy of the bourgeoisie?

Convinced of the need to mend their rift with the workers in order both to legitimize their claims to hegemony and to succeed even in narrow electoral terms, Bradford's entrepreneurial liberals radically changed their course after 1842, recommitting themselves to forge that progressive alliance of 'the people' which had fuelled their earlier reform campaign. To facilitate this populist strategy, party leaders undertook a major internal reorganization, replacing the increasingly oligarchical Reform Society with a new United Reform Club that was designed to be more than a mere bureaucratic political machine. Organized on the voluntary associational principle along the model of the Temperance Society and the Mechanics Institute, the Reform Club was intended to be, at once, a vehicle for electoral and political organization, a focus for its members' cultural and intellectual life, and an agitational agency of evangelical outreach 'to promote the union of the largest possible number of reformers for the accomplishment of all practicable Reforms'.[80] Through 'lectures, public meetings and the establishment of a reading room', the Club's bourgeois founders hoped to promote 'a purer and healthier faith among the people', as well as a renewed commitment to political progressivism on the part of elites.[81]

While 'not sanguine enough to believe that the middle and

---

[79] While this embarrasing loss can, in part, be attributed to the open opposition of disenfranchised Chartists, analysis indicates that 15 per cent of the party's 1837 voters had, four years later, either stayed at home or changed sides. See Koditschek, *Class Formation*, chapter 12. Anon., *Pollbook* (Bradford, 1837); D. G. Wright, 'A Radical Borough. Parliamentary Politics in Bradford, 1832–41', *Northern History*, 4 (1969), pp. 132–66, and J. A. Jowitt and R. K. S. Taylor, eds., *Nineteenth-Century Bradford Elections* (Bradford, 1979).

[80] Bradford United Reform Club, *Annual Report* (Bradford, 1842).

[81] Bradford United Reform Club, *Minutes*, 24 September 1841 (Bradford Reference Library).

working classes have all of a sudden become cordially united', the *Observer*'s editor was pleased to report that 'They have talked over their common wants and common wrongs, they have found that the enemy of one is the enemy of both, and that neither is able to cope with this enemy single handed.'[82] Abandoning their overtly anti-Chartist tactic of attempting to destroy the workers' independent organizations and divert popular politics into the bourgeois-run Anti-Corn Law League, the liberals embarked on a more subtle strategy of negotiated class alliance in which the causes of suffrage extension and free trade would be linked.[83]

However, in December, the failure of the Complete Suffrage Conference revealed the depth of underlying class antagonisms, as mutual suspicion and wrangling over the symbolism of 'the Charter' caused this embryonic coalition to break down. Clearly, workers would no longer submerge their own causes and organizations within entrepreneurial initiatives so long as political progressivism was conceived outside a broader social democratic reform vision which acknowledged that formal equality would be meaningless or impossible so long as material inequalities continued to increase.

Here bourgeois liberals were at a real disadvantage, since their principled commitment to competitive individualism, their penchant for voluntaristic approaches to public organization and their determination to keep industrial production under private control made them hostile, not only towards the collectivism of the workers, but also towards the Tory radicals' schemes for government-sponsored protectionism, or even the Benthamites' proposals for a centralized social service state. Seeking an alternative approach to the provision of public welfare that would neither trammel the production process, stifle voluntary action and local initiative, nor empower distant bureaucrats or reactionary traditional elites, Bradford's liberals looked to the urban environment as an arena to generate new forms of public welfare through the reform of local government and thereby address the worst problems of squalor and suffering without undercutting the predominance of private enterprise in the primary productive sphere.

If urban reform, amidst the crisis of the 1840s, thus became the focal point for liberal efforts to forge a broader, more socially

[82] *Bradford Observer*, 24 February 1842.
[83] *Bradford Observer*, 10 March 1842; Reform Club, *Minutes*, 24 September 1841.

responsible creed, this was because it had always been an important element locally in the party's original anti-aristocratic critique. From the start, the liberal attack on parasitic rural landlords had been accompanied by an assault on what appeared as an even less legitimate oligarchy of entrenched urban Tory elites. The passage of the 1835 Municipal Reform Act had evoked considerable local interest despite the fact that Bradford would obtain no direct benefits from it so long as it remained an unincorporated town. Local government, the *Observer* argued, could provide 'schools of political science', in which the middle and working classes could learn to work together in self-government, because 'they have the closest and most permanent connexion with the well-being of a town'.[84] For the entrepreneurial bourgeoisie, such local self-government would eliminate 'the reproach of our nation that the middle classes are not educated for public life'. As for the workers, 'they will come to the consideration of other and higher affairs with a sounder judgement, with less prejudice, and with a loftier public spirit'.[85]

The implementation in 1837 of the controversial New Poor Law might have seemed to offer a perfect opportunity to put into effect this liberal approach to local self-government. The spread of mass unemployment throughout the workforce whenever the trade cycle bottomed out had become the most serious social welfare problem in Bradford, raising the spectre of a mass destitution which voluntary charity could not relieve. Although the old Poor Law had shown itself to be totally ineffective, the new one, with its aura of bureaucratic rationality, gave promise of a more utilitarian approach. In fact, so far from relieving class tensions, the New Poor Law, with its Malthusian threat of 'less eligibility', did more than anything else to exacerbate them, and the liberals who easily swept the first Bradford Guardians elections seemed almost happy to hand over authority a year later to a new slate of penny-pinching conservatives.[86]

Chastened by their experience with the Poor Law, for the next three years local liberals tried to ignore the social question in the vain hope that it would somehow fade away. Nevertheless, by 1840,

---

[84] *Bradford Observer*, 6 February 1834; 14 August 1845.
[85] *Bradford Observer*, 29 March 1838; 14 August 1845.
[86] Koditschek, *Class Formation*, chapter 14; D. Ashforth, 'The Poor Law in Bradford, *c.* 1834–71' (unpublished Ph.D. thesis, University of Bradford, 1979).

as economic conditions continued to worsen and militant Chartism reached its climax, party leaders began to demonstrate a sense of urgency that something had to be done to avert total class warfare or social collapse. If not in poor relief, then in some other area of local government, it would be necessary to formulate a less ambitious programme of social amelioration around which destitute workers and frightened capitalists could both unite. Perhaps the deep, systemic problems of working-class poverty and exploitation could not be resolved within a liberal reformist framework, but by concentrating on their environmental manifestations, liberals began to diagnose a problem that might, realistically, be addressed. By focusing on the ecological problems of pollution, overcrowding, sanitation and water supply, it might be possible to deflect attention away from the intractable problems of exploitation and primary poverty, relieving misery without restraining industry, and diverting working-class demands for fundamental socio-economic transformation into a limited campaign to clean up the slums.[87]

Thus, in 1840, as the Chartist challenge reached its peak, the *Bradford Observer*, in a stunning reversal of position, suddenly abandoned much of the ideological underpinnings of the original Nonconformist, temperance understanding of working-class dysfunction, and began to explore the possibility that it was the material effects of physical squalor which generated plebeian militancy and immorality rather than the other way around. 'Where wives of the labouring poor are surrounded by puddles and mud . . . they have not', the paper argued, 'a single encouragement to strive for cleanliness and health.' Moreover, working-class demoralization and drunkenness were now to be attributed less to the workers' lack of character than to the inevitable effect of their 'filthy abodes'.[88]

Most significantly, even proletarian radicalism and anti-capitalist hostility were, to some degree, attributed to the experience of urban disamenity, which led the slum-dweller to 'view the possessors of superior comforts with envy and to acquire the notion that might makes right'. Thus, when the wool-combers' trade organization set up its own sanitary investigation of the worst slum districts and presented an analysis which stressed the broadly environmental over the specifically occupational hazards of their

---

[87] Koditschek, *Class Formation*, chapter 18.
[88] *Bradford Observer*, 24 September, 24 December 1840; 27 November 1850.

trade, bourgeois liberals might well feel relief at the prospect that they had discovered an issue which posed no real threat to the economic interest of industrial capitalists, but which conformed to the workers' own social critique.[89]

It was, therefore, a turning-point of considerable significance when, in 1843, the United Reform Club switched its primary agitational focus from the suffrage issue to the incorporation of the town. Seeking to combine 'the purposes of improvement with the principle of liberty', the reformers envisioned the municipal corporation as a vehicle for the achievement of a new kind of consensus based on genuine negotiation and compromise rather than on mere working-class submission to the entrepreneurial ideal. Here, the old cross-class alliance between capitalists and workers that could not be conjured up through a culture of voluntarism, or mobilized through an anti-aristocratic insurgency, might be institutionalized in the form of democratic local government, responsible for providing essential public services and able to regulate the overall pattern of urban growth.[90]

At the outset, many workers, particularly those who were active Chartists, were deeply suspicious of this new liberal campaign. Sceptical as to whether the municipal franchise would really be as democratic as its proponents insisted, they feared that incorporation might simply entrench entrepreneurial capitalists as a new kind of oligarchy invested with formal public powers.[91] In particular, it was widely thought that the only certain consequence of municipal government, the establishment of a beefed-up borough police, would simply reinforce with the power of official compulsion, the behavioural norms of sobriety and work discipline which the bourgeois religious and secular associations had hitherto failed to inculcate through voluntary means.[92]

Nevertheless, by 1846, when a major petition campaign was mounted, it had become clear that a significant number among the better-off skilled workers had been converted to the cause of municipal reform. Even more striking than this erosion of working-class hostility was the sudden evaporation of organized Tory opposition which had united lower-middle-class shopkeepers, hin-

---

[89] *Bradford Observer*, 12 June 1845.
[90] A. Elliott, 'The Establishment of Municipal Government in Bradford, c. 1834–71' (unpublished Ph.D. thesis, University of Bradford, 1979).
[91] Elliott, 'Establishment of Municipal Government', pp. 73–114.
[92] *Bradford Observer*, 3 November 1842; 4, 18 May 1843.

terland property owners and the remnant of the old Anglican oligarchy in an unholy alliance which liberals termed the 'minority of muck'. Not necessarily opposed to urban reform in principle, these groups had been profoundly wary of the prospect of a liberal, entrepreneurially-dominated municipality which they envisioned as an instrument for capitalists to evade their responsibility for industrial pollution by transferring the clean-up costs on to the public rates.[93]

However, since the anti-corporationists had no alternative strategy for grappling with the worsening problems of environmental deterioration, they had little choice but to abandon their resistance and to acquiesce in the organization of a municipal government and town council which, as was expected from the outset, the leading entrepreneurial liberals virtually monopolized. Yet, although bourgeois liberals kept a tight grip over the honorific posts of mayor and alderman, after sweeping, during the first election, 76 per cent of the council seats, this town council became a far more potent and genuinely inclusive symbol of consensus than any of the purely voluntaristic ventures which they had mounted before.[94]

With the exception of a small, diehard reactionary minority, conservatives gradually increased their participation in the council's deliberations, becoming increasingly indistinguishable from the dominant liberal entrepreneurial group. More significantly, the more moderate and better-off among the working-class Chartists gradually detached themselves from the terminally proletarianized and began to participate in local government elections, even electing a few Chartist councillors of their own.[95] Thus, in 1848, when the Chartist militants briefly took to the barricades and 'declared a republic' in their own slum streets, many skilled workers, instead of joining them, enrolled as special constables under the joint command of the liberal Mayor Robert Milligan and the Tory magistrate Joshua Pollard, to ensure that public order would be restored.[96]

---

[93] Elliott, 'Establishment of Municipal Government', pp. 107–14.
[94] *Bradford Observer*, 29 April, 17, 29 June, 12, 19 August 1847.
[95] Elliott, 'Establishment of Municipal Government', pp. 115–31; Cudworth, *Bradford Corporation*, pp. 129–30; *Bradford Observer*, 11 December 1968.
[96] *Bradford Observer*, 13 April, 4, 11, 25 May, 1, 8 June 1848; H. McCarthy, *Chartist Recollections* (n.d.); J. Reynolds, *The Great Paternalist. Titus Salt and the Growth of Nineteenth-Century Bradford* (London, 1983), pp. 135–8, 144.

Of course, mobilizing a cross-class consensus of the respectable to enforce law and order was easier than actively shaping the new instruments of municipal government into an effective vehicle for urban reform. Before the passage of the Improvement Act in 1850 – in large measure a response to the 1849 cholera outbreak – the corporation possessed few regulatory powers of any sort. Thereafter, the council, armed with its new powers and increasingly democratized by the operation of the Small Tenements Rating Act, began to take a more active role in setting minimal standards for building and in establishing policy in relation to public health.[97]

By this time the return of prosperity had diminished the sense of foreboding and urgency that had forced social reform on to the liberal agenda in the first place. Throughout the 1850s, bourgeois liberalism in Bradford exhibited a marked return to the language of market privatism and a renewed reliance on voluntaristic approaches to reform. Within new voluntary organizations like the Bradford Town Mission, bourgeois leaders began a noticeable retreat from the environmentalist diagnosis of working-class misery, returning to older notions that the individual alone bore moral responsibility for his plight.[98]

Once again, the entrepreneurial dream of absorbing urban industrial workers directly, in an unmediated fashion, into a cultural consensus based on individual salvation and secular self-help was manifested in a dramatic resurgence of pre-existing religious, temperance and educational voluntary associations, and in the rise of more specialized associational agencies geared towards working-class savings, rational recreation and even the purchase of one's own home. By the middle of the decade, mass voluntary subscription campaigns for the construction of public buildings and parks suggested that this voluntarist revival was on the verge of coming to dominate social provision even in areas that had hitherto been regarded as belonging to the public sphere.[99]

Yet even during the heyday of mid-Victorian prosperity, when

---

[97] Cudworth, *Bradford Corporation*, pp. 114–17; *Bradford Observer*, 24 January, 25 April, 20, 27 June, 11 July, 29 August, 12 September 1850; 30 September 1852; 11 November 1853; A. Elliott, 'Municipal Government in Bradford in the Nineteenth Century', in D. Fraser, ed., *Municipal Reform and the Industrial City* (Leicester, 1982), pp. 112–61.

[98] *Bradford Observer*, 21, 28 June 1849.

[99] *Bradford Observer*, 15 August, 12 September 1850; 10, 17 February, 1, 8, 22 September 1853; 1 February 1855.

the entrepreneurial world vision seemed to reign unopposed, the new institutions of municipal administration gradually extended their service and regulatory roles. In 1853, the private waterworks company was municipalized, and during the 1860s and 1870s, corporation activism quickened as building codes were tightened, downtown street improvements were co-ordinated, the gas service was brought under public ownership and a subterranean system of arterial sewerage was finally laid.[100] This slow accretion of what came to be known as municipal socialism underlined the difficulty of implementing the positive programme of urban reform envisioned in the 1840s without establishing public authorities and taking action incompatible with the free enterprise organization of the urban space. To devise concrete policies of municipal intervention that were neither so negligible as to be ineffective, so costly as to be rejected by the ratepayers, nor so restrictive of market competition as to be incompatible with the entrepreneurial creed, was to engage in a delicate balancing act in which bold gestures were virtually impossible and progress was almost certain to be slow.[101]

Nevertheless, with the advent of new layers of local government, particularly in public health and education, and with the proliferation of professionals in municipal employ, the stage was set for a substantial increase in size and scope of public action as the nineteenth century drew to a close. With the return in the late 1870s and 1880s of a harsher, more competitive economic climate, voluntaristic fantasies about the possibilities of a seamless, frictionless society along liberal entrepreneurial lines were once again replaced by an aggressive turn towards the infrastructure of public regulation and authority which proved considerably more effective in sustaining the new realism that sought stability not through cultural universalism or some economic miracle, but

---

[100] *Bradford Observer*, 4, 11 November, 23 December 1852; 18 August, 6, 20 October, 11 November 1853; 26 January, 16 March, 20 July 1854; Cudworth, *Bradford Corporation*, pp. 130–3

[101] B. Thompson, 'Public Provision and Private Neglect: Public Health', in Wright and Jowitt, eds., *Victorian Bradford*, pp. 137–64; and 'Infant Mortality in Nineteenth Century Bradford', in R. Wood and J. Woodward, eds., *Urban Disease and Mortality in Nineteenth-Century England* (New York, 1984), pp. 120–47; *Bradford Observer*, 14, 28 July 1853; 17 May 1855; 10 June 1858; 14 June 1860; 21 August, 11 September 1862; 26 February, 24 September, 26 November 1863; 2 November 1865.

through a judicious balance of social provision and political compromise.[102]

V

What general conclusions can be drawn from this account of the rise and crisis of bourgeois liberalism in Bradford, a city whose extraordinarily rapid and volatile course of development generated a degree of instability and trauma in social relations that few other places in nineteenth-century Britain could match? I would contend that this local bourgeois quest for an entrepreneurial society, for all its manifest atypicality, discloses with unusual force and clarity a dynamic of social development that was more pervasive as it worked its way fitfully and indirectly into the fabric of British society as a whole. For Britain was becoming an urban industrial nation in which, by 1821, more people worked in manufacturing than in agriculture and, by 1851, fewer lived in the countryside than in towns.[103] Of course, such figures are, in some ways, deceptive, since a substantial part of the urban and/or manufacturing population still worked and lived in relatively traditional environments, in which capitalist penetration remained incomplete. Nevertheless, by the mid-century, 12 per cent of all Englishmen and women resided in provincial industrial cities like Bradford, while the industrial capitalists, whose enterprise had built them, had risen from virtual insignificance to constitute about 10 per cent of the nation's wealthiest elite (i.e. the 524 individuals who died between 1840 and 1879 with assets estimated to be worth more than £500,000).[104]

Even greater than the quantitative dimensions of urban industrial growth and entrepreneurial capitalist class formation was the qualitative significance of these developments in setting the new terms in which social relations between all groups would, increasingly, have to be enacted. For the phenomena of free market competition, proletarianization and cultural individualism which triumphed in Bradford were fast becoming universal experiences

[102] Bradford Corporation, *Annual Reports* (1854–85).
[103] Calculated from information in A. Weber, *The Growth of Cities in the Nineteenth Century* (New York, 1899), p. 43; and P. Deane and W. A. Cole, *British Economic Growth, 1688–1959* (Cambridge, 1969), p. 142.
[104] Calculated from information in Mitchell, *British Historical Statistics*, pp. 6–7, 24–6, and Rubinstein, *Men of Property*, pp. 60–8.

which, in a slower and less complete manner, would dominate British society at large. The failure during the 1830s and 1840s of Tory paternalism and working-class radicalism to provide coherent alternatives to liberal voluntarism, proved that bourgeois liberalism, in England no less than in Bradford, remained the only viable method through which progress and stability could be reconciled. Although it might be tempered in practice, and would have to win acceptance among hitherto alienated workers and aristocratic elites, the kind of bourgeois liberalism which was emerging in Bradford constituted, in the last analysis, the only satisfactory framework in which a free capitalist society could effectively be organized.

From this perspective, our local evidence tells a rather different story from the tale presented by revisionist historiography of entrepreneurial failure and ideological default. For in Bradford it was not the weakness but the very strength of liberal entrepreneurial identity which both constituted the industrial bourgeoisie's most striking characteristic and ultimately proved to be the greatest impediment in its efforts to stabilize social relations in the town. As we have seen, it was precisely because Bradford's rising bourgeois liberals were determined to remake the urban industrial environment in their own image that the progressive order which their ideology promised slipped even farther from their grasp. Conversely, their confrontation with the mass of proletarianized workers who were being dispossessed by the same forces of economic development which engendered their own entrepreneurial ascent, forced bourgeois liberals to acknowledge the reality of class differences, finally enabling them to recognize the practical limits of hegemony and to seek a species of dominance that was more realistic and less total, within a world that was more than just a projection of themselves.

By the late 1840s, the emergence of an urban reform movement provided the vehicle for this transformation of bourgeois leadership, and the basis on which a more effective liberal consensus could, after 1850, actually begin to take shape. Increasingly accustomed by their experience with municipal institutions to wielding authority in this piecemeal, pragmatic, ultimately administrative way, Bradford's liberal entrepreneurs began to abandon their initial predisposition to envision the social world entirely in competitive market terms. For although bourgeois rule could never be sustained entirely voluntarily through some universal affirmation of popular consent, it could be buttressed by mediating governmental structures which might actually improve the climate for bourgeois liberty by enforcing limited regulations and controls. In the last analysis, particularly during moments of crisis, this more limited, less heroic conception of hegemony, in which culture and politics regained some autonomy in relation to the competitive individualism which properly ruled the market-place, proved more effective in underwriting the social stability that was necessary for entrepreneurship as an economic form to thrive.

Paradoxically then, it was the industrial bourgeoisie's very determination to create a viable entrepreneurial society which forced them to devise new integrative mechanisms and forms of authority that, unlike the classic bourgeois voluntary associations, could acknowledge the irreducibility of non-entrepreneurial groups. Yet, in becoming more sensitive to social complexity, less determined to confront the world in rigidly ideological terms, Bradford's bourgeois insurgents, or at least their late nineteenth-century descendants, lost much of that distinctive personal experience and identity that had set them culturally and politically apart. Perhaps this was the beginning of that historical process in which we still find ourselves involved today, whereby the further bourgeios society continues its expansion, the more the bourgeoisie becomes invisible as a class.

16. The community perspective in family history: the Potteries during the nineteenth century

MARGUERITE DUPREE

Future studies will have to recognize and identify a plurality of competing family options extant within any single society and region.[1]

Women's work in paid industrial employment outside the home and its effects on the structure of family life in Victorian Britain has captured the attention of a long line of investigators.[2] Much of their work, however, has been preoccupied with a debate arising from nineteenth-century anxieties over whether or not factory labour led to the 'disruption' of family life. 'When women work in factories', wrote Engels, 'the most important result is the dissolution of family ties.'[3] In the recent outpouring of literature on family history and women's history,[4] major reorientations in the view of the relation-

This research was funded by a Post-doctoral Research Fellowship from the Economic and Social Research Council (UK). I am grateful to D. Levine, L. Lees, R. H. Trainor and the editors for their comments on earlier versions of this paper.

[1] Lawrence Stone, 'Family History in the 1980s: Past Achievements and Future Trends', *Journal of Interdisciplinary History*, 12 (1981), p. 82.

[2] See, for example, F. Engels, *The Condition of the Working Class in England*, trans. by W. O. Chaloner (Oxford, 1958), especially pp. 145–6, 160–6, 233–5; for a summary of the contemporary debate on industrialism and the family, see H. Perkin, *The Origins of Modern English Society 1780–1880* (London, 1969), pp. 149–53; M. Hewitt, *Wives and Mothers in Victorian Industry* (London, 1958); N. J. Smelser, *Social Change in the Industrial Revolution: An Application of Theory to the Lancashire Cotton Industry 1770–1840* (London, 1959); M. Anderson, *Family Structure in Nineteenth-Century Lancashire* (Cambridge, 1971).

[3] Quoted in Perkin, *The Origins of Modern English Society*, p. 149.

[4] For surveys of recent literature, see M. Anderson, *Approaches To the History of the Western Family 1500–1914* (London, 1980); Stone, 'Family History in the 1980s', pp. 51–87; L. Tilly and M. Cohen, 'Does the Family Have a History? A Review of Theory and Practice in Family History', *Social Science History*, 6 (1982), pp. 131–79; special issue (incorporating nos. 1–3), *Journal of Family History*, 12 (1987); J. W. Scott, 'Women In History: The Modern Period', *Past and Present*, 101 (1983), pp. 141–57; E. Roberts, *Women's Work, 1840–1940* (London, 1988).

ship between family life and industrialization and between women and work have shifted attention away from women in paid industrial employment outside the household. Yet there are a number of reasons to look again at this type of employment and its effects on the social, demographic and economic structure of family life in Victorian Britain.

One reason to focus on women's participation in the factory labour force is that it provides a way to investigate the relationships between families and the economy during the nineteenth century. Surveys of the literature on family history point out major areas of disagreement over what questions to ask, what evidence to use, what interpretations to make. There is, however, agreement that the cohesion of the nuclear family during the Industrial Revolution is no longer an issue; a consensus is emerging that in England the characteristic family structure, based on the principles of economic independence before marriage, nuclear family household afterwards and late age at first marriage, was in place before industrialization (how long before is a matter of controversy). This family structure persisted despite economic development, and it made a significant contribution to the processes of capital accumulation, labour deployment and social welfare.[5]

Coinciding with the theme of continuity is the idea that there was flexibility within the system. As Leonore Davidoff and Catherine Hall remark, 'the variability of family forms cannot be overstressed; there is no essential "family", but always "families"'.[6] For example, there were variations in the co-residence of kin and adolescent children, differences in patterns of family employment and standards of living, and fluctuations in fertility and marriage ages. Conceptually there is agreement that the family and economy are not autonomous; nor is one secondary to the other. The behaviour of families both influences the economy and is in turn

[5] L. Stone, *The Family, Sex and Marriage in England: 1500–1800* (London and New York, 1977); E. A. Wrigley, 'Reflections on the History of the Family', *Daedalus*, 106 (1977), p. 83; P. Laslett, 'Mean Household Size in England since the Sixteenth Century', in P. Laslett and R. Wall, eds., *Household and Family in Past Time* (Cambridge, 1972), pp. 125–58; A. Macfarlane, *The Origins of English Individualism* (Oxford, 1978); R. Smith, 'Fertility, Economy and Household Formation in England over Three Centuries', *Population and Development Review*, 7 (1981), pp. 595–622; D. Levine, 'Industrialization and the Proletarian Family in England', *Past and Present*, 107 (1985), pp. 168–203; Anderson, *Family Structure*; M. W. Dupree, 'Family Structure in the Staffordshire Potteries 1840–1880' (unpublished D.Phil. thesis, University of Oxford, 1981).

[6] L. Davidoff and C. Hall, *Family Fortunes: Men and Women of the English Middle Class 1780–1850* (London, 1987), p. 31.

influenced by it. Furthermore, the mutual influence or 'relative autonomy' needs to be understood historically.[7] Looking at the availability of the 'option' of women's paid employment outside the household and at the family characteristics of those women who did and did not take it up makes it possible to illuminate family decisions and to explore in some detail the relationship between families and the economy.

Second, in recent studies of the experience of women in England during the nineteenth century[8] interest in women factory workers as a special creation of the Industrial Revolution has been replaced by an emphasis on the extent to which women's worlds came to be oriented around their home and family or 'separate sphere'. 'Paid employment was usually taken up at different points in the life cycle in response to crises, as and when the family economy demanded

---

[7] Jane Humphries and Jill Rubery, for example, refer to the 'relative autonomy of social reproduction'. They argue that the family system was not established as 'an interesting, central and dynamic variable for economic analysis' because of the inadequacy of the two opposing methodologies that have been employed to analyse the family system across the whole spectrum of theoretical approaches from neo-classical to Marxist and feminist. The first methodology is 'absolute autonomy', in which social reproduction is independent of the system of production. Here the family system is a 'given' which develops independently of the economy. In the second, 'reductionist–functionalist' methodology, social reproduction is an integrated and adaptable part of the broader system of production and is analysed within the same organizing framework. Here the family system is essentially a dependent variable within the economic system. Instead of either of these approaches, Humphries and Rubery suggest that family behaviour 'develops in response to changes in the productive system but the form of this response must be understood historically. It is neither predetermined nor smoothly accommodating to the demands of the productive system, but depends on the dynamics of social reproduction.' J. Humphries and J. Rubery, 'The Reconstitution of the Supply Side of the Labour Market: The Relative Autonomy of Social Reproduction', *Cambridge Journal of Economics*, 8 (1984), pp. 331–46. Describing developments in population history, E. A. Wrigley makes the same point when he refers to the 'logical status' of population history as both independent of and dependent on the economy. E. A. Wrigley, 'Population History in the 1980s', *Journal of Interdisciplinary History*, 12 (1981), p. 218. Richard Wall recommends the use of the phrase 'adaptive family economy' to emphasize the 'flexibility of family and household patterns among different occupational groups'. R. Wall, 'Work, Welfare and the Family: An Illustration of the Adaptive Family Economy', in L. Bonfield *et al.*, eds., *The World We Have Gained: Histories of Population and Social Structure* (Oxford, 1986), pp. 264–6. For a similar conclusion, see also E. Pleck, 'Two Worlds in One: Work and Family', *Journal of Social History*, 10 (1976), pp. 178–95.

[8] For a wide-ranging collection reflecting recent research, see the companion volumes: A. V. John, ed., *Unequal Opportunities: Women's Employment in England 1800–1918* (Oxford, 1986), and J. Lewis, ed., *Labour and Love: Women's Experience of Home and Family 1850–1940* (Oxford, 1986).

it.'[9] For women there was no dichotomy between work and home or family; instead there was a continuum of women's occupations from paid industrial employment outside the home, to domestic service, to sweated labour inside the home, to unpaid home work. Women's roles were characterized by flexibility which made it possible for families to adjust to circumstances. When women in paid employment are considered, emphasis is placed on the extent and reasons why job opportunities for women contracted in some occupations and expanded in others, and on the gender division of labour with women deliberately confined to the least skilled and worst-paid branches. In addition, domestic servants and women in sweated trades have captured attention because of their large numbers. However, unlike many other types of female occupation, paid industrial employment outside the household can be traced in the census enumerators' books, the most comprehensive source on family history available for the period.[10] As a result, if used with care, evidence is available from the mid-nineteenth century which allows systematic examination of this type of women's employment together with a number of aspects of their family life. It is possible, for example, to look at women's work together with that of their children, husbands and fathers. With this evidence historians can, as Lawrence Stone suggests, consider 'the family as a unit rather than study women or children as isolated groups'.[11]

Third, in discussions of the decline in marital fertility after 1870 women factory workers still have a prominent place.[12] Paid work for women outside the home is seen as a critical variable for determining fertility. Cotton textile workers were the first occupational group within the working class to experience the decline in

[9] J. Lewis, 'Introduction: Reconstructing Women's Experience of Home and Family', in Lewis, ed., *Labour and Love*, p. 19.
[10] For a warning about the pitfalls of using this source for studies of women's employment which recommends its use only with a knowledge of local economic and social conditions, see E. Higgs, 'Women, Occupations and Work in the Nineteenth-Century Census', *History Workshop*, 23 (1987), pp. 59–80.
[11] Stone, *The Family, Sex and Marriage in England*, p. 19.
[12] Hewitt, *Wives and Mothers*, especially pp. 85–97; M. Haines, *Fertility and Occupation: Population Patterns in Industrialization* (London, 1979); L. Tilly, 'Demographic Change in Two French Industrial Cities: Anzin and Roubaix 1872–1906', in J. Sundin and E. Soderlund, eds., *Time, Space and Man: Essays in Microdemography* (Stockholm, 1979), pp. 107–32; S. Szreter, 'The Decline of Marital Fertility in England and Wales c. 1870–1914 ...' (unpublished Ph.D. thesis, University of Cambridge, 1984); M. Teitelbaum, *The British Fertility Decline* (Princeton, 1984); R. Woods, 'Approaches to the Fertility Transition in Victorian England', *Population Studies*, 41 (1987), pp. 283–311.

marital fertility which other groups eventually followed. It was an industry in which women formed a substantial proportion of the labour force. At the same time occupational groups such as miners and ironworkers, which had few women workers and characteristically lived in isolated or homogeneous communities that did not offer paid industrial employment for women outside the home, had exceptionally high fertility.

Finally, despite changing views of the relations among work, women and family life, the main approach to the topics remains the investigation of individual industries, separate occupations or communities dominated by a single industry. Scholars are answering Elizabeth Pleck's call to them to examine 'changes within specific occupational cultures rather than to refer to the "capitalist market place" or to general conditions of poverty'.[13] Women cotton textile workers are especially prominent, but pit-brow lasses, hosiery workers in Leicestershire, women workers in the sweated trades of the East End of London or in Leeds or rural areas, fisher-girls of the Yorkshire coast, domestic servants, teachers and toward the end of the century clerical workers, largely make up our image of Victorian working women.[14] One reason for this concentration on cases of occupational isolation – both geographical and conceptual – is that the Industrial Revolution has been thought of as a series of classic industries or increasingly regionally specialized 'leading sectors' which transformed the economy. Naturally investigators of women's employment and of working-class family life have been attracted to study places and groups that most fit that classic view. Recently a more complex view of the Industrial Revolution has emerged, reminiscent of Clapham, which replaces leading sectors with images of a variegated economy.[15] Studies of women, particularly in the sweated trades and service sector, have both contributed to and reflected this view at the national level. At the same time these and other studies have acknowledged the complexity of the occupational structure within industries.[16] What have

[13] Pleck, 'Two Worlds in One', p. 187.

[14] For the classic study of women cotton textile workers, see Hewitt, *Wives and Mothers*; see also, for example, John, ed., *Unequal Opportunities* and Lewis, ed., *Labour and Love*. For visual images, see M. Hiley, *Victorian Working Women: Portraits From Life* (Boston, 1979).

[15] For a discussion of changes in the historiography of the Industrial Revolution see D. N. Cannadine, 'The Present and the Past in the English Industrial Revolution 1880–1980', *Past and Present*, 103 (1984), pp. 131–72, especially pp. 163–6.

[16] R. Samuel, 'Workshop of the World: Steam Power and Hand Technology in Mid-Victorian Britain', *History Workshop*, 3 (1977), pp. 6–72 has been

received little emphasis heretofore are the interactions between different industrially-based occupational groups within an area.

In what follows, close analysis of women's paid industrial employment outside the household and its effects on the social, demographic and economic structure of family life in an area with a dominant industry reveals surprising complexity in patterns of family employment, fertility and family standard of living. These patterns call into question the method of taking as units of analysis either occupational groups divorced from the localities in which their members lived, or single industry towns which are taken as synonomous with a single occupational group. Instead, the patterns suggest the importance of an emphasis on the local community and the interaction of occupational groups within the local context – even one that appears to be dominated by a single industry. Such an approach, it will be argued, is better suited both to illuminate the complexity of Victorian society and to bring family history into social history as a whole.[17]

I

The Staffordshire Potteries in the middle of the nineteenth century is a particularly appropriate region in which to examine women's work in paid industrial employment outside the home and its effects on the social, demographic and economic structure of family life. First, it was a region in which the dominant industry – pottery manufacture – employed women and children as well as men. This increased the scope for families to mediate between the age-structure and wage-structure on the one hand, and the standard of living on the other. Moreover, because women's and children's work in the potworks was outside the household and is distinguishable in the census enumerators' books, it is possible to analyse systematically patterns of family employment. Second, women's

especially influential; for the pottery industry, see Dupree, 'Family Structure in the Staffordshire Potteries', pp. 44–50, 144–5, 346; for a study which makes this point for the industry in a later period, see R. Whipp, 'Woman and the Social Organization of Work in the Staffordshire Pottery Industry 1900–1930', *Midland History*, 12 (1987), pp. 103–21.

[17] For the need to synthesize specialities and an attempt to overcome the 'balkanizing thrust in social history', see, for example, Pleck, 'Two Worlds in One', p. 178. For the need to integrate family and women's history into general history, see C. Degler, 'Women and the Family', in M. Kammen, ed., *The Past Before Us: Contemporary Historical Writing in the United States* (Ithaca and London, 1980), especially pp. 308, 326.

and children's employment in the pottery industry was not subject to factory legislation until the mid-1860s. So, in the Potteries, unlike the textile areas where the Acts pre-dated useful census material, it is possible to examine patterns of family employment before as well as after the restriction of women's and children's employment through the Factory Acts. Finally, although the pottery industry dominated the region, three industries – coal-mining and iron as well as pottery – were located in the same area. While the pottery industry employed men, women and children, the coal-mines and ironworks employed only men. Thus, the mix of industries allows comparisons of patterns of family employment among different occupational groups in the same area.

Using individual level data from samples of the census enumerators' books for the Potteries in 1861 and 1881,[18] supplemented by information from a wide variety of other sources, it is possible to reveal the extent to which women worked in the pottery labour force and to answer questions about certain aspects of their family background. What was the nature of women's work in the pot-banks? What were the individual and family characteristics of the women who worked there, and were there changes over the life-cycle and over time? Were the wives and children of potters employed or did families diversify employment? Was the employment of women outside the home associated, as in cotton textiles, with low fertility? What was the effect of women's and children's employment in the potbanks on family living standards?

II

Located in the north of England half-way between Birmingham and Manchester, the Potteries was made up of a chain of six towns – Tunstall, Burslem, Hanley, Stoke, Fenton and Longton – which were encompassed in the parliamentary borough of Stoke-upon-Trent (population *c*. 100,000 in 1861). In 1861 over 80 per cent of the British pottery industry was concentrated in the Potteries. Within this relatively self-contained area, seven miles long and two miles wide, there were 180 manufactories (called 'potbanks' or 'potworks') and the residences of 30,000 employees.

---

[18] I have taken a 1 in 15 systematic sample of the enumerators' books for the parliamentary borough of Stoke-upon-Trent in 1861, and a 1 in 24 sample for 1881. The 1861 sample includes information on approximately 6,700 individuals and 1,350 households, the 1881 sample 6,000 individuals and 1,200 households.

During the early 1860s the Potteries as a whole was an area of relatively good housing conditions and comparatively high wages and employment. Moreover, there were unusually low levels of population turnover and migration for pottery workers, who tended to be locally born, though not for miners and ironworkers, who tended to have been born outside the Potteries in other centres of mining or iron-working. Nevertheless, despite general prosperity and relative geographical stability, the Potteries was also an area of exceptionally high mortality rates.[19]

There were two major departments within a pottery manufactory: the potting department, which was made up of the various branches in which clay was prepared and ware formed; and the finishing department, which included the branches in which decorating, sorting and packing the ware took place. Girls and women made up over one-third (37 per cent) of the pottery labour force. However, they did not work in all branches, and their ages and methods of hiring varied among the different branches. In the potting department, girls and women, usually fourteen years or older, worked as assistants to male throwers or turners. Yet, the majority worked in the finishing department, where girls, apprenticed at age eleven or twelve, worked as paintresses, painting earthenware in a room with ten to thirty other girls under the supervision of an older woman. Young girls also worked as paper-cutters in the printing shops, where designs were printed on to tissue paper and then rubbed or 'transferred' on to the ware. In the throwing and turning branches and in the printworks and warehouse, women and girls worked together with men or boys or were interchangeable with them. Otherwise the sexes tended to be employed in different tasks and different places in the manufactory; specific tasks were age- and sex-graded. There were, for example, no female slip-makers, throwers, turners, flat-pressers, hollow-ware-pressers; instead, women were transferrers, paintresses, gilders, burnishers, scourers and warehouse women.

There were several patterns of hiring arrangements. Women in the potting department, paintresses and warehouse girls were hired directly by the employer, while paper-cutters were hired by women who in turn were hired by printers. Girls tended to begin work at a slightly later age than boys. It was exceptional for boys to start before age nine and girls before age eleven. Yet nearly 75 per cent

[19] Dupree, 'Family Structure in the Staffordshire Potteries'.

of the female pottery workers were under thirty years of age, compared with 58 per cent of the male pottery workers. The relatively young age-structure of the female labour force and the fact that only 14 per cent of all married women worked in the pottery industry indicate that women tended to work in the industry for a limited period before marriage but then left the workforce thereafter. Some women, however, did work in the industry after marriage. As in textile areas, married women in the pottery labour force were more likely to have no children, and no children under ten years of age, compared with wives not employed in the pottery industry. Also as in the textile industries, a few women may have worked continuously after marriage, while others, particularly widows and women whose husbands were absent on census night, stopped and restarted work as necessary.

Unlike the cotton textile industry, where married women tended to stop work as soon as children were able to start, mothers with children who worked in the potteries tended to continue to work.[20] For example, twelve-year-old William Bardin, who worked in the biscuit warehouse at the Copeland and Garratt pottery in Stoke, told the Children's Employment Commissioner: 'I got a mother, she is a potter, 6 brothers and sisters, 3 are potters.'[21] This difference between the Potteries and cotton textile areas emphasizes the flexibility of women's roles.

Other evidence of the flexibility of women's participation in paid work outside the home comes from a comparison of women's employment patterns in the Potteries in 1861 and 1881. During this period the extension of factory legislation to the pottery industry, together with the Education Act of 1870, restricted the employment of children in the industry. Alongside the reduction in the number of children, the most striking difference in the pottery labour force between 1861 and 1881 was the increase in the proportion of women from 37 per cent to 44 per cent. The women coming into the labour force included unmarried as well as married women.

One consequence of the gender division of tasks, together with the shorter length of employment over a lifetime for women, was a difference between men and women in their susceptibility to certain diseases. Respiratory diseases such as bronchitis or potters'

[20] *Ibid.*, pp. 136–9.
[21] *Parliamentary Papers* (hereafter *P.P.*), 1843, xiv, p. 249.

asthma were not as prevalent among women as among men employed in the pottery industry, due primarily to the fact that only a small portion of women employed in the industry worked in the potting departments where dust was most prevalent. This is reflected in differential mortality. There was a sharp rise in male mortality rates in the middle decades of life between twenty-five and sixty-four, when female rates were falling. This differential mortality of men and women meant that for families in which the male head was a pottery worker, the industry could both create the 'need' for women and children to work as well as offer an opportunity to meet the need. For example, Benjamin Taylor, aged twelve, who worked for Minton and Boyle earning 4s per week making cockspurs to place ware on when it was baked, told the Children's Employment Commissioner: 'got a mother, but no father; father has been dead ten years; he was a presser, working here; he died of consumption, he was forty-four when he died'.[22]

Another consequence of the sexual division of labour within a potworks was that it left little scope for a nuclear family to remain together as a work group within a potworks. It was possible, however, for members of the same family to work at different tasks within the same factory or industry.

III

Family employment patterns are the result of employers' demand for labour combined with family decisions as to which members supply labour inside and outside the home. A full explanation of the patterns would require an exploration of employers' demand for labour which this essay cannot attempt. Suffice it to say that various economic and social factors produced a strong, continuous and increasing demand for women's labour in the pottery industry.[23] In this context it is possible to explore individual and family characteristics of those employed in the pottery labour force in comparison with the characteristics of those not employed, in order to give some indication of the effect of the 'option' of women's and children's employment on family decisions about labour force participation. The reasons for these decisions will become clearer

[22] *Ibid.*, p. 241.
[23] Dupree, 'Family Structure in the Staffordshire Potteries', pp. 45–50, 281–4, 334–40, 344–8.

below in the course of the investigation of family living standards which acted as a cause as well as a consequence of family employment patterns.

'Occupation' is commonly used as a category of analysis in history and the social sciences. Its use assumes that members of different occupational groups exhibit distinctive social behaviour with regard, among other things, to certain aspects of family life, such as marriage, fertility, co-residence, family employment and mortality. In other studies miners and iron-workers have been singled out for their exceptional behaviour.[24] Due to the nature of the work and its isolated geographical location these occupational groups are associated with strong, homogeneous, 'industrially based occupational cultures',[25] characterized by families headed by a single male wage-earner, little paid employment of women and children outside the home, high fertility and a high degree of role segregation between husbands and wives. Industrially-based occupational cultures also existed in the Potteries. In the early 1860s there were separate unions within the major industries in the Potteries; different occupational groups contained different proportions of migrants; and contemporaries perceived occupational groups as separate.[26] Nevertheless, the fact that the pottery industry offered employment to children and women provides a test[27] of the extent to which the Potteries population was socially segregated by occupation. Given the emphasis in some of the literature relating to textile workers on the evidence that the women employed in the mills were the wives and daughters of textile workers,[28] together with the low labour force participation of wives

[24] Haines, *Fertility and Occupation*; Tilly, 'Demographic Change in Two French Industrial Cities'; Szreter, 'The Decline of Marital Fertility in England and Wales'.

[25] J. Foster, *Class Struggle and the Industrial Revolution* (London, 1974), p. 125.

[26] Dupree, 'Family Structure in the Staffordshire Potteries', pp. 70–1, 255, 390–400.

[27] Other tests undertaken but not included here concern the extent of occupational intermarriage and occupational mobility, both intra-generational and inter-generational, based on an analysis of information from local marriage registers. See *Ibid.*, pp. 180–8.

[28] See, for example, C. Nardinelli, 'Child Labour and the Factory Acts', *Journal of Economic History*, 40 (1980), pp. 739–55; Smelser, *Social Change in the Industrial Revolution*; P. Joyce, *Work, Society and Politics: The Culture of the Factory in Later Victorian England* (Brighton, 1980), p. 117. A. John, 'Introduction', in John, ed., *Unequal Opportunities*, p. 25; for the pottery industry in a later period, see Whipp, 'Women and the Social Organization of Work'.

Table 16.1. *The employment of children and the presence and occupation of fathers: Potteries, 1861*[a]

Father's occupation	Children's occupation				
	Pottery	Other	Scholar	Not employed	All
No father	[23%] 35%	[16%] 9	[9%] 36	[14%] 21	[13%] 100%(101)
Potter	**[40]** 23%	[18] 4	[36] 56	[30] 17	[34] 100%(262)
Miner	**[16]** 33%	[9] 7	[7] 36	[13] 25	[10] 100%(77)
Iron-worker	[4] 12%	[5] 6	[7] 56	[10] 27	[7] 100%(52)
Labourer	[7] 18%	[9] 9	[5] 40	**[12]** **33**	[7] 100%(55)
Other[b]	*[11]* 8%	**[43]** 11	**[36]** **68**	[27] *14*	[29] 100%(222)
All	100% (154) 20%	100% (56) 7%	100% (412) 54%	100% (147) 19%	100% (769)

[] = column %
() = n
numbers in bold = the relationship between the categories is positive and significant at .05 level (Haberman's adjusted residual)
numbers in italic = the relationship between the categories is negative and significant at .05 level (Haberman's adjusted residual)
[a] based on a file of the children aged 8–12 years in the 1861 census sample of the Potteries
[b] 'Other' is a residual category which contains shopkeepers, tradesmen, professional men, etc.

and daughters of miners and iron-workers and their social homogeneity, one might expect that it was the wives and children of pottery workers who worked in the potbanks.

Whose children worked in the potteries? F. D. Longe, the Assistant Commissioner who investigated the area for the Royal Commission on Children's Employment in 1862, suggested that the children employed in the potworks were not the children of healthy, 'respectable' working potters. Instead, they tended to be the children of widows, colliers and fathers who were 'incapable of working or of drunken habits'.[29] It is not possible to discover from the enumerators' books whether fathers were incapable of working[30] or were of 'drunken habits', but it is possible to estimate the extent to which the children aged eight to twelve[31] who were employed in the pottery industry were the children of potters or of widows and miners.

The relationship between the employment of children and the father's presence and occupation is set out in Table 16.1. A relatively high proportion (23 per cent) of the children who worked in the pottery industry lived with their mothers only, compared with 13 per cent of all children aged eight to twelve years. Moreover, it is evident that over one-third of the children aged eight to twelve without fathers living in the household worked in the pottery industry. These relatively high proportions confirm Longe's suggestion that widows' children tended to work in the potworks. Nevertheless, this should not obscure the fact that over

[29] *P.P.* 1863, xviii, p. 99.

[30] Only six, or less than 1 per cent, of the children aged eight to twelve in the sample had fathers who were listed as either 'not employed' or 'retired'. However, it is possible that those 'incapable of working' may have recorded their most recent occupation.

[31] Contemporaries considered 'children' as an undifferentiated category with regard to their employment. The Royal Commissions on the Employment of Children in 1842 and 1862 investigated the employment of both boys and girls, and factory and education legislation applied equally to boys and girls. Although there were well-established differences between the jobs of boys and the jobs of girls within the factory and their age at starting work, the differences were not great enough to jeopardize discussion of them together as 'childen'. In 1861 children made up nearly 20 per cent of the pottery labour force. The Children's Employment Commission divided children into those aged twelve years and below, and those aged thirteen to eighteen; the line between twelve and thirteen corresponded roughly to the age when boys began apprenticeships. Furthermore, the age-group specified in the factory legislation restricting the employment of children was eight to twelve years. Hence, the analysis of children here uses the age category eight to twelve years (inclusive).

Table 16.2. *The employment of unmarried daughters (aged fifteen and over), and the presence of parents and occupation of fathers: Potteries, 1861*[a]

Parent's presence/father's occupation	Daughter's occupation			
	Pottery	Other	Not employed	All
Mother only	[25%] 62%	[17%] 22	[17%] 17	[21%] 100%(79)
Father only	[8] 16%	[3] 3	[17] 13	[9] 100%(32)
Both parents, father's occupation:				
Potter	**[37] 69%**	[19] *18*	[18] *14*	[28] 100%(103)
Miner	**[8] 71%**	[4] 19	[3] 10	[6] 100%(21)
Iron-worker	[2] 33%	[3] 25	[6] 42	[3] 100%(12)
Labourer	[6] 55%	[6] 30	[4] 15	[5] 100%(20)
Other[b]	[14] 28%	**[47] 45**	**[36] 28**	[27] 100%(101)
All	100%(194) 53%	100%(96) 26%	100%(78) 21%	100%(368)

[] = column %
() = n
numbers in bold = the relationship between the categories is positive and significant at .05 level (Haberman's adjusted residual)
numbers in italic = the relationship between the categories is negative and significant at .05 level (Haberman's adjusted residual)
[a] from the Potteries census sample 1861
[b] 'Other' is a residual category which contains shopkeepers, tradesmen, professional men, etc.

three-quarters of the children who worked in the industry lived with both parents.

As might be expected given the high proportion of potters in the population, a large percentage (40 per cent) of the children employed in the potworks were the children of potters. Yet, there is a significant relationship between fathers employed in mining and children's employment in pottery, as well as between fathers employed in pottery and children's employment in pottery. Surprisingly, only 23 per cent of the children aged eight to twelve years whose fathers were potters were employed in the pottery industry, compared with 33 per cent or one-third of the children of miners. Thus, again coinciding with Longe's observation regarding the employment of colliers' children, a child of a miner was more likely to be employed in the pottery industry than was a child of a potter. Therefore, in general, it should not be assumed (as has been done for cotton workers)[32] that the young children of pottery workers also worked in the pottery industry.

Whose daughters and wives were working in the industry? In 1861 (Table 16.2), as expected (given the high proportion of potters in the population), the largest proportion (37 per cent) of unmarried women in the pottery labour force who resided with their parents were the daughters of potters. But although the absolute numbers are small, a slightly higher proportion of the unmarried daughters of miners (71 per cent) were employed in the pottery industry than daughters of potters (69 per cent); furthermore, 55 per cent or over half of the daughters of labourers worked in the potworks. There is a significant relationship between the employment of fathers in mining and daughters in pottery, as well as between the employment of fathers in pottery and daughters in pottery. Thus, an unmarried daughter of a miner who resided with her parents was just as likely to work in the pottery industry as the daughter of a potter.

The relationship between the employment of married women and the occupations of their husbands in 1861 appears in Table 16.3. Although 64 per cent of married women in the pottery workforce were wives of potters, only 21 per cent of the wives of potters were employed in the industry. The latter figure is not much higher than the 13 per cent of the wives of miners who worked in the potteries, even though the relationship between miners and the

[32] See Nardinelli, 'Child Labour and the Factory Acts', pp. 739–55.

Table 16.3. *The employment of wives and occupation of husbands: Potteries, 1861[a]*

	Wife's occupation			
Husband's occupation	Pottery	Other	Not employed	All
Potter	[64%] **21**%	[37%] 5	[34%] 74	[38%] 100%(443)
Miner	[14] 13%	[10] 4	[13] 83	[13] 100%(151)
Iron-worker	[4] 6%	[10] 8	[7] 86	[7] 100%(79)
Labourer	[6] 8%	[5] 3	[10] 89	[9] 100%(108)
Other[b]	[13] 5%	[40] 7	[35] **89**	[33] 100%(381)
All	100%(144) 12%	100%(63) 5%	100%(955) 82%	100%(1,162) 100%(1,162)

[] = column %
() = n
number in bold = the relationship between the categories is positive and significant at .05 level (Haberman's adjusted residual)
numbers in italic = the relationship between the categories is negative and significant at .05 level (Haberman's adjusted residual)
[a] based on a file of the married couples in the 1861 census sample of the Potteries
[b] 'Other' is a residual category which contains shopkeepers, tradesmen, professional men, etc.

employment of their wives in the potworks was not statistically significant.

Thus, the evidence for wives in combination with the evidence for children and unmarried daughters indicates that it is dangerous to assume that the wives and daughters of potters were necessarily employed in the industry. These patterns also indicate that miners, who in other areas seem to be a homogeneous occupational group, displayed a considerable amount of interaction with other occupations in the Potteries. Moreover, the patterns are a further reminder of the flexibility of the roles of wives, mothers and daughters as they responded to needs and opportunities in a particular locality. This flexibility also becomes apparent in another and surprising way, in the relationship between women's factory work and certain aspects of the demographic behaviour of occupational groups.

IV

Studies of occupational differences in fertility associate high female labour force participation in factory occupations with relatively low and declining fertility.[33] The relatively high fertility of coal-mining areas in England, France and the United States and the relatively low fertility in cotton textile areas in England and France have been associated with the low levels of married women's employment outside the home in coal-mining areas and the high levels of industrial employment of married women in textile areas. The Potteries provides a very different kind of area in which to examine these links. The mix of industries in the district allows comparisons of changes in patterns of family employment, in estimates of marital fertility and in marriage ages to be made among different occupational groups in the same area. Do miners' wives continue to have relatively high fertility even in an area where there was an opportunity for female employment? Do potters' wives, like the wives of textile workers, have relatively low fertility?

Given that the levels in the Potteries of women's employment outside the home are similar to those in textile areas and that the proportion of women in the pottery labour force rose between 1861

---

[33] Haines, *Fertility and Occupation*; Tilly, 'Demographic Change in Two French Industrial Cities'; Szreter, 'The Decline of Marital Fertility in England and Wales'.

and 1881, one would expect fertility and marriage patterns in the potteries to be similar to those in textile areas which led the fertility decline among industrial workers and where the average age of marriage for women was rising. What makes the Potteries a critically important area for study is that it does not fit these expectations. The 1911 Fertility Census shows that the potters who married in 1881–5 were one of the groups with the highest fertility in the country. They reached the levels of men in the predominantly male or 'machismo' coal and iron industries.[34] Moreover, within the Potteries a comparison of estimates of marital fertility based on child–woman ratios in 1861 suggests that differences among the occupational groups within the area were small.[35] In an area where there were opportunities for the paid employment of women and children outside the household, there were similarities in the fertility patterns among separate occupational groups, including miners and iron-workers who usually are noted for their exceptional behaviour.

Thus, it is possible that there was a 'community effect' which over-rode the occupational differentials. This is plausible given the evidence of intermixing of occupations in family employment patterns.[36] What is surprising is that the 'community effect' is not that of low fertility, which one would expect given the nature of the industry that dominated the area.

Marriage ages as well as fertility do not appear to fit expectations. The proportions of men and women in the different age-groups in the Potteries who were married or widowed suggest that marriage ages were much younger than those in a textile town such as Preston (where only 28 per cent of women aged twenty to twenty-four were married compared with 45 per cent in the Potteries). Moreover, despite the increasing proportion of women in the pottery labour force between 1861 and 1881, the age of marriage changed little.[37] In short, the pottery workers do not follow the textile pattern. Their experience is contrary to the

---

[34] Dupree, 'Family Structure in the Staffordshire Potteries', pp. 117–19; Szreter, 'The Decline of Marital Fertility in England and Wales', especially pp. 270, 326–7.

[35] Dupree, 'Family Structure in the Staffordshire Potteries', pp. 196–8.

[36] Intermixing among occupational groups is also evident in marriage patterns and in inter-generational and intra-generational occupational mobility. See *ibid.*, pp. 180–5.

[37] For 1861 see *ibid.*, p. 101; for 1881 see PP 1883, lxxx, p. 236, and my sample of the 1881 enumerators' books from the Potteries cited above in note 18.

generalizations associating the relatively high and increasing employment of women in industry with declining fertility and increasing age of marriage.

How women were able to cope with high labour force participation and high fertility is beyond the scope of this essay, but it is plausible to suggest that the solution lay in child care arrangements. Given that pottery employers provided little in the way of child care facilities, it is possible that child care arrangements developed as part of a 'community culture' rather than a single, separate, 'industrially-based occupational culture'. Burslem's municipal day nursery closed after a short period in the 1870s due to its inability to attract working mothers and their children,[38] but there is nothing to suggest that the Potteries differed from Lancashire cotton towns, where a coroner testified in 1871 that children are 'taken care of either by a person in the house or by some neighbour, and my impression is that it is usually done by some neighbour' who might also be a relative.[39] Hence, it is necessary in considering the flexibility of women's roles to look outside as well as inside both the nuclear family unit used in neo-classical economists' analyses of labour force participation and fertility and the co-resident household unit used in some demographic and family history.[40]

V

In order to examine the ways in which the 'option' of women's and children's employment affected the economic structure of families, however, it is useful to turn back to the nuclear family unit and occupation as a category and to examine standards of living.

Among other things, patterns of family employment and fertility such as those emerging above have implications for living standards which in turn help to explain the patterns. It is possible to put the information about labour force participation and family composition together with estimates of incomes and compare the standards of living of families of married men in major occupational groups in the Potteries.[41] In his study of the labour force of a

---

[38] *Staffordshire Sentinel*, 21 December 1872, p. 5; 4 April 1874, p. 5; 17 April 1875, p. 5.

[39] PP 1871 vii, p. 99; Hewitt, *Wives and Mothers*, pp. 128–33.

[40] Anderson, *Approaches to the History of the Western Family*, pp. 17–38, 65–6, 75–84.

[41] For a comprehensive study of changes in living standards in the region which, however, does not undertake the kind of analysis attempted here, see F. W.

paper-making firm and a weaving firm in southeast Scotland in the mid-nineteenth century, John Holley points out that two fairly clear and in some ways opposite models of the determination of family standard of living emerge from the literature.[42] The first model is that of the 'symmetrical' family, in which the family standard of living was governed by the 'pre-industrial' pattern of multiple earners within the family; the second model is that of the 'asymmetrical' family, characterized by the 'industrial' pattern of the adult male head as the sole breadwinner. Young and Willmott among others[43] see these models as two stages in development, and they argue that there has been a change from the 'symmetrical' to the 'asymmetrical' form over the past 200 years. Holley, focusing his study on the effects of technological change, expected to find this change; instead of the asymmetrical replacing the symmetrical, however, he found that both patterns of family income determination appeared at the same time. Family standard of living was correlated with the head's income for highly-paid workers, but with the demographic and labour force participation characteristics of households headed by labourers. Thus, to resolve these issues for the Potteries it is necessary, first, to determine the extent to which the family standard of living of married men within the various occupational groups was determined by the head's income and, second, to compare the family standard of living and its determination among the different occupational groups.

The least squares regression of the head's income against family standard of living (Table 16.4a) shows a moderate to strong correlation (.78) between head's income and family standard of living for iron-workers and a moderate correlation (.53) for those in 'other' occupations. For potters, miners and labourers there was relatively little association. Thus, there is evidence of asymmetry for iron-workers.

The extent to which the standard of living was determined by the head's income or labour force participation of family members can

Botham, 'Working Class Living Standards in North Staffordshire 1750–1914' (unpublished Ph.D. thesis, University of London, 1982); for the second half of the eighteenth century, see E. H. Hunt and F. W. Botham, 'Wages in Britain during the Industrial Revolution', *Economic History Review*, 40 (1987), pp. 380–99.

[42] J. Holley, 'The Re-division of Labour: Two Firms in Nineteenth-Century Southeast Scotland' (unpublished Ph.D. thesis, University of Edinburgh, 1978).

[43] M. Young and P. Willmott, *The Symmetrical Family* (Harmondsworth, 1977); see, for example, Levine, 'Industrialization and the Proletarian Family in England'.

Table 16.4a. *Determinants of family standard of living for families headed by married men in various occupations: Potteries, 1861*

| Occupation of head | Determinants of family standard of living[a] (co-efficients of correlation) | | | |
| | Head's income | Excess of earners over dependants[b] | | (missing values) |
	r	r	n	
Iron-workers	.78	.24	65	(10)
Other	.53	.40	185	(200)
Potters	.31	.39	411	(28)
Miners	.19	.28	149	(2)
Labourers	.22	.69	100	(11)
All (incl. unemployed or retired)	.49	.40	912	(261)

Table 16.4b. *Mean values of each of the three variables used in Table 16.4a for married men in various occupations who headed households: Potteries, 1861*

Occupation of head	Head's income (s/- per week)	Family standard of living (s/- above or below poverty line)[a]	Excess of earners over dependants (adult males=100)[b]
Iron-workers	31	16	137
Potters	27	16	164
Other	26	15	164
Miners	24	12	159
Labourers	15	5	147

[a] 'Family standard of living' = the estimated income minus the minimum standard of family expenditure for each nuclear family. The aggregate income was calculated for each nuclear family headed by a married couple where the income of all family members could be estimated from the figures for the earnings of the different occupations (assuming a full week's work). Information was sufficient for incomes to be calculated for 78 per cent of the families headed by married couples in the Potteries sample. Income from lodgers was ignored, and it was assumed that co-residing children gave all their income to the family. The minimum standard of family expenditure was based on Rowntree's scale of primary poverty expenditure as used by Anderson (*Family Structure*, p. 201), but adjusted for lower rents in the Potteries.

[b] 'Excess of earners over dependants' = the number of earners minus the number of dependants in each nuclear family headed by a married couple where the income of all family members could be estimated. Earners and dependants were weighted in terms of the 'adult equivalent needs' used by Foster (*Class Struggle*, p. 256).

be operationalized as a variable measuring the excess of earners over dependants in terms of needs. This variable with an r = .69 explains the variation in living standard of families headed by labourers better than did the income of the head. Thus, the family composition, i.e. the number of people of working age and the extent of their labour force participation, was far more important for the standard of living of labourer-headed families than was the income level of the head.

Comparisons of the average standard of living among various occupational groups (Table 16.4b) reveal patterns which follow from these correlations. Families headed by potters and iron-workers had similar average standards of living (approximately 16s per week above the poverty line) even though the average pay of a household head who was an iron-worker was higher (over 31s per week versus 27s for potters). In other words, living standards did not decline directly with the differences in the wages of heads. Families headed by potters had a higher rate of labour force participation and fewer dependants than those of iron-workers. Nor was high labour force participation directly related to low earnings by the head; potters, miners and others had higher excesses of earners over dependants and higher head's incomes than did labourers.

The contrast between the living standards of the various occupational groups can be seen more starkly when the pattern of the standard of living over the life-cycle is considered (Fig. 16.1). The pattern for each of the occupations is the same, but the level of labourers is consistently below the rest. To some extent, however, the relatively low standard of living of labourers was alleviated by taking in lodgers which are not included in the previous figures.

To sum up, occupational groups embodying each of the two contrasting principles which determine family living standards co-existed within the Potteries. For iron-workers, family standard of living was related to the income level of the head; for labourers, it was related to the excess of earners over dependants within the household. Among the potters and miners, however, family standard of living was not correlated strongly with either the income of the head or the excess of earners over dependants. Moreover, the average standard of living of various occupational groups could be the same but for different reasons. Iron-workers and potters, for example, had similar mean family standards of living, yet iron-workers had a relatively high income for the head, while potters

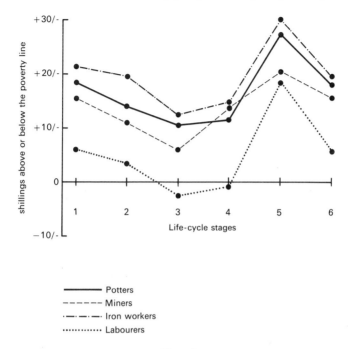

Life-cycle stages
1. Wife under 45, no children at home
2. Wife under 45, one child under 1 yr at home
3. Children at home, but none in employment
4. Children at home, and some, but under half, in employment
5. Children at home, and half or over in employment
6. Wife 45 or over, no children or only children over age 20 at home

Figure 16.1 Standard of living by life-cycle stage for various occupations of husbands: (married couples) Potteries sample, 1861

had a relatively high excess of earners over dependants. Furthermore, all occupational groups displayed a similar pattern of living standards over the life-cycle, but that of labourers was considerably lower.

Thus, the availability of employment for women and children in the Potteries provided increased scope for families to mediate between the wage-structure and the age-structure on the one hand, and the standard of living on the other,[44] since living standards did

[44] Wrigley, 'Population History in the 1980s', pp. 207–8, 225–6; Humphries and Rubery, 'The Reconstitution of the Supply Side of the Labour Market', pp. 331–46.

not decline directly with the wages of heads in different occupational groups. Moreover, the resulting patterns offer evidence of the 'relative autonomy' of families and the economy since relatively high labour force participation was related to low earnings by the head for some but not all occupational groups. Furthermore, at the community level the availability of employment for women and children decreased the inequality in the distribution of income, providing an economic basis for a 'community culture'.

VI

Two general conclusions emerge from this examination of women's work in paid industrial employment outside the home in the potteries and its effect on aspects of the social, demographic and economic structure of family life.

First, the visibility of women and children's factory labour has made it possible, as Lawrence Stone suggests, to 'recognize and identify a plurality of competing family options extant within' a single region. The unexpected variety of responses to employment opportunities in the Potteries provides evidence of variability of employment behaviour which sets up a more complex picture of how family decisions are made about earnings and fertility. Certainly the 'structural context' – social, demographic, economic, ideological, political – imposed constraints on behaviour, but the variations in patterns of family employment, fertility and standards of living in the Potteries highlight the flexibility of the nuclear family and the key position of women – as wives, mothers, daughters and workers – in shaping the responses of families to their circumstances.

Second, this examination of family employment patterns, fertility and standard of living in the Potteries does more than show that patterns were different there from those in other British communities which previously have received attention. More generally, it suggests the need to consider communities rather than single occupations. The family employment and fertility patterns in the Potteries call into question the use of 'occupation' as a category with fixed prior characteristics which can be used as an explanatory variable. Instead, the social characteristics associated with occupations need to be seen as problematic. The family employment patterns in the Potteries reveal a mixing of occupations even among occupational groups, such as miners and iron-workers, usually characterized as relatively homogeneous. They serve as a warning against assuming that it was the wives and children of men in the industry who worked in that industry. Although the largest proportion of women and children employed in the potteries were the wives, daughters and children of male potters, there were substantial proportions of women and children employed in potworks who had husbands or fathers who were either dead or in other occupations. Moreover, the wives, daughters and children of potters typically did not work in the potteries.

In addition, the similarity in fertility in the Potteries among different occupational groups and the relatively high fertility in an area with relatively high married women's labour force participation raise doubts about the use of 'occupation' not only as a category with fixed attributes, but also as a focus for analysis. In particular, it is plausible to argue that urban areas of mixed occupations were more typical of mid- and late Victorian Britain than were homogeneous mining, iron and textile areas; hence, studies of the fertility decline in nineteenth-century Britain have over-emphasized 'occupation' at the expense of studies of particular localities where it is possible to examine fertility behaviour in context.

Even for 'single occupation' communities, where the dominant industry did not employ women and children or where census enumerators' books are not revealing about women's employment or not available for the period in question, the inevitable presence of a service sector means that a community-based rather than an occupation-based methodology is likely to be more appropriate. Such a perspective will also be more useful for any study which approaches families as one of a number of sources of assistance – along with neighbours, the Poor Law, friendly societies, churches, trade unions, voluntary hospitals, civic authorities – which individuals in nineteenth-century towns turned to in times of need.[45] This approach quickly takes family history into the subjects and concerns of social history more generally. The more these are investigated the more important it is that the analysis of family structure itself is community-minded.

[45] Anderson, *Family Structure*, pp. 136–61; Dupree, 'Family Structure in the Staffordshire Potteries', pp. 6–13, 20–6, 349–417.

Epilogue
Lawrence Stone – as seen by himself

This is the story of my intellectual Odyssey over the last fifty-some years through an ocean full of storms, whirlpools and hidden rocks. We can, I think, safely omit the first eight years of life, which are anyway only of interest to dedicated Freudians convinced that the personality is fixed in concrete at this period – and sexual concrete at that. All that might be significant during these years is that this is when I first became a fanatical collector – a collector of anything: postage stamps, butterflies, fossils, cigarette cards. There is obviously a relationship between this early but unfocused collecting instinct, and the adult pursuit by the scholar in libraries and archives of facts and yet more facts to buttress his hypotheses and illustrate and give plausibility – it would be impertinent to say proof – to his arguments.

At eight I went off to an English prep. school and there began to serve what was to prove an eight-year term as a slave in the intellectual salt-mines of intensive training in the classics. As a form of instruction, what I got was whimsically known at the time as 'a liberal education'. In reality it was an intensely narrow programme, a perverted derivative from the educational curriculum worked out 400 years earlier by Vives and Erasmus. By the 1930s it consisted of a mechanical and dreary memorization of the vocabulary and grammar of two long-dead languages. The pronunciation of one of them – Latin – was then taught in England in a manner altogether unintelligible either to the ancient Romans or to the twentieth-century natives of any other country. Thus, whereas my French father-in-law, when in a concentration camp during the Second World War, found it possible to communicate in Latin with Hungarian aristocrats and Polish intellectuals, the Latin I learnt –

the so-called 'old pronunciation' – could have served no such practical purpose.

What I did learn that was useful – though I learnt it the hard way, with blows as a punishment for error – were the rules of Latin grammar, which may perhaps have been helpful in improving my style in English later on. But I am even doubtful about that. Trained in this manner, it is easy to fall into the stately Ciceronian prose of rolling periods perfectly balanced one against the other. Much as I admire the prose of Gibbon and Lord Chesterfield, the style just does not suit me, for by nature I am most at ease in a free-wheeling atmosphere. Let me make the point by analogy. Once, at the age of twelve, I was thought to be a promising cricketer – a batsman. So my school hired a kindly but unimaginative elderly ex-professional cricketer to teach me to hold a straight bat. He succeeded only too well. My bat was forever straight but I never played a successful game again, for he had managed to kill my natural instinct to swipe the ball in a thoroughly unorthodox but effective manner. There is perhaps something to be learnt about teaching in general from this sad little story – a tragedy for me since I used to dream about playing for England one day.

What I acquired – and let me stress that during those eight years from eight to sixteen I was taught little else – was a facility in translating a London *Times* editorial from English prose into Latin prose, from Latin prose into Latin verse, from Latin verse into Greek prose, and from Greek prose back into English prose. You will have guessed that I was not very good at it, partly from natural ineptitude, partly from lack of will. I could not for the life of me see the point of it at all, and I still don't. Even the Latin books we read were dull. Virgil and Livy were, to my perhaps philistine sensibility, a bore. We were never introduced to books that would both stimulate our interest and provide useful information about adult life, such as Tacitus on the court politics of tyranny, or Ovid on the art of heterosexual love.

Like most people, I would imagine, I was eventually taught to love scholarship by a handful of gifted teachers. I will not dwell upon my experiences at an English public school – in my case Charterhouse – because this is a topic that novelists and autobiographers have already made something of a bore. If at the time I had known anything about social anthropology or the political theory of totalitarianism, I could have understood a great deal more. It would have helped, for example, if I had realized that what I was experiencing was merely an extended male puberty rite, very similar to those of many other, more primitive, societies in the world: total segregation from the other sex; regular beatings to be endured in stoical silence; humiliation rituals; a complex formal hierarchy symbolized by elaborate dress codes; inadequate food; sexual initiation by older males; and the learning of a secret language, in this case Latin.

I obtained my freedom from enslavement to the classics thanks to the direct intervention of a new headmaster, Sir Robert Birley, who single-handedly changed my life. He took me under his personal tuition, and in one and a half years of intensive coaching enabled me to obtain an open scholarship in history at Oxford. What made him so dazzlingly successful as a history teacher was his endless fund of enthusiasm for whatever topic happened to be uppermost in his mind.

Birley did not merely pull off the remarkable coup of training me in eighteen months to get a history scholarship to Oxford. He also changed the course of my intellectual development a second time: immediately after the examination, he dispatched me to Paris for six months' exposure to another European culture. There I first encountered (though not in the flesh) that remarkable phenomenon, the Paris mandarin intelligentsia, as well as the great *Annales* school of historians, then represented by Marc Bloch and Lucien Febvre. It was the beginning of a lifelong admiring but critical relationship with French intellectual culture which has deeply influenced my life of learning.

Let me return for a moment to Sir Robert Birley. He was an eccentric figure – half loyal member of England's ruling elite and of the Church of England, and half reforming rebel and idealistic visionary. As a young master at Eton, for example, he openly expressed his sympathy with the strikers during the General Strike of 1926, a position for which some people never forgave him. He was a headmaster first of Charterhouse, then of Eton, sandwiching in between a stint as Educational Adviser to the Deputy Military Governor of the British Zone of Germany after the war. Later he was Professor of Education at the University of Witwatersrand in Johannesburg. He was a conservative radical, whose nickname among the backwoods Etonian Tories was 'Red Robert'. He was not only a great teacher but a great moral reformer. Before the war he had fought Nazism, and spent hours trying to argue me out of my incipient pacifist tendencies. After the war he worked to bring a new generation of liberal Germans back into a federation of Europe. Later still, in the 1960s, he fought to bring education to the blacks of South Africa, personally conducting classes in Soweto; and finally he did his best to humanize and civilize those great barbarian institutions, the English public schools of Charterhouse and Eton.

If Sir Robert Birley provided the inspiration for my scholarly interests, and deeply affected my moral and political attitudes, the second great influence upon me was an Oxford medieval history tutor, John Prestwich by name. He was – indeed, still is – one of those all too common Oxford figures, with a towering local reputation but no international visibility for lack of publications. I studied the Third Crusade under him, as a special subject. At first, I would read my weekly essay, which he would then systematically demolish, leaving me with little but a pile of rubble. I finally decided that my only hope of self-defence was to overwhelm him with data. Since the prescribed texts were entirely taken from the writings of the Christian crusaders, I sought out little-known chronicles by Moslem Arabs, of which I found a fair number in French translation. Artfully, and with studied casualness, I inserted into my essays some recondite facts from these obscure and dubious sources, as a result of which I at least got Prestwich momentarily rattled. I never won the battle, my arguments were always effectively demolished, but even the minor victories improved my self-esteem. The experience taught me the importance of sheer factual information – erudition, if you like – in the cut-throat struggle for survival in the life of learning. I discovered that knowledge is power. It was the experience of that term with John Prestwich which made me decide to be an historian, and an archive-based historian at that.

The third great influence upon my development as an historian was R. H. Tawney. Every one knows about Tawney, the Christian socialist, at once the *eminence grise* and the conscience of the English labour movement in the first half of the twentieth century, the eloquent preacher of equality, the stern denunciator of the evils of unbridled capitalism, the reinterpreter to the Anglo-Saxon world of Weber's ideas about the relation of Protestantism to capitalism, and the great historian of 'Tawney's Century', the period 1540–1640 in England. He was a saintly, if not altogether practical, figure, the only person I have ever met who had a genuine dislike of money. He simply hated the stuff, and tried, as far as humanly possible, to do without it. It was his impassioned book about the sufferings of the sixteenth-century English peasantry from the enclosure of the land by ruthless capitalist landlords, and his equally impassioned denunciations of the evil and corrupt machinations of early modern merchants, entrepreneurs and money-lenders, which drew me to the sixteenth century, and stimulated two of my first forays into print.

I first met Tawney during the war, and I eagerly cultivated his company whenever I came back to London on leave from my ship. Although I was only an ignorant undergraduate from Oxford, and a sailor, he nevertheless always greeted me warmly. By then he had been bombed out of his house and was living in indescribable squalor in a leaky mews in Bloomsbury, surrounded by a chaos of books, papers, cats and left-over plates of food. Draft blueprints for the Labour Party's programme for a more egalitarian post-war Britain were jumbled up with notes on early seventeenth-century English social history and tattered yellowing fragments of jottings about the Chinese peasantry. I had many long talks with Tawney, bundled up in overcoats in these unappetizing surroundings, and I listened carefully to what he had to say, both about the state of the world and how it could be put right, and about seventeenth-century England. Listening carefully, I should add, was not easy, since one had constantly to be on guard lest he set himself on fire. This often happened when the long stalks of wild herbs, which he stuffed loosely into his pipe, caught fire and fell out on to his jacket or trousers, which as a result were always full of black burn holes.

What I learnt from Tawney was that the documents for early modern history were preserved in sufficient quantity to make it possible to enter into the very minds of the actors. This single fact converted me from a medievalist into an early modernist. Second, I learnt that in this period there had taken place in England nearly all the greatest transformations in the history of the West: the shifts from feudalism to capitalism, and from monolithic Catholicism to Christian pluralism, and later to secularism; the rise and fall of puritanism; the aborted evolution of the all-powerful nation-state; the first radical revolution in Western history; the first large-scale establishment of a relatively liberal polity with diffused power, religious toleration, and a bill of rights; and the creation of a society ruled by the landed elite unique in Europe for its entrepreneurship, paternalism, and near-monopoly of political power. Finally I learnt from Tawney, as I had from Birley, that history can be a moral as well as a scholarly enterprise, and that it ought not, and indeed cannot, be disassociated from a vision of the contemporary world and how it should be ordered.

The fourth important teacher to influence my thinking was yet another eccentric, Sir Keith Hancock, whom I did not meet until immediately after the war. It was his scholarly career and conversation which first proved to me that there was something to be said for an interdisciplinary and trans-cultural approach to history. For in his person and his writings he demonstrated that it was possible, and indeed fruitful, to know about such apparently diverse matters as land tenure in Tuscany, the career in South Africa of General Smuts, the economic development of Australia, and the history of modern warfare.

I was very lucky to have been brought at an early stage into contact with four such remarkable men. As a result of them, I survive today as something of a dinosaur, the last of the Whigs, and in many ways still a child of the Enlightenment. I emerged from their tutelage with an abiding faith in reason, in the possibility of limited material and moral progress, in paternalist responsible leadership, and in the rule of laws not men. It is a fading, tattered faith these days, a survival from that older liberal world of the Victorian professional class from which both Tawney and Birley sprang, and the ethos of which the Australian Hancock had absorbed during his long stay at All Souls College, Oxford.

During World War II, I spent five years at sea with the Royal Navy. As anyone who has experienced it knows, war is 99.9 per cent boredom and discomfort, and 0.1 per cent sheer terror. In my case the discomfort was substantially mitigated by occupation of a cabin – admittedly shared – and plentiful and regular supplies of food and, above all, alcohol. If there has ever been a just war in history, then this was it, and I do not regret my five-year diversion from the life of learning.

In fact the diversion was not complete, for I wrote my first historical article while navigator of a destroyer patrolling the South Atlantic. I may not have been a very good navigator of that destroyer – I confess I ran it aground twice – but at least I began my life of learning while on board. The subject of the article was the shameful treatment by the government of the English sailors who had taken part in the Armada Campaign of 1588. The topic was obviously related to my immediate experience, but what is of more interest is whence I got my data. The answer is from that characteristic mid-Victorian institution, the London Library, which right through World War II cheerfully and efficiently dispatched rare and valuable research books to the furthest ends of the earth, which often arrived some three to six months after they had been ordered. The contribution of that private library to the life of learning in Britain, especially during the war, can hardly be over-estimated.

The end of the war found me attached to the American Seventh Fleet off Japan. Immediately after the armistice, I was flown home from the Pacific, since for some unknown bureaucratic reason top priority for demobilization in Britain had been decreed for three classes of persons: coal-miners, clergymen – and students. The flight was one of my most dangerous experiences during the war, since the pilot was a psychological and physical wreck, with trembling hands, as a result of flying fifty missions over Germany. But it got me back to Oxford in early November 1945, just in time to enrol for the year, and so to take the final examination and graduate as a B.A. in June 1946. By paying an extra five pounds I also got an M.A. degree on the same occasion, so that I was a B.A. for only about ten minutes, just time to change my gown and hood. I submit that this may be something of a record, I must also be one of the few people alive today to have bought a degree from a major university for hard cash and no work at all.

I did not proceed to embark on a doctoral dissertation, since in those days this was still something that a graduate of Oxford or Cambridge felt to be beneath his dignity – a peculiar academic *rite de passage* that foreigners went in for, like Germans, or French, or Americans. Instead, I settled down with a research grant, and began, all by myself, to write a book, quite unaware of any foolhardiness in so doing. It was, of course, a terrible mistake, for I badly needed the close discipline and advice that only a conscientious official supervisor can provide. As a result, I had to learn from my own mistakes – and I made plenty.

I chose to write a biography of a late sixteenth-century entrepreneur, a financier of governments, an espionage agent, a diplomat engaged in the recruitment of mercenary armies, a world monopolist of alum (an essential raw material for the dyeing of cloth), and a business tycoon with a finger in many, usually unsavoury, pies. This bizarre figure began life as a member of a distinguished Genoese merchant family and ended it as a Cambridgeshire country squire with a wealthy Dutch wife and an English knighthood conferred by Queen Elizabeth. Urbane and unscrupulous rogue that he was, in the end I found that I got to like him, although the book (*An Elizabethan: Sir Horatio Palavicino*) certainly served my original purpose of illuminating the seamier side of early international finance capitalism.

My next topic was inspired by the seminal articles of R. H. Tawney about the rise of the gentry in the century before the English Civil War – a theory which, if stripped of its Marxist ideology about the rise of the bourgeoisie and some of its dubious statistical props, has in fact turned out to be largely true. My first preliminary foray into this area was a disaster. I published an article claiming that most of the late Elizabethan aristocracy was hovering on the verge of financial ruin. Unfortunately the data were badly handled by me. It was my tutor, Hugh Trevor-Roper, who had first drawn my attention to them, but without pointing out the problems inherent in their interpretation. This mistake of mine provided him with the opportunity for an article of vituperative denunciation which connoisseurs of intellectual terrorism still cherish to this day. What I learnt from this episode – learnt the hard way – is that before plunging into a public archive, it is first essential to discover just why and how the records were kept, and what they signified to the clerks who made the entries.

Before describing how I reacted to this setback, I must pause to explain a peculiar intellectual diversion: in 1946 I also began work on a large text-book on medieval English sculpture in a classic art history series edited by Sir Nikolaus Pevsner. This implausible venture into the field of professional art history came about in the following archetypical English way. First, that passion for collecting everything and anything, to which I have already referred, had somehow driven me in my middle teens to assemble photographs of English Romanesque sculpture. Equipped with a car – which cost all of three pounds – and a Kodak Box Brownie camera – which cost five shillings but happened by some miracle to have a near-perfect lens – I roamed the countryside during the holidays between 1936 and 1939, taking photographs of Romanesque sculpture in English churches. In 1938 I made contact with Sir Thomas Kendrick of the British Museum. He was then engaged on a national survey of Anglo-Saxon sculpture, and in his generous way took me – then still a schoolboy and first-year undergraduate – on his photographic team for two summer expeditions in 1938 and 1939.

After the war, in early 1946, Kendrick had been invited by Nikolaus Pevsner to write the volume on English Medieval Sculpture in his Pelican History of Art Series. He declined, perhaps because he already had hopes of becoming Director of the British Museum, as happened soon after. Asked who could do the job instead, Kendrick, who was *not* a cautious man, named me. I was at that moment a history undergraduate at Oxford; I had never taken a course in art history or written a line about it in my life; and I had only just come back from five years at sea. Trained in the professional German school of art history, Pevsner was understandably horrified by Kendrick's irresponsible suggestion. But he felt he had to give me a contract, for reasons which he explained to me very frankly when we met: 'Tom Kendrick won't do it', he said, 'and there appears to be no one else in the country in the least interested in the subject. Kendrick says that I should give you a contract. I don't trust you at all, for you have absolutely no credentials for the job, but I don't see what else I can do. I would like to see a draft chapter as soon as possible.' On this rather menacing note our interview ended, and a few days later I happily signed the contract. Secretly, I was as uneasy as Pevsner himself about the capacity to pull it off of this ignorant, ill-educated, amateur ex-sailor and now undergraduate. This bizarre episode could only have happened in a society like England, which had remained as profoundly imbued with the cult of the amateur as it had been in the eighteenth-century heyday of the virtuoso. The episode was also only possible in a society which still operated on the eighteenth-century patronage network system, in which a tiny entrenched elite distributed jobs and favours to their clients, friends and protegés.

Before resuming the narrative, something should be said about the intellectual atmosphere at Oxford in those far-off days just after World War II. In the mode of teaching and in the prescribed curriculum for the examination in the School of Modern (as opposed to Ancient) History at Oxford, nothing much had changed since its foundation at the end of the nineteenth century. It was a curriculum stifling both in its national insularity and in its limited late Victorian conception of what subjects were embraced within the canon of historical scholarship. It was perfectly possible and indeed normal to graduate with first-class honours without having studied the history of any continent save Europe and indeed with only minimal knowledge of any country but England – not even Scotland or hapless Ireland. It was also not unusual to have studied little or no social, economic, demographic, cultural, artistic, intellectual, educational or familial history, and to be wholly innocent of any contact with quantitative methodology or the history of the working class. The social sciences were unknown, or if known were cordially despised. On the other hand, under the guidance of gifted and dedicated tutors, the undergraduate education offered by Oxford was unsurpassed in its capacity to teach swift and clear writing, to encourage careful analysis of the evidence, and to produce a mind open to varying interpretations of a single event or set of events. I consider myself extremely lucky to have had that remarkable experience.

In Britain, the post-war period was a time of boundless optimism and confidence – a fact which is hard to remember, much less to comprehend, in these depressed and disillusioned post-imperial times, when England has sunk to the level of a third-rate power in almost all fields of endeavour except those of the pure intellect. To us young men who returned from the war in 1945, the whole world seemed to be our oyster, and all problems of scholarship – to say nothing of those of suffering humanity – were thought to be soluble. Some of this confidence in the future may have been stimulated by close co-habitation with our American Allies during the war. At all events, this was an optimism shared by nuclear physicists, Oxford philosophers, social historians and Keynesian economists, as well as politicians. I well remember a dinner conversation with Peter Strawson, today one of Oxford's most distinguished philosophers, during which he expressed his anxiety about what he would find to do in his late middle age, since it was clear from the way things were going that by then there would be no major philosophical problems left to solve. In history, some of us had much the same hubristic confidence in a wholly new approach. We were dedicated converts to the *Annales* school of history based in Paris, and we were certain that the most intractable problems of history would soon fall to the assaults of quantitative social and economic investigation. The political narrative mode of our elders – 'L'histoire historisante' as it was derogatively called – was beneath our contempt. In time, we believed, such hitherto unsolved problems as the causes of the English or the French Revolutions, or the origins of capitalism and the rise of the bourgeoisie, would be solved by our new tools and new approaches. Bliss it was to be alive and a radical social historian in 1945. We waited breathlessly for each new issue of *Annales* or the *Economic History Review*, every one of which seemed to contain an article which opened up great new vistas of historical exploration and interpretation. I stress this atmosphere of self-confidence and heady excitement, since nothing could be more different from the self-doubt, uncertainty, caution and scepticism about the very existence of truth or about ways to get at it, which afflicts all branches of the humanities today.

Inspired by the mood of optimism of the late 1940s about the possibilities of the new social history, and stung by Trevor-Roper's onslaught on my scholarly credentials, I decided to undertake a large-scale investigation into the economic resources and management, social status and military and political power, lifestyle, values, education and family structure, of the English aristocracy in the century before the outbreak of the English Revolution. My initial assumption had been that the English aristocracy in that period was the epitome of an incompetent, frivolous and decadent ruling class about to be set aside by a rising bourgeoisie. Fifteen years of careful investigation, however, convinced me that this simplistic model failed to fit the facts. The Marxist interpretation of the role of the aristocracy in the English Revolution, with which I had set out, had been shattered by close contact with the empirical evidence.

The solution to my dilemma came from my belated discovery of Max Weber, whose writings, as they slowly appeared in more or less intelligible English translations, have probably influenced me more than those of any other single scholar. Weber's subtle distinction between class and status, and his intense preoccupation with the relationship of ideas and ideology to social and political reality, have guided my thinking and inspired my research from the mid-1950s to the present day.

But the influence of neither Marx nor Weber explains why I have chosen to spend most of my life of learning studying the acts, behaviour and thoughts of a ruling elite, rather than of the masses. One justification for such concentration upon so tiny a minority is that this is the only group whose lives and thoughts and passions are recorded in sufficient detail to make possible investigation in full social and psychological depth. Only this handful were fully literate, in the sense that they wrote continually to each other and about each other, and their writings have been preserved. If one wishes to discover the quirks and quiddities of personality, the intimacies of love and hate and lust, the revelations of financial speculation or rascality, the backstairs intrigues of power and status, one is inexorably forced to concentrate one's attention upon the elite, since the evidence about individuals in the past much below this high social level only rarely exists. Although I have relied heavily upon quantification – most of my books and articles contain graphs and tables – I have always been primarily concerned with people, following the maxim of Marc Bloch: 'Ma proie, c'est l'homme.' In this pursuit I have been inexorably drawn to the elite.

The other justification for concentration on the elite is that it was from this group that for centuries were drawn the political rulers of the country, and the patrons and principal consumers of its high culture. An Englishman, far more than the resident in any other Western country, does not have to read Pareto to learn about the dominance of elites. From his earliest childhood he is made acutely aware of the horizontal layering of the society in which he lives. This elaborate stratification is displayed even today at every moment by such external features as accent, vocabulary, clothes, table manners, and even physical size and shape. I have therefore spent the best part of my life following the trails left in the records by that English landed elite which for so many centuries largely monopolized so much of the three great Weberian entities of wealth, status and power.

As it happened, I could not have chosen a better moment than the late 1940s in which to plunge into the private archives of the English aristocracy, which for the first time had become accessible, thanks to the financial plight of their owners. For fifteen years I enjoyed the dizzy excitement of turning over and reading in archive rooms, cellars and attics great masses of papers which no one had ever examined before. The most dramatic moment always came on first sight of a private archive, which could range from the supremely orderly to the supremely chaotic. At one great house, the late duke had spent a lifetime sorting, cataloguing, and filing his huge collection of family papers, and in his last illness was said to have asked to be taken down to the archive room and laid on the work table in order to die amid his beloved papers. His son was a playboy, too busy chasing girls to bother answering the importunate letters of scholars. But by sheer luck, a telephone call was answered by his aged nanny, who graciously agreed to let me into what turned out to be an amazing and amazingly well-ordered archive, filling several rooms. I believe I was the first person to sit at that table since the removal of the late duke's corpse.

At another great seat I scribbled away in the depths of winter huddled up in an overcoat and blankets at one end of a long freezing room, while at the other end two aged servants sat beside a small flickering coal fire, leisurely polishing the seventeenth-century armour for the benefit of next summer's tourists, and gossiping endlessly – and maliciously – about their master and mistress. When my fingers became too cold to hold the pen, I would join them round the fire for a few moments. It was a scene which could well have occurred in the seventeenth century.

Another house had been gutted by fire some thirty years earlier, but the contents of the archive room had been saved and thrown pell-mell into a room above the old stables, now the garage. Squeezing past his huge Rolls Royce, the owner led the way up the creaking stairs, turned the key in the rusty lock and pushed the door. Nothing happened. Further forceful pushing nudged it partly open, revealing a great sea of paper and parchment covering the whole floor to the height of one to three feet. The only way to enter was to step on this pile, and, as I trod gingerly, seals of all ages from the thirteenth to the nineteenth century cracked and crunched under my feet. Rarely have I felt so guilty, but the guilt was later assuaged by being instrumental in getting the great archive deposited in the local record office for safe-keeping and cataloguing.

Occasionally the owner of the papers would invite me to lunch. The experience was nearly always the same: a spectacularly elegant dining-room with millions of dollars worth of pictures on the wall; exquisite wine; execrable food, so unappetizing that it was often very hard to swallow; and erratic service provided by a bedraggled and sometimes rather drunken butler. Such were the pleasures and pains of the life of learning, as I wrote my book on *The Crisis of the Aristocracy*.

During the late 1950s, the expansion of my interests, which first began with the discovery of Weber, was further stimulated by two events. The first was that in 1958 I joined the Editorial Board of *Past and Present*, which in my – admittedly prejudiced – opinion is one of the two best historical journals in the world (*Annales: Economies, Sociétés, Civilisations*. being the other). At that time the Board was equally divided between Marxists (many of them long-term members of the Communist Party who had only recently resigned after the Russian invasion of Hungary), and liberals like myself. But although it is a very active and contentious board there has never been an occasion, so far as I can recall, in which the division of opinion has been on ideological lines of Marxists versus liberals. This is a small fact about English intellectual history, which is, I believe, worth recording, although I have no explanation to offer for it.

The second event which turned out to have a major influence on my life as a scholar was the shift from Oxford to Princeton in 1963. This move – the most sensible thing I ever did in my life apart from getting married – was made partly as the result of push – I was tired of the insurmountable disciplinary ring-fence erected at Oxford around the core of English political and constitutional history, and also of the crushing burden of many hours of monotonous tutorial teaching; and partly as a result of pull – the open-mindedness to new ideas and new disciplines and new areas of the world which I had observed at Princeton on a visit two years before to the Institute for Advanced Study. At Princeton, I discovered two things. The first was a world of historical scholarship, embracing not only all of Europe, but also America (of whose history at the time of my arrival I knew nothing) as well as the Near East, and East Asia. One of the earliest results of this totally new world view was a joint article, written with my colleague and friend Marius Jansen, comparing education and the modernizing process in England and Japan.

Another area of scholarship which for a few years in the 1960s greatly influenced my interpretation of historical development was the work then being done by American political theorists on the problems of 'modernization' and revolution. In retrospect, I think that my enthusiasm for their model-building was probably exaggerated, but at least they provided me with two valuable tools with which to break open the tough nut of *The Causes of the English Revolution* of the mid-seventeenth century, a book I published in

1972. The first was the somewhat arbitrary but useful division of causes of such an explosion into long-term, medium-term and short-term. The second was the concept of 'relative deprivation', which allowed me to break free from the fallacious necessity of relating observed behaviour to objective conditions of life. But in doing so, I fell into a small puddle of jargon, freely using words like 'pre-conditions', 'precipitants', 'triggers', 'multiple dysfunction', 'J curve' and so on. All this and relative deprivation theory annoyed my English critics, who enjoyed themselves making a mockery of my enthusiasm for these new-fangled transatlantic words and concepts from the social sciences. If I were writing the book today, I would use jargon more discriminately.

Another great discovery made at Princeton was the scope and range of computerized quantitative historical studies then in progress in the United States. In my enthusiasm for this brave new world, I first conceived and then obtained funds for a massive statistical investigation of social mobility in the higher reaches of English society from the sixteenth to the nineteenth centuries. The tasks of directing the researchers, encoding the data, negotiating with the computer programmer and making summary tables from vast stacks of green print-out were fortunately undertaken by my wife, who spent fifteen years working on this project. My own work was interrupted, for reasons I will explain in a moment, and the results were published only last year in our book *An Open Elite? England 1540–1880*.

Political theory and computerized quantification are far from being the only novelties I found on arrival at Princeton. Another influence on my intellectual evolution at that time was the writings of the sociologist R. K. Merton, from whom I learnt, amongst other things, the importance of medium-range generalization. This search for the Aristotelian mean in terms of problems to be solved is, in my view, the best safeguard against shipwreck on the Scylla of unverifiable global speculation, or the Charybdis of empirical research so narrow in scope and positivistic in attitude that it is of little concern to anyone except one or two fellow-specialists, as practised by so many young scholars today.

Although we were colleagues at Oxford, it was only after arrival at Princeton that I first discovered the work of the great anthropologist Evans-Pritchard, and more recently still that I came under the influence of the newer school of symbolic anthropologists whose most eminent and most elegant practitioner is my friend Clifford Geertz. Above all, the contribution of the anthropologists has been to alert historians to the power of 'thick description' – that is, how a close and well-informed look at seemingly trivial acts, events, symbols, gestures, patterns of speech or behaviour can be made to reveal whole systems of thought; and to draw our attention to problems of kinship, lineage or community structures, whose significance would have eluded us without their guidance.

Finally, interest in the history of the family and sexual relations inevitably drew me to psychology. Here I found Freud less than helpful, partly because his time-bound late nineteenth-century mid-European values cannot be projected back on to the past, and partly because of the fundamentally ahistorical cast of his thought which assumes that the human personality is more or less fixed for life in the first few months or years. The developmental models evolved by more recent ego-psychologists, such as Erik Erikson or Jerome Kagan, are much more useful to the working historian interested in the continuous interplay of nature and nurture, of innate drives and over-riding cultural conditioning. Freud certainly admits to such cultural configurations in his *Civilization and its Discontents*, but only in a negative and pessimistic way.

Before summing up, I must explain why it was that I interrupted my quantitative project on elite mobility for some five years to write a large book on *Family, Sex and Marriage in England 1500–1800*. It is a work based almost entirely on non-quantitative printed literary materials mainly from the elite class, and it lays as much stress on emotional as on structural developments. It came about this way. I had long been tinkering with a lecture on the family, when in 1973 I suffered a mild heart attack and was hospitalized for six weeks without telephone, visitors or other contacts with the outside world. I felt perfectly fit and, allowing eight hours a day for sleep, there stretched before me the prospect of being able to read without interruption by anyone for sixteen hours a day for forty-two days. If my mathematics are correct – which some think they rarely are – this adds up to a total of 672 hours of reading. I therefore instructed my wife to remove from the university library shelves all English collections of family letters, autobiographies, advice books, journals, etc. from the sixteenth, seventeenth and eighteenth centuries, and bring them to my bedside, along with a substantial supply of paper. Thus armed, I read and read and read, and emerged six weeks later with almost enough material to write a book. Hence the diversion from the computerized project on social mobility, to which I returned five years later in 1977.

Throughout my time at Oxford and Princeton, I have never wavered in my (always qualified) admiration for the *Annales* school of historians in Paris. But it is a reflection of the change of time and mood that today, while retaining my deep admiration for the *Annales* group as the most talented, innovative and influential historians in the world, I none the less have developed certain reservations about their basic principles and methods, which were expressed in my notorious article on 'The Revival of Narrative', published in 1979. I am unconvinced that their favourite methodological division between static '*structure*' and dynamic '*conjuncture*' is always the best approach. Even less do I accept their three-tiered model of causal factors in history, rising from the economic and demographic base through the middle layer of the social structure to the derivative superstructure of ideology, religion, political beliefs and *mentalité*. This wedding-cake mode of analysis presupposes the predominance of material factors over cultural ones – which I reject – and also precludes the possibility, so well brought out by Max Weber, that the three levels are in a constant state of dynamic interaction, rather than in a hierarchy of domination and dependence.

Finally, there is a strong positivist materialism behind the thirst of the *Annales* school for quantifiable data about the physical world, which even in the immediate post-war period I found impossible to accept without reservations. For example, despite its enormous length, the most brilliant pioneer work of this school, Fernand Braudel's *The Mediterranean in the Reign of Philip II*, barely mentions religion, either Christianity or Islam.

My 1979 article on the revival of narrative was explicitly intended as a statement of observed fact about the way the profession of history was going, and not at all as a prescriptive signpost for the future. It was designed to bring out into the open a subterranean drift back to something I loosely – and I now think misleadingly – defined as 'narrative'. The paper was taken in many quarters, however, as a programmatic call to arms against social science quantification and analytical history. Agitated defenders, fearful for their turf and their grants, criticized my alleged betrayal of the good old cause in almost every journal in the profession. More in sorrow than in anger, my old friend Robert Fogel, in his Presidential address to the Social Science History Association, solemnly excommunicated me from that church. In some quarters I became an instant pariah. And yet in the subsequent few years my prophecy has, I believe, been fully vindicated. Except in economic history, where it still reigns supreme, old-style grandiose cliometric social science history now has its back to the wall. More humanistic and more narrative approaches to history are indeed growing, microhistory of a single individual or an event is becoming a fashionable genre, and a new kind of political history, now firmly anchored in the social and ideological matrix, is reviving. Even intellectual history – no longer that dreary 'History of Ideas' paper-chase that always ended up with either Plato or Aristotle – has undergone an astonishing transformation and resurgence.

All my work has been based on two fundamental hypotheses about how the historical process works. The first is that great events must have important causes, and not merely trivial ones. The second is that all great events must have multiple causes. This eclectic approach towards causation has given rise to a certain amount of negative criticism. Many scholars whose judgement I respect have described the assemblage of a multiplicity of causes for any given phenomenon as 'a shopping list', the mere unweighted enumeration of a whole series of variables of widely different types and significance. This is true, but an argument for multiple causation can be made on the grounds used by Max Weber. They are convincing, provided that they form a set of 'elective affinities', held together not by mere random chance but by a system of logical integration that points them all in the same direction and makes them mutually reinforcing. Despite the criticism, therefore, I still adhere to a feed-back model of mutually reinforcing trends, rather than a linearly ordered hierarchy of causal factors. I do admit, however, that sometimes I have neglected to show just how this glue of 'elective affinities' has in practice worked.

Looking back on it, it is clear that what is peculiar about my intellectual career is that I have never stayed long in one place. Most historians select a single fairly narrow field as their own intellectual territory, and spend a lifetime cultivating that same ground with more and more tender loving care. The advantage of such a procedure is that one becomes the world expert on that patch of turf, building a framework of knowledge, expertise and experience which is cumulative over a lifetime. I have deliberately followed a different course, preferring to roam unusually freely across the historical prairie, although I have confined myself to a single culture, namely that of England, and mostly to a single class, the landed elite. But first, I have ranged over time from the Middle Ages to the nineteenth century. Second, I have jumped from topic to topic, from biography to economic history to art history to social history to cultural history to educational history to family history. Third, conscious from an early age of the provisional nature of historical wisdom, I have moved in a restless quest for theories, concepts, approaches and models more satisfying than the old, and in methodological inspiration from Marx to Weber to some of the modern American social scientists, first sociologists, then political theorists, and more recently anthropologists.

This drift from century to century, this flitting from topic to topic, and these changes in inspiration have inevitably brought their dangers and defects. First, they have meant working very fast, a process which can lead to mistakes, often minor but sometimes serious. Second, the level of my scholarly expertise in any single topic in any single century in any part of England is inevitably less than that of one who has spent a lifetime tilling that particular field. Third, the desire to bring order and shape to a complex problem, such as the causes of the English Revolution or the evolution of the family, has inevitably given rise to overschematization and generalizations which need more qualification. After all, there are no generalizations, in history or any other discipline, which do not need more qualification. And fourth, the fact that my range of expertise is primarily concentrated upon the elite at the top of the social pyramid has sometimes led to rash and ill-informed assertions about the behaviour of the lower classes. These are the reasons why so many more cautious academic reviewers, on receiving a new book of mine, instinctively reach for their pens and write: 'There he goes again.' On the other hand, I have been saved – if saved is the right word – from Parsonian functionalism, French structuralism and linguistic deconstruction, partly by my inability to understand what they are all about, but mainly by a gut feeling that they are too simplistic and must be wrong.

I have always been concerned with public affairs, the effect of which upon the life of learning has taken two forms. First, I have tried to save myself from being trapped in an academic ivory tower by reaching out for a larger audience. This has meant reviewing – often rather critically – a wide range of books for journals with a large national readership. This is of course a high-risk policy that usually brings its punishment, for many of my victims sooner or later find their revenge by savaging a book of mine. In addition to reviewing in national journals, I have tried to make my books accessible to the general public, by following the production of a large-scale academic study in hard covers with that of a cheap paperback abridged version.

One result of this concern with the world outside academia has been more profound in its consequences. Although it was not clear to me at the time, it is obvious upon reflection that the subject matter of my historical interest in the past has tended to shift in reaction to current events and current values. My first article, on the life of seamen in the Elizabethan navy, was written in 1942 on board a destroyer in the South Atlantic Ocean. My next enterprise, a book about a crooked international financier, was largely written in the socialist euphoria of the early days of the first British Labour government after the war. The third, on the aristocracy of the late sixteenth and early seventeenth centuries, was researched at a time when that class was in full financial crisis, and when great country houses were being abandoned and allowed to tumble down by the score. My work on students and faculty at universities began in the 1960s during one of the eras of greatest expansion, and of greatest optimism about higher education, that have ever existed. At that time, I was particularly intrigued by the causes of a similar educational boom between 1560 and 1680. My interest continued, in a more pessimistic vein, after the student troubles of 1968–70, and after the period of heady expansion and affluence had come to an abrupt end. My attention thereafter has been focused on the causes of the dramatic decline of enrolments in grammar schools, universities and Inns of Court between 1680 and 1770. My book on the family, sexuality and marriage was conceived and written in the 1970s, at a time of heightened anxiety about just these issues, provoked by rocketing divorce rates, sharply declining marital fertility, much greater sexual promiscuity, changes in sex-roles caused by the women's liberation movement, and the abrupt rise in the proportion of married women in the labour force.

An Open Elite was written at a time when the demise of the great landed families, and their role in both the rise and the fall of British greatness, were reaching a crescendo of public interest, for example in the phenomenal success of the television version of Evelyn Waugh's *Brideshead Revisited* or of Mark Girouard's book, *The English Country House*. It was begun when the elite who lived in these houses was thought to be in its death-throes, and when critics were blaming English contemporary decline on the absorption of the sons of Victorian entrepreneurs into the idle lifestyle and amateurish value system of the entrenched landed elite.

Although I was not aware of it at the time, I seem to have been constantly stimulated by current events into diving back into the past to discover whether similar trends and problems have occurred before, and if so how they were handled. Whether this makes for better or worse history, I do not know. A serious danger in such a present-minded inspiration for historical inquiry, however unconscious, is that the past will be seen through the perspective of the future and not in its own terms. There is a clear risk of Whiggish teleological distortion if the main question uppermost in the mind of the historian is how we got from there to here. On the other hand, it is just this explanation of the present which is the prime justification for an interest in history. The main safeguard from teleological distortion is to keep firmly in mind that people in the past were different from ourselves, and that this difference must always be investigated and explicated. The further safeguard is always to bear in mind that there is a contingency factor in history, a recognition that at all times there were alternative possibilities open, which might have occurred but in fact did not: the Cleopatra's nose principle, if you will.

This then, for the time being, is the end of my chequered Odyssey through the life of learning. I have constantly been under attack from ogres, dragons and sea-serpents; I have several times been seduced by attractive-seeming sirens; I have made mistakes of navigation, which at least once brought me close to shipwreck. Although I have survived and sailed on, I have not yet set eyes upon the shores of Ithaca. But the story is not, I hope, yet over.

Appendix. Lawrence Stone: a bibliography, 1944–87

BOOKS

Sculpture in Britain: The Middle Ages (Harmondsworth: Pelican Books, 1955; xxi, 297 pp. 2nd edition, revised, London: Penguin Books, 1972; xxii, 297 pp.)

An Elizabethan: Sir Horatio Palavicino (Oxford: Clarendon Press, 1956; xxi, 345 pp.)

The Crisis of the Aristocracy, 1558–1641 (Oxford: Clarendon Press, 1965; xxiv, 841 pp. Abridged edition, Oxford: Oxford University Press, 1967; xiii, 363 pp. Italian edition [trans. Aldo Serafini], Torino: G. Einaudi, 1972; xxiii, 925 pp. Spanish abridged edition [trans. M. R. Alonso], Madrid: Revista de Occidente, 1976; 356 pp.

Social Change and Revolution in England, 1540–1640 (London: Longmans Green & Company, and New York: Barnes and Noble, 1965; xxvi, 186 pp. Introduction revised in chapter 2 of *The Causes of the English Revolution.*)

The Causes of the English Revolution, 1529–1642 (London: Routledge and Kegan Paul, and New York: Harper and Row, 1972; xiv, 168 pp. French edition, Paris: Flammarion, 1974. Japanese edition, Tokyo: Mirai Sha, 1978. Italian edition, 1982. German edition, Berlin: Ullstein Verlag, 1983. 2nd edition, revised, London: Ark Paperbacks, 1986, xv, 185 pp.)

Family and Fortune: Studies in Aristocratic Finance in the 16th and 17th Centuries (Oxford: Clarendon Press, 1973; xvii, 315 pp.)

The Family, Sex and Marriage in England, 1500–1800 (London: Weidenfeld and Nicolson, and New York: Harper and Row, 1977; xxxi, 800 pp. Abridged edition, Harmondsworth, Middlesex: Penguin Books, and New York: Harper and Row, 1979; 446 pp. Italian edition, Torino: Giulio Einaudi Editore; Japanese edition, Keiso Shobo; Spanish edition, Madrid: Fondo de Cultura Economica.)

The Past and the Present (London and Boston: Routledge and Kegan Paul, 1981; xii, 274 pp. Spanish edition, Madrid: Fondo de Cultura Economica, 1986. Italian edition, Bari: Giuseppe Laterza & Figli, 1987. reprinted with six new chapters as *The Past and the Present Revisited.*)

An Open Elite? England 1540–1880 [with Jeanne C. Fawtier Stone] (Oxford: Clarendon Press, 1984; xxv, 566 pp. Abridged edition, Oxford: Oxford University Press, 1986; xv, 320 pp.)
The Past and the Present Revisited (London and New York: Routledge and Kegan Paul, 1987; xii, 440 pp.)

EDITED BOOKS

The University in Society, vol. 1, *Oxford and Cambridge from the Fourteenth to the Early Nineteenth Century*; vol. 2, *Europe, Scotland and the United States from the Sixteenth to the Twentieth Century* (Princeton: Princeton University Press, 1974, and Oxford: Oxford University Press, 1975, ix, 642 pp.)
Schooling and Society: Studies in the History of Education (Baltimore: The Johns Hopkins University Press, 1976; xvii, 263 pp.)

CONTRIBUTIONS TO BOOKS

'Anglo-Saxon Art', in R. B. Pugh and E. Crittall, eds., *A History of Wiltshire* (London: Oxford University Press, 1955), vol. 2, pp. 35–41.
'The Fruits of Office: The Case of the First Earl of Salisbury', in F. J. Fisher, ed., *Essays in the Social and Economic History of Tudor and Stuart England: Essays in Honour of R. H. Tawney* (Cambridge: Cambridge University Press, 1961), pp. 89–116.
'Wroxton', in M. D. Lobel and A. Crossley, eds., *A History of the County of Oxford* (London: Oxford University Press for the University of London, Institute for Historical Research, 1969), vol. 9, pp. 171–88.
'The English Revolution', in R. Foster and J. P. Greene, eds., *Preconditions of Revolution in Early Modern Europe* (Baltimore: The Johns Hopkins University Press, 1970), pp. 55–108. [Revised in chapter 3 of *The Causes of the English Revolution*.]
'Cole Green Park, Hertfordshire', in H. M. Colvin and J. Harris, eds., *The Country Seat: Studies in the History of the British Country House, presented to Sir John Summerson* (London: Allen Lane, 1970), pp. 75–80.
'Country Houses and Their Owners in Hertfordshire, 1530–1879' [with Jeanne C. Fawtier Stone], in W. O. Aydelotte, A. Bogue, and R. W. Fogel, eds., *Dimensions of Quantitative Research in History* (Princeton: Princeton University Press, 1972), pp. 56–103.
'The Size and Composition of the Oxford Student Body, 1580–1910', in L. Stone, ed., *The University in Society* (Princeton: Princeton University Press, 1974), vol. 1, pp. 3–110.
'The Rise of the Nuclear Family in Early Modern England', in C. E. Rosenberg, ed., *The Family in History* (Philadelphia: University of Pennsylvania Press, 1975), pp. 13–57.

'History and the Social Sciences in the Twentieth Century', in C. F. Delzell, ed., *The Future of History: Essays in the Vanderbilt Centennial Symposium* (Nashville: Vanderbilt University Press, 1977), pp. 3–42. Reprinted in chapter 1 of *The Past and the Present* and *The Past and the Present Revisited*.

'The Results of the English Revolutions of the 17th Century', in J. G. A. Pocock, ed., *Three British Revolutions: 1641, 1688, 1776* (Princeton: Princeton University Press, 1980), pp. 24–107.

'The Residential Development in the West End of London in the 17th Century', in B. Malament, ed., *After the Reformation: Essays in Honor of J. H. Hexter* (Philadelphia: University of Pennsylvania Press, 1980), pp. 167–212.

'Social Control and Intellectual Excellence: Oxbridge and Edinburgh 1560–1983', in N. T. Phillipson, ed., *Universities, Society and the Future* (Edinburgh: Edinburgh University Press, 1983), pp. 1–29.

'Passionate Attachments in the West in Historical Perspective', in W. Gaylin and E. Person, eds., *Passionate Attachments: Thinking About Love* (New York: The Free Press, 1988), pp. 15–26.

ARTICLES

'The Armada Campaign of 1588', *History*, 29 (1944), pp. 120–43.

'State Control in Sixteenth Century England', *Economic History Review*, 17 (1947), pp. 103–20.

'The Anatomy of the Elizabethan Aristocracy', *Economic History Review*, 18 (1948), pp. 1–53.

'Elizabethan Overseas Trade', *Economic History Review*, 2nd series, 2 (1949–50), pp. 30–57.

'An Elizabethan Coalmine', *Economic History Review*, 2nd series, 3 (1950–1), pp. 97–106.

'The Political Programme of Thomas Cromwell', *Bulletin of the Institute of Historical Research*, 24 (1951), pp. 1–18.

'The Elizabethan Aristocracy – A Restatement', *Economic History Review*, 2nd series, 4 (1951–2), pp. 302–21.

'The Building of Hatfield House', *Archaeological Journal*, 112 (1955), pp. 100–28.

'The Verney Tomb at Middle Claydon', *Records of Buckinghamshire*, 16 (1955–6), pp. 67–82.

'The Electoral Influence of the Second Earl of Salisbury', *English Historical Review*, 71 (1956), pp. 384–400.

'Inigo Jones and the New Exchange', *Archaeological Journal*, 114 (1957), pp. 106–21.

'The Nobility in Business: 1540–1640', *Explorations in Entrepreneurial History*, 10 (1957), pp. 54–61.

'The Inflation of Honours: 1558–1641', *Past and Present*, 14 (1958), pp. 45–70.

'Companies of Players Entertained by the Earl of Cumberland and Lord Clifford, 1607–39', *Malone Society Collections*, 5 (1960), pp. 17–28.

'The Peer and the Alderman's Daughter', *History Today*, 11 (1961), pp. 48–55.

'Marriage Among the Nobility in the Sixteenth and Seventeenth Centuries', *Comparative Studies in Society and History*, 3 (1961), pp. 182–206 [with reply to W. J. Goode, p. 215].

'The Educational Revolution in England: 1560–1640', *Past and Present*, 28 (1964), pp. 41–80.

'The Howard Tombs at Framlingham, Suffolk' [with Howard Colvin], *Archaeological Journal*, 122 (1965), pp. 159–71.

'Social Mobility in England: 1500–1700', *Past and Present*, 33 (1966), pp. 16–55.

'Theories of Revolution', *World Politics*, 18 (1966), pp. 159–76. Revised in chapter 1 of *The Causes of the English Revolution*.

'Education and Modernization in Japan and England' [with Marius B. Jansen], *Comparative Studies in Society and History*, 9 (1967), pp. 208–32.

'Office Under Queen Elizabeth: The Case of Lord Hunsdon and the Lord Chamberlainship in 1585', *Historical Journal*, 10 (1967), pp. 279–85.

'Literacy and Education in England: 1640–1900', *Past and Present*, 42 (1969), pp. 69–139.

'Prosopography', *Daedalus*, 100 (1971), pp. 46–79. Reprinted in chapter 2 of *The Past and the Present* and *The Past and the Present Revisited*.

'Patriarchy and Paternalism in Tudor England: The Earl of Arundel and the Peasants' Revolt of 1549', *Journal of British Studies*, 13 (1974), pp. 19–23.

'The Revival of Narrative: Reflections on a New Old History', *Past and Present*, 85 (1979), pp. 3–24. Translated by L. Évrard as 'Retour au récit, ou reflexions sur une nouvelle vieille histoire', *Le Debat* (1980) and as 'Il Ritorno alla narrazione: reflessionio su una vecchia nuova storia', *Comunita*, 35 (1981), pp. 1–25. Reprinted in chapter 3 of *The Past and the Present* and *The Past and the Present Revisited*.

'Family History in the 1980s: Past Achievements and Future Trends', *Journal of Interdisciplinary History*, 12 (1981), pp. 51–87.

'Az Angol Forradolom [The English Revolution]', *Világtörténet*, 2 (1981), pp. 19–44.

'Interpersonal Violence in English Society: 1300–1980', *Past and Present*, 101 (1983), pp. 22–33. Revised in chapter 16 of *The Past and the Present Revisited*.

'L'Angleterre de 1540 à 1880: Pays de Noblesse Ouverte?' [trans. J. C. F. Stone], *Annales ESC*, 40 (1985), pp. 71–94.

'The Bourgeois Revolution of Seventeenth Century England Revisited', *Past and Present*, 109 (1985), pp. 44–54.

'A Life of Learning', *American Council of Learned Societies Newsletter*, 36 (1985), pp. 3–22.

'Inheritance Strategies among the English Landed Elite 1540–1880', *Collection de l'École Française de Rome*, 90 (1986), pp. 267–90.

REVIEW ESSAYS

'History A La Mode', review of C. V. Wedgewood, *A Coffin for King Charles*, in *New York Review of Books*, 3 (10 September 1964), pp. 7–8.

'Pieter Geyl', review of Pieter Geyl, *The Netherlands in the Seventeenth Century*, vols. 1 and 2, and *ibid.*, *History of the Low Countries*, in *New York Review of Books*, 4 (8 April 1965), pp. 29–30. Revised in chapter 6 of *The Past and the Present* and in chapter 7 of *The Past and the Present Revisited*.

'England's Revolution', review of C. Hill, *Intellectual Origins of the English Revolution*, in *New York Review of Books*, 5 (26 August 1965), pp. 18–20.

'The Century of Crisis', review of T. Aston, ed., *Crisis in Europe, 1560–1660*; M. Walzer, *The Revolution of the Saints*; P. Laslett, *The World We Have Lost*, in *New York Review of Books*, 6 (3 March 1966), pp. 13–16. Revised in chapter 7 of *The Past and the Present* and in chapter 10 of *The Past and the Present Revisited*.

'That Was the Reformation That Was', review of A. G. Dickens, *Reformation and Society in Sixteenth Century Europe*, and G. R. Elton, *Reformation Europe, 1517–1559*, in *New York Review of Books*, 7 (29 December 1966), pp. 15–18. Revised in chapter 4 of *The Past and the Present* and *The Past and the Present Revisited*.

'News from Everywhere', review of B. Moore, Jr, *Social Origins of Dictatorship and Democracy*, in *New York Review of Books*, 9 (24 August 1967), pp. 31–5. Revised in chapter 5 of *The Past and the Present* and in chapter 6 of *The Past and the Present Revisited*.

'After the Revolution', review of J. H. Plumb, *The Origins of Political Stability: England, 1675–1725*, in *New York Review of Books*, 9 (28 September 1967), pp. 31–3.

'Lo-Marx', review of N. F. Cantor, *The English: A History of Politics and Society to 1760*, in *New York Review of Books*, 10 (1 February 1968), pp. 21–3.

'Revolution Then', review of P. Zagorin, *The Court and the Country*, in *New York Review of Books*, 14 (23 April 1970), pp. 41–3. Revised in chapter 10 of *The Past and the Present* and in chapter 11 of *The Past and the Present Revisited*.

'The Ninnyversity', review of H. F. Kearney, *Scholars and Gentlemen*;

R. L. Greaves, *The Puritan Revolution and Educational Thought*;
I. Berg, *Education and Jobs*; P. Bourdieu and J. C. Passeron, *La Répro-
duction: éléments pour une théorie du système d'enseignement*, in *New
York Review of Books*, 16 (28 January 1971), pp. 21–9. Revised in
chapter 12 of *The Past and the Present* and in chapter 14 of *The Past and
the Present Revisited*.

'The Disenchantment of the World', review of K. Thomas, *Religion and
the Decline of Magic*; A. MacFarlane, *Witchcraft in Tudor and Stuart
England*; C. Hansen, *Witchcraft at Salem*; R. Mandrou, *Magistrates et
sorciers en France au 17e siècle*; H. R. Trevor-Roper, *The European
Witch-craze of the Sixteenth and Seventeenth Centuries*; C. Hill, *Anti-
christ in Seventeenth Century England*, in *New York Review of Books*, 17
(2 December 1971), pp. 17–25. Revised in chapter 8 of *The Past and the
Present* and *The Past and the Present Revisited*.

'How Nasty Was Thomas Cromwell?', review of G. R. Elton, *Policy and
Police: The Enforcement of the Reformation in the Age of Thomas
Cromwell*, in *New York Review of Books*, 20 (22 March 1973), pp. 31–2.
Revised in chapter 4 of *The Past and the Present* and *The Past and the
Present Revisited*.

'The Massacre of the Innocents', review of J. H. van den Berg, *The
Changing Nature of Man* [trans. H. F. Croes]; P. Ariès, *Centuries of
Childhood*; L. de Mause, ed., *The History of Childhood*, in *New York
Review of Books*, 21 (14 November 1974), pp. 25–31. Revised in chapter
13 of *The Past and the Present* and in chapter 17 of *The Past and the
Present Revisited*.

'Whigs, Marxists and Poachers', review of D. Hay *et al.*, *Albion's Fatal
Tree*, and E. P. Thompson, *Whigs and Hunters*, in *New York Review of
Books*, 23 (5 February 1976), pp. 25–8. Revised in chapter 11 of *The Past
and the Present* and in chapter 13 of *The Past and the Present Revisited*.

'The True History of Catholics in England', review of J. Bossy, *The
English Catholic Community 1570–1850*, in *New York Review of Books*,
24 (3 February 1977), pp. 36–8. Revised in chapter 9 of *The Past and the
Present* and *The Past and the Present Revisited*.

'Walking Over Grandma', review of D. H. Fischer, *Growing Old in
America*, and K. Thomas, *Age and Authority in Early Modern England*,
in *New York Review of Books*, 24 (12 May 1977), pp. 10–16. Revised in
chapter 14 of *The Past and the Present* and in chapter 20 of *The Past and
the Present Revisited*.

'The Worst of Times?', review of B. W. Tuchman, *A Distant Mirror*, in
New York Review of Books, 25 (28 September 1978), pp. 3–8.

'Death and Its History', review of P. Ariès, *L'Homme devant la mort*, and
ibid., *Western Attitudes toward Death*, in *New York Review of Books*, 25
(12 October 1978), pp. 22–32 (editor's correction appeared 26 October

1978, p. 54). Revised in chapter 15 of *The Past and the Present* and in chapter 21 of *The Past and the Present Revisited*.

'Death in New England', review of D. E. Stannard, *The Puritan Way of Death*, in *New York Review of Books*, 25 (26 October 1978), pp. 44–5. Revised in chapter 15 of *The Past and the Present* and in chapter 21 of *The Past and the Present Revisited*.

'Goodby to Nearly All That', review of A. Macfarlane, *The Origins of English Individualism*, in *New York Review of Books*, 26 (19 April 1979), pp. 40–1.

'In the Alleys of Mentalité', review of E. LeRoy Ladurie, *Le Territoire de l'historien*, *The Territory of the Historian* [trans. B. and S. Reynolds], and *ibid.*, *Carnival in Romans* [trans. M. Feeney], in *New York Review of Books*, 26 (8 November 1979), pp. 20–5.

'Plebs and Patricians', review of J. Brewer and J. Styles, eds., *An Ungovernable People*, in *New York Review of Books*, 27 (29 May 1980), pp. 45–7. Revised in chapter 11 of *The Past and the Present* and in chapter 13 of *The Past and the Present Revisited*.

'Original Sins', review of T. H. Breen, *Puritans and Adventurers*; T. H. Breen and S. Innes, *'Myne Owne Ground'*; D. G. Allen, *In English Ways*; D. B. Smith, *Inside the Great House*, in *New York Review of Books*, 28 (5 February 1981), pp. 34–6.

'Terrible Times', review of M. St Clare Byrne, *The Lisle Letters*, vols. 1–6, in *New Republic*, 186 (5 May 1982), pp. 24–38. Revised in chapter 5 of *The Past and the Present Revisited*.

'Madness', review of D. P. Walker, *Unclean Spirits*; M. MacDonald, *Mystical Bedlam*; C. Webster, ed., *Health, Medicine and Mortality in the Sixteenth Century*; A. Scull, ed., *Madhouses, Mad-Doctors, and Madmen*, in *New York Review of Books*, 29 (16 December 1982), pp. 28–37. Revised in chapter 15 of *The Past and the Present Revisited*.

'The New Eighteenth Century', review of L. Colley, *In Defiance of Oligarchy*; N. McKendrick *et al.*, *The Birth of a Consumer Society*; P. Kriedte *et al.*, *Industry before Industrialization*; G. Holmes, *Augustan England*; R. S. Neale, *Bath 1680–1850*; P. J. Corfield, *The Impact of English Towns, 1700–1800*; M. Reed, *The Georgian Triumph, 1700–1830*; J. Rule, *The Experience of Labour in Eighteenth-Century English Industry*; L. Bonfield, *Marriage Settlements, 1601–1740*; J. A. Phillips, *Electoral Behavior in Unreformed England*; P.-G. Boucé, ed., *Sexuality in Eighteenth-Century Britain*; R. L. S. Cowley, *Hogarth's Marriage A-la-Mode*; B. English and J. Savile, *Strict Settlement: A Guide for Historians*; R. Porter, *English Society in the Eighteenth Century*, in *New York Review of Books*, 31 (29 March 1984), pp. 42–7. Revised in chapter 12 of *The Past and the Present Revisited*.

'A Demurral', review of F. Braudel, *Civilization and Capitalism, 15th–18th*

Century, vol. 3, *The Perspective of the World*, in *New Republic*, 191 (1 October 1984), pp. 31–4.

'Only Women', review of A. Fraser, *The Weaker Vessel*, and M. Prior, ed., *Women in English Society, 1500–1800*, in *New York Review of Books*, 32 (11 April 1985), pp. 21–3.

'Sex in the West', review of P. Ariès and A. Béjin, eds., *Western Sexuality*; K. J. Dover, *Greek Homosexuality*; E. C. Keuls, *The Reign of the Phallus*; M. Foucault, *L'Histoire de la sexualité*, vols. 1–3, *La Volonté de savoir, L'Usage des plaisirs* and *Le Souci de soi*; P. Veyne, 'La Famille et l'amour sous le haut-empire romain', *Annales ESC*, 33 (1978); P. Brown, *Virginity and Society*; J. Boswell, *Christianity, Social Tolerance and Homosexuality*; L. L. Otis, *Prostitution in Medieval Society*; B. Roy, ed., *L'Erotisme au Moyen Age*; G. Ruggiero, *The Boundaries of Eros*; R. Trexler, 'La Prostitution florentine au XVe siècle', and *ibid.*, 'Le Célibat', in *Annales ESC*, 36 (1981) and 27 (1972); J.-L. Flandrin, *Les Amours paysannes XVIe-XIXe siècles* and *ibid.*, *Le Sexe et l'Occident*; P.-G. Boucé, *Sexuality in Eighteenth-Century Britain*; G. R. Quaife, *Wanton Wenches and Wayward Wives*; R. Thompson, *Unfit for Modest Ears*; A. Bray, *Homosexuality in Renaissance England*; C. N. Degler, *At Odds*, and *ibid.*, 'What Ought To Be and What Was: Women's Sexuality in the Nineteenth Century', *American Historical Review*, 79 (1974); M. Vicinus, *Suffer and Be Still*; P. Gay, *The Bourgeois Experience: Victoria to Freud*, vol. 1, *The Education of the Senses*; B. Barker-Benfield, 'The Spermatic Economy: A 19th-Century View of Sexuality', *Feminist Studies*, 1 (1972); P. T. Cominos, 'Late Victorian Sexual Respectability and the Social System', *International Review of Social History*, 8 (1963), in *New Republic*, 193 (8 July 1985), pp. 25–37. Revised in chapter 19 of *The Past and the Present Revisited*

'Illusions of a Changeless Family', review of Alan Macfarlane, *Marriage and Love in England*, in *Times Literary Supplement*, 16 May 1986, p. 525.

'The Century of Revolution', review of G. E. Aylmer, *Rebellion or Revolution? England 1640–1660*; D. Hirst, *Authority and Conflict: England, 1603–1658*; K. Sharpe, ed., *Faction and Parliament*; D. Underdown, *Revel, Riot and Rebellion*; P. S. Seaver, *Wallington's World*; A. Fletcher and J. Stevenson, eds., *Order and Disorder in Early Modern England*; M. Kishlansky, *Parliamentary Selection*, in *New York Review of Books*, 34 (26 February 1987), pp. 38–44.

'Resisting the New', review of G. Himmelfarb, *The New History and the Old*, in *New York Review of Books*, 34 (19 December 1987), pp. 59–62.

SHORT REVIEWS

Review of B. de Jouvenal, *L'Or au temps de Charles-Quint et de Phillip II*, in *Economic History Review*, 17 (1947), p. 81.

Review of A. Whitworth, *Purveyance for the Royal Household in the Reign of Queen Elizabeth*, in *Economic History Review*, 18 (1948), p. 102.

Review of W. W. Rostow, *British Economy of the Nineteenth Century*, in *Oxford Magazine*, 17 June 1948, p. 552.

Review of the Earl of Cardigan, *The Wardens of Savernake Forest*, in *English Historical Review*, 66 (1951), pp. 132–3.

Review of J. E. Neale, *The Elizabethan House of Commons*, in *English Historical Review*, 65 (1950), pp. 119–22.

Review of A. L. Rowse, *The England of Elizabeth: The Structure of Society*, in *Journal of Education*, 83 (1951), p. 111.

Review of J. E. Morpurgo, ed., *Life Under the Stuarts*, in *Times Educational Supplement*, February 1951, p. 122.

Review of J. A. Williamson, *Hawkins of Plymouth*, in *Oxford Magazine*, 16 February 1950, p. 324.

Review of D. Talbot Rice, *English Art 871–1100*, in *Architectural Review*, 114 (1953), p. 263.

Review of G. Zarnecki, *Late English Romanesque Sculpture 1140–1210*, in *Oxford Magazine*, 1953.

Review of T. S. R. Boase, *English Art 1100–1216*, in *Oxford Magazine*, 19 November 1953, pp. 102–3.

Review of F. Saxl, *English Sculpture of the Twelfth Century*, in *Museum's Journal*, 54 (1954), pp. 138–9.

Review of J. R. Hale, *England and the Italian Renaissance*, in *Oxford Magazine*, 28 October 1954, p. 54.

Review of A. Toynbee, *A Study of History*, vols. 7–10, in *Spectator*, 193 (29 October 1954), pp. 526–8. Reprinted as 'Historical Consequences and Happy Families', in Ashley Montague, ed., *Toynbee and History: Critical Essays and Reviews* (Boston: Porter Sargent, 1956), pp. 111–14.

Review of J. Harvey, *English Medieval Architects* and C. R. Dodwell, *The Canterbury School of Illumination 1066–1200*, in *Spectator*, 193 (31 December 1954), p. 833.

Review of G. Connell-Smith, *Forerunners of Drake*, in *Economic History Review*, 2nd series, 7 (1954–5), p. 265.

Review of F. Barlow, *The Feudal Kingdom of England*, in *Spectator*, 194 (28 January 1955), p. 106.

Review of J. Buxton, *Sir Philip Sidney and the English Renaissance*, in *Oxford Magazine*, 10 February 1955, p. 204.

Review of D. Whitelock, ed., *English Historical Documents*, vol. 1, *c.500–1042*, in *Spectator*, 194 (18 February 1955), p. 196.

Review of W. Ullmann, *The Growth of Papal Government in the Middle Ages*, in *Spectator*, 194 (25 February 1955), p. 236.

Review of D. A. Callus, ed., *Robert Grosseteste*, in *Spectator*, 194 (11 March 1955), p. 300.

Review of H. Swarzenski, *Monuments of Romanesque Art*, in *Spectator*, 194 (22 April 1955), p. 510.

Review of L. E. Elliott-Binns, *Medieval Cornwall*, in *Spectator*, 194 (13 May 1955), pp. 622–4.

Review of G. Davies, *The Restoration of Charles II, 1658–1660*, in *Oxford Magazine*, 24 May 1956, p. 446.

Review of M. B. Donald, *Elizabethan Copper: The History of the Company of Mines Royal, 1568–1605*, in *English Historical Review*, 71 (1956), pp. 151–2.

Review of J. Duffy, *Shipwreck and Empire*, in *Economic History Review*, 2nd series, 9 (1956–7), p. 177.

Review of T. S. Willan, *The Early History of the Russia Company: 1553–1603*, in *Economic History Review*, 2nd series, 9 (1956–7), p. 364.

Review of H.M.S.O., *Calendar of the Close Rolls, Henry VII*, vol. 1, *1485–1500*, in *Economic History Review*, 2nd series, 9 (1956–7), pp. 369–70.

Review of G. D. Ramsey, *English Overseas Trade during the Centuries of Emergence*, in *Oxford Magazine*, 31 October 1957, inside back cover.

Review of J. Marlowe, *The Puritan Tradition in English Life*, in *Gemini*, 2 (1957), pp. 105–6.

Review of G. Zarnecki, *English Romanesque Head Sculpture*, in *Journal of the British Archaeological Association*, 21 (1958), pp. 161–2.

Review of R. H. Tawney, *Business and Politics under James I: Lionel Cranfield as 'Merchant' and 'Banker'*, in *The Cambridge Review*, 22 November 1958, pp. 166–7.

Review of P. Brieger, *English Art 1216–1307*, in *Medieval Archaeology*, 3 (1959), pp. 334–6.

Review of P. McGrath, ed., *I[ohn] B[rowne], The Marchants Avizo*, in *Economic History Review*, 2nd series, 11 (1958–9), pp. 367–8.

Review of C. Hill, *Economic Problems of the Church from Archbishop Whitgift to the Long Parliament*, in *Economic History Review*, 2nd series, 11 (1958–9), pp. 518–19. Revised in chapter 7 of *The Past and the Present*.

Review of P. Handover, *The Second Cecil: The Rise to Power, 1563–1604*, in *Oxford Magazine*, 22 October 1959, p. 40.

Review of G. R. Elton, *Star Chamber Stories*, in *History*, 44 (1959), pp. 58–9.

Review of M. Walker, ed., *Hearth Tax Returns*, vol. 1, *Hemlingford Hundred: Tamworth and Atherstone Divisions*, in *History*, 44 (1959), pp. 64–5.

Review of W. K. Jordan, *Philanthropy in England 1480–1660: A Study of the Changing Patterns of English Social Aspirations*, in *History*, 44 (1959), pp. 257–60.

Review of M. W. Barley, *The English Farmhouse and Cottage*, in *Times Literary Supplement*, 19 May 1961, p. 310.

Review of H. N. Brailsford, *The Levellers and the English Revolution*, ed. C. Hill, in *The Economist*, 15 July 1961, pp. 238–9.

Review of A. F. Upton, *Sir Arthur Ingram*, in *Economic History Review*, 2nd series, 14 (1961–2), pp. 345–6.

Review of H.M.S.O., *Acts of the Privy Council of England: May 1629 to May 1630*, in *Economic History Review*, 2nd series, 14 (1961–2), pp. 558–9.

Review of I. Coltman, *Private Men and Public Causes*; M. Ashley, *Financial and Commercial Policy under the Cromwellian Protectorate*; A. L. Rowse, *Ralegh and the Throckmortons*, in *New Statesman*, 63 (13 April 1962), p. 534–5.

Review of P. Zumthor, *Daily Life in Rembrandt's Holland*, and G. P. V. Akrigg, *Jacobean Pageant*, in *New Statesman*, 64 (24 August 1962), pp. 234–5.

Review of F. S. Fussner, *The Historical Revolution 1590–1640*, in *New Statesman*, 64 (2 November 1962), p. 628.

Review of G. H. Williams, *The Radical Revolution*, in *New Statesman*, 64 (21 December 1962), pp. 903–4. Revised in chapter 4 of *The Past and the Present*.

Review of E. Mercer, *English Art 1553–1625*, in *New Statesman*, 64 (28 December 1962), p. 931.

Review of W. K. Jordan, *The Charities of London: 1480–1660*, in *English Historical Review*, 77 (1962), pp. 327–9.

Review of J. Hurstfield, *Elizabeth I and the Unity of England*, in *English Historical Review*, 77 (1962), pp. 365–6.

Review of S. T. Bindoff, J. Hurstfield, C. H. Williams, eds., *Elizabethan Government and Society: Essays Presented to Sir John Neale*, in *English Historical Review*, 77 (1962), pp. 532–4.

Review of H. Chapman, *Lady Jane Grey*, in *New Statesman*, 65 (18 January, 1963), p. 87.

Review of T. Atkinson, *Elizabethan Winchester*, in *New Statesman*, 65 (10 May 1963), p. 720.

Review of A. R. Hall, *From Galileo to Newton*, in *New Statesman*, 66 (19 July 1963), p. 82.

Review of J. H. Elliott, *The Revolt of the Catalans*, in *New Statesman*, 66 (23 August 1963), p. 228. Revised in chapter 6 of *The Past and the Present*.

Review of H. P. R. Finberg, ed., *Approaches to History*, in *Past and Present*, 24 (1963), p. 103.

Review of J. H. Hexter, *Reappraisals in History*, in *English Historical Review*, 78 (1963), pp. 726–8.

Review of A. Simpson, *The Wealth of the Gentry 1540–1660*, in *English Historical Review*, 77 (1963), pp. 774–5.

Review of J. Webb, *Great Tooley of Ipswich*, in *Economic History Review*, 2nd series, 16 (1963–4), pp. 163–4.

Review of C. Hill, *Society and Puritanism in Pre-Revolutionary England*, in *New Statesman*, 67 (17 April 1964), pp. 605–6. Revised in chapter 7 of *The Past and the Present*.

Review of M. Ashley, *The Stuarts in Love*, in *History*, 49 (1964), p. 226.

Review of M. Dewar, *Sir Thomas Smith: A Tudor Intellectual in Office*, in *Economic History Review*, 2nd series, 17 (1964–5), p. 409.

Review of H.M.S.O., *Calendar of the Patent Rolls, Elizabeth I*, vol. 4, *1566–1569*, in Economic History Review, 2nd series, 17 (1964–5), p. 592.

Review of J. U. Nef, *The Conquest of the Material World*, in *Journal of Economic History*, 25 (1965), pp. 452–3.

Review of M. Girouard, *Robert Smythson and the Architecture of the English Country House*, in *Country Life*, 140 (11 August 1966), p. 326.

Review of P. Collinson, *The Elizabethan Puritan Movement*, L. Boynton, *The Elizabethan Militia 1558–1638*, and R. Howell, *Newcastle upon Tyne and the Puritan Revolution*, in *New Statesman*, 73 (30 June 1967), pp. 911–12.

Review of C. Hibbert, *Charles I*, in *New York Times Book Review*, 22 December 1968, p. 8.

Review of A. Esler, *The Aspiring Mind of the Elizabethan Younger Generation*, in *Journal of Modern History*, 40 (1968), pp. 603–4.

Review of M. P. Schoenfield, *The Restored House of Lords*, in *American Historical Review*, 73 (1968), pp. 812–13.

Review of R. Mousnier, *Problèmes de stratification sociale*, in *American Historical Review*, 74 (1969), pp. 1245–7.

Review of N. Denholm Young, *The Country Gentry in the Fourteenth Century*, in *Speculum*, 45 (1970), pp. 465–7.

Review of P. Seaver, *The Puritan Lectureship*, in *Archive for Reformation History*, 62 (1971), pp. 158–60.

Review of L. B. Smith, *Henry VIII*, in *New York Times Book Review*, 16 December 1971, p. 4.

Review of J. P. Cooper, ed., *The Wentworth Papers 1597–1628, Camden Society*, 4th series, vol. 12 (1973), in *American Historical Review*, 79 (1974), pp. 781–3.

Review of E. Shorter, *The Making of the Modern Family*, in *Times Literary Supplement*, 28 May 1976, p. 637.

Review of M. Girouard, *Life in the English Country House*, in *Times Literary Supplement*, 10 November 1978, p. 1298.

Review of J. Danzelot, *The Policing of Families*, in *New Republic*, 182 (16 February 1980), pp. 32–4.

Review of C. N. Degler, *At Odds: Women and the Family in America* and M. B. Norton, *Liberty's Daughters*, in *New York Times Book Review*, 20 April 1980, p. 9.

Review of P. M. Spacks, *The Adolescent Idea*, in *New York Times Book Review*, 20 September 1981, p. 12.

Review of E. Shorter, *A History of Women's Bodies*, in *New York Times Book Review*, 2 January 1983, p. 6.

Review of J. P. Kenyon, *The History Men: The Historical Profession in England since the Renaissance*, in *New York Times Book Review*, 18 March 1984, p. 22.

Review of M. French, *Beyond Power: On Women, Men and Morals*, in *New York Times Book Review*, 23 June 1985, p. 3.

Review of P. Darmon, *Damning the Innocent*, in *New York Times Book Review*, 23 March 1986, p. 41.

Review of W. Kendrick, *The Secret Museum: Pornography in Modern Culture*, in *New York Times Book Review*, 3 May 1987, p. 3.

NOTES, COMMENTS, REPLIES

'Early Evidence of Golf in England', *Notes and Queries*, 198 (1953), pp. 23–4.

'Notes on British Painting from Archives', *Burlington Magazine*, 96 (1954), p. 323.

'An Early Seventeenth-Century Lining Paper', *Oxoniensia*, 21 (1956), p. 83.

'Lord Montagu's Directions for his Son', *Northamptonshire Past and Present*, 2 (1958), pp. 221–3.

'Oxford Undergraduate Life', *Oxford Magazine*, February 1958.

'College Building Projects', *Oxford Magazine*, 8 May 1958, pp. 413–14.

'The Original Endowment of Wadham College', *Wadham College Gazette*, 146 (1959), pp. 118–19.

'Trevor-Roper's "General Crisis": Discussion of H. R. Trevor-Roper, "The General Crisis of the Seventeenth Century"', *Past and Present*, 18 (1960), pp. 31–3.

'The Case for a Graduate College', *Oxford Magazine*, 26 October 1961, pp. 28–9.

'R. H. Tawney,' *Past and Present*, 21 (1962), pp. 73–7.

Reply to 'Communication from Buttocks', *New York Review of Books*, 6 (28 April 1966), p. 26.

Reply to W. A. Speck, *Past and Present*, 35 (1966), pp. 156–7.

'Foreword' to W. H. Woodward, *Studies in Education during the Age of the Renaissance: 1400–1600* (New York: Teachers College Press, 1967), pp. ix–xix.

'Introduction' to R. H. Tawney, *The Agrarian Problem in the Sixteenth Century* (New York: Torchbook Edition, Harper and Row, 1967 [reprint of London: Longmans, Green and Company, 1912]), pp. vii–xviii.

'A Multidisciplinary Seminar for Graduate Training', *AHA Newsletter*, 6, no. 5 (June 1968), pp. 12–15.

'Two Cheers for the University', *New York Review of Books*, 11 (22 August 1968), pp. 21–3; reprinted in *The University*, 39 (1968–9), pp. 35–7.

Reply to J. C. Maxwell, *New York Review of Books*, 11 (10 October, 1968), p. 41.

Reply to P. Brooks, *New York Review of Books*, 11 (7 November, 1968), p. 37.

Reply to J. H. Hexter, *Journal of British Studies*, 8 (1968), pp. 79–82.

'R. H. Tawney', in *International Encyclopedia of the Social Sciences*, 15 (New York: Macmillan and Company and the Free Press, 1968), pp. 518–20.

'A Faculty View of Student Unrest', *Princeton Alumni Weekly*, 3 November 1970.

'Princeton in the Nation's Service', *New York Review of Books*, 14 (18 June 1970), pp. 7–11.

Comment on C. Hill, 'Newton and His Society', in R. Palter, ed., *The Annus Mirabilis of Sir Isaac Newton 1666–1966* (Cambridge, Mass: the M.I.T. Press, 1970), pp. 48–50.

Reply to M. J. Cullen, *Economic History Review*, 2nd series, 24 (1971), pp. 115–16.

'English and United States Local History', *Daedalus*, 100 (1971), pp. 128–32.

'The AHA and the Job Market for Graduate Students', *AHA Newsletter*, 10 (March 1972), pp. 22–7.

Reply to T. E. Huff, *New York Review of Books*, 18 (4 May 1972), p. 42.

Reply to S. J. Woolf, *Economic History Review*, 2nd series, 25 (1972), pp. 114–16.

Reply to C. Russell, *Economic History Review*, 2nd series, 25 (1972), pp. 121–3.

Reply to C. Thompson, *Economic History Review*, 2nd series, 25 (1972), pp. 131–6.

'The English Revolution of the 17th Century' [discussion with C. Hill and P. Burke], *The Listener*, 90 (4 October 1973), pp. 448–51.

Reply to H. G. Koenigsberger, *Journal of Modern History*, 46 (1974), pp. 106–9.

Reply to N. Stiller, *New York Review of Books*, 24 (14 July 1977), p. 42.

Reply to D. H. Fischer, *New York Review of Books*, 24 (15 September, 1977), pp. 48–9.

'Ages of Admission to Educational Institutions in Tudor and Stuart England: A Comment', *History of Education*, 6 (1977), p. 9.

'Tracing the Evolution of Universities like Princeton', *University*, 73 (1977), pp. 16–21.

'Princeton's Roots: An Amalgam of Models', *Princeton Alumni Weekly*, 12 September 1977, pp. 16–21.

Reply to E. Fox-Genovese, *New York Review of Books*, 25 (7 December, 1978), p. 42.

'Literacy in Seventeenth Century England', *Journal of Interdisciplinary History*, 8 (1978), pp. 799–800.

Reply to D. Neal, *New York Review of Books*, 27 (20 November, 1980), pp. 51–2.

'The New Art of Narrative History', *The Guardian*, 22 November 1980, p. 9.

'The Age of Admission to College in 17th Century England', *History of Education*, 9 (1980), pp. 97–9.

Reply to D. G. Allen, *New York Review of Books*, 28 (30 April 1981), p. 57.

'Illegitimacy in Eighteenth Century England: Again', *Journal of Interdisciplinary History*, 11 (1981), pp. 507–9.

Exchange with M. Foucault, *New York Review of Books*, 30 (31 March 1983), pp. 42–4. Translated as 'Lo Statuto della Folia: Michel Foucault e Lawrence Stone', *Prometeo*, 3, 10 (1985), pp. 94–102. Revised in chapter 15 of *The Past and the Present Revisited*.

Reply to M. Prior and J. W. Scott, *New York Review of Books*, 32 (30 May 1985), p. 53.

Reply to D. and E. Spring, *Albion*, 17 (1985), pp. 167–80.

Rejoinder to J. A. Sharpe in *Past and Present*, 108 (1985), pp. 216–24. Revised in chapter 16 of *The Past and the Present Revisited*.

MISCELLANEOUS

P. Scott, 'Putting Flesh on the Bare Bones of History', profile of Lawrence Stone in *Times Higher Education Supplement*, 23 September 1983, p. 9.

Videotape interview of Lawrence Stone by Keith Wrightson, issued by the Institute for Historical Research, London University, 1988.

Index

Aberdeen, Lord, and Cabinet of, 144
Aberdeen, Royal visitation of
    University of, 409
Ackworth, Reverend, President of
    Bradford Mechanics' Institute, 531
Acts of Parliament:
    act of 1783, correcting minor
        anomalies at Oxford and
        Cambridge, 422
    act concerning a highway from
        Attleborough to Wymondham,
        116
    capital statutes, 307–8
    Catholic Emancipation Act, 1829
    first Conventicle Act, 1668, 463
    Corn Laws, 525; debate on, 143;
        Tory split over, 156
    Corporation Act, 1661, 439, 459;
        repeal of, 417
    Education Act, 1870, 557
    Factory Act of 1833, 537
    Factory Acts, 554–5, 557
    Habeas Corpus Act, 459
    Improvement Act, 1850, 544
    legislation enlarging the use of
        promissory notes, 399
    Marriage Duty Act, 1694, 210
    Mortmain Act, 1736, 417–18
    Municipal Reform Act, 1835, 540
    Newcastle Act, 1690; preamble to,
        375–6
    Occasional Conformity Act, 1711,
        407; repeal of, 1719, 407, 415
    Poor Laws, 1598 and 1601, 203, 238;
        enforcement of, 203, 236, 239;
        implementation of, 226, 234,
        237–8
    Poor Law, 573; of 1601, 236; New
        Poor Law, 534, 537;
        implementation of (1837), 540;
        Old Poor Law, 540
    quo warranto, usage of, 461
    Reform Act, 140; of 1867, 354;
        Third Reform Act, 156
    religious statutes, of the
        Restoration, 463
    Schism Act, 1714, 407; repeal of,
        1719, 407, 415
    Secret Ballot Act, 354
    Small Tenements Rating Act, 544
    Statute of Westminster, 153
    Statute of 1725, concerning arrest on
        mesne, 365–6
    statutes, 474; for relief of insolvent
        debtors, 395; founding courts of
        requests, 373, 375–6; to regulate
        training of attorneys and
        solicitors, 382; to translate legal
        proceedings into English, 382
    Test Act, 101, 416; repeal of, 417
    Toleration Act, 1689, 407
Adams, *see* Phythian-Adams
advertising, by street cries, 487; in
    handbills, 487; in newspapers,
    486–7, 491–508 *passim*; increase in
    volume of, *c*. 1760, 490
Agincourt, battle of, 68
agrarian matters:
    agricultural depression, 370
    agricultural output, 1700–50, 369
    agriculture, 274, 546
    agrarian progress, of Tudor and
        Stuart period, 297
    common, 220, 239
    common rights, 203, 220
    copyhold tenures, 298–9

country, countryside, 203, 209, 216,
224–5, 274, 276, 278–80, 433
crofts, 220, 227
crops, 289; destruction of,
disagreements over, 390
customary lands, 298
damaging of sheep by dogs,
disagreements over, 390
diminishing herds, 220
enclosure and engrossing, 201, 232;
resulting popular uprisings in 1596
and 1607, 232
engrossing, 216
famine, 221; in Ireland, 234
farms, 231, 294
gardens, 204, 220, 227
harvests, 289; poor, 201, 209, 221–4,
229, 231, 235; good, 222
landlessness, 220
middle-sized holdings, 231, 238
pastoral communities, 236
pastoral regions, 220, 231–3
poor corn yields, 220
rural areas, 397, 399
rural settlement, 274
rural society, changes in, 397
smallholdings, 213, 217–18, 220, 231,
238
squatting, 231
subsistence crises, 221, 230
wasteland, 231–2, 234, 236
see also villages
agrarian personnel:
agricultural labourers, 227, 294
cottagers, 203, 217, 231–2;
quasi-landless, 231, 233
cottager/labourer, 238
cottar-miners, of the Stanneries and
Peak District, 227
farmers, 281, 294, 297, 303,
369
freeholders, 220; contentious, in
East Anglia, 371
husbandmen, 206, 231
servants in husbandry, 213, 227
smaller landowners, decline in
numbers of, 375
smallholders, 201, 203, 220, 231,
370, 393; children of, 220
squatters, 220
tenant farmers, 294, 297
villagers, English, 61
villein tenants, 297

yeomen, 206, 231; and husbandmen
farmers, 370; farming families, 516
see also Germany, peasants of and
peasants
Albany, dukedom of, 132
Albert, Prince Consort, 127–65 passim
and education of the Prince of
Wales, 138, 144–5, 148
and marriages of children, 149–50
as improver of the Crown's financial
position, 133
family life of, 129, 134, 146–7, 151
German sympathies of, 149, 164
happy marriage of, 133–4, 149
hard work of, 141, 145
admiration of Peel, 141–3
attitude to ceremonial, 158
disappointment with his eldest son,
138, 147–8, 150
father, 142
ideas on the role of the monarchy,
140–6, 151, 156–8, 163–4
influence upon Queen Victoria, 132,
143
relations with the nation, 132–3, 163
Albrighton Hunt, 182–3
Alcester, War., 229
ale-houses:
licensings of, 103
tallies run up in, 397
keepers' recognizances, 120
see also taverns
Alexandra, Princess of Denmark and
of Wales, 150
Alfred, Prince, son of Queen Victoria,
151
Alleyn, Sir Thomas, 463
Almanack de Gotha, 150
alms, 210
almsbox, 222
almshouses, 202, 212, 228
Ambassador(s),
of France, 78–9
of Venice, 71, 85, 89; see also
Busino, Orazio
Amery, Leopold, Colonial Secretary,
153
Anabaptists, 411
ancestors and ancestry, 36–7, 41, 55,
60; see also property and societies
Anderton, Swithin, 516
Andrew, Prince, son of Queen
Elizabeth II, 160

Angelo, Henry, 324
animals:
  Bactrian camel, 492
  beaver, 493
  crocodile, Mediterranean seal, 493
  Learned Pig, 493
  lions, tigers, kangaroos, opossum,
    ursine sloth from Bengal, 491, 493
  packs of hounds, 498
  rhinoceros (stuffed), 491, 493
  seal, 491
  turtle and cats, 493
Annales:
  school of historians, 577, 584, 591;
    see also Bloch
  journal, 585, 588
Anne, Queen, 115, 118, 230, 407
  and political parties, 139
Anne, Princess, daughter of Queen
  Elizabeth II, 160
anthropology and anthropologists:
  social anthropology, techniques of,
    34; community studies, 37, 39, 60;
    'network approach', network
    analysis, 39–40, 60
  anthropologists, findings of, 38–41
Anti-Corn Law League, 539
apprentice(s), 395
  and labourers, 228
  apprenticed by parish, 206
  apprenticeship, 214
  and service, 212
Arden, parishes of, 232, 239
Arians, 411
Ariès, Philippe, 33
aristocracy, nobility, 35–64 *passim*,
    274, 283, 295–7, 299–301, 303, 386
  continental, western European
    aristocracies, 35, 38, 41; *see also*
    France, nobility of *and* Germany,
    nobility of
  English, 159, 511–12, 522, 547, 582,
    585–7, 594–5; landed elite, 35–6,
    38, 40, 42–3, 59, 61; lesser
    landowners, 55; 'natural' and
    'entrepreneurial' aristocrats, 522;
    noblemen, 73, 789: funerals of,
    87, households of, 87, progresses
    of, 70, public display of, 70, 73,
    87–8; peers, 64, 385–6; economic
    monopoly of, 525; influence over
    elections by, 178; life-style and
    values of, 512, 514; political

dominance and privilege of, 353,
    525; principal seats of, in South
    Staffs, 181; relations with middle
    class, 167–97 *passim*; Scottish
    shootings of, 182; urban business
    interests of, 190
  feudal, 277–9, 281, 302–3; retainers
    of, 278–9, 281
  financial crisis of, 296
  hospitality of, 301
  landed, 277; landed elite, 41, 59
  old, 279, 295
  patrilineal aristocracy, 41
  anti-aristocratic critique and
    rhetoric, 525–6, 537, 540
  see also family *and* kin
Arkell, T., 204n
Arkwright, R., 531
army, armies, 47, 459, 468
  generals, 153
  officers, 44, 46, 386–7, 485
  reform of, in Britain, 137
Arnold, W., *The Important Station of
  an English University,* 422–3
Arthur, King, round table of, 327
Arthur, Prince, favourite son of Queen
  Victoria, 151
asceticism, 518
Ashcroft, Richard, 461, 466
Ashe, John, 445–6
Ashe, Ralph, of Chesterfield, 218
Ashurst, Sir William, 384
Astley, Philip, and circuses, 483
atheism, atheists, 406, 411
Atterbury, Francis, of Christ Church,
  Letter of a Convocation Man, 413
Augustan era, 98, 114, 118, 125, 269
Autry, James David, convicted for
  murder, 305–6
Aylesbury, Bucks,
  and siting of executions, 312–13
  Buckinghamshire County Hall in,
    319
  new charter of, 449
Aylsham, Norfolk, bridewell at, 120

Babergh Hundred, Suffolk, 203, 218
Bacon, Waller, 111
Bagehot, Walter, 139–40, 143, 162,
    164
Bagnalls, iron-makers of West
  Bromwich, 180
  James, 180

John Nock, High Sheriff of Staffs.,
    182
Bagnall, 185
Baker, Joseph, 502
Bakhtin, Mikhail, 339–40, 351
Baldwin, Alfred, 189
Baldwin, Stanley, 153
Balfour Declaration, 153
Balmoral, 134, 136, 146, 149–50
Baptists,
    and Congregationalists, 528
    club of, in London, 467
Bardin, William, 557
Barker, John, ironmaster, 183
Barnes, Michael, 6
Barnstaple, puritan stronghold of, 437
    common council of, 443–4
    fortifications in, 437
    mayors of, 443
Baron, John, Vice-Chancellor of
    Oxford, 416
Barrington, Henry, 452
Bass, M. T., Burton brewer, 179
Bateman, list of 1883 of, 179
Bates, Steven, of High Wycombe, 453
Bath, 96, 506
    architecture of, 506
    as attractor of wealth, 489
Battenburgs, 154–5, 159; see also
    Mountbatten
Beake, Robert, 447
Beattie, J. M., 357, 398
Bedford, magistrates of, 452–3, 455
Bedford, Duke of, 418
Bedworth, War., 226, 236, 239
Behrens, Jacob, German-born
    merchant of Bradford, 516
Beller, Elmer, 22
Belzoni, strongman, 493
Bender, John, 316
Bennett, D., 128
Bennett, G. V., 402
Benning, Ambrose, of Cambs., account
    books of, 380
Bentham, Jeremy, 384
    Benthamites, 539
Berkeley, University of, 25
Berney, John, 102
Bernhardt, Sarah, 134
Berry, Benjamin, 516
Bethal, Sheriff Slingsby, 467, 475
Bethea, Rainey, public hanging of, 306
Bidford, War., 210–12

Bilston, in Black Country, 170 (map),
    184–5
Bingley, Yorks, oratorio performances
    at, 506
Bird, Edward, execution of, 319–20
birds and insects:
    canaries, 496
    emus, ostrich, pelicans, vultures, 493
    turkey-cocks, 493
    centipede, 493
    tarantula, 491, 493
Birmingham, 132, 170, 172, 186, 375,
    489
    as creator of wealth, 489
    club culture of, 489
    court of requests in, 377, 395;
        dipsomaniacal court clerk of, 377
    elite of, 176
    'Change of, 189–90
    iron exchange of, 176
    manufacturers and financiers of, 181;
        see also Watson, J., and
        Hodgetts, T.
    merchants, bankers and lawyers of,
        176
    rioters in, 397
    upper middle class of, 176
    Edgbaston, suburb of, 184, 186
Black Country, West Midlands, 169–97
    passim
    civic life of, 185
    Fair Trade of, 176
    industrialists of, 171–94 passim
    map of, 170
    parliamentary seats of, 177; pressure
        on governments by, 177
    Pleasant Sunday Afternoon
        movement of, 176
    prosperity of, 191
    towns of (unnamed), 184–5
    towns of (named) see Bilston,
        Dudley, Stourbridge,
        Wednesbury, West Bromwich,
        Wolverhampton
Blackstone, William, lawyer, 143, 376,
    383
    his Commentaries on the Laws of
        England, 376
Blake, R., 129
Bloch, Marc, 577, 586
Blum, Jerome, 22–4
Boaz, Herman, magician, 492
Boleyn, Anne, 75–6

Bolton, M., 531
Bonner, Thomas, alderman of
  Newcastle upon Tyne, 446
Book of Orders, 235
Boote, Richard, legal writer, 366, 381,
  383
Borsay, Peter, and 'urban renaissance'
  1680–1760, 485–6, 489, 510
Boston, Lincs.:
  charters of, 445
  continuity in corporation of, 445
Boswell, James, 346–7, 493
Bosworth Field, battle of, 79
Bowen, William G., 25
Bowra, Maurice, 3, 6, 11
Bradford, West Riding, Yorks, 513–48
  passim
  Directories, 1830, 1850, 514
  Guardians' elections, 540
  Mechanics Institute, 530–1, 538
  Bradford Observer, 517, 523, 540–1;
    its editor, 539
  Political Union, 537
  Temperance Hall, 530
  Temperance Society, 529–31, 538
  Town Mission, 544
  churches of, 527, 536
  municipal: franchise, 542;
    government, 543–4; institutions,
    545, 547; socialism, 545
  public: authorities and regulations,
    545; health, 544–5; services, 542,
    545
  urban: environment of, 521, 539,
    541, 543–5; life of, 521, 525;
    industrial growth of, 546;
    industrial revolution in, 514, 516;
    industrial capitalism in, 525–6,
    529; industrial society of, 525–32;
    property in, 514; reform
    movement in, 539, 544, 547
Bradshaw, Nicholas, of High
  Wycombe, 453
Branston, Leics., 233
Braudel, Fernand, *The Mediterranean
  in the Reign of Phillip II*, 591
Bray, Vicar of, 448
Brembre, Sir Nicholas, Lord Mayor of
  London, 477
Brenner, Robert, 465
Breughel, Peter, 341–2
Bridge, James, 217
Brighton, 134, 136

Pavilion at, 131, 158
Bristol, 83, 373, 436
  as creator of wealth, 489
  elite of, 433
  purge of corporation of, 439
Britiffe, Robert, attorney for Viscount
  Townshend, 110
Brockhouse, John, manufacturer of
  West Bromwich, 186
Brooke, George, beheading of, 327–8
Brooks, C.W., 363n
Brosely, Salop, 236
Buckingham,
  Duke of, 86
  Duchess of, 87–8
Buckingham Palace, 135–6, 153
Bunwell, Norfolk, 211, 215
bureaucracies, 241–2; *see also* civil
  service *and* Weber
Burke, Edmund, 424, 428
  *Reflections on the Revolution in
    France*, 423
  on executions, 331–2
Burke, Peter, 12
Burlington, Lord, 499
Burnet, Bishop, 249
Burslem, Staffs, 555
  municipal day nursery at, 567
business matters:
  business affairs, 391
  business deal, 395
  business practices, 387–8; credit,
    369, 373, 383, 388–9, 395, 516;
    extension of, 395
  small-scale borrowing and lending,
    389
  business rivals, 392
  business transactions, 387, 393
  businesses, 242
  businessmen, 389
  see also markets, trade *and* wages
Busino, Orazio, Ambassador of
  Venice, 75, 86
Bute, Lord, 137, 403
Byers, Ann, 391

Cain, Old, 316
California, University of, at Los
  Angeles, 24
Calne, borough of, 442
  constables' accounts of, 442
  guild stewards in, 442
  renewing of charter of, 1655, 442

Calthorpes, old Norfolk family of, 111
Calvin, John, 462
Calvinist or neo-Calvinist sects, 518
Cambridge, 139
Cambridge, duke of, son of George
    III, 131
    the Cambridges, 159
Cambridge, University of, 10, 12, 256
    academic reform at, 414–5, 425–6;
        proposed, 409
    attempted reform of, 401–29 *passim*
        proposed visitation of, 406,
        409–13, 416–21
    alumni of, 1715–60, becoming Tory
        MPs, 427
    behaviour of James II towards,
        404–5
    Chancellor of, 164
    colleges: Emmanuel, 249, 265;
        Christ's, 265; Peterhouse, 249; St
        John's old boys of, 496–7; Sidney
        Sussex, 265; Trinity, alumni of,
        496
    critics of, *see* commonwealthmen,
        radicals, Whigs *and for* clerical
        critics *see* Newton, R., *and*
        Prideaux, H.
    fellowships at, 405
    increasing Whig dominance at, 427
    issue of celibacy at, 421–2
    links with Church of England, *see*
        Church of England
    Jacobism at, 406, 408, 411, 418
    MPs and PMs at, eighteenth
        century, 403
    morality and discipline at, 410, 419,
        423
    non-jurors at, 405
    rise in enrolments at, 425
    senior posts at, 411
Camden, Lord, sometime Whig
    Chancellor, 394
Cannon, J., 401
Cantor, Norman, 28–9
capital punishment and executions:
    abolition of, 1868, 308
    debate on abolition of, 353
    alternatives to, 397–8
    ballad literature about, 325; *see also*
        prints, broadsheets
    parliamentary committee on, 324
    Royal Commission on, 355
    executions: as light entertainment,
323–4, 330; as sacrifice, 340,
    352–3; cart at, 316, 319, 321, 337,
    349, 352; clergymen at, 319;
    commercial sex at, 348, 354;
    condemned at: behaviour of, in
    England, 318–24, 327–9; dress of,
    319, 321, 347–8; 'magical
    properties' of bodies of, 346;
    pardons to, 307, 325, 328–9;
    reprieve of, 342; sermons to, 307;
    state control of behaviour at, in
    Rome and on the Dam, 318
    crowds at: 316, 318–20, 322–5,
    328–9, 338–9, 346, 350–3;
    behavior of, 306–7, 309, 311, 313,
    327–30, 332, 337, 346–8, 351–2,
    354; deaths as result of, in
    Nottingham, 347; helping victims
    to quicker end, 352; in front of
    Buckingham County Hall, 319
    debate about televising, in USA,
    305–6
    drink at, 332, 346, 351, 354
    executioner at, 316, 323, 327;
    assistant, 322–3
    gallows at, 307–8, 311, 318, 328, 337,
    346
    Halbadiers at, 313
    hawkers at, 324
    iconographic associations of, 339,
    342
    Ordinary at, 318, 320–2, 347;
    Accounts of, 320, 348
    in private, 354–5; those present at,
    354
    in public, 308–55 *passim*
    role of state at, 306–13, 316, 322,
    330, 337, 346; in Holland, 330
    sheriff at, 316, 320, 323, 327–9; his
    attendants at, 313; his officers at,
    313
    structural resemblance to carnival
    of, 309, 322, 332, 339–40, 342,
    346–52, 354–5
    venues of, *see* Aylesbury, Newgate,
    Tyburn, Winchester Castle, York
    Castle
    hanging, 398; drawing and
    quartering, 327
    'hanging fair', 319
    'hanging tree', 311, 325
capitalism, 274, 276, 282–3, 293, 301,
    303

agrarian, 302–3
growth of, 238
see also feudalism, transition from
capitalist: competitive life, 526;
development, 524; elite, 514;
mode of production, 526; property-
relationship, 534; social relations,
535–6; society, 547;system, 532;
wage–labour relationship, 533
capitalists, English industrial, 278,
511–48 *passim*; *see also* classes
Capon, William, 310–12
Carlton, Sir Dudley, 326–9
Carlton House, residence of Prince of
Wales, 135
Carlton Miniott, Yorks, 206–8
carnival:
festivals, Italian, 346
Rabelaisian, 351
Carr-Saunders, A. M., and Wilson, P.
A., *The Professions*, 246
Cartwright, Thomas, 1587 survey of,
222
Cataloni, Madame, opera singer, 494
Catnach, 314
Cawston, Norfolk, 205–8
market at, 206
census(es), 1582–1630, 205–9, 211,
214, 222, 237
conducted under the Marriage Duty
Act of 1694, 210
enumerators, books of, 552, 554–5,
561, 573
recording employment, 228
1911 Fertility Census, 566
religious census figures, 1851, 528
Chamberlain, John, 326
Chance, J. H., glass manufacturer, 175
Channon, Henry, 154
chapels, 527–8; chapel membership,
528
Charles I, King, 68, 82–4, 87–93, 436,
439, 450, 452
wife, *see* Henrietta Maria
son, the Prince of Wales, 91; *see also*
Charles II
mother-in-law, 82
intended Spanish match for, 86
investiture as Prince of Wales of, 89
prerogative rule of, 93, 448
Charles II, King, 112, 448, 462, 464, 480
court of, 472–3, 476, 478

government of, 457
reading audience in latter part of
reign of, 462
Charles, present Prince of Wales, 155,
159
Charles, Stuart Prince, 67
Charlton, K., 245, 247
Charterhouse, 576
Sir Robert Birley, headmaster of,
577–8, 580
Chartists, Chartism,
of Bradford: 535, 541, 543;
campaign for universal suffrage,
535; councillors, 543; militant,
541, 543; social democratic policy
aims of, 535
petitions of, 351
Cheshire, Richard, 444
Chilvers Coton, War., 211, 213–14
Chippenham, Cambs., 231–2, 238
Church Clent, Worcs., manor of, 181
Church of England, 96, 182, 252, 462,
466, 468, 527–8
and doctrine of passive obedience
and non–resistance, 405–6
and relations with the state, 401–28
passim
Anglican(s): 514, 543; hierarchy,
413; Tory capitalists, 536
churches, 573
Laudian, 435
links of, with Oxford and
Cambridge, 402–4, 407–9, 413,
416–17, 422–4
patronage, 137
re-establishment of, after 1660, 402
relations with James II and his
ministers, 404
separatists from, 464
clergy of: 206, 241, 245, 249, 268,
402–27 *passim*, 466, 485; sons of,
268; lower (lesser), 412–13, 427;
high-churchmen, 412–13; upper,
249; archbishops, 411, 414; *see
also* Laud, Tenison *and* Wake;
archdeacon, 266; bishops, 252,
256, 406, 412–15; *see also* Burnet,
Fleetwood, Patrick, Sherlock,
Trelawny *and* Norwich, bishop of;
curates, 265, 268; deacon, 248;
deacons and ordinands to
diaconate, diocese of
Peterborough, 241, 252–66;

incumbents, 250; ordinands, 249; priest, 248, 252, 260–1; royal chaplain, 266
clerical: abuses, 258, 269; career, 268; criticism of the universities, 407, 409–16, 418–19; dynasties, 251, 267–8; education, 248–9, 254–9, 265; employment, 262–6; labour market, 256, 258; livings, 252; marriage, 250–1; positions, 248, 250, 266; profession, 248; proletariat, 248; supporters of the Tories, 407; wealth, 250
abolition of minor and clerical orders, 248
benefice holders, 252
diocesan authorities, 256, 258, 262
ordinations, 412
parishes, and parochial matters, 202, 204, 206, 230, 232, 234–6, 248–9, 252, 266, 268
'parson's freehold', 268
preaching, 248–50
scripture, 248
visitation articles, 248
Commissioners for Ecclesiastical Causes, 404
Convocation, 412–13; crisis, 413
laity, 249, 251, 403, 418, 425; laicization of society, 248
Churchill, Winston, 153
civil service, 249
mode of appointment to, 426
clan, 39
Scottish and Irish, 41
sippe (sib, clan), 41n
Clapham, Sir John, 553
Clarence, Duke of, eldest son of Edward, Prince of Wales, 154
Clarendon, Lord, 137, 145–6
Clark, J. C. D., 460, 486, 510
Clark, Sir James, 137
Clark P., 433n, 434n
class(es):
bourgeois: 279; commercial and industrial, 282; landed, 296; liberal, liberalism, 530, 535, 539, 543–4, 546–7; petit bourgeois businessmen, 530
bourgeois hegemony, 513, 525, 547–8
bourgeois revolution, theory of,

271–4, 278–81, 283–5, 294–7, 302–3
bourgeoisie: 55, 133, 243, 278–80, 282, 295–6, 302, 528, 538, 540; nineteenth-century industrial, 511, 513, 547–8; urban patriciate, rich widow from, 58
capitalist landed, 297
elites, 60; *see also* aristocracy
English governing, 403, 418, 420–1, 423–4, 426–8
exploiting, 273, 288–90
feudal, 279, 282, 285, 295
landed, 43, 271–2, 300, 302, 304; *see also* aristocracy
landed feudal, 282, 296
lordly, 291
lower: 36, 38, 43, 97–8, 396; *see also* agrarian personnel *and* Germany, peasantry of; and the labouring poor, in Lancs., 377
industrial capitalist, 278
merchant, 291
middle: 161, 167–97 *passim*, 483, 490, 494, 507, 509, 511–48 *passim*; industrialists within, 167–9, 171–7, 179–81, 183–96; 'gentrification' of, 167–97 *passim*; rural migration of, 169, 171, 179–86, 188–94; leaders of, 174–8, 181, 184–6, 191–2; lower, 174–5, 517, 521, 542; non-industrialists within, 167–8, 171, 173, 176–7, 192, 194–6; substantial, 516; upper, 160, 172, 175–6, 180, 184–6, 188–9, 192, 195
of peasant producers, 273
of tenant farmers, 294; *see also* farmers, tenants
parliamentary, 422
ruling, pre-capitalist, 287
upper, 268
urban; 283; lower middle, 515; middle, middling sort, 393–4, 397, 399, 435; patriciate, 58; proletariat, 354, 372–3, 375;
working: proletariat, 278, 294, 375; of Bradford, 513–47 *passim*; of the Black Country, 174–5, 178, 191; semi-skilled, 277
see also gentry and landlords
class: conflict, 284–5; evolution of, 287; formation, 511–48 *passim*;

legislation, 523; in patrilineal
societies, 37; relations, 284
Clendinnen, Inga, 27
Clifden, Nellie, 138, 150
Cliffe, Thomas, shipwright, 449
cloth and cloth-making:
broadcloth: producers, 226, 229;
white and coloured, of Leeds
hinterland, 488; workers, 231;
exports, 229; North European
markets' collapse, 229
cotton textiles: female workers in,
553, 557, 559; fertility in areas of,
552–3, 555, 565–6, in France, 565;
of Lancs., 520; young children of
workers in, 563
luxury cloth: brocade, 71;
embroidered, 88; gold and silver
lace, 89; of Arras, 69; of gold,
69–70; silks, 70–1; tapestry,
69–70
woollen cloth: manufacture of,
228; finishing, in Leeds, 488;
industry of Norwich, 371; industry
of West Riding, 488; kerseymeres,
of Huddersfield, 488; mills, 521,
536; mill-owners, 514, 536;
steam power in manufacture of,
489; textile handicraftsmen, 521,
534; wives' and children's
earnings, 521
worsteds: businesses, 516; combing,
520–1, 531, 534, 541; handicraft
proto-industry and trade, 513;
industry, 513–14, 517, 519–21; of
Bradford, 520; and Halifax, 488;
spinning machinery, 520;
mechanization of spinning, 513;
weaving, 520; workers in, 519,
521–3; female and adolescent
operatives in, 520
clothiers: large-scale capitalist, 513;
middlemen-clothiers, 228; old
style putting out masters, 514
domestic and foreign exchanges, 229
knitters, 229
new draperies, of Essex, 229
spinners and clothworkers: of
Coventry, 225; of Devizes, 225; of
Devon, 225
textile centres, 234; decline of, 235,
238
Clydeside, 193

coalmining, 226, 236, 239; *see also* the
Potteries, coalmining in
high fertility in areas of, 553, 559,
565–6; in France and USA, 565
workers in, 553, 559, 565
Cobham, Lord, intended execution
and reprieve of, 327–8
Coburg:
German house of, 131
Leopold of, King of Belgium, 130–2,
140–3, 145, 149, 155; Charlotte,
his wife, 130, 149; his nephew, *see*
Albert, Prince Consort
Victoria of, Duchess of Kent, 130–1,
149; her husband, *see* Kent, Duke
of; her daughter, *see* Queen
Victoria
influences upon the British
monarchy, 132, 138, 140, 143, 149,
155
influences upon the German
monarchy, 157
Colburgs (unnamed), 140, 154–5
Cockayne experiment, 229
Coke, Sir Edward, 371
Colchester, 434
charters of, 452
free burgesses of, 452
struggle within corporation of, 451–3
Cole, Stephen, 184
Coleridge, Samuel Taylor, 493
commissions, commisioner(s):
of the peace, *see* legal personnel
for courts of requests, 376–8
appointed under the Corporation
Act, 439
of Children's Employment, 557–8
of Queen Anne's Bounty, 250
Commonwealth, the, 445
civic leaders of, 463–4
commonwealthmen, 407–10, 414,
423–4, 462; *see also* Gordon, T.,
Onslow, A., Trenchard, J.
commune, urban, 277
communal jurisdictions, 375
medieval communal movement, 283
Congo, Belgium, 230
Connaught, dukedom of, 132
conscription, 221
Conservatives, 178, 182; *see also*
Tories
constitution, 140, 143, 401, 417, 428
ancient, 474–5

and parliamentary confrontations,
467
and royal intervention, 157
in church and state, 424
Restoration, 462
unreformed, 403
Cooke, Sir George, chief prothonotary
of Court of Common Pleas, 362–3
Cooper, J. P., 21
Cooper, John, execution of, 321
co-operatives, 533–4
Cornish, Henry, 475
Cornwall, duchy of, 133
Cotes, John, will and inventory of,
219–20
Cotton, R. W., 443n
country house(s), 95, 181
and estate, 119
and fashions in landscaping, 97
changes in architecture of, 96,
506
walled parks and extensive gardens
of, 97
manor-house hall or parlour, 98
court(s), 297, 379, 404, 452
assize(s): 363; 381, 390; Middlesex,
391; Norfolk, 371–2; 'articles for
the assizes', 110; grand jury of,
service on, 123; semi-annual, 97;
and lieutenancy meetings, in
Norfolk, 110; see also York,
assizes in
civil, 425
commissions of the peace,
magistracy, bench, 98–101, 107,
109, 116–17, 122, 124, 182, 236,
379; in Norfolk, 99–101, 105–6,
109–10, 112–15, 117–20, 122–4
common law, 359–60, 366–8, 378,
382–3, 387–90, 395, 397, 399
Council of the North, 361, 372
county, 99
criminal, system of, 392
ecclesiastical, 248
established urban small-debt, 376–7,
379
local: 373–5, 377; borough, 375–6;
manor, 375
of Chancery, 358–64, 380–1, 385–6,
388, 399
of Common Pleas, 358–72 passim,
385, 387–90
of Exchequer of Pleas, 364

of King's Bench, 358–72 passim,
388–90, 476
of Star Chamber, 361
urban courts of requests, 360, 373–8,
395–7, 399; commissioners on
tribunals of, 376–8; customary law
of, 377
quarter-sessions: 97, 102, 109,
117–19, 178, 210, 225; in Norfolk,
101–9, 112–15, 118, 120, 123–4; in
Yorks and the West Country, 379;
and assizes, 98–9; in Norfolk,
107–12, 117–18; sessional orders,
1698–9, 101–2
petty sessions, 97–8, 101–3, 119
court procedure: arrest on mesne,
365–7, 384, 396; nisi prius, 358–9,
363, 390
routinization of court business, 99,
122
court(s), of kings or princes, 298, 300
English, 67, 69–71, 73–4, 92, 301–2;
ceremonies in, 85
German, 46–7, 52–4
Scottish, lack of ceremonies in, 85
court favours, 303
court offices, 279, 296, 302
Courvoisier, François, execution of,
351
Coventry, 83, 217, 447
poor of, 204, 209
Cowden, Kent, 235
Cowper, Lord Chancellor, 413
crafts, 533
industrial, 72
rural cottage handicrafts, 513
craftsmen, see occupations
Cranbrook, Kent, 235
Cranworth, Lord, 354
Cressy, David, 35, 40, 43, 52, 61
his 'Kinship and Kin Interaction in
Early Modern England', 40n, 43n,
52n
crime:
concern over rising levels of, by
1750, 397
studies of, 369
victims of, 398
criminal(s), 97, 358, 398
criminal matters: 119; armed raids,
49, 51; criminal interlopers, 97;
game offences and felony charges,
99; highway robbery, 42, 50

law and order, 543–4
Crompton, Lancs., 211, 215, 217
Crompton, Robert, and his wife, 217
Cromwell, Oliver, Lord Protector, 439, 451–2
   government of, 449, 451
   Protectorate of, 448, 455
Crondall, parish in Hants, 223–4
crowd(s), 65, 490; *see also* capital punishment and executions *and* London, ordinary citizens of
culture, 95, 98
   British culture elite, 512
Cumberland, parts of, 372
Cumberland, Duke of, son of George III, 131
   dukedom of, 132
Curtis, M., and theory of 'alienated intellectuals', 265

Daily News, 355
Dalton, R., 494
Damien, would-be regicide, public dismemberment of, 306, 309
Darnton, Robert, 25
Dartmouth, Earls of, 185
   fifth Earl of, 178–9
   sixth Earl of, 182
   Earl and Countess of, 191
   Lord, and his heir, 178
Davidoff, Leonore, 550
Davis, Natalie Z., 25
Davy, Henry, 111
Dawson, Henry, 466
   clique of, at Newcastle, 448
debts, debtors, 49, 113, 357–9, 365–6, 369, 373–7, 379, 382–3, 386–90, 393–8
   'debt on speciality', 390
   payment of debts by instalment, 377, 389, 397–8
   imprisoned debtors: charitable foundations for the relief of, 396; petitions for the relief of, 396
   see also courts, urban courts of requests
Defoe, Daniel, 348, 499
deists, 408, 411; *see also* Tindal
Dellany, S., 'Monody on his late Majesty', 492
Derby, 437
Derby, Lord, PM, 134
Derbyshire, 236

Desborough, Major-General, 439, 447
Devizes, Common Council of, 225
Devonshire, Duke of, 403
D'Ewes, Sir Simonds, 84
Dewick, Francis, alderman of Hull, 445
Dickens, Charles, 332, 349, 351, 354
   his *Oliver Twist*, 349–51
Disraeli, Benjamin, 144–5
dissent, dissenters, 458–60, 462, 465, 479, 481
   abolition of civil penalties for, 401
   excluded from degrees and fellowships at Oxford and Cambridge, 402
   London dissenters, 460, 462–6, 482
   dissenting academies, 407
   see also Non-conformists
Docker, Dudley, 188
Dodd, Dr, execution of, 325
Doll, Tiddy, ballad-singer, 349
Doncaster, 233, 502
   assemblies in, 506
Donne, John, attorney, 385–6
Doughty, Mr, Norfolk gentleman, 110
Douglas, Mother, Covent Garden Bawd, 349
Doves, Thomas, 'Arminian', 265
Drake, F., 499–500, 502
Draper, George, Herts. attorney, 382
Drayton, Staffs., 143
drink, drunkenness, 529, 533, 541; *see also* temperance
Drury, alderman of Nottingham, 437
Dryden, John, 462
Dubois, John, Whig merchant of London, 471, 478
Duby, Georges, 41, 44
Dudley, improved facilities of, 178
Dudley, Earls of, 189
   first Earl of, and his son, 178
   second Earl of, 186
   Lord, 178, 186
duel, 51
Durham, proposed college at, 446
Durham, Lord, 160
   his Canadian report, 160
Durkheim, E., 242
Duval, Claude, 348
Dyck, Van, 93

Eagle, John, attorney of Bradford, 382
Ealing, 211, 213
East Anglia, 371

East Indiaman, ship's mate of, 392
economy, the:
  bourgeois, 279
  commercial, 281
  natural, 281
  subsistence, 281
  urban, 279
economic matters:
  Bank of England, 125, 368
  capital: 291; accumulation of, 517;
    investment, 290
  conspicuous consumption, 296
  decline of British economy, 171–2
  division of labour, 242, 247
  economic determinism, 280
  economic trends, early
    eighteenth-century, 369–70, 387;
    effect of, on litigation levels,
    368–9
  employers' lock-out and blacklist,
    534
  extra-economic compulsion
    (coercion), 273, 292, 294, 296–7
  financiers, 512
  integration of parts of northern
    counties into the national
    economy, 372
  investment in government stocks,
    368–9
  labour costs, 250, 253
  labour market, 524, 533
  market freedom, 525, 546
  mid-Victorian prosperity, 544
  prices, 221, 223, 227
  producers: 288–9; direct, 285–6,
    289–90, 292–3; individual, 280;
    pre-capitalist, 288
  production: 275–8, 280–2, 286, 290,
    296–7; means of, 277, 285–6,
    293–4; mode of, 272–3, 279, 292;
    units of, 275, 277–8, 284;
    productive forces, 272–3, 275–6,
    279–80, 283–5, 287, 291;
    productivity, 289, 299
  raw materials, 291
  recoinage of money, 1695–6, 368
  reinvestment of surpluses, 299
  shortage of specie, 1690s, 368
  standards of living, sixteenth and
    seventeenth centuries, 230–1
  unemployment, 521; mass
    unemployment, 540
  unit costs, 520
  see also business matters, inflation,
    markets, rents, trade, wages
Economic History Review, 6, 585
Edinburgh, dukedom of, 132
Edinburgh, University of, 24
education, 517, 545
  factory schools, for child textile
    workers, 536
  for the working class, 530–1
  formal schooling, 517
  German university, 54
  grammar school, 188
  Oxbridge, 188
  public schools, 177, 187–8; see also
    Eton
  technical, 188; see also Mason's
    College see also law and legal
    matters, legal training
Edward VI, King, 248
Edward VII, King, 152–4, 157–8
  as Prince of Wales, 138–9, 147–8,
    154
  and his relations with his parents,
    147–8
  adolescence of, 138
  education of, 138, 144–5, 148
  Hanoverian characteristics of, 138–9,
    151–2
  marriage of, 150
  personality and physique of, 138
  statecraft of, 156
  wife, see Alexandra, Princess of
    Denmark
  daughter, 159
  sisters, 158
Edward VIII, King, 152–3, 158
  as Prince of Wales, 153, 160
  abdication of, 160
  as Duke of Windsor, 152
Edwards, Thomas, of Dunchurch, 212
Eldon, Lord, 353
election(s), 99
  of London sheriffs, 114–15
  of sheriffs for London and
    Middlesex, 1682, 461, 470–1,
    475–7
  hustings, 477
  polls, 477
  see also parliamentary matters,
    elections
Elizabeth I, Queen, 66, 69, 71, 74,
  77–8, 80–1, 83, 85–7, 90, 301
Elizabeth, II, Queen, 156–7, 164

as Princess, 153; accession of, 153
Elizabeth, Princess, daughter of James
  I, 87
  wedding of, 89
Elwells, iron-makers of Wednesbury,
  184
Empire, British, 137, 145, 153, 160
  colonies, 162, 278, 303, 398
  era of imperial aggrandisement, 162
Encounter, 5
Engels, Friedrich, 549
Enlightenment, the, 280
entertainments:
  masques, 65–6, 88, 93
  portraits and outdoor
    entertainments, 65
  pageants, 66–7, 70, 78, 81, 83, 158;
    of the Lord Mayor of London, 75,
    83
  plays, pastimes and pleasures, 80
epidemics, 209, 216, 221, 224
  of cholera, 1849, 544
  of fever, ague and influenza, 225
  of plague, 221, 224–5, 229;
    quarantines, 224
  contagious sickness, 225; *see also*
    prisons, gaol fever
Erikson, Erik, 590
Escott, T. H. S., 163–4
Esher, Lord, 156
Essex, 224, 233
Essex, University of, 12
estates, 42, 44–5, 48, 51–2, 54, 56–7,
  167, 279, 290, 294, 299–300
  confiscation of, 50–1
  exchange of, 57
  recovery of, through lawsuits, 47
  renunciation of claims to, 57
  sale of, for payment of debts, 49
  estate economies, 278
  estate management, 300
Estmead, Arthur, of Calne, 442
Eton, public school, 577–8
Eulenburg, 157
Europe, 33
  areas settled by Germanic tribes, 41
  barbarian invasions of, 274, 281–2
  Celtic fringe of, 41
  western, 40
  the tour of, 119
Evans-Pritchard, 589
Evett, William, sheriff of Worcester,
  440, 450

Exclusion Crisis, *see* James II
Exeter, Devon, 216
Exhibition, the Great, 133, 149
Eyck, F., 128

fairs, 489–90
  decline of, 485
  see also Leeds *and* York
Fakenham, Norfolk, 103, 105
family, the, 550–73 *passim*
  aristocratic: 36, 39, 42–3, 59;
    bilateral and patrilineal elements
    in, 42; German, 35, 36n
  authority within: clan heads,' 37;
    patriarchal, 33–4; patriarchal
    head's, 36
  characteristic structure of, 550
  comprehensive source for the study
    of, *see* census (es), books of
    enumerators of
  descent groups in: corporate, 37, 39;
    formally organized, 39, 41;
    patrilineal, 41, 49
  knightly, German, 51
  living standards of, 568; *see also*
    Potteries, the, living standards in
  local community with mixed
    occupations as unit of study of,
    554, 566, 572–3
  noble, German, 46
  nuclear: 33–6, 38, 40, 44, 48–9, 55,
    60–1; households of, 40; members
    of, 38
  'open Lineage', 33, 35–6, 59
  family: archives, 300; chronicles, 55
    and n; *see also Zimmerische
    Chronik*; councils, 37, 54;
    fortunes, 113; obligation, *see* kin;
    strategy, 42–3, 47; unity and
    disunity, 50, 56–7; *see also*
    relationships
  see also kin *and* lineage
'Famous African', *see* Hottentot
'fanatic', 461–2, 466
Farley, Reuben, iron-founder of West
  Bromwich, 179, 185, 187
  his sons' careers, 187
Fawcetts, industrial capitalist dynasty
  of, 516
Febvre, Lucien, 577
Fenton, *see* Potteries, the, towns of
Ferrers, Lord, execution of, 323
Fessler, A., 236n

feudalism, 274, 276, 278–9, 280–2, 295, 300–1
    agrarian, 285
    English, 296
    dissolution of, 273
    transition from, to capitalism, 272–304 *passim*
    see also society
fiefs, regulation of succession to, 43
Fielding, Henry, playwright and theatre-manager, 330–2
Fife, Earl of, 159
Filmer, royalist myth of, 475
Fisherton Anger, Wilts., debtors in gaol at, 365
Fison, William, 516
Fitzgerald, Scott, 165
Fleet, prison, 113, 387
Fleetwood, Whig Bishop of Ely, 416
Flegg, East and West, Norfolk, 102
Fletcher, A., 116, 235n
Florence, city of, 479
Fogel, Robert, 592
food, 223, 227, 291
    berries, nuts and seed, 220
    ox roast, 96
    supplies, 221, 289
    see also agrarian matters, harvests
Foord, Henry, 440
Forbes, Henry, 516
Forman, Robert, of Calne, 442
Forster, W. E., 516, 518
Foster, James, iron-maker of Stourbridge, 187
    his grand-nephew, 187
Foster, W. O., ironmaster, 175, 183
Foucault, Michel, 306, 309
Fowler, Henry Hartley, Viscount Wolverhampton, 183, 190
    'Woodthorne', his home, 183, 190
Foxe, J., *Book of Martyrs*, 322
France, 41, 44, 50
    northern, 221
    nobility of, 41, 43–4
Frank, Francis, 440
Frankfurter, Justice, 355
Franz Joseph, Emperor, 145
Frederick, Prince of Wales, and defence of Oxford, 420
Frederick, Sir John, 463, 465
Frend, William, Unitarian and Fellow of Jesus College, 424–5
    his *Peace and Unity Recommended*
    to the Associated Bodies of Republicans and Anti-Republicans, 424
Freud, 590
    his *Civilization and its Discontents*, 590
friendly societies, 532–3, 573
Frogmore, mausoleum at, 131
fruits and flowers:
    gooseberries, 496–7
    carnations, 495–6
    hyacinths, tulips, ranunculuses and carnations, 496
    pinks, 496
Fryer, W. F., Wolverhampton banker's son, 179
functionalism, 243–4
'Funny Joe', half-wit, 349
Fürstenberg, Count Johann von, 51
    Fürstenbergs, 51

Gainsborough, Lincs., 234
Gandhi, K. M., 153
Gardner, Ralph, 446, 449
Garnett, James and Richard, 516
Garrick, staging of 'Macbeth' by, 330
Garter, the:
    Order of, 152
    banners of, 159
Gash, Norman, 129
Gawdys, old Norfolk family of, 111
Gay, John, *The Beggar's Opera*, 325, 348
Geertz, Clifford, 65–7, 590
genealogy, geneaologies, 46–7, 55, 62, 64
    genealogical ties and relationships, 39, 53, 61
    genealogists, 36
Gentleman's Magazine, The, 384, 386n, 421–2
gentry, the, 64, 96–100, 122, 124, 231, 268, 296–7, 385–6, 393, 397, 399, 433, 485, 503, 506–7, 511, 516; *see also* Norfolk, gentry participation in local government of, York, citizens of *and* Yorkshire, gentry of
    lesser, 107, 122, 387, 427
    upper, greater, 107, 119, 122, 124–5, 511; of Norfolk, 99, 106–7, 111, 119, 123–5, 511
    country house owners, of Northants. and Herts., 95

knights and baronets, of Norfolk, 111
squire, 96, 392, 399; of Norfolk, 113
agents of, 99
gentlemen, 95–6, 206, 379, 385–6, 425; of Norfolk, 106, 110
national genteel class, 124
George I, King, 135–8, 408, 411, 415, 418–20
accession of, 109, 115
George II, King, 135–8
George III, King, 130, 132–3, 136–8, 140–1, 152–3, 161–3
and political parties, 140
his children, 148; *see also* George IV, William IV, *and* Cambridge, Cumberland, Kent, Sussex, Dukes of
George IV, King, 130–3, 136, 138, 152
as Prince Regent, 130
George V, King, 141, 152–4, 156, 158–9
his wife, Queen Mary, 152, 154, 159
his daughter, the Princess Royal, 159
his Greek relatives, 159
George VI, King, 152–3, 158
Germany, 41, 44, 49–50, 53, 55, 64, 157; *see also* political authority
emperor and territorial princes of, 53
Emperor of, 52; imperial ban, 49, 52; imperial commissioners, 50, 51n; imperial judge, 57; Charles V, 49
personal rule of Kaiser of, 157
royal family of, 159
princely courts of, 54
princely houses of, 44
smaller princes of, 44
obscure princelings of, *see* Battenburgs *and* Coburgs
German nobility: 35, 36n, 41, 43–5, 47, 49, 55; of Austria, 44, 48; of the Rhineland and south-west Germany, 44–5, 48; of south-west Germany, 45–64 *passim*; children of, entering the Church, 45, 47–8, 55; daughters of, 45 and n, 54; guardianship of children of, 53–5; sons of, securing places at courts, 46–7, 52–4; and customary law, 45; and ecclesiastical prebends, 44, 47, 57; Bavarian nobleman, unnamed, 159

knights of, 46; Hessian, 36n; 'hedge-knights', 45
peasants of, 36n, 44
unification of, under Prussian leadership, 149
German Reichstag, 51
Germanic societies, 41
Germanic tribal obligations, 50
Germanic tribes, 41
Germans, 187
Berlin, capital of, 157
see also Prussia, Schleswig-Holstein, Heidelberg
Gibbon, Edward, 428
Gibbs, R., 319n
Gilmour, Gary, 355
Ginzburg, Carlo, *The Cheese and the Worms*, 27
Girard, René, 340, 342n
Girouard, Mark, *The English Country House*, 595
Gladstone, W. E., 141, 144, 156
his Home Rule policy, 137, 144
Gleane, Sir Peter, 111, 113
Glorious Revolution, the, 401, 404–7, 420, 425, 428, 460–1, 466, 481
institutional restructurings following, 457
revolutionary settlement, 406, 425, 427
Gloucester, 373, 435
St Aldate's parish in, 234
purge of the corporation of, 439
Gloucester, Duke of, son of George V, 152, 159
Godwin, J. V., 518
Godwin, Reverend, 527
Goode, W. J., 245
Gordon, Thomas, commonwealthman, 417
Gowan, John, execution of, 320
Gower, Lord, 418
Grain, Kent, 206–8, 222
Grant, Alexander, 387, 395
Grantham, Lincs.,
Graves, Mr, dancing school of, 500
Great North Road, *see* transport matters
Great Yarmouth, Norfolk, 102, 235
Green, Ann, hanging of, in Oxon., 352
Greenblatt, Stephen, 329
Greville, 136, 163

Grey, Lord, of Wilton, intended excution and reprieve of, 327–8
guilds, 72, 277, 291, 293, 387, 473
  religious, 202
  livery companies, 72
  guildsmen, 481
Guizot, François, 278
Gurdon, Thornhagh, Tory magistrate of Norfolk, 102, 111
Gurney, Sir Richard, Lord Mayor of London, 477

Hacket, Thomas, mayor of Worcester, 450
Haiti, 230
Halifax, Yorks., concerts and theatre in, 506
Hall, Catherine, 550
Hall, Edward, 69, 79–80
Hampden, John, 462
Hampton Court, 135
Hancock, Sir Keith, 580
Hanley, see Potteries, the, towns of
Hanover, 114
  King of, 131
  House of, 418
  Hanoverian: ascendancy, 96; dukedoms, 132; dynasty, 420; influences upon the British monarchy, 129, 135–9, 151–5, 160, 165; names, 131, 158; past, break with, 160; period, 97; regime, 414, 418–20; succession, 130, 404, 407, 409–10
  Hanoverians, 130–8, 140–1, 148–9, 152–3, 155, 158, 161–3
  later, debaucheries of, 130, 133; debts and finances of, 130, 133; divorces of, 130
Harbison, E. Harris, 22
Harbord, Harbord, 110
Hardwicke, Lord, 418, 421
Hare, Sir Ralph, Norfolk justice, 113
  his son and grandson, 113
Harper, John, 184
Harrison, Brian, 12, 529
Harvard, University of, Charles Warren Center for Studies in American History at, 26
Hastings, Sussex, freemen of, 441
Hastings, Flora, 134
Hatherton, Lord, 178
Hay, Douglas, 307–9, 325, 357

Hay, Sir James, 329
Heal, F., 250
Heidelberg, 89
Hemlingford, Hundred of, War., 239
Henderson, G. B., 129
Henneset, Dr, reprieve of, and resulting riot, 325
Henrietta Maria, Queen, 91
Henry V, King, 68
Henry VI, King, 82
Henry VII, King, 79–80
Henry VIII, King, 373
  and his Queen, coronation of, 69
Henry, Prince, son of James I, 82
  his installation as Prince of Wales, 87
Henry, Louis, 33
heraldry, 55
  coats of arms, 57
  personal arms, 57
heralds, 36
Herlihy, David, 41–2
Heron, William, of Harbury, Yorks., 381
Hertfordshire, 233
Hesse, Anna of, 150
Hexter, J. H., 21–2, 27, 29
  his 'Storm over the Gentry', 21
Heylin, Peter, former chaplain to Archbishop Laud, 90–1
Hickman, Sir Alfred, steel giant, 175, 182–7, 189
  home at Wightwick, 182
  sons' careers, 187
High Wycombe, Bucks., 434, 452
  split in corporation of, 453
Hill, Christopher, 271, 295
Himmelfarb, Gertrude, 29
Hingley, family of, 187
  Sir Benjamin, and his nephew, 187
historians,
  bourgeois, 293
  Cambridge group of, for historical demography, 33
  conservative, 511
  English medievalist, 44
  liberal French, 278, 302
  Marxist, 511
  nineteenth-century legal, 43
  psycho-historian, 56
  see also Annales
historical materialism, 274, 285, 287, 302

historicism, Whiggish and Marxist variants of, 241
historicist approach, 247
historiography:
French liberal, 283
of Tudor–Stuart England, 271–4
revisionist, 547
Hitler, Adolf, 153
Hobart, Sir John, Whig knight, 111–12
his son and grandson, 112
Hobbes, Thomas, 322, 393
Hobhouse, H., 128
Hodgetts, Thomas, Birmingham land surveyor, 181
Hodsons, brewers, 185
Hogarth, William, 332–3, 337, 342, 348–9, 483
Holden, Isaac, 516, 518
and Lister, S. C., mechanical wool comb of, 521–2
Holland, 330
a Dutchman, unnamed, 392
the Dutch, 394
Holland:
Sir John, first baronet and veteran of the Long Parliament, 112, 121
Sir John, his grandson, second baronet, privy councillor and Controller of the Household, 102, 104, 111–12
Holley, John, and the determining of family living standards, 568
Holmes, G., 259, 363n
Holmes, Sherlock, 401
Holstein, 157
Holt, Norf, sessions at, 105–6
honour, concept of, 70
Hoskins, W. G., 203, 208, 218, 223, 237
his critics, 219
hospitals, 202
voluntary, 573
Hotham, Sir John, 438
Hottentot, 491
Houlbrooke, Ralph, 34–5, 37–41, 43, 48–9, 59–61
his *The English Family 1450–1700*, 34–5
households:
possessions of: 218; brass, 219; candlesticks, 219; 'consumer boom', Elizabethan and early Stuart period, 218–19, 231; flock

beds, 218–19; other furniture, 219; kitchen equipment, 219; 'luxury' possessions, 227; pewter, 218–19, 237; pillows, sheets, blankets, 219
rural, 276
housing, 239
model cottages, for some textile workers, 536
shacks, 234
sub-standard, 216
substantial Elizabethan house in Warwick, 219
improved, for working classes, 133
see also country house(s)
Huddersfield, Yorks., theatre in, 506
Hull, 438
aldermen of, 445
oratory performances in, 506
theatres at, 502, 504
Humberside, 193
Hume, David, 283, 302
Hunt, Thomas, *Defence of the Charter, and Municipal Rights of the City of London*, 473
Hurst, William, of Warwick, will and inventory of, 219–20
Husbands, C., study by, 205 and n
Hustlers, industrial capitalist dynasty of, 516
Hutchinson, Colonel, burgess of Nottingham, 437
Hutton, William, Birmingham commissioner, 377–8, 395, 397
his *Courts of Requests: Their Nature, Utility, and Power Described...*, 378n
Hythe, 440

Illingworth, Yorks., oratorio performances at, 506
Illingworth, Daniel, 516
impressment, 392
and billeting, 125
India, 153
and Morley-Minto reforms, 153
independence of, 153
individualism, 37–8, 56, 59
affective, 33
competitive, 515, 526, 529–30, 532, 548
cultural, 546
liberal, 527
self-help, 536

individual's self-interest, 38, 50,
58–61
individualistic set of values, 40
Independents, 411
Industrial Revolution, 196, 247, 368,
553
and creation of women factory
workers, 551
and family structure, 550
effect of, upon the middle class, 173
industry, 278, 283; see also coalmining,
cloth-making and Potteries, the,
industries of
high fertility in areas of, 553, 559,
566
iron, 553, 559; see also Potteries,
the, iron industry in
inflation, 44, 297
price revolution, sixteenth-century,
88, 219, 295
inflationary pressures, 433
inheritance, 36n, 41, 298
and division of estates, 47–8, 51,
56–8
and parental selection of heirs, 48
and patrilineal line of descent, 56
systems of, 44, 48; English
aristocratic, 43; mixed system,
45–6, 48
partible, 36n, 41, 43–5, 48, 57–8,
220
impartible, 42, 44, 48, 59;
primogeniture, 42–4, 46, 48, 58–9
fines, 298
Interregnum, the, 122, 252, 268
upheavals of, 428
the major-generals, 439, 446–7, 451,
455
Ipswich, Suffolk, 205, 211, 215, 228
Ireland, 131, 234; see also Gladstone,
home rule policy of
'Irish Giants', freak show, 492

James I, King, 66, 69, 76, 82, 84,
86–90, 301, 326, 328–9, 380
as King of Scotland, 84–5
court of, 328–9
pro-Spanish policies of, 75, 86
James II, King, 100–1, 104, 112, 420
and 'evil counsellors', 404
and Exclusion crisis, 457–82 passim;
revisionist views on, 457–9, 481
deposition of, 405

his appointees to Norfolk
commission, 117
his Commissioners for Ecclesiastical
Causes, 404
James, R. Rhodes, 128
Jansen, Marius, 588
Jefferson, Thomas, 493
Jeffrey, William, and his son, of Calne,
442
Jeffries, John, attorney of Bath, 382,
394
Jerningham, Sir Francis, of Costessey,
100–1
Jesuits, 86
jewels, 71
John Hopkins University, 24
Johnson, Mr, trick-riding act of, 491
Johnson, Samuel, 396
Jones, J. R., 457–9
Jordan, Professor W. K., 250
Joseph II, Emperor, 145
Josselin, Ralph, clergyman, 34
Justices of the Peace, see legal
personnel

Kagan, Jerome, 590
Keevil, Wilts., 231, 238
Kemble, Charles, 311, 505
Kemp, Sir Robert, kt; 113; his son, 113
Kendrick, Sir Thomas, 583
Kenilworth, War., 225
Kenricks, Black Country family of, 186
Kensington Palace, 135
Kent, 116, 235
justices of, 97, 109
petty sessions of, 103
three villages of, 205; see also Grain,
Shorne, Strood
various parishes of, 211, 215
Kent, University of, 12
Kent:
Duke of, son of George III, 130,
137–8; his wife, see Victoria of
Coburg
Duke of, son of George V, 152
Kent, J., Professor, 233
Kenyon, J. P., 457–9
Keregan, Thomas, actors and theatre
of, 502
widow of, 502; her successor, see
Joseph Baker
Kerridge, Eric, 298–9
Kew, royal residence at, 135

Kidd, Captain, execution of, 320, 323
Kielmansegge, Frederich, 316n
kin, kinship, 33–64 *passim*
  'kin' (living relatives): 41, 49, 58–60;
    extended, 34–40, 42–3, 49–50,
    59–60; 'friends', 50; kindred,
    kinsfolk, 38–9; functions and
    obligations of, 39, 42, 50, 53–4,
    60–1; interaction, behaviour of,
    34, 59–60; ties of, 35–6, 38–9, 43,
    49, 60–1
  kinship: aristocratic system of, 44;
    bilateral and patrilineal elements
    in, 44–5, 49, 59–60; bilateral
    system of, 35, 37–42, 48–9, 53, 55,
    59–60; *freundschaft* (bilateral
    extended kin group), 49–50, 54–5;
    English system of, 35, 37, 39–40,
    43, 50, 59; German system of, 41;
    patrilineal system of, 35–6, 39,
    41–2, 48, 59; 'patrilinear' system,
    36; terminology of, 40 and n;
    today's, 39
King, Gregory, his 'Scheme' of
    national incomes, 204, 208, 210
King, William, principal of St Mary's
    Hall, Oxford, 418
Kings' Bench prison, 395–6
King's Lynn, Norfolk, 101, 103
  kinship:
    autocratic tendencies within, 85–6
    effects of Reformation upon, 69
    in pre-colonial Bali and
      nineteenth-century Morocco, 66
    and royal entries into London, 65–93
      passim; and concept of
      goodlordship, 78; cost of, 87–9;
      decline of, 82–9; in Spain and
      France, 85; medieval ritual
      surrounding, 68, 72, 83; in France,
      68n; religious elements in, 79–81;
      in post-Reformation England,
      80–2; Stuart attitude towards, 84,
      88
    and royal progresses, 66–7, 69–70,
      77, 83, 88, 90
    acclamation, 74, 78
    see also monarchy *and* courts
Kinver, Staffs., 187
Kirchbergs, 51
  Count Philip von, 51–2; his first
    cousin, *see* Johann Werner von
    Zimmern

Countess Anna von, 51; her first
    husband, *see* Johann von
    Fürstenberg; her second husband,
    see Werner von Zimmern
Kite, Mr, circus of, 493
Kittle, Police Inspector, 347
Klingenberg, knightly family of, 51–2
  Albrecht and Wolfgang von, 51–2
Know, Vicesimus, 421
Knowle, War., 217
Knox, J., 462
Kobos, Don, reporter for Channel 13,
    Houston, Texas, 305

labour, 275–7, 284, 287–8
  division of, 242, 247, 272–3, 275–7,
    281–2, 285, 287, 291
  product of, 276
  labour discipline, 290
  labour process, 275, 277, 284;
    semi-skilled, 277
labourers, 290
  agricultural, *see* agrarian personnel
  wage, 290, 294; wage labour, 513,
    529
Lancashire, 224, 236
  child care in cotton towns of, 567
  access to Westminster by, 195
  factory towns of, 193
  links between aristocracy and middle
    class of, 194–5
  textile masters of, 194
  middle-class elites of, 194
Lancaster, 224
  petition by sheriff of, 1792, 377
Lancaster, University of, 12
land:
  competition for, 299
  demand for, 300
  land market, 386
  see also estates
Landau, N., 98n
landlord(s), landowners, lords, 43,
    96–8, 271–2, 278–9, 287–9, 290–2,
    294–5, 297–300, 302, 304, 389–90,
    359, 511–12, 514, 540
  rent rolls of, 524
  enclosing and rack-renting, 201
  feudal lords, 277–8, 280, 282–3, 296
  rural lords, 296, 298
  landed elite, 97–8
  landed income, 44
  landed society, 387

see also aristocracy, nobility *and* gentry
Landseer, 135, 161
Laslett, P., 206 and n, 217
Latin, 379
Laud, Archbishop, 91
Laudians, 260
law and legal matters:
law: 294, 354; critics of, 378, 386, 396–8; debate on the role of, 357; English compared with Prussian, 384; literature calling for the reform of, 383–4; reformers, 382
by-laws, 210
civil law, 357–99 *passim*
common law, 358, 360, 366–8, 378, 382–3, 387–90, 397, 399, 474–5
establishment, 375
courts, *see* courts, common law
criminal law: 357, 360m, 397–8; criminal accusations, 391; criminal trials for felonies, 398; reformers, 308; *see also* courts *and* crime
contention, contentiousness, 359–60, 384–5, 392–4, 396–7
legal costs, 366, 375–6, 378–85, 398
legal disputes: settlement of; arbitration, 382, 391, 396; informal means, 376; out of court settlements, 365
legal documents: bills and pleadings, 380; case paperwork, 380; contracts, 357; (conditional bond, 388, 391, 393; replacement of, 394, enforcing promises, 393–4; making and enforcing promises, 390; promissory notes, 391, 399, and bills of exchange, 389); deeds, wills and warrants for gamekeepers, 386; docket rolls and books, of Common Pleas and King's Bench, 358; fee books, of attorneys, 383; *see also* Travers, Henry and Benning, Ambrose; leases, 281, 294, 298–9, 303; letters, 381; plea rolls, of Common Pleas and King's Bench, 358–9; probate, documents of, 174, 218–20, 227; quarter-session rolls, of Lancs., 235; Rolls of Warrants of Attorney, of Common Pleas, 359; summonses, 365; wills and legal transactions,

39–40; writs (documents and procedural steps, 376, new, 365, London, 382, of summons, 395); written obligations under seal, 388, 393
legal proceedings, complexity of, 378, 384
legal training, 111, 116; Inns of Court, 246; Inns of Chancery, 381
legal work: actions on the case, 369, 389–90, 393; assault, 390–2; ejectments, 369, 385, 390, 393; fraud, 394 (and contention, 390); law suits, 50, 56, 358–72 *passim* (indictments and disfranchisements, 476, with regard to the keeping of promises, 360); litigation about debts and contracts, 390; litigation over mortgages, 386; loans or other financial arrangements, 388; malfeasance, 390; negligence, 390, 357; non-litigious work, of attorneys and solicitors, 381; prosecution of man aiding gaol-break, 385; slander, 357, 391–3; trespass, 369, 390–3
other legal matters: appeal, 107; appeals of justice's orders, 120; bail, 365; dedimuses, 107, 112–13; depositions in case of acused theft, 114; difficulty of using the law to recover property, 384; disputed titles to land, 390–1; informal written or verbal contracts, 389; judicial routine, 124; law of contract, 388; legal renunciation of claims, 45; mortgages, 386; oaths of the peace, 110; plea of minority, 395; property conflicts, reduction in, 386; property rights, 357; settlement appeals, 119; verbal contracts, promises, 393–4
Lecky, W. H., 162
Leeds, 133, 229, 483–510 *passim*
as creator of wealth, 489
cloth-making of, 488–9
elite of, 489, 503, 507
fairs in, 490, 493
Gentleman Cricket Players of, 497–8
growth in population of, 488
lack of gentry and professional men in, 489, 507

lack of 'season' in, 500, 503, 507
merchants of, 488–9
new charter of, 449
newspapers of, 486–7, 491n, 492n,
  493n, 494n, 495, 497, 501n, 505n,
  506n, 508
races in, 491–2
sweated labour of women in, 553
theatre in, 494, 502–3
'Assembly Room' in, 500; 'Leeds
  New Assembly', 501
Briggate in, 492
'Music Hall' in Albian Street in, 501
Rose and Crown Inn at, 501
see also leisure and sports
legal personnel:
attorneys: 381, 383; country, 381;
  local, 376–8; and solicitors, 380–1;
  and court officials, 379
bailiffs, 120
barristers, 380
clerical justices, urban trading
  justices, stipendiary magistrates,
  99
complainants, witnesses and
  suspected culprits, 98
constables: 120, 391, 399; accounts
  of, Norfolk, 116; chief, Norfolk,
  121
coroner, 567
counsellor at law, 100
court employees, Norfolk, 121
court officials, 380; in London,
  399
defence lawyer, 392
executors of wills, 53
lawyers, 359, 376, 378, 380, 398–9,
  485
Lord Chancellor, unnamed, 331, 411
judge(s): 391, 404, 409; and juries,
  463; disputes over the
  independence of, 459; from
  Westminster, 398; pronouncing
  the death sentence, 307
jury, juries: 359, 377, 390–2;
  Middlesex Grand Jury, 384;
  petition by some Aylesbury
  citizens to Grand Jury, 312–13;
  trial by, 376
jurors, 120, 392–3; of Middlesex, 392
justices, magistrates: 97–8, 100–1, 106,
  109–10, 114, 117, 123, 379, 391
  399; in Norfolk, 99–118, 120–1,

123–4; in Somerset, 235; clerks of,
  120; minor, 118
prothonotaries: of Common Pleas,
  358, 362–3; of King's Bench, 358
sergeant-at-law, Norfolk sessions,
  104
treasurer(s): Norfolk, 121; and
  session chairmen, 111, 115, 120;
  auditor for, 121; clerks for, 121
medieval legalists, 42
the legal profession, 57, 377, 382,
  385–6, 394, 398
criticism of, 378, 382, 399
witnesses, 391
see also professions, the
Leicester, purge of corporation of, 439
Leicester House, 135
Leicestershire, women hosiery workers
  of, 553
leisure and sports:
'commercialisation of', 483–510
  passim; and growing print trade,
  483, 509; see also Leeds,
  newspapers of and York,
  newspapers of
development of a more private,
  domestic culture, 506–7
balls and assemblies, 506
clubs, convivial banquets and
  reunions, in Leeds and York, 487,
  489, 495–8, 500–1, 507–8; and
  fraternal orders, 487, 489
hunting, in Leeds and York, 498
musical performances: 483, 489, 491,
  494–5, 501, 506; and assemblies,
  499; decline of, 506; and cards,
  503; and dancing, 487, 490; and
  card-playing, 499–500
new northern leisure centres, 506
popular science: growing strength of,
  484–5; audience for, 489–90;
  peripatetic scientific lectures,
  490–2, 494
professionalization of horse-racing,
  boxing and cricket, 483
races, 488–92
shows, in Leeds and York, 489–97
showmen, lectures and virtuosi, 508
sports: travelling shows and
  circulating libraries, 487; rural,
  189
theatre(s), 483, 487, 490, 501–5, 506
Lenthall, William Speaker, 445

Leominster, Heref., new charter of, 449
Leopold I, King of the Belgians, see Coburg, Leopold of
Leopold, Prince, son of Queen Victoria, 151
L'Estrange, old Norfolk family of, 111
Sir Roger, 466
Levellers, 243; see also radicals
Liberals, Liberal Party, 183, 189
Liberal Unionists, 191
liberals, liberalism, 525–48 passim
Lichfield, Staffs., 211, 213–14
Lilburne, Major-General, 446
Limpurg, Schenk, Albrecht von, 52, 54
Lincoln:
purge of mayor and corporation of, 439
town charter of, 439
town clerk of, 439, 446
Lincolnshire, 235
Lincolnshire, Lord, 147
lineage, 33–64 passim
definition of, 37
geschlecht, 49, 55–7, 59
'lineage consolidation' in the nobility, 41, 43–4, 59
lineage loyalty, 38, 50, 57–8, 60
'houses', 37, 41, 55
Lister, S. C., later Lord Masham, 516, 518
and Holden, Isaac, mechanical wool comb of, 521–2
'Little Devil', and his acrobats, 505
Liverpool, 133, 375
'Liverpool Museum', 493
Lloyds, manufacturing and banking family, 176
Locke, John, radical, 426, 461, 480
lodgers,
of the poor, 206
of the working class, 570
London, 66–93 passim, 96, 98–9, 113–15, 119, 123, 158, 175–6, 194, 196, 216, 233, 249, 312, 316, 323, 328, 346, 366, 372–3, 375, 381–2, 392, 396, 398–9, 445, 460–82 passim, 485, 487, 493, 498–9, 504, 579
and the south-east, 168
apprentices of, 75
areas of: Billingsgate, 337; Blackheath, 69; East End,

sweated female labour in, 553; Kensington, 186; Shoreditch, 79; Southwark and Tower Hamlets, 373; West End, 186; Westminster, 69; Whitehall, 90
arms of, 70
Cathedral church of St Paul in, 80–1
charter(s) of, 461, 473–4, 478
citizens of: 461, 467, 470–3, 476–7; churchwarden of, 392; freemen, 472–4, 469–70; glazier of, 392; leading, 68–9, 91–2; ordinary, 70, 72–4, 76–7, 80, 90–3; (behaviour of, 67, 74–6, 78, 83, 85–6, 91–2; 'baser sort' of, 92–3)
civic ritual of, 473; changes in, at Reformation, 83
Corporation or Magistrates of; 72–3, 79, 83, 86, 92, 462–82 passim; and magisterial or royal authority, 475; constitution of, 469; institutes and personnel of, 468; officers of, 476; court of aldermen (Senate), 68–70, 72–4, 79, 463–5, 469–70, 477, 479 (vetoes by, 464, 469; Tory alderman of, 464, 469; Whig aldermen of, 463, and sheriffs, 477); court of Common Council: 462–4, 469–70, 472–3; common councilmen of, 462–4, 470; Whig, 462, 469; court of Common Hall: 469–74, 476–9; annual meetings of, for election of sheriffs, 474–5; and lord mayor, 470; lord mayor: 68–70, 72–4, 79, 91, 469–72, 474, 476–9; and right of nomination in shrieval elections, 470–1, 474; see also entertainments, pageants of the lord mayor of London; Recorder: 92; and two sheriffs, 72
crafts of, 73; goldsmiths of, 69
grand jurors of, 1681, 463
Guildhall in, 92, 467
Library, 581
livery companies of, 69–70, 73, 467; livery men of, 471–2, 476, 469–70
loyalists of, 466, 478–9
MPs of, in Exclusion Parliaments, 463
merchants and professionals of, 171; and finance of, 173
militia and lieutenancy of, 463
mounted guards in, 92

non-industrial middle-class elites of, 196
Old Bailey in, 323
Old Change in, 69
palace in, of Bishop of London, 80
parish churches of, 74; St Sepulchre's Church in, 316
River Thames through, 69, 89
St James's Palace in, 82
'season' in, 96, 498; influence of, 508–9
society of, 177
street demonstrations in, 91
streets of: Connaught Circle, 311; Edgeware Road, 311; Fleet Street, 81; Horsemonger Lane, 324; Lombard Street, 467; upper Seymour Street, 311
Temple Bar in, 81
theatre in: in Drury Lane, 311; stars of, *see* 'Little Devil', Siddons, Sarah *and* Kemble, Charles
trading interests of, 465–6
trumpeters in, 70
whifflers or guards in, 70, 73, 92
London, University of, 10, 12
Long, Francis, Whig magistrate of Norfolk, 101–2, 111
Long, Mr, and his lecture on electricity, 492
Longden H. Isham, his study of the clergy of diocese of Peterborough, 252–3, 268
Longe, F. D., Assistant Commissioner for Children's Employment, 1862, 561
Longton, *see* Potteries, the, towns of
Lorne, Marquess of, 159
Louis XIV, King of France, 85
Louise, Princess, daughter of Queen Victoria, 159
Love, William, 463, 465
Low Countries, 221
Lowe, Mr, magician, 492
Ludlow, Salop, 234, 238
luxury goods, 227, 291

Macdonald, R., 153
Macfarlane, Alan, 34–5, 37–41, 48–9, 59–61
his *Origins of English Individualism*, 34
McFarlane, K. B., 12–13

McGowan, Randall, 306
Mackay, Sarah, 391
Madely, Salop, 236
'Magic Oak, The', pantomime, 505
Maidstone, Kent, 441
Maldon, Essex, 434
Manchester, 132, 194, 375
as creator of wealth, 489
Chamber of Commerce in, 195
Manders, families of, 185
household of, at Wightwick Manor, 185, 191
S. Theodore, mayor of Wolverhampton, 191
Mandeville, Bernard, 313, 317, 332
Manning, B., 435n
manors,
manorial customs, 210, 298; disputes over, 359
manorial records, 204
manorial rights, 174
Margaret, Princess, 160
marriage to Armstrong-Jones, 160
Snowdon divorce, 160
Marius, John, 387
markets, 272, 275, 277–9, 288–9, 291–2, 294, 299–300
market forces, 297
marketing, 288
see also trade
Markham, Sir Griffin, intended execution and reprieve of, 327–9
marriage, 46–8, 50, 54
alliances, 42, 48, 50, 53–4n
delayed, 517
negotiations, 64; women and, 47
settlement, 42
partners, 39
'prohibited degrees of', 42
property through, 42
regulation of, 42
relations by, 52–3
intermarriage, 46
remarriage, 53
unmarried children, 45
Marshall, Sherrin, 34n
Martin, Theodore, 163
Marx, Karl, 238, 272, 274–95, 302, 585, 593
his *Capital*, 272, 285–6, 291–4
his *Communist Manifesto*, 272, 274, 278
his *Grundrisse*, 272, 285–6

his *Poverty of Philosophy*, 272
his *The German Ideology*, 272, 275
Marxian theory, 272–304 *passim*
Mary, Queen, 74–5, 79, 81, 92
    priests and bishops of, 75
Mason, Tim, 12
Mason's College (later University of
    Birmingham), 188
Massachusetts Institute of Technology,
    24
Matthews, N. L., 451n
May, Erskine, 162
mechanics institutes, 532–3; *see also* of
    Bradford
Mediterranean, the,
    ancient commercial society of, 282
    ancient world of, 281
Melbourne, Lord, 132, 134, 137
Melcombe Regis, 439
    elections at, 445–6
    purge of corporation of, 450
merchants, *see* trade
Merton, R. K., 589
Methodists, lower-middle-class, 538
Middleton, Conyers, fellow of Trinity
    College, Cambridge, 417
Midlands, three parishes of, 233; *see
    also* West Midlands
Midon, F., scientific lecturer, 491
Mignet, François, 278
militia, administration of, 125
Miller, John, 457–9
Milligan, Robert, stuff merchant, 516,
    518
    as liberal mayor of Bradford, 543
Milton, Lord, MP for Yorkshire,
    497
Mitchel, Mr, 311
Mitford, Nancy, 5
modernization theory, 241; *see also*
    Weber
Molesworth, Robert, common-
    wealthman, 408–9, 411, 413–14
    and marks of royal favour, 408
    his *Account of Denmark*, 408
    his *Count Patkul*, 408
monarchy, 281, 291, 296, 301, 479
    absolute or arbitrary, 278–9, 303,
    477
    constitutional, English, 127–65
    passim; financial situation of, 133
    residences of, *see* Balmoral,
    Brighton, Buckingham Palace,

Carlton House and Leicester
    House (homes of successive
    Princes of Wales), Hampton
    Court, Kensington Palace, Kew,
    St James's Palace, Windsor; their
    administration and staffing, 133
    the succession question, 1690s, 125;
    earlier succession problem, *see*
    James II
    see also courts *and* kingship
monasteries, dissolution of, 202
monopolies, *see* trade
Montaigne, Michel de, 318
Montgolfiers, 492
Moore, Sir John, Tory Lord Mayor of
    London, 470–1, 476–8
    his chamber at Guildhall, 477
Morley-Minto reforms, *see* India
Morris, William, 185
mortality,
    infant, 230–1
    crises, 221, 223, 225, 230
    levels, 221–2
    burials, 225
    life-expectancy, 230–1, 237
    'mortality regime', Elizabethan and
    Stuart, 230
Mountain, Mrs Rosoman, singing and
    reciting by, 494
Mountbatten(s), 155, 159
    Lord, 155; Philip, his nephew, 155,
    157, 164; Amanda Knatchbull, his
    grand-daughter, 155
Mountbatten-Windsor, royal house
    of, 155
    see also Battenburgs
municipal government, *see* towns
Munn, Thomas, execution of, 320
Mussolini, B., 153
Myddle, Salop, 232, 236

Napoleon, 441
National Trust, 185
navy:
    Royal, 158, 580; officers, 386–7,
    485
    marines, 391; military
    quartermasters, 391
Negus, Henry, 102
neighbours, 36, 96, 393
New York, University of, 28
New York Review of Books, The, 28
Newbery, John, entrepreneur

(medicines and children's books),
483, 509
Newcastle-under-Lyme, purge of
corporation of, 439
Newcastle-upon-Tyne, 434, 441
disturbances at, 1633, 434
elite of, 433; counter-elite of, 441
corporation of, 446, 448–9
court of requests, in, 374
growth of, 374–5
petition to parliament from, 373
puritans in, 435
town courts of, 373–4; records of,
early eighteenth-century, 373
Newcastle, Duke of, 114–15
Claremont, country home of, 115
Newcastle, Earl of, 67
Newgate, prison, 311, 313, 316, 318,
320, 324, 332, 347, 428
newspapers, the press, 386, 509; *see
also* of Leeds *and* of York
Newton, Isaac, 426
Newton, Richard, principal of Hart
Hall, Oxford, 418–19
his articles in *General Evening Post*,
419
Newtonian System, The, by 'Tom
Telescope', 509
Nicholson, John, animal trainer, 493
Nietzsche, F., 319, 340
Non-conformists, 402, 462–6, 479, 481
of Bradford: 515, 529;
congregations, 527;
denominations, 529, 533;
entrepreneurs and clergymen, 530;
liberal bourgeois culture of, 528
Non-conformity, 189, 191
see also Dissenters, Baptists,
Congregationalists, Methodists,
Puritans, Quakers
Norburie, George, Chancery official,
393
Norfolk, 101, 205, 213, 220
assize circuit of, 371–2
committees in the magistracy of,
116, 118, 121–2
county treasury of, 103
gentry participation in local
government of, 95–125 *passim*
orders regulating county pensions of,
103–5; review of, 121–2;
pensioners, 121–2
lord lieutenants of, 100, 103, 111,

113–14, 123; deputy, 112; agent
of, 123; and militia of, 123
magistracy and lieutenancy of, 99;
see also legal personnel
sheriff of, 108
Diss and Depwade hundreds in, 102
four south-eastern hundreds of, 101
redefinition of boundaries of
thirty-three hundreds of, 102
see also gentry *and* legal personnel
North, Dudley, 471
North, Francis, Chief Justice, 365
North, Roger, *Examen*, 457, 464
Northampton, 441
Northamptonshire, 216
villages of, 217
Northumberland, parts of, 372
Norwich, 172, 205, 228, 371, 373, 434
bridewell at, 120
political elite of, 444
sessions at, 101, 103–6, 111, 113,
120, 122
Norwich, Bishop of, 110
Nottingham, 434, 437
governor and corporation of, 437
principal inhabitants of, 437
town clerk of, 450
Castle, 437
petition of, 1644, 437
Nottingham, University of, 24

Oastler, Richard, 536–7
occupations:
artisans, artificers; 117, 282, 291,
387, 504, 506, 521; and
journeymen, 72; and small
masters, 489; and tradesmen, 467;
and wage-labourers, 369
builders, 227
civil servants, 485
craftsmen: 206, 227, 231, 485;
building, 227, 237; master, 276–7
distillery-worker, 392
doctor, of West Bromwich, 183
domestics, 227
gamekeepers, 386
journeymen, 276–7
labourers: 231–2; labouring families,
232; wage-labourer, 369, 523;
urban, 395
laundresses, 504, 506
mantua-maker, 391
organ-maker, 391

professionals: 511; in municipal
employ, 545
retailers and overseas merchants,
467
servants: 96; and retainers, 70, 87
shopkeeper(s): 395, 369, 485, 521,
542; families of, 516
skilled mechanics, 521
tradesmen: 206; and artisans, 217
victuallers, 102; victualler, of
Wallington, 391
warehousemen, 531
typology of, 243
see also agrarian personnel, Church
of England, clergy of, civil
servants, cloth-making,
workforce, of Leeds, legal
personnel, professions, trade,
merchants and of York
O'Day, R., 247, 250–1, 253, 260
her The English Clergy: the
Emergence and Consolidation of a
Profession 1558–1642, 247
Oettingen, Count Wolf von, 52, 54
his sister, Margarette von, 51–2; her
husband, see Johann Werner (I)
von Zimmern
Old Noll, 462
old regime, English, 421, 425, 428
Old Sarum, 428
'Oliverian', 461
Onslow, Arthur, 'true Whig' and
speaker of the House of
Commons, 417–18, 420–1
Orange, house of, 131; William of, see
William III, King
Orgel, Steven, 326
Orpen, P. K., 247
Orwell, Cambs., 231–2, 238
Osborne, royal residence of, 134,
136, 146, 150, 158–9
Outhwaite, R. B., 220n
Owensboro, Kentucky, USA, 306
Oxford, city of, 23
Oxford, University of, 11–13, 15, 24,
401–29 passim, 577, 579, 581,
583–4, 588–9, 591
academic reform at, 414–15, 425–6;
proposed, 409
behaviour of James II towards,
404–5; expulsion of President and
fellows of Magdalen, 404
colleges at:

All Souls, 580, warden of, 406;
Christ Church, 6; University, 9;
Wadham, 3–6, 9–11, 22
critics of, see radicals,
commonwealthmen, Whigs; for
clerical critics, see Prideaux, H.,
and Newton, R.
election of Chancellor of, 420
fellowships at, 405
issue of celibacy at, 421–2
Jacobitism at, 404, 406, 408, 411,
418, 420; and resulting garrisoning
of city, 1715, 408, 418
links with established church, see
Church of England
MPs and PMs at,
eighteenth-century, 403, 427
morality and discipline at, 410, 419,
423
New Examination Statute of, 1801,
426
non-Jurors at, 405
opening of Radcliffe Camera at, 418
proposed visitation of, 406, 409–13,
416–21
Reformation visitation of, 409
relations of, with Hanoverian
regime, 418–20
rise in enrolments at, 425
senior posts at, 411
Toryism of, 427
'Oxford Magazine', 11
Oxford University Press, 22
Oxfordshire,
north, 232
unnamed inhabitant of, 391

pageants, see entertainments
Paley, William, his views on capital
punishment, 331–2
Palliser, D. M., 201n, 221n, 230n
Palmer, Robert R., 22
Palmerston, Lord, 134, 144, 156
Papillon, Thomas, 465, 469, 471, 475,
478
Paris, France, 577, 584, 591
parish(es), unnamed, see Church of
England, parishes and parochial
matters
Parker, Lord Chief Justice (later Earl
of Macclesfield), 413–14
his 'A Memorial Relating to the
Universities', 413–14

Parkes, Ebenezer, manufacturer and
MP, 185
Parliament(s), 93, 153, 178, 186, 218,
303, 362, 378, 386, 403, 415,
424–6, 428, 457–8, 467, 475, 480
Addled, 1614, 236
Exclusion, 463
Long, summoning of, 90
Oxford, 469
of 1620s, 457
of 1621, 236
Rump, 439
agitation in, for legal reform, 378,
382
annual sessions of, 101, 114
commission(s) of: 186, 354; on legal
fees, 379, 382
committees of: of 1819, 347; on
small debts, 1823, 383; resident at
Nottingham Castle, 437
influence upon, of Black Country
manufacturers, 177
inquiries and investigations in:
358–9, 364, 375, 379–80, 383–4,
399; reports of, 383
opening of, 84, 87
petitions to, 373, 375, 377, 379, 383
parliamentary matters:
bill(s): for Catholic Emancipation,
401; for establishing small debt
courts, 379, 382; for reform of
universities, 1709, 406; for reform
of the two universities, 1719, 404,
413–17; Great Reform, 401, 537;
reform campaign, 538; of 1780, to
prevent abuse by courts of
requests, 377; Sunderland's
Peerage, 415
business, 125
cabinet(s): 145; appointments, 143;
decisions, 156; ministers, 142–3,
145, 152–3; papers, 143;
policy-making, 144
candidates, selection of, 174
elections, 99, 104, 409, 446, 488;
reform of, 1872, 354
extremism, 458
foreign affairs: 154; disputes over,
459, 468
Foreign Office: 143; diplomatic
despatches of, 144
government expenditure, 368
government(s): 104, 109, 144;

coalition, 140, 153; first Labour,
152; Liberal, 153; Tory, 1852, 134;
Whig, 537; expenditure, 368;
issues, 124–5; records of (relating
to commissions of the peace,
107–8, pipe rolls, 108); workings
of, 145
Hansard, 353n
Home Office report, 1844, 347
houses of parliament: Commons,
140, 143–4, 364, 375, 377, 379,
405–6, 411, 424, 475; Speaker of,
438; Lords, 153, 190, 409, 411,
415; disputes between, 459
impeachment, 476
legislation, 412; *see also* Acts of
Parliament
liberties, 296
lord keeper, 411
MPs: 111, 114, 403, 420, 378;
Cavalier, 479; gentry, 399
ordinances, 439, 448–9, 450
parties, party politics, 99–100,
103–6, 115–18, 125, 132, 139–42,
144, 153, 156; *see also* Tories *and*
Whigs
peers, 420
PMs, 140–1, 403; *see also* Baldwin,
Bute, Derby, Devonshire,
Disraeli, Gladstone, Macdonald,
Melbourne, Palmerston, Peel,
Rosebery, Russell, Salisbury,
Walpole
politicians: 140, 142, 153; 'Old
Gang', 153
representation, 433, 525
Westminster: 458, 479; and
Whitehall, politics of, 467;
communities represented at, 467;
hall(s) of, 406, 525
see also Acts of Parliament
Parry, John, harp concerts of, 491
Past and Present, 588
paternalism, 295, 512
employer, 536–7
Tory, 537
Patrick, Bishop of Ely, 409
Pattingham, Staffs., 233
Pauletts, wealthy Somerset family of,
385
Lord Paulett, 386
garden of, at Hinton St George,
385

peasants, peasantry, 231, 237, 273–4,
    278, 286–96, 303
  customary, 299
  free, 279
  unfree, 297
  see also serfs and Germany, peasants
    of
Peck, John, 111
Peckovers, industrial capitalist dynasty
    of, 516
pedlars, children of, 516
Peel, Sir Robert, 141–3
  his police force, 353
Pelhams, 419
  Thomas, Duke of Newcastle,
    Chancellor of Cambridge, 419,
    421
Peterborough, Ordination Books of,
    252–3
  study of clergy of diocese of, see
    H. Isham Longden
Peter, Hugh, 462
Petro, Signior, firework display of, 492
Pevsner, Sir Nikolaus, 582–3
Philip II, King of Spain, 145
Philipstal, Mr de, 494
'Philonomos', 352
Physicians, Royal College of, 246
Phythian-Adams, C., 83, 205n, 209n,
    218n
Pierrepont, Mary, 499
Piers, William, 260, 269
Pilkington, Thomas, Alderman of
    London, 463, 465, 470, 476
Pittsburgh, University of, 24
Plakans, Andrejs, 39–40
  his Kinship in the Past, 39–40
Player, Sir Thomas, Chamberlain, 463
playing cards, 461
Pleck, Elizabeth, 553
plots, conspiracies:
  Arabella Stuart, plot surrounding,
    326, 329; resulting executions, 327
  'bye' or 'priests', 326, resulting
    executions, 327
  Cato Street, conspirators in the, 322,
    324
  Powder, 76, 86
  Rye House, 463
Plumb, J. H., 113n, 483, 509
Poems of Affairs of State, Yale ed.,
    461–2
political authority,

  in England, 43; see also kinship
  in Germany, 49, 60
Polito, Menagerie of, 493
Pollard, Joshua, Tory magistrate, 543
Pollnitz, Baron Charles Louis de,
    313n, 352n
Pond, Arthur, entrepreneur
    (engravings), 483
Pontefract, Yorks., 502
poor, the, 96, 201–39 passim, 353
  age groups among: adolescents, 228;
    and young adults, 210–14, 237;
    adult, 212, 214, 228; over-forties,
    212–13; aged, ageing, 209–12;
    children, 206, 209–10, 213–14,
    228; pensioners, 235
  ages of, 211–15
  and beggary, begging, 209, 222,
    224–5, 228; permission to beg, 234
  and settlements, 210; disputes, 236;
    examinations, 213
  charity and, 202, 236
  employment and: by-employment,
    203, 216, 239; employment, 228;
    in the home, 214; wage-earning,
    203, 213, 228; unemployment,
    unemployed, 225–6, 228–9, 232;
    underemployment, 238
  gradations among, 205–9, 222, 237
  goods of, 203, 218–20, 237
  illness and death amongst, 221–2,
    224–5
  migration of: 'subsistence', 201,
    231–4, 237–8; migrants, 209,
    232–4, 236, 239; in-migration,
    231–3, 238; out-migration, 231–2,
    238; pauper immigrants, 210;
    pauper immigration, 216, 222,
    232, 238
  life-cycle of, 208, 213, 237
  mortality rates of, 214, 221, 230; and
    fertility rates of, 212
  numbers of: 201–39 passim; of
    Restoration period, 209; in reign
    of Charles II, 204; in late sixteenth
    and early seventeenth centuries,
    208; in late seventeenth-century,
    204
  official records of, 204, 210, 212–13,
    233
  officials and: 209, 212, 222, 224, 235;
    churchwardens, 233; constables,
    233; deputy-lieutenants, 224;

justices, 235; magistrates, 202,
235; parish overseers, 210, 223,
237; accounts of, 102; *see also*
Bradford, guardian elections of
oppression of, 377
relief of: 201–39 *passim*, 453, 541;
means-testing, 209, 237; poor box,
248; poor rates, 205–8, 216, 222–5,
228, 234–7; relief rolls, 204;
workhouse, 224
size of households of: 204, 206, 226,
237; lodgers in, 206; servants in,
203, 217, 237
types of: able-bodied, 210;
borderline groups, 222; demobbed
soldiers, 233; destitute, 209–10,
234, destitute workers, 541;
families, 233; foreigners, 233;
gypsies, 233; 'impotent', 202, 210;
in suburbs, 214, 216, 224;
labouring, 213, 222; poorer
people, 396; 'potential', 213–14;
'secondary', 210, 217, 225; those
'ready to decay', 205, 222; those
who 'neither give nor take', 208,
222; urban, 395, 397–8, in
suburbs, 214, 216, 224; widows,
widowhood, 210, 213–14, 221;
wives and children, deserted or
left through conscription, 221;
women, 233; vagabonds, 202, 233;
vagrants, vagrancy, 212, 216–17,
224, 233; *see also* agrarian
personnel, agricultural labourers,
cottagers, servants in husbandry,
smallholders, squatters *and*
occupations, labourers
variations between sexes of, 208,
214–15, 237
population, the:
and growth in proportion living in
towns, 1670–1800, 372
growth of: 201, 216–17, 221, 229,
232, 299, 360, 367–69, 384; and
Malthusian crisis, 232; and
'Malthusian trap', 201, 221
stagnation of, 1650–1700, 367, 369
de-population, in south Warw., 216
see also Wrigley *and* Schofield
Porter, Roy, 486
portraitists:
Elizabethan, 71
see also Van Dyck

Potteries, the, Staffs., region of,
554–5, 565–8, 570, 572
coal industry of: 555; miners in, 556,
568–70, 573 (birthplace of, 556;
children and young daughters of,
working in pottery industry, 563;
wives of, working in pottery
industry, 563–4)
high mortality rates in, 556
iron industry of: 555; ironworkers in,
566, 568–70, 573 (birthplace of,
556; wives of, working in pottery
industry, 564)
labourers in: 568–70; unmarried
daughters of, working in pottery
industry, 563; wives of, in pottery
industry, 564
marital fertility in population of,
565–7, 572–3
percentage of potters in population
of, 563
pottery industry of: 554–72 *passim*;
age-structure of workers in, 556–7;
birthplace of workers in, 556;
children and adolescent girls
working in, 555, 557–9, 561–3,
567, 571, 573; child care
arrangements, 567; hiring
arrangements in, 556; industrial
disease amongst workers in,
557–8; mortality rates in, 558;
'potworks' in (numbers of, 555;
number of residences of
employees in, 555; Copeland and
Garnett pottery, Stoke, 557;
Minton and Boyle pottery, 558);
types of work involved in, 556;
women working in, 555–8, 563–4,
573
segregation in population of, by
occupation, 559
standards of living in, 567–72
towns of, 555
poverty, 201–39 *passim*, 541
geographical variations in incidence
of, 208, 214–15, 237
Povey, Thomas, 441
Presbyterians, 411, 514
Prest, W. R.,
his *The Rise of the Barristers*, 247
Preston, Lancs., 224
ages of women at marriage in, 566
Prestwich, John, 578

Prideaux, Humphrey, dean of
    Norwich, 410–14, 418
    his 'Articles of Reformation for the
    Two Universities', 410–12
Priestman, John, 516
primitive accumulation, 273, 293–5,
    302–3
Princeton, Hospital, 28
Princeton, University of, 9, 11–12,
    15–20, 22–5, 588–91
    Shelby Cullom Davis Center for
    Historical Studies at, 18, 25–9
    Institute for Advanced Study in, 22,
    26–7, 588
    Prospect (faculty club) at, 27
prints, 461
    of executions, 316–17, 325, 332,
    334–8, 342, 349; see also Capon,
    Catnach, Hogarth, Rowlandson
    printers: 420; broadsheets of, 313,
    324–5, 337–40, 342, 344, 461
prison(s), penitentiary, 107, 308,
    365–6, 395, 399; see also Fisherton
    Anger, Fleet, King's Bench,
    Newgate
    debtors', 387
    gaol fever, 321
    gaolers, 120
    imprisonment, 377, 395, 398
    prisoners: 358, 395; for debt, 365,
    395–8
professions, the:
    'ancient', of law, medicine and
    divinity, 242
    characteristics of, 242–3
    rise of, 241, 246
    sociology of, 241
    clerical profession, 241–69 passim
    professional lawyers, 245
    professional police force, 391
    professionalism, 241–69 passim
    professionalization, 241, 246
progressivism, 538
propaganda, Ricardian socialist and
    syndicalist, 534
property, 276, 287
    capitalist, 278, 282
    feudal, 218
    landlord, 273
    preservation of landed, 41–2
    protection of, 277
    transmission of, 43
    see also estates

Protestant:
    concepts of salvation, 81
    creed and the spirit of capitalism, 518
    England, 249
    ideal of discipline, 83
    society, early, 248
Prussia:
    King of, 384
    King of, another, 149; Prince
    Frederick, nephew and eventual
    heir of, 149
    Berlin, capital of, 150; see also
    Germany, Berlin, capital of
Puritan(s), 435, 437, 459–60, 462
    London Puritan revival, 463–4
    Restoration puritanism, 482
Pym, John, 462

Quakers, 514
Quellien, 318

Rabb, Theodore K., 24
radicals, radicalism, 460–1, 466–7,
    478–82
    Interregnum, 402
    London: 466–7, 469–70, 474, 481;
    Levellers, 469 (and concept of a
    'Norman York', 475)
    political and religious: 422, 424, 428;
    anti-clericalism of, 424
    working-class, 541, 547
Radzinowic, Leon, 308
railways, see transport matters
Raleigh, Sir Walter, trial of, 329
Rand, John and William, 516, 536
rates, 543; see also poor rates
    ratepayers, 545
rationalization, process of, 241–2; see
    also Weber
Reading, corporation of, 439,
    443–3
Reason, Age of, 367
rebellion(s):
    Catholic: and foreign invasions,
    threats of, 76, 86
    Jacobite, of 1715, 408, 418
    Jacobite, of 1745, 404, 418
    Scottish, 459
    Wyatt's, 75–6, 92
Reform Society, 538
    United Reform Club, 538, 542
    Reformation of Manners, Societies
    for, 96

Reformation, the, 248, 251
  effects of, upon the poor, 202
regicides, 462
relationships,
  affective, 33–4, 36–7, 39
  family: 43, 48–9; strains and tensions
    within, 44; sibling affection,
    estrangement and rivalry, 43–4, 48
relatives:
  affines, 54, 61
  blood, 52–4
  collateral, branches and lines, 38,
    44–6, 51, 53, 61
  maternal and paternal, 51, 63
  schwager ('brother-in-law', used for
    any relative by marriage), sibling
    group, 41, 49
  vetter ('cousin', used for any blood
    relative), 55
religious practice, 79, 83
rents, 203, 217–18, 237, 295–6, 298–301
  customary, 298
  fixed, 44
  in kind, 217
  rack-rent, 300; rack renters, 295
  rentiers, 514
  entry fines, 300
republicans, republicanism, 467,
  479–80, 482
Restoration, the, 96, 109, 250, 252,
  258, 361, 439, 445, 472
  oaths, of allegiance and supremacy,
    459, 463
  order; 475, 481; challenge to, 460
  polity, challenge to, 465
  state, 479
  Settlement: 114, 481–2; Religious,
    459, 479
  post-Restoration Church, 257
  post-Restoration period, 266
Revolution(s):
  American, 137, 153, 162
  English, 272, 274, 283, 285, 295,
    302–3, 435–6, 440–2, 444, 447–8,
    454–5, 457, 459, 472, 482; *see also*
    War(s), English Civil
  French; 424, 428, 480; and
    American, 421, 425
  see also Glorious Revolution *and*
    Industrial Revolution
Reynolds, Thomas, clothier of
  Colchester, 452
Richard II, court ministers of, 477

Richardson, Samuel, author, 321, 330,
  332, 488
riot(s), 353, 435
  election, 354
  Gordon, 331
  Spa Fields, execution of rioter at,
    323
Ripley, Henry, 516, 518
Ripon, Yorks., balls in, 506
Robinson, Francis, execution of, 320
Robinson, Sir John, alderman of
  London, 464
Rogers, John, alderman of Hull, 445
Roman Catholics, 86
  co-religionists of James II, 404–5
  emphasis of, on charity and
    communality, 83
  seminary training of clergy, 249
  popery, 422; popish designs, 466
Rome, 479
Root and Branch Petition, time of, 250
Rosebery, Lord, 156
Rossell, Samuel, 307n
Rossendale, valley of, 232
Rouse, William, 516
Rowington, War., 232
Rowlandson, Thomas, 315–16, 332,
  337
Rubenstein, W. D., 167, 172–3, 176,
  179, 181, 196, 512
Russell, Lord John, 143–5
Russell, Lord William, 351
Russia, royal family of, 155, 159
Ryder, Sir Dudley, 391–2
Rye, tensions in, 445

Sacheverell, trial of, 413
St James, Palace of, 135
'saints', *see* London Whigs
Salisbury, 205, 216, 228, 234, 238
  dean and chapter lands of, 449
  St Edmund's parish in, 210
  St Martin's parish in, 228
Salisbury, Lord, 155–6
Salt, Titus, manufacturer, 516, 518
Sand, Mr, Museum of Animals of, 493
Sand Hutton, Yorks, 206–7
Sankey, J. W., metal manufacturer of
  Bilston,
Saville, William, execution of, 347
Saxe-Coburg, Duke Ernest II of, 163
Saxe-Coburg-Gotha, royal house of,
  159

Scaglioni, Signior, and his dancing dogs, 505
Scandinavia, royalty of, 155
Scarborough, 444–5
  as attractor of wealth, 489
  continuity in town government of, 445
  oratorio performances at, 506
Schleswig-Holstein, 144, 156
Schmid, Karl, 41, 44
Schofield, R. S., 214n, 229–30
Schorske, Carl, 25
Schumpeter, J. A., 243
Scotland, 32, 83, 85, 90–1, 221, 476, 516
Scott, Reverend, 531
Scott, W., 229
self-help organizations, secular, 529; see also mechanics' institutes and temperance societies
Semon, Charles, German-born merchant of Bradford, 516
serfs, serfdom, 276, 278–9, 293–5, 297, 300
Sewall, Samuel, execution of, 319
Shaftesbury, Lord, 458
Shakespeare, William, Henry VIII, 71
Shapiro, Harold, 25
Sharpe, J. A., 306, 357
Sheffield, steel masters of, 195
Shenstone Moss, near Lichfield, 182
Sheppard, Jack, famed escape from gaol of, 342
Sheppard, William, 451, 455
  his Of Corporations, Fraternities and Guilds, 451
Sherlock, Thomas, Bishop of London, 419
Shorne, near Gravesend, Kent, 205, 207–8, 222–3
Shrewsbury, 216, 234, 450
  as attractor of wealth, 489
  governing body of, 439, 443–4
  mayor of, 436
  new charter of, 444
  St Chad's parish in, 223
Shropshire, 183
  rural parishes of, 235
Siddons, Sarah, 505
Sieder, Reinhard, 44, 48
Simpson, Mrs, 160
Skipp, V., 232, 239
Skipton, Yorks., balls in, 506

Slack, P., 224–5, 433n, 434n
Smiles, Samuel, 522
Smith, A. H., 125n
Smith, Adam, 272–3, 280–5, 288, 291–2, 302, 394
  his Book I of the Wealth of Nations, 280–1
Smith, Frederick, one-time chief agent of Lord Dudley, 180
Smith, John, execution of, 342
Snyder, Ruth, 355
social and property relations, 272–3, 275, 282, 284–5, 288–90
  capitalist, 278, 293, 299
  feudal, 274, 278, 284
  pre-capitalist, 286–93
society, societies:
  types or forms of: 279–80, 282–3; ancient, 274; bourgeois, 272–3, 277, 279–81, 283, 285; capitalist, 187, 302; feudal, 272–3, 296, 302 (see also feudalism); pre-capitalist, 287, 292–3; rural, 296
  ancestor-orientated, 37
  Asian and Eastern European, 37–8
  bilateral, 40
  Germanic, 41
  patrilineal: 37, 39; non-western, 37, 41
  western European, 40
socinians, socinianism, 406, 411
Solihull, West Midlands, 231
Solley, Edward, royalist, 451
Somers, Lord, 406
Somers, Walter, ironmaster of Halesowen, 188
Somerset, 235–6
Southampton, 223
Sowerby, Yorks., 206–7
Sowerby, Robert, scientific lecturer, 491
Spain, 75, 86
  Spaniards, 86
  Spanish embassy in London, 86
Spelmans, old Norfolk family of, 111
  Spelman, 371
Spencer, H., 242
Spencer, J. Ernest, barrister and iron merchant, 177
Spilsbury, John, entrepreneur (jigsaw puzzles), 483
sport, see leisure and sports

Staffordshire:
south, affairs of, 183
brewers of, 183
rural grandees of, 186
Stallybrass, P., 340
Stamford, transport town of, Lincs., 489
Stanhope, Lord, Whig politician, 419
state(s), 276, 537
absolutist, 277, 279, 285
capitalist, monarchical, 304
centralized, 303
centralized social service, 539
city, 278
corporate, 537
national, 277, 302–3
Tudor, 300; and early Stuart
paternalistic, 201
Stockmar, Baron, 131–2, 137–8, 140–4,
149, 155, 163
Stoke, *see* Potteries, the, towns of
Stourbridge, Worcs., 170, 187
Strachey, Lytton, 127, 164
Strawson, Peter, 584
strike(s), 534
of 1911 and 1926
Stone, Jeanne, 7, 11, 18, 23–4, 29,
95–6, 167–8, 172, 589–90; her joint
work with Lawrence, *see below*
Stone, Lawrence, 3–30 *passim*, 33–9,
41, 43, 48–9, 56, 59–60, 87, 95–6,
167–8, 172, 202, 241, 256, 268,
271, 295, 297, 299–303, 357, 385,
395, 397, 403, 426–7, 433, 459–60,
511, 513, 552, 572, 575–95 *passim*
his *An Elizabethan: Sir Horatio
Palavicino*, 12, 582
his *The Family, Sex and Marriage in
England 1500–1800*, 28, 33–4, 36,
56, 590
his 'The Anatomy of the Elizabethan
Aristocracy', 21, 301
his *The Causes of the English
Revolution*, 10, 588
his *The Crisis of the Aristocracy*,
11–13, 22, 24, 36–7, 271, 274, 297,
299–303, 587
his 'The Revival of Narrative', 591
his *Sculpture in Britain: The Middle
Ages*, 12
with Jeanne Stone, *An Open Elite?
England 1540–1880*, 589, 594
Stout, William, tradesman, 387
Strood, north Kent, 206–8, 222–3

Stuart, C. H., 129
Stuart(s):
government, 116
later, 455
political and religious conflict, 481;
see also War, English Civil
regime, 479
see also individual Stuart monarchs
Stubbes, on luxurious dress, 71
Suffolk, 110, 220
study of imprints of, 509
suffrage, 539, 542
Complete Suffrage Conference, 539
see also Chartists
Sugden, Jonas, 518
his biographer, 518–19
Summers, his execution at Aylesbury
in 1693, 346
Sunderland, third Earl of, 415, 419
Supple, Professor B. E., 225
surname(s), 37, 55–6
patrilineally-inherited, 37, 56
stam und nam, 56, 59
surveys:
'Midland Captains of Industry', 180
'New Doomsday', 179
Sussex, 180
parishes of, 235
land purchase in West, 180
Sussex, University of, 12
Sussex:
Duke of, son of George III, 131
dukedom of, 132
Swaffham, Norfolk, bridewell at, 120
Swift, Jonathan,
his *Sentiments of a Church of
England Man*, 406–7
his *Tale of a Tub*, frontispiece to,
342, 345
Swynoke, Samuel, 464

tavern(s), 410
Salutation, in London, 467
see also ale-houses
Tawney, R. H., 21, 201, 271, 295, 299,
578–80, 582
his *The Agrarian Problem in the
Sixteenth Century*, 298
taxes and taxation, 279, 294, 296
government stamp duties, 380, 383
Henry VIII's assessments, 237;
Assessment of 1522, 205, 217
Hearth Tax(es): 205, 216, 218, 231,

237, 239; exemption from, 203–4, 209–10, 216, 218, 220, 225, 231–2; records of, 212
income tax, 174
Lay subsidies of 1524–5, 205, 218
levies of the absolute state, 279
Ship money and assessments, 125
local rates and tax burdens, 117
high levels of, associated with the War of the Grand Alliance, 368
records of, 212, 237
rise in, on newspaper advertisements, 1712–89, 487
taxpayers, 239
Taylor, Benjamin, 558
Teck, family of, 159
Princess Mary of, 154; as Queen Mary, 152, 159
temperance, 529–30
societies and associations for the promotion of, 532–3, 544
see also Bradford
tenants, 282, 301–21, 359, 385, 390
commercial, 278, 290, 299, 303
customary, 281, 299
free, 296
tenant right, 299
tenants' unfreedom, 300
see also agrarian personnel
Tenison, Whig Archbishop, 406
Terling, Essex, 231–2, 238
Tewkesbury, purge of corporation of, 439
Texas, USA:
Attorney General of, 305
Board of Corrections of, 305
resumption of capital punishment in 1983 by, 355
Thackeray, W. M., novelist, 349, 351–2
theology, 518
Protestant, 248
theological training, 249
Thierry, Augustine, 278
Thirsk, Yorks., 205–7, 209–11, 215
Thistle, Order of, 152
Thistlewood, A., execution of, 324
Thomas, J. H., 434n
Thomas, Keith, 28
Thompson, A. F., 3, 11
Thompson, E. P., 27–8, 357
Thompson, Matthew, 536
Thurloe, John, 439

Thurmond, John, his 'Harlequin Sheppard', 342–3
Times, The, 130, 352
Tindal, Matthew, deist, 406
Tiverton, purge of corporation of, 439
Toland, John, commonwealthman, 408, 411, 413–14
his Memorial presented to a Minister of State . . ., 409
his State Anatomy, 409
Tory, Tories, 115–16, 118, 125, 156, 407, 415, 420, 458, 538
Anglicans, 183
capitalists, 536
MPs, 1715–60, 427
ministry, 1852, 134
radicals, 536, 539
urban elite, of Bradford, 540
writers, 479
conceptions of rule of state and church, 427
mishandling of the succession issue, 407
paternalism, 537, 547
of London, 461, 466, 469–71, 473, 476, 478–9
aldermen, 478
sheriffs and lord mayor, 478; see also Moore, Sir John
see also Conservatives
towns, boroughs, unnamed, 96, 174–6, 202–5, 209, 214, 216, 231–2, 234, 239, 274, 276–7, 279–81, 291, 387, 433, 435–42, 444, 446–8, 452, 454–5, 458–9, 481, 485–6, 498–9, 509
attracting or creating wealth, 489, 508
charters of, 433–4, 439; calling in and revising of, 449, 451, 455
civic authorities in, 573
civic government of, 478; protests about, 434–5
civic processions, 72; effect of Reformation upon, 83
corporations, magistracy of, 72, 433, 438–9, 446–51
employment in manufacturing in, 204
freedom of, 434, 454; and unprivileged residents, 434, 441
garrison, 437
growth in population of, 485, 510

immigration to, 216, 222, 520–1 (*see also* poor, migration of);
immigrants, 210, 515, 517, 528
libraries, reading clubs and learned societies in, 509–10; *see also* of Leeds *and* of York
magistrates of, 434–6, 438–41, 445, 448, 451–5; godly, 447, 451
military governors in, 437–8
neutral stance of, in Civil War, 436, 447
provincial papers, 509; *see also* of Leeds and of York
purges of municipal governments, 438–9, 448–50, 455; use of force against towns resisting, 440
suburbs of, 214, 216, 224; slums in, 224
townsmen, 277
urban: communities, culture of, 387; elite, 506; (political, during English Revolution, 433–55 *passim*; factors in the maintenance of, 447–55; counter-elite, 440–1, 448, 453–4; league table, 375)
urbanization, 201, 372–3, 397
Townshend:
Horatio, first Viscount, 103–5, 114; his son, Charles, second Viscount, 105, 114–15; tenants or relatives of 123; his grandson, the third Viscount, 105–6
Lord, 410
trade, 272–3, 280–3, 285, 287–9, 292–2, 295–6, 303, 384, 459, 465, 473
free, 278, 539
foreign, of England, 125, 238
and manufacturing, 440
companies: Levant, East India, Royal African, 465
cycle, 515, 521, 540
depressions, slumps: 209, 221, 225, 229, 237, 239; of 1625, 225, 231; in cloth trade, 229, 234, 521, 534, 540
routes, 278
merchants: 277, 282, 291–2, 387–8, 511–12; and tradesmen, 372, 376, 387; of Leeds and York, 488–9; of London, 465 (and retailers, 467); Merchant Adventurers, 445; merchant community, 385, 388; merchant manufacturers, 227; mercantile elite, 515

monopolies, 276–9, 291, 296, 435
tradesmen: 383, 386; clubs of, 387
protectionism, 524, 539
see also markets
trade unions, 533–4, 573
textile workers', 534
transport matters:
carriages, 501
coach(es), 82, 87, 321, 506; coaching network, 506; coachmen, 75
railways, 308, 352
bridge repair(s), 116, 119
causeway committee, 119
public thoroughfares, 67, 70
roads: 98; main, 489; turnpikes on, 489, 506; Great North Road, 491; highway maintenance, 116; highway surveys, 119
transportation, 398
Travers, Henry, King's Bench attorney, account books of, 380
Treby, Sir George, Recorder, 470
Trelawny, Bishop, 406
Trenchard, John, commonwealthman, 417
Trent, river, 372
Trevelyan, George Otto, 162
Trevor-Roper, Hugh, 6, 21–2, 582, 585
Trimmer, Mrs, 493
Tunstall, *see* Potteries, the, towns of
Turner, Sir Charles, 101
Turner, Thomas, tradesman, 387
Turner, Victor, 76–7
Turpin, Dick, 346
Tyas, Sir Daniel, 450–1
Tyburn, 311, 313, 316, 320–1, 330, 332, 347–9
Tyneside, 193

United States of America, 16, 18, 23–4, 28, 33
Americans, 584, 588
Seventh Fleet of, 581
see also Owensboro, Revolution(s) *and* Texas
Universal Spectator, The, 384
uprisings, of 1715 and 1745, *see* Rebellions, Jacobite
Upton, Notts., 233
use value, 292

Valbourg, Mission de, 321n

values:
  class, 526, 532
  genteel, conservative, 512
  liberal, of self-reliance and self-help,
    515
  traditional cultural, 514
  see also individualism, self-help
    organizations, voluntary
    associations
Vendor, Mr, 320
Venn, John, MP for London, 92
Victoria, Queen, 127–65 passim
  accession of, 130, 161
  attitude to ceremonial of, 158
  family life of: 128–9, 134, 146–7,
    151; and attitude to Prince of
    Wales, 138, 148, 150 (education
    of, 144–5, 148); and deaths in the
    family, 148–9, 137; and marriages
    of children, 149–50
  grandfather of, 137; see also George
    III
  Hanoverian characteristics of, 129,
    135–9, 151, 160, 164
  happy marriage of, 133–4, 149
  husband of, see Albert, Prince
    Consort
  Jubilees of, 161–3
  parents of, 130–1, 137–8, 148; her
    mother, 149
  personal and political preferences of,
    132, 137, 143
  physique and personality of, 137
  uncles of, 131, 135, 138–9, 144
  view of the monarch's role in the
    constitution, 140, 144–6
  views on Irish problem of, 137, 144
Victoria, Princess, daughter of Queen
  Victoria and Prince Albert, 146–7,
  149–50, 157
Victoria, Princess, mother of Queen
  Victoria, see Coburg, Victoria of
villages, 96, 205, 217, 231–2, 238
  open-field, 201
village communities, 34
violence:
  armed force, 50
  feuds and blood money, 42, 50
  see also crime
voluntary associations, 526–7, 531–2,
  535, 544, 548
voluntarism: 527, 532–3, 538–9,
  542–5; liberal, 547–8

voluntarist revival, 544
voluntary charity, 540

wages, 201, 227–8, 237, 369, 372
  falling, 534
  high real, 369, 374
  low, 213, 227, 369
  weavers', 520; disputes over, 379
  payment in kind, 203, 227
  wage-earners, 227
Wake, William, Archbishop of
  Canterbury, 412–16, 419
Wakefield,
  concerts in, 506; theatre in, 502
Wales, 236
Walford, E., 181
Walker, Adam, and orrery, 492
Walker, Robert, entrepreneur
  (newspapers), 483
Walpole, Horace, 420
  his Delenda est Oxonia, 420
Walpole, Sir Robert, 101, 105–6,
  113–15, 403, 417–18
  Robert, his father, MP, 113–14
Walsh, John, entrepreneur (published
  music), 483
Walsingham, Little, Norfolk, 102, 110,
  120
Waltham-on-the-Wold, Leics., 233
Ward, Sir Patience, 463, 475
Warren, George, 111
war(s), 225–6, 229, 369, 396
  civil, 300
  English Civil, another, 229, 234,
    252, 263, 265, 271, 273–4, 358,
    360–1, 436–43, 445, 452; see also
    Revolution(s), English
  Thirty Years', 229
  finance during Elizabethan conflict
    with Spain, 301
  against Spain, 1625, 229
  of the Grand Alliance, 1689–97, and
    associated revolution in finance,
    368
  of the Reformation era, 64
  of 1702–13, 1739–48, 1756–63, 368;
    financing of, 368–9
  World War I, 152, 159
  World War II, 3, 153, 575, 579–81
  virtues of land as against sea war,
    125
warfare, 229, 278
warriors, 274

military men and equipment, 291
Warwick, 205, 213, 222
    High Pavement in, 214, 216
    St Mary's parish in, 206–9, 211, 215,
        219, 222; West Street of, 214, 216
Warwickshire, 187, 205, 216, 218, 236
    parishes of, 220
    feldon south of, 216, 232
    north-east, 226
    northern plateau of, 216
Washington, University of, 21–2
Watson, James, cheesemonger of
    Birmingham, 181
Watt, J., 531
Waud, Christopher, 516
Waugh, Evelyn, *Brideshead Revisited*,
    595
Weavor, Mr, lecturer, 492
Webb, Sidney and Beatrice, 243
Weber, Max, 241, 518, 578, 585, 588,
    591–3
    Weberian model of 'ideal-type' of
        profession, 244; Weberian
        modernization theory, 247
Wedel, von, 78
Weintraub, Stanley, 128, 146
Wells, Norfolk, 100
Werdenberg, noble family of, 51, 53,
    56
    Hugo von, 49, 53, 56
    a Werdenberg, 52
West Bromwich, 185–7
    constituency of, 178
    Council of, 179
    manufacturers and coalmasters of,
        180
West Country, 238, 379
West Midlands, 170, 180–1, 184, 192–4
    access to Westminster of, 195
    commercial, financial and
        professional leaders of, 192
    country houses of, 181
    directories of, 175, 180
    elites of, 175, 194
    fluidity of landed society in, 190
    industrialists and businessmen of,
        180–1, 189, 192, 194; *see also* of
        the Black Country *and* of
        Birmingham
    land sales in, 179
    see also the Black Country *and*
        Birmingham
West Riding *see* Yorkshire

Westcote, 225
Westmorland, parts of, 372
Weymouth, 439
    elections at, 445–6
    purge of corporation of, 450
Whalley, Major-General, 439, 446–7
Whig(s), 105, 114–16, 118, 125, 406–7,
    409–10, 413, 415–16, 419–21,
    458–82 *passim*
    anti-clerical, 404, 406, 410, 414–19,
        423–5, 427
    clerical, 407, 416; *see also* Tenison,
        Trelawny, Wake
    parliamentary, 475
    'true', *see* commonwealthmen
    ministry, 411, 413, 415–16, 418, 421
    of London: 460–3, 466–81; leaders
        of, 460, 469–70, 475–6, 479;
        radical, 467, 471–8, 480–1;
        liverymen, 476; sheriffs, 463, 471,
        477
    pamphleteers, 470, 473–5
    politicians, *see* Bedford, Gower,
        Hardwicke, Parker, the Pelhams,
        Stanhope, Sunderland,
        Townshend, Walpole
    writers, 471–2, 479
    'Good Old Cause', 466, 482
    Independent Whig, 417
Whiston, William, Cambridge don, 405
Whitchurch, Salop, 235, 238
White, A., 340
White, Charles Thomas, execution of,
    323
Whitely, James, theatre company of,
    502
Wied, Elizabeth of, 150
Wiener, M. J., 167, 172–3, 176, 184,
    196, 512
Wild, Jonathan, thief-catcher, 342
Wilde, Edward, 217
Wildenstein, family of, 57
Wildman, John, 467
Wilhelm II, Kaiser of Germany, 157
    his parents, 157; *see also* Victoria,
        Princess *and* Prussia, Prince
        Frederick of
Wilkinson:
    Tate, theatres of, 502–5
    John, 502, 504–5
William I, King, 474
William III, King, 96, 115, 117, 143,
    405

as William of Orange, 404
and Mary, 164
and political parties, 139
William IV, King, 130–1, 133, 149
and political parties, 140
Willingham, Cambs., 232
Willmott, P. 568
Wilson, P. A., *see* Carr-Saunders,
A. M., 246
Wiltshire, 233
Winchester, 233, 238
Castle, great hall of, 327–9
Windermere, Westmorland, 194
Windham, Mr, Norfolk gentleman, 110
Windsor,
royal resident of: 135, 150, 157; Park
at, 147; St George's Chapel at,
131, 159
royal house of, 155, 159
Winterhalter, 135, 161
Wiseman, Thomas, 91n
Wollstonecraft, Mary, 493
Wolverhampton, 170, 178, 182–3,
185–6, 191
Tettenhall, suburb of, 182, 184–5
Tettenhall Towers, near, 189
Wolverhampton, Viscount, *see* Fowler,
Henry Hartley
women:
education and improvement of lot
of, 137
in paid industrial labour outside the
home: 549–73 *passim*; *see also*
Potteries, the, women workers in
industries of; effect of, on age at
marriage, 565–8; effect of, on
marital fertility, *see* Potteries, the,
marital fertility in
Wood, John, 536–7
Woodforde, Parson, 493
Woodham-Smith, C., 128
Woodstock, Oxon., 434
Worcester, 437–8
elite of, 440
garrison in, 437
mayor and corporation of, 450–1
Worcestershire, 205
Wordsworth, W., 493
Worfield, Salop, 233
workforce,
feminization of, 521
proletarianization of, 521–2, 531–2,
534–5, 543, 546–7

see also class, working, *and*
occupations
reduction in working day of the, 536;
workers' ten hour movement, 537
Wrightson, Keith, 34–5, 37–41, 48–9,
59–61
his *English Society 1580–1680*, 34,
37n
Wrigley, E. A., 214n, 229–30
Wriothesley, 79
Wrott, John, steward to Robert
Walpole, 110
Wyatt, *see* rebellions
Wyeth, George, initial reprieve and
later hanging of, 317, 338
Wymondham, Norfolk, bridewell at,
120

Yale, University of, 24
Yardley, West Midlands, 231
York, 346, 483–510 *passim*
as attractor of wealth, 489
as legal, administrative and social
centre, 488
as legal and religious centre, 495
as social centre, 499
assizes of, 488, 490, 496, 500
buildings in: Assembly Rooms, in
Blake Street, 499–500, 507;
coffee-house in, 492; 'George', in
Coney Street, 495; theatre, 502–5
citizens of: alumni of Charity
Schools, 496; craftsmen and
shopkeepers, 488–9; clergy,
lawyers and physicians, 508;
gentry, 489; merchants, 488–9;
professional men, 489, 495, 508
continuity in government of, 444
election dinners in, 496
elite of, 433
execution at Castle of, 322
fairs in, 496
fashionable season of, 488, 503, 507,
509
growth in population of, 488
horse-races of, 488, 490–1
lack of large-scale industry in, 488
newspapers of, 1720–1807, 486–7,
491n, 492n, 493n, 494n, 495–7,
499–500, 502n, 505n, 506n, 508
promenade in, 507
societies and clubs of: Agricultural
Society, 496; Masonic Lodges,

496; Musical Society, 497;
Rockingham Club (political),
495–6; Royal Society of Gardeners
and Lovers of a Garden, 495;
Society of Florists, 496
see also leisure and sports
York, University of, 12
York:
Duke of, later James II, 459, 476
Duke of, son of George V, 152,
159
Duke and Duchess of, 191
dukedom of, 132
Yorkshire, 110, 379, 509
clothing districts of, 379
gentry of, 488
hinterland of, 516
Law Society of, 496
North, 205
parts of, 372, 379
East Riding of, 438
West Riding of, 193, 238, 379
Young, Francis Brett, 189
Young, M., 568

Zimmerische Chronik, 35, 45, 49–64
passim
Zimmern, family of, 46, 49–64 *passim*;
genealogy, 62
legendary ten brothers, 56–7
Werner von, 51; his wife, *see* Anna
von Kirchberg; Gottfried, his
brother, 51–2
Froben Christoph von, 49–52, 54,
56–9, 64; his brothers, 58
Gottfried Werner von, 54, 57–9;
Anna, his daughter, 58
Johann Werner (I): 49–50, 52–3; his
wife, *see* Margarethe von
Oettingen; his sons, 49–50, 52,
56
Johann Werner (II), 54, 56–9
Wilhelm Werner von, 54, 57–9
Wilhelm Werner von, jurist and
historian, 64
estates of, 49–52, 54, 56–8
seat of, 64
Zoffany conversation pieces, 161
Zollern, Eitelfriedrich von, 51

Past and Present Publications

General Editor: PAUL SLACK, *Exeter College, Oxford*

Family and Inheritance: Rural Society in Western Europe 1200–1800, edited by Jack Goody, Joan Thirsk and E. P Thompson*

French Society and the Revolution, edited by Douglas Johnson

Peasants, Knights and Heretics: Studies in Medieval English Social History, edited by R. H. Hilton*

Towns in Societies: Essays in Economic History and Historical Sociology, edited by Philip Abrams and A. E. Wrigley*

Desolation of a City: Coventry and the Urban Crisis of the Late Middle Ages, Charles Phythian-Adams

Puritanism and Theatre: Thomas Middleton and Opposition Drama under the Early Stuarts, Margot Heinemann*

Lords and Peasants in a Changing Society: The Estates of the Bishopric of Worcester 680–1540, Christopher Dyer

Life, Marriage and Death in a Medieval Parish: Economy, Society and Demography in Halesowen 1270–1500, Zvi Razi

Biology, Medicine and Society 1840–1940, edited by Charles Webster

The Invention of Tradition, edited by Eric Hobsbawm and Terence Ranger*

Industrialization before Industrialization: Rural Industry and the Genesis of Capitalism, Peter Kriedte, Hans Medick and Jürgen Schlumbohm†*

The Republic in the Village: The People of the Var from the French Revolution to the Second Republic, Maurice Agulhon†

Social Relations and Ideas: Essays in Honour of R. H. Hilton, edited by T. H. Aston, P. R. Coss, Christopher Dyer and Joan Thirsk

A Medieval Society: The West Midlands at the End of the Thirteenth Century, R. H. Hilton

Winstanley: 'The Law of Freedom' and Other Writings, edited by Christopher Hill

Crime in Seventeenth-Century England: A County Study, J. A. Sharpe†

The Crisis of Feudalism: Economy and Society in Eastern Normandy c. 1300–1500, Guy Bois†

The Development of the Family and Marriage in Europe, Jack Goody*

Disputes and Settlements: Law and Human Relations in the West, edited by John Bossy

Rebellion, Popular Protest and the Social Order in Early Modern England, edited by Paul Slack

Studies on Byzantine Literature of the Eleventh and Twelfth Centuries, Alexander Kazhdan in collaboration with Simon Franklin†

The English Rising of 1381, edited by R. H. Hilton and T. H. Aston*

Praise and Paradox: Merchants and Craftsmen in Elizabethan Popular Literature, Laura Caroline Stevenson

The Brenner Debate: Agrarian Class Structure and Economic Development in Pre-Industrial Europe, edited by T. H. Aston and C. H. E. Philpin*

Eternal Victory: Triumphal Rulership in Late Antiquity, Byzantium, and the Early Medieval West, Michael McCormick†

East-Central Europe in Transition: From the Fourteenth to the Seventeenth Century, edited by Antoni Mączak, Henryk Samsonowicz and Peter Burke†

Small Books and Pleasant Histories: Popular Fiction and its Readership in Seventeenth-Century England, Margaret Spufford‡

Society, Politics and Culture: Studies in Early Modern England, Mervyn James*

Horses, Oxen and Technological Innovation: The Use of Draught Animals in English Farming, 1066–1500, John Langdon

Nationalism and Popular Protest in Ireland, edited by C. H. E. Philpin

Rituals of Royalty: Power and Ceremonial in Traditional Societies, edited by David Cannadine and Simon Price

The Margins of Society in Late Medieval Paris, Bronisław Geremek†

Landlords, Peasants and Politics in Medieval England, edited by T. H. Aston

Geography, Technology, and War: Studies in the Maritime History of the Mediterranean, 649–1571, John H. Pryor

Church Courts, Sex and Marriage in England, 1570–1640, Martin Ingram

Searches for an Imaginary Kingdom: The Legend of the Kingdom of Prester John, L. N. Gumilev

Crowds and History: Mass Phenomena in English Towns, 1780–1835, Mark Harrison

Concepts of Cleanliness: Changing Attitudes in France since the Middle Ages, Georges Vigarello†

The First Modern Society: Essays in English History in Honour of Lawrence Stone, edited by A. L. Beier, David Cannadine and James M. Rosenheim

* Published also as a paperback
‡ Published only as a paperback
† Co-published with the Maison des Sciences de l'Homme, Paris